CONGRESS VOLUME

GÖTTINGEN 1977

SUPPLEMENTS

TO

VETUS TESTAMENTUM

EDITED BY

THE BOARD OF THE QUARTERLY

VOLUME XXIX

LEIDEN
E. J. BRILL
1978

CONGRESS VOLUME

GÖTTINGEN

1977

TUTA SUB AEGIDE PALLAS
EJB

LEIDEN
E. J. BRILL
1978

ISBN 90 04 05835 4

PRINTED IN THE NETHERLANDS

CONTENTS

PREFACE

The University of Göttingen was a highly suitable place in which to hold the Ninth Congress of the International Organization for the Study of the Old Testament from 21 to 26 August 1977. It is the University at which the President, Professor Walther Zimmerli, has taught for many years. It is also a University that has had among its teachers many other distinguished Old Testament scholars since it was founded in 1737 by Georg August, Elector of Hanover, better known to the English-speaking world as King George II, who reigned over the United Kingdom as the second of the Hanoverian dynasty. There were such men as J. D. Michaelis, J. G. Eichhorn, H. Ewald, J. Wellhausen, B. Duhm, R. Smend (whose grandson is now a professor at the same University), and H. Gunkel, to name but a few, and the exhibition "Zur Geschichte der alttestamentlichen Wissenschaft in Göttingen" reminded us how many well-known Old Testament scholars had taught at the University in which we were meeting.

Those who attended the Congress will remember the opportunities it provided to meet scholars from many countries, and to hear and discuss papers. They will remember the welcome and the hospitality given in the Rathaus by the authorities of Lower Saxony and the City of Göttingen, and in Braunschweig by the Confederation of Evangelical Churches of Lower Saxony and the Roman Catholic Diocese of Hildesheim. The reception in Braunschweig came after a journey by rail to Wolfenbüttel, where Professor Rudolf Smend spoke in Holy Trinity Church about Lessing and biblical scholarship and Professor P. Raabe described the work of the Herzog-August-Bibliothek, and where visits were paid to the Schloss and to the famous Library close to Lessing's house. There was much else that members of the Congress will recall with gratitude, including the exhibition at the City Museum of Göttingen on "Propheten-Gestalten und Propheten-Visionen. Das Alte Testament im Spiegel zeitgenössischer Graphik", the maps and pictures of Palestine in Professor L. Perlitt's house, and also the highly efficient work of Dr E. Noort, the Secretary of the Congress, and his helpers.

The present volume contains all but two of the papers read at the Congress together with the paper that Professor S. Wagner would have read if circumstances had not made it impossible for him to get to Göttingen. Professor P. A. H. de Boer's paper, "Bemerkungen zu Jesaja XIX 24, 25", is not included, because the author wishes to carry his researches further before publishing the results of his investigation. The other paper that is not included is Professor O. Keel's study of "Jahwe und die Tiere in Ijob XXXIX vor dem Hintergrund der zeitgenössischer Glyptik", but it is hoped that it will be published in expanded form as a separate monograph.

J. A. Emerton

Postscript

Professor O. Keel's monograph has now been published as *Jahwes Entgegnung an Ijob. Eine Deutung von Ijob 38-41 vor dem Hintergrund der zeitgenössischen Bildkunst* (Göttingen, 1978).

WAHRHEIT UND GESCHICHTE IN DER ALTTESTAMENTLICHEN SCHRIFTPROPHETIE

von

W. ZIMMERLI

Göttingen

Alle wissenschaftliche Arbeit ist umgetrieben von der Frage nach Wahrheit. Auch die wissenschaftliche Arbeit am Alten Testament, der dieser Kongress in seiner Weise in der Vielfalt seiner Fragestellungen dienen möchte, ist letztlich von der Frage nach vollerer Erkenntnis von Wahrheit in Atem gehalten. Woher eigentlich dieser für den bewusst gewordenen Menschen unaufhaltsame Drang der Frage nach Wahrheit? Dahinter steht wohl die Empfindung, dass mehr Erkenntnis von Wahrheit vollere Begegnung mit der Wirklichkeit des Daseins und dann auch die Bewältigung desselben ermöglicht. Begegnung mit der wahren Wirklichkeit erschliesst den Weg zum Leben. Wir fragen nach der Wahrheit, weil wir nach dem Leben fragen.

Aber "was ist Wahrheit?" (Joh. xviii 38). Diese Pilatusfrage ist der bedrängende Schatten, der alle wissenschaftliche Mühe um die Erkenntnis der Wirklichkeit begleitet. "Eine böse Mühe, die Gott den Menschenkindern auferlegt hat, dass sie sich darin abmühen", sagt Kohelet, wo er davon redet, dass er "sein Herz darauf richtet, in Weisheit zu suchen und zu erspähen alles, was unter dem Himmel geschieht".[1] Kohelet steht im Bereich der "Weisheit", dieser in ihren internationalen Bezügen immer voller bekannt gewordenen alten Welt des Fragens nach den Dingen der Welt, wie den Ordnungen menschlichen Lebens, in denen der Mensch sich bewegt und die es zu kennen und zu befolgen gilt, damit wirklich "Leben" gewonnen werden kann. Die alttestamentliche Weisheit redet ganz offen von dem hohen Ziel der Gewinnung von "Leben" durch Weisheitserkenntnis. "Ein Baum des Lebens ist sie für die, welche sie ergreifen", sagt Prov. iii 18. "Wer mich findet, findet Leben", formuliert die personifizierte Weisheit Prov. viii 35 in aller Direktheit. Sie ist der

[1] Koh. i 13. Statt "Himmel" ist hier vielleicht mit einer Reihe von Textzeugen zu lesen "Sonne".

Meinung, dass das Finden von Weisheit und Leben keine Unmöglichkeit sei, während der kritische Prediger vom Geheimnis des Geschehens reden muss. "Tief, tief ist es, wer findet es?" (Koh. vii 24).

Aber nun soll es in dieser Stunde nicht um das weisheitliche Suchen nach dem Geheimnis der wahren Wirklichkeit gehen. Es soll von dem ganz anderen Bereich der alttestamentlichen Schriftprophetie die Rede sein. Nicht im ruhigen, geschichts- und Israel-abgewandten Bedenken der Ordnungen von Welt und Menschenleben steht die Schriftprophetie, sondern mitten im Sturm der Geschichte Israels—jenem Sturm, der die Staatlichkeit des Jahwevolkes mit all seinen Institutionen, mit Königtum, Tempeldienst und politischer Verfassung weggefegt hat. Es ist die Eigentümlichkeit der Schriftprophetie des Alten Testamentes, dass sie zeitlich ganz in diese härteste Sturmzeit Israels fällt. Mit Amos setzt sie ein, am unmittelbaren Vorabend des Sturmes, in dem dann wenige Jahre später Tiglatpileser III. nach Syrien-Palästina hineinfährt. Über dem Trümmerfeld der selbständigen Staatlichkeit und dem verhaltenen Versuch des Neubaus eines vom persischen Oberherrn abhängigen Kirchenstaates, in dem dann nochmals messianische Hoffnung aufflammt,[2] endet es. Was in dem Unbekannten des Buches Maleachi, im Joelbuch, sowie den späteren anonymen Zusätzen zu den älteren Prophetenschriftsammlungen noch folgt, ist nur mehr Nachhall, der schliesslich voll ins apokalyptische Schrifttum hinüberführt. Die eigentliche grosse Schriftprophetie fällt in jene zwei Jahrhunderte grösster geschichtlicher Umbrüche, welche Syrien-Palästina als leidender Weltbereich erfährt. Diesem Äusseren aber entspricht das innere Wesen der Schriftprophetie. Sie ist, was auch da und dort an Weisheits- und Psalmelementen in ihr entdeckt werden mag, inhaltlich voll auf dieses Geschehen bezogen. Da ist von Amos, Hosea über Jesaja und Micha, Jeremia und Ezechiel, Deuterojesaja bis hin zu Haggai-Sacharja nirgends etwas von jener völkergeschichts- und Israel-abgewandten Haltung zu erkennen, wie sie der Weisheit eigen ist. Das prophetische Reden ist voll beteiligt auf eben dieses Geschehen bezogen. Dieses Geschehen geht in die Inhalte des prophetischen Worte ein.

Das prophetische Wort aber beansprucht, meist in polemischer Leidenschaft, Wahrheit auszusagen. Mehr als einmal steht die Verkündigung der Schriftpropheten gegen die Verkündigung anderer Verkündiger, die in anderer Weise von kommender Geschichte reden,

---

[2] Bei Haggai und Sacharja.

als es die Schriftpropheten tun. In Schärfe wird jenen entgegengehalten, dass sie "Lüge" verkündigen.[3] Damit aber stehen wir mitten in der Thematik, die in dieser Stunde zur Sprache kommen soll: "Wahrheit und Geschichte in der schriftprophetischen Verkündigung". Was hat in der Wahrheit, welche die Schriftpropheten im Gegensatz zur Lüge jener zu verkündigen beanspruchen, die Geschichte, von der und in die hinein sie reden, zu tun? Oder andersherum gefragt: Inwiefern hat die stürmische Geschichte, in der sie drinstehen und aus der heraus und die hinein sie reden, etwas mit "Wahrheit" zu tun?

Es gilt, gleich zu Beginn scharf hinzusehen, in welcher Weise die Schriftpropheten von "Wahr" und "Falsch" reden. Dieses Fragen geschieht sehr anders als das Fragen des durch die Schule des Historismus gegangenen modernen Geschichtsforschers, das ohne Zweifel vieles in unserem Kongress zu Besprechende kennzeichnen wird. Es ist nicht die auf vergangene Geschichte ausgerichtete Frage, wie es denn wohl damals genau gewesen ist — die Frage nach der "Richtigkeit" von Überlieferung vergangenen Geschehens. Es ist auch nicht die Frage nach den immanenten genetischen Beziehungen, der "Entwicklung" einer Geschichtsstufe zur anderen hin — etwa die Frage, wie es aus der Richterzeit durch geschichtliche Notwendigkeiten zur Bildung des Königtums in Israel gekommen ist.[4]

Dabei wäre es durchaus falsch zu sagen, dass die Propheten an dem, was einst gewesen ist, nicht interessiert wären. Die mancherlei Untersuchungen über geschichtliche Überlieferungen bei den Propheten,[5] im besonderen die traditionsgeschichtliche Erforschung der Prophetie, die heute eine wichtige Fragerichtung der Prophetenforschung darstellt,[6] hat auf diese Elemente in besonderer Weise aufmerksam gemacht. Es ist auch nicht so, dass geschichtliche Übergänge, die in der Überlieferung eine Rolle spielten, für den Propheten bedeutungslos gewesen wären. Hosea redet eindrücklich davon, wie Jahwe Israel durch einen Propheten aus Ägypten herausgeführt habe und vergleicht dieses Geschehen mit dem, was einst

---

[3] *šaeqaer*, dazu vgl. vor allem M. Klopfenstein, *Die Lüge nach dem Alten Testament* (Zürich/Frankfurt, 1964), S. 95-129.

[4] Vgl. dazu etwa die klassische Darstellung von A. Alt, *Die Staatenbildung der Israeliten in Palästina*, Reformationsprogramm der Universität Leipzig 1930 = *Kleine Schriften zur Geschichte des Volkes Israel* II (München, 1953), S. 1-65.

[5] Vgl. etwa J. Vollmer, *Geschichtliche Rückblicke und Motive in der Prophetie des Amos, Hosea und Jesaja*, *BZAW* 119 (Berlin, 1971).

[6] Vgl. etwa die Prophetendarstellung in der *Theologie des Alten Testaments* II (München, 1965[4]) von Gerhard von Rad.

beim Ahnvater Israels geschah (Hos. xii 3f., 13f.) Er beleuchtet sehr scharf den Übergang des von der Wüste herkommenden Volkes ins Fruchtland und weiss den Ort Baal Peor als Stelle dieses Überganges zu nennen (ix 10). Jesaja redet von dem frühen Jerusalem als der Stadt, in der "Gerechtigkeit" wohnte—man meint in seiner Formulierung den Namen des frühen, vorisraelitischen Königs Melchisedek anklingen zu hören[7] — und von dem Übergang in das Jerusalem seiner Gegenwart. Amos und Jesaja kennen die Form des Strophengedichtes,[8] in dem Phasen früherer Geschichte geschildert werden und dessen Kehrreim jeweils hüben und drüben eine gewiss verschieden gewendete *šûb*-Formulierung enthält: "Ihr seid nicht umgekehrt zu mir" bei Amos, "In alledem hat sich sein Zorn nicht umgekehrt und noch ist seine Hand ausgestreckt" bei Jesaja. Geheime Verbindungslinien zwischen der Verkündigung dieser beiden Propheten des 8. Jahrhunderts sind hier und an anderen Stellen kaum zu übersehen.[9] Nicht anders ist es mit den grossen Geschichtsentwürfen, die etwa in Jer. iii 6ff. und Ez. xxiii die Geschichte des Nordreiches und des durch jene nicht gewarnten Südreiches unter je verschieden "sprechenden" Decknamen zum Ausdruck bringen. Bei Jeremia wird die *mešubāh* (Israel) der *bāgōdāh* bzw. *bōgēdāh* (Juda) gegenübergestellt, bei Ezechiel die Ohola der Oholiba. Wieder wird man bei aller Verschiedenheit der Benennung: hier offene Tadelsbezeichnungen, dort verhüllende, auf die Wüstenzeit und ihre Zeltwohnung zurückweisende Beduinen-Mädchennamen[10] um die Annahme einer heimlichen innerprophetischen Traditionsbeziehung nicht herumkommen. So schauen die Propheten in alte Geschichte zurück und erwähnen sie in ihrem verkündigenden Wort. Die Belege dafür wären leicht noch zu mehren.

Man wird sogar noch einen Schritt weitergehen und feststellen müssen, dass in dieser Betrachtung alter Geschichte die Kategorien Wahrheit und Lüge durchaus eine Rolle spielen. Aber eben in ganz anderer Weise als in der nach der historischen "Richtigkeit" alter Überlieferung fragenden modern-wissenschaftlichen Geschichtsforschung. Wahrheit und Lüge liegen auf einer tieferen Ebene als jener der objektiven Feststellung von Geschehensein oder Nicht-Geschehensein.

---

[7] Jes. i 21-26, vgl. das *ṣaedaeq jālîn bāh* von V. 21b.
[8] Am. iv 6-12; Jes. ix 7-x 4 (v 25).
[9] R. Fey, *Amos und Jesaja* (Neukirchen, 1963).
[10] Dazu *BK* XIII (Neukirchen, 1969), S. 541f.

Die spezifisch prophetische Frageweise nach Wahrheit und Unwahrheit in dieser Zitierung von überkommener Tradition soll aber zunächst zurückgestellt werden. Das die Schriftprophetie recht eigentlich kennzeichnende Reden zur Geschichte ist ja das auf Kommendes ausgerichtete Reden. Es ist nicht nur Zufall, dass das προφήτης, das in seinem ursprünglichen griechischen Verständnis, wie dann in der Übertragung auf die ägyptischen Tempelfunktionäre den "Verkündiger", den "Heraussager" der geheimen Gottesbotschaft etwa am Heiligtum der Pythia in Delphi meinte,[11] in unserem Vulgärverständnis unter dem Eindruck der alttestamentlichen Prophetie zur Bezeichnung des Zukunftsverkündigers geworden ist. Die Verkündigung der Schriftpropheten im Blick auf die eingangs erwähnte erregte Zeitgeschichte ist zentral Ankündigung des unmittelbar bevorstehenden geschichtlichen Geschehens. Noch die späte Lehrgeschichte des Jonabüchleins formuliert den einzigen Teilvers, der hier prophetische Verkündigung enthält, in dieser Form: "Noch 40 Tage, dann wird Ninive zerstört sein" (iii 4bß).

So ist es denn wohl richtig, zunächst darauf zu achten, wie "Wahrheit" und "Geschichte" in der Ankündigung kommender Geschichte aufeinander bezogen sind und inwiefern dann die im Zukunftswort angesagte Geschichte etwas mit "Wahrheit" zu tun hat.

Auch hier möchte sich zunächst der Gesichtspunkt der "Richtigkeit" anbieten. Was vom Propheten richtig angesagt wird — so nämlich, dass seine Ansage stimmt und das von ihm Angesagte nachher geschichtlich eintrifft —, daran möchte sich seine Wahrheit legitimieren. Die durch das folgende Eintreffen bestätigte Geschichtsankündigung wäre danach "wahre" Verkündigung und die so im voraus angesagte Geschichte käme danach in ein Verhältnis zu "Wahrheit" zu stehen. Es fehlt in der Schriftprophetie nicht an Stellen, welche dieses Verständnis der "Wahrheit" von prophetischer Verkündigung zu legitimieren scheinen. In Jer. xxviii 9 ist bei dem dramatischen Zusammenstoss zwischen Jeremia und Hananja im Tempel in dem warnenden Wort Jeremias an Hananja das Kriterium zu hören: "Am Eintreffen des Prophetenwortes wird erkannt werden, ob Jahwe ihn in Wahrheit (*bae'aemaet*) gesandt hat". Es ist das Kriterium, das ganz so auch im Prophetengesetz des Deuteronomiums zu hören ist: "Wenn der Prophet im Namen Jahwes redet und das Angesagte geschieht nicht und es kommt nicht — das ist das Wort,

[11] E. Fascher, ΠΡΟΦΗΤΗΣ. *Eine sprach- und religionsgeschichtliche Untersuchung* (Giessen, 1927).

das Jahwe nicht geredet hat. In frevler Eigenmächtigkeit hat der Prophet es geredet. Fürchte dich nicht vor ihm" (xviii 22). Wer in der Aussage von Jer. xxviii nur eine sekundäre deuteronomistische Bearbeitung meint sehen zu müssen, kann die gleiche Argumentation aus den Worten der Leute heraushören, die Jesaja nach v 19 mit der Aufforderung entgegentreten: "Er beeile doch, er beschleunige sein Tun, dass wir es sehen. Es möge sich nahen, eintreffen der Plan des Heiligen Israels, dass wir es erkennen". Wer hier sagen möchte: Das sind ja nur die von Jesaja in seinem Weheruf angegriffenen Leute, die so denken, der mag die ganz verwandten Stellen Ez. xii 21-25 und 26-28 bedenken, wo dem Propheten ganz analog entgegengehalten wird: "Die Tage ziehen sich in die Länge und die ganze Schau wird zunichte", d.h. das Prophetenwort trifft nicht ein, oder etwas variiert: "Die Schau, die er sieht, geht auf lange Tage und auf ferne Zeiten prophezeit er", hier aber der Prophet selber in schroffen Jahwewort formuliert: "Ich, Jahwe, rede. Das Wort, das ich rede, wird geschehen ... In euren Tagen, Haus Widerspenstigkeit, rede ich ein Wort und tue es". Dieses ist wohl auch ganz im Sinne Jesajas geredet.

Es ist in all diesen Aussagen nicht zu verkennen, dass das prophetische Wort, das auf kommendes Geschehen hinweist, den Anspruch macht, vollen Wirklichkeitsbezug zu haben, nicht leeres, sondern Geschichte wirkendes und dadurch wahres Wort zu sein. Wenn die erste Strophe von Jesajas Strophengedicht mit der Aussage anhebt: "Ein Wort hat der Herr nach Jakob gesandt und es ist niedergefallen in Israel", und dann nachher ausführt, wie das sich stolz erhebende Volk von seinen Feinden angefallen wird: "Aram von vorn (von Osten), die Philister von hinten (von Westen) und sie frassen Israel mit vollem Maul" (ix 7-11), dann ist hier, wenn schon in der Rückschau geredet wird, doch deutlich ausgesprochen, dass Jahwes Wort — und das gilt ganz so für das vorauslaufende Wort — ganz Geschichte wird und Geschichte wirkt. Besonders eindrücklich ist das bei Deuterojesaja festgehalten, dessen Wortsammlung—wer immer die Sammlung vollzogen haben mag — ganz im Sinne des Propheten von Hinweisen auf das Geschichte wirkende Wort Jahwes gerahmt ist. Redet Jes. xl 8 von dem Wort Jahwes, das im Unterschied zu aller Hinfälligkeit des "Fleisches", das wie die Blume des Feldes welkt, bestehen bleibt, so führen lv 10f. es in einem schönen Bilde aus, wie dieses Wort in der Welt wirkendes Wort ist. "Denn wie der Regen und der Schnee vom Himmel herabkommt und nicht dorthin zurückkehrt, er hätte denn die Erde bewässert, sodass sie fruchtbar wird und sprossen lässt und dem Sämann Samen und dem Essenden Brot gibt, so ist mein Wort, das aus meinem Munde geht. Es kehrt nicht leer zu mir zurück, sondern wirkt, woran ich Gefallen habe und lässt zum Erfolg gelangen, wozu ich es gesendet". Das Naturbild von Regen und Schnee veranschaulicht hier, wie das ausgehende Wort — und dabei ist an die Sendung des Propheten zu denken — Geschichte wirkt. Die Wahrheit des jahwegesandten prophetischen Wortes ist im Geschehen leibhaft geworden.

So führt all dieses auf die Formulierung: Durch den Propheten vorausgesagte Geschichte ist Wahrheit? Und umgekehrt: Wahrheit ist nach des Propheten Wort in der Geschichte zu finden? Führt dieses dann nicht stracks auf das Geschichtsverständnis Hegels, wonach der absolute Geist, der Logos in der Geschichte zu sich selber kommt und somit Wahrheit aus der Geschichte zu entnehmen ist, oder, um ein auch in der alttestamentlichen Diskussion vertretenes Programm aufzunehmen: Geschichte als Offenbarung, Offenbarung als Geschichte? [12]

Aber nun steht unter den Prophetenschriften wieder jenes Lehrbüchlein Jona. "Noch 40 Tage, dann wird Ninive zerstört", so hatte das einzige vom Propheten Jona in diesem Büchlein berichtete Verkündigungswort gelautet. Und dann wird das Ninive, das Busse tut, nicht zerstört — zum Ärger und Zorn des Propheten Jona. Wir brauchen aber nicht beim Jonabüchlein allein stehenzubleiben. "Das Ende ist gekommen für mein Volk Israel", lautet die Botschaft der 4. Amosvision (viii 1). Sollte einer sagen: Hier ist gegen Nordisrael geredet, das dann ja auch 722 aus der Geschichte ausgelöscht worden ist, so kehrt die gleiche Botschaft in der für Ezechiel bezeichnenden predigtartigen Ausweitung textartig in Ez. vii wieder: "Das Ende ist gekommen. Gekommen ist das Ende . . . Jetzt steht das Ende über dir und ich lasse meinen Zorn auf dich los und richte dich nach deinem Wandel und bringe über dich alle deine Greuel" (vii 2f.). In diesem Wort, das in Gen. vi 13 seinen auffallenden Nachhall in der priesterschriftlichen Sintfluterzählung hat: "Das Ende alles Fleisches ist .... gekommen", muss unwidersprechlich das Restisrael in Juda gemeint sein. Dann aber ist die Katastrophe von 587 unverkennbar nicht das Ende gewesen. Ezechiel selber schaut in der späteren Phase seiner Verkündigung in den Tagen, in denen das Ende be-

---

[12] W. Pannenberg, *Offenbarung als Geschichte* (Göttingen, 1961).

siegelt zu sein schien, wie Gott die toten Gebeine wieder zum Leben erweckt. Er hört die Verheissung, dass Jahwe das Volk wieder in sein Land zurückbringen werde, ja, er muss mit seiner Verkündigung selber dazu mitwirken, dass das Ende des Hauses Israel nicht sein Ende ist. Wir können auch an Mi. iii 12 denken, wo das Prophetenwort dem Tempelberg ansagt, dass er zur Waldeshöhe werden soll, — und dann ersteht in den Tagen von Haggai und Sacharja auf jener Höhe der zweite Tempel, und dieses erneut unter ausdrücklichem prophetischem Wort.

Diese wiederum mühelos zu vermehrenden Wahrnehmungen nicht oder dann ganz anders erfüllten Prophetenwortes[13] verbieten es, Wahrheit und Geschichte nach dem Wort der Schriftpropheten einfach direkt zu verbinden. Die Wahrheit, welche die Propheten meinen, ist unverkennbar nicht so einfach aus dem Geschichtsverlauf abzulesen. Geschichte ist nicht per se Enthüllung von Wahrheit, so intensiv auch die Schriftprophetie auf Geschichte hin redet.

Man wird in diesem Zusammenhang die Worte, in denen auch die schon erwähnten Propheten von der Verborgenheit Gottes zu reden wissen, nicht übersehen können. Lothar Perlitt hat in der Festschrift für Gerhard von Rad im Gefolge von Äusserungen von Rads von der "Verborgenheit Gottes" gehandelt.[14] Die Erfahrung dieser Verborgenheit kommt beim ersten Jesaja etwa da zum Ausdruck, wo er nach dem syrisch-ephraimitischen Krieg seine prophetische "Weisung" in seinen Jüngern "versiegelt", das gegebene Zeugnis einbindet und von sich selber bekennt: "Ich harre auf Jahwe, der sein Angesicht vor dem Hause Israel verborgen hat" (viii 16f.). Sie verdichtet sich beim zweiten Jesaja geradezu zu dem rätselhaften, staunend-anbetenden Wort, das den von Jahwe herangeholten Fremdvölkern in den Mund gelegt ist: "Fürwahr, du bist ein verborgener Gott, Gott Israels, Retter" (xv 15). Beide Propheten, die doch so voll in die Geschichte hinein ihr Wort, zu dem sie von Jahwe her legitimiert sind, sprechen, wissen von der Verhülltheit Jahwes, dessen Tun und Wesen sich nicht einfach aus der Geschichte ablesen lässt.

Aber damit sind wir, ohne es bisher voll formuliert zu haben,

---

[13] E. Jenni, *Die politischen Voraussagen der Propheten* (Zürich, 1956), ist der Frage der "Erfüllung" des Prophetenwortes einmal im Einzelnen nachgegangen.

[14] L. Perlitt, "Die Verborgenheit Gottes", in *Probleme biblischer Theologie. Gerhard von Rad zum 70. Geburtstag*, herausgegeben von H. W. Wolff (München, 1971), S. 367-82.

schon auf der rechten Spur zur Erkenntnis der Beziehung von Geschichte und Wahrheit nach der Sicht der grossen Schriftpropheten. Es darf hier, ohne dass es voller entfaltet würde, für die alttestamentliche Prophetie im Sinne einer unzweifelhaft gültigen These angenommen werden, dass auf jeden Fall Wahrheit und Jahwe für die Schriftpropheten unlöslich zusammengehören.

Dann aber besagen alle diese Aussagen über die Verborgenheit Jahwes in dem Geschichtshandeln der Tage der Propheten, dass Geschichte keinesfalls in sich als der Offenbarer Jahwes verstanden werden kann. Sie bleibt Jahwe gegenüber. So sehr die Propheten, die von Jahwes Tun künden, auf das geschichtliche Geschehen ihrer Tage weisen, so sehr wissen sie, dass Jahwe über, hinter der Geschichte, die sie erfahren, steht, von ihr erwiesen, aber von ihr auch immer wieder verhüllt wird.

Jes. xiv 24-27, ein Wort, das man dem Propheten angesichts der unnachahmlichen Dichte seiner Sprache, die ganz der Sprache Jesajas entspricht, nicht absprechen sollte, redet vom majestätischen Plan Jahwes in der Geschichte, den keiner zu zerbrechen vermag — dem Plan, Assur zunichte zu machen. Und Jes. viii 9f., das sprachlich ebenfalls genuin jesajanisches Gepräge trägt, ruft in die erregte Völkergeschichte hinein aus, dass alles Planen der tobenden Völker an Jahwes Plan zerbrechen wird. Zugleich aber weiss der Prophet, dass der göttliche Plan für den Menschen Geheimnis bleibt. Fremdartig ist Jahwes Tun (xxviii 21), wunderbar, für menschliches Auge undurchdringlich, sodass "die Weisheit seiner Weisen zunichte wird und der Verstand seiner Verständigen sich verbergen muss" (xxix 14). Nur, wer Jahwe nicht kennt, meint ihn direkt in der Geschichte fassen zu können. Er steht mit all seinem geschichtlichen Planen über, jenseits aller Möglichkeit des menschlichen Errechnens seines Tuns. In dem scheinbar so durchsichtigen Gleichnis vom Tun des Bauern, das in all seinem Wechsel voller verborgener Weisheit ist (xxviii 23-9), hält Jesaja diese verborgene, nur seinem eigenen Planen folgende Weisheit Jahwes fest. Am wechselnden Tun des Bauern ist die Freiheit Jahwes, hinter der doch tiefer Sinn verborgen liegt, zu erkennen. "Wunderbar ist sein Plan, gross seine Weisheit". Nur, wo beides gesagt ist: Geschichte ist für den Propheten Ort des Handelns Gottes, und zugleich: Geschichte ist für ihn Ort der Verhüllung Gottes, ist recht von Jahwe geredet. Mit dieser Aussage entlässt uns Jesaja, der wohl gewaltigste Geschichtsprophet unter den Schriftpropheten.

Aber führt dieses nun nicht in ein unauflösbares Dilemma, wenn wir nach Wahrheit und Geschichte bei den Schriftpropheten fragen?

Richtiger erkennen wir darin ein anderes. "Geschichte" ist für den Propheten sichtlich nicht ein Organon, das als Ganzes in eigener Geschlossenheit — und dann auch Verschlossenheit gegenüber Gott — Jahwe erkennen liesse. Der Raum "Geschichte" darf auch für das Alte Testament nicht dogmatisiert werden. Es ist mit Recht in neuster Zeit, etwa durch die wichtige Arbeit von B. Albrektson,[15] darauf hingewiesen worden, dass auch ausserhalb Israels göttliches Handeln in der Geschichte gefunden wurde, und dass nicht etwa eine Exklusivbeziehung "Jahwe und Geschichte" für Israel reklamiert werden darf. Auf der anderen Seite ist ebenso, besonders nachdrücklich von J. Barr,[16] mit Recht darauf hingewiesen worden, dass etwa in den Psalmen und der Weisheit im Alten Testament auch das Naturgeschehen Ort göttlicher Wirksamkeit ist. Dieses ist dann zweifellos ganz ebenso auch immer wieder Ort der Verhüllung Jahwes. Geschichte ist, das gilt über die Prophetie hinaus für das Ganze des Alten Testamentes, nicht als ein exklusiv in sich geschlossener Ort göttlicher Selbstenthüllung verstanden. Sie ist Werkzeug, Schauplatz göttlichen Handelns — gewiss in der älteren Schriftprophetie zentraler, fast ausschliesslich bedeutsamer Platz dieses Handelns. Deuterojesaja mit seiner starken Einbeziehung des Schöpfungsgeschehens warnt dann davor, in ihr — auch für die Prophetie — den streng ausschliesslichen Ort göttlichen Handelns zu sehen.

In dieser Relativierung will darum "Geschichte" auch da gesehen werden, wo es um die Frage "Wahrheit und Geschichte in der alttestamentlichen Schriftprophetie" geht. Als Schauplatz, Werkzeug göttlichen Handelns will Geschichte auch in der intensiven Geschichtsbezogenheit prophetischer Rede verstanden sein.

In dieser Geschichte nun allerdings, wo des Menschen Entscheidungen gefordert sind, wo über seine Entscheidungen hinaus der Mensch Verfallenheit in Katastrophe und Bewahrung erlebt, hier soll durch der Propheten forderndes und deutendes Wort auch Begegnung mit Wahrheit — der Wahrheit Jahwes erfahren werden. In der Geschichte und ihrem Geschehen lässt die prophetische Verkündigung Israel seinem Gott begegnen.

---

[15] *History and the Gods. An Essay on the Idea of Historical Events as Divine Manifestations in the Ancient Near East and in Israel* (Lund, 1967).

[16] *Old and New in Interpretation. A Study of the Two Testaments* (London, 1966), bes. 3, "The Concepts of History and Revelation", S. 65-102.

So ist es schon bei Amos, wenn er im Hinblick auf die von ihm als nahe bevorstehend erschaute Katastrophe das Jahwewort formulieren kann: "Auf allen Plätzen Klage, auf allen Strassen ruft man: Wehe, Wehe! Und man ruft den Ackersmann zur Klage und zur (Toten-) klage die, welche sich auf (Toten-)klage verstehen. Und in allen Weinbergen schallt Klage, wenn ich durch deine Mitte hindurchschreite" (v 16f.). Dieses "Ich, Jahwe", dem Israel in seinem geschichtlichen Erleben als dessen eigentlicher Wahrheit begegnen soll, ist leidenschaftlich bei Hosea zu vernehmen, wenn er dem Volk, das seine Hilfe bei Assur, beim Grosskönig, sucht, im Jahwewort entgegenhält: "Ich bin wie ein Löwe für Ephraim und wie ein Junglöwe für das Haus Juda. Ich, ich reisse und gehe davon, trage davon und keiner entreisst (mir)" (v 14).

Dieses Ich Jahwes, dem Israel in allem Geschehen, das ihm in seiner Geschichte widerfährt, begegnet, hat sich sprachlich in der spezifisch prophetischen Redeform, für die ich die Bezeichnung "Erweiswort" vorgeschlagen habe,[17] niedergeschlagen. Sie mag ihren ursprünglichen Sitz im Leben im Fremdvölkerwort, wie es etwa in Ez. xxv in einer Mehrzahl von Beispielen begegnet, haben. Sie ist dann auch in die Worte an Israel eingedrungen. So kann es in dem zuvor zitierten Wort vom Tag des Endes, der von Ezechiel verkündet wird, abschliessend heissen: "Ich will deinen Wandel über dich kommen lassen und deine Greuel sollen sich in deiner Mitte auswirken, und ihr sollt erkennen, dass ich Jahwe bin" (vii 4). Diese auffallend eckige Formulierung, die nicht einfach akkusativisch vom Erkennen Jahwes redet,[18] enthält in sich das formgeschichtlich festgeprägte Element: "Ich bin Jahwe".[19] Diese Selbstpräsentation hält eine unumkehrbare Reihenfolge fest, nach welcher Jahwe selber sich in seinem Namen vorstellt und als Person heraustritt. Auch für das geschichtliche Tun Jahwes soll damit diese unumkehrbare Reihenfolge festgehalten werden. Jahwe lässt sich nicht als Objekt fassen. Wohl aber tritt er selber in seinem geschichtlichen Tun aus seinem Geheimnis heraus. Sollte die Vermutung zu Recht bestehen, dass der ursprüngliche Sitz

---

[17] W. Zimmerli, "Das Wort des göttlichen Selbsterweises (Erweiswort), eine prophetische Gattung", *Mélanges Bibliques rédigés en l'honneur de André Robert* (Paris, 1957), S. 154-64 = *Gottes Offenbarung. Gesammelte Aufsätze* (München, 1969²), S. 120-32.

[18] So ist es bei Hosea und Jeremia zu finden.

[19] W. Zimmerli, "Ich bin Jahwe", *Geschichte und Altes Testament. Festschrift für A. Alt* (Tübingen, 1953), S. 179-209 = *Gottes Offenbarung. Gesammelte Aufsätze* (München, 1969²), S. 11-40.

des *'ᵃnî Jhwh* im Leben in der göttlichen Selbstvorstellung in der kultischen Epiphanie zu finden ist, die sich noch im Dekalogeingang spiegelt, so hätten wir hier in revolutionärer Weise das Heraustreten Jahwes in seinem freien Sich-Kundmachen, oder nun eben Sich-Erweisen in den Bereich des unmittelbar vom Propheten angesagten geschichtlichen Geschehen hinaus vor uns.

Wichtiger ist für unseren Zusammenhang die Erkenntnis, dass die Wahrheit der Geschichte, welche die Propheten ankündigen, nicht in einem abstrakt zu erfassenden Wahrheitsgehalt, aber auch nicht in einer ebenfalls neutral verstehbaren, objektivierbaren Weltordnung liegt, sondern in dem in diesem Geschehen Begegnenden. "Wahrheit als Begegnung" hat Emil Brunner seine, wie mich dünkt, schönste kleine Schrift,[20] die ihre Anregungen nicht zufällig dem von alttestamentlichem Wissen her bestimmten Martin Buber verdankt, überschrieben. Die Wahrheit der von den Propheten angekündigten geschichtlichen Ereignisse besteht, so wollen die Propheten sagen, in der Begegnung mit dem in diesen Ereignissen kommenden Jahwe. So ist es in den Gerichtsworten, so aber gleichermassen auch in den scheinbar ganz gegenläufigen Ankündigungen heilvoller Geschichte zu hören. Ezechiels Ankündigung der Wiederbelebung des toten Volkes, die in der Schau der Wiederbelebung des Feldes voller Totengebeine enthalten ist, mündet in die Aussage aus: "Ich lege meinen Geist in euch, dass ihr Leben bekommt, und setze euch in euer Land, und ihr sollt erkennen, dass ich, Jahwe, geredet habe und es tue" (xxxvii 14). Aber auch Deuterojesaja kann das Wunder, dass die Könige der Völker die unter die Völker zerstreuten Israeliten zurückbringen werden, im Gotteswort ausmünden lassen in die Formulierung: "Und du sollst erkennen, dass ich Jahwe bin — dass nicht zuschanden werden, die auf mich harren" (xlix 23). Ja, das unmittelbar darauf folgende Wort kann den Kreis der darin Gott Erkennenden ausweiten: "Und alles Fleisch soll erkennen, dass ich Jahwe, dein Helfer bin, und der Starke Jakobs dein Erlöser" (xlix 26).

Von hier aus hellt sich nun auch das eigentümliche Dilemma auf, dass, der hier Richter war, dort zum Erlöser wird. Dahinter steht keine allgemein zu erschliessende Regel, ein neutral zu fassender Ordnungsgedanke, sondern die Freiheit des Herrn, der nicht unter Regeln gebunden ist, sondern nur an seinen freien Entscheid. So nur

---

[20] *Wahrheit als Begegnung. Sechs Vorlesungen über das christliche Wahrheitsverständnis* (Berlin, 1938).

erklärt sich bei dem Geschichtspropheten Jesaja, dass er, der seinen Sohn Schear-Jaschub genannt hat, worin zunächst die unheimliche Ankündigung des Amos nachhallt, dass nur ein dezimierter Rest die Katastrophe durchstehen wird (Am. v 3), dass der Verkündiger des nahen richtenden "Tages Jahwes" (Jes. ii 11-17) im syrisch-ephraimitischen Krieg, wo das drohende Gericht Gestalt anzunehmen beginnt, dem König Ahas mit der apodiktischen Ankündigung im Namen Jahwes entgegentreten kann: "Hüte dich und bleibe ruhig, fürchte dich nicht ... das wird nicht geschehen noch sich ereignen" (Jes. vii 4, 7). Und dann wird in der Folge der Assyrer als Gerichtswerkzeug Jahwes angesagt — ein Gerichtswerkzeug, das nach späteren Worten des Propheten selber dem Gericht verfallen wird. Noch bei Ezechiel ist auch in den Völkerworten etwas von diesem eigentümlichen Wandel des Gotteswortes zu sehen, wenn die Drohung gegen Tyrus in dem spätesten, ins 27. Jahr Jojachins datierten, deutlich nachgetragenen Wort xxix 17-20 gegen Ägypten gewendet wird. Die Krieger Nebukadnezars, die sich vergeblich an Tyrus abgemüht haben, sollen ihren Lohn in dem Nebukadnezar preisgegebenen Ägypten bekommen.

Wer hier nach einer allgemeinen ratio der Geschichte sucht, wird vergeblich nach ihr suchen. Wer aber in alledem erkennt, dass die Propheten ihr Volk nicht mit einem Logos der Geschichte, sondern mit dem in der Geschichte kommenden freien Herrn konfrontieren wollen, der im Geheimnis seines Planes wohl Macht hat, hier im Gericht, dort in der Errettung seines Volkes sich zu erweisen, der wird auch diesen Wandel, den Jesaja sich mit dem weisheitlichen Bauerngleichnis selber zu verdeutlichen suchte, demütig von der Freiheit des auch im Geheimnis sich selber treuen Herrn her, der selber die Wahrheit ist, verstehen.

All dieses ist kaum richtig verstanden, wenn man etwa Jesaja nun einfach zum Umkehrprediger macht, der dann im Grunde eine konditionale Geschichtsankündigung lautwerden lässt und sich einfach der jeweiligen Situation anpasst.[21] So hat der dtr. Geschichtsschreiber das Phänomen der Prophetie hinterher zu verstehen gesucht. Ansätze dazu finden sich auch beim frühnachexilischen Sacharja (i 3f.). Die tatsächliche Verkündigung der vorexilischen Schriftpropheten ist härter gewesen. Sie hat kommendes Gericht ankündigen müssen. Aber sie hat in dieser Verkündigung den kommenden Herrn

[21] So etwa H. W. Hoffmann, *Die Intention der Verkündigung Jesajas*, *BZAW* 136 (Berlin, 1974).

angekündigt, der wohl Macht hat, wenn es ihm gefällt, das Angekündigte anders einzulösen, als der Prophet selber es meinte. Nochmals ist hier die Gestalt Jonas mit seiner apodiktischen Ankündigung zu nennen. In seinem Ärger, dass Gott sich durch die Umkehr der Niniviten zur Vergebung bewegen lässt, spiegelt sich die Anfechtung des Propheten, der auch in seiner Verkündigung seinen Gott nicht mit einem festen Programm in Händen hat.

Aber ist dieser Gott dann nicht die personifizierte Unberechenbarkeit — kein Gott, vor dem ein Mensch leben kann? In seinen hermeneutischen Erwägungen zu "Wahrheit und Methode" hat H. Gadamer[22] im Gefolge hermeneutischer Einsichten Heideggers herausgestellt, wie alles Verstehen des Menschen, der nun einmal nicht aus der Geschichte aussteigen kann, von einem geschichtlichen Vorverständnis bestimmt ist. Bei der Erwägung der Frage, ob die grossen Schriftpropheten als Wahrheit der Geschichte, die sie ankündigen, nicht lediglich einen Gott des Zufalls und der Laune kennen, darf vielleicht — mit aller vorsichtigen Behutsamkeit — etwas von dieser Sicht hier eingebracht werden. Wir müssen dabei nochmals auf das zurückblenden, was in früherem Zusammenhang bei den Propheten an Wissen um ältere Geschichte erwähnt worden ist. Zu dem von den Propheten eingebrachten Vorverständnis gehört das Wissen um ältere Geschichte Jahwes mit Israel. Schon bei Amos ist zu sehen, dass er von anfänglicher Zuwendung Jahwes zu Israel weiss, der dieses Volk "allein aus allen Völkern" erkannt (iii 2) und die Amoriter, "deren hoher Wuchs wie Zedern und deren Stärke wie Eichen" war, vor ihnen vertrieben hatte (ii 9). Hosea und Jeremia wissen von einer hellen Anfangs-Liebeszeit zwischen Jahwe und Israel zu reden (Hos. xiii 5f; Jer. ii 2f.). Bei Ezechiel reduziert sich dieses Wissen in scharfer theologischer Zuspitzung auf die nur von einer Seite her zu formulierende Aussage, dass Jahwe in den Anfängen Jerusalems bzw. Israels diesem Liebe erwiesen hat, was Israel von seinen Anfängen her mit Undank lohnte (xvi, auch xx). Die Propheten wissen dann auch von schon zuvor ergangenen Gerichten zu reden, die Israel erfuhr, sich aber nicht zur Warnung dienen liess.

Soll man hier von einem Vorwissen, einem eingebrachten Vorverständnis des göttlichen Tuns reden? Beides, das Vorwissen um gnädige, aber dann auch um die eifernde Wendung zu seinem Volk, das dann in den zwei verschiedenen Dekalog-Selbstpräsentationen

---

[22] *Wahrheit und Methode. Grundzüge einer philosophischen Hermeneutik* (Tübingen, 1975[4]).

Jahwes seine klassische Ausformung erfährt (Ex. xx 2/5b), wann immer diese ihre vorliegende Gestaltung erfahren haben mögen, ist im Vorwissen des Propheten beschlossen. Dieses Vorverständnis hat Raum für Gericht und Zuwendung Jahwes gegenüber Israel. Aber der Rückgriff auf dieses Vorwissen vermag zweifellos das Geheimnis der aktuellen prophetischen Ansage nicht aufzuhellen. Wir können nur konstatieren, dass auch die Sendung mit sich wandelnder Botschaft — am deutlichsten bei Jesaja — den Propheten nicht in seinem Gottwissen zerreisst, oder ihn zum Relativisten oder skeptischen Gottesverehrer macht. An der Einheit des Planes des Herrn, der seine Boten zu verschiedener Zeit mit verschiedenem Auftrag aussendet, besteht für ihn nie ein Zweifel. Jenes Bauerngleichnis, welches das Rätsel des göttlichen Planes zu umgreifen sucht, endet in derHaltung der Anbetung des göttlichen Geheimnisses und seiner alle Menschenweisheit übergreifenden Weisheit.

Damit aber rückt die Prophetie mit ihrer Gotteserkenntnis ganz in die Nähe der Gotteserkenntnis der im übrigen scheinbar so ganz anderen, geschichtslosen Weisheit, deren Summe in dem thematisch die Proverbien einleitenden Satz: "Die Furcht Jahwes ist der Weisheit Anfang" befasst ist (i 7). Die Sprüche, Kohelet, Hiob und die Weisheitspsalmen akzentuieren diesen Satz je auf ihre eigene Weise. Neben die zurückhaltende Scheu des Kohelet tritt das leidenschaftliche Sich-Anklammern an den Verborgenen, den Hiob seinen "Zeugen" im Himmel (xvi 19) und seinen *gō'ēl* "Löser" (xix 25) zu nennen wagt, und der sich dann im Sturmwetter seinem Knecht in seiner Majestät antwortend zuwendet (xxxviii 1ff.). Proverbien und Weisheitspsalmen aber mahnen zum Vertrauen, das in der Gottesfurcht beschlossen ist, wobei die Zerreissprobe angesichts des Geheimnisses des Verborgenen nur selten, etwa in Ps. lxxiii erkennbar wird.

Von dem im Geheimnis Verborgenen, und sich dann doch je neu seinem Volke Zuwendenden redet auch die grosse Schriftprophetie als der verborgenen "Wahrheit" der erregten Welt- und Israelgeschichte, in die hinein zu reden sie in den Geschichtsstürmen des 8. bis 6. Jahrhunderts aufgeboten ist. Die Geschichte ihrer Tage wird ihnen in ihren Katastrophen, aber dann auch ihrer erneuten Lebenseröffnung Wahrheit, weil sie in ihr der Wahrheit des lebendigen Gottes begegnen, der im Gericht tötet, aber durch das Gericht hindurch lebendig zu machen vermag, und der es auch tut.

ISAIAH I-XII: PRESENTATION OF A PROPHET

by

PETER R. ACKROYD

London

The completion in 1972 of the first part of Hans Wildberger's commentary on Isaiah, extending to nearly 500 pages for the first twelve chapters of the book,[1] would suggest a measure of impertinence on my part in proposing in this relatively short discussion to deal with the same group of chapters. On a pro rata basis, it might be thought more judicious for me to devote the whole of my time to the consideration of one half verse! But the task which I have set myself is not that of commentary. It involves some wider considerations regarding the nature and function of Isa. i-xii. It also involves questions which go beyond not only i-xii but also i-xxxix, and which indeed raise doubts about the propriety of a method which makes the assumption, as so many commentaries and works of introduction do, that it is possible to consider Isa. i-xxxix as a book separate from the whole in which it is now contained. Such an assumption is so commonly made that it is well to examine once again its propriety and justification.

I

James Barr in his book *Fundamentalism*, in the context of considering how what he terms "residual fundamentalism" survives, points to the belief in such circles that "the whole book of Isaiah is still somehow linked to the prophet of that name".[2] Elsewhere he discusses what he terms "maximal conservatism", that process by which, if it is forced upon the conservative scholar that, for example, Moses really cannot be responsible for the book of Deuteronomy as it stands, then that view of its origin is to be preferred which takes it

---

[1] *Jesaja 1-12* (Neukirchen, 1972).

[2] *Fundamentalism* (London, 1977), p. 157. The same phrase is used by R. F. Melugin, *The Formation of Isaiah 40-55*, *BZAW* 141 (1976), p. 176, in the context of some sensible concluding comments to his discussion of the structure of those particular chapters. Cf. also below.

back nearest to his authorship (pp. 85-9). So too what he says about the view of the book of Isaiah as "somehow linked to the prophet" may be seen as an example of the way in which traditional authorship and hence traditional authority may be regarded as upheld, even where the findings of critical scholarship inevitably force the recognition that the book of Isaiah is really not all of one piece.

The problem arises when we begin to attempt a definition of that phrase "somehow linked". So much of critical scholarship is still geared to the classic formulations that it is sometimes felt to be hardly necessary to concern ourselves with such apparently outmoded lines of thought. I propose to raise some of these questions because I consider them important; I do not for one moment fear that anyone will suppose that I am thereby disclosing myself as a biblical fundamentalist, though I may have to accept the dubious distinction of being misquoted as having abandoned one of the key points of critical scholarship.[3]

The divison of the book of Isaiah into two major sections, i-xxxix and xl-lxvi, has withstood the test of time; the further subdivision of the latter into xl-lv and lvi-lxvi less well, and the problem of interrelationship between those two sections remains unresolved.[4] The points of linkage between chapters (xxxiv) xxxv and xl-lv or xl-lxvi raise important questions;[5] much of the more recent work on i-xxxix has pointed to very considerable difficulties in the way of the oversimple subdividing of that part of the book.[6]

---

[3] For the quotation of critical scholars by fundamentalist writers, to undergird a position not intended by the scholar quoted, cf. e.g. R. K. Harrison, *Introduction to the Old Testament* (Grand Rapids, 1969), and E. J. Young, *An Introduction to the Old Testament* (London, 1960). Both books contain numerous examples of this procedure, designed to suggest that fundamentalist scholars take critical work seriously, and by implication that critical scholars do not trouble to read the fundamentalist works. At least Barr's volume gives the lie to the latter contention.

[4] Cf. e.g. O. Kaiser, *Einleitung in das Alte Testament* (Gütersloh, 1969), pp. 222-24; ([3]1975), pp. 247f.; E.T. by J. Sturdy, *Introduction to the Old Testament. A Presentation of its Results and Problems* (Oxford, 1976), pp. 268-71.

[5] Cf. e.g. C. C. Torrey, *The Second Isaiah* (New York, 1928); J. D. Smart, *History and Theology in Second Isaiah: A Commentary on Isaiah 35, 40-66* (Philadelphia, 1965).

[6] For the presence of elements in i-xxxix akin to xl- lv, cf. e.g. O. Kaiser, pp. 175f.; E.T. pp. 225f. The presence of other late elements is commonly assumed: cf. e.g. H. Barth (see n. 9), and G. Fohrer, "The Origin, Composition and Tradition of Isaiah I-XXXIX", *ALUOS* 3 (1962), pp. 3-38, see pp. 6-23; German text "Entstehung, Komposition und Überlieferung von Jes 1-39", *BZAW* 99 (1967), pp. 113-47, see pp. 117-34. More generally, cf. J. H. Eaton, "The Origin of the Book of Isaiah", *VT* 9 (1959), pp. 138-57.

So far as the formation of the whole book is concerned, it is impossible to be satisfied with what we may term the "accident" theory. It is mere supposition to suggest that, assuming a normal lower and upper limit for the length of a scroll, there were four prophetic scrolls containing respectively Isa. i-xxxix, Jeremiah, Ezekiel, and the Twelve, and that of these texts the first, being so much shorter in compass, resulted in a large empty space, and that this was filled, arbitrarily, by the insertion of another collection of prophecy, eventually to be known as chapters xl-lxvi.[7] A more careful expression of this by O. Eissfeldt runs as follows: "... our book of Isaiah, in addition to the sections which are at least in the main concerned with the prophet of the second half of the eighth century B.C. who bears this name (or are regarded as concerned with him), namely i-xxxix, contains also the two complexes xl-lv and lvi-lxvi. These belong to a substantially later date, and ... were only secondarily added to i-xxxix and so came to be ascribed to the eighth-century prophet".[8] There is some question-begging here. It is, of course, true that the two complexes xl-lv and lvi-lxvi are of "a substantially later date" than the prophet Isaiah whose activity belongs to roughly 740 to 700 B.C. But study of i-xxxix has shown how complex a structure this is, and even if extremes of late dating are dismissed -partly now because of the Qumran scrolls—it can hardly be supposed that its compilation really antedates the compilation of the one or two further complexes in xl-lxvi. This could be shown by a consideration of a whole range of recent literature, but it will be convenient to point to the study of H. Barth [9] which attempts to trace aspects of the process by which i-xxxv (xxxix) reached its present form. His main concern is with an "Assyrian" redaction which he associates with the period of Josiah's successes and the collapse of Assyria, 621-614 or 616 B.C. But in the process, he suggests (and illustrates diagrammatically) stages in the evolution of i-xxxv down to the post-exilic period. The whole discussion works from the assumption that such a division of the book is a primary datum for its examination. At the very end of his study, he expresses the "accident" theory in a

[7] Cf. R. H. Pfeiffer, *Introduction to the Old Testament* (New York, 1941), pp. 447-48. O. Eissfeldt, *Einleitung in das Alte Testament* (Tübingen, [3]1964), pp. 465f.; E.T. by P. R. Ackroyd, *The Old Testament: an Introduction* (Oxford, New York, 1965), p. 346—a view that Eissfeldt sets out but rejects as improbable.

[8] p. 406, see also p. 466; E.T., pp. 302, 346.

[9] *Israel und das Assyrerreich in den nichtjesajanischen Texten des Protojesajabuch* (Diss. Hamburg, 1974).

new manner, in the form of a question to which further research is invited. "The redaction-history of the book of Isaiah was not indeed at an end with the formation of the complex i-xxxv. Along with the historical appendix of xxxvi-xxxix there were added xl-lxvi, and it is a difficult question to decide on what grounds this last extension was undertaken. Is it possible—and this final point is put forward with the utmost caution as one for discussion—that we here have an attempt at structuring the book of Isaiah in the familiar three parts known already from Ezekiel and Jeremiah (LXX): i (ii)-xii doom for his own people; xiii-xxxv (xxxix) themes concerning foreign nations; xl-lxvi salvation for his own people?" (p. 232—my translation). This represents an attempt at giving some sort of rationale for the accident theory; but that is what it remains. The motivation for the addition of xl-lxvi is external to the book, based here, very tentatively, on the analogy of the book of Ezekiel and one form (LXX) of the book of Jeremiah. But is the analogy valid? Granted that the LXX form of the book of Jeremiah places the foreign nation oracles in the middle, it is very difficult to maintain that the division of the book really corresponds to such a schema as is often proposed for such a tripartite form. Indeed one may wonder whether the two forms of the book of Jeremiah, whichever may be held to have priority, do not indicate rather the existence of two basic Jeremianic collections, totally different in kind, to which the foreign nation oracles have been added in two different manners: (1) Jer. i-xxv which is in character much more like other prophetic books, and which reaches its climax in the pronouncement of judgement on Babylon and on the nations (xxv)—the LXX form provides in part a substitute for this last point and in part a very elaborate extension of it; and (2) Jer. xxvi-xlv, which consists of a collection of narratives illuminating the disaster (xxvi-xxxvi) plus an appendix which is a variant form of the end of 2 Kings (xxxvii-xliv) [10] plus a colophon in xlv which is closely linked to xxxvi. The MT form of the book apparently has no regard for the supposed tripartite division. Why does the MT ignore the pattern, if indeed such a pattern exists?

The book of Ezekiel comes nearest to the pattern, but it must be noted that even here i-xxiv is not totally doom and xxxiii-xxxix is certainly not totally salvation; and the appendix in xl-xlviii does not come satisfactory within that term. An analogy for the supposed

---

[10] Cf. my "Historians and Prophets", *SEÅ* 33 (1968), pp. 18-54, see pp. 43-53.

tripartite arrangement may be sought in the book of Zephaniah where we may divide i 2-ii 3 as doom to Judah; ii 4-iii 10 as doom for the nations; iii 11-20 as salvation for Judah: but this too is less than certain.[11] Amos has the foreign nation oracles at the beginning; Nahum, if it may be included, has its one such complex at the end; Obadiah has a pattern of doom on Edom followed by restoration for Judah. Is there really adequate evidence for such a supposed pattern at all? And certainly in the book of Isaiah, while it is true that there is a collection in xiii-xxiii (xxvii) which is primarily concerned with foreign nations, it is not in fact so limited, having, uniquely among such collections, two passages—xx and xxii 15-25 (and possibly we should add also xxii 8b-13 and the curious and problematical xiv 28) [12]—which introduce the direct activity of the prophet (not actually mentioned in xxii but implied because of the reference to the contemporaries Shebna and Eliakim);[13] nor can it be properly said that i-xii is really entirely doom on Judah, nor that xiii-xxxv (xxxix) is concerned only with the nations, and even xl-lxvi has elements of doom, particularly in lvi-lxvi. These generalizations do little that is satisfactory in the categorizing of prophetic material. The whole tripartite pattern appears to be a modern invention.

There is a further supposition which needs a question. It is the commonly affirmed belief that, to quote Eissfeldt again, "... The presence of xxxvi-xxxix ... shows that at one time the book of Isaiah must have ended with xxxv. The narratives have been appended at the end of a book" (p. 408; E.T., p. 304). There is one analogy and one only for this: the presence of Jer. lii as a historical appendix at the end of the book of Jeremiah. But this differs in a marked respect from Isa. xxxvi-xxxix. Jer. lii contains no reference to the prophet; it is an extract from the last part of the books of Kings, in a recension slightly different from that which we have there.[14] It does not show that remarkable intertwining of the activity of the prophet with the course of events which is so important a part of Isa. xxxvi-xxxix. This equally is an extract from a particular recension of the books

---

[11] So A. van der Woude in the discussion of this paper, referring also to W. Rudolph, *Micha-Nahum-Habakuk-Zephanja* (Gütersloh, 1975), p. 255.

[12] The proposed emendation *wāʾeḥ^e^zeh* (J. A. Bewer) would introduce the prophet here.

[13] Cf. xxxvi 3, 22, xxxvii 2. The relationship between these passages and xxii is by no means clear.

[14] The reason for the addition of Jer. lii is not at all clear.

of Kings; equally it shows important differences.[15] But here the figure of the prophet has already come to occupy a primary place, and the passage is much closer in form and style to Jer. xxxvii-xliv which may itself be regarded as such an extract, but from a fuller and more elaborate recension of Kings than that which we know directly (see n. 10). The analogies we have for the insertion of prophetic narrative material, in prophetic books, suggest their placing at significant points, designed to illuminate the context into which they are put. The function of Isa. xxxvi-xxxix must be discussed separately;[16] I have elsewhere examined some aspects of the function of Amos vii 9-17.[17] Some further comments will be made below on Isa. vi 1-ix 6. A consideration of the Isaiah narrative material in chs. xx and xxii could throw light on why those passages stand where they do and what function they may be held to perform. There is a possible connection here between the structuring of the prophetic books and the function of prophetic narratives in the Deuteronomic history.[18]

II

These considerations are preliminary to the asking of a fundamental question: Why is there so substantial a book associated with the prophet Isaiah? The accident hypothesis is in reality ruled out partly by the various critical considerations just raised, but also by the fact that the interrelationship between the various elements in the book is such as to point to some degree of affinity or influence or connection of thought and language.[19] It is not in any way to concede the fundamentalist position if we recognize that the arguments for the unity of Isaiah, inadequate as they are, are not mere figments

[15] Cf. e.g. B. S. Childs, *Isaiah and the Assyrian Crisis* (London, 1967); P. R. Ackroyd, "An Interpretation of the Babylonian Exile: A Study of 2 Kings 20, Isaiah 38-39", *SJT* 27 (1974), pp. 329-52.

[16] Cf. my paper "Isaiah xxxvi-xxxix: Structure and Function" read at the January 1978 meeting of the Society for Old Testament Study. Cf. also Melugin, op. cit., p. 177.

[17] "A Judgment Narrative between Kings and Chronicles? An Approach to Amos 7:9-17", in G. W. Coats and B. O. Long (ed.), *Canon and Authority: Essays in Old Testament Religion and Theology*, presented to Professor W. Zimmerli (Philadelphia, 1977), pp. 71-87. Reference may also be made to significantly placed narrative material in Hosea, Jeremiah, Ezekiel and Haggai.

[18] Cf. the article by I. L. Seeligmann in this volume.

[19] Cf. e.g. D. R. Jones, "The Traditio of the Oracles of Isaiah of Jerusalem", *ZAW* 67 (1955), pp. 226-46, see p. 245. I should express the relationship less precisely than in terms of knowledge on the part of Deutero-Isaiah of a definable Proto-Isaianic collection.

of conservative imagination. There are linkages between all parts of the book.[20] I do not propose to pursue the matter here, but simply cite as examples two points: (1) the often noted use of the expression *q^edôš yiśrā'ēl*. If we follow Wildberger's analysis (p. 23), we may observe four occurrences in i-xii (two "genuine", two doubtful or later), one in xiii-xxvii (doubtful), five in xxviii-xxxv (four "genuine", one doubtful—all in fact in xxix-xxxi), one in xxxvi-xxxix (also in 2 Kings); eleven in xl-lv; two in lvi-lxvi. This expression occurs otherwise only in Jer. l 29 and li 5 in the Babylon oracles, virtually certainly later than Jeremiah and perhaps to be associated in some degree with the Deutero-Isaianic circle,[21] and in three psalms—lxxi 22, lxxviii 41 and lxxxix 19. We may agree with the view that the expression belongs to the Jerusalem cultus, but its marked use in Deutero-Isaiah points strongly to a degree of affinity between that part of the book and Proto-Isaiah. (2) The relationship between xxvii 2-5 and v 1-7, and that between xi 6-9 and lxv 25 demand a recognition of the interrelatedness of otherwise quite widely disparate sections. If such alternative uses of the same themes are deemed to be unrelated we may still, as a very minimum, argue for the propriety with which later material—whether in the so-called apocalypse of xxiv-xxvii, or in the collection in lvi-lxvi, or in the glossing, if such it is, of xi 1-5 with xi 6-9—has been associated with already existing material whether Isaianic in the sense of "genuine" prophetic oracles or in the sense of already belonging to an Isaianic tradition. I shall consider a third type of link later.

But the problem still remains: Why, alone among the eighth century prophets, has Isaiah acquired so enormous a prophetic collection now associated with his name and "somehow" linked to him? It is begging this question to say, as G. Fohrer does; "... in the later period, Isaiah was often considered the prophet par excellence".[22] That he was so considered is likely itself to derive in part

---

[20] Cf. e.g. J. A. Soggin, *Introduction to the Old Testament*, translated by J. Bowden (London, 1976), pp. 318f.; O. Eissfeldt, p. 466; E.T. p. 346. Also J. Becker, *Isaias—der Prophet und sein Buch* (Stuttgart, 1968), pp. 33ff.; L. J. Liebreich, "The Compilation of the Book of Isaiah", *JQR*, N.S. 46 (1955/56), pp. 259-77; 47 (1956/57), pp. 114-38.

[21] Cf. e.g. A. Weiser, *Das Buch Jeremia* (Göttingen, [6]1969), p. 427. W. Rudolph, *Jeremia* (Tübingen, 1947), p. 256, suggests links with Isa. xiii-xiv and notes *q^edôš yiśrā'ēl* (l 29, li 5) as Isaianic. It is, of course, frequent in later material in the book of Isaiah (see above).

[22] *Einleitung in das Alte Testament* (Heidelberg, 1965), p. 411; E.T. by D. Green, *Introduction to the Old Testament* (Nashville, 1968; London, 1970), p. 375.

from the very attribution to him of so large a collection; and the fact that traditionally the book of Isaiah heads the "latter prophets" may be held to contribute to this or to follow from it. We need some evidence to suggest why he came to be so regarded and why this attribution of material to him actually came about. It is towards the answering of this question that I propost now to devote some attention, first in general terms and second in relation to i-xii.

It is of course arguable that Isaiah was the most significant of that astounding group of four men—Amos, Hosea, Micah and Isaiah. But on what basis can such an assertion be made, except by a circular argument from the book itself? The Isaianic corpus itself suggests his greater status, the other collections are modest in extent. But a consideration of the material which may with reason be treated as "genuine"—a very precarious method, but still a fashionable one—does not immediately mark him out as more remarkable than his near contemporaries. A sober assessment would neither exaggerate nor depreciate his status in that period. But there are some further factors to take into account.

We may perhaps give weight to the fact that Amos and Hosea belong by their message to the now defeated northern kingdom. Yet this disaster to the north could be seen to confirm the validity of their message and this may provide one clue to the process by which that message came to be handed down in a more tangible form than those of their predecessors in the preceding century. Why can we see some indications of continuing influence—Hosea on Jeremiah and Ezekiel, Amos possibly on Isaiah[23] and Zephaniah, but only a modest extension of the collections of oracles associated with them? Micah, associated with a place outside Jerusalem, is often depicted as a prophet of the countryside, set in contrast to the capital. Isaiah is said to be close to the court and the temple, though the evidence for both has been questioned. Did this give him a status, independent of whatever might be his official position, if any, which assisted both the preservation of his message and its amplification? Yet in making this comparison we must take account of the claim made by the tradition preserved in Jer. xxvi 17-19.[24] Here appeal is made by "certain of the elders of the land", clearly men of status, to the effect that it was when Micah of Moresheth prophesied in the reign of Hezekiah

[23] Cf. R. Fey, *Amos und Jesaja. Abhängigkeit und Eigenständlichkeit des Jesaja* (Neukirchen, 1963).

[24] Cf. also the comments of H. W. Wolff in this volume.

of Judah, pronouncing doom on Jerusalem and its shrine, that the king, so far from putting him to death, in fact feared Yahweh and propitiated him, so that Yahweh repented of the calamity which he had pronounced against them. Since we have elsewhere a tradition of reform by Hezekiah, simply stated in 2 Kings xviii 4-5 and greatly elaborated in 2 Chron. xxix-xxxi, but in neither case in any way associated with Isaiah, we might tentatively draw the conclusion that in the tradition utilized by Jer. xxvi, that reform was associated with the activity of Micah. Equally we might postulate some other situation in the reign of Hezekiah, entirely unknown to us, and associate that with Micah's words. But in either case it is evident that for this tradition the status of Micah is extraordinarily high, that is, when we compare it with the status which is suggested by the quite small collection of prophecies associated with his name. Other traces of a broader Micah tradition have been lost except perhaps for the curious association of his message with a stylized judgement:

> and one kept the statutes of Omri,
> even all the deeds of the house of Ahab,
> and you walked in their counsels (vi 16)

a judgement which looks suspiciously like an alternative form to that which becomes the stereotype for Deuteronomic judgement of the northern kingdom.[25] By contrast, the status of Isaiah, while unaltered by the Micah tradition, since the reform is not associated with Isaiah anywhere, is put into a clearer perspective. It was to Micah not to Isaiah that later tradition was to attribute a major alleviation of threatened disaster for Jerusalem and its temple.

Now this is a very remarkable fact. It suggests that whatever the ultimate assessment of these two prophets was to be, there was a moment when it could have been Micah who acquired the greater reputation rather than Isaiah. To redress the balance, we must set over against this the important fact that alone among the prophets, with the sole exception of Jonah ben Amittai in 2 Kings xiv 25—an exception which by its equivocal character serves to prove the rule—Isaiah appears in a narrative series in 2 Kings xviii-xx which has a variant form in Isa. xxxvi-xxxix. I would myself qualify this statement

[25] Cf. J. L. Mays, *Micah* (London, Philadelphia, 1976), p. 148. Note also the extension of the Micah tradition implied in 1 Kings xxii 28 which cites Mic. i 2, thus claiming identity for Micaiah and Micah, a point which might be linked to this curious element in Mic. vi 16.

by reiterating that in fact Jer. xxxvii-xliv provides us with another such integrated narrative, in which the prophet appears bound up with the account and interpretation of the events of Judah's downfall (see no. 10), and more tentatively I would point also to Amos vii 9-17 for yet a further clue.[26] But neither of these alters the fact that in the form of the Kings text which has come down to us it is the prophet Isaiah who is given a commanding position in relation to crucial events in the reign of Hezekiah: a significant part in the sequence which traces the threats and withdrawal of the Assyrians, and a yet further importance as the prophet of life and death and of ultimate disaster in the exile (see n. 15). We can see in 2 Kings xviii-xx = Isa. xxxvi-xxxix the growth of a significant Isaiah tradition, generally recognized as providing us with little information of substance about the actual figure of the prophet, but undoubtedly a vital link in the growth of the concept of his status as prophet. That growth we may associate with his place in relation to the Davidic house and the Jerusalem temple; we may understand it in relation to the evidently historical fact that in spite of siege and the imminent threat of total disaster, Jerusalem did not actually suffer the fate of Lachish. The Isaiah tradition of these chapters in fact conflicts rather sharply with the doom-laden oracles of what are generally held to be genuine Isaianic material, such as the relentless judgement of vi, the impression created by i 4-8 with its possibly appended alleviation in i 9, though even that is dire enough, the dark message of xxix 1-8 with Jerusalem brought low, speaking from the earth. Its growth may be in part associated with that aspect of the modification of the Isaianic message which Barth attributes to the Assyrian reaction; the downfall of Assyria, seen in actuality in the latter part of the seventh century, is here projected into the moment of Isaiah's triumphant message to Hezekiah and his taunt-song over the king of Assyria. It provides at the same time a link between that and the moment of judgement in the Babylonian conquest, thus providing for an undergirding both of the prophet's message of doom—it was not to be at the hands of Assyria but at those of Babylon—and pointing beyond to a moment of new life in the use of the illness and recovery, death and life theme, given fuller point in the Isaiah text by the inclusion of the psalm which emphasizes just these themes.[27]

[26] See my article on this (see n. 17).
[27] See my article in *SJT* (see n. 15), p. 345.

III

Here then we have an important factor in the understanding of how Isaiah acquired status. It is, I believe, of further importance in relation to xl-lxvi, but that I shall not now explore (see n. 16). Before moving on to the next main point that I want to make, I would like to comment briefly on two other lines of thought which may be used to account for the Isaianic corpus and the enhanced status of the prophet.

(1) In a number of recent studies, R. P. Carroll has judiciously examined the value which dissonance theory may have for the interpretation of the prophetic literature.[28] The failure of the prophetic message, the non-fulfilment of pronouncements of doom or promise, invite the response of transposition of these to a new level, the reinterpretation of particular sayings with reference to situations further into the future. Carroll makes particular use of the book of Isaiah in examining the usefulness of this approach, drawing attention to the totality of judgement in vi 9-13, contrasting this with the salvation oracles attributed to Isaiah and also to the call to turn from evil in i 16f.[29] He understands vi as providing mature reflection on the nature of the prophet's call, suggesting that the failure of his proclamation has been resolved by the affirmation that it was indeed his mission to produce precisely this effect. He further observes that "this general failure of preaching eventually led Isaiah to retire from active proclamation and to seal up his teaching among his disciples" (viii 16-18).[30] Carroll here contributes to the discussion of the nature of reinterpretation, whether this is undertaken by the creator of the oracles himself or by later editors. He suggests how we may see that the recognition of failure, the non-fulfilment of the message, may itself be a criterion of later success, of confirmation of the validity of the message. Yet it is evident that there must be more to the matter than this. There must be some underlying acknowledgement of the status of the prophet—a status which is not under-

---

[28] "Prophecy, Dissonance and Jeremiah XXVI", *TGUOS* 25 (1973-74 [1976]), pp. 12-23; "Ancient Israelite Prophecy and Dissonance Theory", *Numen* 24 (1977), pp. 135-51. Dr Carroll has also kindly lent me the first draft of a chapter entitled "Text and Interpretation" from a proposed book, provisionally entitled *Prophecy, Dissonance and Hermeneutic*, and I am glad here to acknowledge the stimulus of his discussion.

[29] So op. cit. (*TGUOS*), p. 19; (*Numen*), p. 144. On the theme of repentance in Isaiah, cf. H. W. Hoffmann, *Die Intention der Verkündigung Jesajas*, *BZAW* 136 (1974).

[30] Loc. cit. (*Numen*).

mined by failure, but which can lead to reinterpretation so that ultimately a pronouncement will be seen to be fulfilled. In other words, the original status of the prophet is a necessary element in the continuing reinterpretation of his words; at the same time that continuing reinterpretation itself contributes to the enhancement of his status by providing confirmation in eventual fulfilment of the validity of what he said. Such an approach contributes to our understanding of the processes of thought by which both the prophet himself and his later editors may be motivated in their handling of material which is problematic; by reinterpretation the prophetic word is given new impetus and the prophet's status is raised. For Isaiah, it would be important to show that the prophet had a recognized status, from which vantage point it became desirable for him and for his successors to offer such an enhancing reinterpretation. To some extent we may recognize the presence of the same problems in the other prophets of the period, particularly in Micah. The approach does not therefore deal fully with the question of why Isaiah is so much enhanced and not Micah.

(2) Allusion is made also by Carroll to a point which has much engaged other interpreters of Isaiah, namely the committal of his words to disciples in viii 16-18. For Carroll, this is a good example of withdrawal on the part of one whose message has been found to be unfulfilled, "of recourse to social support among a group of sympathetic followers whose agreement with the prophet could stimulate him and detract from his failure".[31] I would not wish to quarrel with the contention that support from others is a necessary element in dealing with the problem of religious isolation. We may see it in the narratives of Elijah, where the claim to total loneliness in his allegiance to God is countered by the evidently symbolic reference to 7000 faithful (1 Kings xix 14, 18). We may see it in the indications of the tension between isolation and support in the Jeremiah tradition: certain aspects of that tradition stress the dereliction of the prophet, other elements show the degree to which there were those who were on his side—Uriah a like-minded prophet, Baruch a scribe turned associate, the politically powerful family of Shaphan, and even at times the vacillating king Zedekiah. In the case of Isaiah, the evidence is less than clear. Of associates we know of Uriah the priest and Zechariah ben Jeberechiah, "reliable witnesses" (viii 2) but perhaps

[31] Loc. cit. (*Numen*).

"associates" is too strong a word for these. We know of the "*y^e^lādîm* whom Yahweh has given me" (viii 18), but not whether *y^e^lādîm* actually means "children"—such as Shear-jashub and Mahershalal-hashbaz—or "associates, followers, disciples". The reference in viii 16 to "bind the testimony,[32] seal the instruction *b^e^limmūdāy*" is also obscure. It does not for our purpose matter whether the actions are real or symbolic.[33] The similar expression in xxix 11-12 does not clarify the matter, and in any case looks suspiciously like a reinterpretation of the former. The further usages of *limmūd* in l 4 and liv 13 point to the meaning "instructed", as does also Jer. xiii 23. The negative interpretation of LXX (*tou mē mathein*) does not help resolve the problem of why the preposition is *b^e^*, and its negative sense "so that they are not taught" looks suspiciously like an interpretation in line with vi 9f.

We are confronted here with two elements of interpretation. There is the commonly held notion that Isaiah withdrew from public ministry. But this is not warranted by the evidence of the text. The fact that we have no historical references in the Isaianic material for the period between the Syro-Ephraimite war in the reign of Ahaz (so vii and viii) and the threat to Ashdod in 713-711 (so xx) is no basis for the supposition that Isaiah did not speak publicly during that period. We have little basis for allocating prophetic oracles to precise occasions anyway, even if we accept as correct such historical attachments as are provided. There is also here the point of attachment for the often elaborated view that there was a "school of Isaiah", responsible ultimately for the handing on of his prophetic message, for its elaboration, and in the fullest view of this, providing a context for the activity of his successors in Deutero- and Trito-Isaiah.[34] But such

[32] Or "message", cf. H. M. I. Gevaryahu (see n. 34).

[33] Cf. Wildberger, p. 345, who makes use of O. Eissfeldt's suggestion (*Der Beutel der Lebendigen* [Berlin, 1960], pp. 26f.), that the reference is to a bundle or bag tied up, and hence a metaphor for preservation. This would in fact make it clear that there are here two distinct metaphors—the tied bag and the sealed document—both emphasising preservation intact. For other comments, cf. e.g. D. R. Jones, op. cit., pp. 232ff. Cf. also viii 1 and xxx 8 which indicate the actual writing of brief statements, though direct deductions cannot be made from this to the interpretation of viii 16.

[34] Cf. e.g. S. Mowinckel, *Profeten Jesaja. En bibelstudiebok* (Oslo, 1928); *Jesajadisiplene. Profetien fra Jesaja til Jeremia* (Oslo, 1926); *Prophecy and Tradition* (Oslo, 1946); D. R. Jones, op. cit.; and cf. his "Exposition of Isaiah Chapter One Verses One to Nine", *SJT* 17 (1964), pp. 463-7, see p. 465: "...the book of Isaiah... is the corpus of oracles of a school of prophets, brought into being by Isaiah ben Amoz and therefore standing under his name". J. H. Eaton, op. cit.; O. Eissfeldt,

a school is in reality a deduction from the present form of the book.[35] It may find a point of attachment in viii 16; even if that passage is partly discounted because of uncertainty, we are still in some degree forced both with Isaiah and with other prophets into the view that there must have been those who heard the message and preserved it. There must have been a succession within which the message could be reapplied and reinterpreted. All the discussions of the gradual shaping and reshaping of the Isaianic material, as of other prophetic traditions, point to the existence of such tradents, editors, glossators, and the like. It is to such activity that we owe the prophetic books. But when all that has been said it is evident that this applies to all the prophetic books, and it still provides no real answer to the problem of why the Isaiah tradition grew to such immense proportions.

I want to suggest that a clue may be found in the actual structure of i-xii, and that this section, separable from what follows, provides a presentation of a prophetic figure and validates his authority in a particular manner.

IV

The structure of the book of Isaiah raises many questions to which answers can be given only very tentatively. The conventional divisions are not entirely satisfactory, with the one clear exception of xxxvi-xxxix, where the fact that these chapters appear in another form in 2 Kings makes their demarcation obvious. The conventional division after xxxix raises difficulties because of the admitted links between the following chapters and xxxv at least and probably xxxiv too.[36] Evidence from structure as distinct from content could prompt a division of xl-lxvi not as is normally made into xl-lv and lvi-lxvi, but into xl-xlviii, xlix-lvii, lviii-lxvi, on the grounds that each of these three sections has an identifiable colophon: xlviii 22 *ʾên šālôm ʾāmar yhwh lārᵉšāʿîm*; lvii 21 identically, except for *ʾᵉlôhāy* for *yhwh*; and

Einleitung, p. 466; E.T., p. 346; J. Becker, op. cit. p. 40. For a similar attempt, cf. also H. M. I. Gevaryahu, "The School of Isaiah: 'Biography', Transmission and Canonization of the Book of Isaiah", a lecture delivered at New York University, April 1976, of which the author has kindly lent me a copy. He hopes to publish this shortly.

[35] Cf. also the criticisms of Fohrer, *Einleitung*, p. 410; E.T., p. 375, though these are weakened by his arbitrary excision of the word *bᵉlimmūdāy*.

[36] The strength of the position maintained by Torrey and Smart (see n. 5) derives from their recognition of this relationship, though the arguments for a literary unity consisting of (xxxiv) xxxv + xl-lxvi are by no means strong.

lxvi 24, admittedly different, yet making more elaborately the same point that those who rebel against God will know no rest.[37] It is relatively easy to affirm that these colophons are the work of a later editor; less easy to discover what particular purpose was being served by them. It may be more appropriate to ask whether they may not shed light on the structure of the book at one stage of its formation, being markers at the ends of sections.

Division within i-xxxiii(xxxv) is again clear at certain points only. Titles at i 1, ii 1 and xiii 1 have been seen as indicating the beginnings of sections. I shall consider the first two of these in a moment. The title at xiii 1 coincides with a very marked break in content, introducing the well-defined section which begins here and which is characterized by the repeated use of the technical term *maśśā'*.[38] But where this section ends is open to debate. Conventionally it has been thought that xiii-xxiii offers the foreign nation oracles collection, followed by an "apocalyptic" section in xxiv-xxvii. This is then followed by another collection xxviii-xxxiii (xxxv), built around an Isaianic nucleus.[39] But it must be admitted that there are no very clear lines of demarcation. The so-called foreign nation section includes a number of odd elements: xiv 28 (if the text is correct)

[37] Cf. B. O. Banwell, "A Suggested Analysis of Isaiah xl-lxvi", *ET* 76 (1964-65), p. 166, who proposes a division xl-xlviii, xlix-lvii, with xl as introduction; and lviii-lxvi as a third unit. Cf. F. Rückert, *Hebräische Propheten* (Leipzig, 1831). (I have not been able to consult this, but cf. J. Muilenburg, "Isaiah 40-66", *IB* 5 [Nashville, 1956], p. 384). Cf. also A. Schoors, *Jesaja* (Roermond, 1972), ad loc., and especially p. 346: "...at a certain stage in the redaction, someone wished to articulate the point at lxviii 22 and lvii 21 so as to anticipate lxvi 24. This last verse is differently formulated, but expresses the same idea in an even stronger form" (my translation). Cf. the further comment by Schoors on p. 391.

[38] *maśśā'* occurs in xiii 1, xiv 28, xv 1, xvii 1, xix 1, xxi 1, 11, 13, xxii 1, xxiii 1, also in xxx 6. This last occurrence, introducing the oracle on Egypt of xxx 6-7, may point to a misplacement from the original context in xiii-xxiii, but it equally suggests the possibility that the arrangement of the whole complex from xiii to xxxiii is not simply to be understood in the neat subdivisions often proposed. On a link between xiii-xxiii and xxviii-xxxiii, cf. O. Kaiser, *Der Prophet Jesaja, Kap. 13-39* (Göttingen, 1973), p. 3; E.T. by R. A. Wilson (London, 1974), p. xi.

[39] So e.g. H. Barth, op. cit., p. 362, n. 2, who accepts as assured the commonly held view (cf. B. Duhm, *Das Buch Jesaja* [Göttingen, [5]1968], pp. 17, 64) that there are two Isaianic nuclei: vi 1 - viii 18* (ix 6); xxviii (1)7b - xxx 17. Even O. Kaiser (op. cit., [3]1975, pp. 205f.; E.T., pp. 234-6), with his more radical critique of the Isaianic corpus, holds that the latter contains a nucleus of Isaianic sayings; Kaiser (*Introduction*, p. 224; cf. *Einleitung*, [3]1975, p. 208) now holds that the former does "not contain any genuine Isaianic material". Cf. also O. Kaiser, "Geschichtliche Erfahrung und eschatologische Erwartung. Ein Beitrag zur Geschichte der alttestamentlichen Eschatologie im Jesajabuch", *NZSThR* 15 (1973), pp. 272-85. On this section, see some further comments below.

introduces a *maśśā'* associated with the moment of the death of king Ahaz; xvii (especially verses 4-11) contains elements of judgement on Israel and Judah and an attack on irreligious practices akin to i 29-31, and in verses 12-14 a theme suggestive of the onslaught and overthrow of the nations not unlike both psalm passages which deal with this (e.g. Ps. xlvi) and the narrative of the overthrow of Assyria in xxxvii; xviii 4 introduces an oracle described as delivered to the prophet presented in the first person: "Thus Yahweh said to me"; xx describes a symbolic action performed and interpreted; xxii is a very complex section in which any specific reference is absent in the opening verses, and which then moves over to reflection on Jerusalem's lack of trust in God and reliance on preparations for siege; in xxii 15-25 there are two sections concerned with particular individuals, Shebna and Eliakim. While it is true that xxiv-xxvii lack any specific reference, so that various suggestions have been made for identifying particular elements, it can hardly be maintained that this is necessarily more "apocalyptic" than some of what precedes. And a division between these chapters and xxviii-xxxiii (xxxv) is again not entirely satisfactory (cf. Kaiser—see n. 38). While we here return to the more specific, in judgements on the north, on Judah and Jerusalem, and in words of promise, we find another of the *maśśā'* type passages in xxx 6-11, perhaps deliberately transposed to this point. It is difficult not to feel that some passages, particularly in xxx-xxxiii, are again as much like apocalyptic as are parts of xxiv-xxvii.

By contrast, i-xii or i + ii-xii stand out as clearly marked off. But here there is a further problem. This is the occurrence of titles both at i 1 and ii 1. The often propounded view that i is introductory to the prophecies of Isaiah [40] has certain attractions; yet it may be wondered whether it really is such an introduction, or whether it may not be better understood as a coherent collection of sayings, built of various small units into a structure which can stand alongside other such structures discernible within i-xii.[41] The title at i 1 may be

[40] Cf. G. Fohrer, "Jesaja 1 also Zusammenfassung der Verkündigung Jesajas", *ZAW* 74 (1962), pp. 251-68, and further references there.

[41] All the arguments adduced by Fohrer (see n. 40) to explain the content and arrangement of the material in this chapter appear to be equally valid to the view that this chapter, together with ii 2-5 as he believes to be proper—as I do also—, form a small coherent collection. It does not summarize the teaching of Isaiah as that was traditionally understood any more than the other small collections in i-xii might be supposed to do; and it is introductory only in the sense that it stands first. For a presentation of Isa. i 1-31 as a coherent structure, cf. A. Mattioli, "Due schemi letterari negli oracoli d'introduzione al libro d'Isaia Is. 1, 1-31",

designed to cover the whole book—we have seen the uncertainty attaching to the supposition that there was an earlier complete book ending at xxxv; or it may cover simply the first section, ending at xii.[42]

The title at ii 1 complicates the issue. Its presence allows the supposition that i is a preface added later; it may then be regarded as the title to a small collection, though opinions differ as to how far this collection extends—to some point in iii, iv, v or even later.[43] The argument of this discussion would not in fact be fundamentally affected if we were to treat the unit as ii-xii rather than i-xii, but I should like nevertheless to look a little more closely at the occurrence of this title at ii 1 since I believe it may serve to underline the point which I wish to make.

I have argued elsewhere, and still believe rightly, that the title in ii 1 is intrusive, breaking the more natural link between the oracle of ii 2-4(5) and the groups of sayings which form i.[44] So far as I am

Rivista Biblica 14 (1966), pp. 345-64; L. G. Rignell, "Isaiah Chapter 1. Some exegetical remarks with special reference of the relationship between the text and the book of Deuteronomy", *StTh* 11 (1957), pp. 140-58, affirming complete unity and close links especially with Deut. xxviii-xxxii; R. J. Marshall, "The Structure of Isaiah 1-12", *Bibl. Res.* 7 (1962), pp. 19-32, see p. 28 on i 2-20.

[42] There are many interesting comments on titles and colophons in H. M. I. Gevaryahu, "Biblical Colophons: A Source for the 'Biography' of Authors, Texts and Books", *VTS* 28 (1975), pp. 42-59, and cf. also the lecture noted in n. 34. But the marked differences between the titles in the prophetic books and the colophons adduced as parallels, as well as the lack of real evidence of the transfer of "colophons" to become "superscriptions", make me very doubtful about the fuller extension of his investigations. Cf. the useful critical comments by G. M. Tucker, "Prophetic Superscriptions and the Growth of a Canon" in *Canon and Authority* (see n. 17), pp. 56-70, esp. pp. 66f.

[43] The variety of views here is considerable. Fohrer (in the article cited in n. 40, pp. 252f.) allows for it having originally referred to ii-iv and subsequently, with addition of v-x, to ii-x. Wildberger, p. 81, leaves the question open, noting only that xiii begins a new collection. Kaiser (commentary p. 17; E.T., p. 23) considers that the agreement of content suggests that the collection contained the various sections of v, ix 8-21 and x 1-4, and even that it contained the substance of x 5ff. and xiii-xxxii. Schoors, pp. 35f., thinks of ii-xii or ii-x, but also suggests that it originally belonged to ii-v, while i 1 formed the original heading to vi when, as he supposes, this chapter stood at the beginning of the book. But the arguments for this are not strong.

[44] "A Note on Isaiah 2 1", *ZAW* 75 (1963), pp. 320-21. L. G. Rignell, op. cit., p. 141 considers that the title at ii 1 refers only to the prophecy which follows in that chapter, while treating i 1 as title to i-xii. Cf. also R. B. Y. Scott, "The Literary Structure of Isaiah's Oracles", H. H. Rowley (ed.), in *Studies in Old Testament Prophecy presented to T. H. Robinson*, (Edinburgh, 1950), pp. 175-86, see p. 177, who thinks it a possible view that the "editor is claiming for Isaiah what he knows is also credited by others to Micah".

aware, only Wildberger has devoted some space to refuting this contention (p. 77), but I do not think his arguments are convincing. He makes three points: (1) I suggested that the title is in reality a marginal note, the affirmation of what I described as "one of the first literary critics", that this oracle, occurring also in Mic. iv, is really Isaiah's. Wildberger thinks that "such a 'literary critic' would have made his meaning clear". It is not evident to me how, lacking the modern practice of footnoting and cross-reference, he could have done this more clearly. The annotator would simply be providing an introduction to the oracle that it is "the word (*dābār*) which Isaiah ben Amoz spoke concerning Judah and Jerusalem". It uses *dābār* which makes a good reference to a single oracle [45] rather than *ḥāzôn* (i 1) which clearly here designates a whole prophetic corpus or message. (2) Wildberger considers that such an annotator "would hardly have mentioned Isaiah yet again with his father's name". But we may note that such apparent superfluity of reference is to be found in 2 Chron xxxii 20, 32; xxvi 22, as also in Isa. xiii 1; xx 2, and in the parallel texts of 2 Kings xix 2, 20; xx 1 = Isa xxxvii 2, 21; xxxviii 1. It would appear that it was more natural to refer to Isaiah with the patronymic than without. The name Isaiah alone, without patronymic, appears in narratives which continue from a mention of the name with patronymic (so 2 Kings xix 5, 6 = Isa. xxxvii 5, 6; 2 Kings xx 4, 7 = Isa. xxxviii 4, 21; 2 Kings xx 11; xx 14 (+ *hannābî'*) = Isa. xxxix 3; 2 Kings xx 16, 19 = Isa. xxxix 5, 8). The only exception is Isa. vii 3, but this too stands in the middle of a narrative, though it is one in which the prophet has not so far been mentioned.[46] On the evidence, it would have been more surprising if the father's name had not been mentioned. (3) Wildberger contends that "the links of subject-matter between ii 2-4 and i prove nothing, since the theme 'Zion' is so very frequent in Isaiah". This latter statement is true enough, and I did in fact myself point to the not altogether dissimilar structure in iii-iv where a more complex passage dealing with Jerusalem leads up to the promise in iv 2-6 of what Zion is

[45] But, as in Hos. i 1, it can evidently denote a collection.

[46] On the opening verses of vii, see below. The material which directly concerns Isaiah begins with verse 3, but it is evident that this does not mark the original opening of a narrative, since the unexplained presence of Isaiah's son Shear-jashub presupposes that some other account, offering an explanation of the origin of that evidently symbolic name, must originally have preceded this. It remains one of the unexplained oddities of the Isaianic material that this particular element has not survived.

eventually to be. This does not, however, affect the point that the passage ii 2-4(5) stands adjacent to i where the Jerusalem theme is used, and that this theme does not reappear in the remainder of ii. The question may, in fact, be put another way round by asking why this particular oracle was placed here. It does not properly serve to introduce the rest of ii, [47] but it may be seen to perform a function here in the book of Isaiah not unlike that which it performs in the book of Micah. In Micah the oracle provides a counter to the doom oracle on Jerusalem which reaches its climax at the end of Mic. iii; the same oracle in Isa. ii provides both a counter to the doom sayings of i and a climax to the promises of a new and faithful Jerusalem which appear there in verses 26-28.

It still seems to me to be more natural to suppose that a later scribe, aware of the double occurrence of the oracle, claimed it for Isaiah by the simple device of attaching to it a heading almost identical to that in i 1, without the chronological information and using *dābār* rather than *ḥāzôn*. But I would wish now to take this further and to qualify my own suggestion somewhat. This insertion may be seen not so much in terms of the activity of a "first literary critic", but—since I am less than sure that such questions arise except in relation to concerns with authority—rather as part of a process of claiming a particular kind of status for the prophet and a particular kind of authority for this collection as a whole. It is, I believe, geared to the presentation of the prophet as authoritative spokesman.[48]

V

The collection in Isa. i-xii is circumscribed by both its beginning and its end. The title in i 1 makes this clear, using *ḥāzôn* in a way characteristic of the later handling of the prophetic material. Here the relevance of the same phrase in 2 Chron. xxxii 32 is clear: the remaining deeds of Hezekiah are recorded in the *ḥāzôn* of Isaiah, within the book of the kings of Judah and Israel. This is the under-

---

[47] F. E. Deist, "Notes on the structure of Isa. 2:2-22", *Theologia Evangelica* 10/2-3 (1977), pp. 1-6, attempts a structural analysis of the whole chapter, but in fact treats verses 2-5 as a "liturgical quotation", so that unity is only partially assumed. No relationship between 2-5 and 6-22 is really established in either case. R. Lack, *La Symbolique du Livre d'Isaïe. Essai sur l'image littéraire comme élément de structuralisme* (Rome, 1973), pp. 36f., links ii 2-5 to ii 6-iv 1 by the use of images. Cf. also J. Becker, op. cit., pp. 46f.

[48] Cf. also G. M. Tucker, (n. 42), p. 70.

standing of the whole message and activity of the prophet in one term.[49]

The end of the collection is marked by the appearance in xii of psalm material. An examination of this suggests some points of interest and relevance. Whatever may need to be said about the earlier stages in the formation of the Isaianic material—and here I have in mind those many studies which have attempted to describe more precisely redactional or interpretative activity and to explore the contexts in which such activity took place [50]—the placing of this psalm material at this point and the clearly indicated new start in xiii 1 invite us to look back over what precedes as a whole. It is also clear that we need to take account of other aspects of the structure of i-xii in considering this, for if, as seems likely, we may trace within those chapters a number of smaller groupings, even if some are now dislocated, we may need to recognise xii as having originally formed the climax to such a smaller unit rather than to the whole of i-xii. Such small units may be detected in i 2—ii 4(5), as just suggested; in ii 6-22 where the final obscure verse invites contemplation on the frailty and ephemeral quality of human life, contrasted with the immediately preceding recognition of the sole exaltation of Yahweh, using one of the refrain or echo elements of the probably complex structure of this passage;[51] iii 1-iv 6 forms another such unit, though it is also possible to divide at iii 15, where iii 13-15, with their partial reminiscence of Ps. lxxxii provides a picture of Yahweh as the exalted judge. The structure of the following chapters is more involved,[52]

---

[49] Against Schoors, op. cit., p. 26, who argues that the title "vision" is not suitable for the whole collection i-xii. "The great vision of Isaiah is chapter vi. It is thus evident that this title originally introduced that chapter. Later chapters i-v were inserted between the title and vi-xii so that i 1 came to function for the whole of i-xii" (my translation). But this overlooks the point that whereas *ḥāzôn* is used in i 1, as indeed it is used also in Obad. 1 and Nah. i 1 and in 2 Chron. xxxii 32, of a total prophetic collection, the vision in vi is described with the use of *rā'āh* not *ḥāzāh*.

[50] Cf. e.g. H. Barth, op.cit.

[51] Deist (see n. 47) describes this verse as a concluding "liturgical plea", but it appears to have a moralising tone rather than a liturgical form.

[52] An alternative approach is to treat the units in i-xii as being i-vi and vii-xii, the latter sometimes being described as the "book of Immanuel". A recent study is that of E. Testa, "L'Emmanuele e la Santa Sion", *Studii Bibl. Franc. Lib. Ann.* 25 (1975), pp. 171-92; but his analysis into Zion themes and David themes leaves considerable gaps in the material of these chapters. R. J. Marshall, op.cit., argues for a greater unity noting correspondence between ii, iv (exaltation of Jerusalem and the temple) and ix, xi (the theme of David), and suggesting the insertion of vi-viii (21). He sees verbal links between v 30b and viii 22 and notes also the link of *nēś* in v 26, xi 10 and xi 12.

though it has most often seemed proper to see a central unit, vi 1—viii 18 or better vi 1—ix 6, which breaks an already interwoven "woe" complex (v 8-24 + x 1-4) and a doom poem v 25-30 + ix 7-20), introduced by v 1-7 and concluded in x 4b by the refrain of the doom poem. A convenient link is provided in the "woe" opening of x 5 for a section which extends to xi 16: judgement on Assyria issues in the theme of new Davidic monarchy, of the gathering of the dispersed, and a second exodus comparable with the first (xi 16); it is to this last that it is possible to see xii as original colophon, and the exodus echoes make the particular passage appropriate, but we may see a further appropriateness in the passage as linked to the whole presentation of the message of Isaiah in i-xii.[53]

It is commonly held that xii consists of two short psalms or sections of psalms: xii 1b-3 and 4-6. This division is based largely on the opening of verse 4 which appears to introduce the second extract just as verse la introduces the first. We may note, however, that these introductory phrases, if that is what they are, differ: 1a has the singular verb *wᵉʾāmartā*, 4b the plural *waʾᵃmartem*.[54] We might have expected two such introductory phrases in the same section to have the same form. The plural of 4a might be by attraction to the plural verb of verse 3 (*ûšᵉʾabtem*), but then we may wonder whether an alternative division could not be made: 1b-2 as one unit in the first person singular, 3-5 a unit in the second person plural. But this leaves us with an isolated verse 6 which uses the second person feminine singular (referring to Zion). Such attempts at analysis strongly suggest that we should better treat the whole passage as a unit, introduced only by the summons of 1a. As so often in the psalms, there is a progressive shift in the thought: it moves from the first person spokesman of 1b-2, however he may be designated, to the summons to the peoples in 3-5, and from this again to the summons to Zion in 6. Such a progression occasions no real surprise

---

[53] Cf. O. Procksch, *Jesaja I* (Leipzig, 1930), p. 161; "it appears. . . . that (Isaiah's) book is evaluated as a *maʿyan hayyᵉšûʿāh*"; L. Alonso-Schökel, "Is. 12: De duabus methodis pericopam explicandi", *VD* 24 (1956), pp. 154-60, see p. 160; J. Steinmann, *Le Prophète Isaïe. Sa Vie, Son Oeuvre et Son Temps* (Paris, 1950), pp. 342f.; P. Auvray, *Isaïe 1-39* (Paris, 1972), p. 149; J. Becker, op.cit., p. 52.

[54] Alonso-Schökel, p. 156 compares *ʾāmartā* with the use of comparable formulae in xxiv-xxvii (xxv 9; xxvi 1; xxvii 2) and suggests that the same redactor might be responsible for the addition of this psalm as added psalm material there. But in fact only xxv 9 is really comparable so far as formula is concerned.

and no awkwardness when the poetic structure and thought are appreciated.[55]

We may then ask whether there is any particular significance in the choice of this psalm passage to stand here, now as colophon [56] to i-xi. We may observe that the passage taken as a whole has some marked similarities to other psalms,[57] notably in verses 2 and 5 to that in Exod. xv [58] and that verse 3 could continue the exodus theme of verse 2 by alluding to that of water from the rock,[59] though it may be proper to see here also a reference to the water rituals of Tabernacles.[60] Verses 4-5 utilize the common psalm themes of the exaltation of God and his glorification among the nations; what he has done for Israel is to be of significance for the whole earth. The climax in verse 6 of the rejoicing of Zion uses yet another familiar theme, emphasizing the presence in Zion of the "holy one of Israel". A consideration of these themes in relation to the preceding chapters shows some points of interest.[61] The exodus theme is not an Isaianic one, though it is to be found in the clearly later material in xi 16.[62] We may observe, however, that the final passage in xi 11-16 which speaks of the gathering of the scattered remnant provides an echo to the indications of judgement at the hands of both Assyria and Egypt in the preceding material—Assyria most prominently, either directly or by implication, Egypt clearly in vii 18-19.

---

[55] Alonso-Schökel finds the unity of the psalm by his "artistic analysis". His sensitive treatment of the literary structure and of the various motifs and their development contrasts very sharply with the view of the psalm as a "mosaic" (so Duhm) and with that of Steinmann (op.cit., pp. 342f.) who regards it as "un type de prière passe-partout".

[56] The term is used loosely rather than precisely.

[57] Links also with Ps. cv 1, cxlviii 13, Isa. xxxv 10, lv 1 are suggested by Duhm; but it must be admitted that some of the links depend on common psalm phrases and others are not really very close.

[58] On the text here, cf. S. Talmon, "A Case of Abbreviation Resulting in Double Readings", *VT* 4 (1954), pp. 206-8; "Double Readings in the Massoretic Text", *Textus* 1 (1960), pp. 144-84, see p. 163, comparing MT and IQIsa[a] for Isa. xii, MT and Sam for Exod. xv.

[59] Cf. Schoors, p. 96, who sees allusion to the theme of Yahweh as living water and to the stream in Jerusalem (cf. Isa. viii etc.).

[60] Cf. S. Mowinckel, *Psalmenstudien* II (Oslo, 1922), pp. 100f.; *The Psalms in Israel's Worship*, translated by D. R. Ap-Thomas (Oxford, 1962), I, pp. 123, n. 58, 131, 187.

[61] So Alonso-Schökel, pp. 159f.; R. Lack, p. 57, suggesting links of xii 2, 4, 5, to ii 6ff.; xii 3 to viii 6ff., xii 6 to vi 11, iii 25f.; and also clues here to xxiv-xxvii and a link between xii 1 and xl 1.

[62] Cf. R. J. Marshall, pp. 24ff. on the process by which, with this psalm, the "Jerusalem theology" of Isaiah is modified by references to "covenant theology".

The Zion theme of xii 6 is a clearly Isaianic one, and such a climax to the section if very fitting. The themes of the sole exaltation of Yahweh and of acknowledgement of him and his deeds by the nations, are again used directly or indirectly in i-xi—the former clearly in ii 6-22 and elsewhere, the latter in ii 2-4(5) and in xi 10 and 11-16. If, observing the usage of the psalms, we see in the first person singular forms of xii 1b-2 the figure of the king, acknowledging the moment of divine anger which is now past and the restoration which is thus implicit, there is a link to ix 1-6 and xi 1-9, as well as to the whole structure of the section vi 1—ix 6.

But quite apart from these rather generalized points, there are two which are more specific. (1) The one is the divine title *qᵉdôš yiśrāʾēl*. We have already noted the significance of this title, traceable to Isaianic material and providing a link to the later elements in the book, particularly to xl-lv. Here, to be placed alongside the three psalms in the Psalter which use the expression, is another psalm which further exemplifies the context of its use. (2) The other point is the threefold occurrence in verses 2-3 of the noun *yᵉšûʿāh*, with its clear link to the name of the prophet *yᵉšaʿyāh*, *yᵉšaʿyāhû*.[63] The statistics of the use of the root *yšʿ* show a considerable preponderance of use in the Psalter and in the book of Isaiah, with Judges, Samuel and Jeremiah as the other books in which there is substantial use.[64] Bald statistics are misleading. The frequent occurrence of the root in Judges and Samuel is clearly geared to the presence in those books of numerous narratives which stress how God delivered his people.[65] Usage in the book of Isaiah needs to be described more exactly: the root *yšʿ* is entirely absent from i-xii aprt from xii 2-3 and the prophet's name. The noun *yᵉšûʿāh* occurs in xxv, xxvi and xxxiii, none of which can be considered to be genuine Isaiah; it then occurs in xl-lxvi. The hiphʿil of the root occurs in Isa. xix, xxv, xxxiii (xxxvii-xxxviii), xxxv + xl-lxvi. Only the nipḥʿal occurs in Proto-Isaiah (xxx 15).

[63] Schoors, p. 97, states: "certain writers even contend that the frequent occurrence of *yᵉšûʿāh* in verses 2-3 contains an allusion to the name of Isaiah". He refers only to Alonso-Schökel, op.cit., who refers to Procksch. A similar point is made by Auvray, p. 151.

[64] *TWAT* I (1971), p. 786, (F. Stolz) notes 354 occurrences of the root, not including proper names: 136 in Pss., 56 in Isa., 22 in Judg., 20 each in 1 Sam., 2 Sam. and Jer. There are small numbers of occurrences in other books. For a much fuller discussion of *yšʿ* and related words, cf. J. F. A. Sawyer, *Semantics in Biblical research. New Methods of Defining Hebrew Words for Salvation* (London, 1972).

[65] 2 Sam. xxii (Ps. xviii) contains a number of these.

The noun *yešaʿ* occurs in xvii 10 (hardly Isaianic) and in xl-lxvi. Two points may be made about this distribution and its significance. First, it must be observed that the root *yšʿ* is very much a word belonging to psalm-language, and its appearance in Isa. xii, probably also in xxv, xxxiii, xxxviii, and fairly clearly in xxxv + xl-lxvi may be seen as derivable from the psalms which are so clear an influence in these texts. Second, we may ask legitimately whether the large-scale use of the root in the book of Isaiah, outside the genuine Isaianic material (other than the single example of xxx 15 where the word is used in fact in a secular sense "be safe" rather than with any reference to the idea of divine salvation) may not owe something at least to the actual name of the prophet. How far may we associate one aspect of the development of the Isaiah tradition with the consideration of the significance of that name just as the tradition already contains interpretation and/or reinterpretation of the names Shear-jashub, Immanuel and Mahershalalhashbaz? [66] We have no means of knowing how the prophet himself viewed his name; the negative evidence of his non-use of the words associated with it implies that it did not enter his thought patterns. But for certain stages of the Isaiah tradition, may we not see here an element in the process by which this one prophet of the eighth century acquired a status which owed something to theological reflection, and thus contributed, alongside

[66] The general significance of names is clear from many narratives of name-giving. In the case of Isaiah, there is the additional point that there are three symbolic names in vii 3—Shear-jashub, unexplained but reinterpreted in x 21 as part of the unit x 20-22 (23), and there may be a further stage of reinterpretation in xi 11, 16, though the root *šûb* is not used there; vii 14—Immanuel, reinterpreted in viii 10; viii 1—Mahershalalhashbaz, not alluded to except in the short account of this symbolic naming. (Cf. R. Lack, pp. 42-52, on v 25 - ix 6 as a unit on this basis). We may therefore consider it not improbable that such a reinterpretation also took place in relation to Isaiah's own name (Cf. Alonso-Schökel, p. 159, commenting on his view that chapters vii-xii are "sub signo nominum", with the persons involved as signs (viii 18), the interpretation of the sons of the prophet; "yet, while all the names are explained, the name of the prophet alone lacks an interpretation". He notes also the emphasis on the name of God in verse 4, as also on the titles of the deity in verse 2). Name-interpretation is also marked in later material in the book, e.g. lx 14; lxii 4. In relation to the root *yšʿ* we might also consider the possible degree to which the name *yᵉhôšūaʿ*, in view of its links to exodus and land themes, might have contributed to the development of *yšʿ* usage in Isa. xl-lxvi, though the name of Joshua itself hardly occurs outside the books from Exodus to Joshua. A comparable link might be sought in the use of the root *ḥzq* in relation to Ezekiel in iii 14, cf. also iii 7-9, ii 4, though the relatively frequent use of this root in other passages in the book, unrelated to the prophet himself, makes this much less striking.

other elements, to the eventual primacy of position which he occupied? [67]

If there is validity in these contentions, there is strong inference that xii provides an interpretative comment on what precedes, drawing out in a final poetic statement the broadest significance of the prophet's person and message. Title and colophon together make a claim for his status, and the inserted note at ii 1 then stands as an additional underlining of the appeal back from the present structure to the prophet who stands as a shadowy figure of authority in the background.

VI

It must be observed that the information provided by these chapters about the prophet himself is minimal. A typical opening to a commentary [68] on a prophetic book is to attempt an outline of the prophet's life and activity. But certainly in the case of Isaiah, and in fact this is true even of Jeremiah where much more information appears to be available, there is too little tangible evidence, and any presentation of the figure of the prophet is only possible as the one who stands behind the present structure. The information provided by xxxvi-xxxix cannot be satisfactorily co-ordinated with what else is known, and it is this in part which provides problems for the interpretation of the prophet's personality and status. Outside those chapters, only the barest information is available in xx, and even less in xxii. No other direct indication is given of the prophet, who is not mentioned by name after xxii. In i-xii, apart from the titles, the only section which provides some tangible points of contact with the context of his activity is vi 1—ix 6. This provides an authenticating statement of his divine commission in vi;[69] a brief account of controversy with Ahaz in vii, where we may probably detect two separate elements in verses 3-9 and 10-17; a symbolic action witnessed, performed and interpreted in viii 1-4; and an allusive passage in viii 11-18 which indicates at the outset a moment at which Yahweh

---

[67] Cf. also Ben Sira xlviii 20: *wayyôšîʿēm beyad yešaʿyāhû.*

[68] So e.g. Schoors, pp. 11-14. The title of Steinmann's volume (see n. 53) suggests a degree of knowledge that we do not possess.

[69] The literature on this topic is immense, but I would refer here to B. O. Long, "Reports of Visions among the Prophets", *JBL* 95 (1976), pp. 353-65, see pp. 360f., and his comment: "The traditions and the literary form of vision-report work together to legitimate the claim of Isaiah to a prophetic office and to give a documentary explanation for his message of evil". Also his "Prophetic Authority as Social Reality", in *Canon and Authority* (see n. 17), pp. 3-20, esp. pp. 11-13.

"spoke to me at the taking of the hand", which most naturally suggests a moment of commissioning, and which subsequently, as we have seen, deals with the preservation of the message of the prophet and the status of himself and the *yelādîm* as signs and portents in Israel.

We may observe that this central section provides some historical attachment: it is in the year that king Uzziah died (vi 1);[70] it is in the days of Ahaz, at the time of the Syro-Ephraimite coalition's threat (vii 1-2), a situation also envisaged in the interpretation of the symbolic action in viii 1-4. While the first of these provides only the barest chronological note—and its precise significance in relation to the material which follows in vi remains a matter of debate [71]—the reference to the period of Ahaz in vii 1-2 is of a different kind, being a shorter and variant form of the account of Ahaz' reign which appears in 2 Kings xvi 1-5. We may note a number of points in this section vi 1 - ix 6: (1) the complex nature of the material in vi, with its probable reflection on the interpretation of the prophetic activity of Isaiah;[72] the structure of vii 1 - viii 10 in which there is a twofold theme of encounter between Ahaz and Isaiah and a twofold statement of speedy judgement on Aram and Israel in that double material on the one hand and the opening of viii on the other; (2) the further reflection on the nature of the prophetic commission and message in viii 11-18, followed by the very obscure passage in viii 19-23; (3) the final element in this section in ix 1-6 which may well have been

[70] I may here acknowledge that the stimulus for some elements in this discussion derives in part from A. Schoors, "Isaiah, the Minister of Royal Anointment?", *Oudt. Stud.* 20 (1977), pp. 85-107. This was read at the joint meeting of the Dutch and British Old Testament Societies in Leuven in 1976. Dr Schoors kindly supplied me with a copy of the proof of this article which has enabled me to take more exact note of a number of the points which are relevant here. For the historical attachment, cf. his discussion on pp. 99-101, and also his reference to H. Cazelles, "Jesajas kallelse och kungaritualet", *SEÅ* 39 (1974), pp. 38-58 (cf. L.-M. Dewailly, *RB* 82 [1975], p. 455). The association of vi with the anointing of Uzziah's successor by the prophet Isaiah is followed on pp. 102-6 with a consideration of wider Davidic elements in the following chapters.

[71] Cf. Schoors, *Oudt. Stud.*, pp. 99f.

[72] Schoors, *Oudt. Stud.*, p. 92, n. 27, mentions my own conviction that vi is a complex structure, "composite as to its literary origin". Attempts at categorizing the chapter (see n. 69) suggest that it is by no means easy to find a satisfactory form-critical or literary analysis. If Schoors is right in contending that Isaiah is here presented as "the minister of royal anointment", then it would hardly appear likely that the doom material of verses 9-13 belongs originally to such an occasion. As the chapter now stands, the expected pronouncement of blessing and hoped for well-being, appears to be lost, replaced by words of doom; it might be found in ix 1-6, whether that is Isaianic or not, as a counter to the indications of unfaithfulness in the Davidic house in vii 1 - viii 23. Cf. also below.

placed thus because it was thought to provide a comment on the status of Hezekiah, already perhaps in this passage beginning to acquire the exalted character which appears more fully in xxxvi-xxxix and still more clearly in 2 Chron. xxix-xxxi and especially in xxxii.[73] All these suggest that this section of the complex i-xii is already a highly stylized structure, directed towards establishing the relationship between the prophet Isaiah and successive rulers of the Davidic house. Relationships may be suggested to the themes of the Davidic dynasty as these are set out in 2 Sam. vii and xxiii 1-7.[74]

VII

It falls beyond the scope of this discussion to attempt more than a brief characterization of the other main sections of Isa. i-xii, and any such sketch will inevitably do less than justice to the content and function of such smaller units. Nor is it possible here to consider in greater detail indications of the ways in which the units are built up, the separable elements within them, and the problems which arise immediately any attempt is made at judging what parts of the material may be associated more rather than less directly with the prophet of the eighth century. We may observe something of the main elements, treating of larger rather than smaller units for this purpose.

The opening section, which I delineate as i 2 - ii 5,[75] stands now as an appeal and a promise: Jerusalem the unfaithful and judged city of God, over which the lament of i 21ff. is pronounced, is to be the true and faithful city, the centre of the religious life of the world. The incorporation in this section of judgement oracles on Jerusalem and Judah, of radical questions regarding the nature and status of the worship of the temple, of attacks on idolatrous practice, makes it appear much more than the often supposed introduction to the book (cf. nn. 40 and 41). Without attempting to resolve the questions which would be raised by pointing to the inclusive structure of the whole book of Isaiah, I would point to the number of points of

---

[73] For the later stages, cf. my discussion in *SJT* (see n. 15), pp. 351-2, with some reference to relevant rabbinic material.

[74] Cf. Schoors, *Oudt. Stud.*, pp. 102-6.

[75] So too Fohrer, *ALUOS* (see n. 6), pp. 8f. = *BZAW* (see n. 6), pp. 118f. While ii 5 can be seen as a link phrase to ii 6ff.—and the verbal link of *bêt yaᶜaqōb* may be a factor in the present arrangement of the text—the parallel and significantly different text of Mic. iv 5 strongly suggests that the form of the poem here used is designed to reach a climax in appeal to the whole community, *bêt yaᶜaqōb* understood as all Israel, to accept the way of true religion in allegiance to Yahweh.

resemblance between this opening chapter with its appeal and lxvi, the closing chapter to the whole book, in which comparable radical questions are asked about the temple, about worship: in which judgement is pronounced and a summons issued to the nations to gather to see the divine glory and to acknowledge Yahweh. The final compilers of the book appear to have been sensitive to the import of this opening section and to have echoed it in their conclusion.[76]

The overarching theme of the second section, ii 6 - iv 6, is that of judgement upon human pretensions, both in general terms—so especially in ii 6-22—and in specific reference to the leadership of Jerusalem and of the supremacy of Yahweh in judgement and his presence in glory in a future purified Zion. The section is punctuated at ii 22 in a moralizing comment on man, at iii 13-15 in a judgement scene like Ps. lxxxii but directed specifically to the rulers of his people for their despoiling of the vineyard which is that people (cf v 1-7), and in iv 2-6 which provides a counterpart to the themes of ii 2-5, here expressed not as appeal but as confident statement of the divine will.

As the material now stands, the next elements in the book are broken into two, as has already been noted. The generalized indictment of v 1-7 is exemplified in the woes of v 8-23 where specific evils are identified and judged, and this is resumed in a general and totally black judgement statement in v 24-30, where the opening two verses show the clear links with the remainder of the poem in ix.[77] What follows in vi 1 - ix 6 traces both the consistent theme of failure on the part of the royal house and hence of the people, of their disregard of the prophetic message (so in vi 9-10, vii 10-17, viii 5-10, and perhaps also in viii 19-23a). Such royal failure and lack of response is answered in ix 1-6 in the presentation of a promise of the overthrow of the enemy in a climactic event, and the establishment of a final ruler of the Davidic line. Here is the core of the whole section, in which the question of the status of the prophet and hence the validity of his message is set out; and to this I shall return.

The judgement themes of v are resumed at ix 7 in a combining of

---

[76] Cf. L. J. Liebreich, (see n. 20), see 46 pp. 276f.; 47, pp. 126f. In the latter passage, Liebreich also links lxv with i.

[77] The suggestion that v 25-30 should be transposed to follow x 4 (so e.g. *BHS*), or that v 24-25 should be so transposed (so e.g. *NEB*), is without textual basis. We have to accept that elements, probably of a long poem, have been used deliberately to underline the judgement theme of v 1-22 and must be interpreted in their present context. Cf. D. R. Jones, p. 244.

stanzas of a long poem of judgement (ix 7-20), with a final woe on the leadership (x 1-4). This in its turn is followed by the interweaving of the theme of divine judgement by the agency of Assyria, and divine judgement upon Assyria. The passage incorporates elements of material picturing the divinely ordered advance of the Assyrians on Jerusalem (so x 6-7, (27d) 28-32), other elements linked to the depicting of the Assyrians' boastful claims (x 8-11, 13-14—cf. xxxvi and xxxvii for comparable material), now incorporated [78] in a woe-theme on Assyria (x 5), reflection on its hybris (x 7, 15), and judgement on it (x 12, 16-19, 24-26). With these too is incorporated the theme of the restoration of the survivors of the people of God, with their trust now to be absolutely in God himself rather than in the alien power (x 20-23, and also in 24-26). The section reaches its climax in the contrasting of the overthrow of the most exalted trees (x 33-34 cf. ii 13) and the establishment of the Davidic shoot (*ḥōṭer* and *nēṣer*, xi 1), in a new age of peace and well-being (xi 2-9); this in its turn leads to the summoning of the nations (xi 10), interpreted in terms of the gathering of the dispersed of Israel (xi 11-16) in a new exodus from Assyria. If we look at the whole section, now divided by the inclusion of vi 1 - ix 6, we may see that the picture of the vineyard of God's planting which has failed to produce true fruits is answered at the end in themes of total restoration of the people.

To the whole there then comes the colophon of the psalm in xii which has already been considered.

VIII

The overall impression created by Isa. i-xii is of a great wealth of very varied material. There are points at which a good case can be made out for genuine Isaianic sayings; but it is everywhere clear that the words of the prophet have been ordered and amplified to bring them into relationship with subsequent situations. It is not my intention to try to sort out either the genuine from the non-genuine, or the possible situations—reign of Manasseh, period of Josiah's supremacy, moment of Jerusalem's overthrow, loss of the Davidic monarchy as a present political reality, experience of defeat and dispersion, prospect of restoration with the overthrow of the alien power—to which this or that passage may belong, or in which reapplication has been made. I am concerned rather to observe how, in

[78] For fuller discussion, cf. H. Barth, op.cit.

these twelve chapters as they now stand, there is a presentation of the prophet, initiated by the claim of the heading in i 1 of the whole message which was delivered, the *ḥāzôn*, which "Isaiah ben Amoṣ saw concerning Judah and Jerusalem" tied to the period of four kings, Uzziah, Jotham, Ahaz and Hezekiah. That the formula as here presented is late has been clearly demonstrated.[79] Its effect is to direct the reader back from the situation in which he is confronted with the present collection to the moment of the prophet's activity. It is the Isaiah of that historic period who stands behind the message. The presence in these chapters of much that is dark, directed to the theme of judgement and depicting the prophet as himself directly involved in the description of his people as made unable to respond, provides a verifying basis most clear to us in our recognition of the enormous impact on the life and thought of the community of the disaster of the sixth century B.C. But in ii 1, stressing the Isaianic authority of the message of promise of ii 2-5, and in the colophon, with its emphasis on the salvation of God, echoing the prophet's name, and linked to the variety of hopeful words which intersperse the chapters, there is drawn out most clearly the significance of this prophet, the messenger of doom, now fulfilled, as he is also presented as messenger of salvation. Again, the question whether Isaiah himself was solely a prophet of doom, or whether in the context of the involvement which we may detect in him with the themes of Zion and Davidic kingship there was confidence in a nearer or a more distant salvation, remains open to debate. There can be no simple *a priori* judgement of the matter. But as the prophet is presented in these chapters, there is clear evidence of the chiaroscuro by which the prospect of the future is set out against the background of a recognition of failure and doom. Whether the prophet himself or his exegetes were responsible, the prophet appears to us as a man of judgement and salvation.

In the central section of this collection, as we have seen, the prophet is presented as authenticated by his commissioning directly from God, with a message geared to disaster. The obscure word of promise at the end of vi 13 now provides a pointer forward to the hopeful statements of ix 1-6.[80] Similarly we are left with an ambivalent impression from the obscurity of the Immanuel sign, which contains both

---

[79] Cf. e.g. D. R. Jones, pp. 239f., and G. Fohrer, *ALUOS* (see n. 6), p. 6, and n. 9 = *BZAW* (see n. 6), p. 116, and n. 9.

[80] Cf. Cazelles, op. cit. (see n. 70).

gloomy and hopeful overtones, the former being particularly drawn out in the group of sayings now attached to that sign in vii 18-25. The emphasis on prophetic commission is again made clear in the allusive wording of viii 11, and implicit in the preservation of the message envisaged in viii 16. The prophet himself and his associates or children become signs to Israel (viii 18).

The question posed earlier in this discussion—Why did so great a tradition come to be attached to this particular prophet?—may in part at least be answered. He has been given that status by the presentation in i-xii. Both the confirmation of his message of doom and the affirmation of the salvation theme associated with his name, provided for the period of exile and its aftermath, with the continuing experience of deferred hope, a clear picture of the reality of the divine word associated with this particular figure.

IX

In a paper in the volume *Beiträge zur Alttestamentlichen Theologie* presented to Professor Zimmerli in celebration of this year, Brevard Childs has offered some reflections on the merely historical tendency of endeavouring to recover "the *original* meaning of the text as it emerged in its pristine situation".[81] It is not simply the uncertainties of reconstructing the original situation, the form and impact of the original utterance, which make for the weakness of such a historifying approach, though the difficulties are all too apparent. It is the presence of an underlying assumption about the authority of the divine word which cuts through the problems of discussing how such a divine word can be known to be mediated by assuming the authoritative quality of what is believed to be original. When the ultimate compiler of Isa. i-xii invites his readers or hearers to look back to the prophet, it is not with the aim of providing them with some kind of picture of the prophet's activity—for which indeed only minimal information is to be found here—but to show the basis for the acceptance of the present application of what is associated with the prophet to lie in a view of his authoritative status, tied on the one hand to the record of a particular commissioning and on the other hand to the authenticating of the prophet's word in the sequel—that is, in the fulfilment

[81] "The Sensus Literalis of Scripture: An Ancient and Modern Problem" in H. Donner, E. Hanhart, R. Smend (ed.), *Beiträge zur Alttestamentlichen Theologie. Festschrift für Walther Zimmerli zum 70. Geburtstag* (Göttingen, 1977), pp. 70-93; see p. 89.

of his word in events, in the continued vitality of that word in new situations. It is in such a perspective that authority for the prophetic word can be claimed; it is, of course, not without its uncertainties, but in that it may be compared with the original situation of the prophet whose claims to speak the word of God do not validate themselves. Indeed the original moment of the prophetic utterance is open to question because of the inevitably unverifiable nature of the prophet's claims.[82] Authentication rests then neither in the reconstruction of the original moment nor in the claim for the particular validity of a subsequent moment of reinterpretation. It rests rather in the continuing process by which prophetic word and receptive hearing interact.

It is clear that there must be a relationship between what is claimed about the prophet and his status here in i-xii and what may be seen or detected in other literary constructions—in chapters xiii-xxxiii with their attachment only very briefly to moments of the prophet's activity or, much more precisely, in the interweaving of narrative and prophetic activity depicted in xxxvi-xxxix. The full impact of that will not be found by harmonization, but by the recognition that the impact of the prophet is to be assessed ultimately through the differing, even contradictory, presentations which are made. Beyond this there will be the whole book now associated with his name, some aspects of which have been briefly touched on in this discussion. It is clear here that questions about the ultimate canonical status of the finished product cannot be satisfactorily resolved without a regard for the stages through which that status was brought about, the appeal in a whole variety of situations, more clearly detectable or only dimly discerned, in which the words of the prophet have been seen to be immediately meaningful. There can be no limiting of the discussion to either end of the process, however much we are forced to recognize the degree to which our discussion is limited by the final form or forms of the text through which alone we have access to the earlier stages. In this, I find myself sympathetic to the re-emphasis in recent years on concern for the status of the canon, but also to the attempts at uncovering some of the stages in the process which have marked a good deal of recent writing on the Old Testament.[83] Canon-criti-

---

[82] For a specific instance, cf. R. P. Carroll, "A Non-Cogent Argument in Jeremiah's Oracles against the Prophets", *StTh* 30 (1976), pp. 43-51.

[83] Cf. e.g. a number of recent studies by J. A. Sanders: "Adaptable for Life: the Nature and Function of Canon", in F. M. Cross, W. E. Lemke, P. D. Miller

cism, as a distinct area of discussion, involves a sensitive appraisal of both the final stages of the according of authority to the biblical writings, and the awareness of the different levels at which this has operated in the eventual determining of the texts which have come down to us, stamped with the hallmark of experiential testing in the life of the community to which they belonged.

(ed.), *Magnalia Dei. The Mighty Acts of God. Essays on the Bible and Archaeology in Memory of G. Ernest Wright* (New York, 1976), pp. 531-60; "Hermeneutics in True and False Prophecy" in *Canon and Authority* (see n. 17), pp. 21-41; "Biblical Criticism and the Bible as Canon", *USQR* 32/3-4 (1977), pp. 157-65. Cf. also my "Original Text and Canonical Text", *USQR* 32/3-4 (1977), pp. 166-73. *Additional note*: I have been unable to consult J. Vermeylen, *Du Prophète Isaïe à l'Apocalyptique. Isaïe, I-XXXV, miroir d'un demi-millénaire d'expérience religieuse en Israël* 1 (Paris, 1977), 2 (1978).

[The article by H. Cazelles (see n. 70) has appeared in French as "La vocation d'Isaïe (ch. 6) et les rites royaux" in *Homenaje a Juan Prado* (Madrid, 1978), pp. 89-108.]

REFLECTIONS ON THE EMERGENCE OF A STANDARD TEXT OF THE HEBREW BIBLE

by

BERTIL ALBREKTSON

Uppsala

One of the most important and interesting features in the history of the Hebrew Bible is the emergence of a standard consonantal text. The variety of text-types attested by the discoveries in the Judaean Desert and by the ancient versions disappeared at the beginning of the Christian era, and later manuscripts reflect one single text-type which superseded all others. Diversity was replaced by unity.[1]

This development from a plurality of text-types to a single standard version of the sacred text is commonly regarded as a conscious and controlled process. In the profound and difficult crisis of Judaism after the destruction of the temple in the year A.D. 70 and the emergence of the Christian Church, the Pharisees managed to preserve and strengthen the national unity of the Jews by establishing a definite canon of the Holy Scriptures and, we are told, by establishing and promulgating a normative standard recension of the text of these writings. The rabbis are often pictured as having constituted a kind of editorial committee, carefully selecting variants from different manuscripts and fixing an authoritative text, which was to serve as the official norm.[2]

---

[1] For a general survey see, e.g., E. Würthwein, *Der Text des Alten Testaments* (Stuttgart, [4]1973), pp. 15ff.; G. Fohrer, *Introduction to the Old Testament* (Nashville and New York, 1968; London, 1970), pp. 489ff. = *Einleitung in das Alte Testament* (Heidelberg, 1965), pp. 538ff.

[2] See, e.g., P. Kahle in H. Bauer and P. Leander, *Historische Grammatik der hebräischen Sprache des Alten Testaments* (Halle, 1922; reprinted Hildesheim, 1962), p. 74; R. H. Pfeiffer, *Introduction to the Old Testament* (New York, 1941), p. 78; F. M. Cross, Jr., *The Ancient Library of Qumran And Modern Biblical Studies* (New York, [2]1961), pp. 171ff.; D. Barthélemy, "Text, Hebrew, history of", *The Interpreter's Dictionary of the Bible, Supplementary Volume* (Nashville, 1976), pp. 881f. Similar views are also found in S. Talmon, "The Old Testament Text", *The Cambridge History of the Bible* 1 (Cambridge, 1970), pp. 159, 168f.; cf. however below, n. 34.

My purpose is simply to call in question the current idea that the emergence of the standard text must have been the result of a conscious and deliberate text-critical activity with the purpose of creating a normative recension. I shall first attempt a brief discussion of the validity of the evidence commonly adduced in favour of the current view (I); I shall then indicate certain difficulties which this view seems to involve (II); and finally I shall try to sketch—very tentatively—a possible alternative (III).[3]

I

First, then, something about the evidence for the view that the rabbis created an official recension using the methods of textual criticism.

One important aspect of this problem is the question whether the Jewish sages responsible for the biblical text were influenced by the principles and practices of textual criticism pursued by Greek scholars, especially the famous grammarians attached to the Museum at Alexandria.

At the beginning of the Hellenistic period many texts of the classical Greek authors were in a state of corruption: in a number of passages in Homer, in lyric poetry and in the works of the great tragedians, different copies of the same text showed considerable discrepancies.[4]

The large collection of books which was brought together in the library at Alexandria may have contributed to making this state of affairs more conspicuous; at any rate it was here that methods were developed to put the text in order. This important work, which went on for many generations and which "led to a great advance in learning and scholarly methods",[5] was not restricted to the problem of textual criticism proper. The aim of the great Alexandrian scholars was not merely to restore the literary creations of the past but also to explain them, and so they interpreted difficult passages and commented on all kinds of problems found in the classical texts.

Practically no book of any Hellenistic scholar has survived, but enough can be reconstructed from fragments and quotations, in-

---

[3] For an earlier version (in Swedish) of some of my arguments see *SEÅ* 40 (1975), pp. 18ff.

[4] L. D. Reynolds and N. G. Wilson, *Scribes and Scholars. A Guide to the Transmission of Greek and Latin Literature* (Oxford, ²1974), pp. 5ff.

[5] Reynolds and Wilson, p. 7.

cluded in marginal commentaries known as *scholia* and preserved in medieval manuscripts, to give us a reliable picture of the methods and achievements of the Alexandrian scholars.[6]

Their attempts to restore the text of Homer and other poets seem in many cases to have been based on manuscript evidence: they examined copies in the library and collected variant readings, which were then sifted and evaluated and used to remedy the deficiences of the manuscript selected as a basic text.[7] The scholars also introduced corrections without support in the available manuscripts: some of their alterations were evidently conjectures of their own.[8] They also worked out a system of critical signs (such as the *obelos* and the *asteriskos* later used by Origen); these were used to mark corrupt or spurious verses, to indicate noteworthy points of language or contents, or to denote passages in which the lines were thought to be in the wrong order, and they could refer the reader to a separate volume containing a commentary on the text.

The critical and editorial work of the Alexandrian scholars was not without influence on the ordinary texts in circulation:[9] the later "vulgate" manuscripts of the Iliad, for instance, show a text which is in several respects superior to that of the pre-Alexandrian papyri (though it seems to be an open question whether the credit for this purification of the text is due more to the labours of the scholars than to the demands for uniformity of the booksellers).[10] It is important to note that the critical recensions produced by the Alexandrian grammarians were not edited for the general public in a large number of copies: their so-called "editions" (ἐκδόσεις) were in fact "individual copies of the poetical work in question—normally only one copy, and thus not available on the market" [11]—"there is no reason to suppose that copies were multiplied by the book trade".[12] And so many of their corrections and proposals seem to have remained in the commentaries without ever being incorporated in the current

[6] R. Pfeiffer, *History of Classical Scholarship from the Beginnings to the End of the Hellenistic Age* (Oxford, 1968), pp. 266, 276; Reynolds and Wilson, pp. 10f.

[7] R. Pfeiffer, pp. 110, 114; P. M. Fraser, *Ptolemaic Alexandria* I (Oxford, 1972), pp. 451, 457, 464.

[8] R. Pfeiffer, pp. 110, 114, 276; Fraser, pp. 459, 464; see also M. van der Valk, *Researches on the Text and the Scholia of the Iliad* 2 (Leiden, 1964), pp. 13ff., 90ff., 201ff.

[9] See Reynolds and Wilson, p. 8.

[10] Fraser, p. 477.

[11] Fraser, p. 447.

[12] Fraser, p. 476.

manuscripts of the text. P. M. Fraser, in his monumental work *Ptolemaic Alexandria*, summarizes the effects of the text-critical endeavours of the grammarians in the following words: "not only did the work of Alexandrian scholars mostly survive only for a short time, but even when it did its influence outside the learned world seems to have been restricted" (p. 477).

Now it seems indisputable that Palestinian Judaism of the first century A.D. was deeply influenced by Hellenism,[13] and so from a general point of view there is nothing *a priori* unreasonable in the conception of "the influence of the Alexandrine philologists' ideas of textual criticism upon Jewish circles".[14] But a possibility is not a fact and on closer inspection there is little to make such an influence certain or even likely.

The main evidence for Jewish dependence on the methods and practices of the Alexandrian grammarians was collected by Saul Lieberman, who discussed in great detail a number of interesting parallels and traced "Hellenistic influence in the behavior, rites, practices, conceptions and literary methods of the Jews" (op. cit., p. 20). It is, however, essential to observe that the correspondences between the early rabbis and the Alexandrian grammarians pointed out by Lieberman belong in two distinct areas: that of purely scribal procedures concerning the copying of texts and the terminology used in this connection, and that of principles of interpretation and exegesis. Lieberman's parallels do not fall in the area of textual criticism and recensional endeavours in any strict sense. In fact Lieberman, who otherwise tends to make the most of the similarities, expressly denies Alexandrian influence on the Jewish scribes in this respect: "The Rabbis never suggest a correction of the text of the Bible. In the entire rabbinic literature we never come across divergencies of opinion regarding Biblical readings. It is therefore obvious that the textual corrections of Greek classics practiced by the Alexandrian grammarians have no parallels in the rabbinic exegesis of Scripture" (p. 47; cf. also p. 37).

Lieberman seems to be right: there are no valid reasons to think that the methods used by the Alexandrian scholars in their recensional

---

[13] See, e.g., S. Lieberman, *Hellenism in Jewish Palestine* (New York, 1950); M. Hengel, *Judentum und Hellenismus* (Tübingen, [2]1973); id., *Juden, Griechen und Barbaren* (Stuttgart, 1976).

[14] C. Rabin, "The Dead Sea Scrolls and the History of the O.T. Text", *JTS*, N.S. 6 (1955), p. 182.

work on Homer and other classical authors were ever applied to the biblical texts by the Jewish scribes. There is no detailed evidence to prove such a dependence; and there are general differences which seem to tell against it. In the Hebrew material the striking and important thing is the emergence of a standard text, whereas questions of textual criticism with scholarly discussions of variant readings and proposals of conjectural emendations are conspicuously absent from the rabbinical literature. But it is precisely these problems that are the focus of interest at Alexandria: the emphasis is on learned treatments of textual difficulties, whereas less importance seems to be attached to the task of influencing the current text and enforcing a single, authoritative recension; producing a critical edition for a limited circle of scholars (which is what the grammarians did) is something different from standardizing all existing manuscripts (which is what the rabbis are alleged to have done). In the absence of further and more decisive evidence of rabbinical activities in the sphere of textual criticism, general references to a possible influence from Alexandrian textual methods remain inconclusive.

It is a common argument that the method of exegesis practised by R. Aqiba and his school, involving arguments from details of the text such as the presence or absence of certain particles or even variations in the spelling of individual words, presupposes a text that has been unified in its slightest details.[15] A characteristic formulation of this argument can be found in an article by M. Greenberg, who maintained that the "prevalence of the standard . . . is the necessary precondition of the highly literal exegesis which flourished in the Tannaitic academies. Such an exegesis, undertaken in all seriousness by earnest men is inconceivable had the text not been hallowed in its letter well beforehand".[16] Another version of this argument makes the standardization not a precondition but rather a consequence of Aqiba's exegetical methods; it is represented for instance by O. Eissfeldt: "Rabbi Akiba . . . darf, wenn nicht geradezu als Anfänger, so doch als der erste überragende Vertreter der Schriftauslegung gelten, die auf den Buchstaben Wert legte und damit die textliche Sicherung eben auch des kleinsten Buchstabens erforderlich machte".[17]

---

[15] See, e.g., R. H. Pfeiffer (above, n. 2), p. 77; N. M. Sarna in *Encyclopaedia Judaica* 4 (Jerusalem, 1971), col. 835.

[16] "The Stabilization of the Text of the Hebrew Bible Reviewed in the Light of the Biblical Materials from the Judaean Desert", *JAOS* 76 (1956), p. 166.

[17] *Einleitung in das Alte Testament* (Tübingen, ^{3}1964), p. 929.

Now it is certainly true that in his exegesis Aqiba argues from insignificant grammatical or orthographical details of the text.[18] But the question is whether the conclusions drawn from this fact are really necessary. Superficially it may seem reasonable to maintain that Aqiba's and his followers' interpretation of minor formal peculiarities of the Bible text "presumes"—to quote G. F. Moore—"a standard text, copies of which consistently agreed in these peculiarities".[19] Further reflection shows, however, that this is not necessarily the case. Strictly speaking this kind of interpretation does not in itself presuppose that everybody else has got exactly the same text: the only *necessary* requirement is that there is *a* text which can serve as a starting-point for the hermeneutic exercises. Moreover—and this is more decisive—it can be shown that certain exegetical arguments of this type in the rabbinic literature are in fact based on a text which deviates from the standard text of the masoretes. Precisely in cases where, according to the usual argument as stated by Moore and others, the detailed exegesis ought to require absolute uniformity in all manuscripts, the rabbis do in fact sometimes rely on a spelling which is at variance with that found in the MT.

A case in point is a rabbinical exposition intended to supply scriptural proof for the rule that the phylacteries worn on the head should consist of four sections, each containing a scriptural passage (TB Men. 34b; cf. TB Sanh. 4b). The words *w^ehayû l^eṭôṭapot bên ʿênêka* "they shall be as frontlets between your eyes" occur—with minor variations—three times in the O.T.: Ex. xiii 16; Deut. vi 8, xi 18. The rabbinical argument for the number four is based on the spelling of the plural ending *-ôt* in the word *ṭôṭapôt*: in one case it is written *plene* and in two cases *defective*, and if it is written without the letter *waw*, these forms can be read as singular forms, and so, according to this subtle calculation, the result is $1 + 1 + 2 = 4$. Now the interesting thing is that the word is in fact written *defective* in all three cases in our *textus receptus*—and so the argument which is supposed to require a text standardized down to the very use of *matres lectionis* is in this case based on a text which deviates from the standard precisely on the crucial point.

This is not the only passage where a rabbinical argument is based

---

[18] On Aqiba's exegesis see, e.g., D. Barthélemy, *Les Devanciers d'Aquila*, *SupplVT* 10 (Leiden, 1963), pp. 3ff.

[19] *Judaism in the First Centuries of the Christian Era* I (Cambridge, Mass., 1927), pp. 100f.

on deviations from the standard text, and this phenomenon seems to take the force out of the argument that an exegesis based on single letters of the words of Scripture presupposes a rigidly uniform text. It is difficult to maintain that a method of interpretation requires a state of affairs which demonstrably did not exist when the method was being used.

A few passages from rabbinic literature are sometimes adduced as evidence for the idea of the rabbis as textual critics, collating manuscripts and weighing variant readings. The text which is most frequently invoked is probably the tradition of the three scrolls in the temple. Already Abraham Geiger in his *Urschrift und Übersetzungen der Bibel* quoted this report as testimony of how the rabbis proceeded when fixing the standard text.[20] The tradition is found in several rabbinic writings, and the versions differ from one another in certain respects.[21] We are told that three scrolls were found in the temple court, called *sepær meʿônî* (*meʿônā*, *-îm*), *sepær zăʿaṭûṭê* and *sepær hîʾ*. In one of these was written *maʿôn*, and in the other two was written *meʿônā*; so they adopted the reading of the two scrolls and discarded that of the one. In one of the scrolls was found the reading *zăʿaṭûṭê benê yiśraʾel*, and in the other two it was written *năʿarê benê yiśraʾel*; in this case too the majority reading was retained and the reading of the single witness was abandoned. Some similar procedure seems to have been adopted in the third case, but here the four versions differ more markedly, and it is difficult to get a clear picture: in one passage (TJ Taʿan. IV 2) it is said that one manuscript had *hîʾ* nine times and the two others eleven times; in another text (Soferim VI 4) it is stated that one scroll had *hûʾ* eleven times and two scrolls had *hîʾ* eleven times; a third passage (Aboth de R. Nathan, B, 46) is almost unintelligible on this point, and in the fourth version of the story (Sifre 2, 356) this item is missing altogether.

From this ancient tradition it is frequently inferred that the rabbis carefully compared manuscripts to produce a critically revised text of

[20] *Urschrift und Übersetzungen der Bibel in ihrer Abhängigkeit von der innern Entwicklung des Judentums* (Breslau, 1857; reprinted Frankfurt am Main, 1928), p. 231ff. See also C. D. Ginsburg, *Introduction to the Massoretico-Critical Edition of the Hebrew Bible* (London, 1897; reprinted New York, 1966), pp. 408f.; Kahle (above, n. 2), p. 74.

[21] See L. Blau, *Studien zum althebräischen Buchwesen und zur biblischen Litteraturgeschichte* (Strassburg, 1902), pp. 101ff.; J. Z. Lauterbach, "The Three Books Found in the Temple at Jerusalem", *JQR*, N.S. 8 (1917-18), pp. 386ff.; S. Talmon, "The Three Scrolls of the Law that were found in the Temple Court", *Textus* 2 (1962), pp. 14ff.

the Bible and that they proceeded more or less like Nestle in his edition of the Greek text of the New Testament: when the authorities disagree, the reading of the majority is mechanically followed. The question is, however, whether the tradition is really able to carry the burden of proof which has been laid upon it.

A comparison between the four versions shows that we must allow for different strata in the story: the original notice, and later additions and embroideries. This is agreed by the scholars who have analysed the texts, even if their assessments of what is original and what is secondary differ in details. Ludwig Blau is of the opinion that the kernel of the tradition is the notice about three scrolls in the temple and their names, whereas the explanations of the names are a typical talmudic development of the tradition.[22] Blau, like Talmon in his discussion of the subject, regards the scrolls as manuscripts of the Torah, but all do not agree on this point: according to Lauterbach the original report referred to books "containing the genealogical lists of various classes of the people, or family records" (p. 401), which were kept in the temple at Jerusalem, and the idea that it speaks of copies of the Torah is a mistake made in the commentaries by the later teachers (pp. 413, 416ff.). Blau also emphasized that it is inconceivable that a Torah scroll in the temple, serving as a model manuscript, would have contained the reading *ză‘*^{a}*ṭûṭê b*^{e}*nê yiśra’el* in Ex. xxiv 5 instead of *nă‘*^{a}*rê b*^{e}*nê yiśra’el* "the young men of Israel", *ză‘*^{a}*ṭuṭê* not even being a Hebrew word.[23]

Thus we may establish that the story is probably composed of an original record and later explanations and additions, that the information about the collating of manuscripts and the variant readings is likely to belong to the rabbinic embroidery, and that it is even disputed whether the original report concerned biblical manuscripts at all. In view of all this it seems to me that one must use this tradition with far greater caution than has usually been the case. Source criticism seems seriously to reduce its value as a principal witness, and it is difficult to see how it could serve as decisive evidence for the thesis that the scribes at the beginning of the Christian era created an eclectic recension of the Hebrew scriptures using text-critical methods.

There are a number of rabbinic traditions about certain persons entrusted with the task of checking newly written manuscripts, and

---

[22] pp. 101ff.; cf. Lauterbach, pp. 385, n. 1, 398ff.

[23] p. 102. The derivation and meaning of the word are disputed.

these talmudic passages have been interpreted as evidence of the existence of "an authoritative text by which the accuracy of other scrolls was measured".[24] In TB Keth. 106a it is recorded that the book correctors in Jerusalem received their fees from the Temple funds. A similar statement is preserved in the Palestinian Talmud (TJ Sheq. IV 3): those who corrected the Torah scroll kept in the temple were paid in the same way. That the copy of the Torah in the temple was used for the checking of other scrolls appears from TJ Sanh. II 6.

It is however important to notice precisely what these talmudic passages tell us and what they do not tell us. Here, as so often in traditional material of this kind, it is sometimes difficult to decide which period the statements refer to. But above all it is hard to see how they could really prove an official standard text common to all Jewry. It is evident from these passages that new manuscripts of the sacred scriptures, especially more or less official copies, were carefully checked to ensure their complete agreement with the *Vorlage*. But as far as I can see, they do not imply that this *Vorlage* had to represent an authorized standard text. Accuracy in transcription and collating of the copy is one thing; the claim that the copy must not only be faultless but also reproduce a certain type of text is another. The rabbinic traditions testifying to the importance of flawless copying are in themselves compatible with the existence of different types of text. In TB Meg. 18b it is reported that R. Ḥisda found R. Ḥananel writing scrolls without any *Vorlage* and admonished him: you are quite qualified to write the whole Torah by heart, but according to the Sages it is forbidden to write one single letter except from a copy. The point of R. Ḥisda's reproof is that it is necessary to write a biblical manuscript from another copy; there is not a word to indicate that this copy had to represent the official and authoritative recension.

The manuscripts found at Murabbaʿat have frequently been adduced as decisive proof of a standardization of the text during the decades following the fall of Jerusalem. As is well known, the biblical manuscripts from Qumran include several different text-types and exhibit a great number of variant readings, whereas the manuscripts found at Wadi Murabbaʿat represent in all essentials the textual tradition which is later attested by the medieval masoretes. Now the Qumran texts belong in the period before the destruction of the

---

[24] Sarna (above, n. 15), col. 834.

temple, while Murabbaʿat was a last place of refuge for Jewish patriots of the Second Revolt. In the view of many scholars this leads to the conclusion that the rabbinic standardization of the consonantal text must have been carried out in the period between the two revolts, between A.D. 70 and 132. This view is cautiously adumbrated already in R. de Vaux's first presentation of the material from Murabbaʿat in the *Revue Biblique* in 1953,[25] and it has since been formulated with ever increasing confidence: one might for example quote the article in *RGG* by C.-H. Hunzinger, stating that the "Konsonantentext nun also nachweislich zwischen den beiden Aufständen fixiert worden ist".[26]

It is difficult to see how this argument could be conclusive. First, there is a certain tendency to overstate the agreement with MT, which is certainly striking but not complete. In particular ms 88, the well-known scroll of the Twelve Prophets, contains some variants which make it difficult to speak of a strict standardization affecting every detail.[27] Second—and this is more important—the proto-masoretic character of the Murabbaʿat manuscripts, however impressive, does not prove that the rabbis must have carried out a deliberate standardization in the period between the Jewish revolts. We know that the ancestor of the standard text is found already in Qumran, and the fact that all manuscripts from Murabbaʿat belong to the same type could be due to their origin in a certain group, namely followers of the rebel leader Bar Kochba, who was closely connected with the master of "normative" Judaism, R. Aqiba. The fact that these circles used the Bible text which was to become prevalent cannot tell us much about textual conditions elsewhere and it does not allow any definite conclusions about successful rabbinical efforts at textual unification. M. H. Goshen-Gottstein has called for caution on this point, and there is no doubt that his appeal is justified.[28]

---

[25] "Les grottes de Murabbaʿat et leurs documents. Rapport preliminaire", *RB* 60 (1953), p. 264.

[26] *RGG*³ 5 (Tübingen, 1961), col. 755. Cf. also P. W. Skehan, "The Qumran Manuscripts and Textual Criticism", *SupplVT* 4 (1957), p. 148; Cross (above, n. 2), p. 171.

[27] See the list of variants in P. Benoit, J. T. Milik and R. de Vaux, *Les grottes de Murabbaʿat. Texte, Discoveries in the Judaean Desert* 2 (Oxford, 1961), pp. 183f., 205.

[28] "The History of the Bible-text and Comparative Semitics.—A Methodological Problem", *VT* 7 (1957), p. 200, n. 1 (= *Text and Language in Bible and Qumran* [Jerusalem and Tel-Aviv, 1960], p. 161, n. 1).

II

A scrutiny of the grounds commonly given for the current view thus shows that they are not as solid as one might have expected, and that the evidence is not conclusive. But it seems possible to go a step further and maintain that there are reasons which tell against the idea that the Jewish scribes created a normative recension through a careful sifting of manuscript readings.

The main argument is simply that the MT displays certain characteristics which are hard—if not impossible—to reconcile with such a theory. We all know that the MT is not a flawless text. On the contrary it has a number of peculiarities and deficiencies: there are inconsistencies of spelling and transpositions of letters, there are haplographies and dittographies, there are erroneous word-divisions and faulty joining of words. Some of these deficiencies are of such a kind that it is virtually inconceivable that they could have been allowed to stand if the text had really been subjected to thorough and deliberate recensional activities. Is it at all plausible to picture the MT of the Books of Samuel as the outcome of a careful comparison of manuscripts and textual traditions, when it is obvious that it is an inferior text, full of errors and lacunae which could easily have been remedied with the aid of contemporary manuscript material? Could the traditional text of the Book of Jeremiah, notoriously marked by expansion, conflation and harmonizing, really have been deliberately preferred on *text-critical* grounds to the type of text found in the Septuagint and in 4QJer^{b}, far superior to the MT? Is the inconsistency in the use of *matres lectionis* found in the MT compatible with the idea of a thorough-going recension, which is supposed to have affected precisely details of this kind?

It is most instructive to observe how adherents of the current theory run into difficulties when trying to reconcile their knowledge of the actual characteristics of the MT with the thesis of a conscious textual recension of the rabbis. Let me quote a telling description of the "recensional endeavours" of the scribes, written by no less an authority than F. M. Cross:

> The principles which guided the scholars who prepared the recension were unusual. The recension was not characterized by wholesale revision and emendation, nor by eclectic or conflating procedures. Nor was a single, local textual family chosen. In the Pentateuch the current Palestinian text-type was rejected, ... Rather the conservative, superb text of Babylonian origin, recently introduced into Palestine,

> was selected for the standard text. In the Former Prophets, the same pattern was followed, a Babylonian text was chosen, despite the existence of the superior Old Palestinian textual family. ... In the Latter Prophets, the scholars shifted textual families. In these books a Palestinian text was chosen, perhaps because Babylonian texts were not available. However that may be, the orthographic type chosen was not the new *plene* style common in many Palestinian manuscripts beginning in Maccabaean times.
>
> The process of recension was basically one of selecting traditions deriving from two old textual families available in Palestine in the first century A.D.
>
> There was some leveling through, not always successful, of the conservative orthographic style chosen, and some revision, within narrow limits, was undertaken.[29]

The principles of this recension seem to have been "unusual" indeed: readings from different traditions were not adopted; instead one single text-type was chosen for entire parts of the canon—but so that in one case a good text was selected and in another an inferior text, in spite of a better one being available; a certain orthography was decided on but never consistently carried out. The crucial question is: how could one distinguish a text which has been revised according to such principles from a text which has not been revised at all? As soon as we rid ourselves of the preconceived notion that an official textual recension must have taken place, it becomes clear that what Cross describes is in fact a text which has not been subject to recensional and text-critical activities.

Now of course some scholars have seen that we have no conclusive evidence of a recensional work in the sense that a new text-form was created. Already John Allegro, in his well-known book on the Dead Sea Scrolls, wrote that the rabbis who fixed the authoritative text "did not compose a standard text, or even make an eclectic version from many traditions, but settled on one particular textual tradition as the norm for all time".[30] But though Allegro did not think of a rabbinic recension in the ordinary sense, he still adheres to the traditional idea of an authoritative fixing of the text, even if it consisted in the promulgation of an already existing version. The distinction

---

[29] "The Contribution of the Qumrân Discoveries to the Study of the Biblical Text", *IEJ* 16 (1966), p. 94. See also his "The History of the Biblical Text in the Light of the Discoveries in the Judaean Desert", *HTR* 57 (1964), pp. 288f.

[30] J. M. Allegro, *The Dead Sea Scrolls* (Harmondsworth, 1956), p. 51. See also, e.g., B. J. Roberts in *The Interpreter's Dictionary of the Bible* 4 (New York and Nashville, 1962), pp. 582f.

between the idea of text-critical activity on the part of the rabbis and the concept of an official promulgation of a normative text is important, but I would suggest that it is possible to dispense with the latter hypothesis as well. There is no clear evidence in its favour, and it does entail difficulties: the character of the MT in, say, the Books of Samuel tells not only against the theory of a text-critical recension but also against the idea of a conscious selection among different text-types: who would deliberately have preferred this inferior version to other and better manuscripts which were available?

One might also ask the question whether we are really justified in taking for granted that absolute uniformity must have been an ideal for the tannaitic scholars. There is a risk that our arguments may be somewhat anachronistic, based on a modern approach which was not necessarily shared by the ancient rabbis. With our historical way of looking at the matter, we tend to assume that a text has one and only one original meaning which it is the task of the exegete to recover (with the obvious exception of intentionally ambiguous statements), and by the methods of textual criticism we endeavour to reconstruct the original wording of a text or at least to identify which reading has the best claim to represent the oldest attainable stage in the history of the text. When we speak of the standardization of the text, it sometimes sounds as if we believed the rabbis to share our outlook and our ideal: Aqiba is pictured as the leader of a Hebrew Text Project pretty much as Professor P. A. H. de Boer is the leader of the Peshiṭta Project. But what to us is an embarrassment, the multitude of incompatible readings, does not seem to have been so regarded by the rabbis themselves. Our views about the meaning of a text were not theirs: Scripture contained many strata and many meanings, and one did not exclude another. For them the ideal was not to find one and only one signification but to discover the entire fulness of divine truths which lay hidden in the sacred writings.[31] Variety was not primarily a problem but an asset. Is it unreasonable to imagine that those who approached the texts with such assumptions regarded the multiplicity of readings and variants differently from us, did not feel our need of recovering *the* correct reading but could even see the pluralism as something positive, or at least did not find it necessary to enforce absolute unity, to single out one possibility while discarding all others? After all they

[31] For the rabbinic striving to produce multiple meanings see J. Barr, *Comparative Philology and the Text of the Old Testament* (Oxford, 1968), p. 44.

were capable of freely using both *Kethib* and *Qere* in their expositions, regarding the two variants as equally authoritative.[32] They even invented variants, the so-called *'ăl-tiqre'*-readings, to broaden the basis for their ingenious expositions.[33] Perhaps it is symptomatic that the remarkable readings found in R. Meir's copy of the Torah seem to be reported not only with equanimity but even with appreciation and with not a little of that playful temper which is an essential element in rabbinic hermeneutics. In Gen. iii 21 we read that God made garments of skin for Adam and his wife, but in R. Meir's Torah it was found written "garments of light", *'ôr* instead of *'ôr* (Gen. R. 20:12). And this obvious mis-spelling of a guttural is simply made the basis of a new interpretation, without a word of criticism of the deviation from the standard text. The same is the case with another variant in the same scroll: "death was good" instead of "it was very good", reading *mawæt* instead of *me'od* (Gen. R. 9:5): the reaction is not a condemnation of a faulty reading but a grateful acceptance of another lesson taught by the inexhaustible Torah. Such an attitude to variant readings would not seem to have been particularly fertile soil for tendencies towards a rigidly fixed recension.

III

To my mind there is much to be said for the view that the crystallization of a standard consonantal text is not primarily the outcome of conscious and deliberate measures taken by the rabbis but, to a much greater extent than is usually thought, the result of historical coincidences, of a number of concurrent factors which are not in the main of a textual kind.[34]

The two revolts against the Romans led to a radical change in the conditions of life of the Jewish community. Before the downfall we have a broad spectrum of different religious movements and groups,

---

[32] Cf. Lieberman, p. 26; W. Bacher, *Die exegetische Terminologie der jüdischen Traditionsliteratur* 2 (Leipzig, 1905; reprinted Darmstadt, 1965), pp. 92f.

[33] A. Rosenzweig, "Die Al-tikri-Deutungen. Ein Beitrag zur talmudischen Schriftdeutung", M. Braun und J. Elbogen (hrsg.), *Festschrift I. Lewy* (Breslau, 1911), pp. 204ff.

[34] Occasionally remarks can be found which point in this direction: see, e.g., H. M. Orlinsky, "Prolegomenon: The Masoretic Text: A Critical Evaluation", in the reprint of Ginsburg's *Introduction* (above, n. 22), p. XX. This happens even in authors who elsewhere would seem to subscribe to the current view: see, e.g., Sarna (above, n. 15), col. 836; Talmon (above, n. 2), pp. 194, 198f.

but only the Pharisees survive the disasters and have the strength to reorganize in new and changed conditions. Religious diversity is replaced by unity: the Pharisees alone dominate the development. Similarly before the revolts there is a diversified textual tradition, but afterwards one single text-type gradually becomes predominant. It is tempting to connect these parallel developments and to suggest that the victorious text was one which had been used by Pharisaic scribes and that it came to supplant other texts because the Pharisees supplanted other religious groups.

Such a view might explain the partly paradoxical properties of the MT: it is at the same time a good text—as a whole it is clearly superior to other textual traditions like the LXX or the Samaritan—*and* an uneven text with obvious and in places rather embarrassing defects. If the text which was to hold the field in the future was what Pharisaic scribes happened to have left after the defeats imposed by the Romans (to put it briefly and perhaps to oversimply), this might explain both the merits of the text and its deficiencies. It had been handled in circles which devoted much care and attention to the word of Scripture, and so it is plausible that on the whole it should have an archaic and authentic character, lacking many of the defects which are typical of the so-called vulgar texts. But at the same time it is not the result of a thorough-going recension, it is based on manuscripts which happened to be preserved after the downfall, and its dominating position is not based on text-critical grounds—and therefore in places it does display lacunae and errors which would not be found in a thoroughly revised text.

Thus facts which are difficult to fit into the current view seem to fall into place in this pattern. Another fact of this kind is the silence of the rabbinic sources. The process of the fixing of the canon can be documented in the Talmud: it is reported that the rabbis discussed the canonical status of certain biblical books, and it seems quite natural that such an important and far-reaching procedure should have left its traces in the traditions. It is all the more remarkable that an equally important and far-reaching procedure, the alleged official standardization of the text, has not left corresponding traces. It is a notable fact that in the rabbinic writings we never come across cases where the sages disagree about the wording of the Bible or base conflicting arguments on variant readings affecting the consonants proper. Though arguments from silence have a limited value, it seems reasonable to adduce this one to cast doubt on the theory of an organized and official recensional activity.[35] After all a development towards unification without official and determined action would not be entirely unparalleled. There did exist a number of rival systems of vocalization, but in the end one such system prevailed, the Ben Asher variant of the Tiberian punctuation, and all others were superseded. And this seems not to have been the result of an official decision: rather it was a case of one tradition gaining prestige and ousting the others in a gradual process of development in which the decisive factors are not always easy to discern. I would suggest that similar mechanisms may have been at work in our case as well: a textual tradition may have supplanted all others not because it was carefully constructed on the basis of the best manuscripts and given official sanction but because it happened to belong to a leading group, was favoured by famous rabbis (many of them were, of course, scribes) or had become authoritative in some similar way. Recently S. Talmon has stressed, to my mind rightly, what he calls "the social and societal aspects of the preservation of literature",[36] and this is certainly a relevant aspect of this problem as well.

I am not saying that there were no conscious measures to ensure a safe and unitary manuscript tradition—on the contrary the scribes systematically aimed at a deliberate and methodical preservation of the text, and obviously this must have been an important factor in the development towards the predominance of a single standard text. But to reckon with these elements in the scribal procedures is something different from imagining that "the Jews refined their texts on the basis of what they judged to be the best available manuscripts and the best attested readings";[37] there seems to be little reason to believe that this was ever the case.

In conclusion I should like to emphasize how limited our infor-

---

[35] Cf. the similar argument in B. Gerhardsson, *Memory and Manuscript. Oral and Written Transmission in Rabbinic Judaism and Early Christianity* (Lund and Copenhagen, 1961), p. 53. For Gerhardsson the silence of the rabbinic sources is an indication that the standardization must have occurred much earlier. This is however unlikely: see my paper "Josefus, Rabbi Akiba och Qumran. Tre argument i diskussionen om tidpunkten för den gammaltestamentliga konsonanttextens standardisering", *TAik* 73 (1968), pp. 201ff.

[36] "The Textual Study of the Bible—A New Outlook", in F. M. Cross and S. Talmon (ed.), *Qumran and the History of the Biblical Text* (Cambridge, Mass., and London, 1975), p. 325.

[37] Greenberg (above, n. 16), p. 166.—I ought to add that, when I read this paper in Göttingen, Professor Greenberg's contribution to the discussion made it clear that this quotation from 1956 does not reflect his present views.

mation really is in these matters: there is little we know for certain, much less than confident talk about "the promulgation of the official textual recension of the rabbis" [38] would seem to presuppose. And so I may perhaps be allowed to end—as seems most fitting in this place—with a quotation from Julius Wellhausen It is taken from the end of his sketch of the history of Old Testament scholarship written for the 4th edition of Bleek's *Einleitung*, 1878. There Wellhausen expressed three wishes for the future; the last wish was for "etwas mehr Nichtwissen".[39]

[38] Cross, *The Ancient Library of Qumran*, p. 173.

[39] "Kurze Übersicht über die Geschichte der alttestamentlichen Wissenschaft", in R. Smend (hrsg.), *Grundrisse zum Alten Testament*, (München, 1965), p. 119.

THE EXEGETICAL SIGNIFICANCE OF CANON FOR THE STUDY OF THE OLD TESTAMENT

by

BREVARD S. CHILDS

New Haven, Connecticut

This article will defend the thesis that an important historical force in the composition of the Hebrew Bible has been widely disregarded by critical Old Testament research in its failure to deal adequately with the process and effect of canonization.

Largely as a result of the early critical investigations of Semler and Eichhorn on the formation of the Hebrew canon, canonization came to be regarded as a late, external act of ecclesiastical validation without any significant historical influence on the composition of the biblical books. Whereas Eichhorn at least dealt with canon in the first volume of his multi-volumed *Einleitung*, scholars who succeeded him up to the present day have generally placed their brief treatment of canon at the end of their book. The impression given is that the fixing of a canon was an unfortunate historical accident, based on false criteria of authorship, with which both the synagogue and the church have been burdened ever since. For the historical study of the Old Testament the concept of canon is irrelevant. H. Gunkel[1] offers a classic expression of this position: "Zum Schluss dann die Tragödie der israelitischen Literatur: der Geist nimmt ab; die Gattungen sind verbraucht; Nachahmungen häufen sich; an Stelle der selbständigen Schöpfungen treten die Bearbeitungen; die Sprache stirbt als Volkssprache aus. Aber schon hat die Geschichte der Sammlung der Sammlungen begonnen: der Kanon entsteht".

In my judgement, this negative attitude toward canon reflects a fundamental misunderstanding of the historical development of the Old Testament. However, before I attempt to describe the influence of canon on the formation of the Hebrew Bible, a clarification of a few issues regarding definitions and critical methodology is called for.

---

[1] "Die Grundprobleme der israelitischen Literaturgeschichte", *Reden und Aufsätze* (Göttingen, 1913), p. 36.

I. *Issues of Exegetical Methodology*

The first issue to be faced is to define "canon", which remains a highly controversial subject. I am using the term "canon" to refer to that historical process within ancient Israel—particularly in the post-exilic period—which entailed a collecting, selecting, and ordering of texts to serve a normative function as Sacred Scripture within the continuing religious community. In the transmission process, traditions which once arose in a particular milieu and were addressed to various historical situations were shaped in such a way as to serve as a normative expression of God's will to later generations of Israel who had not shared in those original historical events. The crucial canonical move occurred when occasional oracles were rendered into the form of Scripture to be used authoritatively by another generation.

In defining the term broadly I am consciously rejecting the sharp distinction between Scripture and canon advocated by several recent scholars[2] who argue that the term Scripture designates a body of authoritative writings, whereas canon implies a closed collection to which nothing more can be added. In my judgement, to conceive of canon mainly as a dogmatic decision regarding the scope of the literature is to overestimate one feature within the process which is, by no means, constitutive of canon. Moreover, the sharp distinction obscures some of the most important features in the development of canon by limiting the term only to the final stages of a long and complex process which had already started in the pre-exilic period. Essential to understanding the growth of canon is to see the interaction between a growing corpus of authoritative literature and the community which treasured it. The formation of the canon was not a late extrinsic sanctioning of a corpus of writings, but involved a lengthy series of decisions deeply affecting the shape of the material. Although it is possible to distinguish different phases within the canonical process—the term "canonization" should be reserved for the final fixing of the limits of Scripture—the earlier decisions were not qualitatively different from the later ones.

How does the canonical process relate to the literary history of the formation of the Old Testament? Although the position of biblical

[2] A. C. Sundberg, *The Old Testament of the Early Church* (Cambridge, 1964); T. N. Swanson, *The Closing of the Collection of Holy Scriptures: A Study in the History of the Canonization of the Old Testament*, Diss., Vanderbilt University, 1970. Cf. also the important earlier work of G. Hölscher, *Kanonisch und Apokryph* (Leipzig, 1905).

criticism represented by Wellhausen and his school sharply distinguished between these two historical processes, several recent studies have sought to identify the literary and the canonical history.[3] In my opinion, the two processes are not to be identified, although they belong closely together. The development of Hebrew literature involved a much broader history than that of the canon. The former process resulted from many complex forces such as are reflected in the laws of saga growth, the use of inherited literary patterns of prose and poetry, the social setting of multiple institutions, and changing scribal techniques, whereas the latter process of canon was much more closely defined by those forces which affected the literature's collection, transmission, and usage. Although non-religious factors (political, social, economic) certainly entered into the canonical process, these were largely subordinated to the religious usage of the literature by a particular religious community for some authoritative role.

How does the canonical process relate to the redactional history of a book? The method of redactional criticism seeks to discern from the peculiar shape of the biblical literature signs of intentional reinterpretation of the material which can be related to an editor's particular historically conditioned perspective. A canonical method also makes use of the peculiar shape of the literature, often in direct dependence upon redactional analysis. However, the models by which the seams in the literature are interpreted differ markedly. Canonical analysis focuses its attention on the effect which the different layers have had on the final form of the text, rather than using the text as a source for other information obtained by means of an oblique reading, such as the editor's self-understanding. A major warrant for this approach is found within the biblical tradition itself. The tradents have consistently sought to hide their own footprints in order to focus attention on the canonical text itself rather than the process.

Of course, the crucial question is immediately posed from the side of tradition and form criticism: why should one stage in the process be accorded a special status? Were not the earlier levels once regarded as canonical as well? I recognize the force of these questions, but feel that they have not fully grasped the methodological issues at

[3] Cf. D. N. Freedman, "Canon of the Old Testament", *The Interpreter's Dictionary of the Bible, Supplementary Vol.* (Nashville, 1976), pp. 130-36; M. G. Kline, *The Structure of Biblical Authority* (Grand Rapids, 1975).

stake in canon. The reason for laying such emphasis on the canonical form of Scripture lies in the peculiar relation between text and community which is constitutive of canon. The shape of the biblical text reflects a history of encounter between God and Israel. Canon serves to describe this peculiar relationship and to define the scope of this history by establishing a beginning and an end to the process. It assigns a special quality to this particular segment of human history which became normative for all future generations of this community of faith. Canon implies that the witness to Israel's experience with God lies not in the process, which has usually been lost or purposely blurred, but is testified to in the effect on the biblical text itself.[4]

Again, to take canon seriously is also to take seriously the critical function which it exercises in respect to the earlier stages of the literature's formation. A critical judgement is evidenced in the way in which these earlier stages are handled. At times the original material is passed on unchanged; at other times the tradents have selected, rearranged, or expanded the received tradition. The role of canon is to bring to bear a critical theological judgement on the process which it exercised in fixing a final shape to the literature. The dimension of depth gained by a critical reconstruction of the literary history aids in understanding the interpreted text, but, from a canonical stance, does not serve independently of it. To distinguish the Yahwist source from the Priestly within the Pentateuch often allows the interpreter to hear the combined text with new precision. But the full, combined text has rendered a judgement on the shape of the tradition which continues to exert its authority on the community of faith.

Finally, the canonical form of the text performs a crucial hermeneutical function in establishing the peculiar profile of a passage. Its shaping provides an order in highlighting certain elements and subordinating others, in drawing some features to the foreground and in pushing others into the background. To work from the canonical shape is to resist any method which seeks critically to shift the canonical ordering. Such an exegetical move occurs whenever an overarching category such as *Heilsgeschichte* subordinates the peculiar canonical profile, or a historical critical reconstruction attempts to

[4] This distinction sets my canonical method apart from that proposed by J. A. Sanders in "Adaptable for Life: The Nature and Function of Canon", *Magnalia Dei. Essays...in Memory of G. Ernest Wright* (Garden City, N.Y., 1976), pp. 531-60. I am also critical of understanding canon chiefly in terms of identity crisis as suggested by E. Jacob, "Principe canonique et formation de l'Ancien Testament", *SVT* 28 (1974), pp. 101-22.

refocus the picture according to its own standards of historical accuracy.

II. *The Canonical Shaping of Old Testament Literature*

It is now time to turn from these methodological considerations to the biblical text itself in order to describe the exegetical significance of canon for the interpretation of the Old Testament. The effect of the canonical shaping of the literature reveals an enormous variety in the manner by which the traditions were rendered as Sacred Scripture. A few examples can be sketched:

1. *A collection of material has been detached from its original historical mooring and provided with a secondary, theological context.*

The classic example of this canonical move is so-called Second Isaiah. I do not have the time to rehearse the history of research on this problem, but the reasons for assigning chapters xl-lv to a different author from the 8th century prophet appear to me incontrovertible. Yet it is extremely short-sighted simply to disregard the present context as a historical fiction. Rather, there is much evidence to suggest that the present context, while secondary, is a highly reflective, intentional setting which was considered so important that the original 6th century context was almost totally obliterated by those who transmitted the material. What is left of the original historical context is, at best, scattered vestiges, which accounts for the fact that the repeated attempts to interpret these chapters on the basis of a critical historical reconstruction have proven so unsatisfactory and hypothetical. Even though the message of Second Isaiah was once addressed to real people in a particular historical situation, the canonical shape of these chapters has drained them of their historical particularity and has subordinated the original message to a new role within the canon. These chapters begin with no superscription; there are no dates given and few concrete historical personages addressed. Even the figure of Cyrus has become such a theological projection that his role blurs into the description of Abraham (cf. xli 8ff.).

What is the effect of the new context on the interpretation of this material? By placing the message of Second Isaiah within the context of the 8th century prophet his message of promise has become a prophetic word not tied to a specific historical referent, but directed to the future. The process toward canonization has thus sharply transformed the original prophetic tradition, allowing the message to function as Scripture for every successive generation of Israelites.

2. *The original historical setting of a tradition has been retained, but it has been placed within a framework which provided the material with an interpretative guideline.*

The epilogue to the Book of Koheleth (Ecclesiastes) provides an excellent example of an appendix serving as a rule-of-faith. From the canonical perspective the crucial issue lies in determining the effect on the interpretation of the book for the religious community which used Koheleth as Scripture.

xii 9 first characterizes Koheleth as "wise". His sayings are not just pessimistic utterances of a discouraged old man, but are designated as part of Israel's wisdom. Moreover, his words are put into the larger context of a teaching office within the community, and the nature of his role is described as a critical one: weighing, studying, ordering. His literary critical role is then explicitly characterized as "truthful". In *v.* 11 the epilogue sets Koheleth's work into the larger context of other wisdom teachers. The "sayings of the *ḥakamim*" stand in parallel to their "collected sayings". The role of these wisdom collections is then succinctly evaluated. They act as "goads" to stimulate, and together they function as firmly fixed nails, points of reference, which stake out an area in which wisdom is found. In spite of this variety of function the source of all wisdom is from God, "the one Shepherd". This characterization thus legitimates the Book of Koheleth as divine wisdom and rules out any individualistic interpretation. In additon, there is a warning against other books which the editors explicitly exclude from the community as a distraction from the canonical collection. The final two verses offer the community of faith a material guide, a practical rule-of-faith, from which to read the whole book: "fear God and keep his commandments". In the end, God's hidden wisdom relativizes all human strivings.

In sum, the canonical shaping in this instance did not consist in a heavy reworking of the original sayings of the sage, but provided a new perspective for interpretation.

3. *A body of material has been edited in the light of a larger body of canonical literature.*

There has been a wide consensus ever since Mowinckel's initial impetus in seeing different layers of material comprising the Book of

Jeremiah. Again, without rehearsing the whole history of exegesis, we may say that the critical discussion in recent years has focused in establishing the historical and literary relationships between the poetic tradition of the layer "A" and the prose tradition of "C". The divergent theories of composition proposed by Duhm and Mowinckel, on the one hand, and Weiser and Bright, on the other hand, need not be pursued. If one translates this debate into canonical terminology, the editors of the Book of Jeremiah have attributed to Jeremiah two different modes of preaching. The one in oral form extended from Josiah's reign through Jehoiakim's. The other consisted of a written condensation of the oral threats in scroll form during the fourth year of Jehoiakim. According to this prose tradition Jeremiah saw himself standing in the line of a series of prophets (xxv 4) who preached the law and called for repentance. This role as a preacher of judgement in the mode of Deuteronomy became the dominant pattern into which his entire prophetic message was shaped.

From a historical-critical perspective the authentic poetic traditions of Jeremiah were transformed into the prose language of the Deuteronomic school. From the perspective of the canonical process a new understanding of Jeremiah emerged from the events of history which confirmed the prior words of Scripture. The canonical shaping of the Book of Jeremiah accepted the Deuteronomic framework as an authentic interpretation of Jeremiah's message which it used to bracket the earlier poetic material. Jeremiah's words were preserved in conjunction with a commentary which sought to understand his ministry as part of a chain of prophetic messengers who were loyal to the law of Moses and who warned of Jerusalem's coming destruction. Thus, the ordering of Jeremiah's message by means of the larger canonical corpus provided the later Jewish community with an interpretation of how the law and the prophets should properly function together.

4. *An original historical sequence of a prophet's message was subordinated to a new theological function by means of a radically theocentric focus in the canonical ordering of a book.*

The Book of Nahum is introduced by a hymn; the Book of Habakkuk concludes with one. The effect on the material is similar. This shaping process did not require a de-historicizing of the original oracles. Although the material was left virtually untouched, a new role was assigned the oracles. They now function as a dramatic illustration of the eschatological triumph of God over his adversaries whose divine nature is celebrated in hymnic form. In Nahum the destruction of the enemy is explicitly derived from the nature of Yahweh—a "jealous God", "avenging and wrathful", "keeping wrath for the enemy"—who claims dominion over the entire world. The threat against Nineveh does not arise from the personal hatred of a Hebrew prophet against Assyria, nor is it evoked by some particular historical event of the 7th century. Rather, the biblical tradents use the initial psalm, even shattering its earlier acrostic form to establish the true canonical context for understanding the significance of the prophecy. Nineveh has become a type of a larger recurring phenomenon in history against which God exercises his eternal power and judgement.

The editing of the Book of Ezekiel reflects a similar canonical shaping process. The innumerable problems of the book are well-known. The traditions of Ezekiel appear to lack the sharp contours of a definite geographical locality with a concrete group of hearers fixed in time. The prophet oscillates back and forth between Babylon and Jerusalem. Oracles from pre-exilic and post-exilic periods seem indiscriminately intertwined. The traditional forms of prophetic oral speech are largely missing, but the book abounds in allegory, sign acts and visions. The canonical key for understanding this unusual book lies in the radical theocentric perspective of the prophet which has deeply affected the final literary shape of the book. Thus, even though his oracles are fixed within a chronological framework, these temporal moorings are immediately transcended when the prophet testifies to the activity of God in terms freed from any such human limitations. Similarly, the spacial distinction between Babylon and Jerusalem is completely relativized whenever the people of God are viewed from the divine perspective as one theological entity.

5. *The shaping process altered the semantic level on which a passage originally functioned by assigning it a less-than-literal role within the canonical context.*

One example of this process derives from the combining of the Priestly creation account in Gen. i 1-ii 4a with the Yahwist's in Gen. ii 4b - iii 24. Again, the time is insufficient to rehearse the complex problems of source, tradition, and redactional analysis associated with these well-known chapters. In my judgement, the striking differences between these chapters affecting language, style, and theology which the literary critics of the 19th century first pointed out have been completely sustained. Under continued scrutiny the differences in the prehistory of the two chapters have continued to grow. Nevertheless, in their present canonical shape the original integrity of two parallel creation accounts has not been maintained. Rather, the original Yahwist account has been assigned a new role in the Book of Genesis different from its original one because of its new position in relation to chapter i.

The *toledot* formula in ii 4 offers the first indication of the shift. The formula "these are the generations of the heavens and the earth" denotes the genitive of the progenitor and never that of the progeny. It serves as a superscription to the Yahwist account which follows and can neither be shifted to a position preceding i 1, nor treated as a subscription of the Priestly account. Rather, the formula functions to link J's account to the preceding chapter. What now follows in ii 4ff. proceeds from the creation in the analogy of a son from his father. In spite of the partial overlapping in the description of the creation, ch. ii performs a basically different role from ch. i in unfolding the history of mankind as the intended offspring of the generations of the heavens and earth.

When the sequence of events in ch. ii differs from ch. i, the structure of the newly formed composition guides the reader to accommodate the friction by recognizing a literary device somewhat akin to poetic paraphrase by which to illuminate the relationship between creation and offspring. However, by this move the semantic level of ch. ii is altered by assigning to the chapter a degree of figurative interpretation once-removed from the literal sense of the original language. To speak of the two "parallel" creation accounts of Genesis is to disregard the canonical shape of the book according to which each passage performs a discrete role.

Another example of an analogous effect of canonical shaping which changed the level on which an original passage functioned is found in the Book of Hosea. The original message of Hosea was directed to the inhabitants of the Northern kingdom in the mid-eighth century. The prophet's word constituted a sustained attack on Israel's syncretistic religious worship which had changed the worship of Yahweh into a fertility cult. Hosea appropriated the language of his opponents in laying claim on all the areas of fertility, land, and kinship for Yahweh, Israel's faithful lover. The sign acts of chapter one functioned as a history-creating act of divine judgement which actualized the threat in the giving of names of judgement.

However, in its present canonical form the original material has been arranged to reflect an important semantic shift in the function of Hosea's witness. The prophet's realistic language is now understood metaphorically. Regardless of the prehistory behind the sign acts in chapters i and iii, the present shape of these chapters has given the material a symbolic interpretation. It is now quite impossible to reconstruct a history of Hosea's marriage from these two chapters. Rather, the intent that the sign acts be understood metaphorically is made explicit in both chapters i and iii (cf. i 2, 4f., 6f., 9, iii 1, 4, 5). Moreover, the placing of chapter ii between these two chapters to serve as an extended metaphor provides additional evidence of the editor's intent in interpreting the marriage in a less-than-literal fashion within its canonical context.

There is one final redactional element to be observed which affects the canonical shaping of the material. The Book of Hosea concludes with a wisdom saying (xiv 9): "Whoever is wise, let him understand these things . . . for the way of Yahweh is right . . .". Although many prophetic books show signs of wisdom influence, the wisdom material is not on the final redactional level, but usually belongs to the primary proclamation itself. Only in Hosea does a wisdom saying function in a role which has its closest parallel in Prov. xxx 5 and Eccl. xii 13. What is the canonical effect of this final verse on the reading of Hosea?

The verse functions as a directive to the reader to instruct in the proper understanding of the collection. The reader is admonished "to be wise", and "to discern" the ways of God which are surely right, but not obvious. Reflection and meditation are required to penetrate their meaning. By characterizing the collection of Hosea's words as wisdom, thus tying it to the mysteries of God's purpose, the editors offer another indication of the metaphorical function of the prophet's language. His message was true and faithful for subsequent generations within Israel, but the reality of the symbolic language requires the insight and penetration of the wise in order to discern.

6. *Prophetic proclamation has been given a radically new eschatological interpretation by shifting the referent within the original oracles.*

Scholars have long recognized that the visions in Zech. i-vi appear once to have functioned independently of each other and to have been addressed to particular historical situations both preceding and following the return from the exile.[5] But the tension between the original visions and their present framework does not derive from a historical confusion but rather points to an intentional theological shaping. The prophetic visions of Zechariah are now set in the 2nd year of Darius, that is to say, some twenty years after the return from Babylon. The deliverance from the exile now lies in the past. Although the traditional language of the Second Exodus has been retained, it has been given a new referent. The language of hope now points to a still future event in which Israel's deliverance lies. The original focus has been eschatologized and projected once more out into the future. The community of faith which lived after the return still anticipates the future in the language of the past. Thus Israel will still "flee from the land of the north", "escape to Zion", and God will dwell in her midst (ii 6ff.).

The Book of Daniel offers another example of creating a new interpretation by shifting the referent from that of the original oracle. Historical-critical scholarship has made out a convincing case for holding that at least the visions of chapters vii-xii were written about the year 165 B.C. shortly before the death of Antiochus IV Epiphanes at the moment of great persecution. In the form of visions a Maccabean author described the last great convulsion of the nations before the end. He focused on the final "indignation" of the fourth kingdom and described the developments leading up to its destruction by tracing the detailed history of the Hellenistic era step by step. There seems little doubt but that the writer of chapter xi understood Antiochus to be that last "contemptible person" who would desecrate the temple, take way the burnt offerings, and commit the final blasphemy before the moment in which God would cut him down in order to usher in the new age (xi 36).

But how was the message of Daniel understood by the generations after Antiochus and what shape was it given in its canonical context? How was a message to serve future generations as a sacred writing which appeared to be so securely anchored to the Maccabean age?[6]

---

[5] K. Galling, "Die Exilwende in der Sicht des Propheten Sacharja", *VT* 2 (1952), pp. 18-36.

[6] In my judgement, the typical response from the side of liberal Protestantism, such as is represented by H. H. Rowley, *Darius the Mede and the Four World Empires in the Book of Daniel* (Cardiff, 1935; reprinted 1964), pp. 178-82, does not come to grips with the basic theological issues.

First of all, the form in which the message originally functioned in the Maccabean crisis and the form within its canonical context appear to be essentially the same. All the historical particularity of chapters viii, ix, and xi remains untouched. The canonical text still speaks of Media, Persia, and Greece, of the cutting off of an Anointed One after 62 weeks, and of the cessation of burnt offerings. However, there is strong evidence to suggest that the interpretation of the Book of Daniel has been sharply altered by those who edited it. Although the original author of the visions appeared to have identified the fourth kingdom with the tyranny of Antiochus, this interpretation was no longer held, and the visions of Daniel continued to function authoritatively even after the death of Antiochus. The author of 2 Esdras xii 10ff. is aware that his interpretation differs from the original since Esdras identifies the fourth kingdom with Rome. How did the book's canonical shaping allow for this shift of referent?

One might have expected that the portrayal of the entrance of the kingdom of God would have been separated from the end of the fourth kingdom and then projected into the future. Instead of this move, the original sequence of the destruction of the last world power and the immediate entrance of the kingdom of God was retained unaltered in all its Hellenistic particularity. Then both the period of the fourth kingdom and the coming of God's kingdom were projected into the future to mark the end of time. Obviously a major hermeneutical move has been effected within the canonical text. The description of the "period of indignation" which reflected the policy of Antiochus against the Jews was now understood typologically. The pattern of the original referent was made normative within the canonical context. Antiochus had simply become a representative of the ultimate enemy, but he himself was not the fulfillment of the vision. For the canonical editor the Book of Daniel still spoke truthfully of the end of the age, and Israel was still called upon to "discern the times".

To summarize: an attempt has been made to describe the effect of the canonical process on the shaping of the biblical literature. It is clear that no single redactional technique was used, nor was any one dominant theological position represented. Rather, great freedom and remarkable diversity was employed in the process of rendering Israel's sacred traditions into Sacred Scripture.

III. *Theological Implications of Canon for Exegesis*

If the preceding analysis of the canonical process at work in the shaping of the Old Testament is in any measure accurate, there are some important theological implications to be drawn. I shall attempt to outline only a few of them.

1. A recovery of the true historical dimension of the Old Testament is possible only when one takes seriously the biblical text as religious literature of a community of faith. Its peculiar features must be handled in a way compatible with the literature itself. A corpus of religious writing which has been transmitted within a community for a thousand years cannot be properly compared to inert sherds which have lain buried in the ground for centuries. The frequent assumption at work in much critical study that each Old Testament text must be established with an ostensive historical reference in order to recover its correct interpretation fails to reckon with the historical forces generated from within the community of faith which often transformed an original role into one more suitable for a canonical function. The attempt to bring a biblical passage into sharper focus by means of historical reconstruction runs the acute danger of destroying those very features which reveal how the historical tradents understood the tradition. The task of exegesis involves taking seriously the historical dimension of the biblical text in tracing the effect of the community upon the text and conversely examining the force of the text on the community. This historical interaction between text and community is constitutive of canon.

2. The exegetical implication of canon is crucial in dealing with the problem of the actualization of the biblical text. In the recent hermeneutical debate, the term actualization (*Vergegenwärtigung*) denotes that process by which an ancient text was rendered religiously accessible to a later generation of users. An axiom of much recent redactional criticism is that the layering of a biblical text derives chiefly from a need to "update" an original tradition. Although this description occasionally applies, the chief point to be made by the canonical approach is that actualization is by no means limited to this one model. Rather, it is an essential function of canon to seek to transmit the tradition is such a way as to prevent its being moored in the past. Actualization derives from a hermeneutical concern which was present during the entire canonical process. It is built into the

structure of the text itself and reveals an enormous richness of theological interpretation by which to render the text religiously accessible. The modern hermeneutical impasse which found itself unable successfully to bridge the gap between the past and the present has arisen in large measure by its disregard of the canonical shaping. The usual critical method of biblical exegesis is often to reconstruct an original historical setting by stripping away those very elements which constitute the canonical shape. Little wonder that, once the biblical text has been securely anchored in the historical past by decanonizing it, the interpreter has difficulty applying it to a modern religious context.

3. The recent history of the discipline of Old Testament Theology has been dominated by the concern to find suitable categories by which to do justice to the full diversity within the literature. There is a wide consensus that extrinsic dogmatic or philosophical categories which are foreign to the material itself are incapable to describing the historical theology of ancient Israel regardless of how existential they are to the modern interpreter.

The importance of canon for Old Testament theology is that it establishes a perspective from which the literature was understood by historic Israel. It fixes the object of its study as the collection of authoritative writings in an established form with fixed parameters.[7] In my judgement, the continuing confusion between writing a theology of the Old Testament and a history of Israel's religion which has plagued the discipline since Wellhausen cannot be successfully resolved by appeals to kerygmatic theology, *Heilsgeschichte*, or sociology of religion, but the solution rather lies in coming to grips with the canonical shape which Israel gave to its Scriptures. The high level of subjectivity within the discipline occurs because the modern interpreter feels at liberty to pick and choose whatever historical level of the tradition he deems to be theological significant. The appeal to the canonical form of the Scriptures at least seeks to establish a common text as the grounds for theological reflection.

To take the canon seriously is by no means a return to a flat, one dimensional reading of the Old Testament. We have already sought to

[7] The problem of the different order and extent of the Greek canon lies beyond the scope of this paper. Briefly, the issue at stake turns on relating the Hebrew Scriptures to other bodies of religious tradition, some equally ancient, which also claim differing degrees of authority for certain communities. In my judgement, this important problem belongs to the wider field of Biblical Theology rather than Old Testament Theology as such.

give evidence of the diversity within the canonical process. Canon serves to stake out the arena in which the theological task is to be pursued. By insisting on viewing the exegetical task as constructive as well as descriptive, canonical exegesis forces the interpreter to confront the text of Scripture in an continuing and creative theological dialogue.

EBLA, UGARIT AND THE OLD TESTAMENT

by

MITCHELL DAHOOD

Rome

In the title of this paper the name "Ugarit" is intended as a double-duty modifier or two-way middle, looking back to Ebla and ahead to the Old Testament. Dating to *circa* 1375-1190 B.C., the Ugaritic tablets, found on the North Syrian shore about 85 kilometers from Ebla lying inland to the northeast, furnish the chronological and geographical link that considerably facilitates discourse attempting to relate the finds at Tell Mardikh-Ebla to the text of the Old Testament. With its 27 consonants the Ugaritic alphabet permits a precision in writing that enables one to identify roots and words in Eblaite, whose use of the Sumerian syllabary results in a very imprecise and ambiguous representation of the Semitic sounds and roots.

In recent press interviews and articles the director of the Italian archaeological mission in Syria, P. Matthiae, has been decrying the efforts of biblical scholars to find in the Ebla tablets material relevant for the interpretation of biblical data. To cite but one of his recent onslaughts, "L'engagement de la Mission italienne, tout à fait étrangère aux mystifications pseudo-scientifiques concernant une signification présumée d'Ébla comme élément de contrôle de la véracité des traditions bibliques, consiste à obtenir de la continuation des fouilles de Tell Mardikh un documentation de première importance . . .".[1] In an accompanying footnote he continues the broadside, asserting "La Mission considère déplorable la présentation populaire de l'importance des découvertes d'Ébla protosyrienne sur cette base dans une perspective anti-historique typique de l'archéologie biblique, dont on peut voir un example dans *The Observer*, 8 janv. 1977".[2] Of course one of the principal reasons for Matthiae's (and others') refusal to see any connection between Ebla and the Bible is the chronological chasm of more than a millennium separating the two cultures, but on

---

[1] *Comptes rendus de l'Académie des Inscriptions et Belles Lettres* (Jan.-March 1977), p. 172.

[2] *ibidem.*

the same page of the cited article we find him writing thus about the continuity of cultures in Syria, "enfin, les aspects de continuité des cultures de la Syrie depuis cet épanouissement initial dans le troisième quart du IIIe millénaire av. J.-C. jusqu'aux développements plus tardifs des royaumes araméens à la fin du VIIIe siècle av. J.-C." This cultural continuity in Syria can also be traced from the Ebla tablets through the Ugaritic texts straight into the Bible, and while one can sympathize with Matthiae's deploring the unjustifiable extrapolations *vis-à-vis* the Bible that have appeared in some press reports, he does himself no service by taking such an adamant anti-biblical stance. It is much too early to judge how much bearing these new finds will have on biblical research, but, from what little of the Ebla material has been published to date, the harvest is going to be much ampler than Matthiae suspects.

Since our subject is "Ebla, Ugarit and the Old Testament", we would be well advised to discuss first the linguistic classification of Eblaite. The position taken on its classification bears considerably on the relevance of Eblaite for Ugaritic and the Old Testament. This has been true of the linguistic classification of Ugaritic and its consequent pertinence or less for biblical studies. Those who consider it a Canaanite dialect tend to use it for biblical research with fewer inhibitions than those who classify Ugaritic as an independent language whose prime cognates are Akkadian, Amorite or some other Semitic language. A similar development can be expected with regard to the language emerging from the Ebla records.

On the basis of his study of the first 42 tablets and fragments discovered in 1974, G. Pettinato[3] concluded in April 1975 that "the language of Ebla as it is attested in our texts is sharply distinguished both from Old Akkadian (because of the lexicon and the verbal system) and from Amorite (because of the pronominal and verbal systems). For these reasons, in addition to its very close kinship with the languages of Canaan in the first millennium, especially with Phoenician and Hebrew, I would propose to define it as Paleo-Canaanite" (translation mine). In subsequent articles and basing his position on the study of some 400 of the 15,000 tablets unearthed in October, 1975, Pettinato has continued to propound the same classi-

[3] In a lecture delivered 23 April 1975 at the Pontifical Biblical Institute in Rome and subsequently published under the title "Testi cuneiformi del 3. millennio in paleo-cananeo rinvenuti nella campagna 1974 a Tell Mardikh=Ebla", in *Orientalia*, N.S. 44 (1975), pp. 361-74.

fication, writing in July, 1975, "The archive of 42 tablets discovered in 1974 already permitted in 1975 the identification in the Ebla texts, especially in the onomastica, of a new and very ancient West Semitic language, different from those nearest in time, namely Old Akkadian and Amorite. This language had already shown such strict affinities with Ugaritic and even more with Phoenician and Hebrew as to suggest the classification 'Paleo-Canaanite'. The attestation of the term 'Canaan' in the Eblaite texts precludes the accusation of using an anachronistic designation.[4] What is more, the 1975 archives so confirm the relationship with the languages of Canaan in the 2d and 1st millennia that the generic designation 'Paleo-Canaanite' for the language of Ebla appears fully justified".[5]

While fully agreeing with Pettinato's classification, I would prefer to stress more the kinship of Eblaite with Ugaritic; after all, the two cities were only 85 kilometers apart, Ugarit on the North Syrian coast and Ebla inland to the northeast. In fact, Ugarit may well have been the Mediterranean port for Ebla in its trade with Cyprus, mentioned as Alashiya. Being the nearest point on the mainland, just fifty nautical miles from Cyprus, Ugarit may have been the port of arrival for the Cypriote copper destined for Ebla and the port of departure for the textiles and manufactured goods shipped by Ebla to Cyprus. The Canaanite classification has been challenged by G. Garbini,[6] who finds the designation "Paleo-Canaanite" scarcely justifiable for a language used, according to him, hundreds of kilometers distant from Canaan. The same quandary arose at the time of the Ras Shamra discoveries in 1929. C. Virolleaud, the epigrapher of the French mission at Ugarit, at first tended to believe that the strange script of Ugarit, so different from the Akkadian syllabary employed in those areas during the First International Period, was introduced by the Mycenaeans, impressed as he was with the archaeological remains at Minet el Beida which displayed so many Mycenaean-Minoan features. At the same time he had possibly not reconciled himself to

[4] And, one might add, upsets the thesis of J. D. Muhly, *JAOS* 97 (1977), p. 65, who claims that "the term 'Canaanite' is of even more questionable legitimacy; the name has no real historical meaning before the Late Bronze Age. More important the whole idea of Amorite and Canaanite invasions, and of the latter group being a distinct entity, separate from the former, makes little sense either as ethnology or linguistics". The Ebla tablets frequently call Dagan "the Canaanite" to emphasize his origins in the west; the people of Ebla were evidently conscious of Canaan as a geographical entity as early as 2500 B.C.

[5] In *Biblical Archeologist* 39 (1976), p. 50.

[6] *Annali* (Naples) 36 (1976), p. 222, n. 3.

the fact that a major settlement in the northern extremity of Syria could be attributed to Phoenicians or Canaanites. Further research quickly dissolved this difficulty and for the next forty years Virolleaud championed the Canaanite classification of Ugaritic which today has gained the largest number of supporters. But Garbini is not among these and this may help explain his position *vis-à-vis* the language of Ebla.[7]

After a preliminary evaluation entitled "Thoughts about Ebla", I. J. Gelb[8] concludes from the material available to him that Iblaic, as he terms the language, must be considered not as a dialect of West Semitic but rather as a new Semitic language closer to Akkadian and Amorite than to Ugaritic and Hebrew. This is consistent with his practice of disregarding all such divisions as "eastern" and "western", "northwestern" and "southwestern", and of simply listing in chronological order the eight attested Semitic languages (Akkadian, Amorite, Ugaritic, Canaanite, Aramaic, [classical] Arabic, South Arabic, and Ethiopic) with their dialects. In his opinion Eblaite should be added to that list as a ninth Semitic language having closest relationships with Old Akkadian and Amorite. It will be noticed that Gelb does not consider Ugaritic as Canaanite, following A. Goetze's rejection of the traditional classification of Ugaritic as a member of the Canaanite branch of Semitic. Gelb claims that Goetze's arguments set forth in 1941 have never been rebutted, and that those who support the Canaanite classification continue to rely on such non-linguistic arguments as mythology, traditions, and literary genres. Here I sharply take issue with Gelb and at several points in this article shall have occasion to show how Gelb's misunderstanding of the linguistic position of Ugaritic impairs his interpretation of the Ebla material.

My thesis is that the safest and most rapid route to understanding the forms and contents of the new tablets lies along the Ebla-Ugarit-Palestine axis. The result achieved here will in turn facilitate the task of sorting out the Northwest Semitic names and forms in Old Akkadian texts from Mesopotamia but have remained dimly understood because their provenance was not divined.[9]

---

[7] See also A. R. Millard in D. J. Wiseman (ed.), *Peoples of Old Testament Times* (Oxford, 1973), p. 36, who believes that Canaanite and Ugaritic are contemporary and related, but distinct languages. Eblaite promises to contribute much linguistic and lexicographical matter to the discussion.

[8] The full title being *Thoughts about Ibla*: *A Preliminary Evaluation March 1977* (Syro-Mesopotamian Studies 1/1, May 1977; Malibu), 30 pp.

[9] See the brief remarks of W. von Soden, *ZA* 66 (1976), pp. 136-7, who in his review of A. Westenholz's edition of third-millennium documents from

In the present stage of enquiry, Ebla studies resemble much Mari research where the knowledge of Amorite derives almost exclusively from personal and place names. To be sure, the Ebla archives include bilingual vocabularies in Sumerian and Eblaite, letters, commercial treaties, and literary texts with many words in the local language, but these have not been published and the current administrative and organizational problems besetting La Missione Archeologica Italiana in Siria do not augur well for the speedy publication of these much awaited texts. But a sufficient number of personal names with significant phonetic and morphological features appear in TM.75.G.336, published in 1976 by G. Pettinato and P. Matthiae,[10] to permit the corroboration of the Canaanite affiliation propounded by Pettinato on the basis of the evidence furnished by the 42 tablets unearthed in 1974.

Fascinating from the phonetic and biblical point of view is the PN *wa-na* (TM.75.G.336 III 3), where biblical scholars will recognize at once the same name as that borne many centuries later by the Prophet Jonah, a name unattested outside the Bible till the Ebla discoveries. This preservation of *primae waw*, as in the Ebla conjunction *wa* (*Or* N.S. 44 [1975], p. 365, n. 17; *RSO* 50 [1976], p. 13), might suggest a South Semitic affiliation, but a re-examination of the early Northwest Semitic evidence shows that the preservation of initial *waw* was more a matter of chronology than of genetic relationship. Ebla also witnesses *primae waw* in the qal active participle *wa-ti-nu*,[11] which in turn sheds welcome light on much-disputed *wtn* in *UT*, 51 V 70-71, *wtn qlh b'rpt* / *šrh larṣ brqm*, "He gave forth his voice from the clouds/his bolts of lightning traveled toward earth". Parsed as qal perfect, *watana* suggests that parallel *šrh* is also a verb whose subject is *brqm*, hence to be vocalized *šarahū*, a verb probably related to the *mediae waw* verb in Hebrew, *šûr*, "to travel". The identity of *šrh* with Job xxxvii 3 *yišrēhû* has long been noted: *taḥat-kol-haššāmayim yišrēhû* / *weʾôrô ʿal-kanpôt hāʾāreṣ*, "Beneath all the heavens it [his voice] travels / and his illumination is upon the wings of earth". In addition to *wtn*,

---

Nippur and Fara, observes that one must now in the light of the Ebla material separate Old North Semitic from Old Akkadian.

[10] "Aspetti amministrativi e topografici di Ebla nel III millennio av. Cr." in *Rivista degli studi orientali* 50 (1976), pp. 1-30.

[11] See *Orientalia*, N.S. 44 (1975), p. 372. The name is obviously a hypocoristicon with the name of the god omitted. Compare the composite divine title *ʾēl*/ /*yōtēn* as reconstructed by D. N. Freedman and myself in M. Dahood, *Psalms I* (Garden City, N.Y., 1966), p. 114, on Ps. xviii 33.

Ugaritic preserves vestigially initial *waw* in the conjunctions *w* and *wn*, *wld*, "child", *wpṯ*, "to spit", *wṯb*, "to sit", in *UT*, 51 IV 104, and in the PNN *wql* and *wry*. Hebrew examples include *wāzār*, "guilty", in Prov. xxi 8; *weled*, "child", in Gen. xi 30 and 2 Sam. vi 23 (usually emended to *yeled*); *weqar rûaḥ*, "slow to anger", in Prov. xvii 27;[12] *wōšebêhā* (MT *wešābêhā*), "her inhabitants", in Isa, i 27;[13] *whb*, "the Benefactor", in Num. xxi 14;[14] and possibly *wd*ʿ, "knowledge", if one reads Prov. xiv 33 as follows: *belēb nābôn tānûaḥ ḥokmāh / ûbeqereb kesîl yāmūt wēdāʿ* (MT *kesîlîm tiwwādēaʿ*), "In the heart of the intelligent man wisdom rests / but in the bosom of the fool knowledge dies".

Another Eblaite PN preserving initial *waw* is *we-du-lum* (= **weḥdu-lum*), "God is one" or "God is unique" (TM.75.G.336 II 10), which elicits the *Shemaʿ Yiśrāʾēl* in Deut. vi 4. *Wêdum*, "single, unique", probably occurs in Sargonic and Ur III PNN, as well as in PNN from Mari.[15]

As in Ugaritic, *ā* does not become *ō* at Ebla, at least as a general rule. This can be deduced from the PNN *wa-na* (Heb. *yônāh*), *wa-ti-nu* (Heb. *nōtēn*), *da-sí-ma-ad* (Heb. *meʾōd*), *en-na-da-ru* (Heb. *dôr*),[16] *ar-en-num* (Heb. *ʾôr*), the infinitives *a-ḫa-zu-um* and *ma-ḫa-ṣi*, and from the negative particle *la*, to be discussed below. The divine name *ka-ša-lu/ru* (*BA* 39 [1976], p. 48, equals Ugar. *kṯr*, and underlies the *hapax legomenon kôšārôt* im Ps. lxviii 7.

The consonantal phonemes *ʿayin* and *ḥet* influence the *a* > *e* change in some words but not in others. Gelb[17] claims that the change takes place in some *positions* and not in others and cites the examples *ib-du-ma-lik* (*ʿebd-malik*), *ib-du-ra-sa-ap* (*ʿebd-rašap*), *en-na-ì-li* (*ḥennā-ʾil*), and as examples of the non-change in the final position *iš-ma-il* (*yišmaʿ-il*), "Il has heard me", and *ištamamalik*, "Malik heard". He concludes that "this single isogloss places the language of Ibla

---

[12] H. Limet, "Grammaire des anciennes tablettes de Mari", *Syria* 52 (1975), pp. 37-52, esp. 50-51, is at a loss to explain the PN *a-ḫu-wa-qar*, which he thinks was borrowed from Babylonia without phonetic change. The name might also be West Semitic, though Ugaritic attests this root as *yqr*, "precious".

[13] D. N. Freedman, "The Twenty-third Psalm", in L. L. Orlin (ed.), *Michigan Oriental Studies in Honor of George G. Cameron* (Ann Arbor, 1976), pp. 139-66, esp. 162-63, correctly sees in Ps. xxiii 6 *wšbty* the verb *wšb* with the initial *waw* preserved; he reads *wāšabtî*, "I will dwell".

[14] Consult D. L. Christensen, *Transformations of the War Oracle in Old Testament Prophecy* (Missoula, 1975), p. 51, n. 81.

[15] See I. J. Gelb, *Glossary of Old Akkadian* (Chicago, 1957), p. 2.

[16] *Orientalia*, N.S. 44 (1975), p. 370.

[17] Gelb, *Glossary*, p. 18.

squarely with the Akkadian of the Sargonic period (*beʿlum*, *rēʿijjun*, and *jišmaʿ*), and not with any West Semitic language". But Gelb's conclusion appears premature, being based on too scanty evidence. The Eblaite preposition "upon" is *al*[18] and not *e-lu*; *ʿam*, "people", appears as *am* in the construct phrase *é-am*, "the people's palace",[19] in contradistinction to *é-en*, "the king's palace". Pettinato entertained the idea of relating *am* to *ʿam*, "people", but discarded it because, in the light of the then present knowledge, the *ʿayin* at the beginning of a word should be reproduced by *é*. The PNN *a-lum*, "the Most High" (cf. Heb. PN *ʿēlî*) (TM.75.G.336 V 13), and *a-lu-a-ḫu*, "the Most High is (my) brother" (TM.75.G.336 rev. I 7), conspire with *am* to show that the presence of *ʿayin* does not always produce the *a* to *e* shift. The divine name Baal appears both in the abbreviated form *be* in PN *en-na-be* (= *Ḥannibaʿal*) in TM.75.G.336. II 15 but as *ba-al* in some personal names to be published soon by Pettinato. Since the verb *bāṣaʿ*, "to cut, decide", is predicated of God in Job vi 9, xxvii 8, and Lam. ii 17, it becomes possible to explain PN *ba-ṣa-a* in TM.75. G.336 VI 10 as a hypocoristicon denoting "(God) has decided", in which the presence of the third radical *ʿayin* does not produce the vowel change characteristic of Akkadian.

The morphologically interesting names *ti-ra-il*, "Il sees",[20] and *ti-dì-nu*, "He judges" (TM.75.G.336 I 4), draw back into the third millennium possible evidence for the existence of the third masculine singular with preformative *t*-. That El Amarna and Ugaritic employ preformative *t*- alongside preformative *y*- with masculine plural subjects[21] is generally accepted, but that preformative *t*- was used with masculine singular in the Northwest Semitic dialects finds scholars sharply at odds.[22] The promising Eblaite examples require a brief review of the evidence; the evidence marshalled in the past

---

[18] *Rivista Biblica* (Italiana) 25 (1977), p. 237.

[19] *Rivista degli studi orientali* 50 (1976), p. 13.

[20] *Rivista Biblica* (Italiana) 25 (1977), p. 240, and for the thought compare Heb. PN *reʾāyāh*, "Yah has seen", and for the form, Old Akkadian PN *dar-ti-bu* which Gelb, *Glossary*, p. 22, interprets "She compensated"; now also possible would be "He compensated".

[21] For rapid orientation consult C. H. Gordon, *Ugaritic Textbook* (hereafter *UT*), § 9.14.

[22] On the *status quaestionis* and for recent bibliography, see H. J. van Dijk, "Does Third Masculine Singular TAQTUL Exist in Hebrew?" in *VT* 19 (1969), pp. 440-47, who cites among biblical attestations Isa. vii 20, xlii 20, liii 10; Ezek. xii 25; Hab. i 14; Pss. x 13, 15, xlii 2; Qoh. x 15. Van Dijk's thesis has been accepted by R. Degen, *Die Welt des Orients* 6 (1971), p. 62.

several decades and the convincing new biblical instances leave little doubt that this form was employed in all the major Canaanite dialects. Thus alongside Ugaritic PN *ygrš* one finds *tgrš* (*UT*, 321 II 24), while unexplained *bn tran* (*UT*, 2046:3) can be compared with Eblaite *ti-ra-il* and interpreted "the son of 'he (God) sees me' ". Ugar. PN *tdn* can scarcely be dissociated from Eblaite *ti-dì-nu* and El Amarna 71:5; 86:4 where the verb *ti-di-nu* is predicated of a god. In fact, a good number of Ugaritic PNN become morphologically understandable on this hypothesis: *tan*, *tiyn*, *tbšn*, *tkn*, *tlbr*, *tldn*, *trdn*, *trn*, *ttn*, etc. The place name *tbq* (*UT*, 1098:10) looks etymologically related to Heb. *yabbōq*; both probably derive from **nbq*, "to gush forth", Arab. *nabaqa*, cognate with *nbk* and *nbʿ* with the same meaning, rather than from *bāqaq*, "to split", as older lexica propose.

In his study of this form in Hebrew, N. M. Sarna[23] claimed to identify it in Job xviii 14-15, xx 9; his position was challenged by W. L. Moran[24] but convincing new examples from Job sustain Sarna's contention. Thus Job xxxiv 17, *haʾap śônēʾ mišpāṭ yaḥ*^{a}*bôš*/ *w*^{e}*ʾim ṣaddîq kabbîr taršîaʿ*, "Can an enemy of right bind up / or pronounce guilty the Venerable Just One?" The Targum and 2 Mss do read third-person *yršyʿ* for MT *taršîaʿ*, since there is no apparent motive for an unexpected shift from third to second person. Following two third singular verbs in vs. 25, *yakkîr* and *hāpak*, Job xxxiv 26 becomes intelligible when pointed *tāḥīt* (MT *taḥat*) *r*^{e}*šāʿîm sōp*^{e}*qīm* (MT *s*^{e}*pāqām*) / *bim*^{e}*qōm rōʾîm*, "He shattered the wicked as they clapped in mockery/in the place where men look on". Job xv 24, *y*^{e}*baʿ*^{a}*tūhû ṣar ûm*^{e}*ṣûqāh* / *titq*^{e}*pēhû kīmelek* (MT *k*^{e}*melek*) *ʿātîd lakkîdôr*, "Distress and anguish terrify him / the King himself (Death) overwhelms him / readier than a vulture". In Isa. xlii 20, the balance with *yišmāʿ* shows that *tišmōr* is also third masculine singular, and the masculine gender of *kûš* imposes a similar analysis in Ps. lxviii 32,

---

[23] In *JBL* 82 (1963), p. 318.

[24] In his attempt to refute the thesis of Sarna, W. L. Moran, *Biblica* 45 (1964), p. 82, n. 1, conceded that he had no explanation for Job xx 9, *t*^{e}*šûrennû m*^{e}*qômô*, other than the possibility than in this unique instance *māqôm* is feminine. But a glance at Job vii 10 and Ps. ciii 16 discountenances such a possibility. Others have applied similar reasoning to Aḥiram, line 2, *tḥtsp ḥṭr mšpṭh* / *thtpk ksʾ mlkh*, "May his judicial rod be stripped / may his royal throne be overturned", where *ḥṭr* and *ksʾ*, masculine in other Semitic languages but here construed with *tḥtsp* and *thtpk*, were claimed to be dialectically feminine. Mounting evidence in the Canaanite dialects for preformative *t-* with third masculine singular dispenses one from recourse to such explications. See the apposite remarks of H. Vincent, *Revue biblique* 34 (1925), p. 186, concerning the Aḥiram usage.

kûš tārîṣ yādāyw lē'lōhîm, "Cush speeds his wares to God". Good parallelism facilitates the reading and analysis of Ezek. xxvi 11, *'ammēk baḥereb yahᵃrōg / ûmaṣṣᵉbôt 'uzzēk lā'āreṣ tōrīd* (MT *tērēd*), "Your people he will slay with the sword / and the pillars of your fortress he will bring down to the ground". Other biblical attestations of this form can be seen in Deut. xxxii 14, *tišteh*;[25] Pss. vii 10, *tᵉkônēn*; xvii 14, *tᵉmallē'*; xlviii 8, *tᵉšabbēr*; xlix 20, *tābô'*; cvii 25, *tᵉrômēm*; Lam. ii 22, *tiqrā'*; iii 17, *tiznaḥ*.

Qal Passive

The qal passive perfect seems to be attested in PNN *pù-tá-be*, "He has been ransomed by Baal" (TM.75.G.336 rev V 15), and *pù-ta-yà*, "He has been ransomed by Ya" (TM.75.G.rev V 10).[26] Compare the Hebrew PNN *pᵉdāyāh*, *pᵉdāyāhû*, *pᵉdā'ēl*, Pss. xxxiv 23, xlix 16 and Isa. xxxv 10. Qal passive participles are reflected in PN *a-bù-sí*, "Well-fed" (TM.75.G. 336 rev V 15), and *ḫa-zu-ru*, "Encompassed (by God)" (*ibid.* II 2).[27] Witnessed only in Ugaritic[28] and Hebrew, the root *'bs* occurs only twice in the OT and both times as qal passive participle: 1 Kings v 3, *barbūrîm 'ᵃbûsîm*, "fatted fowl", and Prov. xv 17, *šôr 'ābûs*, "a fatted ox". The appositeness of such

[25] See L. H. Brockington, *The Hebrew Text of the Old Testament: The Readings adopted by the Translators of the New English Bible* (Oxford and Cambridge, 1973), p. 28. Other modern translations also construe *tišteh* as third masculine singular, without however obliging us with a textual note; the "Chicago Bible" (AT) to name one.

[26] In his review of H. Limet, *Études de documents de la période d'Agadé* in *JCS* 27 (1975), p. 182, M. A. Powell writes, "There is a similar problem with the name read *Pú-ta*, for which I would prefer *PÚ-ta*, since the underlying word may in reality be / *burt* / from Akk. *burtum*. The true reading of this abbreviated Sumerian name, like many others contained in this volume, can only be determined when the full form of the name is known". The Ebla onomasticon has happily provided the full form of the name now seen to be Canaanite and not Sumerian.

[27] Read *ḫa-zu-EN* by Pettinato, *RSO* 50 (1976), p. 6. P. Matthiae, *Archaeology* 30 (July, 1977), p. 253, continues to defend the reading A.EN.GA.DU, and to see a reference to king of Akkad, a reading long discarded by Pettinato in favor of *a-ru-ga-du*, a city in the neighborhood of Ebla. Pettinato's reading of the sign EN as *ru* appears to be correct here since the resultant city-name turns out to have a good Canaanite etymology in *'rk*, "to restore"; cf. Heb. feminine noun *'ᵃrûkāh*, "healing" and "restoration" when describing the restoration of walls of temple (2 Chron. xxiv 13) and of the walls of Jerusalem (Neh. iv 1). Hence the city-name *a-ru-ga-du* would mean "Restored City", just as Carthage means "New City" and Utica "Old City".

[28] In the place-name *ᵃˡú-bu-sú/i* (*PRU* III, 11.830:11; 15:11; 15.20:1). The Ugaritic form exhibits a vocalic harmony not witnessed in either the Eblaite or Hebrew forms. Thus far I have collected six features common to Hebrew and Eblaite but differing from Ugaritic.

personal names emerges from comparison with literary texts expressing the Canaanite ideal, as in *UT*, 51 VII 49-52, where the duties of the supreme deity are thus set forth: *aḥdy dymlk ʿl ilm | lymru ilm wnšm|dyšbʿ hmlt arṣ*, "He alone who will reign over the gods / who will indeed fatten gods and men / who will sate the multitudes of the nether world". The second name *ḫa-zu-ru* contains the root underlying Heb. *ḥāṣēr*, "courtyard", as well as the name of the ancient Canaanite city *ḥāṣôr*, appearing in Ebla geographical lists as *ḫa-zu-ru.*[29]

The qal passive participle with *mediae waw* root is found in names apparently deriving from *ʾwš*, "to donate, bestow", as in *iš-a-bù*, "Donated by the Father",[30] and *iš-i-lum*, "Donated by Il"[31] (compare the Latin name Donatus). Both names accord with the sentiments voiced by *UT*, Krt 135-136, *udm ytnt il | wušn ab adm*, "Udum is the gift of El/and the donation of the Father of Mankind". Here one sees in *ušn*, *il* and *ab* the same roots witnessed in Eblaite *iš*, *a-bù* and *i-lum*. This root in qal active is predicated of El the creator (*bny bnwt*) in PN *aš-ba-ni*, "the Creator has donated" (TM.75.G.336 rev I 1). Also instructive is *iš-la-yà*, "Donated by Ya" (TM.75.G.336 I 9, 12), which sheds light on Job xii 9-10, where one finds in the dialogues the only mention of Yahweh: "Who does not know from all these / that the hand of Yahweh has made this? That from his hand is the soul of every living being/ and the spirit in all flesh is his donation" (reading *ʾîšō* for MT *ʾîš*).[32] Here *yhwh* and *ʾîšō*, when derived from *wš*, manifest the elements evidently collocated in PN *iš-la-yà*, "Donated by Yà", where *la* marks the *lamedh* of agency with a passive form an exclusively Northwest Semitic usage.[33] Comparable biblical

---

[29] As reported by Pettinato in a conference given at the Istituto Geografico Italiano in Rome in June, 1976, and repeated in newspaper interviews.

[30] Understood as "A man is the father" by Pettinato in *BA* 39 (1976), p. 50.

[31] Pettinato, *ibid.*, renders this name "A man is the god", an unlikely proposition in Canaan but not improbable in Mesopotamia.

[32] Consult my article "Ugaritic *ušn*, Job 12, 10 and 11QPsaPlea3-4" in *Biblica* 47 (1966), pp. 107-8, where I pointed out that where the *textus receptus* reads *ʾyš*, Qumran has *ntth*, "you have given". Today I would vocalize MT *ʾîš* as *ʾîšō*, "his gift", and explain the form as qal passive participle of *ʾwš*. See also P. Bordreuil, *Syria* 52 (1975), p. 116 and n. 3. The equation *ʾwš=ntn* already occurs in Old Akkadian synonym lists where *ḫa-a-šu = na-da-nu*; see Gelb, *Glossary*, p. 122.

[33] For an analysis of this usage with the verb *nāšāʾ*, "to deceive", in Hos. i 6, see W. Kuhnigk, *Nordwestsemitische Studien zum Hoseabuch* (Rome, 1974), p. 4, an analysis now sustained by the same idiom in Isa. ii 9 where MT *ʾal tiśśāʾ lāhem*, usually considered corrupt, yields sense when pointed *ʾal tuššāʾ lāhem*, "Be not deceived by them". Cf. also Gen. ii 20, *ûleʾādām lōʾ mūṣāʾ* (MT *māṣāʾ*) *ʿēzer kenegdô*, "But by Adam no helpmate was found like himself".

instances of the passive participle of *'wš* occur in PN *'ešba'al*, "Donated by Baal", to be equated with Ugar. PN *išb'l*,[34] and in the hitherto unexplained place-name in Josh. xv 32, *'eš'ān*, "Donated by (the god) 'An".[35]

The Ebla PNN containing *'wš*, "to donate", promise to shed light on the PN *uš-mi-il* attested at Abū Ṣalābīkh in southern Mesopotamia. In an article published in 1967 and entitled "Semitic Names in the Fara Period",[36] R.D. Biggs noted that many of the names of the scribes mentioned in the colophons to Sumerian tablets bear Semitic names. By about the 26th century B.C. Semites were well established at Abū Ṣalābīkh (the name of the ancient city remains to be identified) and were active in the intellectual life. It turns out that the overwhelming majority of scribes who actually copied the tablets have West Semitic names. Some of these such as *en-na-il*, "Have mercy, O Il", now appear at Ebla. Though not yet found at Ebla, PN *uš-mi-il* may be interpreted "Donate, O Il", on the basis of Northwest Semitic syntax. The first element *uš* can parse as imperative singular, *-mi-* as the emphatic particle known from Ugaritic-Hebrew *-mi* and Akk. *-ma*, but here with the function of a vocative.[37] Of the same formation (imperative +*mi* + divine name) are Heb. PNN *ḥᵃnameʾēl*, "Have pity, O God!", usually explained as dissimilated from *ḥᵃnanʾēl*, a solution that can no longer be accepted in view of *uš-mi-il*, and Neh. vii 7, *ra'amᵉyāh*, "Shepherd, O Yah!", but in Ezra ii 2 reproduced as *rᵉ'ēlāyāh*, where vocative *-lā-* replaces vocative *-mi-*. The Hebrew precative particle *bî*, "I beseech you", heretofore documented in standard Babylonian, can now be identified in the PN from Abū Ṣalābīkh *uš-bi-a-ḫa*, "Donate, I beseech you, a brother!"

Imperatives

When giving names to their children, parents often ask a blessing of the god; hence personal names are a rich lode for imperative forms. Thus PN *ri-da-li-im*, "Come down, O Lim", illustrates the

---

[34] As proposed in my *Ugaritic-Hebrew Philology* (Rome, 1965), p. 52.

[35] W. Baumgartner, *Hebräisches und aramäisches Lexikon zum Alten Testament* I, p. 93b, rightly question's Borée's derivation from *š'n*, "to support". Doubtless the male counterpart of 'Anat, the god *'n* is well attested in Ugaritic texts; see *UT*, Glossary, No. 1881.

[36] In *Orientalia*, N.S. 36 (1967), pp. 55-6.

[37] Most clearly in UT, 51 II 30, *'n mkṯr*, "Look, O Kothar!" when compared with 51 VII 53-54, *'n [gpn] wugr*, "Look, O Gapnu and Ugaru". Cf. further 1 Aqht 86, *abšrk mdn[il]*, "I announce to you, O Daniel!".

energic imperative of *yārad*; compare Ugar. *rd*, Heb. *rid* > *rēd*; energic *ridā* > *r^edāh*.[38] Like some of the Ebla names cited above, *ri-da-li-im* can be illustrated from a literary text expressing a similar sentiment: *UT*, Krt 35-7, *wbḥlmh il yrd / bḏhrth ab adm*, "and during his dream El came down / during his vision the father of mankind", and 77-9, *šrd bʿl bdbḥk / bn dgn bmṣdk*, "With your sacrifice make Baal come down / with your game-offering the son of Dagan".[39] PN *si-piš-ar*, "O Sun, shine!" (TM.75.G.336 rev V 15) contains the simple imperative *ar*, Heb. impr. *'ôr*, "shine!" whereas *ar-ra-si-piš* (TM.75.G.336 rev I 2) exhibits the energic imperative *ar-ra*.[40] Biblical in both of its components is PN *en-na-ma-ni*, "Have pity, O Mani" (TM.75.G.336 rev I 4) with energic *en-na* = Heb. *ḥannāh*, "Have pity!" and the god of destiny known from Isa. lxv 11, "who prepare for Fortune the table/who fill for Destiny (*m^enî*) the crater". Ebla and the Bible combine to clarify unexplained Ugar. PNN *pmn*, "the utterance of Destiny", and *mny*, "My destiny is Ya". Cf. Ps. xvi 5.

The El Amarna-Hebrew particle of entreaty *-nā'*, placed after imperatives, can be seen in PN *sí-mi-na-yà*, "Hear, I pray, O Ya" (TM.75.G.336 IV 16). This name helps interpret Ugar. PN *šmʿy*, "Hear, O Ya!", which is now seen to be formally identical with the biblical PN *š^emaʿyāh*, "Hear, O Yah!"[41] Compare also Ebla PN *sí-mi-na-be*, "Hear, I pray, O Dagan!"[42]

Another morphologically significant name is *ṣi-la-be*, being published by Pettinato in a forthcoming article on Dagan and his cult at Ebla.[43] Analysed into *ṣi*, imperative of *yāṣā'*, followed by vocative *la* and *be*, "master", Dagan's title at Ebla, the name signifies "Go forth,

[38] G. Pettinato, *Or*, N.S. 44 (1975), p. 372a and n. 91, derives *ri-da* from *ridday*, (*rdy*, "to govern"), but this etymology appears unlikely because *ridday* should become *ri-dē*, not *ri-da*.

[39] Ugaritic PN *trdn* may now be interpreted "He/You came down to me", with the final *-n* expressing dative suffix. It might also mark the energic ending, "Indeed He/You came down". Heb. PN *yaḥat* may now be derived from *nāḥat*, "to descend"; hence "May (God) descend". The imperfect of *nāḥat* occurs with (Ps. xxxviii 3) and without (Jer. xxi 13; Prov. xvii 10) initial *nun*. On Isa. li 6, see M. Dahood in E. Testa (ed.), *Studia Hierosolymitana in onore di P. Bellarmino Bagatti* (Jerusalem, 1976), p. 18.

[40] And helps appreciate the polemical tone of Isa. lx 19, "No more will the sun be your light by day".

[41] F. Gröndahl, *Die Personennamen der Texte aus Ugarit* (Rome, 1967), p. 194, hazards no interpretation of *šmʿy*.

[42] In this name *-be* designates Dagan as argued by Pettinato in his forthcoming article "Dagan ed il suo culto ad Ebla" in *Revue d'Assyriologie*.

[43] I express my gratitude to Prof. Pettinato for having given me an advance copy of his article.

O Dagan!" Here *ṣi* probably means to go forth in a military sense, though this cannot be proved. This name resembles in thought the Mari PNN *ya-ṣí-^{d}IM*, *ya-ṣì-AN*, and also clarifies the Old Akkadian names *ẓé-la-da-ad*, *ẓé-la-^{d}IM*. Not appreciating the vocative function of *la*, Gelb[44] subsumes these names under *ṣll*, *ṣillum*, "shade, protection". That *la-* in *ẓé-la-^{d}IM* represents the vocative particle is evident upon comparison with PN *ẓé-^{d}IM*.

The imperatives cited thus far all come from personal names and, being addressed to a god, are singular in number. The two following occur in a proverb and are plural in number. The proverb appears to be pure Canaanite, containing not a word of Sumerian.[45]

ù-šu la kà-la	Donate without measure,
ù-šu la ti-li	Donate without weighing;
gú-šu la kà-la	Make presents without measure,
gú-šu la ti-li	Make presents without weighing.

If *ù-šu* parses a plural imperative of *ùš*, "to donate", just as *uš* in PN *uš-mi-il*, "Donate, O Il", from Abū Ṣalābīkh parses as the singular imperative, then *gu-šu* must be read as *gu-šu*, imperative plural of *qw/yš*, "to present". In Akkadian one finds *qiāšum*, "to present", *qištum* and *qišum*, "a present".[46] The biblical PNN *qušāyāhu*, "Present, O Yahu!", in 1 Chron. xv 17 but *qîšî* in 1 Chron. vi 29, and *qîš*, "Presented (by Yahu)", the father of Saul, have long been derived from the root *qûš*, "to present, donate".[47] Thus *qîš* may be parsed as the qal passive participle of *qûš*, just as Eblaite *iš-a-bu* has been explained above as "donated by the Father". In *la* may be recognized the negative particle, here with the nuance "without", while *kala* may tentatively be derived from *kwl*, "to measure",[48] and *tili* from *talaya*,

44 *Glossary*, pp. 243-4. For vocative *lamedh* in Hebrew PNN, see Dahood, *Orientalia* 45 (1976), pp. 328, 332.

45 In *Rivista biblica*, 25 (1977), p. 232, "anche se non oso tradurlo".

46 Consult Gelb, *Glossary*, pp. 222-3. The recognition of this root in Hebrew opens up a new possibility in much-disputed Isa. xxix 21, *maḥ^{a}ṭî'ê 'ādām b^{e}dābār / w^{e}lammokîaḥ baššaʿar y^{e}qūšûn* (MT *y^{e}qōšûn*), "who cause a man to sin in speech / and then hand him over to the prosecutor at the gate". Jer. xviii 18 seems to allude to a similar practice.

47 So T. C. Vriezen, *OTS* 14 (1965), p. 333, and M. Noth, *Die israelitische Personennamen* (Stuttgart, 1928), p. 171, n. 3. The *hapax* gentilic in Nah. i 1, *hā'elqōšî* "the man from Elqosh", apparently contains this root.

48 See Baumgartner, *HAL* II, p. 442a, with bibliography. Comparison with Isa. xl 12, *mî-mādad* ... *w^{e}kāl* "Who has gauged ... and measured?" perhaps uncovers the sense of the feminine PN *mîkāl*, the daughter of Saul. Appreciation

"to hang, suspend"; the form *tili* may be piel, which is witnessed in Ezek. xxvii 10. Latin *suspendere*, "to hang, weigh", illustrates the possible semantic range of Semitic *talaya*, while the two ideas purportedly juxtaposed in this proverb find a counterpart in Isa. xl 12, *wᵉkāl baššālīš ʿᵃpar hāʾāreṣ / wᵉšāqal bappeles hārîm*, "(Who) has measured with a cup the earth's soil / and weighed the mountains with a balance?"[49] At first blush the proverb sounds incomplete—some sort of reward should accompany such behavior—but as it stands it looks like a direct invitation to altruistic generosity.

Piel participle

The hypocoristicon *ma-gal-lu* (TM 75.G.336 VI 8), with the doubled final consonant, looks like the Heb. piel participle *mᵉkalleh*, "the one who annihilates", predicated of God in Jer. xiv 22 and Job ix 22. It is doubtless to be identified with the Ugar. PN *mkl*[50], as well as with the Phoenician god *mukal* of Bethshan in the 13th century B.C. who is equated a millennium later at Cyprus with the god of the plague Resheph; hence *mukal* and Eblaite *magallu* refer to destroying deities. Semantically, *magallu* compares with *PN ḫabil*, "the Destroyer" (TM.75.G.336 rev V12), which in turn evokes the name of the Ugaritic goddess *ʿnt ḫbly*.

Infinitive absolute

Two examples have been published to date: *a-ḫa-zu-um*, "to seize", and *ma-ḫa-ṣí i-da*, "to smite with the hand". Gelb[51] terms the latter "questionable", but it appears to conform to the *qaṭāli* model of infinitive absolute studied by W. L. Moran in 1950.[52] To be sure, most of the examples come from the Byblos Amarna letters, but Ebla too may have used this form, if *ma-ḫa-ṣi* is a true indication.It might be noted here that the ending of *i-da* may mark the accusative

---

of the A:B::B:A chiasmus recovers this root in Prov. xvi 11, *peles ûmōʾznê mišpāṭ layahweh / maʿᵃśēhû kol-ʾabnê-kîs*, "Scales and just balances are from Yahweh / his work is the size of the stones in the bag".

[49] See M. Dahood, *Biblica* 48 (1967), p. 435, who proposed for Sirach xvi 23 (25) the untraditional version "I will pour out my spirit without weighing / and without restraint I will expound my knowledge".

[50] Contrast *UT*, Glossary, No. 1474, and Gröndahl, *Personennamen*, pp. 156-7, who both subsume PN *mkl* under the root *mkl*.

[51] Gelb, *Thoughts about Ibla*, p. 22, terms *ma-ḫa-zi* as a "questionable" attestation of the infinitive. Within a Northwest Semitic framework it can find a suitable classification as an infinitive absolute.

[52] In *JCS* 4 (1950), pp. 169-72.

of means ending, while the entire phrase recalls *UT*, 1 Aqht 220, *yd mḫṣt*, "the hand that smote", and Job v 18, *yimḥaṣ weyādāw tirpênāh*, "He smites but his hands heal".

Infixed -T- conjugation

This conjugation is witnessed in the historical text TM.76.G.344, *is-ta-ma-a-ta*, "you have heard" (Pettinato), which may be compared with the Ugar. imperative *ištmʿ*, "hear!", and the biblical place-name *ʾeštemōaʿ*. It is also present in the PN *iš-ta-a-nu*, "I am at ease" (TM.75. G.1863 rev VII 13), from the root *šʾn*. Its verbal attestation in Jer. xlviii 11; Job iii 18, etc. with the final consonant doubled, *šaʾanān*, is well known but the assimilation of the final *nun* may be responsible for its non-recognition in Gen. iv 7, *halôʾ ʾim têṭîb šāʾattā* (MT *śeʾēt*) / *weʾim lōʾ têṭîb* / *lappetaḥ ḥaṭṭāʾt rōbēṣ*, "Look, if you have behaved well, you will be at ease. / But if you have not/sin will be lurking at your door". Just as *nātantā* becomes *nātattā*, so **šāʾantā* becomes **šāʾattā*. The parallelism between **šāʾattā* and *rōbēṣ* is unexceptionable and brings out the poetic character of the verse.

The divine name read ^{d}NI.DA.KUL by Pettinato[53] may also be read ^{d}*ì-tá-kul*, an infixed *-t-* form of *yākōl*, "to be able, prevail", and interpreted "I prevail", a name recalling Baal's standing epithet *aliyn bʿl* in Ugaritic. Cf. Heb. PN *yekolyāhû*, "Prevail, O Yahu!", and Prov. xxx 1, *leʾitîʾēl weʾūkāl*, "I, El, have triumphed" and "I prevail".[54]

Construct chain with enclitic -ma

Long recognized in Akkadian and in certain South Semitic dialects, the enclitic *mem* was unsuspected in Hebrew until its discovery in the north Canaanite dialect of Ugaritic. The chances are that it exists even farther north and as early as 2500 B.C. The diplomatic letter recently published by Pettinato[55] begins *en-ma ì-bù-bū*$_6$. agrig *é* en *lí-na* sukkal-du$_8$, "The grace of Ibubu, the superintendent of the palace of the king to the ambassador", and ends *en-ma ti-ra-il*

[53] See *Archiv für Orientforschung* 25 (1977), p. 27.

[54] On the parallelism of the roots *lʾy* and *ykl* in Ps. cxxxix 6, see Dahood, *Psalms III* (Garden City, N.Y., 1970), p. 288. Gelb, *Thoughts*, p. 22, writes, "Outside of personal names, parallels to this usage of BT (infixed *-t-*) are found in Akkadian and Ugaritic, but not, to my knowledge, in Aramaic (Hebrew)". I have found a good number of infixed *-t-* forms in Hebrew and have discussed them in disparate places, but a monographic study on this conjugation in Hebrew is badly needed.

[55] *Rivista biblica* 25 (1977), pp. 238-42.

dub-sar *ik-tub lí-na* sukkal-du$_8$ (zi-zi) ì - na - sum, "the grace of Tirail the scribe who wrote and gave the letter to the ambassador of Zizi". Found *passim* in Old Akkadian letters, *en-ma* has been connected by Assyriologists[56] with *um-ma*, "thus", and Pettinato also translates it *così*. But the beginning of Ugaritic letters with the formula *tḥm PN 1 PN*, literally "the consoling word of *PN* to *PN*", suggests that *en-ma ì-bu$_3$-bu$_6$*, is also a constructc hain. In its 50-odd occurrences, Ugar. *tḥm*, which I derive from *nḥm*, "to console",[57] stands as the construct followed by a PN as the genitive. Thanks to Eblaite PNN such as *en-na-yà*, "Have mercy, O Ya!", *en-na-ma-ni*, *en* can readily be identified with Heb. *ḥēn*, "grace". Thus when St. Paul employs at the beginning of some of his letters the formula *charis hymīn*, "Grace to you" (1 Cor. i 3; Col. i 2), and variations thereon, he is probably continuing a tradition reaching back to 2500 B.C. in Ebla. The LXX, it might be noted, almost exclusively renders Heb. *ḥēn* by *charis*. Finally, the preposition *lí-na*, "to", has a counterpart in Ugar. *ln*.[58]

The superlative

Pettinato[59] has noted that Sumerian 1 tug-NI.NI in TM.75.G.1789 II 7 could signify, if read 1 tug *ì-lí*, "1 garment of god" in the generic sense of "precious" and finds support for this interpretation in corresponding kinds of materials such as *gada dingir-ra*. In the light of Ugaritic phrase such as *hdm il*, "gorgeous footstool", *nʿl il*, "precious sandals"[60] and biblical *ʾarzê ʾēl*, "lofty cedars", in Ps. lxxx 11, and *hareré ʾēl*. "towering mountains", in Pss. xxxvi 7 and l 10

---

[56] The most recent discussion being that of F. R. Kraus, "Einführung in die Briefe in altakkadischer Sprache", *JEOL* 24 (1975-1976), pp. 74-104, esp. 98. I am indebted to G. Pettinato for this reference. See also Gelb, *Glossary*, p. 47, who relates *en-ma* to Heb. *hinnē-ma*. *CAD*, E, p. 169a, curtly describes *enma* as "particle introducing direct speech; see *umma*". A much more adequate and documented treatment can be found in W. von Soden, *Akkadisches Handwörterbuch* I, p. 218. Thus *en-ma PN ana PN iqabbi* is seen to equal the Ugaritic formula.

[57] Though scholars still dispute the etymology of *tḥm*, a derivation from *nḥm*, "to console", seems the most feasible. As shown above concerning the root *nḥt*, "to descend", the *primae nun* does sometimes assimilate or disappear even when followed by laryngal *-ḥ*. On biblical *tanḥūmôt* with similar connotation, see M. Dahood in W. A. Ward (ed.), *The Role of the Phoenicians in the Interaction of Mediterranean Civilizations* (Beirut, 1968), p. 144, n. 16.

[58] Cf. *UT*, § 12.9, and for biblical examples, M. Dahood, *Psalms* I, p. 116, and *Psalms III*, p. 292.

[59] *Or Ant* 15 (1976), p. 12 and n. 7.

[60] Cf. *UT*, Glossary, No. 163, p. 357; Dahood, *Psalms I*, p. 220.

(when *-p* of *'lp* is joined to the following word as the conjunction), one can readily accept this explanation. Compare also the hapax phrase in El Amarna, *kasap ilāni*, "the finest silver".

In a syncretistic list of correspondences between Mesopotamian and Syrian divinities, the head of the Sumerian pantheon Enlil is equated with no West Semitic god. Instead of an equation, the apparently simple syllabic transcription *i-li-lu* is given.[61] Still one might hazard the guess that this writing is an attempt to express the superlative *il-ilu*, "god of gods", corresponding to Heb. *'ēl 'elōhîm* or **'ēl 'ēlîm*

Double negative ma-in

The international treaty between Ebrium, the king of Ebla, and Dudya, the king of Assur, dealing with commercial questions, closes with a series of curses directed toward the Assyrian king should he violate any of the stipulations. One of them reads *ma-in* tuš, "May you have no stable abode!" The sense of the mysterious new vocables *ma-in* emerged from the comparison with the double negative *mā'ên* (MT *mē'ên*) in Jer. x 6-7, which I had occasion to study a few months before the Ebla phrase cropped up.[62] Since then several other biblical instances have come to light and these have been duly discussed elsewhere.[63] These include Isa. lxiii 3 (cf. 1QIs[a]), xli 24; Jer. xxx 7; Ps. xxxviii 11; Job vi 13; Lam. iii 49; Sirach xiii 17.

The use of a double negative can also be seen in Phoenician *'bl*, Punic *'ybl*, comprised of negative *'y* and negative *bl*;[64] El Amarna *ù-ul la-a* combines two negative particles to emphasize the negation.[65] In the Alalakh tablets of the early second millennium the double negative *ūlā* occurs once.[66] Thus the use of double negatives is documented in five different sources distributed over the whole Northwest Semitic area between 2500-150 B.C.[67]

---

[61] So Pettinato in *BA* 39 (1976), p. 49.

[62] "Emphatic Double Negative *m'yn* in Jeremiah 10:6-7", *CBQ* 37 (1975), pp. 458-9.

[63] See *Orientalia*, N.S. 45 (1976), p. 347, and my article in *Biblica* 59 (1978), pp. 174-97, "New Readings in Lamentations", where Lam. iii 49 is treated.

[64] S. Segert, *A Grammar of Phoenician and Punic* (Munich, 1976), § 55.83, p. 159.

[65] Cf. F. M. T. Böhl, *Die Sprache der Amarnabriefe: Mit besonderer Berücksichtigung der Kanaanismen* (Leipzig, 1909), § 34f., p. 72.

[66] See D. J. Wiseman, *The Alalakh Tablets* (London, 1953), p. 22.

[67] On the Greek double negative in John xx 25, see Dahood, *CBQ* 37 (1975), p. 458, n. 1.

Vocative lamedh

Unknown till the discovery of the Ugaritic tablets, vocative *lamedh* is now largely accepted in some texts of the Psalter and has gained entrance into W. Baumgartner's *Hebräisches und aramäisches Lexikon zum Alten Testament*, Fasc. II (1974). If properly interpreted, the Ebla PN *ṣi-la-be*, discussed above in connection with imperatives, would add a thousand years to its history. Another possible example is PN *ti-la-yà*, "Come, O Ya!" (TM.75.G.336 rev V 7; 2075 rev VII 14), in which *ti* might parse as the imperative of *'ty/w*, "to come", with the elision of the initial *aleph*. The vocative *lamedh* is probably to be identified in the Ugaritic PNN *ldn*, "O Judge!", *lḫsn*, "O Mighty One!" (cf. Ps. lxxxix 9, *mî kāmôkā ḥ*ᵃ*sîn yāh* "Who is mighty like you, Yah?"), and *lkn*, "O Honest One!"

Prepositions lí-na and ší-in

As noted above, *lí-na*, "to", exhibits afformative *-na* that characterizes some prepositions in Ugaritic, Hebrew, and South Arabic.[68] The completely new but widely documented preposition *ší-in*[69] "to, toward", may derive from the root *s'n* found in Ugar. *sin*, "boot", and Isa. ix 4, *kol s*ᵉ*'ôn sō'ēn*, "every boot of booted warrior". From the verbal meaning "to tramp, tread", to prepositional "to, toward", there are good and varied analogies in *dārak*, "to march", and *derek*, "toward"; *bô'*, "to come", and *bô'*ᵃ*kā*, "in the direction of"; *'ādāh*, "to advance", and *'ad*, *'*ᵃ*dê* (Eblaite *a-dè*); [70] Ugar. *aṯr*, "to proceed", and *aṯr*, "toward", in *UT*, 49 II 29-30, *km lb 'nt aṯr b'l*, "Such was the heart of Anath toward Baal".

Parallel word—pairs

C. H. Gordon introduces his sample list of synonymous pairs in Ugaritic and Hebrew with the affirmation, "Nowhere does the proximity of Heb. and Ugar. manifest itself more plainly than in the pairs of synonyms used parallelistically in both languages".[71] Of course the discussion should include not only synonyms but antonyms and other categories (such as meristic pairs) as well; hence the more general term "word-pairs" adopted here. To date more than a thou-

---

[68] For ampler documentation, K. Aartun, *Die Partikeln des Ugaritischen* 1 (Neukirchen-Vluyn, 1974), pp. 64-5.

[69] See Pettinato, *Rivista biblica* 25 (1977), p. 237.

[70] *Ibid.*, p. 237.

[71] *UT*, p. 145.

sand word-pairs common to Ugaritic and Hebrew have been identified,[72] and now Ebla begins to weigh in with its contribution, a further manifestation of the tenacity of literary usages in Canaan.

The geographical text TM.75.G.1860 lists the following sequence of cities: *si-da-mu*, *è-am-ra*, *ad-ma*, *ṣi-ba-iy-um*, *be-la*, the same sequence as in Gen. xiv 2; cf. also Gen. x 19 and Deut, xxix 22 which list the first four cities. In Deut. xxxii 32; Isa. i 9-10, xiii 19; Jer. xxiii 14; Zeph. ii 9 biblical poets took the names of the first two cities to form a poetic pair in parallelism, but Hos. xi 8 shows greater originality when reaching down to numbers three and four in the list: *ʾêk ʾettenᵉkā keʾadmāh* / *ʾaśîmᵉkā kiṣᵉbōʾyīm*, "How can I make you like Admah/treat you like Zeboim?" TM.75.G.1426 III 8-13 lists two words denoting "rod" and "mace" respectively: *ḫi-ṭum* and *ma-ṭì-um*. These two nouns serve a poetic function in *UT*, 52:32, *il ḫṭh nḥt*/*il ymnn mṭ ydh*, "El-his rod sinks / El-the mace of his love subsides".[73]

The religion of Ebla

Writing more than 30 years ago, W. F. Albright[74] observed that one of the two things that strike the student at once when dealing with the Canaanite deities is the extent to which the gods receive etymologically transparent names and appellations. The same may be said about the principal gods of Ebla simply because many of them can be identified with deities known from the Ras Shamra tablets whose names and titles are remarkably transparent. From this quality Albright concluded that Canaanite religion was in this respect, at least, more primitive and nearer its fountainhead than either Mesopotamian or Egyptian religion. What would Albright say about the religion of Ebla were he alive today?

While the Ugaritic pantheon numbers some 255 gods, two dozen of them of some importance, the Ebla tablets studied to date count more than 450 deities. The head of the pantheon in northern Syria was Dagan, who is called *ᵈbe-kà-na-na-um*, "the Lord of Canaan", and *ᵈbe-ka-na-im*.[75] Other top-flight gods were Baal, Resheph and

---

[72] See L. R. Fisher (ed.), *Ras Shamra Parallels* I, II (Rome, 1972-1975). Volume III with some 350 new pairs, most of them *hapax legomena* in Ugaritic and in Hebrew, is scheduled for press in 1978.

[73] One may now read Ps. lxxxix 45, *hišbattā maṭṭe hārô* (MT *miṭṭᵉhārô*), "You have caused his conception rod to fail", a fine parallel to vs. 46, "You shortened the days of his prime".

[74] *Archaeology and the Religion of Israel* (Baltimore, 1946), p. 71.

[75] See Pettinato in the forthcoming article cited in note 42.

Sipiš. The patron god of Ebla was, surprisingly, *da-bi-ir* (spelled thus) the god of pestilence known in Ugaritic, Hebrew and doubtless preserved in the Southern Palestinian city-name *d^e^bîr*. Since the god of pestilence could keep the plague distant from the city, his choice by the king and people of Ebla as their guardian becomes readily understandable. Another popular god was Rasap, also a god of pestilence, well documented in the ancient Near East.[76] Both these major Eblaite deities were demoted by Hab. iii 5 to mere attendants of Yahweh: *l^e^pānāyw yēlek dāber/w^e^yēṣē' rešep l^e^raglāyw*, "Before him walks Pestilence/ and Plague lights up his feet".[77]

Among other texts, TM.75.G.1560 rev C 15-17 contains the phrase *é-^d^ra-sa-ap gú-ni ^ki^*, "the temple of Rasap of the town Guni", which equals *UT*, 1088:3, *bt ršp gn*.[78] Though a millennium apart, the tablets from Ebla and Ugarit may well be referring to the same temple; after all, these two cities are only 85 kilometers apart.

The gender of "sun" is fluid in Semitic. In Akkadian it is masculine, but in Ugaritic it is feminine; in Hebrew it oscillates between the two.[79] At Ebla the sun appears to be masculine to judge from the PN *sipiš aḫu*, "Sun is a brother".[80] The popular artisan god at Ugaritic, Kothar, appears as *ka-ša-lu*, whose final syllable may also be read *-ru*, and the second half of the double-barrelled name *kṯr w ḫss* turns up as *ḫa-si-su*, "intelligent", in a bilingual vocabulary as the equivalent of Sumerian geštu, "understanding".

Many of the personal names preserved at Ebla provide insights into popular beliefs and aspirations. They normally consist of verbs, participles or nouns combined with the name of a god or goddess, though sometimes the divine element is omitted, thus resulting in a hypocoristicon or abbreviated name. Of the nearly ten thousand PNN recorded thus far, only a few will be discussed here, and usually

---

[76] The material has been conveniently gathered and competently evaluated by W. J. Fulco, *The Canaanite God Rešep* (New Haven, 1976).

[77] The parallelism of two Canaanite deities in the same verse can also be seen in Isa. lxv 11.

[78] Cf. M. Dahood-G. Pettinato, "Ugaritic *ršp gn* and Eblaite *rasap gunu(m)* ^ki^", in *Orientalia*, N.S. 46 (1977), pp. 230-32.

[79] Cf. the relevant observation of C. H. Gordon, *Or*, N.S. 22 (1953), p. 247, on a cylinder seal from the Babylon I period.

[80] The Eblaite vocalization *si-piš* has occasioned surprise in some quarters in view of Akk. *šamaš*, Heb. *šemeš*, etc. But forms such as *šimšēk*, "your sun" (Isa. lx 20), *šimšāh*, "her sun" (Jer. xv 9) and PN *šimšôn*, "Samson", also preserve the first-syllable *-i-* found in *sipiš*.

those with some biblical relevance.[81] Thus *kà-ra-ba-ìl*, "Il is near", brings to mind *UT*, Krt 37-38, *wyqrb bšal krt mat*, "and (El) drew near while Kirta requested a hundred times"; Jer. xxiii 23; Pss. lxix 19 and lxxv 2, "We give you thanks, O God (*'elōhîm*)/we praise you, O Near One!" (the *we* of *weqārôb* parsing as vocative *waw*). In the PN *dìl-ḫa-il*, "Il is strength"[82] one recognizes the elements that concur in 1 Sam. ii 3-4; Job xx 15, and Ps. xviii 33, *hā'ēl hame'azzerēnî ḥāyil*, "the God who girded me with strength". The components of *il-dra-mu*, "Il is the High God" (TM.75.G.522 rev II 2), are distributed over the parallel cola of Job xxi 22, *hale'ēl yelammed-dā'at/wehû' rāmîm yišpôṭ*, "Will he teach God knowledge/or judge the Most Exalted?"[83] Biblical too is the sentiment expressed by PN *en-na-ni-il*, "Have pity on me, O Il!", which evokes Heb. *ḥannî'ēl* and *ḥanan'ēl*, while *en-na-be*, "Have pity, O Baal!" (TM.75.G.336 II 15), equals Punic Hannibal! Cf. also Ugar. PNN *ḥnil*, *ḥnn*, *yḥnn*, the divine name *ḥnn il*, and Ps. xxx 9, *'ēlêkā yhwh 'eqrā' / we'ēl* (MT *'el*) *'adōnāy 'etḥannān*, "To you, Yahweh, I cry / O El my Lord, I plead for mercy".[84] The national god of Moab, Chemosh, turns out to be a member of the Canaanite pantheon, thanks to the information supplied by three tablets published in *Ugaritica V* (see p. 605) and now confirmed by PN *i-ti-dkà-mi-iš*, "Come(?), O Kamish" or "With me is Kamish" (TM.75.G.336 rev III 4) as well as by the place-name *kār-kamiš*, "Quay of Kamish".[85]

The divine element in PN *da-sí-ma-ad*, probably "He-goat of the Grand One" (TM.75.G.366 I 3), arrives at an opportune moment in view of the debate over biblical *me'ōd* employed as a divine appel-

---

[81] This biblically oriented approach will be looked at askance by M. Sznycer, *Journal asiatique* 264 (1976), p. 219, who complains that Northwest Semitic studies have been scientifically hampered by being controlled by biblical scholars intent mainly on "mieux comprendre la Bible". To correct this imbalance Sznycer plans to contribute a regular "Chronique des études nord-sémitiques" prepared by a pure Semitist with no biblical prejudices. While deploring over-zealous use by biblicists of Northwest Semitic material, one should never lose to sight the centrality of Biblical Hebrew for an understanding of ancient Canaan, and a mastery of same remains the best preparation for the interpretation of the Ebla Canaanite texts.

[82] See Pettinato, *BA* 39 (1976), p. 50.

[83] Cf. A. M. C. Blommerde, *Northwest Semitic Grammar and Job* (Rome, 1969), p. 94; M. H. Pope, *Job*[3] (Garden City, N.Y., 1973), pp. 156, 160.

[84] For further details, *Biblica* 58 (1977), p. 218.

[85] For the numerous Canaanite linguistic features in the Mesha Inscription from Dibon, see my study "The Moabite Stone and Northwest Semitic Philology" in the forthcoming S. H. Horn *Festschrift*.

lative. The first element may equal Heb. *tayiš* "he-goat", Akk. *daššu*, Arab. *tays*; *ma-ad* (illustrates retention of *ā* which becomes *ō* in Hebrew) is also attested in Old Akkadian PNN *en-na-ma-ad* "Have pity, O Grand One", and *i-dur-ma-ad*, "Everlasting is the Grand One".[86] These names sustain the position of those who claim to find in MT adverbial *mᵉʾōd* the divine appellative in some biblical passages, though the syllabic writing *ma-ad* makes it unnecessary to repoint to stative *māʾēd* on the analogy of *kābēd*; one may equally well retain *mᵉʾōd* or read *māʾōd* on the analogy of *gādōl*.[87] Because of the complete chiasmus, Ps. xlvi 2 illustrates clearly the usage of this title: *ʾᵉlōhîm lānû maḥᵃseh wāʿōz* / *ʿezrat bᵉṣārôt nimṣāʾ māʾōd*, "God for us is refuge and stronghold/the liberator from sieges have we found the Grand".[88] Note that the other strophic verses of this psalm, vss. 8 and 12, also begin and end with divine names and titles. Equally instructive is Ps. lxxviii 59, *šāmaʿ ʾᵉlōhîm wayyitʿabbār* / *wayyimʾas māʾōd* (MT *mᵉʾōd*) *bᵉyiśrāʾēl*, "God heard them and was enraged / and so the Grand rejected Israel",[89] when the second colon is compared with Jer. ii 37 *māʾas yhwh bᵉmibṭaḥayik*, "Yahweh rejected those in whom you trust", and with the preceding verse (Jer. ii 36) *mah tāzēllî* (MT *tēzᵉlî*) *māʾōd* (MT *mᵉʾōd*), "Why have you despised the Grand One?"

The form and analysis of theophoric *da-sí-ma-ad* grant a new insight into the unexplained Ugar. PN *kry*[90] which now may be separated into *kr*, Heb. *kār*, "lamb", and the divine name *-ya*, hence "Lamb of Ya", which naturally brings to mind NT "Lamb of God". When imposing such names, Canaanite parents may have thought of the sacrificial relationship between the goat or lamb and the divinity.

Since H. S. Nyberg's studies in 1935 and 1938 on *ʿal*, "Most High", many scholars have discussed this title and its cognates *ʿēlî* and *ʿelyôn* in the Bible.[91] At Ebla *alu* appears as the name of a

---

[86] Cf. Gelb, *Glossary*, p. 167.

[87] For full discussion with bibliography, see L. Viganò, *Nomi e titoli di YHWH alla luce del semitico del Nord-ovest* (Rome, 1976), pp. XIII, 63-4, 70-80. It was the adjectival use *mid*, "great, grand", in Ugaritic that triggered the search for similar usage in Hebrew.

[88] For further details, M. Dahood, *Psalms III*, p. XXVI.

[89] Cf. D. N. Freedman, "God Almighty in Psalm 78, 59", in *Biblica* 54 (1973), p. 268.

[90] Gröndahl, *Personennamen*, pp. 151, 237, proposes no interpretation. The occurrence of *krm*, "lambs", in *UT*, 51 VI 47 shows that the word was known in Ugaritic.

[91] Cf. Viganò, *Nomi e titoli*, pp. 34-62, for a thorough review of the evidence.

god in PN *a-lu-a-ḫu*, "the Most High is a brother" (TM.75.G.336 rev I 7),[92] the semantic equal of Phoen. *ʾḥrm*, biblical *ʾaḥîrām*, "My brother is the Exalted". For the form *a-lu* compare 1 Sam. ii 10, *yhwh yēḥattû meribāw* / *ʿālû* (MT *ʿālāw*) *baššāmayim yarʿēm*, "Yahweh—his adversaries are terrified/the Most High thunders from the heavens". The hypocoristicon *a-lum* occurs in TM.75.G.336 V 13, and may be compared with biblical PN *ʿēlî*, "Eli", also an abbreviated name. In addition to the divine epithet *ʿly*, Ugaritic witnesses the form *ʿl* (= Eblaite *a-lu*) in the PNN *šdʿl* and *adʿl*.

PN *ṭù-bí-si-piš*, "My good is the Sun" or "My Good One is the sun" (TM.75.G.336 VII 6), recalls the phoenicianizing Qoh. xi 7, *ṭôb laʿênayim lirʾôt ʾet haššāmeš*, "It is good for the eyes to see the sun". Where Pettinato[93] reads the PN *ṭù-bí-da-lu* I propose to read *ṭù-bí-da-ru*, "My good is the Everlasting", since the *lu* sign must often be read as *ru*; e.g., *ka-ša-lu* equals *ka-ša-ru*, Ugar. *kṯr*. In the bilingual vocabularies one encounters *da-ri da-ru* "generation upon generation", Ugar. *dr dr*, Heb. *dōr dōr*. Compare also the Old Akkadian PN *šu-da-ri*, "the one of the Everlasting",[94] and Ps. lxxxix 2, *ḥasdê yhwh ʿôlām ʾāšîrāh* / *ledōr wādōr ʾôdîaʿ ʾemûnāteka*, "Let me sing your mercies, Yahweh Eternal / O Everlasting, let me proclaim your fidelity".

In the PN *lé-é-ì-lu*, "Il is the Victor" (TM.75.G.336 VII 8),[95] appears the root best known from the Ugaritic divine epithet *aliyn*, "I am the Victor". Thanks to the Ugaritic attestation of the root *lʾy*, scholars have been able to recover many instances of this title camouflaged by the Masoretes under negative *lōʾ* which in numerous poetic texts is now preferably read as stative *lēʾ* or possibly active participle *lōʾē* defectively written.[96] To cite but one example, 1 Sam. ii 3, *kî ʾēl dēʿôt yhwh* / *welēʾ* (MT *lōʾ*) *nitkenû ʿalîlôt*, "For a God of knowledge is Yahweh/ and by the Victor actions are weighed".[97] Since the

[92] In his forthcoming article "ʾ*AHL* 'Gruppo Gentilizio' nell'onomastico eblaita di TM.75.G.336", Pelio Fronzaroli does not even consider the identification of *a-lu* with "Most High". Instead he opts for the identification with Akk. *ālu*, "city", while admitting at the same time that West Semitic *ʾahl* means "tent" and not "city".

[93] *Orientalia*, N.S. 44 (1975), p. 370.

[94] Gelb, *Glossary*, p. 106, cites PN *šu-da-ri* which I would interpret "the one of the Everlasting" and compare with Ugar. PN *šbʿl*, "the one of Baal".

[95] Pettinato, *RSO* 50 (1976), p. 5, reads *ni-é-ì-lu*, but the first sign also carries the values *lé* and *lí*.

[96] An examination of the relevant passages can be found in Viganò, *Nomi e titoli*, pp. 80-106.

[97] No one seems to have called attention to the merismus implicit in *ʾēl dēʿôt*, "a God of knowledge", and *ʿalîlôt*, "deeds". Yahweh evaluates both the inward

epithet *lē'* is associated with knowledge,[98] one would be authorized to read TM.75.G.336 rev V 13 *i-da-lé*, "the Victor knows", instead of Pettinato's *i-da-NI* since the Sumerian sign NI has also the syllabic value *lé*. Cf. Prov. xxx 3 which connects the two components of *i-da-lé*: *w^{e}lē' lummadtî* (MT *lō' lāmadtî*) *ḥokmāh* / *w^{e}da'at q^{e}dōšîm 'ēdā'*, "But by the Victor have I been taught / and so I know the knowledge of the Holy One".

The first king of the dynasty of Ebla brought to light by the discovery of the archives bears the good West Semitic name Igrish-Ḫalam,[99] "Drive out, O Ḫalam", in which *ḫalam* apparently derives from the root *ḫlm* in Ugaritic PN *bn ḫlm*, Heb. *ḥālam*, "to be healthy".[100] The verbal element *igriš* can be interpreted in the light of *UT*, 126 V 20-21, *my bilm ydy mrṣ* / *gršm zbln*, "Who among the gods will expel the sickness/driving out the malady?" Thus Ḫalam would be the god of health, who drives out sickness, and in Isa. xxxviii 16 *taḥlîmēnî*, "You restore me to health", is predicated of Yahweh. Interesting for the literary background of Job is the use of this uncommon verb (four occurrences) in xxxix 4: *yaḥl^{e}mû b^{e}nêhem*/*yirbû babbār* / *yāṣ^{e}'û w^{e}lō' šābû lāmô*, "Their young are healthy / they grow more quickly than wheat / they go forth and do not return to them".[101]

The name of the second king of the dynasty, Ar-ennum, can be understood as "the Sun (Light) is mercy", when *ar* is identified with Heb. *'ôr* employed as a divine title in Job xxiv 13, and *ennum* derived from *ḥnn*, "to be merciful". Both components concur in Ps. cxii 4, *zāraḥ baḥōšek*/*'ôr lay^{e}šārîm*/*ḥannûn w^{e}rāḥûm w^{e}ṣaddîq*, "In the Darkness will dawn / the Sun for the upright / the Merciful and Compassionate and Just One!" [102] Finally, the PN *i-da-pa-lil* (TM.75.G.336 rev I 12) may be understood as "the Mediator knows", and aligned with the poetic quatrain usually printed as prose in 1 Sam. ii 25:

---

thoughts and outward deeds of men. This verse is not discussed by Jośe Krašovec, *Der Merismus im Biblisch-Hebräischen und Nordwestsemitischen* (Rome, 1977).

[98] Cf. also Isa. xi 3; Job xxxii 14, xxxix 17; and Ps. cxxxix 6 as read and interpreted in *Psalms III*, p. 288.

[99] Gelb, *Thoughts*, p. 21, renders Yigriš-Ḫalam "Halam has come?" Both *grš*, "to drive out", and *ḫlm*, "to be healthy", are exclusively West Semitic roots.

[100] W. Baumgartner, *HAL* I, pp. 307-8, would seem to err when subsuming *ḥlm*, "to be healthy", and *ḥlm*, "to dream", under the same root. In Ugaritic the verb "to dream" is *ḥlm*, but "to be healthy" is *ḫlm*, if our interpretation of PN *bn ḫlm* is correct. The Heb. PN *ḥēlem* in Zech. vi 14 may be of the same derivation and its emendation with Baumgartner to *ḥeldāy* may be gratuitous.

[101] Compare Ezek. xvi 7, *r^{e}bābāh k^{e}ṣemaḥ*, "Grow like a plant in the field!"

[102] See Dahood, *Psalms III*, pp. 126, 127-8; Viganò, *Nomi e titoli*, pp. 169-70.

ʾim yeḥeṭāʾ ʾîš leʾîš
ûpilelô ʾelōhîm
weʾim layhwh yeḥeṭāʾ ʾîš
mî yitpallel lô

If a man sin against a man,
God will mediate for him;
but if a man sin against Yahweh,
who will mediate for him? [103]

Old Akkadian witnesses PNN *ib-lul*-DINGIR and *ib-lul-il* which Gelb[104] subsumes under *balālum*, "to pour out" (or the like), leaving open the possible derivation from *palālum*. Eblaite *palil*, Ugar. *bn pll*, Ammonite PN *pll*,[105] the Heb. PN *pelalyāh* and its use of *pālal* with God the subject all conspire to support a West Semitic interpretation of the name *ib-lul-il* in Old Akkadian.

The God Ya at Ebla

In his book *BC The Archaeology of the Bible Lands*,[106] Magnus Magnusson writes that one aspect of the Ebla finds that is bound to provoke endless debate in the future are the personal names ending in *-yà*. Is this name related to biblical Yah and Yahweh? The problem stands out in the juxtaposition of such names as *mi-ka-il* and *mi-ka-yà*; *iš-ma-il* and *iš-ma-yà*; *en-na-il* and *en-na-yà*. That *-yà* is a divine element corresponding to the divine element *-il* seems at once to be obvious, but a number of scholars urge caution here since *-yà* might also be understood as the diminutive ending, much as Mickey is the diminutive of Michael. The problem is not a new one but has only been dramatically highlighted by the Ebla revelations. Back in 1909 in his monograph *Die Sprache der Amarnabriefe*, F. Böhl briefly—and cautiously—addressed himself to the problem created by the ending found in PNN *la-ab-a-ya*, *ad-da-ya* and *bi-ri-di-ya*[107] asking whether

---

[103] Some of the more obvious poetic elements are the pairing of the dative suffix in *pilelô* with prepositional *lô*; the breakup of the composite divine name, and the double chiasmus *yeḥeṭāʾ* ... *leʾîš*/ / *layhwh yeḥeṭāʾ* and *pilelô ʾelōhîm* / / *mî yitpallel lô*.

[104] *Glossary*, p. 96.

[105] Cf. E. Puech, "Deux nouveaux sceaux ammonites", *RB* 93 (1976), pp. 59-62.

[106] (London, 1977), p. 30.

[107] Which may be translated "Ya is my coolness/refreshment", giving expression to the *refrigerium* motif that would later become so popular in early Christian

the divine name Yahweh would be thinkable in the Amarna period. The problem is further complicated by the Ugaritic onomasticon which contains a host of names with the ending *-y*, which may be taken in several different ways, but which, when compared with biblical names, are most simply interpreted in the same way.

First, the juxtaposition of Ugaritic PNN creates the same impression as the juxtaposition of Eblaite names. Thus *amril*, "El sees", *amrbʿl*, "Baal sees", and biblical *ʾamaryāh* strongly suggest that Ugar. *amry* means "Ya sees". Similarly, *ḏmrbʿl*, "Baal is my sentinel", *ḏmrhd*, "Haddu is my sentinel", make it difficult to avoid concluding that *ḏmry* signifies "Ya is my sentinel", especially when the biblical refrain in Exod. xv 2, Isa. xii 2 and Ps. cxviii 14 is brought into consideration: *ʿozzî weẓimrāt yāh*, "My strength and sentinel is Yah". Alongside *yrmʿl*, "Alu is exalted", and *yrmbʿl*, Baal is exalted", *yrmy* is readily rendered "Ya is exalted", and compared with the prophet's name *yirmeyāhû*. PNN *ʿbdil*, "slave of El", *ʿbdy*, "slave of Ya", evoke biblical *ʿabdeʾēl*, *ʿōbadyāh*, and Eblaite *eb-du-yà*. PN *mlky* appears syllabically as *milkiya* in Akkadian texts from Ugarit[108] and closely resembles Heb. *malkiyāh*, "my king is Yah". Ugar. *bdil*, "from the hand(s) of El",[109] and Phoen. *bdbʿl*, "from the hand(s) of Baal", express the gratitude that underlies such Eblaite names as *iš-la-yà*, "donated by Ya", and *iš-la-bé*, "donated by Dagan", discussed above. The name of the Prophet Elijah was borne by the Canaanite *ily*, if our analysis of this ending is not perverse. Cf. also Ugar. *ḏkry*, the equivalent of Zachariah. Surely *iltm*, "El is perfect", is related to *tmy*, "Ya is perfect". Of course, the problem of the ambiguous ending *-y* would be neatly solved if some good examples of *yā* could be found in the initial position. To date the most promising candidate is Ugar. *ytm* which may well be identical with biblical *yôtām*, "Jotham", or "Yo is perfect".[110]

Ugaritic place-names such as *mgdly*, "Tower of Ya" (cf. Heb. *migdal-ʾēl*), *ṯmry*, "Watchtower of Ya", and *hry*, "Mountain of Ya",

---

liturgy and literature. The root is well known from Arab. *baruda*, "to be, become cold", Heb. *bārād*, "hail", and in the doubly dissimilated form *perāt*, the biblical name for the Euphrates, "the Cold River". The river creating today the oasis of Damascus is called *Il Barada*.

[108] Cf. J. Nougayrol, *Le palais royal d'Ugarit* VI (Paris, 1970), p. 140.

[109] See M. Dahood, *Biblica* 47 (1966), pp. 107-8, n. 4; *UT*, Glossary, No. 445.

[110] In *Beth Miqra* 63/64 (1975), pp. 530-35, J. L. Benor cites a number of Biblical texts indicating that Yahweh was worshipped by peoples other than the Israelites. Cf. also C. H. Gordon, *Midstream* (February, 1977), p. 49.

may also illustrate the divine element since the explanation of *-y* as the caritative or diminutive ending scarcely fits in these cases.

A comparison with Job xxii 25 and xxxi 24 suggests a fetching explanation for the Ugar. name *aktmy*. It is patient of at least three interpretations, but I would prefer "I consider Ya my fine gold". Witnessed as *kutim* at Ebla, *ketem* occurs some ten times in Hebrew poetry. In the PN *aktmy* it would form the basis of a piel verb of consideration. In Job xxii 25, Eliphaz, whose name means "my God is gold", puns on his own name when assuring Job *wᵉhāyāh šadday bᵉṣārêkā*, "then Shadday will be your gold", while in xxxi 24 Job denies *wᵉlakketem 'āmartî mibṭaḥî*, "or I called fine gold my object of trust".

How does this pre-Abrahamic designation of God as Ya square with biblical tradition? In this regard there are two traditions preserved in the Bible. Gen. iv 26 reports that in the second generation after Adam "man began to call upon the name of Yahweh", and with this tradition the new Canaanite material from Ugarit and Ebla would seem to be in accord. That Moses and his followers were unfamiliar with this name (Exod. iii 15) finds a plausible explanation in the long sojourn of the Israelites in Egypt where this divine name does not figure in the onomasticon. But even Exod. iii 15 does not create a problem if the final bicolon is translated as poetry: *zeh ššᵉmî lᵉʿôlām/wᵉzeh zikrî lᵉdōr dōr*, "This has been my name from eternity/ and this will be my title throughout all generations".[111]

Pan-Eblaitism

In recent interviews P. Matthiae has tended to minimize the bearing of the Ebla tablets on the OT. The London *Times* with 14 January 1977 dateline from Rome writes, "Professor Matthiae dismisses as 'silly' current press reports that the archives in some way support parts of the Old Testament". He concedes that Professor Pettinato had deciphered the names of two cities which appear similar to those of Sodom and Gomorrah. In his opinion this may mean that the biblical story about their wickedness and destruction may refer to two cities which actually existed. For the sake of com-

[111] It is interesting to notice that the 1939 edition of *The Complete Bible: An American Translation* ("Chicago Bible") renders Exod. iii 15 "This has always been my name, and this shall remain my title throughout the ages", ascribing to *lᵉʿōlām* the meaning "from eternity", whereas the first edition of 1927 read, "This is my name for all time, and this is my title for age after age". Cf. also Ps. cxxxv 13 for a similar poetic construction.

pleteness Matthiae should also have mentioned that Pettinato had by October 1976 already deciphered on one tablet all five names of the cities of the plain and that these cities are listed in the same order as in Gen. xiv 2, namely, Sodom, Gomorrah Admah, Zeboiim, and Bela.

To the same newspaper Professors E. Ullendorff of London and A. Malamat of Jerusalem addressed a letter in March, 1977, which emphasized the importance of exercising caution in the interpretation of the finds and their relation to the OT. Finally, Prof. Pettinato ends his article "Gli archivi reali di Tell Mardikh-Ebla: Riflessioni e prospettive"[112] with a paragraph entitled "Paneblaitismo?" Here he complains that newspaper reports as well as scholarly interventions especially in the United States (he uses the term *oltreoceano* which translated in context = U.S.A.) have manifested a tendency and a danger from which he feels obliged not only to dissociate himself but to put other scholars on their guard. The fact that names in the onomasticon of Ebla reappear in the Bible does not authorize us to make the Eblaites the forefathers of Israel. And to wish to restudy the OT in the light of Ebla, Pettinato concludes, would be a methodological error destined to repeat errors already committed in the past. How must Pettinato's warnings be evaluated?

The OT itself partially supplies the answer. While not mentioning Ebla, the OT does point to this region as the fatherland of the Israelites. The patriarchs came to Canaan from Haran, and after Abraham left Haran for the Promised Land, some of his kinsmen stayed behind. Genesis xxiv reports that, when Abraham wanted a bride for his son Isaac, he sent his trusted servant to Haran to seek a girl from among his relatives. Haran stands to the north of Ebla, not far away, and is often mentioned in the new tablets, which also list a city called Ur in the territory of Haran.[113] Hence biblical scholars have an obligation to deepen their understanding of patriarchal traditions[114] by exploiting the fresh information placed at their disposal by the Tell Mardikh excavations. To be sure, mistakes in the application of the new data to the biblical text are going to be

---

[112] *Rivista biblica* 25 (1977), pp. 242-3.

[113] *Ibid.*, p. 236.

[114] In his review of Thomas L. Thompson, *The Historicity of the Patriarchal Narratives: The Quest for the Historical Abraham*, in *JNES* 36 (1977), pp. 222-3, D. G. Pardee asserts, "Genesis 14 is clearly unhistorical and probably the latest of the major patriarchal narratives (exilic)", a position that will become difficult to maintain as the Ebla evidence begins to unfold.

made, but this does not mean we should adopt the attitude of the nervous nellies and claim that the chronological gulf separating the two cultures absolves us of the duty of undertaking a painstaking examination of the evidence. Most discoveries from the ancient Near East, especially those epigraphic,[115] oblige scholars to re-examine the biblical text and its data. Our purchase on biblical Hebrew poetry is so uncertain that we should welcome the opportunity to check our current assumptions and translations against independent data from a new and more ancient source. Who during the past two thousand years ever suspected that Biblical Hebrew possessed a vocative *lamedh* until the Ras Shamra tablets emerged from the dust in 1929—and taught philologists to distinguish between prepositional and vocative *lamedh*? When Ebla prose and poetic texts get published, they will surely reveal forms and usages that will enable biblical grammarians to give a better account of the text before them. Already a number of obscure and downright unintelligible *hapax legomena* in Hebrew have turned up in the Sumerian-Eblaite bilingual vocabularies with clear definitions that will warm the cockles of the Bible translator's heart.

On the other hand, the OT itself bids fair to elucidate, to judge from the rapprochments with Ebla already effected, many words and names in the Ebla tablets.[116] Those archaeologists, P. Matthiae to name one, who in their claim to maintain objectivity by prescinding from the biblical record, and facetiously distinguish between "real archaeologists" and "Abraham chasers", do themselves and Near Eastern scholarship a disservice.

General consequences

In the preceding pages some particular points of contact between Ebla and the OT have been spelled out. It remains now to discuss briefly two possible general implications. The first concerns Ugaritic

[115] By way of illustration, the publication in 1924 of the two-line Aḥiram Inscription with its clear attestation of two infixed *-t-* forms, of two verbs with probable *t-* preformative with third masculine singular, and the use of *ʿl* in the sense of "from", has enabled Hebraists to improve the translation of more than a score of biblical texts as well as to facilitate the analysis of numerous puzzling roots and verb forms.

[116] As well as in Old Akkadian. Thus Gelb, *Glossary*, p. 267, postulates the root *ŠKB*? (perhaps Sum.) to account for the PNN *sag-gu-bí*, *šà-gú-bi*, and *šà-gú-ba*, when all of them can readily be explained by West Semitic *śgb*, "to be high, inaccessible", witnessed in the Heb. PN *śᵉgûb*, "Exalted", and in the verb *śāgab*, which in a number of texts is predicated of God and his name.

and what may be called the closing of the chronological chasm. Over the past twenty years, when reviewing in the pages of *Revue biblique* my work or that of my students, Père R. Tournay has without fail warned against the danger of employing second-millennium writings from Ugarit on the North Syrian coast to explain first-millennium difficulties in poems presumably from Palestine. Or when reviewing M. Pope's *Job* in the Anchor Bible, he writes, "L'écart de près de dix siècles qui sépare Ugarit du livre de *Job* accentue le caractère très hypothétique des contacts supposés entre la langue de ce livre saint et celle de Râs Shamra".[117] F. C. Fensham voices the same preoccupation in his review of L. Sabottka's *Zephanja*: "One must, however, be very cautious in comparing Ugaritic material from the 14th to 12th centuries B.C. with the Hebrew of Zephaniah (ca. 612 B.C.) with the interval of about 600 years in which the meaning of a word or a literary device could have changed enormously. In cases where one has no choice but to compare Ugaritic and Hebrew so far apart, it would be wise to put a question mark after one's solution".[118]

The striking and illuminating linguistic and cultural correspondences between Ebla and the OT now upset the neat and impeccable logic of Tournay and Fensham and others who have voiced similar difficulties. Between Ebla and the Bible the chronological gap runs from 13 to 22 centuries, between Ugaritic and the Bible only 2 to 8 centuries. Instead of being too early to be much pertinent, the Ras Shamra documents now appear, *vis-à-vis* Ebla, to be much too recent to be of much help! Not the least of Ebla's contributions to biblical research will be the gradual demolition of the psychological wall that many scholars have erected on the foundation of the relatively slight chronological difference between the Ugaritic tablets and the OT. That a word could have changed its meaning over the course of centuries few would deny, but preliminary study of the bilingual vocabularies reveals that recognizable Eblaite words here witness the same meaning as in the Book of Job some 18 centuries later! A biblical scholar who now accepts the definition of a Ugaritic word as still obtaining in Zephaniah can scarcely be considered reckless if he fails to put a question mark after his equation. In years to come the importance—or better, the centrality—of Ugaritic for Northwest Semitic research will, paradoxically, continue to grow, thanks to the discovery of the nearly 15 thousand tablets at Tell Mardikh.

[117] *RB* 74 (1967), p. 128.
[118] *JBL* 92 (1973), p. 598.

The second general development resulting from these finds may be a gradual change of attitude toward the literary and mental capacity of the biblical authors. A hundred years ago Reuss and Wellhausen had convinced a large segment of the academic community that writing came to Israel with the monarchy, and that it was unscientific to maintain that the patriarchal traditions could have been written down before that period. Rather, the floruit of biblical composition was, according to these scholars, during the exile in the sixth century B.C. The discovery in 1887 of the El Amarna tablets dating to the middle of the 14th century, some of them originating in Jerusalem, Shechem, and Megiddo, shook but did not shatter this article of faith. Only after 1929 when the Ras Shamra tablets came to light did the idea that writing was not a latecomer in Israel make serious headway; the close linguistic and literary kinship between Ugaritic and Hebrew showed that the latter had roots in Canaan in the second millennium. Though found on the North Syrian shore, the elegant, intricate, and sophisticated Ugaritic poetry reflects the religion and mythology prevalent in Canaan which includes Palestine, Lebanon, and Northwestern Syria. Hence the existence in Palestine of a written alongside an oral tradition in the second millennium becomes a reasonable assumption. Now the Ebla discoveries reveal a literary tradition in Canaan reaching back into the first half of the third millennium. This means that biblical poets and writers fell heir to a long and sophisticated tradition of writing; to picture them as neophytes struggling with the rudiments of poetic composition now becomes a caricature. In October 1975 I gave a lecture at Cambridge University on the formal techniques of Hebrew poetry. After the lecture one of the professors commented that it was too clever by half because it ascribed to biblical poets a greater technical capacity and mental subtlety than he was willing to concede for that period. One conversant with the refined poetic devices employed by the Canaanite poets of Ugarit, who presumably inherited some of them from their third-millennium ancestors, would hesitate to raise such an objection.

In his book *L'eau, sa vie, et sa signification dans l'Ancien Testament* Philippe Reymond translates Job xxxvi 27, "Il attire les gouttes d'eau; il filtre la pluie (c'est-à-dire ce qui sera plus tard la pluie) pour son fleuve", with the comment, "Au fond, le verset décrit, comme *à l'envers*, le trajet de la pluie et montre comment elle a son origine dans les courantes celestes".[119] So far so good. Then Rey-

[119] *VTS* 6 (Leiden, 1958), pp. 205-6.

mond proceeds to examine "il attire" and asks if evaporation is intended here. One cannot prove this, he states, and such an explanation seems to exceed the scientific knowledge available at the time of Job. The encyclopedic lists of birds, fishes, beasts, stones and metals compiled at Ebla offer an insight into how carefully these people observed and recorded nature, and authorize the exegete to accept Job's description at face value. A knowledge of evaporation need not have been beyond his grasp unless of course there had been a sharp cultural decline in Canaan during the interval.

In his comments on Job xxix 18, *ʿim qinnî ʾegwāʿ/wᵉkaḥôl ʾarbeh yāmîm*, "Like its nest I will perish/ and like the phoenix I will multiply my days" (my translation), the late H. H. Rowley observes that "the phoenix is a symbol not merely of longevity, but of immortality, and it is impossible that Job dreamed of this".[120] Recent philological studies [121] and fresh research on the phoenix myth [122] confute the limitations set by Rowley on the range of Job's dreams. In the light of one of the bilingual vocabularies listing the phoenix, the Eblaite PN *aḫ-ḫa-lum* (TM.75.G.336 V 3) may well be interpreted "the Phoenix is my brother", a name indicating that the sacred bird had already been divinized. Thus the phoenix myth may date back to the third millennium while the very name of this symbol of immortality betrays the Phoenician-Canaanite provenience of the myth.

The complex social structure of Ebla itself, where 11,700 functionaries administered the royal palace and its archives, the intricate relationships binding together its extensive commercial empire and given expression in detailed commercial treaties, the dedication nearly obsessive to the keeping of written records of multiple genres, the existence of a scribal school where bilingual vocabularies and encyclopedic lists were compiled and copies of the Creation and Flood stories prepared, all bespeak a level of culture in Northwestern Syria, the homeland of the Patriarchs, hitherto unsuspected. Our esteem for them and their culture cannot but affect our attitude toward their descendants in Canaan in the second and first millennia B.C.

---

[120] *Job*: *New Century Bible Series* (London, 1970), p. 239.

[121] Cf. M. Dahood, "*Ḥôl* 'Phoenix' in Job 29:18 and in Ugaritic", *CBQ* 36 (1974), pp. 85-8. That *ḥôl* here signifies "phoenix" is further confirmed by the mention of *ṭāl* in the next verse. Both classical and Judeo-Christian sources report that the phoenix fed on the life-giving dew from heaven; see the next note.

[122] Cf. the thoroughly-documented study of R. van den Broeck, *The Myth of the Phoenix according to Classical and Early Christian Traditions* (Leiden, 1972).

THE TARGUMISTS AS ESCHATOLOGISTS [1]

by

R. P. GORDON
Glasgow

If the Targums were first committed to writing in the late intertestamental period—an unexceptionable premise in our present state of knowledge—then it should cause no surprise that they are found to reflect the interests and preoccupations of those formative years. And one of the outstanding features of the intertestamental period was the popular predilection for subjects with an eschatological flavour. Furthermore, speculative interest was sharpened by sectarian contention, and the Targumists were unwaveringly on the side of those who maintained a lively eschatological hope, with its promise of God's imminent intervention in the affairs of a disordered world. The Targumists were, of course, in a privileged position since they stood at the headwaters of biblical exposition and could easily, if they were so minded, make the biblical text conform to their own *parti pris*. But their endeavours in this field were well-intentioned and normally in the interests of what was considered to be doctrinal orthodoxy.

There were many occasions, let it be said, when the Targumists felt justified in their liberal interpretation of their duties as translators and paraphrasts. If the plain sense of a verse seemed to contradict the general tenor of scripture they would feel duty-bound to harmonize, and there were not a few ways of accomplishing this. M. L. Klein has recently drawn attention to the technique of "converse translation" by which even the most refractory text could be made pliant.[2] "Converse translation" involves saying the exact opposite of

---

[1] "Targumist" properly denotes the author of a written Targum. Behind the written Targum there lies, of course, the oral composition of the synagogal *meturgeman*. The following symbols have been used: F (Fragment-Targum, ed. M. Ginsburger); N (Targum Neofiti, ed. A. Díez Macho); P (Palestinian Targum; in the case of the Pentateuch this symbol indicates the agreement of at least two of the group F-N-Ps); Ps (Targum Pseudo-Jonathan, ed. M. Ginsburger).

[2] "Converse Translation: A Targumic Technique", *Biblica* 57 (1976), pp. 515-37.

what the text intends, for example by the insertion or omission of a negative particle. Now when the Targumists came to deal with certain O.T. passages which speak of the afterlife they were only too glad to take refuge in the device of "converse translation". What else could be done with those sections in Job and Ecclesiastes in which the ideas of resurrection and immortality are expressly repudiated? That some of these agnostic sentiments might have been made *argumenti causa* was not likely to be appreciated by the man in the street. Job xiv 11f., for example, was in urgent need of attention because of its espousal of annihilationism.

11 As waters fail from a lake,
and a river wastes away and dries up,
12 so man lies down and rises not again;
till the heavens are no more he will not awake,
or be roused out of his sleep.

To render these verses innocuous the Targumist had recourse to a type of "converse translation" which we may dignify with the title of "alternative attribution". Not men in general, but the wicked in particular, will suffer the fate described by Job:

till the heavens are no more *the wicked* shall not awake,
or be roused from their place of sleep.[3]

Eccles. iii 18-22 is treated in similar fashion, so that it is not "the sons of men" but the wicked who experience the same fate as the beast, and "the advantage of *a sinner* over the unclean beast is nothing but the burial-place".[4]

The resolution of rhetorical questions was, as Klein observes, another method by which dissident texts could be brought into line. But the Targumists not only resolved rhetorical questions, they might also create them, as in Eccles. ii 16. "How the wise man dies just like the fool!" exclaims the Preacher; the Targumist achieves a completely different effect with his rhetorical question: "And why, then, *say the children of men* that the end of the righteous is like that of the wicked?" This contortion was necessary because the option of "alternative attribution" was foreclosed by the Preacher's specific reference to the wise man.

[3] In the light of this and the examples which follow it is surprising to find that the Targumist rendered Job vii 9f. quite literally.

[4] Tg Ps. xlix 19 (Heb. 20) introduces the same distinction between the fate of the righteous and the fate of the wicked.

G. F. Moore claimed that "the primary eschatological doctrine of Judaism is the resurrection",[5] and it is certainly the case that the Targums make frequent mention of the resurrection and of the related themes of reward and retribution. Apart from the many general references to the resurrection there are also more specific statements as to who would, or would not, participate in it. Adam, for example, was told by God, "You shall return from the dust and shall arise and give an account and a reckoning of all that you have done" (P Gen. iii 19).[6] For her disobedience Lot's wife was turned into a pillar of salt "until the time when the dead are brought to life" (P Gen. xix 26), which implies that she herself would be resurrected. On the other hand, it is said of the Egyptians who perished at the Red Sea that they would not be resurrected on the day of judgement (P Exod. xv 12). Exceptions of this kind are made in texts as far apart in time as 2 Maccabees and the Mishnah, to go no further.[7]

The apocalyptic literature of the intertestamental period displays no consensus in its references to the classes of people expected to have a part in the resurrection. Three main views are represented: a resurrection of righteous Israelites, or of all Israelites, or of all mankind.[8] Each of these view-points can be illustrated from the Targums.

The Targum to Ps. lxviii 22 (Heb. 23) teaches that nothing will be able to stand in the way of the righteous on the day of resurrection. Whereas the MT declares that God will bring his enemies from Bashan and from the depths of the sea in order to requite them, the Targumist inserts a word of hope for the righteous who had not been buried in the normal way and who might therefore fear exclusion from the resurrection.

> As for the righteous who died and were consumed by the beasts of the field, says the Lord, I shall bring (them) back from Bashan, I shall bring back the righteous who were drowned in the depths of the sea.[9]

---

[5] *Judaism in the First Centuries of the Christian Era* 2 (Cambridge, Mass., 1927), p. 379.

[6] The same text furnished proof of the doctrine of resurrection for later Samaritan theologians, who, however, based their argument on a reading ("and to *your* dust you shall return") peculiar to the Samaritan Pentateuch; see M. Gaster, *Samaritan Oral Law and Ancient Traditions* (London, 1932), p. 137; J. Macdonald, *The Theology of the Samaritans* (London, 1964), pp. 374f.

[7] Cf. 2 Macc. vii 14 (referring to Antiochus Epiphanes); Mish. San. x 1-4.

[8] See the references in R. H. Charles, *Apocrypha and Pseudepigrapha of the Old Testament* 2 (Oxford, 1913), p. 218; G. W. E. Nickelsburg, *Resurrection, Immortality, and Eternal Life in Intertestamental Judaism* (Cambridge, Mass., 1972), p. 143.

[9] Cf. Rev. xx 13; 1 Enoch lxi 5.

This positive statement about the resurrection of the righteous does not necessarily imply that the wicked will not be raised, yet it is worth recalling that the MT is actually speaking about the fate of those who oppose God. It could therefore be significant that their resurrection to judgement does not come into the picture.[10] Any suggestion that Tg Psalms is late and therefore unlikely to reflect the earlier view that only the righteous would be raised has to be put alongside the fact that the quotation of verse 18 (Heb. 19) of this same Psalm in Eph. iv 8 betrays its obvious indebtedness to the Targum.

The resurrection of all deceased Israelites is taught in Targum Pseudo-Jonathan to Num. xi 26. The MT says no more than that Eldad and Medad prophesied in the camp of Israel; the Targumist reveals that their prophecies were concerned, in the main, with the end times. We are informed that, after the destruction of the armies of Gog, "all the dead of Israel will be raised and will enjoy the good things hidden for them from the beginning, and will receive the reward of their deeds". Here it is probably the resurrection of the dead of Israel at the beginning of the Messianic age which is in view; Neofiti and the Fragment-Targum credit the Davidic Messiah with the defeat of the invading armies. This interpretation appears to be supported by the reference to "the good things hidden for them from the beginning", for this is probably an allusion to the monsters Behemoth and Leviathan which were supposed to have been created on the fifth day (cf. Gen. i 21) and to have been reserved for the Messianic banquet of the last days.[11]

There is at least one explicit statement of a general resurrection of mankind in the Targums. In the prayer of Hezekiah the king addresses God with the words, "O Lord, by these things men live, and in all these is the life of my spirit" (Is. xxxviii 16). Whatever is meant by "these things" (possibly "the words and works of God" [12]), the Targumist saw an opportunity to raise the subject of resurrection: "O Lord, thou hast declared that thou wilt bring all the dead to life, and before them all thou hast revived my spirit". It is the insertion

[10] A resurrection of the righteous only seems to be implied in the conditional promise made to Joshua the high priest in Tg Zech. iii 7.

[11] Cf. P Gen. i 21; Tg Ps. l 10; 1 Enoch lx 7-10; 2 Bar. xxix 3f.; 4 Ezr. vi 48-52. Other references in Moore, pp. 363-5; M. J. Mulder, *De targum op het Hooglied* (Amsterdam, 1975), p. 113. Tg Cant. viii 2 speaks of the old wine which was also thought to have been set aside (same verb (*ṣnʿ*) as in Ps Num. xi 26) from the creation (cf. also TB San. 99a).

[12] So J. Mauchline, *Isaiah 1-39* (London, 1962), p. 236.

of the word "all" in the first clause which calls for comment. This affirmation of a universal resurrection is deliberate; the Targumist's choice of words was not dictated solely by the underlying Hebrew text. Unequivocal teaching about a general resurrection is rare in the apocalyptic literature and seems to have gained currency only in the first century A.D.[13]

There was one point on which there was general agreement among the ancient rabbis and that was the rôle of the land of Israel in the resurrection.[14] Israel was, in an eschatological sense, "the land of the living", the land of everlasting life. Some obscure Hebrew in Hos. xiv 7 (Heb. 8) becomes the vehicle for expressing this conviction. In its Targumic form the verse reads: "They shall be gathered in from their dispersion, they shall dwell in the shadow of their Messiah, the dead shall live, and goodness shall abound in the land". Israel was, then, the land in which the resurrection life was to be enjoyed. But it also came to be regarded as "the land of the living" in the sense that only there could the dead entertain hope of being raised from their graves. Some authorities held that even a righteous Israelite could be denied a part in the resurrection if he had been buried beyond the borders of Israel (so R. Eleazar in TB Ketub. 111a). Conversely, the hope of resurrection was extended to non-Israelites whose only merit was their interment within the holy land. The resulting concern for the fate of Jews who had died in exile partly accounts for the widespread practice of *ossilegium*, or secondary burial, especially in the first three or four centuries of the Christian era.[15] Secondary burials in Palestine have a long prehistory, but the belief that resurrection was a favour reserved for those buried in the land can only have ensured the continued popularity of the custom.

In recognition of this problem, and in order to preserve the unique status of Israel as the land of resurrection, a highly fanciful solution was proposed. It is expounded in the Targum to Cant. viii 5:

> Solomon the prophet said, When the dead come to life the Mount of Olives will be split asunder and all the dead of Israel will come out from beneath it; and also the righteous who died in exile will come by way of channels under the ground, and will debouch from under

---

[13] Cf. Nickelsburg, *loc. cit.*

[14] Cf. W. D. Davies, *The Gospel and the Land: Early Christianity and Jewish Territorial Doctrine* (Berkeley, 1974), pp. 61-5.

[15] See E. M. Meyers, "Secondary Burials in Palestine", *BA* 33 (1970), pp. 1-29; *idem*, *Jewish Ossuaries: Reburial and Rebirth* (Rome, 1971).

> the Mount of Olives. But the wicked who died and were buried in the land of Israel will be ejected just as a man throws a stone with a sling.

The Targum's picture of subterranean channels issuing at the Mount of Olives is no isolated exegetical quirk, for there are similar representations of the resurrection in rabbinic literature.[16] While the connection of the Mount of Olives with the resurrection has no biblical basis the notion of the cleaving asunder of the hill is obviously derived from Zech. xiv 4.[17] Direct reference to the resurrection is made in the Reuchlinianus Targum text of this verse: "At that time the Lord shall take in his hand a great trumpet and shall blow ten blasts on it to resurrect the dead". Although it is not expressly said that the dead will issue from the Mount of Olives we are a step nearer the tradition preserved in the Targum to Cant. viii 5.

A quite fundamental reinterpretation of the various passages which speak of the subterranean travels of the righteous Israelites was mooted by Herbert Loewe in an extended note in *A Rabbinic Anthology*.[18] Behind the references to underground burrowings, suggests Loewe, there lies the Greek concept of metempsychosis. Each of the terms which serve to depict the resurrection in this highly fanciful manner can be shown to have had a totally different significance originally. For example, the notion that the righteous will "roll" (*mitgalgᵉlîn*) [19] through the ground is the result of a misunderstanding of the term *gilgûl*, meaning "transmigration". In fact, says Loewe, two ideas have become intertwined: the practice of removing corpses to Palestine for re-burial and the concept of metempsychosis which was little understood among Jews and was quite unacceptable in any case.

Loewe's thesis is nothing if not original, but it suffers from a couple of basic weaknesses. First, it is hard to conceive of the rabbis so misunderstanding the idea of metempsychosis as to link it in some way with the institution of secondary burials. Loewe's reinterpretation had arisen out of the conviction that there was a limit to the fantasies in which the rabbis indulged, and that the view of resurrection presented in Tg Cant. viii 5 was beyond that limit. But is anything gained by substituting rabbinic stupidity for rabbinic fantasy? The

---

[16] Some parallels are given in Strack-Billerbeck, III, pp. 828f.

[17] Cf. V. Aptowitzer, "Arabisch-Jüdische Schöpfungstheorien", *HUCA* 6 (1929), p. 227.

[18] Ed. C. G. Montefiore and H. Loewe (London, 1938), pp. 660-3.

[19] The word used in TJ Ketub. xii 3 and TB Ketub. 111a.

second possible objection was anticipated by Loewe himself. There is not good evidence to show that metempsychosis was seriously considered by Jewish thinkers until the time of Saadia. Loewe counters by pointing out that although the concept was not discussed the terminology was known in the earlier period. However, the fact that the root *gālal*, from which the later *gilgûl* ("transmigration") derives, was used in connection with the incubation of an egg and the rolling of dough is hardly conclusive for the argument. Nor can Philo's acquaintance with the idea of transmigration be taken as an index of knowledge or opinion in Palestine and Babylonia. And it is noticeable that the examples of metempsychosis quoted from Josephus and the Talmud are of "retrogressive transmigration": the souls of the wicked become demons, the men of Babel are transformed into apes, and so on. Such conjectures about the fate of the wicked may owe nothing at all to Greek concepts.[20]

On the other hand, it would seem that the idea of underground burrowing on resurrection day was already current in Babylonia in the mid-third century A.D. The evidence comes from the Dura-Europos synagogue where a large fresco (no. 21) portrays the resurrection, largely in terms of Ezek. xxxvii but also incorporating features from Zech. xiv. There need be little doubt that the action revolves round the Mount of Olives which is shown split in two, the two halves separated by a deep valley whence human heads and limbs are issuing.[21] We cannot really tell whether this valley, or channel, was thought to extend under the ground to regions beyond Israel, but there are several reasons for thinking that this was the case. (i) How would the bodies of the righteous who died *in* Israel be conducted from their graves to the Mount of Olives, if not by "subterranean traction"? (ii) It is unlikely that a painting in Babylonia would represent the resurrection in such a way as to exclude from participation in it the very people by whom and for whom the fresco was made. (iii) It is probable that the group of ten men in Greek garb on the right of the panel are representatives of the ten tribes of

---

[20] Similar developments are traceable in Islam; cf. J. Macdonald, "Islamic Eschatology - V: The Day of Resurrection", *Islamic Studies* 5 (1966), pp. 159f. See also Quran v 60f., etc.

[21] See H. Riesenfeld, *The Resurrection in Ezekiel xxxvii and in the Dura-Europos Paintings* (Uppsala, 1948), esp. pp. 28-34 (this study is reprinted in J. Gutman (ed.), *No Graven Images, Studies in art and the Hebrew Bible* (New York, 1971); E. R. Goodenough, *Jewish Symbols in the Greco-Roman Period* 10 (New York, 1964), pp. 179-96; also plate XXI in vol. 11.

the northern kingdom. The artist indicates clearly enough that the group had taken part in the resurrection (cf. Pes. R. 147a).

There was a particular reason why the vision of Ezek. xxxvii should enjoy prominence at Dura-Europos. In his account of the vision the prophet mentions only that he was set down in a valley. Several rabbinic sources, Targums included, assert that it was the valley of Dura which Ezekiel saw.[22] Dan. iii 1 gives the only biblical mention of the valley of Dura, in connection with Nebuchadrezzar's erection of his great image. Not only was the valley of Dura in Babylonia, the word "valley" in Dan. iii 1 is the Aramaic cognate of the Hebrew *biqʿāh* used in Ezek. xxxvii 1. This easy association of Ezekiel's vision with the valley of Dura was probably made long before the painting of the Dura-Europos frescoes and the inhabitants of the town will have regarded themselves as being, in a special way, the heirs of the promise.

Panel no. 21 represents, therefore, a conflation of two resurrection traditions, the one based on Ezek. xxxvii and the other traceable to Zech. xiv. The fresco reflects, in our opinion, that view of the resurrection presented in the Targum to Cant. viii 5 and its rabbinic parallels. And because the Dura-Europos paintings are known to have been made between A.D. 245-256 we can plot this point with rare accuracy.

In the fragment of Palestinian Targum to Ezek. xxxvii published by A. Díez Macho in 1958 [23] the problem of the fate of the diaspora Jews is also addressed. The fragment reproduces Ezek. xxxvii 1-14 in a form which differs considerably from the standard Targum. There are what Díez Macho calls "incrustations" on the earlier text of the passage, and these are easily identified. Apart from these additions,

---

[22] Cf. P Exod. xiii 17; Tg Cant. vii 10; TB San. 92b; *PRE* xxxiii. In the fragment of Palestinian Targum to Ezek. xxxvii (see next note) the vision is again located in the valley of Dura. Because the next verse there proceeds to identify the dead bones of Ezekiel's vision with the remains of those who took part in a supposititious Ephraimite exodus from Egypt thirty years before the main body of Israelites Díez Macho (p. 203n.) concludes that this must be a different Dura from that mentioned in Dan. iii 1. Instead he nominates Dor, situated between Carmel and Caesarea (cf. 1 Kg. iv 11; 1 Macc. xv 11, 13, 25, etc.). But this is to treat the reference to the Ephraimite exodus as if it were an integral part of the Targum, whereas it is probably a later insertion in the text. The identification of the valley of Ezek. xxxvii 1 with Dura will have been made independently of the tradition of the Ephraimite exodus, as the references at the beginning of this note, which know nothing of that tradition, would indicate.

[23] "Un segundo fragmento del Targum Palestinense a los Profetas", *Biblica* 39 (1958), pp. 198-205.

however, there are still major differences from the Babylonian standard version. The latter, as commonly, follows the MT closely, and therefore portrays the resurrection as a revival of national fortunes. In the Palestinian fragment it is the resurrection of those who have died outside Israel which is in focus.

> Son of man, from what I have done to these bones you can know what I shall do[24] to those of the children of Israel who die in captivity. For, behold, the children of Israel are saying, When we die and do not see the deliverance which the Lord will accomplish for Israel, our bones will be dry and our expectation will cease and our confidence perish (verse 11).

Clearly the Targumist is endeavouring to correct that view which denied the blessing of resurrection to those buried beyond the borders of Israel.

Without doubt the most discussed aspect of Targumic eschatology hitherto has been the subject of Messianism.[25] For that reason, and because it is such a large field in any case, our observations will be restricted to a few points of general interest. We shall not be misrepresenting the Targumists if we say that, in their estimation, the primary task of the Messiah was to remove the yoke of the Gentiles from the land of Israel. The Targumic version of Is. liii 8 expresses this conviction very aptly:

> From chastisements and from punishment he shall bring our exiles near. Who shall be able to recount the wonderful things which shall be accomplished for us in his days? For he shall remove the sovereignty of the nations from the land of Israel;[26] the sins which my people have committed he shall transfer to them.

In the days of the Messiah Israel would recover its status as a nation and there would be a great ingathering of its exiled sons and daughters. But an element of confusion is introduced into all this by the fact that the Targums actually speak of two Messiahs, a Messiah son

---

[24] The Aramaic actually has the perfect.

[25] See, for example, P. Humbert, "Le Messie dans le Targum des Prophètes", *RTP* 43 (1910), pp. 420-47; 44 (1911), pp. 5-46; S. H. Levey, *The Messiah: An Aramaic Interpretation* (Cincinnati, 1974).

[26] For the same emphasis cf. Tg Is. x 27; Ps. Sol. xvii 25; TB San. 99a; Shab. 63a. Cf. the rôle of the Messiah in the eschatology of the Qumran sect: "This [*sc.* the smiting of the nations] is almost the sole function which is certainly ascribed to the Messiah in the Scrolls. Their Messiah is therefore the Messiah of the 1st century A.D. coming to make their nation the rulers of the world" (G. R. Driver, *The Judaean Scrolls* [Oxford, 1965], p. 468).

of David and a Messiah son of Ephraim. Targumic references to the Messiah son of Ephraim are few in number, and the same is true of the rabbinic literature as a whole. All that we are told about him is that he would be killed while doing battle with that eschatological character Gog, the leader of Gentile resistance to the Messianic rule. This information is provided by our two main sources, TB Sukk. 55a and the Reuchlinianus marginal variant to the Targum of Zech. xii 10. In the words of the latter, "the Messiah son of Ephraim shall go out to do battle with Gog and Gog shall kill him before the gate of Jerusalem . . .". Evidently it was expected in some quarters that the golden age of the Davidic Messiah would be preceded by the appearance, and the death, of a secondary Messianic figure.[27] It is all the more surprising, then, and an illustration of the doctrinal pluralism of the Targums, that Targum Pseudo-Jonathan to Exod. xl 11 attributes the defeat of Gog to the hand of the Messiah son of Ephraim.

It is impossible to discover how the tradition of the Ephraimite Messiah came into being. Christian Messianism seems an unlikely source of influence.[28] Perhaps the most attractive solution is that which sees it as the product of bitter historical experience in the first two centuries of the Christian era, when one and another Messianic hero fell before the seemingly invincible might of Rome.[29]

The Targums do not represent the Messiah as being personally involved in the raising of the dead. Hos. xiv 7 (Heb. 8), already quoted, comes as near as any Targumic text to linking the Messiah with the resurrection. But here the Targumist does not actually say that the Messiah will himself perform the miracle of resurrection, only that it will take place during his reign of peace.[30] This approximates to the situation in all but the very late rabbinic writings. Mish. Soṭ. ix 15 says that "the resurrection of the dead shall come through Elijah of blessed memory". In a few places such as Is. xxvi 19 and

---

[27] The death of the Messiah is anticipated in 4 Ezr. vii 29f.

[28] Nor is it easy to relate Targumic Messianism, in its hybrid aspect, to the question of "the Messiahs of Aaron and Israel" mentioned in the Qumran Discipline Scroll (ix 11). On this latter see G. R. Driver, pp. 462-86; W. S. LaSor, *The Dead Sea Scrolls and the New Testament* (Grand Rapids, 1972), pp. 98-103.

[29] Cf. Levey, p. 16: "Such a personality was probably built up as a psychological reaction to the death of Bar Kokhba". The concept of dual Messiahship itself is rather older and probably owes its inspiration to the complementary figures of Zerubbabel and Joshua in the early post-exilic period.

[30] Cf. Humbert, p. 10: "C'est le seul passage de tout le Targum des prophètes qui place pendant l'époque messianique une résurrection des morts".

Zech. xiv 4 (Reuchlinianus variant) the Targumists see the resurrection as being directly the work of God himself.[31]

In the thinking of the earlier apocalyptists no distinction was made between the Messianic age and "the world to come". But already in the first century B.C. it was being propounded that the Messianic age would be of limited duration and but the prelude to "the world to come" (1 Enoch xci 12-17). Seldom do the Targumists commit themselves *in expressis verbis*; when they do it is, as we should expect, to expound the later view. Targum Pseudo-Jonathan to Exod. xvii 16 announces that God will destroy the Amalekites from three generations: "from the generation of this world, and from the generation of the Messiah, and from the generation of the world to come". The Hebrew phrase thus dilated is *middōr dōr*, "from generation to generation", an expression which might more naturally have been enlisted in support of a two-age scheme of history if such had been in vogue when the Targum was composed. The same tripartite arrangement is presupposed in the Targum to Ps. lxi 7 where it is affirmed that the Messiah would not be subject to death but would live on into the age of "the world to come".

From time to time the Targumists saw fit to make their own positive declarations concerning the principles of reward and retribution. So the message of the watchman in Is. xxi 12, "Morning comes, and also the night", is metamorphosed to become "There is a reward for the righteous and there is punishment for the wicked". A similar explanation of this rather cryptic utterance of MT is given in the Jerusalem Talmud (Taʿan. i 1): "Morning for the righteous, and night for the wicked; morning for Israel and night for the peoples of the world". By means of a pun on the word *rāzî* in Is. xxiv 16 the same theme is introduced[32] and here the Targum stands as close to the apocalyptic literature as anywhere. "The prophet said, 'The mystery of the reward of the righteous has been shown to me, the mystery of the punishment of the wicked has been revealed to me'." The association of "mystery" with the theme of reward and punish-

---

[31] Cf. N Gen. xxx 22: "There are four keys which are given into the hand of Yahweh, the lord of all ages, and they are not handed over either to angel or to seraph". One of these keys is the key (so F; N "keys") of the sepulchres. On Messiah and the resurrection see Strack-Billerbeck, IV, p. 819; on Elijah and the resurrection see Moore, p. 384.

[32] G. Bornkamm suggests (*TDNT* 4, p. 814n. = *TWNT* 4, p. 820n.) that the Massoretic pointing of *rāzî* is intended to associate the form with *rāz*, "mystery" (cf. TB San. 94a).

ment is noteworthy. There are various parallels in the apocalyptic literature. Equally, there is nothing in the MT which would have inclined the Targumist to formulate his "mystery" in these terms.[33] It may also be regarded as a felicitous circumstance that MT is expressed in the first person singular ("But I say . . ."). Whether by accident or design, the form of words which the Targumist attributes to the prophet is on a par with "I know a mystery" in 1 Enoch ciii 2 (cf. civ 10, 12, cvi 19) and "He made known to me the mystery of the times" in 2 Bar. lxxxi 4. The first person references by the apocalyptists were not made simply to preserve esotericity, they were also supposed to assure the reader of the reliableness of the information being conveyed. It was doubtless the latter case in Tg Is. xxiv 16.

Gehenna and the Second Death are familiar features of New Testament eschatology whose closest parallels on the Jewish side are to be found in the Targums. This holds especially for the use of the term "Second Death" which does not figure in early rabbinic literature, though the concept was known and expressed in other ways.[34] Twice in the Targum to Jeremiah it is said of the Babylonian spoliators of Jerusalem that they would "die the Second Death and not live in the world to come" (li 39, 57), but the Targumists are customarily less specific and prefer to direct their strictures against "the wicked" (cf. Is. xxvi 15, xxxiii 14; Hos. xiv 10). This expression, as may be deduced from various texts, certainly included the ungodly within the community of Israel. Upon such the sentence of Tg Is. xxii 14 is passed: "This sin shall not be forgiven you until you die the Second Death, says the Lord God of hosts". Tg Is. lxv 5 is in similar vein and again it is ungodly Israelites who are the object of the Targumist's attack: "their punishment shall be in Gehenna where the fire burns all the day". An apparent historical allusion in the preceding verse adds to the interest of this particular commination. Is. lxv 3f. outlines certain obnoxious practices which have still to be explained fully. For the more part the Targum is faithful to the Hebrew, but there is one notable deviation in the translation of verse 4a where MT speaks of those "who sit in tombs, and spend the night in secret places". Whereas the MT may be alluding to an in-

---

[33] The temptation to relate the Targumic expansion to MT *ṣ^e^bî laṣṣaddîq* (taken in the sense of "glory for the righteous") is checked somewhat by the fact that these words are given an independent rendering by the Targumist ("a song of praise for the righteous").

[34] Cf. Strack-Billerbeck, III, p. 830.

cubation rite, this is plainly not the case in the Targum. In the latter the guilty party "sit in houses which they build from the dust of graves, and dwell with the corpses of men". And there is much to be said for P. Churgin's suggestion that the Targumist had in mind the building of the town of Tiberias by Herod Antipas.[35] In the earliest phase of its history Tiberias was regarded with disdain by observant Jews since it was supposed to have been built partly on the site of a cemetery. The tradition of the unseemly origins of Tiberias was no closely-guarded secret and it appears highly probable that the Targumist has introduced a contemporising reference to the town. If so, we have a *terminus post quem* and the makings of a *terminus ante quem* for this snatch of Targum. Tiberias was founded about A.D. 20, so that any allusion to its location must be placed after that date. However, in spite of its inauspicious beginnings Tiberias before long acquired a reputation *nulli secundus* as a centre of rabbinic scholarship, and there are hints of its respectability being acknowledged in the mid-second century A.D. Some years after the Hadrianic persecutions Simeon ben Yochai took the springs at Tiberias and "declared either a part or the whole of Tiberias to be clean".[36] Judah ha-Nasi took up residence there and, all in all, it would seem that by A.D. 200 its period of disfavour had come to an end. A jibe such as we have in Tg Is. lxv 4 is unlikely to have been coined after this date, and probably not in the decades immediately preceding it.

What would be the duration of the punishment meted out to the wicked in Gehenna? To this question the rabbis gave varying answers. According to one view the wicked, whether belonging to Israel or to the nations generally, would be punished for twelve months, while heretics and apostates would suffer unending torments (Cf. TB R.H. 17a; Tos. San. 13 4f.). The Targumists do occasionally speak of the unquenchable nature of the fire of Gehenna in such a way as to suggest belief in punishment of infinite prolongation for rebellious Israelites (cf. P Gen. xxxviii 25; Is. xxxiii 14 may refer to Israelites or, if the wider context is determinative, to Gentile oppressors). Tg Is. lxvi 24, on the other hand, is noteworthy because of the way in which it introduces the idea of limited punishment. The MT says that in the end-time those who rebel against God will be a *dērā'ôn*, an abhorrence,

[35] *Targum Jonathan to the Prophets* (New Haven, Conn., 1927), p. 25. See the relevant article by M. Avi-Yonah, "The Foundation of Tiberias", *IEJ* 1 (1951), pp. 160-9.
[36] *Jewish Encyclopedia* 12, p. 143.

to the rest of humanity: "their worm shall not die, their fire shall not be quenched, and they shall be an abhorrence to all flesh". The last clause is expanded considerably in the Targum: "and the wicked shall be judged in Gehenna until the righteous say of them, We have seen enough". To achieve this interpretation the word *dērā'ôn* has been read as *day* (or *dê*) *rā'înû*, "we have seen enough". Such a treatment of the MT, no matter about its artificiality, was possible only in an atmosphere in which differing estimations of the significance of Gehenna were current.[37]

The Targumist's midrashic interpretation of *dērā'ôn* emphasizes a feature of the judgement of the wicked which occasionally receives notice in the apocalyptic writings, viz. the expectation that those consigned to Gehenna would be a spectacle to the righteous as the latter enjoyed the delights of paradise (cf. Jub. xxiii 30; Ass. Mos. x 10; 4 Ezra vii 93).[38] It is an idea which could have had any one of a number of Old Testament texts as its starting-point (e.g. Ps. xci 8, not to mention Is. lxvi 24 itself) and it finds expression in other texts which have been similarly remodelled by the Targumists (e.g. Ps. xlix 10 [Heb. 11]; Is. xxxiii 17).

Finally, we come to a consideration of the possibility of sectarian controversy having left its mark upon the eschatology of the Targums. The passage most discussed in this connection is Gen. iv, which tells of Abel's death at the hand of Cain.[39] Now in *Myth, Legend and Custom in the Old Testament* (New York, 1969), pp. 53-5, T. H. Gaster voiced his suspicion that an earlier form of the story of Cain and Abel contained some account of a conversation, of the *débat* type, between the two brothers. Support for this view he found in the words which the major versions supply in addition to the MT's "And Cain said to Abel his brother" (verse 8). (The MT is truncated and has obviously suffered in transmission.) But the major versions, with the exception of the Palestinian Targums, have nothing more than

---

[37] Is. lxvi 24 is quoted in TB R.H. 17a to show that the exceptionally wicked will suffer unending torment in Gehenna.

[38] Cf. also 1 Enoch xxvii 2f., xlviii 9, lxii 12. It is a familiar conceit among the church fathers; cf. Tertullian, *De Spectaculis* 30; Cyprian, *Ad Demetrianum* 24.

[39] See A. Marmorstein, "Einige vorläufige Bemerkungen zu den neuentdeckten Fragmenten des jerusalemischen (palästinischen) Targums", *ZAW* 49 (1931), pp. 235-9; P. Grelot, "Les Targums du Pentateuque—Étude comparative d'après Genèse, IV, 3-16", *Semitica* 9 (1959), pp. 59-88; R. Le Déaut, "Traditions targumiques dans le Corpus Paulinien?", *Biblica* 42 (1961), pp. 30-6; G. Vermes, "The Targumic Versions of Genesis iv 3-16", *ALUOS* 3 (1961-2, published 1963), pp. 81-114 (= pp. 92-126 in *Post-Biblical Jewish Studies* [Leiden, 1975]).

"Let us go into the field" (or variants) to represent what Cain said. The authors of the Palestinian Targums evidently shared Gaster's hunch, for they introduce their own form of *dèbat* in which the brothers argue the question of theodicy in several of its aspects. Cain is made to say: "There is no judgement, there is no judge, there is no other world, there is no gift of good reward for the just and no punishment for the wicked", and Abel contradicts him in similar terms.

It would seem that Cain and Abel have representative functions so far as the Palestinian Targums are concerned. For L. Finkelstein [40] and G. Vermes [41] the dialogue is a distillation of the controversy between the Pharisees and the Sadducees. S. Isenberg has sought to reinforce this position by showing that, as early as the second century A.D., Cain's assertions were being used as a *topos* to be placed in the lips of others who were also held to be heretical.[42] He goes on to link the Targumic *haggadah* to the non-Massoretic reading which the Palestinian Targums share with the other versions, in such a way as to conclude that the *haggadah* must antedate the standardization of the consonantal Hebrew text.

H. A. Fischel interprets the *haggadah* differently, seeing it as a rebuttal of Epicureanism rather than of Sadduceeism.[43] In fact, the first words attributed to Cain ("there is no judgement, there is no judge") are to be regarded as an Epicurean *sententia*, according to Fischel. The argument is that it cannot be Sadduceeism which is being repudiated, since Cain "denies any kind of compensatory judgement", and not just the notion of judgement after death. Cain's insistence that "there is no other world" is also claimed as a positively Epicurean sentiment. And as further illustration of his point, Fischel attempts to show that the speeches by Cain and Abel betray the influence of Greek rhetorical structures.

It might appear as one of the strengths of Fischel's case that he is able to give full weight to Cain's assertion that "there is no judge". On the surface this is an absolute rejection of the idea of human accountability, in the present life as much as in any future existence. This, Fischel contends, more truly reflects Epicureanism than Sad-

---

[40] *The Pharisees*³ (New York, 1962), pp. 762ff.

[41] p. 103 (= p. 116).

[42] "An Anti-Sadducee Polemic in the Palestinian Targum Tradition", *HTR* 63 (1970), pp. 433-44.

[43] *Rabbinic Literature and Greco-Roman Philosophy* (Leiden, 1973), pp. 35-50 (footnotes on pp. 128-38).

duceeism. But this is not all that can be said on the matter. Unfortunately, our knowledge of the Sadducees is largely derived from hostile sources in which no attempt at an unbiassed exposition of their beliefs is ever made. In view of the tone of many of these references it is well within the bounds of possibility that in Gen. iv the Palestinian Targums are also indulging in overstatement in order to score points off the opposition. It is possible, too, that Cain's seeming denial of accountability in any shape or form has to be read in the light of his rejection of belief in a future life, the point then being that there is no judgement after death because there is no life after death. It is also relevant to mention that the epigrammatic "there is no other world", described by Fischel as "a well-known and widely fought tenet of Epicurus", was precisely that feature of the Palestinian Targum to Gen. iv 8 which led Finkelstein to conclude that the life-setting of the *haggadah* was the doctrinal controversies involving the Pharisees and the Sadducees (p. 769). Finkelstein was influenced by the fact that the comparatively uncommon expression "other world" (*'wlm 'ḥr*) appears in *Aboth de-Rabbi Nathan* ch. 5 in the account of the schism between the Pharisees and the Boethusians/Sadducees.

Fischel, however, lays particular stress on the rhetorical, formulaic nature of the Epicurean *sententia* which he claims to have discovered in the Palestinian Targum. That the *sententia*, whether Epicurean or Sadducean, enjoyed a long and varied life in the Talmudic and Midrashic literatures is very evident from his study. It is also undeniable that similar coinages are to be found in Greco-Roman literature, but whether the similarities between these and their Hebrew-Aramaic counterparts are sufficient to justify a theory of a common, in this case Greco-Roman, origin is a different matter. It could be argued that the correspondences upon which Fischel builds his case are nothing more than coincidence. Challenges to items of traditional belief in any culture are naturally couched in negatives,[44] and it is this feature of the coinages which more than anything gives them the appearance of sharing a common origin.

If the case for the influence of Greek rhetorical patterns is insubstantial then we must inquire whether the carefully structured utterances of Cain and Abel draw their inspiration from some other identifiable source. In point of fact Ps. lviii 11 (Heb. 12) seems to

---

[44] The point hardly needs substantiation but cf. "there is no God, no hereafter, no punishment" (R. Wurmbrand, *Tortured for Christ*[2] [London, 1970], p. 49, quoting his Communist torturers).

throw light on the genesis of the dicta attributed to Cain and Abel by the Targumists.

w^eyō'mar 'ādām 'ak p^erî laṣṣaddîq 'ak yēš 'elōhîm šōp^eṭîm bā'āreṣ

Men will say,
Surely there is a reward [45] for the righteous,
Surely there is a God who judges on earth.

There are several things to be noted about the verse. First, it contains the basic components of the dialogue between Cain and Abel: reward and divine retribution. Again, in the second stich the verbal particle *yēš* is used. All occurrences of the *sententia* in Hebrew and Aramaic sources are marked by the use of such a particle: *yēš/'ît* in positive formulations, *'ên/lêt* in negative. Thirdly, as Fischel observes, all Talmudic (and Targumic) formulae of this type have word repetition at the beginning of each "stich". This feature is also present in the biblical text, in the repetition of the asseverative *'ak*.[46] In short, it is easier to relate the speeches of Cain and Abel to Ps. lviii 11 than to their supposed Greco-Roman prototypes. We would therefore conclude that the whole case for interpreting the Palestinian Targumic version of Gen. iv 8 as a repudiation of Epicureanism rests on questionable premisses.

A more direct challenge to prevalent heterodoxy in the area of eschatology is presented in Tg Mal. iii 6. There the MT's "I the Lord do not change; therefore you, O sons of Jacob, are not consumed" has been transformed into "I the Lord have not changed my covenant which is from of old; but you, O house of Israel, you think that if a man dies in this world his judgement has ceased". This is certainly not a matter of an alien philosophy on the periphery of Judaism; it is, on the contrary, a heresy which has become deep-rooted among a section of the population and which requires controverting in plain language. It is not now a question of putting a *topos* in the mouth of a heretical figure like Cain or Esau (see P Gen. xxv 32, 34), but of confronting a significant proportion of the 'house of Israel' in the manner of P Ezek. xxxvii 11 ("the children of Israel"). "Such a situation seems to have existed in these proportions only in the

---

[45] *p^erî* clearly means "reward" here. The Targum has *'gr ṭb*, "good reward", the expression used in P Gen. iv 8.

[46] In *'elōhîm šōp^eṭîm* we even have an instance of *parēchēsis* (repetition of sound), a feature of which Fischel (e.g. pp. 38f.) makes a great deal.

period when the Pharisees and Sadducees co-existed and before strict pronouncements on Minim in general began to be made by the rabbinical authorities." [47]

Targumic eschatology will not readily submit to schematizing in the ways which we might consider appropriate. It is too tolerant of variation and dissonance for that to be the case. But there is one feature which remains a constant throughout and that is the Targumists' insistence on human accountability in the face of the doctrines which they uphold. Tg Mal. iii 6 is illustrative of the point. The Targumists were not content with the mere repetition of eschatological credenda; they set themselves the more rewarding task of encouraging the faithful, and of rallying the wavering, to orthodoxy of belief and to rectitude of conduct.

---

[47] A quotation from my, as yet, unpublished dissertation, *A Study of Targum Jonathan to the Minor Prophets: From Nahum to Malachi* (Cambridge, 1973), pp. 49f.

THE USE OF THE ANCIENT VERSIONS FOR INTERPRETING THE HEBREW TEXT

A sampling from Ezekiel ii 1 - iii 11

by

MOSHE GREENBERG
Jerusalem

I

I feel honored by the invitation of our President, Professor Walther Zimmerli, to deliver a paper to this learned audience. I wish to acknowledge this feeling at the outset because the argument I shall put forward, though critical of much that is being done in textual work today, is yet one which only colleagues in scholarly training and endeavor can judge; the opportunity of presenting it to such an audience is therefore precious to me. Since my argument originated in work on a commentary to the Book of Ezekiel, I wish further to acknowledge my special debt to Professor Zimmerli for his monumental contribution to the understanding of every facet of that difficult book. If I seem to be directing an inordinate measure of criticism at Zimmerli, it only that no one else since Cornill has stated his reasoning in text-critical and exegetical matters in comparable detail. Through his careful justification of his decisions it is possible to study the axioms of OT criticism at large. If I believe that in some matters I can move beyond the point reached by the present consensus, it is only because I have started from the advance positions won by the patient and erudite labors of such predecessors.

II

Modern scholarly interpretation of Ezekiel [1]—as of all biblical books—works with a text restored as far as possible to the form of

[1] Modern works on Ezekiel referred to in this article are (in alphabetic order): C. H. Cornill, *Das Buch des Propheten Ezechiel* (Leipzig, 1886); and the commentaries of W. Eichrodt (*ATD* Göttingen, 1965-66; Eng. trans. *OTL* London, 1970); G. Fohrer (*HAT*, Tübingen, 1955); J. W. Wevers (*Cent. Bible*, NS, London, 1969); W. Zimmerli (*BK*, Neukirchen Kreis Moers, 1955-69).

The commentary of (R. David) Kimhi is cited as printed in standard rabbinic Bibles (*Miqra'ot Gᵉdolot*).

Ezek. ii 1 - iii 11

ii 1 ויאמר אלי בן אדם עמד על־רגליך ואדבר אתך 2 ותבא בי רוח כאשר דבר
אלי ותעמדני על־רגלי ואשמע את[a] מדבר אלי 3 ויאמר אלי בן־אדם שולח אני
אותך אל־בני[b] ישראל אל־גוים המורדים אשר מרדו־בי המה ואבותם פשעו בי עד
עצם היום הזה 4 והבנים קשי פנים וחזקי־לב אני שולח אותך אליהם ואמרת אליהם
כה אמר אדני ה׳ 5 והמה אם־ישמעו ואם־יחדלו כי בית מרי המה וידעו כי נביא
היה בתוכם 6 ואתה בן־אדם אל־תירא מהם [-c]ומדבריהם אל־תירא[c-] כי [-d]סרבים
וסלונים[d-] אותך ואל־עקרבים אתה יושב מדבריהם אל־תירא ומפניהם אל־תחת כי
בית מרי המה 7 ודברת את־דברי אליהם אם־ישמעו ואם יחדלו כי[e] מרי המה
8 ואתה בן־אדם שמע את אשר־אני מדבר אליך אל־תהי־מרי כבית המרי פצה
פיך ואכל את אשר־אני נתן אליך 9 ואראה והנה יד שלוחה אלי והנה־בו[f]
מגלת־ספר 10 ויפרש אותה לפני והיא כתובה פנים ואחור וכתוב אליה קנים[g] והגה
והי iii 1 ויאמר אלי בן־אדם את אשר־תמצא אכול אכול את־המגלה הזאת ולך
דבר אל־בית ישראל 2 ואפתח את־פי ויאכלני את המגלה הזאת 3 ויאמר אלי
בן־אדם בטנך תאכל ומעיך תמלא את המגלה הזאת אשר אני נתן אליך ואכלה ותהי
בפי כדבש למתוק 4 ויאמר אלי בן־אדם לך־בא אל־בית ישראל ודברת בדברי
אליהם 5 כי לא אל־עם עמקי שפה וכבדי לשון אתה שלוח אל־בית ישראל
6 לא[h] אל עמים רבים עמקי שפה וכבדי לשון אשר לא־תשמע דבריהם אם־לא
אליהם שלחתיך המה ישמעו אליך 7 ובית ישראל לא יאבו לשמע אליך כי־אינם
אבים לשמע אלי כי כל־בית ישראל חזקי־מצח וקשי־לב המה 8 הנה נתתי
את־פניך חזקים לעמת פניהם ואת־מצחך חזק לעמת מצחם 9 כשמיר חזק מצר
נתתי מצחך לא־תירא אותם ולא־תחת מפניהם כי בית־מרי המה 10 ויאמר אלי
בן־אדם את כל דברי אשר אדבר אליך קח בלבבך ובאזניך שמע 11 ולך בא אל
הגולה אל־בני עמך ודברת אליהם ואמרת אליהם כה אמר אדני ה׳ אם־ישמעו
ואם־יחדלו

not in LXX ______	a אתו Z	e +בית ZEF LXX
‘’ Fohrer __ __ __	b בית ZE (LXX)	f בה ZF (LXX)
[] Eichrodt _ _ _ _ _	c-c ואל תחת מפניהם Z (LXX)	g קינה F (LXX)
[] Zimmerli - - - - - -	d-d סבבים וסולים EF	h ולא ZEF (LXX)
	סלונים סבבים Z	

"the lost original"; as Eichrodt writes, "Exegetical work during the last few decades . . . displays increasing certainty in penetrating to the original text. . ." (p. 11). The method of restoration has been to collate the ancient versions—among which G(reek) has chief importance—with the Hebrew, and (1) when the Hebrew is unintelligible or looks corrupt or awkward, to correct it by recourse to the versions or conjecture; (2) where the Hebrew is different from or not represented in the versions, to decide in each case which reading is closer to the original, or make a conjecture based on the divergence. (3) On the assumption that the M(asoretic) T(ext) is considerably removed from the original, the work of restoration continues even where it and the versions agree; e.g., on theoretical grounds, matter may be deleted which is attested in all or most witnesses—repetitions, synonymous or explanatory phrases may be declared secondary or editorial. The necessity of step 1 is here granted; the legitimacy of steps 2 and 3 as now practiced must be questioned, on the ground that the stated goal of textual criticism is, in reality, obscure.

Consider the treatment of Ezekiel's commissioning (11 1 - iii 11) in three recent commentaries—those of Fohrer (1955), Eichrodt (1965-6), and Zimmerli (1955-1969). The wording of G differs from that of MT, mostly by minuses, in 10% of the passage. F(ohrer) reconstructs a text diverging from MT by over 20%, mostly in minuses; the texts of E(ichrodt) and Z(immerli), though not identical, diverge similarly from MT by 14%. "Restoration of the original text" is manifestly more an art than a science; let us study the state of the art as displayed in our specimen. See the Hebrew text.

Our critics are unanimous in deleting, in ii 2 *ka'^{a}šer dibber 'elay*; in ii 4a *w^{e}habbanim q^{e}še panim w^{e}ḥizqe leb*; in iii 1 *'et '^{a}šer timṣa '^{e}kol* and in iii 6 *lo*—all these are not in G. However, though *'^{a}šer '^{a}ni* in ii 8 is likewise not in G, not one of our critics proposes to delete it. On the other hand, several items evidenced in G are nonetheless deleted by all of them: in iii 5 *'el bet yiśra'el*, and in iii 5-6 *kibde lašon* twice and *'imqe śapa* once. A theoretical model of a short "original" evidently exists, although this is not followed absolutely. For not only is G's minus in ii 8 *'^{a}šer '^{a}ni* not adopted, but all our critics insert G's plus (*bet*) in ii 7, and add the copula with G and other versions to *lo* in iii 6. We must proceed to cases in order to learn what guiding principles are at work.

The most extensive divergence between MT and the restored text is the deletion, with G, of ii 4a. Here is the reasoning: F and E regard it as a gloss "quoted" from iii 7 [*ḥizqe meṣaḥ uqᵉše leb*]; Z takes it as a secondary explanation of the text: *banim* is not used anywhere else in Ezekiel for the status of the people *vis-à-vis* YHWH, while it is a favorite expression of Isaiah and Jeremiah. On the other hand, *qᵉše panim* will be a free variation of the formula found in iii 7f. ii 4b attaches best to ii 3.

Beside the basic fact of G's not evidencing these words, two or three reasons are offered for disregarding them. First, their similarity to phrases in iii 7 which, though not identical, are close enough to be judged as their inspiration. F (followed by E) uses "gloss" here not in the normal sense of "a brief explanation of a difficult or obscure word or expression", but—as Z puts it better—an explanatory expansion. But what needed explanation? In the end our critics mean only that 4a is an expansion suspiciously similar to words found in iii 7; as repetitious and lacking in G, it is adjudged unoriginal. Indeed, many repetitions and parallelisms have suffered at the hand of our critics, whether attested in G or not; see the various fates of *marᵉdu/pašᵉʿu* (ii 3), *ʾal tira/ʾal tira* (ii 6), *middibrehem ʾal tira umippᵉnehem ʾal teḥat* (ii 6), *ʾᵉkol, ʾᵉkol ʾᵉkol* (ii 8, iii 1), *hammᵉgilla hazzot, hammᵉgilla hazzot, hammᵉgilla hazzot ʾᵃšer ʾᵃni noten ʾeleka*, (iii 1-3), *ʿimqe śapa wᵉkibde lašon* [twice] (iii 5-6). On the other hand, others have survived: the repetitions of *ʾim yišmᵉʿu wᵉʾim yeḥdalu* (ii 5,7, iii 11), *ki bet mᵉri hemma* (ii 5, 7; but not unanimously in ii 6, iii 9); the parallelisms *biṭnᵉka taʾᵃkel umeʿeka tᵉmalle* (iii 3), all of iii 8, and *qaḥ bilᵉbabᵉka ubᵉʾozneka šᵉmaʿ* in iii 10. A criterion for deleting does not emerge.

Before leaving this matter, it is worth noting that *qᵉše panim* in ii 4a is not merely a "free variation of the formula of iii 7f." It is unique. It does not mean "hard, unyielding" (Ges.-Buhl), but in the light of iii 7's *ḥizqe meṣaḥ* must be comprehended as an original play on *qᵉše ʿorep* (which does mean "unyielding"), with *panim* substituted for *ʿorep* and a consequent shift in sense to "impudent" (if anything had to be glossed, it was *qᵉše panim* itself!).

A second reason for disregarding ii 4a is given by Z: *banim* is not used anywhere else in Ezekiel to represent Israel's status *vis-à-vis* God. That is true, but it applies here as well. For *banîm* in ii 4a means "the sons"—the present generation of Israelites. Cornill, who likewise rejected these phrases, argued better when he asserted that "the whole [of ii 4a] is spun out of the simple *hemma waʾᵃbotam* [of the preceding verse]"; for Cornill, it was only "the striking vacillation in the existing mss. of G [with respect to MT's ii 4a that] shows it to be unoriginal".

Thirdly and last is Z's observation that the words are not missed, since ii 3 is best followed by ii 4b.

The judgement that the words *wᵉhabbanim qᵉše panim wᵉḥizqe leb* are unoriginal rests then on the following grounds: foremost, their absence in G; then, their repetitiveness, the uncommon usage of *wᵉhabbanim* (a ground that fails here), and their dispensability.

Before weighing these grounds, we must give our attention to a small item in ii 3: for MT *bᵉne yiśra'el* G reflects *bet yiśra'el.* F renders *Israeliten*, staying with MT, but E and Z choose G. Z defends the choice: *bet yiśra'el* agrees with the dominant usage of Ezekiel; moreover, it is the point of departure for the following *bet mᵉri* (vs. 5). MT is a pale [i.e., commonplace] substitute, the fault of a copyist.

At first glance, this divergence seems to be a meaningless variant.[2] On second thought a question arises: is it meaningless that G which reads *bet yiśra'el* in ii 3 does not read *wᵉhabbanim* etc. in vs. 4a, while MT which reads *bᵉne yiśra'el* in vs. 3 does read *wᵉhabbanim* etc. in vs. 4a? Considering these correlations, has the divergence no exegetical import? Is MT merely more verbose? G and MT certainly agree on the gist of God's speech: Ezekiel is sent to a hard audience. But what is only hinted at in *hemma wa'ᵃbotam* of vs. 3 (which G has) is a veritable subtheme of the paragraph in MT. Israel's evil character is hereditary and hence hopeless. The prophet is forewarned that he is sent not to "vinegar son of wine"—to use a talmudic phrase—but to "vinegar son of vinegar". The impudence and unyieldingness of his audience is the product of a generations-long blemish. Moses called his generation of Israelites *bᵉne meri* "sons of rebelliousness" (Num. xvii 25); Ezekiel's generation, descendents of these, are called by God in the next vs. *bet meri* a "house"—that is, a dynasty and a line [3]—of rebelliousness. The correlation in MT of *habbanim/bᵉne* has a consequence for translation. *bᵉne yiśra'el* must be rendered not

[2] As seem to be, at first glance, the five other cases of G reflecting *bet* where MT has *bᵉne* listed in the *Biblia Hebraica Stuttgartensia* (K. Elliger, ed., 1971) at ii 3 note a (cf. iii 1 note b, where MT *bet* corresponds to a G reflection of *bᵉne,* and BHS note b thereto listing four other such cases). The following argument for the meaningfulness of this particular variation is based on correlations uniquely present in the passages under discussion. This argument is without prejudice to the other listed cases in which the variation may or may not turn out to be meaningful.

[3] That this is the nuance of *bayit* here was suggested to me by Prof. Jacob Milgrom.

"Israelites" (*Israeliten*) but precisely "sons of Israel" so that one can pick up the point of vs. 4, "And the sons, impudent and stubborn, etc."

It is an acute observation of Z that G's *bet yiśra'el* is, in its context, a point of departure for *bet meri*—a pejorative twist of the name. But it turns out, upon an alert reading, that MT has its own message, conveyed precisely by its differences from G; in its context of *habbanim*/ *b*^{e}*ne*, *bet meri* evokes *b*^{e}*ne meri*, which it converts into a hereditary line, fully in accord with a view taken elsewhere in Ezekiel of Israel's ingrained sinfulness (e.g., chs. xvi, xx). The two versions thus convey different messages in this paragraph, for which their distinctive formulations are the necessary vehicles. Can one message be made a criterion for the other? Which one is more original? On what ground will the decision be made?

Two features of the MT of this passage have been mentioned that now may be enlarged upon. First, the variety of double expressions that permeate the passage: (a) apposition—"to the sons of Israel, to the rebellious nations" (ii 3) at the opening of the speech; "to the exiles, to the sons of your people" (iii 11) at its end; (b) synonymy and parallelism—"rebelled/transgressed" (ii 3), "do not be afraid of them/ of their words do not be afraid" (ii 6), "hard-faced / tough-hearted" (ii 4), "feed your belly / fill your stomach" (iii 3), "of obscure speech/ of unintelligible language" (iii 5-6), "tough browed/ hard-hearted" (iii 7), "do not be afraid of them / do not be dismayed by their faces" (iii 9), "take in to your heart / hear with your ears (iii 10). Chiastic alternation occurs frequently, always indicating interrelation, often resumption: in ii 3-4 *šole*^{a}*ḥ '*^{a}*ni* / *'*^{a}*ni šole*^{a}*ḥ*; in ii 6 *'al tira mehem umiddibrehem 'al tira*; in ii 8, iii 1 *'*^{e}*kol 'et '*^{a}*šer '*^{a}*ni noten* / *'et '*^{a}*šer timṣa '*^{e}*kol* / *'*^{e}*kol 'et hamm*^{e}*gilla*; in ii 4, iii 7 *q*^{e}*še*... *w*^{e}*ḥizqe* / *ḥizqe* ... *uq*^{e}*še*; in ii 3, iii 11 *'el b*^{e}*ne yisra'el 'el goyim hammor*^{e}*dim* / *'el haggola 'el b*^{e}*ne ʿammeka* (these last two, at the beginning and the end of the passage call attention to the interrelation of these separated phrases), and finally, *qaḥ bil*^{e}*bab*^{e}*ka ub*^{e}*'ozneka š*^{e}*maʿ* (iii 10). A feature of the parallel expressions is that one member almost invariably displays a semantic innovation or is unique while the other is commonplace: *q*^{e}*še* panim *w*^{e}*ḥizqe leb*; *ʿimqe śapa* w^{e}kibde lašon—the second phrase means, uniquely, "of unintelligble speech", ḥizqe meṣaḥ *uq*^{e}*še leb*, biṭn^{e}ka ta'^{a}kel *umeʿeka t*^{e}*malle*—on the first, unique phrase, see ahead; qaḥ bil^{e}bab^{e}ka *ub*^{e}*'ozneka š*^{e}*maʿ*—the first phrase has the unique sense "take into your haert".

This feature of repetition and parallelism, occurring throughout MT, is exhibited in several items which have been deleted by one critic or another, although most have versional support. If MT exhibits such a uniform texture, on what ground other than arbitrary canons of taste can some of these items be retained, others deleted?

The second feature of the commissioning scene, which has been in a way observed by critics who supposed that ii 4a was an outgrowth of iii 7, is the close interrelation of its parts. The chiastic reversal of the adjectival parts of the phrases in ii 4a and iii 7 shows that the two are indeed interrelated, and that the interrelation was intended to be felt. A survey of the entire passage shows that such interrelation extends over the whole, and the key to the overall design is precisely the two adjectival phrases of ii 4a—*q^{e}še panim*—an exterior figure, and *ḥizqe leb*—an interior one. These play a thematic role in the sequel.

In the immediately following paragraph (ii 6-7), the exterior image is taken up by *umipp^{e}nehem ’al teḥat*, which must be rendered, not by the conventional "do not be dismayed by them", but "do not be dismayed by their faces"—so as to bring out the connection with *q^{e}še panim*. But the main burden of this paragraph is indicated by the threefold *’al tira* and the threefold occurrence of *d^{e}barīm*: it is the fortification of the prophet against the stinging speech of his audience. This is directly related to the interior image *ḥizqe leb*, since *leb* means not only "heart" but also "source of speech" (i.e. chest), as in Prov. xxiii 33 *‘eneka yir’u zarot w^{e}libb^{e}ka y^{e}dabber tahpukot* which, with H. L. Ginsberg (*Encyc. Judaica*, s.v. "Heart") is to be rendered "Your eyes will see strange things and your throat will utter garbled things."

In the next paragraphs the prophet is equipped for his hard task interiorly and exteriorly. In ii 8-iii 3 he is fed a scroll in order to fill his inside with messages of doom. In iii 4ff. the theme of speech leads into the exterior image: the prophet is equiped to *outface* his impudent audience. Note that the final exhortation in iii 9 differs from the similar ones in ii 6 in that *dibrehem* (which belongs to the interior image) is missing; only *mipp^{e}nehem* is mentioned, in accord with the reference to the exterior figure.

The alternation of exterior and interior themes, the stylistic effects (chiasm) employed to interrelate the parts of the passage—these add to the impression of the integralness of MT. By deleting entire elements or altering them to accord with G, the integral effect is diminished when not destroyed. On what ground? In ii 6a MT has a monotonous but emphatic parallelism *'al tira mehem umiddibrehem 'al tira*; the second monotonous clause is deleted by F ("a variant gloss, after 6b") and replaced by Z with G's commonplace *we'al teḥat mippenehem*. Why is G's commonplace variant preferable to MT's monotonous emphasis on the—for it—key elements *'al tira* and *debarim*? is one text explicable as a corruption of the other, or do we have simply variants spontaneously arising, unconnected with each other and creating different effects?

We turn now to another plus of MT over G, unanimously judged to be secondary: *'et 'ašer timṣa 'ekol* of iii 1. F, who takes out all of iii 1 as "an explanatory gloss to ii 9b," regards this clause as even more derivative—"a more closely defining gloss to the scroll"; E declares it a gloss, after Jer. xv 16, a point enlarged upon by Z, who reasons as follows: "The clause overloads the verse, and, materially, it is unsuitable; the scroll has already been shown to Ezek., so he has nothing more to 'find' [this argument comes from Cornill]. At this juncture, we expect a command regarding the object just shown, and it appears in the second half of the verse—*'ekol 'et hammegilla hazzot*. the gloss is valuable because it is obviously spun out of Jer. xv 16's *nimṣe'u debareka wa'okelem*; Ezek's act was thus explicitly illuminated from Jer. . ."

We begin our discussion of this passage with the observation that *maṣa* means not only "find" but "find there" (BDB p. 593a; cf. F *vorfindest*) the command of MT means, then, "What you find (= see) there, eat!" (NEB "eat what is in front of you"). In this clause *maṣa* has nothing to do with discovery.

As for G's minus, it is important, again, to see how the data of MT and G correlate. In MT, *'et 'ašer timṣa 'ekol* correlates with two prior clauses of identical construction: in ii 8 *šema' 'et 'ašer 'ani medabber 'eleka* and *peṣe pika we'ekol 'et 'ašer 'ani noten 'eleka*. Each of these three clauses subjects the prophet to an ever more defined command of God. First, a comprehensive demand for unconditional obedience expressly contrasted with the disobedience of Israel: "Listen to *'et 'ašer* I speak to you! Do not be rebellious like the rebellious house! Open your mouth and eat *'et 'ašer* I give you!" Then, after the display of the object to be eaten (a leather scroll!), a chiastic, resumptive command, "*'et 'ašer* you find there, eat!". One wonders whether *'et 'ašer* here does not carry a meaning particularly fit for expressing unconditional submission to a command, namely, "all that, whatever". A survey of its usage, consulting other translations to preclude self-serving, idiosyncratic interpretation, turns up evidence for just this meaning. TJ at Num. xxxii 31 (*'et 'ašer dibber YHWH 'el 'abadeka ken na'aśe*) and Deut. xxix 14 (*'et 'ašer yešno . . . we'et 'ašer 'enenu*) renders the combination *yat kol di*, and NEB at the last verse and at Gen. xviii 19, xxxiv 28, and Exod. xxxiv 34 renders "all that, everything that". The Ezekiel passages may be interpreted accordingly: in all three commands the object is left vague in order to express the unconditional submission of the prophet (Z understands the idea well but does not perceive how the formulation of the sentences expesses it). After "Listen to whatever I speak to you" comes the command, "Eat whatever I give you"; the prophet had, of course, no notion of what was to be offered. He (and the reader) might well expect some kind of food. Then the scroll is displayed, and we can imagine the prophet's amazement. God's third command answers the prophet's unspoken, incredulous question, "Am I supposed to eat that?" to which God's retort is, "Whatever you find there, eat!" and then, with complete specificity, "Eat this scroll".

In iii 2 the narrative continues: "I opened my mouth (showing myself ready to obey) and He offered me the scroll to eat, saying 'Feed your belly [a strange, unique expression] and fill your stomach. . .'" Kimhi aptly glosses, "so as not to vomit it out of your mouth". The unusual terms of the fresh command answer the apprehension of the prophet that, though he take the scroll into his mouth and even chew it, he will never be able to swallow the indigestible mass. Accordingly God commands, "Feed your belly", that is, get it down there. Thereupon, "I ate it"—meaning I chewed it and gulped it down—"and (a miracle!) in my mouth it turned sweet as honey" (Kimhi: "and so I fed my belly and did not vomit it").

MT thus has a graduated series of interlaced commands and acts, revealing by means of interrupted monologue the unexpressed reactions of the prophet to the strange demands of God. The gradation from a blanket demand of absolute obedience to the specific, outragous imposition upon Ezekiel's alimentary system is skillfully drawn in MT; essential elements in it are the three commands with *'et 'ašer* in ii 8 and iii 1.

Turning to G, we note that the absence of *'et 'ašer timṣa 'ekol* in iii 1 correlates with the absence of the first *'ašer 'ani* in ii 8. The beginning of ii 8 in G reads "Hear the one talking to you"—exactly the way G renders the end of ii 2, "I heard the one talking to me". For G, ii 8 echoes as it were the beginning of the audition; not obedience is called for in G's rendition but attention: "Hear what the speaker is to say". Nothing of the graduated series of commands in MT is reflected in G, though, to be sure, it gives a perfectly intelligible, if flatter text. Once again, we have two versions, each with its own quality and its own coherence; is a decision to be made between them? How?

Let us recapitulate: We have tried to show through study of two examples that divergences between MT and G in Ezekiel (and by implication elsewhere) may constitute alternative messages, each with its own validity. Exegetical rewards came, in each case, by asking not which reading was the original one, but what effect did the divergence work on the messages of the respective versions. That question alerted us to correlations between divergences within each version, and stimulated a more thorough investigation of the content and language of each, particularly of MT, whose divergences were largely pluses. That question focused exegetical work where it belongs, on the working out of the meaning of the texts. Instead of hurrying to decide which of two readings is original, we tarried at the threshold of an anterior question: what does each reading mean in its own context. Experience has taught us that every divergence must be approached as possibly significant. Of course, not every one may in fact be so; but unless one is predisposed to find significance, one cannot hope to discover it if it should be there. In this way, divergences between the versions and the MT can be turned into a powerful heuristic resource; scarcely one has proven sterile in our labors on the commissioning scene.

III

Suppose, then, that the versional messages have each been worked out; is it not now necessary to press on and ask which of these comes closest to the original? Several preliminary questions arise: What is meant by "the original" and what are the criteria for recognizing it? What is the likelihood that, given the present state of evidence, the quest for "the original" can meet with any measure of success?

E. Würthwein (*The Text of the Old Testament* [Oxford, 1957], p. 70) defines the aim of textual criticism thus: ". . . to restore the oldest text which can be recovered. This does not mean the recovery of the actual form in which the individual sentences were first conceived, but the form of the text which the OT books had when they had already attained their present shape, as regards extent and content, and were becoming canonical, which happened . . . from the fourth century B.C. onwards." In a similar vein, M. Noth writes (*The Old Testament World* [London and Philadelphia, 1966], p. 359): "By 'Original Text' . . . we have in mind . . . the hypothetical textual form of the OT which the Palestinian canon produced as it was taking shape . . . from about the fourth century B.C." The features of this hypothetical text are unknown, but that is not a fatal obstacle to inquiry, as we read on: "It must be definitely assumed that the 'Original Text' of the OT has been corrupted . . . at a time to which no remaining textual witness extends, not even the Septuagint translation which came into being very early; furthermore we must assume that a number of original readings which had been maintained for some time were not assimilated either in M[T] or in any of the translations. Therefore, there is basically the right of free conjecture. . . , which means an assumption about the original wording which is not supported by any available old textual witness" (p. 361).

This conception of the task of textual criticism will not stand up under scrutiny. The notion of "the hypothetical textual form" (in the singular) that existed at the time of canonization posits an identity between canonization and text standardization which is flatly contradicted by all the evidence we have.[4] The only part of Hebrew Scriptures about which anything of the process of text-standardization is known is the Pentateuch. An informed scholarly guess is that at some time during the Hasmonean period the Pentateuchal text was subjected to critical sifting, and that in the subsequent century or so until the destruction of the Temple a "Scroll of the Temple Court", described by tannaitic sources as a model-text, was in existence. Not only did such standardization of the text occur centuries after the Pentateuch became canonical, it occurred (according to our best guess) after the Septuagint was made. Now if scholars aimed their textual criticism at the recovery of the standard text of the Temple Court, they at least could claim to be aiming at a target known to have

[4] See the fine summary by Sh. Talmon, in P. R. Ackroyd and C. F. Evans (ed.), *The Cambridge History of the Bible* I (Cambridge, 1970), pp. 159-99 ("The Old Testament Text"); reprinted in F. Cross and Sh. Talmon (ed.), *Qumran and History of the Biblical Text*, (Cambridge, Mass., 1975), pp. 1-43.

existed, and thus, in theory at least, attainable. But no scholar I know makes that his goal; all unhesitatingly use the Septuagint to emend and improve on MT, without knowing—indeed without caring—whether such restorations reflect the Scroll of the Temple Court or not. To what "Original Text" of the Pentateuch are they, then, aspiring? To the one Ezra may have brought with him from Persia? But for that early age there is absolutely no evidence of standardization! Presumably, several text forms circulated simultaneously. The Septuagint though it may have originated before the Scroll of the Temple Court does not *ipso facto* reflect an "older" text form. The age of text forms is not determined by the time their vehicles were produced, but by their lineage and characteristics. Judging by these, the MT—in all probability a lineal descendant of the Scroll of the Temple Court—has less vulgar characteristics than the Septuagint, despite its lateness, and thus represents a text-form at least as old as that of the *Vorlage* of the Septuagint. But this means that in the 3rd century BCE, when the Septuagint was made, several text-forms were extant and considered authoritative.[5] Which of these is the "Original Text" which criticism aims to restore?

In the rest of the Hebrew Scriptures the situation is worse. For the Prophets and Hagiographa, evidence of text-standardization does not antedate the 2nd century CE, when revision of the Septuagint was undertaken (e.g. by Aquila) to bring the old G into line with the recently established Hebrew standard. Tannaitic literature (to the end of the 3rd century) attests massively to a standard text of all of Scriptures (not fully made to prevail, but the ideal was there). However no scholar aims at recovering the standard text of tannaitic times when he applies text-criticism to the MT—despite the at least theoretical possibility of attaining such a goal. Instead, we hear of "the text form when the books became canonical" as the goal, though as a criterion this is meaningless. Even according to the conventional (and improbable) view that Prophets and Hagiographa attained to canonical status only at the end of the 1st century, canonization and standardization were still not simultaneous in the Prophets and Hagiographa any more than in the Pentateuch. It is virtually

[5] See the studies by M. H. Segal (*JBL* 72 [1953], pp. 35-47), M. Greenberg (*JAOS* 76 [1956], pp. 157-67), and Sh. Talmon (*Textus* 2 [1962], pp. 14-27); reprinted in S. Leiman, *The Canon and Masorah of the Hebrew Bible* (New York, 1974), pp. 285-326, 455-68. Though old, the positions put forward in these articles respecting the Pentateuch still merit attention.

certain, however, that canonization of the rest of Scripture occurred well before the Christian era;[6] the authority of Scripture in the intertestamental literature is warrant enough for that. Qumran fragments and G make it equally certain that before the end of the Second Temple, centuries before, variant versions of canonical books were extant. Not a scrap of evidence exists for a standardization of Prophets and Hagiographa before the 2nd century CE.[7] What, then, is the "Original Text" which textual criticism aims at here? Suppose we had, not the G of the commissioning scene in Ezekiel, but the Hebrew *Vorlage* of G (which, let us grant, we have correctly reconstituted in the preceeding discussion); suppose it was datable to the mid 2nd centary BCE. How much better off would we be than now? By what criterion would the shorter *Vorlage*, which, in chronological terms, would be older than MT, be recognizable as more "original"? To be sure, it would be a shorter text, but a poorer one too in literary values. Mere oldness is no sign of originality unless it is joined by other features known to be associated with the original. Do we know enough about the original to decide between shortness and literary richness as its hallmark? It is affirmed that shortness is a feature of originality (see Wevers, p. 35), and on that basis the minuses of the versions are combined, other subtractions ("glosses") are proposed, and a text shorter than any in evidence is "restored" as "original to the prophet". But even if the prophet spoke tersely (and there is no evidence that this was the rule), we are, after all, working with written texts; is there any reason to think that the first written form of prophecies, whether at the dictation of the prophet or by deposition from

[6] The carefully reasoned conclusion of S. Leiman, *The Canonization of Hebrew Scripture* (Hamden, 1976), is that the mid-2nd century BCE is the time of the closing of the biblical canon (pp. 131ff.).

[7] L. Blau, *Studien zum althebräischen Buchwesen* (Budapest, 1902), pp. 110f., thought that Tosefta Kelim II 5.8 (584[10]) alluded to a standard Temple text of the Prophets. The passage is wholly obscure; see Leiman, *Canonization*, pp. 104f., and notes thereto.

The fundamental difference between the Torah and the rest of Scripture with respect to text-stabilization has not hitherto been adequately noticed. It was Prof. Elias Bickerman who called it to my attention, observing that since the Torah was the constitution of the Jewish polity, the fountainhead of law of the religious community, there was a special urgency in establishing its text and standardizing it for the entire people. This will account for the evidence that only for the Torah was any editing work done, as well as for the decided superiority of the MT of the Torah (presumably a direct descendent of the Scroll of the Temple Court) over the other ancient versions. As is known, outside the Torah, MT often has no such superiority (as in the text of Samuel).

the memory of his devotees, was also terse? Considering the palor of the written word relative to the rich color of the spoken, it is intrinsically probable that reduction to writing entailed from the first compensatory verbal elaboration. Do we know that there was, from the first, just one collection of the prophet's speeches, from which all others descended? Was a collection completed at once, or were new finds and variants added, so that by the time it was completed it contained "authenticated" variants that diverged from and mutually contaminated each other? Were the several collections themselves sealed off from influencing one another? Is it not possible, nay probable, that within a couple of generations of the prophet's death there were already in existence not only the ancestors of the various text-forms of Jeremiah and Ezekiel that underlie our MT and G, but other texts and mixed forms? Does not this probability militate against the working assumption of "the (single) hypothetical original" from the 4th century onward from which all our witnesses derive and toward the reconstruction of which all text-criticism must aspire? If we further admit, with Noth and all others, that this hypothetical original was already corrupt; if we license, accordingly, free conjectural restorations we end up in pursuit of a chimera—"the original words of the prophet" for whose identification not a single objective criterion is available.[8]

[8] Talmon (in the article cited above, note 3) raised the possibility, on the basis of the correlation of antiquity and variety in the textual evidence that "individual variants, and also groups or even types of variants, which have been preserved in the ancient versions both in Hebrew and in translations, may derive from divergent pristine textual traditions" (p. 162 [reprint 4]). Accordingly, at the end of his study, "the investigator may carefully conclude that with the available evidence no 'first' text form can be established. Or else, . . . he may attempt to reconstitute the presumed pristine texts of each of the major versions individually. It then still remains to be debated whether these proto-texts of the extant versions can be reduced to one common stem, or whether, at least in part, they must considered to represent intrinsically independent textual traditions. . ." (p. 163 [5]). Since the situation varies from book to book, generalization is not very useful except for alerting one to alternatives. I am pleading against the working hypothesis of an "original" where available evidence runs against it, as seems to me to be the case in many of the variants between MT and G I have so far found in Ezekiel. This hypothesis here has simply short-circuited the exegetical process.

It may be noted, incidentally, that F. M. Cross's conviction that the rise of divergent text-types requires geographic dispersion and local isolation is not well grounded; some random counter examples from ancient Near Eastern literature have been adduced by M. Tsevat in "Common Sense and Hypothesis in OT Study", *SVT* 28 (1975), pp. 225f. (for a recent reiteration by Cross of his conviction see *Qumran and the History of the Biblical Text*, p. 309).

The question of "original texts" takes on an altered aspect in the light of

What, then, should be the object of text criticism and of exegesis based on it? We recall the facts: Extensive mss. of Hebrew Scripture start only from the 9th century CE, and they all represent a single text-form, MT, though with many very minor variations which scarcely affect the sense. Before then, only very partial mss. and scraps fill the interval to the Qumran fragments from the turn of the era. Excepting the Samaritan Pentateuch, these all show the standard text attested in the Talmud and Midrash, again with insignificant variations. Contemporary with this fragmentary Hebrew evidence of, basically, a single text type, and a few centuries earlier than it are translations of varying fidelity, the earliest parts of G reaching back to the 3rd century BCE. The study of the early translations in order to reconstruct their Hebrew *Vorlagen*, though over a century old, has still far to go until its principles are worked out systematically and

---

the inner-biblical variant, synonymous, and double readings (see Talmon's latest, suggestive contribution to the understanding of these phenomena in the just-cited work, pp. 321-400), but especially in the light of the theory of an oral substratum that underlies them. Perhaps the earliest grappling with the problem is Ibn Ezra's (d. 1164), in his comment at Exod. xx 1 on the double tradition of the Decalogue: "It was the custom of speakers of Hebrew sometimes to speak at length, sometimes to say what they had to tersely, but so as to enable the hearer to grasp their meaning. Understand that words are like bodies and meanings like souls, and the body is to the soul like a vessel; hence it is the custom of all wise men in speaking any language to preserve the meanings while not being concerned over changing the words, so long as their meaning is the same". R. B. Coote ("The Application of Oral Theory to Biblical Hebrew Literature", *Semeia* 5 [1976], pp. 51-64) proposes that oral theory suggests a way to account for "hyparchetypical, or irreducible variants (zero variants, parallel variants, synonymous readings and the like)". "It can be argued that there must have been a first writing down of a composition, somewhere, some time. But if the tradition of its transmission accepted or produced reformulations and preserved its multiforms, why should greater importance be imputed to the hypothetical original than the ancients thought it had? Their indifference to verbatim fidelity to an original makes the recovery of a single original text an elusive and possibly mistaken goal" (pp. 60-61). Post-biblical Jewish literature offers a large field for observing the practice of written transmission of an originally oral literature; particularly relevant is J. Heinemann's discussion of "The development of prayers and the problem of 'the original text' ", chapter 2 of his *Prayer in the Talmud* (Berlin, 1977).

I am aware that the argument for multiple "originals" can be turned against me: if the transcribers and transmitters exercised such freedom so long as it did not alter the meaning, what justifies poring over their products in order to extract significance from their variations? The answer is that "meaning" is a broad term; there are several ways to "say" something, and their effects may not be the same. It is precisely the exegete's task to determine whether the various ways of saying a given thing have all the same significance. His results will gain in persuasiveness to the extent that they are based on combination and correlation of several items in a given version, as I have tried to show in the examples from Ezekiel.

extensively enough to command confidence.[9] What is clear today, owing to the agreement of Qumran fragments with the Samaritan Hebrew Pentateuch and the G, is the existence in pre-Christian times of text-forms of biblical books diverging from contemporary ancestors of MT. The evidence is still too meager for constructing stemmata, for at best we have (for Isaiah and Samuel) only another one or two extensive texts with which to compare a single book of MT.[10] But it is enough for assuming that not all versional divergences from MT derive from the translators; some demonstrably go back to ancient non-MT-types.

Such meager resources make the task of the Hebrew text critic fundamentally different from that of the NT, the Septuagintal, or the classical text critic. For all practical purposes, the first operation of those critics lies outside his scope—the operation called "recension" (*recensio*). "Unless the manuscript tradition depends on a single witness, the function of recension is to establish the relationships of the surviving manuscripts to each other, to eliminate from consideration those which are derived exclusively from other existing manuscripts and therefore have no independent value . . . and to use this stemma or family tree to reconstruct the lost manuscript (or manuscripts) from which the surviving witnesses descend" (L. D. Reynolds and N. G. Wilson, *Scribes and Scholars* [Oxford, 1968], p. 137). The Hebrew text critic starts, for the greatest part of the literature, by examining the relation of the MT—the single text-form in which the Hebrew has reached us—to the reconstituted *Vorlagen* of the early translations, in order to test its authenticity. Where MT shows corruption, emendation by reference to the versional *Vorlagen* and conjecture is surely a task of text criticism. It is where the Hebrew is perfectly intelligible that the present practice is, as I see it, in need

[9] See the excellent cautions of J. Barr, *Comparative Philology and the Text of the Old Testament* (Oxford, 1968), pp. 238-72; much new light on the nature of the Peshitta as a translation, and, hence, on how to judge it as a reflection of a Hebrew *Vorlage* is contained in Y. Maori, *The Peshitta Version of the Pentateuch in its Relation to the Sources of Jewish Exegesis* (Jerusalem [Heb. Univ. diss.], 1975). For detailed illustration of the extreme care taken by the editor of the Heb. Univ. Bible Project to avoid pitfalls in retroversion, see M. Goshen-Gottstein, "Theory and Practice of Textual Criticism", *Textus* 3 (1963), pp. 130-58.

[10] L'Abbé Jean Carmignac informs me that for the Book of Chronicles he has been able to construct a stemma, combining the evidence of the Hebrew (Chronicles and Kings) and the Greek, going back to a single archetype. It is much to be desired that at least samples of chapter length be published for the inspection and edification of fellow workers in the field.

of revision. If the *Vorlagen* show a divergence, too often critics have supplanted the Hebrew by it without realizing that what is at stake is not an isolated reading, but an entire context and message, or without awareness that they may be contaminating the text of one edition by that of another.[11] Elsewhere, even without versional evidence, the Hebrew has been tailored to fit a literary theory before its message has been adequately deciphered. How much may be missed by such license I have tried to show in a small specimen.

To avoid premature text-alteration, exegesis and text-criticism must proceed together, each illuminating the other. The exegete, whose task is to interpret text in hand, must work on the hypothesis that every element in his texts has significance—contributes to the meaning of its context. Only such a hypothesis keeps him alert to discover significance and design if it is there, and he will cling to it until he is baffled (at which point he may be inclined to think that some flaw exists in the text). While he notes the particulars of the versions, his focus is the MT, not because it is the best or oldest, but because it is the only complete text of the Hebrew Bible, and only through it can sound exegesis, interpreting the Hebrew by the Hebrew, be achieved.

But for illuminating the MT, no external help comes near the ancient versions, correctly used. Every divergence from the MT in a translation made from the Hebrew (like G, S, or T) calls for explanation, whether or not it is adjudged a reflection of a differing *Vorlage*. Where MT is degenerate, the value of *Vorlage* variants of the versions is undisputed. But even where MT is sound—indeed especially there—the versions are cardinal help. For where MT is sound, the exegete glides easily onward, often without noticing hidden problems (contradictions with far and near passages), interrelations, verbal assonance and other devices which are of the essence of ancient composition. Here the versions offer a powerful stimulus: a substitution, a small omission or addition may point up a carrier of

[11] On the latter danger, see the sober strictures of E. Tov in his "Studies in the methods and limitations of biblical text criticism" (Heb.), to appear in the Loewenstamm *Festschrift*; in that article (whose proofs Dr Tov kindly allowed me to read) he develops some points summarized in his entry "Septuagint. Contribution to OT Scholarship", in the *Supplementary Volume* of the *IDB* (Nashville, 1976), pp. 807-11. Tov recognizes recensions of biblical books, identifiable by systematic stylistic or doctrinal characteristics (e.g. the short and long recensions of Jeremiah, the divergent chronological systems of the G and MT of Kings); he regards recensions as lineally related. He does not consider the possibility of irreducible variants going back to plural primary versions.

meaning that would otherwise go unobserved. Wider divergences may suggest differences in conception (of the translators or the *Vorlage*) that illuminate the Hebrew by their very contrast with it. The first question to be asked when a divergence appears is, What is its effect on the respective messages of each version? This often entails laborious lexical, syntactic and stylistic inquiry, sometimes over new ground, but here is where discovery and excitement reward the patient exegete. Nor can he content himself with isolated readings, but he must seek correlations within each of the versions of divergences that add up to a pattern of meaning. After seeking the sense of each version in its own terms he will end up in each case with or without design, integrality, and regularity. With such results in hand, he is qualified to ask the final question: in cases of versional divergences that seem to reflect a different *Vorlage*, which reading is the best?

Given the problems of our evidence, what is a useful definition of "the best reading"? I submit: that reading by which the other(s) can be explained. If the critic can identify (or reconstruct) the reading from which the variant(s) in the other witness(es) can be derived, and if he can indicate how the variant(s) came into being according to the documented ways in which texts become corrupted or altered, he will have established the best reading that the extant witnesses make available. This is, to be sure, a relative gain only, and it leaves the "lost original" beyond the scope of text-critical inquiry, where it belongs. Sometimes (as I believe is the case in the examples shown above from Ezekiel), the critic will not be able to derive one version from the other(s). He must then be content with having reached the limit of his understanding of the witnesses—a praiseworthy, if limited, result. But to recognize and stay within one's limitations is a sign of responsibility, and it is as a call for responsibility in text-critical and exegetical work, for abandoning illusory goals in favor of the proper tasks that summon us, that my argument is advanced.

VERSUCH EINER NEUEN INTERPRETATION DER ZIONSHYMNEN [1]

von

STANISŁAW ŁACH

Lublin-Kraków

H. Gunkel hebt aus den Psalmen eine Gruppe von sechs Zionsliedern heraus. Dazu gehören: Pss. xlvi, xlviii, lxxvi, lxxxiv, lxxxvii und cxxii.[2] Diese Psalmen handeln von der Hoheit des Zion und der Stadt Jerusalem, die Jahwe vor den Feinden schützt und denen er alles Heil schenkt. Die Auslegung der Psalmen ist jedoch problematisch. Die bisherigen Interpretationen, d.h. die geschichtliche, die eschatologische und die kultische, bieten keine angemessene Erklärung und suchen zudem die Lösung des Problems außerhalb des Psalmenbuches. Die erste, geschichtliche Auslegung stützt sich dabei auf die Erzählung der Belagerung Jerusalems durch Sanherib (2 Kön. xviii 13, xix 36; Jes. xxxvi 1 — xxxvii 28), die zweite, eschatologische auf die Worte der Propheten über das zukünftige Zion (z.B. Jes. xxvi 1, xxvii 2-6; Dtjes. lxi 10; Jer. xxxi 23), die dritte endlich auf entsprechende Lieder zur Ehre der Kultstätten verschiedener Götter außerhalb Israels.[3]

Mir scheint, daß die theologische Auslegung der Zionshymnen der

---

[1] Der Artikel berücksichtigt hauptsächlich die polnische exegetische Literatur, die wegen der Sprachbarriere sonst weniger bekannt ist.

[2] H. Gunkel/J. Begrich, *Einleitung in die Psalmen* (Göttingen, ²1966), S. 50 und 80. Die späteren Exegeten schwanken in der genauen Bestimmung der Zionslieder. So zählen J. Schreiner, *Zion-Jerusalem, Jahwes Königssitz* (München, 1963), S. 220, und G. Wanke, *Die Zionstheologie der Korachiten*, *BZAW* 96 (1966), S. 4f,. den Ps. xlvi zu den Vertrauenspsalmen des Volkes. Einige Gelehrte nehmen überhaupt keine besondere Gruppe von Hymnen an, sondern zählen sie entweder zu den Thronbesteigungsliedern Jahwes (H. Schmidt, *Die Psalmen* [Tübingen, 1934], S. VIII) oder zu den gewöhnlichen Hymnen (O. Eißfeldt, *Einleitung in das Alte Testament* [Tübingen, ²1956], S. 128, Anm. 2, und P. Auvray, in A. Robert/A. Feuillet, *Introduction à la Bible* I [Tournay, 1957], S. 500). S. zu den Meinungen der übrigen auch E. Lipiński, "Les Psaumes", in *DBS* 48 (1973), S. 23ff., und S. Łach, "Ksiega Psalmów", in *Wstęp do Starego Testamentu* ["Das Buch der Psalmen", in *Einleitung in das Alte Testament*] (Poznań/Warszawa, 1973), S. 547-630, bes. 577, 580-81.

[3] Vgl. A. Erman, *Die Literatur der Ägypter* (Leipzig, 1923), S. 327f. und 363f.; A. W. Sjöberg/E. Bergmann, *The Collection of the Sumerian Temple Hymns* (Glückstadt, New York, 1969).

Wahrheit am nächsten kommt. Sie stimmt mit den Aussagen über Gott überein, die das Psalmenbuch enthält.

Zunächst werden wir uns mit Hilfe der diachronischen Methode darum bemühen, zumindest die wichtigsten Bezeichnungen Jahwes in den sechs Zionshymnen abzuheben. Sie scheinen in diesen Hymnen die Grundlage zum Lob des Zion darzustellen, als der Stadt Jahwe Zebaots (xlviii 9), zu dem Israel im Augenblick der Gefahr ruft: Unser Gott ist uns Zuflucht und Stärke (xlvi 2:) *ʾ^{ae}lōhîm lānû maḥ^{a}saeh wāʿōz*[4]), ein lebendiger Gott (lxxxiv 3: *ʾēl ḥāj*), ein ewiger Gott (xlviii 14b:) *ʾ^{ae}lōhîm ^{e}ôlām*), der die Tore Zions liebt lxxxvii 2: *ʾōhēb šaʿ^{a}rê Ṣijjôn*) als einen Ort, an dem sich der Thron Davids befindet (cxxii 5: *kis^{e}ʾôt l^{e}bēt dāwîd*), und auch der Tempel des Herrn (lxxvi 3 und lxxxiv 11). Danach müssen wir mit Hilfe der synchronen Methode[5] überlegen, ob sich diese Bezeichnungen Jahwes, die einen Einfluß auf die Entstehung der Hymnen zu Ehren des Zion haben konnten, nicht auf eine von ihnen zurückführen lassen. Wenn das aber gelingt, dann denken wir weiter darüber nach, welche dieser Bezeichnungen Jahwes die älteste ist, aus der die anderen abgeleitet worden sein könnten. Zum Schluß werden wir die Frage stellen, ob die älteste Bezeichnung Jahwes in den Zionsliedern nicht die Grundlage für eine Theologie der Psalmen, oder gar des gesamten Alten Testaments, bilden könnte.

1. Am häufigsten stoßen wir auf die Bezeichnungen Jahwes in den ersten drei Zionshymnen, d.h. in der ersten Gruppe dieser Hymnen und besonders in den Pss. xlviii und lxxvi. Denn während der Psalmist in Ps. xlvii den Zion als Zuflucht seines Volkes und als seine Stärke ansieht, blickt er in Ps. xlviii auf die wunderbar gerettete Stadt — allen Gefahren zum Trotz (vgl. VV. 5-8) und entdeckt die Ursache der Errettung in der göttlichen *ḥaesaed*.[6] Das bringt er auch in V. 10 zum Ausdruck:

---

[4] Vgl. P. Hugger, *Jahwe, meine Zuflucht, Gestalt und Theologie des 91. Psalms* (Münsterschwarzbach, 1971); W. Ziemba, *Wyznania ufności oraz ich teologiczne uzasadnienia w lamentacjach indywidualniych Psałterza* [*Die Äußerungen des Vertrauens und ihre theologische Begründung in den individuellen Klageliedern*] (Lublin, 1974; Maschinenschrift), bes. S. 201-59.

[5] T. Donald, "The Semantic Field of 'Folly' in Proverbs, Job, Psalms, and Ecclesiastes", *VT* 13 (1963), S. 285-92; Vgl. J. Chmiel", Mozliwości zastosowania pola semantycznego w egzegezie biblijnej" ["Die Möglichkeiten für die Untersuchung des Wortfeldes in der biblischen Exegese"], *Analecta Cracoviensia* 4 (1972), S. 181-90; derselbe, "Nowa semantyka biblijna" ["Die neue biblische Semantik"], *Ruch Biblijny i Liturgiczny* 27 (1974), S. 319-27.

[6] Vgl. Józef Łach, *Ḥesed a ḥāsîd w Psalmach* [*Ḥesed und ḥāsîd in den Psalmen*] (Kraków, 1977), bes. S. 31ff. (maschinenschriftliche Dissertation).

Wir bedenken, o Gott, deine Huld (*ḥasdaekā*)
in deinem heiligen Tempel.

Das, was sie einst gehört hatten und wiederholten — Jahwe Zebaot ist mit uns (*Jahwe ṣᵉbā'ôt ʿimmānû* — xlvi 8, lxxvi 3, lxxxiv 5) —, das wurde in Salem Wirklichkeit. Denn

Seine Wohnstatt erstand in Salem (*bᵉšālēm sukkô*)
Sein Haus auf dem Zion (*ûmᵉʿōnātô bᵉṣijjôn* / Ps. lxxvi 3).

Aus diesen Worten läßt sich schwer entnehmen, an welche Rettung Jerusalems der Psalmist denkt: ob an eine vor- oder an eine nachexilische. Bei dieser Errettung Jerusalems erschien, wie der Psalmist sogleich in Ps. xlviii 11 erläutert, der göttliche Ruhm, und vor allem seine Gerechtigkeit. Der Psalmist beschreibt das so:

Wie dein Name, Gott, so reicht dein Ruhm
bis an die Enden der Erde;
deine rechte Hand ist voll von Gerechtigkeit (*ṣaedaeq*).

Aus dem Kontext geht hervor, daß das Wort *ṣaedaeq* die Rettung Israels und die Bestrafung seiner Feinde bezeichnet, die die heilige Stadt stürmen wollten. *Ṣaedaeq* begegnet uns in den Psalmen 49 mal — das verwandte Substantiv *ṣᵉdāqāh* nicht mitgerechnet — und hat in den Psalmen eine zweifache Bedeutung. *Ṣaedaeq* bezeichnet wie im besprochenen Hymnus die Huld gegenüber Zion oder die Bestrafung seiner Feinde.[7] Von der Bestrafung der Feinde des Zion handeln die VV. 5-8, während von der dem Zion erwiesenen Huld in V. 12 gesprochen wird:

Der Berg Zion freue sich,
die Töchter Judas
sollen über deine gerechten Urteile (*mišpāṭækā*) jubeln.

Das hebräische Wort *mišpāṭîm* in Bezug auf Gott kann auch zweierlei Bedeutung haben: Rettung oder auch Bestrafung.[8] Offenkundig beinhalten die *mišpāṭîm* in Ps. xlviii 12 die Befreiung, denn der Psalmist läßt den Zion sich über die Bestrafung der Feinde freuen.

---

[7] Vgl. A. Z. Kończak, *ṣᵉdāqāh w Psalterzu* [*ṣᵉdāqāh im Psalter*] (Lublin, 1974), bes. S. 60-123 (maschinenschriftliche Dissertation). Die älteren Exegeten hielten *ṣædæq* und *ṣᵉdāqāh* für identisch in ihrer Bedeutung. Die neueren Exegeten meinen, daß *ṣædæq* ein konkreterer Ausdruck als *ṣᵉdāqāh* ist. Vgl. A. Jepsen, "*Ṣdḳ* und *ṣdḳh* im AT", in *Festschrift H. W. Hertzberg* (Göttingen, 1965), S. 78.

[8] Vgl. J. Warzecha, *Znaczenie terminu mišpât w Psalterzu* [*Die Bedeutung von mišpâṭ im Psalter*] (Lublin, 1977), bes. S. 144-55 (maschinenschriftliche Dissertation).

Die Verwendung von *mišpāṭîm* im Plural scheint freilich auf eine mehrfache Errettung vor den Feinden und nicht nur auf eine einzige hinzuweisen.

Vom göttlichen *mišpāṭ* spricht der dritte Hymnus der ersten Gruppe jener Psalmen, die die Unbezwingbarkeit des Zion besingen, und zwar Ps. lxxvi. Dieser Psalm preist Jahwe dafür, daß er den Feinden des Zion eine Niederlage bereitet hat. In den VV. 9f. beschreibt er das so:

> Vom Himmel her machst du das Urteil bekannt;
> Furcht packt die Erde, und sie verstummt,
> wenn Gott sich erhebt zum Gericht (*lammišpāṭ*),
> um allen Gebeugten auf der Erde zu helfen (*l*^e^*hôšîa*ʿ).

In den zitierten Versen ist *mišpāṭ* gleichbedeutend mit dem Heilshandeln Gottes, worauf der Parallelismus zwischen *lammišpāṭ* und *lehôšîa*ʿ hinweist.

Solche Bedeutung hat auch der dreimal in diesem Hymnus auftretende Ausdruck *nôrā*ʾ[9] (VV. 8 und 12f.). Wir müssen hier darauf aufmerksam machen, daß *nôrā*ʾ in den Psalmen fünfzehnmal auftritt und immer als Attribut Gottes als Jahwe (xcvi 4, 5), als El (lxxxix 8), als Eljon (xlvii 3) oder Elohim (lxvi 5, lxviii 36) dient. Mitunter wird die Bezeichnung Gottes als ʾ*Ēl nôrā*ʾ auch durch verschiedene Suffixe ersetzt. Zweimal bezeichnet *nôrā*ʾ auch den handelnden Gott (Pss. cvi 22 und cxxxix 14). In den Hymnen, zu denen Ps. lxxvi gehört, taucht *nôrā*ʾ noch viermal auf, außerdem zweimal in den Jahwe-König-Hymnen (xlvii 3 und xcvi 4) sowie zweimal in gewöhnlichen Hymnen (lxxxix 8 und xclv 4). In allen diesen Hymnen bezeichnet *nôrā*ʾ Jahwe als mächtigen Herrscher, der die Feinde Israels mit Furcht erfüllt, sein Volk jedoch erfreut. Diese Bedeutung hat *nôrā*ʾ ebenso eindeutig auch in Ps. cxlv 5-6, wo der Psalmist alle Stämme Israels auffordert, von den Taten Jahwes zu erzählen, von seinen Wundern (*niflāʾôt* / *nôrāʾôt* / *g*^e^*dullôt*) Die zwischen den Ausdrücken *niflāʾôt* und *g*^e^*dullôt* stehenden *nôrāʾôt* müssen eine ähnliche Bedeutung haben. Auf eine solche Bedeutung von *nôrā*ʾ weist auch Ps. xlvii 3 hin, wo der Psalmist die Aufforderung an alle Völker, Jahwe zu loben,so begründet:

---

[9] S. Łach, "Podstawy nowotestamentalnej bojaźni Bozej w Psalmach" ["Die Grundlagen für die neutestamentliche Gottesfurcht in den Psalmen"], in *Obietnica i wypełnienie* 4 (Lublin, 1977), S. 30f.; Vgl. S. Plath, *Furcht Gottes. Der Begriff jrʾ im AT* (Berlin, 1963); J. Becker, *Gottesfurcht im AT* (Rom, 1965).

Denn furchtgebietend ist Jahwe, der Höchste (*'aeljôn nôrā'*),
ein großer König über die ganze Erde.

Diese Bedeutung läßt sich vielleicht am deutlichsten in Ps. lxxxix 8 erkennen. Darauf weist der aktuelle Kontext dieses Verses hin: Jahwe kommt seinem Volk zu Hilfe, das sich in einem beklagenswerten Zustand befindet. Denn er ist ein *'ēl nôrā'*. In dem besprochen Ps. lxxvi hat der Ausdruck *nôrā'* — ähnlich wie *ṣaedaeq* oder *mišpāṭ* — zwei Aspekte: zum einen bedeutet *nôrā'* Bestürzung für die Feinde des Zion, zum anderen Freude für die Bewohner des Zion.

Aus dieser allgemeinen Übersicht über die ersten drei Zionshymnen ergibt sich bereits, daß von den vier Bezeichnungen Jahwes in diesen Hymnen — seinem *ḥaesaed*, seinem *ṣaedaeq*, von *mišpāṭ* und *nôrā'* — *ḥaesaed* die allgemeinste ist, denn sie präzisieren allein alle anderen.

Weniger ergiebig für die Bestimmung Jahwes sind die drei weiteren Zionshymnen (Pss. lxxxiv, lxxxvii und cxxii). Sie preisen den Zion als einen Ort, der besonders reich von Jahwe beschenkt worden ist. Nur in Ps. lxxxiv 12 scheint sich eine vergleichbare Bestimmung Jahwes zu finden:

Denn Jahwe Gott ist Sonne und Schild.
Er ist Gnade und Herrlichkeit (*ḥēn wekābôd*).

Schon die Bilder im ersten Glied des Verses 12 enthalten den Gedanken, daß Jahwe für den Zion das ist, was die Sonne für die Erde und der Schild für den Menschen ist, der von Feinden überfallen wird. Ohne die Sonne erlischt das Leben auf der Erde. Ohne den Schild könnte sich der Mensch nicht vor den Feinden schützen, die ihn angreifen. Ebenso wäre der Zion ohne Jahwe durch die Feinde zerstört und nicht im Besitz der Güter, die er nun hat. Auf andere Weise drückt das zweite Glied von V. 12 diesen Gedanken aus: Gott ist für den Zion *ḥēn* und *kābôd*. Es ist die Frage, ob sich die beiden Ausdrücke in diesem Halbvers *ḥēn* und *kābôd* auf Gott beziehen und zum Ausdruck bringen, daß Jahwe diese Attribute in Bezug auf die Menschen offenbart (so A. J. Kraus), oder ob sie sich auf die Menschen beziehen, denen Jahwe *ḥēn* und *kābôd* gewährt (so B. Duhm und A. Weiser). Es ist wohl eher anzunehmen, daß sich die beiden Ausdrücke auf Gott beziehen und den Gedanken enthalten, daß Jahwe ein Gott von *ḥēn* und *kābôd* ist. Das Substantiv *ḥēn*[10] begegnet uns im

[10] K. W. Neubauer, *Der Stamm CHNN im Sprachgebrauch des AT* (Berlin, 1964; & Dissertation), S. 73-105. Vgl. W. F. Lofhouse, "Ḥen and Ḥesed in the Old Testament", *ZAW* 51 (1933), S. 29-35; W. L. Reed, "Some Implications of

Buch der Psalmen nur zweimal (außer im zitierten Ps. lxxxiv 12 noch in Ps. xlv 3), obgleich es sonst im Alten Testament hinreichend oft (69 mal) erscheint. Häufiger wird in den Psalmen die gleiche Wurzel in der Verbform *ḥānan* verwendet: dreißigmal in den Psalmen und 55 mal im gesamten Alten Testament. Darüber hinaus gebraucht man auch das Adjektiv *ḥannûn*: dreizehnmal im Alten Testament und davon sechsmal in den Psalmen.

Das Substantiv *ḥēn* erscheint in der Einzahl vor allem in erzählenden Texten und in der Formel *māṣā' ḥēn b^e'ênê*. Diese Formel zeigt an, daß es hier nicht so sehr um einen Segenserweis als vielmehr um ein Verhalten zueinander — im Unterschied zum Begriff *ḥaesaed*, der eher für verschiedene Segenserweise steht. Ein anderes Kennzeichen zur Unterscheidung des *ḥēn* von *ḥaesaed* liegt darin, daß sich *ḥēn* vorwiegend auf Menschen bezieht (Jahwe ist seltener ausdrücklich Subjekt von *ḥēn*). Eine Ausnahme stellen die Gebete des Mose dar, der sich fragt, ob er Gnade bei Gott gefunden habe (Ex. xxxiii-xxxiv). Auf jeden Fall ist der, der in den Augen eines anderen Menschen Gnade gefunden hat, tiefergestellt. Am häufigsten ist der Höherstehende der König (1 Sam. xvi 22, xxvii 5; 2 Sam. xiv 22, xvi 4; 1 Kön. xi 19; Est. v 28, vii 3), der Thronfolger (1 Sam. xx 3,29) oder der königliche Wesir (Gen. xlvii 25). Daran ist zu erkennen, daß diese Formulierung ihren Ursprung im Hofstil hat. Wenn sie auch im Laufe der Zeit einer Demokratisierung unterlag, bleibt dennoch der, der "Gnade gefunden hat" niedriger als jener, bei dem er sie gefunden hat (der Vorgesetzte in Gen. xxxix 4, 21 oder der mächtigere Bruder in Gen. xxxii 6). Wenn der Höhergestellte dem Tieferstehenden *ḥēn* erweist, dann erniedrigt er sich.

Da *ḥēn* am Anfang sich aus dem guten Verhalten des Königs gegenüber seinen Untergebenen ableitet, enthält *ḥēn* in Bezug auf Gott den Gedanken der Fürsorge für die ihm Unterstellten, besonders für diejenigen, die seiner speziellen Hilfe bedürfen. Somit müssen wir *ḥēn* mit "Gunst", "Berücksichtigung" oder "Zuneigung" übersetzen. Diese drei Begriffe bilden das Bedeutungsfeld des Ausdruckes *ḥēn*. Wenn Gott Israel *ḥēn* erweist, dann hebt er es aus der grauen Masse der anderen Völker heraus, dann kennt er dieses Volk bzw. jemanden aus diesem Volk beim Namen (vgl. Ex. xxxiii 12).

Die Beschreibung des auf dem Zion wohnenden Jahwe mit Hilfe

Ḥēn for OT Religion", *JBL* 73 (1954), S. 36-41; J. Homerski, "Księga Zachariasza" ["Das Buch Sacharja"], in *Księgi Proroków Mniejszych* XII/2 (Poznań, 1968), S. 426f.

des Terminus *ḥēn* beinhaltet zunächst die große Gunst Jahwes gegenüber diesem Ort, sodann die Beachtung aller seiner Wünsche und schließlich seine besondere Zuneigung zu ihm.

Im Psalter ist auch oft genüg, ungefähr fünfzigmal, von *kābôd* die Rede. *Kābôd* steht dabei parallel zu einem anderen göttlichen Attribut wie z.B. zur Gerechtigkeit — *ṣaedaeq*. Im Jahwe-Königs-Psalm xcvii 6 lesen wir:

> Seine Gerechtigkeit (*ṣidqô*) verkünden die Himmel,
> seine Herrlichkeit (*keḇôdô*) schauen alle Völker.

Was unter *keḇôd Jahwe* zu verstehen ist, wird diskutiert.[11] Wahrscheinlich bezeichnet dieses Wort jene Eigenschaften Jahwes, die er während der Theophanie zu erkennen gab. Solche Eigenschaften können die Güte und die Macht Gottes sein, die Israel nicht nur an der Wiege seiner Geschichte, auf dem Sinai, sondern auch des öfteren im Verlauf seiner Geschichte und der Geschichte der Stadt Jerusalem erfuhr.

Beide Bestimmungen Jahwes treten aber in den beiden letzten Zionshymnen nicht auf: weder in Ps. lxxxvii noch in Ps. cxxii. Diese Hymnen enthalten jedoch die gleiche Idee, die in den oben genannten Bestimmungen Jahwes zum Ausdruck kommt. So ist in Ps. lxxxvii die Rede davon, daß Jahwe den Zion als seinen Aufenthaltsort liebt, und das mehr als alle anderen Stätten in Israel. Denn es handelt sich um die Stadt des gesamten Gottesvolkes, das bis in die fernsten Länder zerstreut wohnt (ebd. VV. 4-6). In Ps. cxxii ist die Huld Gottes gegenüber dem Zion nicht weniger unterstrichen. Hier ist das Haus des Herrn, von dem aus Jahwe seinem geliebten Volk Frieden zu gewähren vermag, und dabei handelt es sich um Frieden (*šālôm*) ohne Ende.

2. Nachdem wir die wichtigsten Bestimmungen Jahwes in den Zionsliedern zusammengetragen haben, haben wir zu erwägen, welche von ihnen die grundlegende ist, aus der die anderen hervorgegangen sein könnten. Wir haben bereits betont, und zwar auf der Grundlage einer Analyse des Ps. xlviii, daß die dort erscheinende Bestimmung Jahwes *ḥaesaed* die grundlegende Bestimmung Jahwes zu sein scheint. Denn sie enthält in sich bereits hier in diesem Psalm zwei andere Bestimmungen Jahwes — den göttlichen *ṣaedaeq* und den göttli-

[11] Vgl. J. Synowiec, "Historyczny szkic dyskusji na temat kebôd Jahwe" ["Ein Abriß der Diskussionen um die kebôd Jhwh"], *Roczniki teologiczno-Kanonicne* 19 (1968), S. 33-45.

chen *mišpāṭ*. Wir müssen noch hinzufügen, daß die Beschreibung Jahwes mit Hilfe des Ausdrucks *ḥaesaed* die häufigste in den Psalmen ist. Denn sie erscheint hier 127 mal, also einige Male häufiger als in allen übrigen Büchern des Alten Testaments. Diese Bestimmung bezieht sich nur zweimal auf Menschen (Ps. cix 12 und cxli 5).[12] Über die Bedeutung von *ḥaesaed*, sofern es Gott zuerkannt wird, gibt es eine Diskussion. Während die einen meinen, daß diese Bestimmung die Realisierung der von Gott gegebenen Versprechen im Bund bezeichne,[13] verleihen andere dem Begriff eine weitere Bedeutung und übersetzen ihm durch "Gunst", "Güte".[14] Wahrscheinlich muß man *ḥaesaed* eine noch weitere Bedeutung einräumen. Darauf weist die semantische Beschreibung dieses Ausdrucks mit Hilfe anderer Termini im Kontext hin. Im poetischen Psalmenbuch läßt sich der Parallelismus ausnützen, um bei der Suche nach der ureigenen Bedeutung von *ḥaesaed* zum Ziel zu kommen. Wendet man diese Methode an, dann ergibt sich, daß *ḥaesaed* nicht immer mit *b^erît* verbunden ist. Denn *b^erît* ist nur eine Art der Offenbarung der göttlichen *ḥaesaed*. Es stimmt in seiner Bedeutung jedoch auch nicht mit solchen Attributen wie Barmherzigkeit, Güte, überein. *Ḥaesaed* ist vielmehr die Quelle für alle göttlichen Attribute, die *ḥaesaed* nach den Bedürfnissen der Adressaten modifizieren. Mannigfaltige parallele Bestimmung, die im synonymen Parallelismus zusammen mit *ḥaesaed* auftreten, unterstreichen die weite Bedeutung. Am häufigsten erscheinen im Parallelismus des Psalters neben *ḥaesaed* die Worte *'aemaet* und *'^aemûnāh*.[15] Wir übergehen die Texte, in denen *ḥaesaed* mit *'^aemaet* und *'^aemûnāh* im gleichen Glied nebeneinander stehen. Wir berücksichtigen nur die, in denen diese Termini in den beiden Gliedern parallel stehen. In den Psalmen bezeichnet *'^aemaet*, insofern es parallel zu *ḥaesaed* gesetzt ist, die Beständigkeit, Treue und Wahrhaftigkeit des göttlichen *ḥaesaed*. Das ist eine gewisse, zumindest formale Ausweitung des Begriffes *ḥaesaed*. Denn an und für sich

---

[12] Józef Łach, S. 35-45.

[13] N. Glueck, *Das Wort Ḥesed im alttestamentlichen Sprachgebrauch als menschliche und göttliche gemeinschaftsgemäße Verhaltensweise*, *BZAW* 47 (1927), S. 47ff. Vgl. M. Filipiak, "Przymierze w Piśmie świetym" ["Der Bund in der heiligen Schrift"], *Ruch Biblijny i Liturgiczny* 25 (1972), S. 145-55.

[14] H. J. Stoebe, *Gottes hingebende Güte und Treue. Bedeutung und Geschichte des Begriffes* (Münster, 1950); derselbe, "Die Bedeutung des Wortes *ḥäsäd* im AT", *VT* 2 (1952), S, 244-54; derselbe, *ḥæsæd*, in: THAT I, 600-21.

[15] Vgl. A. Tronina, *'El 'Emet, Wiernośc Boga w świetle Psalterza* [*'El 'Emet. Die Treue Gottes im Lichte des Psalters*] (Lublin, 1977), bes. S. 35-84 (maschinenschriftliche Dissertation).

drückt es nur das göttliche Wohlwollen aus, unabhängig von seiner Dauer, während *ʾ^{ae}maet* die göttliche Beständigkeit zum Ausdruck bringt. Und so begründet der Psalmist in Ps. xxvi 3 seine Bitte an Gott so:

> Denn mir stand deine Huld (*ḥasd^{e}kā*) vor Augen,
> ich ging meinen Weg in Treue zu dir (*baʾ^{a}mittaekā*).

In einer Reihe von Psalmen richten die Autoren ihr Lob an die Adresse von *ḥaesaed* und *ʾ^{ae}maet*. So preist der Psalmist in Ps. xxxvi 6 die beiden Eigenschaften Gottes:

> Jahwe, deine Güte (*ḥasd^{e}kā*) reicht, so weit der Himmel ist,
> deine Treue (*ʾ^{ae}mûnāt^{e}kā*), so weit die Wolken ziehn.

Ähnlich drücken sich die Autoren von Ps. lvii 11 und cvi 5 aus. In Ps. lxxxviii 12 stellt der Psalmist fest, daß der Verstorbene die beiden göttlichen Attribute nicht mehr preisen kann. Er sagt:

> Erzählt man im Grab von deiner Huld (*ḥasdækā*),
> von deiner Treue (*ʾ^{ae}mûnāt^{e}kā*) im Totenreich?

Nur der Lebende kann den göttlichen *ḥaesaed* und *ʾ^{ae}maet* preisen, wie der Psalmist in Ps. xcii 3 sagt:

> ... am Morgen deine Huld (*ḥasd^{e}kā*) zu verkünden
> und in den Nächten deine Treue (*ʾ^{ae}mûnāt^{e}kā*).

Beide Bestimmungen Gottes haben in Ps. cxvii 2 ähnliche Prädikate:

> Denn mächtig waltet über uns seine Huld (*ḥasdô*),
> und Jahwes Treue (*waeʾ^{ae}maet Jhwh*) währt in Ewigkeit.

Aus den zitierten Psalmtexten geht klar hervor, daß *ḥaesaed* das Wohlwollen Jahwes gegenüber dem Menschen zum Ausdruck bringt. Es handelt sich dabei um ein beständiges Wohlwollen, wie man am synonymen Parallelismus in einer Reihe von Psalmen erkennen kann, in denen *ḥaesaed* durch *ʾ^{ae}maet* und *ʾ^{ae}mûnāh* näher bestimmt wird. Der Ausdruck *ḥaesaed* bezieht sich auf Jahwe selbst, der in Ps. lix 9 und 18 ein Gott des Wohlwollens genannt wird. Es handelt sich hier um ein individuelles Klagelied, in dem sich der Autor über seine Feinde beklagt, die ihm in irgendeiner Weise zu schaden versuchen. Der Psalmist vertraut jedoch auf Gott, daß er ihn nicht verläßt, sondern zu Hilfe kommt. Denn er ist doch — wie es in V. 11 heißt — ein Gott seiner Güte (*ʾ^{ae}lōhê ḥasdô*: so das Ketib) bzw. ein Gott meiner Güte (*ʾ^{ae}lōhê ḥasdî*: so das Qere). Wir müssen uns wohl für die letztere Lesart entscheiden, denn sie wird noch einmal in V. 18 bezeugt. Die Bezeichnung Gottes als *ʾaelōhê ḥasdî* bildet die Grundlage des Vertrauens, das der Psalmist zu Gott hat.

In Ps. lii 10 bestimmt der *ḥaesaed* ebenfalls Gott selbst:

> Ich aber bin im Haus Gottes wie ein grünender Ölbaum;
> auf Gottes Huld (*beḥaesaed ʾaelōhîm*) vertraue ich immer und ewig.

Ein andermal bedeutet *ḥaesaed* dasselbe wie der Name Jahwes, der den Erretter bezeichnet.[16] Denn der Autor von Ps xxi stellt in V. 8 folgendermaßen den Sieg des Königs über seine Feinde vor:

> Denn der König vertraut auf den Herrn,
> die Huld des Höchsten (*ûbeḥaesaed ʿaeljôn*) läßt ihn niemals wanken.

Unter einem anderen Aspekt bringen zwei andere, parallele Ausdrücke — nämlich *ṣaedaeq* und *mišpāṭ* — das zur Sprache, was *ḥaesaed* beinhaltet. Schon am Kontext von Ps. xlviii, wo die beiden Ausdrücke auftauchen, war abzulesen, daß sie die Bestimmung Jahwes mit Hilfe von *ḥaesaed* näher erläutern. Während *ṣaedaeq*[17] ein Verhalten bezeichnet, das mit einer Rechtsnorm übereinstimmt, und *mišpāṭ*[18] ein bestimmtes beständiges Verhalten, bezeichnen die beiden zusammen auftretenden Ausdrücke *ṣaedaeq ûmišpāṭ* ein beständiges Verhalten, das mit der göttlichen Norm in Übereinstimmung steht. Das gleichbleibende Verhalten in Übereinstimmung mit einer Norm ist also ein Synonym zu der bereits besprochenen Bestimmung Jahwes *ḥaesaed waeʾaemaet*. Das bringt der Psalmist in Ps. lxxxix 15 zum Ausdruck, wenn er Gott so preist:

> Recht und Gerechtigkeit (*ṣaedaeq ûmišpāṭ*)
> sind die Stützen deines Thrones,
> Huld und Treue (*ḥaesaed waeʾaemaet*)
> schreiten vor deinem Antlitz her.

Folglich ist der beständige göttliche *ḥaesaed* ein Synonym der Gerechtigkeit und des Rechts. Er besagt, daß Gott nicht spontan handelt, sondern sein Wohlwollen dann erweist, wenn Menschen dessen bedürfen und ihn zum Handeln bewegen. Dann nimmt der *ḥaesaed* die Form des Erbarmens an (*raḥamîm*: vgl. Ps. xxv 6, li 3 u.ö.), bisweilen auch des göttlichen Versprechens, wobei *ḥaesaed* dann parallel

---

[16] S. Łach, "Imię Boze Jahwe" ["Der Gottesname Jahwe"], in *Ksiega Wyjścia* (Poznań, 1964), S. 300ff.

[17] A. Z. Kończak, S. 219.

[18] J. Warzecha, S. 20f.

zu *b^erît* auftritt (z.B. Ps. cvi 25), mitunter auch die Form der moralischen Haltung des Menschen (Ps. xviii 26), wenn der König für den Sieg dankt, den er mit Gottes Hilfe davongetragen hat, und das Bekenntnis ablegt: Gegen den Treuen zeigst du dich treu — *ʿim ḥāsîd titḥassād. Ḥaesaed* bedeutet, wie uns schon die ersten drei Zionshymnen gezeigt haben, die Erlösung von den Feinden. *Ḥaesaed* begegnet uns in den Psalmen auch relativ oft parallel zu soteriologischen Ausdrücken wie *ješaʾ* (lxxxv 8), *j^ešûʿāh* (xiii 6) oder *t^ešûʿāh* (cxix 41), die Hilfe und Befreiung bedeuten.[19] In Ps. lxxxv 8 bittet das klagende Israel Jahwe um Erlösung aus dem Unglück, das ihm widerfahren ist:

> Erweise uns, Jahwe, deine Huld (*ḥasdækā*)
> und gewähre uns dein Heil (*jaeš^{ʿa}kā*).

Manchmal ist die Befreiung so gewaltig, daß sie Staunen erregt, und dann tritt *ḥaesaed* in Parallel zu *niflāʾôt*, d.h. zu den Wundern (z.B. Ps. cvi 7 und cvii 8). In Ps. cvi 7 stellt der Autor den Sünden Israels verschiedene Wohltaten und Hulderweise Jahwes gegenüber und sagt zu Gott:

> Unsere Väter in Ägypten begriffen deine Wunder (*nifl^eʾôtaekā*) nicht,
> dachten nicht an deine reiche Huld (*ḥ^asādaekā*).

Hier wird das Substantiv *ḥ^asādîm*, das im Plural erscheint, durch "Wunder" (*niflāʿôt*) näher bestimmt. Das zeigt an, daß es um die Offenbarung göttlicher Hulderweise geht, wie es die Plagen waren. In dem ähnlichen Ps. cvii 8 ruft der Psalmist sein Volk auf, Gott für die Befreiung aus der babylonischen Gefangenschaft Dank zu sagen, die er gleichfalls für ein Wunder hält. Deshalb spricht er auch hier einmal von *ḥaesaed* und das andere Mal von *niflāʾôt*. Hier der Text: Diese Worte bilden einen Refrain, auf den verschiedene Ereignisse aus der Geschichte Israels folgen, die Hulderweise Jahwes, wunderbare Wohltaten sind.

> Sie alle sollen Jahwe danken für seine Huld (*ḥasdô*)
> für sein wunderbares Tun an den Menschen (*nifl^eʾôtāw*).

[19] W. Michalski, "Idea soteriologiczna w Starym Testamencie" in *Christus Soter* (Warszawa, 1934), S. 3-44 ["Der soteriologische Gedanke im Alten Testament"]; W. J. Rosłon, *Zbawienie człowieka w Starym Testamencie* [*Die Erlösung des Menschen im Alten Testament*] (Warszawa, 1970); A. Kubik, "Terminologia soteriologiczna w Starym Testamencie. Jahwe - Zbawca" ["Die soteriologische Terminologie im Alten Testament. Jahwe als Erlöser"], *Ruch Biblijny i Liturgiczny* 18 (1965), S. 321-8.

Nirgends im Psalter stoßen wir freilich auf einen Parallelismus zwischen *ḥaesaed* und *nôrāʾ*, d.h. jener Bestimmung Gottes, die dreimal im Zionslied Ps. lxxvi erscheint. Eine Verwandtschaft zwischen *nôrāʾ* oder *nôrāʾôt* und *ḥaesaed* ist jedoch nicht auszuschließen. Der parallele Ausdruck *niflāʾôt* zu *ḥaesaed* taucht, wie wir schon hervorgehoben haben, auch im synonymen Parallelismus mit *nôrāʾôt* auf, und zwar in Ps. cvi 21-22. Hier der Text:

> Sie vergaßen Gott, ihren Retter,
> der einst in Ägypten Großes vollbrachte,
> Wunder (*niflāʾôt*) im Lande Hams,
> furchterregende Taten am Schilfmeer (*nôrāʾôt*).

Vgl. dazu Ps. cxxxix 14. Wir können auch die letzte Bestimmung Gottes in Ps. lxxxiv 12, nämlich *ḥēn*, in das semantische Feld von *ḥaesaed* einbeziehen. Es gibt dafür zwar keine Beispiele in der substantivischen Form. Denn im Gegensatz zu dem zahlreichen verwendeten *ḥaesaed* tritt das Substantiv *ḥēn* in den Psalmen, wie wir schon gesagt haben, nur zweimal und davon nur einmal auf Jahwe bezogen auf. Zwischen diesen Wurzeln gibt es jedoch eine Verwandtschaft. Darauf weist zunächst der Parallelismus zwischen *ḥaesaed* im Sinne von menschlichem *ḥaesaed* in Ps. cix 12 und dem Menschen hin, der durch das Partizip *ḥōnēn* bestimmt wird. Der Parallelismus findet sich in einem Fluch:

> Niemand sei da, der ihm die Gunst bewahrt (*mōšēk ḥāsaed*),
> keiner, der sich der Waisen erbarmt (*ḥōnēn*).

Auf die Verwandtschaft mit der Wurzel *ḥ-s-d* weist auch hin, daß in den Psalmen oft die Bitte an Gott gerichtet wird: Erbarme dich nach deiner Huld (so Ps. li 3: *ḥånnēnî ... keḥasdaekā*). Die schon besprochenen Synonyme zu *ḥaesaed* in den Psalmen haben uns gezeigt, wie weit das Bedeutungsfeld von *ḥaesaed* ist. Es ist zumindest nicht möglich, *ḥaesaed* auf die Erfüllung der Verpflichtungen einzuschränken die sich aus dem Bund ergeben. Wir können *ḥaesaed* auch nicht mit *raḥamîm*, d.h. der Barmherzigkeit, gleichsetzen. *Ḥaesaed* ist vielmehr die Summe der göttlichen Attribute, noch besser: ihre Quelle. Aber nicht allein die parallelen Substantive, sondern auch die Adjektive, mit denen die Psalmisten den göttlichen *ḥaesaed* beschreiben, werfen viel Licht darauf, daß *ḥaesaed* die Quelle der göttlichen Eingenschaften ist. Zunächst wird Jahwe als *ʾēl gādôl* beschrieben (Ps. lxxvii 14; vgl. xcix 2 usw.). Das unterstreichen auch die Zionshymnen (Ps. xlviii 2 und lxxvi 2). Groß ist auch sein *ḥaesaed* (Ps. lvii 11 = cviii 5, lxxxvi 13, cxlv 8; vgl. auch 1 Kön. iii 6 und 2 Chr. i 8). So hören wir z.B. in Ps. lxxxvi 13, daß der Fromme Jahwe verspricht, seine große Huld zu preisen, weil er ihm das Leben neu geschenkt hat:

> Du hast mich den Tiefen des Totenreichs entrissen,
> denn groß (*gādôl*) ist über mir deine Huld (*ḥasdᵉkā*).

Während das Adjektiv *gādôl* die Größe des göttlichen *ḥaesaed* hervorhebt, soll das mit dem Substantiv verbundene Adjektiv *rôb* ihren Reichtum unterstreichen. In Ps. v 8 betet der Psalmist:

> Ich aber darf dein Haus betreten
> dank deiner großen Güte (*bᵉrôb ḥasdᵉkā*).

Ähnlich spricht der Psalmist in Ps. lxix 14:

> Erhöre mich in deiner großen Huld (*bᵉrôb ḥasdᵉkā*).

In Ps. lxxxvi 5 und 15 wendet sich der Beter an Gott und nennt ihn *rôb ḥaesaed*, d.h. jederzeit bereit zur Güte, so oft er angerufen wird. Ähnlich ist es in Ps. ciii 8.

Wie also das Adjektiv *gādôl*, das *ḥaesaed* beigefügt wird, die Aufmerksamkeit auf die Größe des *ḥaesaed* lenken sollte, so sollte das Adjektiv *rôb* die Kontinuität der *ḥaesaed* hervorheben.

Wieder einen anderen Aspekt des *ḥaesaed* unterstreicht das Eigenschaftswort *ṭôb* in Ps. lxix 17 und cix 21. Wie Gott sich als gut erweist in seiner Offenbarung (vgl. Pss. xxv 8, xxxiv 9, lxxiii 1, lxxxvi 5, cxxxiii 5 und cxlviii 9), so ist auch der göttliche *ḥaesaed* gut (*kî ṭôb ḥasdᵉkā*). Vgl. auch Ps. cix 21, der ganz ähnlich über den Namen Gottes sagt:

> Du aber, Jahwe, mein Gebieter,
> handle an mir, wie es deinem Namen entspricht.
> Nach der Güte deiner Huld (*kî ṭôb ḥasdᵉkā*).

Die Autoren der Psalmen bedienen sich aber zur näheren Bestimmung von *ḥaesaed* nicht allein der Adjektive *gādôl*, *rôb* oder *ṭôb*, sondern verwenden auch das beigefügte *ʿôlām*, um die Beständigkeit von *ḥaesaed* zu unterstreichen. Am häufigsten erscheint das Wort *ʿôlām* innerhalb der Psalmen in der Formel: "denn ewig währt seine Huld" (*kî lᵉʿôlām ḥasdô*: Pss. c 5, cvi 1, cvii 1, cxviii 1-4, cxxxvi 1-26 und cxxxviii 8).

Genau dieselbe Bedeutung wie *lᵉʿôlām* hat das bloße *ʿôlām* (vgl.

Pss. lxxxix 2, 3 und 38). Wie Gott selbst immer bleibt (Pss. xcii 8 und cii 12f.), so sind auch seine Huld und die Treue des Bundes ewig (Pss. xxv 6, xxxiii 11, ciii 17, cv 8, 10, cxi 5, 8, 9, cxvii 2, cxix 89, 142, 144, 152, 160, cxxv 2, cxxxv 13, cxxxviii 8 und cxlvi 6). Gott gewährt sein *ḥaesaed* jeden Tag (Ps. xcii 3). Darum schätzen sie die Psalmisten auch höher als das Leben (lxiii 7).

So wie die Adjektive, die im Psalter mit *ḥaesaed* verknüpft werden, viel dazu beitragen, diese Eigenschaft als Quelle aller übrigen Attribute Jahwes zu erkennen, so sind unter diesem Aspekt auch die Verben eine große Hilfe, deren sich die Autoren der Psalmen bedienen, um die verschiedenen Funktionen eben dieses *ḥaesaed* zu bestimmen. Zunächst kann Gott selbst den Menschen seine Huld erweisen. So bittet der Psalmist in Ps. cxix 124 Gott voller Demut:

> Handle an deinem Knecht nach deiner Huld (*ʿaśēh keḥasdaekā*),
> und lehre mich deine Gesetze.

In Ps. xviii 51 trägt Jahwe die Bezeichnung *ʿōśaeh ḥaesaed*, d.h. der, der den Menschen Huld erweist. Der Gebrauch des zeitlosen Partizips zeigt an, daß Jahwe immer — in Vergangenheit, Gegenwart und Zukunft — seine Huld erwiesen hat, erweist und erweisen wird. Durch die ununterbrochene Gewährung seines Wohlwollens, das in der Befreiung besteht, wird der König groß (*magdîl*).
In Ps. lxi 8 betet der fromme Israelit für seinen König:

> Er throne ewig vor Gottes Angesicht.
> Huld (*ḥaesaed*) und Treue mögen ihn behüten (*yinṣerûhû*).

Denselben Gedanken bringt der Autor von Ps. lxxxix in V. 29 zum Ausdruck, wenn er dort die Worte Jahwes anführt, mit denen er einmal dem David und seinen Nachkommen, insbesondere dem Messias, das Versprechen gab:

Auf ewig werde ich ihm meine Huld bewahren (*ʾaešmôr ḥasdî*). Der *ḥaesaed* schützt aber nicht nur den König und seine Dynastie, sondern auch die Hauptstadt, den Zion (Ps. xlviii 10), und das gesamte auserwählte Volk. So heißt es in Ps. xxxiii 22:

> Laß deine Güte (*ḥasdekā*) über uns walten, o Jahwe,
> denn wir schauen nach dir aus.

Denn die Huld Jahwes erfüllt die ganze Welt (vgl. Ps. xxxiii 5b und cxix 64), besonders das Land Israels.

Die göttliche Funktion des *ḥaesaed* würden wir noch besser erkennen können, wenn wir die verschiedenen Gattungen der Psalmen berücksichtigen würden, in denen vom *ḥaesaed* Gottes die Rede ist. In den individuellen Klageliedern[20] ist er der Ursprung der Hilfe für die verfolgten Beter, für die Heilung der Kranken und für die Vergebung der Sünden. In den Volksklageliedern[21] hingegen ist der *ḥaesaed* identisch mit der Bitte um Heimkehr aus der Gefangenschaft und der Hilfe Gottes beim Aufbau des zerstörten Jerusalem, sofern Israel zur Buße bereit ist. In den individuellen Dankliedern[22] ruft der *ḥaesaed* dazu auf, die in der Not abgelegten Schwüre zu erfüllen. In den Hymnen[23] schreiben die Psalmisten dem *ḥaesaed* sowohl die Schöpfung der Welt als auch die Lenkung der Völker, besonders Israels, zu. In den Lehrgedichten (Pss. lii und cxix) schließlich belehrt der *ḥaesaed* uns über das Verhalten Gottes gegenüber einem jeden Menschen.

Wenn aber das Wortfeld von *ḥaesaed* so weit ist, dann kann es keinem Zweifel unterliegen, daß eine solche Bestimmung Gottes die Grundlage zur Entstehung der Zionslieder als der Hymnen über den Wohnort Jahwes, des *'ēl ḥasdô*, bilden kann. Es erhebt sich freilich noch die eine Frage, ob es diese häufig in den Psalmen anzutreffende Bestimmung Gottes zur Zeit der Komposition der Zionshymnen schon gab. Auf diese Frage können wir nicht unter Berufung auf die Psalmen selbst antworten. Denn uns ist die Entstehungszeit eines Großteils der Psalmen nicht bekannt. Eine gewisse Hilfe kann uns jedoch die sog. biblische Literatur der historisch-prophetischen Bücher liefern. Auf Grund dieser Literatur wissen wir, daß die Bestimmung Gottes mit Hilfe von *ḥaesaed* in Israel schon seit den ältesten Zeiten bekannt war. Das kennt bereits die älteste Tradition des Pentateuchs, der Jahwist. In dem jahwistischen Gebet des Eliëser, des Knechtes Abrahams, in Gen. xxiv 12-14 stoßen wir auf die Bitte: "Gott meines Herrn Abraham ... zeig meinem Herrn Abraham dein Wohlwollen" (*'ᵃśēh ḥaesaed*: V. 12). Als Jahwe seine Bitte erhört hat, dankt Eliëser Jahwe mit den Worten: "Gepriesen sei Jahwe, der Gott meines Herrn Abraham, der es meinem Herrn nicht an Wohlwollen und Treue (*ḥasdô wa'ᵃmittô*) fehlen ließ" (V. 27). Dieser Text ist deshalb so wichtig, weil hier *ḥaesaed* zusammen mit *'ᵃᵉmaet* genannt

[20] In achtzehn individuellen Klageliedern ist von der *ḥæsæd* Jahwes die Rede, und zwar: Ps. v, vi, xiii, xvii, xxv, xxvi, xxxi, xlii, xliii, li, lxiii, lxix, lxxxvi und cxliii.

[21] Pss. xliv, cvi, und Fragmente der Psalmen lxxxv, xc, und xciv.

[22] Pss. xxxii, xl 1-12, xcii, cxviii, und cxxxviii.

[23] Pss. xxxiii, c, ciii, cvii, cxxxvi, cxlii, und die Pss. xlviii sowie cxviii.

wird, das die Beständigkeit des *ḥaesaed* Gottes gegenüber Abraham bezeichnet.

In 2 Sam. vii 14-15 bezeichnet der biblische Autor mit dem Terminus *ḥaesaed* das Versprechen, das Jahwe dem David und seiner Dynastie durch Natan[24] gegeben hat und das den besonderen Schutz und die Beständigkeit der Dynastie zusicherte: "Ich will für ihn Vater sein, und er wird für mich Sohn sein. Wenn er Unrecht tut, werde ich ihn nach Menschenweise mit Peitschen und Ruten züchtigen. Meine Gnade aber (*ḥasdî*) will ich ihm nicht entziehen". *Ḥaesaed* bezeichnete hier wie in 1 Kön. iii 6 und viii 25 das große Versprechen Gottes gegenüber David und seinen Nachkommen auf dem Königsthron.

In der prophetischen Literatur bezeichnete *ḥaesaed* nicht nur das Wohlwollen Jahwes für Israel, sondern auch umgekehrt die Zuneigung Israels zu Jahwe und der Israeliten untereinander (s. Hos. iv 1, vi 4 sowie Jer. ii 2).[25]

Wenn aber der Gedanke des *'aelōhê ḥaesaed* (Ps. lix 11) bis in die Anfänge des biblischen Schrifttums zurückreicht, konnte er auch seinen Einfluß ausüben, und zwar nicht nur auf die immer neue Bestimmung Gottes,[26] sondern auch auf die Aussagen der Autoren der Zionslieder, der Hymnen über die Unbesiegbarkeit des Zion also und über den Reichtum an Hulderweisen, mit denen Jahwe den Ort überhäuft und auch in Zukunft überhäufen wird. Denn der *ḥaesaed* des Jahwe, der auf dem Zion wohnt, ist ein *ḥaesaed le'ôlām*.

Am Schluß meines Vortrags möchte ich mich an die hier versammelten Alttestamentler aus der ganzen Welt mit der Frage wenden: Wäre es nicht möglich, in Anlehnung an die bekannte Anrufung des Psalmisten in Ps. xviii 26 *'im ḥāsîd titḥassād* eine Theologie der Psalmen oder vielleicht sogar des gesamten Alten Testaments zu schreiben? Mir scheint, daß dieser Text als Grundlage zu einer solchen theologischen Synthese geeignet ist.

---

[24] Vgl. Jan Łach, *Ksiegi Samuela* [*Die Samuelbücher*] (Poznań, 1973), S. 82-96.

[25] Vgl. J. Kudasiewicz, "Miłoserdzia chce a nie ofiary (Oz 6,6; Mt 9,13; 12,7)", ["Barmherzigkeit will ich, nicht Opfer: Hos 6,6; Mt 9,13; 12,7"], in *Powołanie człowieka* 4 (Poznań, 1975), S. 125-43.

[26] Vgl. L. R. Stachowiak, "Bóg w St. Testamencie" ["Gott im Alten Testament"], in *Encyklopedia katolicka* II (Lublin, 1976), S. 902-9; S. Grzybek, "Obraz Boga w Starym Testamencie" ["Das Bild Gottes im Alten Testament"], *Ruch Biblijny i Liturgiczny* 30 (1977), S. 2-18; Jan Łach, "Obraz Boga w Księgach Kronik" ["Das Bild Gottes in den Büchern der Chronik"], ebd. S. 18-26.

L'ÉPIGRAPHIE PALÉO-HÉBRAÏQUE ET LA BIBLE

par

ANDRÉ LEMAIRE

Paris

L'épigraphie paléo-hébraïque est une science relativement jeune. C'est en 1870 que Ch. Clermont-Ganneau découvrit les deux premières inscriptions en écriture paléo-hébraïque datant de l'époque royale israélite. Depuis cette date, cette science n'a cessé de progresser, en particulier grâce aux nombreuses fouilles archéologiques de ces dernières années: chaque année produit au jour de nouvelles inscriptions sur pierre ou sur plâtre, inscriptions sur vase ou ostraca, sceaux ou estampilles . . . Nous dresserons ici un rapide bilan d'un siècle d'épigraphie paléo-hébraïque; nous essaierons ensuite de préciser le principal écueil à éviter dans la conception des rapports entre l'épigraphie paléo-hébraïque et la Bible; enfin, de manière positive, nous montrerons, par quelques exemples concrets, ce que ces inscriptions peuvent apporter à l'exégèse biblique . . . Nous tenons à préciser, dès maintenant, que nous ne considérons ici que l'épigraphie paléo-hébraïque de l'époque royale (Xe-VIe siècle av. J.C.), sans tenir compte des inscriptions de l'époque postérieure.

I. *Bilan d'un siècle d'épigraphie paléo-hébraïque*

Un premier dénombrement des inscriptions paléo-hébraïques en vue de la publication de la *Pars Hebraica* du *Corpus Inscriptionum Semiticarum* nous a conduit à un total d'environ 2000 inscriptions. Ce chiffre global recouvre des réalités très diverses; en effet, sur ces 2000 numéros, on distingue:

— environ 1000 estampilles royales,
— environ 300 sceaux ou estampilles dites privées,
— un peu moins de 300 poids inscrits,
— un peu plus de 400 autres inscriptions diverses.

Cette statistique approximative ne doit pas donner le change: les quelque 1000 estampilles royales ne représentent l'utilisation que d'une vingtaine de sceaux différents, tandis que les sceaux et estampilles dites privées ne comportent, le plus souvent, qu'un ou deux noms propres reliés, ou non, par *bn*, "fils de", c'est dire que leur apport est essentiellement paléographique et onomastique. Bien plus, à part quelques cas spéciaux, les poids inscrits peuvent se classer en une vingtaine de types différents qui ne comportent, tout au plus, qu'un seul mot inscrit. Dès lors, on réalise facilement que ce sont les 400 autres inscriptions diverses qui ont surtout retenu l'attention des épigraphistes et des biblistes. Parmi ces dernières inscriptions, on peut distinguer quatre grandes catégories:

1) Les inscriptions sur pierre. Elles sont relativement peu nombreuses: outre la tablette de Gézer et la fameuse inscription du canal de Siloé,[1] on connait aussi maintenant plusieurs inscriptions tombales (Silwan,[2] Khirbet Beit-Lei,[3] Khirbet el-Qôm [4]) presque toujours gravées ou incisées dans le roc, ainsi qu'une inscription écrite à l'encre sur la paroi d'une grotte à Naḥal Ishaï, près de Ein-Gedi.[5] Sauf un petit fragment trouvé à Samarie et ne contenant que le mot *'šr*, le sol de la Palestine n'a, jusqu'à ce jour, révélé aucune stèle monumentale, du type de la stèle de Mésha par exemple. Il ne semble donc pas y avoir lieu de distinguer une écriture monumentale d'une écriture cursive comme semble le confirmer l'écriture de l'inscription de Siloé, dans laquelle le graveur a reproduit fidèlement les pleins et déliés de l'écriture cursive à l'encre.

---

[1] Cf. J. C. L. Gibson, *Textbook of Syrian Semitic Inscriptions, I, Hebrew and Moabite Inscriptions* (Oxford, 1971), pp. 1-4 et 21-23; cf. aussi E. Puech, "L'inscription du tunnel de Siloé", *Revue Biblique* (*RB*) 81 (1974), pp. 196-214.

[2] Cf. S. Moscati, *L'epigrafia ebraica antica, 1935-1950* (Roma, 1951), p. 115; N. Avigad, "The Epitaph of A Royal Steward from Siloam Village", *Israel Exploration Journal* (*IEJ*) 3 (1953), pp. 137-52; *id.*, "The Second Tomb-Inscription of the Royal Steward", *IEJ* 5 (1955), pp. 163-6; J. C. L. Gibson, pp. 23-24; D. Ussishkin, "On the Shorter Inscription from the 'Tomb of the Royal Steward' ", *BASOR* 196 (1969), pp. 16-22.

[3] Cf. J. Naveh, "Old Hebrew Inscriptions in a Burial Cave", *IEJ* 13 (1963), pp. 74-92; F. M. Cross, "The Cave Inscriptions from Khirbet Beit Lei", dans J. A. Sanders (ed.), *Near Eastern Archaeology in the Twentieth Century, Essays in Honor of Nelson Glueck* (New York, 1970), pp. 299-306; J. C. L. Gibson, pp. 57-8.

[4] Cf. W. G. Dever, "Iron Age Epigraphic Material from the Area of Khirbet El-Kôm", *Hebrew Union College Annual* (*HUCA*) 40-41 (1969-70), pp. 139-204; D. Barag, "Note on an Inscription from Khirbet El-Qôm", *IEJ* 20 (1970), pp. 216-18.

[5] Cf. P. Bar-Adon, "An Early Hebrew Inscription in a Judean Desert Cave", *IEJ* 25 (1975), pp. 226-32.

2) Les ostraca.[6] Ils représentent le groupe le plus important (environ 250). Les trois plus abondantes collections d'ostraca sont celles de Samarie, d'Arad et de Lakish. Il s'agit essentiellement de messages administratifs ou militaires, de listes de noms propres ou de comptes économiques. Leur état de conservation est extrêmement variable; ils sont parfois incomplets, parce que brisés, ou à demi-effacés, parce que généralement écrits à l'encre; leur lecture est donc souvent incertaine. La longueur de leur texte est très variable, depuis un seul mot (un nom propre, comme dans plusieurs ostraca d'Arad) jusqu'à 21 lignes, comme dans l'ostracon 3 de Lakish. Un des derniers ostraca découverts récemment, l'ostracon 88 d'Arad, est une déclaration royale, malheureusement très fragmentaire.[7] Cependant cette dernière découverte montre bien l'importance et la variété des ostraca paléo-hébreux.

3) Les papyrus. Même si le nombre des ostraca montre clairement l'emploi courant de tessons de poterie comme support de l'écriture, il ne faut pas oublier que de nombreux documents administratifs officiels devaient être écrits sur papyrus comme le montrent les diverses bulles servant à sceller ces papyrus découvertes à Lakish et ailleurs. Malheureusement, le papyrus est un matériau qui devait coûter assez cher et, surtout, il ne s'est généralement pas conservé à cause du climat humide de la Palestine. Le seul papyrus paléo-hébreu de l'époque royale connu à ce jour a été découvert dans le désert de Juda: c'est le palimpseste de Murabbaʿât publié par J. T. Milik.[8]

4) Les inscriptions sur vase. Alors qu'un ostracon est un texte écrit sur un tesson d'un vase déjà brisé, l'inscription sur vase a été écrite alors que ce vase était complet et en usage; il y a donc un lien fonctionnel entre l'inscription et le vase: le texte en indique le plus souvent le propriétaire, parfois le contenu ou la contenance ou encore son utilisation. Ces inscriptions sur vase peuvent être écrites à l'encre ou incisées; dans ce dernier cas, elles peuvent être incisées avant ou après cuisson. L'inscription elle-même est tantôt écrite sur la panse du vase, tantôt, pour certaines jarres, sur les anses (inscrip-

[6] Cf. A. Lemaire, *Inscriptions hébraïques. I, Les ostraca* (Paris, 1977).

[7] Cf. Y. Aharoni, *Arad Inscriptions* (Jerusalem, 1975), pp. 103-4; Y. Yadin, "The Historical Significance of Inscription 88 from Arad: A Suggestion", *IEJ* 26 (1976), pp. 9-14; D. Conrad, "On *zᵉrōʿa* = 'Forces, Troops, Army' in Biblical Hebrew", *Tel-Aviv* 3 (1976), pp. 111-19; A. Lemaire, pp. 220-21.

[8] Dans P. Benoît *et alii*, *Les grottes de Murabbaʿât*, *DJD* II (Oxford, 1961), pp. 93-100; J. C. L. Gibson, pp. 31-2.

tions d'el-Jîb [9]) comme les estampilles privées ou royales dont elles se rapprochent par leur fonction. Généralement très courtes, ces inscriptions intéressent surtout l'onomastique et, moins souvent, la topographie historique.

Cet aperçu général sur les diverses catégories d'inscriptions donne déjà une première idée de leur variété typologique et de leur importance relative. Un coup d'oeil plus précis sur leur datation, même approximative, révèle immédiatement un phénomène important: à part la tablette de Gézer, quelques inscriptions sur jarre et quelques ostraca d'Arad, la quasi-totalité de ces inscriptions date de la deuxième partie de l'époque royale: du début du VIIIe siècle au début du VIe siècle av. J.C. Cette constatation semble indiquer un développement important et assez général de l'emploi de l'écriture à partir du VIIIe siècle. On pourrait rapprocher ce développement d'une civilisation de l'écriture et l'apparition des premiers "prophètes écrivains", Amos et Osée, dans la première moitié du VIIIe siècle. Ce premier rapprochement avec les textes bibliques en appelle beaucoup d'autres, mais avant de les étudier, il importe de préciser quelques problèmes de méthode dans la comparaison entre l'épigraphie paléo-hébraïque et la Bible.

II. *Rapports entre l'épigraphie paléo-hebraïque et la bible*

Qu'il y ait de nombreux rapports entre les textes paléo-hébreux de l'époque royale et les textes bibliques est incontestable et nous allons en donner plusieurs exemples tout à l'heure; cependant il importe de faire ces rapprochements avec discernement et méthode. En effet, les exégètes ou archéologues qui ont publié ou étudié les inscriptions paléo-hébraïques n'ont pas toujours échappé à la tentation d'un certain *concordisme* entre l'épigraphie paléo-hébraïque et la Bible; ils ont souvent cherché à retrouver le texte même de la Bible dans des passages ou allusions des inscriptions paléo-hébraïques et, pour mieux prouver cette identification, ils n'ont pas hésité parfois à "corriger" aussi bien le texte épigraphique que le texte biblique. Deux exemples concrets suffiront à montrer que cette tentation du concordisme n'est pas illusoire:

---

[9] Cf. J. B. Pritchard, *Hebrew Inscriptions and Stamps from Gibeon* (Pennsylvania, 1959); *id.*, "More Inscribed Jar Handles from el-Jîb", *BASOR* 160 (1960), pp. 2-6; F. S. Frick, "Another Inscribed Jar Handle from El-Jîb", *BASOR* 213 (1974), pp. 46-8.

1) A la suite de la découverte d'un certain nombre d'estampilles royales et d'estampilles privées portant des noms attestés dans les chapîtres ii et iv du premier livre des Chroniques, R. A. S. Macalister [10] n'a pas hésité, en 1905, à proposer de corriger la graphie de certains noms bibliques afin de pouvoir les identifier avec les noms propres nouvellement découverts et montrer par là l'apport possible de l'épigraphie à l'exégèse biblique. Il va sans dire que ces rapprochements n'ont rien prouvé et que les corrections proposées, purement conjecturales,[11] n'ont pas été retenues par les biblistes.
2) Lors de la publication des ostraca de Lakish, H. Torczyner [12] avait à peu près bien lu, aux lignes 14-16 de l'ostracon 3:

> *yrd šr hṣbʾ knyhw*[13] *bn ʾlntn lbʾ mṣryhm.*
> "Le chef d'armée (général) Konyahu fils d'Elnatan est descendu pour entrer en Égypte",

et il en avait aussitôt rapproché Jérémie xxvi 22:

> "Le roi Yehoyaqîm envoya en Égypte Elnatan fils d'Akbor et ses hommes...".

Pour lui, ce rapprochement conduisait à une identification: H. Torczyner, et plusieurs autres commentateurs après lui,[14] ont proposé d'identifier l'ambassade mentionnée dans l'ostracon avec l'ambassade mentionnée dans la Bible, en corrigeant au besoin le texte biblique. En fait, ces deux ambassades sont différentes: d'une part, elles ont probablement eu lieu sous des rois différents et, d'autre part, "Konyahu fils d'Elnatan" n'est pas "Elnatan fils d'Akbor", tout au plus pourrait-il en être le fils [15]...

Ces deux exemples suffisent à montrer le danger du *concordisme* dans les rapprochements entre les textes épigraphiques et les textes bibliques. Il est donc important de procéder de manière critique et

---

[10] "The Craftsmen's Guild of the Tribe of Judah", *Palestine Exploration Fund Quarterly* (*PEFQS*) 37 (1905), pp. 243-53 et 328-42; *id.*, "The Royal Potters of 1 Chron. IV, 23", *Expository Times* 16 (1905), pp. 379-80.

[11] R. A. S. Macalister le reconnaissait d'ailleurs lui-même: "I am conscious that the foregoing paper is little but a string of conjectures" (*PEFQS* [1905], p. 341).

[12] *Lachish I, The Lachish Letters* (London, 1938), pp. 51ss, spéc. pp. 62-7.

[13] Ici Torczyner lisait [*y*]*kbryhw* mais la lecture *knyhw* nous semble assurée.

[14] Cf. encore A. Malamat, *Yediot* (*BJPES*) 14 (1948), pp. 7-8, et *Journal of Near Eastern Studies*(*JNES*) 9 (1950), p. 222.

[15] Cf. A. Lemaire, pp. 107-8.

avec méthode dans l'utilisation de ces rapprochements, tant de la part de l'épigraphiste que de la part du bibliste: tous deux ne doivent pas chercher à voir la Bible partout:

—L'épigraphiste doit d'abord étudier l'inscription pour elle-même, s'efforcer d'en établir le texte de façon aussi précise et nuancée que possible, en utilisant, si nécessare, plusieurs photographies et en vérifiant les lectures sur les originaux. Il distinguera ensuite, avec nuance, ce qu'il considère comme une lecture certaine et ce qui l'est beaucoup moins et s'efforcera alors de comprendre le texte pour lui-même en tenant compte de son genre littéraire et des parallèles attestés dans d'autres inscriptions. Enfin seulement, il pourra rapprocher le texte de l'inscription de tel ou tel passage biblique qui présente un contenu analogue ou se réfère au même évènement historique et, dans ce rapprochement, tiendra compte du genre littéraire et de la datation probable du texte biblique considéré. Ainsi, si l'épigraphiste peut être amené parfois à corriger le texte des inscriptions—les scribes et les graveurs peuvent commettre des fautes par inadvertance ou incompréhension — il le fera en s'inspirant essentiellement du contexte de l'inscription et des textes parallèles attestés dans d'autres inscriptions.

— De son côté,— est-il besoin de le rappeler? — le bibliste doit d'abord étudier le texte biblique pour lui-même avant de le confronter aux données épigraphistes. Ainsi, s'il propose de corriger le texte biblique, il utilise essentiellement le témoignage des divers manuscrits, des passages bibliques parallèles et des versions. Dans la confrontation avec les données épigraphistes, le bibliste restera prudent en tenant compte, en particulier, du caractère plus ou moins assuré de certaines lectures ou de certaines interprétations.[16]

Ces quelques remarques ne prétendent pas proposer un traité méthodologique détaillé. Ce bref rappel de quelques principes généraux était cependant nécessaire car la tentation d'un certain concordisme non critique est d'autant plus forte que, souvent, l'épigraphiste et le bibliste sont confondus dans la même personne.

III. *Apport de l'épigraphie paléo-hébraïque à l'exégèse biblique*

L'écueil d'un concordisme facile entre les données épigraphiques et les données bibliques ne doit pas empêcher le rapprochement des deux *corpus*. Le *corpus* des textes paléo-hébreux de l'époque royale et

[16] Cf. par exemple, les commentaires sur la lecture *yrḫ ṣḥ* proposée par Y. Aharoni pour l'inscription n° 20 d'Arad (cf. A. Lemaire, p. 185).

une bonne partie des textes bibliques proviennent, en effet, du même milieu, sont écrits dans la même langue et reflètent l'histoire d'un même peuple: il est donc normal qu'ils puissent et doivent s'éclairer l'un par l'autre. D'ailleurs, dans cet échange, c'est vraisemblablement le *corpus* le plus petit, celui des inscriptions paléo-hébraïques, qui retirera le plus grand bénéfice! Cependant, le nombre des inscriptions découvertes s'accroissant chaque année, les cas où l'épigraphie paléo-hébraïque éclaire les données bibliques deviennent de plus en plus nombreux. Nous voudrions en donner quelques exemples dans les divers domaines de la philologie, de l'onomastique, de la critique littéraire, des institutions, de la topographie historique et de l'histoire politique et religieuse de l'ancien Israël.

1) Philologie.

Le sens de certains termes bibliques assez rares, qui ne sont parfois attestés qu'une seule fois, peut être précisé par de nouvelles occurences. Ainsi *ẓāmīr* n'est attesté qu'une seule fois dans la Bible, en Cantique ii 12 et sa signification a été discutée; or ce même terme apparait à la ligne 6 de la tablette de Gézer où il s'agit très clairement d'une activité agricole, très probablement de la vendange. C'est donc aussi dans ce sens qu'il faut probablement comprendre *ẓāmīr* dans le Cantique des Cantiques.[17]

2) Onomastique.

Les inscriptions paléo-hébraïques, spécialement les sceaux et les listes des ostraca contiennent beaucoup de noms propres; la plupart sont déjà connus par la Bible mais certains sont nouveaux et peuvent éclairer tel ou tel passage biblique. Ainsi le nom propre *ṣmḥ*, attesté dans l'inscription 49 d'Arad,[18] montre que le prophète Zacharie qui, en iii 8 et vi 12, joue, pour transmettre son message, sur la signification de *ṣemaḥ*, "rejeton", a très bien pu utiliser un nom propre réel.

3) Critique littéraire.

Les inscriptions paléo-hébraïques sont généralement assez bien datées, au moins à environ cinquante années près d'après la paléographie; elles peuvent donc servir de référence chronologique précise

[17] Cf. A. Lemaire, "*Zāmīr* dans la tablette de Gézer et le Cantique des Cantiques", *VT* 25 (1975), pp. 15-26.

[18] Cf. Y. Aharoni, *Arad Inscriptions* (Jerusalem, 1975), pp. 82ss.

pour l'emploi de telle ou telle expression, de telle ou telle tournure, de telle ou telle phraséologie. Ainsi, dans l'ostracon 17 d'Arad, qui date probablement de 597 av. J.C.,[19] la datation est indiquée par "*b* + chiffre + *lḥdš*"; or cette manière de dater se retrouve dans la finale du deuxième livre des Rois (2 Rois xxv 1, 3, 8, 27), dans la finale du livre de Jérémie (Jérémie xxxix 2, lii 4, 6, 12, 31) et, surtout, dans le livre d'Ezéchiel (sauf Ezéchiel xlv 21, 25); cette référence phraséologique tend donc à confirmer l'authenticité des dates du livre d'Ezéchiel (sauf Ezéchiel xlv 21, 25 probablement à rattacher à la rédaction sacerdotale) dont la valeur historique a été récemment mise en relief par A. Malamat.[20]

Soulignons cependant ici la nécessité d'être prudent dans l'utilisation de ce critère phraséologique: ainsi, ce n'est pas parce que l'expression *ḥy yhwh* se retrouve probablement deux fois dans les ostraca de Lakish (ostracon 3, ligne 9 et ostracon 12, ligne 3 [21]) que cette formule est caractéristique du début du VIe siècle av. J.C.; en fait, une telle formule a pu être utilisée plus longtemps, avant et après cette période.[22]

4) Institutions.

Les inscriptions paléo-hébraïques nous donnent de nombreux renseignements sur l'administration royale, tout specialement sur le fonctionnement des magasins royaux.[23] Cependant nous voudrions ici attirer l'attention sur une autre institution de l'époque royale: celle des "écoles", que des découvertes récentes éclairent peu à peu. Ainsi la découverte d'au moins deux abécédaires à Lakish [24] constitue un indice important en faveur de l'existence d'une école dans cette ville fortifiée; les différences de formules de salutation utilisées

[19] Cf. A. Lemaire, *Inscriptions*, pp. 176 et 232.

[20] "The Twilight of Judah in the Egyptian-Babylonian Maelstrom", dans *Congress Volume Edinburgh 1974*, *Sup. to VT* 28 (Leiden, 1975), pp. 122-43, spéc. p. 141; cf. aussi M. Weitzman, "The Dates in Ezekiel", *The Heythrop Journal* 17 (1976), pp. 20-30.

[21] Cf. A. Lemaire, pp. 101 et 130.

[22] La même prudence s'impose pour l'emploi de la formule *dbr* + *ʾšr* + verbe *ṣwh* (cf. A. Lemaire, p. 181) et nous avons du mal à comprendre la remarque de G. Garbini, *AION* 37 (1977), p. 243, qui ne semble pas avoir compris que l'argument stylistique ne peut servir à dater que lorsqu'on peut saisir une évolution chronologique ou que l'expression employée est caractéristique d'un auteur ou d'une couche littéraire.

[23] Cf. en particulier A. Lemaire, pp. 228-32.

[24] Cf. A. Lemaire, "A Schoolboy's Exercise on an Ostracon at Lachish", *Tel-Aviv* 3 (1976), pp. 109-10; cf. aussi "Abécédaires et exercises d'écolier en épigraphie nord-ouest sémitique", à paraître dans *Journal Asiatique* (1979).

dans les ostraca de Lakish et dans ceux d'Arad s'expliquent probablement par le fait que les scribes d'Arad et de Lakish étaient formés dans deux écoles différentes; [25] les découvertes récentes d'inscriptions à Qadesh-Barnéa [26] et à Kuntilat-Ajrud,[27] en cours de publication, permettront probablement d'avoir une idée plus précise de ce qui était enseigné dans ces écoles: écriture (abécédaires), rédaction (formulaires de débuts de lettres), dessin (reproduction de motifs iconographiques classiques)... Dans ces conditions, l'hypothèse de l'utilisation de certains textes bibliques comme "manuels" scolaires des écoles judéennes [28] pourrait bientôt prendre une forme plus concrète.

5) Topographie historique.

Les inscriptions paléo-hébraïques contiennent de nombreux noms de lieu dont certains, attestés déjà dans la Bible, étaient, jusqu'ici difficiles à localiser avec précision. La comparaison des données bibliques et épigraphiques permet souvent de proposer de nouvelles identifications ou de confirmer celles qui étaient déjà proposées. Ainsi, utilisant les données des ostraca de Samarie, nous avons pré-présenté une carte administrative des clans ou cantons de la tribu de Manassé.[29] Bien plus, en localisant le clan d'"Asriel" (*śr'l* dans les ostraca) au coeur de la montagne ephraïmite, près de l'ancien sanctuaire de Silo, nous proposons d'y voir le clan originel qui a donné son nom à toute la confédération israélite.[30]

---

[25] Cf. A. Lemaire, *Inscriptions*, pp. 225-226.

[26] Cf. R. Cohen, "Kadesh-Barnea, 1976". *IEJ* 26 (1976), pp. 201-2.

[27] Cf. Z. Meshel, "Ketuvôt miymêy Yedudâh bekuntilat-Ajrud", *Ḥadashôt Archeologiôt* 56 (1975), pp. 51-2; *id.*, "Kuntilat-Ajrud", *Ḥadashôt Archeologiôt* 57-8 (1976), pp. 43-5; S. Singer, "Cache of Hebrew and Phoenician Inscriptions Found in the Desert", *The Biblical Archaeological Review* 2 (1976), pp. 33-4; Z. Meshel-C. Meyers, "The Name of God in the Wilderness of Zin", *The Biblical Archaeologist* (*BA*) 39 (1976), pp. 6-10; Z. Meshel "Kuntilat-Ajrud—An Israelite Site on the Sinai Border", *Qadmoniot* 9 (1976), pp. 119-24; *id.*, "Kuntilat-Ajrud, 1975-1976", *IEJ* 27 (1977), pp. 52-3.

[28] Sur le problème des écoles dans l'ancien Israël et de leur relation avec les écrits de sagesse, cf. T. N. D. Mettinger, *Solomonic State Officials* (Lund, 1971), spéc. pp. 140-57; J. P. J. Olivier, "Schools and Wisdom Literature", *Journal of Northwest Semitic Languages* (*JNSL*) 4 (1975), pp. 49-60; R. N. Whybray, *The Intellectual Tradition in the Old Testament* (Berlin, 1974); B. Lang, *Frau Weisheit, Deutung einer biblischen Gestalt* (Düsseldorf, 1975), *passim*.

[29] Cf. A. Lemaire, pp. 59-65.

[30] Cf. A. Lemaire, "Asriel, *śr'l* et Israël et l'origine de la confédération israélite", *VT* 23 (1973), pp. 239-43; *id.*, *Inscriptions*, pp. 283-6. L'objection de H. Seebass, "Landverheißung an die Väter", *Evangelische Theologie* 37 (1977), p. 211, n. 5, ne nous semble pas fondée: il faut partir du fait que *'aśrî'ēl* est écrit *śr'l* dans les ostraca de Samarie: le "aleph" de *'aśrî'ēl* est donc prosthétique, comme vraisem-

6) Histoire politique.

Certains ostraca de Lakish et d'Arad, se référant directement à la situation politique de la Shephélah et du Négev au début du VIe siècle av. J.C., permettent de mieux comprendre l'atmosphère trouble des dernières années du royaume de Juda. Cependant nous préférons plutôt ici mettre en valeur un sceau et une bulle publiés récemment pour illustrer l'apport possible de l'épigraphie paléo-hébraïque à l'histoire d'Israël:

— La bulle est celle de "Yehozaraḥ fils de Ḥilqi(ya)hu serviteur de Ḥizqi(ya)hu".[31] Ḥizqiyahu, précédé ici de *ʿbd*, est presque certainement un nom de roi et la datation paléographique permet de l'identifier: c'est le roi "Ezéchias". Dès lors, "Yehozaraḥ fils de Ḥilqi(ya)hu serviteur (ou "ministre") d'Ezéchias" est très probablement le frère d'"Elyaqim fils de Ḥilqiyahu maître du palais (*'šr ʿl hbyt*)", mentionné en 2 Rois xviii 18 et Esaïe xxxvi 3. Cette découverte confirme donc le rôle politique important joué par la famille de Ḥilqiyahu à la fin du VIIIe siècle.

— Le sceau est un sceau inscrit sur les deux faces et dont le revers porte l'inscription "(A Ze)karyaw, prêtre de Dor" (*[lz]kryw khn d'r*).[32] Cette inscription, qui date approximativement du milieu du VIIIe siècle av. J.C., peut être rapprochée du titre de l'adversaire du prophète Amos: "Amaṣyah prêtre de Béthel" (Amos vii 10). Ces deux personnages devaient occuper des fonctions analogues, l'un à Béthel et l'autre à Dor, à l'époque de Jéroboam II, et ce dernier contrôlait probablement aussi bien le sanctuaire de Dor que celui de Béthel.

7) Histoire religieuse.

L'apport des inscriptions à l'histoire religieuse d'Israël est très divers, comme le montrent les quatre exemples suivants:

1 — L'onomastique semble révéler une différence importante de situation religieuse entre le royaume du nord et celui du sud. Alors

blablement celui de *ʾaśarʾēl* (1 Chron. iv 16) et *ʾaśarʾēlāh* (1 Chron. xxv 2); dans ce dernier cas, le caractère prosthétique du "aleph" est confirmé par l'alternance *ʾaśarʾēlāh* et *yeśarʾēlāh* (1 Chron. xxv 2 et 14). Pour ces trois noms, il faut donc rejeter l'étymologie proposée, non sans hésitation d'ailleurs, par M. Noth, *Die israelitischen Personennamen im Rahmen der gemeinsemitischen Namengebung* (Stuttgart, 1928), pp. 167, 183, et qui n'était, tout au plus, qu'une hypothèse.

[31] Cf. R. Hestrin - M. Dayagi, "A Seal Impression of a Servant of King Hezekiah", *IEJ* 24 (1974), pp. 26-9.

[32] Cf. N. Avigad, "The Priest of Dor", *IEJ* 25 (1975), pp. 101-6. L'interprétation proposée par N. Avigad nous semble beaucoup plus naturelle que celle de M. Haran, "A Temple at Dor?", *IEJ* 27 (1977), pp. 12-15.

que dans ce dernier, jusqu'à maintenant, les inscriptions ne nous ont fourni aucun nom propre comportant l'élément théophore *bʿl*, les ostraca de Samarie révèlent une onomastique dans laquelle il y a à peu près autant de noms baalistes que de noms yahvistes.[33] Ce fait confirme l'importance de l'affrontement entre Baal et Yahvé dans le royaume du Nord, affrontement dont nous n'avons pratiquement aucune trace dans le royaume de Jérusalem.

2 — La crise nationale et religieuse qu'a traversée le royaume de Juda lors de l'expédition de Sennachérib en 701 av. J.C. nous est racontée dans plusieurs passages bibliques. On peut désormais l'illustrer par les graffiti de Khirbet Beit Lei contenant des prières et des malédictions écrites très vraisemblablement au cœur même de cette crise, une des malédictions visant vraisemblablement Sennachérib "l'insulteur" de Yahvé.[34]

3 — En Genèse xiv 18, 19, Melkisédeq roi de Salem est présenté comme prêtre de "El Elyon. . . créateur du ciel et de la terre". Or une inscription sur jarre, mise au jour par les fouilles du Professeur N. Avigad à Jérusalem, doit probablement être lue "(El) créateur de la terre" ([*ʾl*]*qnʾrṣ*),[35] confirmant ainsi l'existence du culte de El créateur de l'univers à Jérusalem[36].

4 — La finale de l'inscription nº 3 de Khirbet el-Qôm [37] est difficile à lire. Pour la comprendre, il faut probablement tenir compte d'une erreur du graveur qui a déplacé une expression. Si l'on admet cette correction, on lit alors la formule suivante:

brk ʾryhw lyhwh wlʾšrth.
"Béni soit Ouryahu par Yahvé et par son ashérah".

Cette formule, que l'on peut rapprocher d'expressions similaires attestées dans les inscriptions découvertes à Kuntilat-Ajrud,[38] aiderait à clarifier la nature de l'ashérah de Yahvé tout en montrant le danger de personnification idolâtrique de son culte.[39]

[33] Cf. A. Lemaire, pp. 47-55.
[34] Cf. A. Lemaire, "Prières en temps de crise: les inscriptions de Khirbet Beit Lei", *RB* 84 (1977), pp. 558-68.
[35] Cf. N. Avigad, "Excavations in the Jewish Quarter of the Old City of Jerusalem, 1971", *IEJ* 22 (1972), pp. 193-200, spéc. pp. 195-6.
[36] Cf. N. C. Habel, "Yahweh, Maker of Heaven and Earth, A Study in Tradition Criticism", *Journal of Biblical Literature* (*JBL*) 91 (1972), pp. 321-37.
[37] Cf. W. G. Dever, *HUCA* 40-41 (1969-70), pp. 159ss.
[38] Communication orale de Z. Meshel.
[39] Cf. A. Lemaire, "Les inscriptions de Khirbet el-Qôm et l'ashérah de Yhwh", *Revue Biblique* 84 (1977), pp. 595-608.

Ces quelques exemples que nous venons d'énumérer ne prétendent pas être exhaustifs : ils veulent simplement montrer tout l'intérêt de l'épigraphie paléo-hébraïque pour une meilleure compréhension de la Bible et, donc, l'utilité de la publication d'un *corpus* des inscriptions paléo-hébraïques de l'époque royale. Cependant, et il importe de le souligner, ce *corpus* ne sera jamais clos définitivement : de nouvelles découvertes, comme celles de Kuntilat-Ajrud en cours de publication,[40] pourront révéler de nouveaux aspects inattendus de l'apport de l'épigraphie paléo-hébraïque à l'exégèse biblique.

[40] Cf. *supra*, note 27.

GENESIS IV 6-7 — EINE JAHWISTISCHE ERWEITERUNG?[1]

von

ILSE VON LOEWENCLAU

Berlin

"Eine Erklärung dieser beiden Verse ist bisher nicht gelungen", bemerkt C. Westermann zu Gen. iv 6-7 (S. 406). Für das Verständnis der Erzählung scheint sie ihm nicht unbedingt notwendig zu sein, da die Verse in ihrem Zusammenhang wie ein Fremdkörper wirken. "Man muß mit der Möglichkeit rechnen, daß das Stück ihr nicht ursprünglich angehört" (S. 407; vgl. auch S. 410). Der neueste Aufsatz zu unserem Kapitel von W. Dietrich sieht gleichfalls in unseren Versen eine Hinzufügung (S. 98f.). Wohl auch deshalb wird eine Diskussion ihrer textlichen und inhaltlichen Schwierigkeiten vermieden (S. 99, Anm. 23). Nun scheint mir gerade die berechtigte Vermutung, daß es sich in unseren Versen um einen *Zusatz* handle, umso mehr Anlaß zu sein, ihnen *besondere Aufmerksamkeit* zu widmen. Zusätze werden nicht von ungefähr eingebracht. Sie zeigen, wie ein vorliegender Text verstanden und weitergeführt wurde. Als Zeugnis eines Gespräches mit der Überlieferung haben sie hermeneutische Relevanz.

---

[1] Eine erschöpfende Auseinandersetzung mit der Literatur kann hier nicht gegeben werden (erst kurz vor Fertigstellung des Vortrages wurde mir noch dankenswerterweise der Aufsatz von Dietrich zugänglich gemacht). Ich beschränke mich darauf, ausdrücklich angeführte Werke zu nennen, auf die im Folgenden dann nur mit Verfassernamen und Seitenzahl verwiesen wird. Außer den bekannten Kommentaren von A. Dillmann (*KeH*, 1892[6]), H. Gunkel (*HK*, 1922[5]), H. Holzinger, (*KHC*, 1898), O. Procksch (*KAT*, 1924$^{2}/_{3}$), G. v. Rad (*ATD*, 1972[9]), C. Westermann (*BK*, 1974) handelt es sich um folgende Monographien bzw. Aufsätze: W. Dietrich, " 'Wo ist dein Bruder?' Zu Tradition und Intention von Genesis 4", *Beiträge zur alttestamentlichen Theologie* (Göttingen, 1977), S. 94-111; H. Heyde, *Kain, der erste Jahwe-Verehrer* (Berlin, 1965); B. Stade, "Beiträge zur Pentateuchkritik 1) Das Kainszeichen", *ZAW* 14 (1894), S. 250-318; F. Stolz, Artikel *nś'*, *panīm*, *THAT* II (München/Zürich, 1976), S. 109-17; S. 432-60; R. de Vaux, *Das Alte Testament und seine Lebensordnungen* I (Freiburg-Basel-Wien, 1964[2]) = *Les Institutions de l'Ancien Testament* I (Paris, 1958); G. Wallis, "Die Stadt in den Überlieferungen der Genesis", *ZAW* 78 (1966), S. 133-48; J. Wellhausen, *Die Composition des Hexateuchs und der historischen Bücher des alten Testaments* (Berlin, 1963-Nachdruck).

Die Überlieferung, der unsere Verse angehören und die zunächst bedacht werden muß, ist die bekannte Geschichte von Kain und Abel. Kain, ihre Hauptgestalt, ist Ahnherr der in Nachbarschaft zu den Judäern lebenden Kenitern, eine Gestalt also, die stammesgeschichtlich eingeordnet werden kann.[2] Anders Abel, dessen Name "Hauch" sein Schicksal innerhalb der Erzählung andeutet und — als Variante zu Jabal, dem Hirten — auch nur in ihr beheimatet sein wird.[3] Auf die Geschichte von Kain und Abel folgt in V. 17-22 eine Genealogie der Kainabkommen, die vermutlich in V. 1 beginnt. Sie dürfte in kenitischen Kreisen beheimatet sein, wofür schon die Gattung spricht, die im Leben der Sippe ihren Ursprung hat.[4] Sie wird in V. 23f. abgeschlossen durch das Prahllied eines kenitischen Verbandes, das sich nach Lamech nennt (Dietrich, S. 103). Die der Genealogie eingefügten "Errungenschaftsnotizen" weisen einerseits auf verschiedene Gruppen einer nicht bodenständigen Schicht innerhalb der städtischen Gesellschaft — Musikanten und Schmiede,[5] andererseits auf viehzuchttreibende Nomaden.[6] Jene setzen also durchgehend ein Leben ohne Bindung an das Kulturland voraus. Zweifellos wird dieses Leben von den Kenitern bejaht und nicht als Fluch gesehen.

Einer fundamental anderen Sicht begegnen wir in der Geschichte von Kain und Abel. Sie deutet das Leben fern vom Ackerboden, der *ʾᵃdāmā* als Fluch (V. 11f.) und kann deshalb unmöglich auf kenitische

---

[2] Hierfür ist immer noch auf den grundlegenden Aufsatz von Stade hinzuweisen, an dessen Sachverhalt Westermann bei seiner Deutung von Gen. iv vorübergeht (mit Recht von Dietrich, S. 101, Anm. 36, angefragt). Insofern ist es nicht mehr "ein einheitliches Ergebnis der neueren Forschung..., daß die Erzählung von Kain mit dem Volksstamm der Keniter zu tun haben muß" (Heyde, S. 7).

[3] "Für den Erzähler war es vermutlich ein Name, der das Schicksal seines Trägers bezeichnet, der wie ein Hauch dahinschwand" (Holzinger, S. 46). Wellhausen, S. 8, sieht in diesem Namen eine Reminiszenz an den iv 20 genannten Jabal, andere Ausleger folgen ihm hierin. Treffend sagt Dietrich, S. 101: "Abel... mußte erfunden werden, damit Kain zum Brudermörder werden konnte".

[4] Vgl. dazu grundsätzlich de Vaux, S. 20f. Dietrich, S. 104, weist auf die "Anzeichen einer langen (kenitischen) Überlieferungsgeschichte", anders Westermann, S. 438ff.

[5] Damit ist eine Verbindung zu der Aussage von Kain, dem Städtegründer (V. 17) herzustellen — vgl. hierzu den Aufsatz von Wallis, der auch die kenitischen Gruppen im einzelnen charakterisiert (S. 139f.).

[6] Im Gegensatz zur herrschenden Auslegung, die in iv 20 "eine eindeutige Bestimmung des Nomaden- oder Beduinenlebens" (Westermann, S. 449), sieht, will Wallis, S. 135, in den Viehzüchtern vor der Stadt Jabals Nachkommen sehen. Der viehzuchttreibende Nomadenstamm sei ja schon in Abel vorhanden. Wenn Abel jedoch — wie dargetan — nur eine Variante zu Jabal ist, wird gerade die herrschende Auslegung bestätigt!

Überlieferungsträger zurückgeführt werden.[7] Nur an einem Punkt ist sie von deren Selbstverständnis abhängig: sie weiß, daß der in ihr geschilderte Kain ein besonderes Verhältnis zu Jahwe hat (vgl. V. 1), und deshalb ist Jahwe sein einziges sprechendes Gegenüber.[8] In welchen Kreisen mag unsere Geschichte aufgekommen sein? Es gibt nur eine Antwort: bei Leuten, die den Sinn menschlicher Existenz mit der Bearbeitung der *ʾadāmā* verbinden (ganz im Einklang übrigens mit Gen. ii 5 und iii 23), die also das tun, was Kain anfangs tat, die Jahwe als Herrn der *ʾadāmā* Opfer darbringen. *Israelitische Bauern* sind es, die zum erstenmal die Geschichte von Kain und Abel erzählen.[9] Sie sind im judäischen Raum zu lokalisieren, wo ihnen immer wieder verschiedene Gruppen von Kenitern begegnen mögen, wo ihnen zugleich im Süden die weite Wüste vor Augen liegt — dem seßhaften Bauern ein Ort des Grauens.

Das Phänomen der Keniter, die sich zu Jahwe bekennen und sein Zeichen tragen, gibt diesen Bauern eine Frage auf. Wie kommt es, daß einer, der zu Jahwe gehören will, nicht dort wohnt und seine Arbeit verrichtet, wo Jahwes Altäre stehen — auf der *ʾadāmā*? Die Umwelt des israelitischen Bauern kennt Geschichten von Schuld und Vertreibung, sie weiß zu erzählen, daß die Menschen einst in einem schönen Garten lebten, aus dem sie durch ihre Schuld vertrieben wurden.[10] Könnte nicht auch Kains unstetes Leben fern von der *ʾadāmā* ähnlich zu deuten sein? Welche Verschuldung mag ein so furchtbares Los nach sich ziehen? Jeder weiß es — niemand ist ruheloser als der Brudermörder, der aus seiner Sippe ausgestoßen wird und dem keine andere Sippe Asyl gewähren darf,[11] er ist der Prototyp des "Unsteten und Flüchtigen". Kain hat seinen Bruder erschlagen, das ist seine Verschuldung. Trotzdem bleibt er der von

[7] Ich stimme hier ganz mit Dietrich, S. 102, Anm. 43, überein. Die dort genannte Literatur müßte durch den Hinweis auf die Studie von Heyde ergänzt werden: Nach ihm war in einer Urfassung die Sage bei jenen Kenitern lebendig, die vor den Israeliten Jahweverehrer waren, um dann in der Überarbeitung durch den Jahwisten den Glauben der Jahweverehrer aller Zeiten und Zonen zu kennzeichnen (S. 22).

[8] Was ist schon das akzeptierte Opfer Abels im Vergleich zu dem ausgeführten Dialog zwischen Jahwe und Kain? Die "unbefangene, häufige Erwähnung Jahwes in Gen. 4" (Dietrich, S. 102) dürfte sich am ehesten erklären, wenn Kain tatsächlich "der erste Jahwe-Verehrer", die sog. Keniterhypothese im Recht ist.

[9] Ihre (beschränkte!) Sicht wird besonders in V. 16 deutlich, der zweifellos den Sinn hat: Jahwe ist nur im Kulturland anzutreffen.

[10] Wesentliche Elemente aus Gen. ii und iii sind mit ihrer Vorgeschichte in der bäuerlichen Welt Kanaans anzusiedeln.

[11] Wallis, S. 138, erläutert das an den Bräuchen arabischer Beduinen.

Jahwe Bewahrte, gegenwärtig in seinen Nachfahren mit ihrem "Kainszeichen".[12]

Wenn die Kainüberlieferungen zwei verschiedenen Tradenten zuzuweisen sind (wodurch sich zu einem Teil die bekannten Widersprüche klären!), dann dürfte ihre Zusammenarbeit im jetzigen Text relativ spät erfolgt sein. In jedem Falle hat sie schon literarischen Charakter und ist deshalb am ehesten als Werk des *Jahwisten* zu begreifen.[13] Der Geschichte von Kain und Abel hat er besondere Aufmerksamkeit gewidmet und die darin schon angelegte Beziehung zu den vorangehenden Kapiteln verstärkt. Das geschieht vor allem dadurch, daß er Kain zum Sohn des Adam und seiner Frau macht (V. 1a), deren Name Chawwa vermutlich der Kenitergenealogie entstammt.[14] Durch diesen Eingriff, dessen Bedeutsamkeit schwer zu überschätzen ist, wird eine *Sippenüberlieferung zur Menschheitsüberlieferung*. Mehr noch: Vergegenwärtigt man sich, daß nach semitischem Verständnis das Blut eines Stammes am reinsten und stärksten im Erstgeborenen fließt,[15] so wird Kain beim Jahwisten zum exemplarischen Repräsentanten des Menschengeschlechtes.

Ein älterer genealogischer Anschluß zu iii 24, der in Seth Adams Erstgeborenen sieht, kann jetzt nicht mehr stehen bleiben (V. 25). Durch entsprechende Ergänzungen im Text wird Seth zum Ersatzsohn für den erschlagenen Abel.[16] Über Seth geht dann die Linie der Menschheit weiter. Er zeugt einen Sohn "Enosch" (Mensch!) und

---

[12] Dagegen vermag ich unserer Erzählung keine antikenitische Tendenz zu entnehmen, wie sie Dietrich, S. 101ff., zu sehen meint. Es geht allerdings auch nicht schlechthin um den Gegensatz von Seßhaften und Nomaden (vgl. ebd., S. 102, Anm. 42): der Seßhafte ist konkret als *ʿōbēd ʾᵃdāmā* gesehen (der Urstand des Kain), dem in den Kenitern verschiedene Gruppen gegenüberstehen, die sämtlich durch ihre Lebensweise von der *ʾᵃdāmā* gelöst sind.

[13] Eine ähnliche Sicht bestimmt die Studie von Heyde — nur ist sie nicht so selbstverständlich wie er S. 7 annimmt. Das zeigt auch wieder der jüngste Aufsatz zu unserem Text von Dietrich. Vor der letzten Hand des Jahwisten nimmt er zwei aufeinanderfolgende Gruppen israelitischer Tradenten an: die erste habe die schon mit dem Urmenschen beginnende kenitische Genealogie durch eine Kurzfassung der Kain und Abel-Geschichte ergänzt, die zweite eine erweiterte Fassung eingebracht, erst diese sei dann durch den Jahwisten ergänzt worden.

[14] Auch sonst erscheinen in der Kenitergenealogie die Stammütter (Stade, S. 268). Vielleicht war Chawwa ursprünglich die Mutter des Städtebauers Kain, die mit Adams Frau erst sekundär identifiziert wurde (Stade, ebd.). Die Identifikation mußte erfolgen, als die Kenitergenealogie mit Kapitel iii verbunden wurde: "der Mensch" in iv 1 ist dann dem dort erwähnten Menschen gleichzusetzen (danach wurde iii 20 eingefügt).

[15] Das verdeutlichen Gen. xlix 3 und Deut. xxi 17.

[16] Dietrich, S. 97, hat sie (nach Stade, S. 263) noch einmal zusammengestellt: *ʿōd, ʾaḥēr taḥat hābel ki hᵃrāgō qajin.*

der fängt an — als habe es Kain nie gegeben! — Jahwe anzurufen (V. 26). Dabei ist der reinste Vertreter des Menschengeschlechtes keineswegs von der Bildfläche verschwunden. Kain ist da, denn er begründet ein Geschlecht, auf das sich in der Gegenwart bestehende Gruppen zurückleiten. Damit gewinnt die Genealogie für den Jahwisten eine neue Funktion: sie sichert die Präsenz Kains unter den Menschen. Ist sie mit dem Lamechlied verbunden, in dem der Kainnachkomme schon wegen einer beigebrachten Wunde einen Mann zu Tode schlägt, dann heißt das für den Jahwisten: der Geist Kains verlöscht nicht mit seiner Vertreibung, er flammt immer wieder neu auf und hat sichtbare Auswirkungen.

Es liegt auf der Hand, daß die den Kontext derart bestimmende Geschichte von Kain und Abel auch in sich eine andere Intention gewinnen muß, als ihr ursprünglich innewohnt. Für ihn ist Kain ja nicht so sehr Stammvater der Keniter, Kain vertritt den Menschen schlechthin in seinem Umgang mit dem Bruder. War es dem judäischen Bauern selbstverständlich, daß *er* mit Kain nichts zu schaffen hatte, ihn mit leichtem Grausen gewissermaßen aus der Ferne betrachten konnte, so hat der Jahwist durch seine Sicht Kains als erstgeborenen *Menschen* eine derartige Distanzierung ausgeschlossen. Damit wird bei ihm die Geschichte von Kain und Abel zu einer jeden Menschen unmittelbar betreffenden und anredenden Geschichte, die ins Hinhören und Nachdenken ruft. Deshalb erscheint auch Kain in ihr sehr betont als der *einzelne* (nur jeweils der einzelne kann hören und nachdenken!); es scheint geradezu vergessen, daß er als Stammesheros ein Volk vertritt (Gunkel, S. 49). Darüber hinaus treten wesentliche Züge, die in einer Urfassung unserer Erzählung wichtig gewesen sein müssen, in den Hintergrund (Gunkel, ebd.). Woran erkennt Kain die Verschmähung seines Opfers? Wann, wo und wie spricht Jahwe zu ihm? (Man erinnere sich, wie anschaulich Entsprechendes in Gen. iii ausgeführt ist!) Worin besteht eigentlich das Kainszeichen? Auf das alles kommt es für den Jahwisten offensichtlich nicht mehr an. Mit Sicherheit unterdrückt er den Anfang der ursprünglichen Erzählung, als er sie in die eingangs überarbeitete Kenitergenealogie einfügt — schon dadurch anzeigend, daß ihm hier erzählerische Details weniger bedeutsam sind. Am klarsten tritt das in V. 9 zutage, wenn Jahwe unmittelbar nach dem Brudermord (letztes Wort in V. 8!) Kain befragt: "Wo ist dein Bruder Abel?" Es fehlt unbedingt ein erzählerisches Zwischenstück des Inhalts, daß der Mörder die Leiche verscharrt, Jahwe aber gleich die Stimme des Blutes von der Erde her hört (in V. 10b vorausgesetzt!) und sich aufmacht, um Kain zur Rede zu stellen. Die erzählerische Härte akzentuiert jedoch genau das, worauf es dem Jahwisten ankommt: das Geschehen zwischen Jahwe und Kain, wie es sich in den *Reden* widerspiegelt. Sie treten umso mehr in den Vordergrund, als Erzählelemente unterdrückt werden.[17] An einer Stelle hat der Jahwist den überlieferten Redentext sogar *erweitert*: in den Versen 6 und 7. Sind wir darauf aufmerksam geworden, daß für ihn gerade die Reden Gewicht haben, dann muß ein noch hinzugefügtes Redestück für sein Gesamtverständnis wohl von entscheidender Bedeutung sein (womit sich unsere eingangs angestellte Erwägung zu Zusätzen in besonderer Weise bestätigen würde). Folgende Argumente sichern V. 6 und 7 als Hinzufügung: 1) Die Analogie vergleichbarer Erzählungen zeigt, daß Jahwe erst nach geschehener Tat mit seinem Wort zur Stelle ist. Unsere stellt eine Ausnahme dar.[18] 2) Jahwes Erscheinen ist für den eigentlichen Erzählungsablauf ohne Bedeutung — die Tat wird dadurch nicht verhindert (Dietrich, S. 98), 3) Im Gegensatz zu den folgenden Redestücken findet Kain auf Jahwes Anrede keine Erwiderung. Als "Antwort" soll offenbar die in der Erzählung vorgegebene Tat angesehen werden. 4) Der Anschluß der Tatschilderung in V. 8 an V. 5 unter Fortlassung von V. 6-7 ist ausgezeichnet und erzählerisch folgerichtig. Lediglich V. 8a scheint auffallend knapp zu sein. Nach "Und Kain sprach zu seinem Bruder" müßte eine Angabe dessen folgen, was er sagt.[19] Da der Brudermord auf dem Felde geschieht (V. 8b) und nicht am Altar vielleicht: "Wir wollen aufs Feld gehen" — Worte, die bekanntlich im Samaritanus und den alten Übersetzungen eingefügt sind. Sicher waren diese oder ähnliche Worte

[17] In der Forschungsgeschichte haben die Reden — nach Gunkel, S. 49, ein Zeichen später Zeit — öfter die Beweislast für ein Spätdatierung unseres Textes tragen müssen. Wenn V. 6 und 7 in der ursprünglichen Fassung entfallen, werden die Redestücke wesentlich reduziert. Es bleiben auf Seiten Jahwes die aus Gen. iii bekannte Rechenschaftsforderung und das Fluchwort, es bleiben auf Seiten Kains die freche Antwort und das Erschrecken über die Strafe, es bleibt das bewahrende Handeln Jahwes im Vollzug der Strafe (auch dieses Element findet sich in Gen. iii, allerdings als Erzählstück: V. 21). Das sind — wie vor allem die Parallelität zu Gen. iii zeigt — denkbare Bestandteile einer vom Jahwisten übernommenen älteren Erzählung.

[18] Wieder ist besonders auf Gen. iii hinzuweisen (vgl. die Synopse bei Dietrich, S. 98): Jahwes erstes Wort lautet "Wo...". Vgl. ferner Gen. xi 5 und xii 17 (hier ohne Wort, aber nach der Tat mit einem entsprechenden Eingreifen).

[19] Dietrich, S. 105, will dem Hiat dieses Verses entnehmen, daß V. 8b ursprünglich zu V. 2 gehörte und eine erste Kurzfassung der Geschichte von Kain und Abel darstellte.

Bestandteil unserer Erzählung, ehe der Jahwist sie überarbeitete. Da er aber gerade erzählerische Details gekürzt hat (V. 9!), kann das sehr wohl — zumal unmittelbar nach der Jahwerede — auch hier geschehen sein, und spätere Tradenten haben sinngemäß ergänzt. 5) Form und Inhalt der Jahweworte in V. 6 und 7 sind nicht einer alten Erzählung gemäß (vgl. Westermann, S. 406f.). *Zwei Fragen*, die das in V. 5 berichtete Empfinden Kains voraussetzen, leiten zunächst zur Selbstbesinnung an (V. 6). Dann folgt eine offenbar grundsätzliche *Erläuterung* hierzu (V. 7), deren warnende Funktion trotz des unsicheren Textes unverkennbar ist, und eine damit in Zusammenhang stehende *Aufforderung*. Diese Strukturelemente geben der jahwistischen Hinzufügung von vornherein *belehrenden Charakter*.

Wir setzen mit der Interpretation des textlich einwandfrei erhaltenen V. 6 ein: "Und Jahwe sprach zu Kain: Warum bist du zornig, und warum ist dein Gesicht gefallen?" Jahwes Fragen betreffen ein psychisches Phänomen, das in seiner Komplexität bereits von der alten Erzählung angesprochen wird. Kain kocht vor Zorn, zugleich aber ist er niedergeschlagen und enttäuscht (vgl. Holzinger, S. 47). Der umstrittene hebräische Ausdruck *npl pānīm* kann schon von seiner Grundbedeutung her nicht die Widerspiegelung des Zorns im Gesicht meinen (= finster blicken). Wer vom Zorn gepackt wird (beachte das Verb *ḥrh*!), wendet sich seinem Gegenüber sofort und sehr direkt zu, er senkt nicht das Gesicht.[20] Bis in das Bild hinein entspricht unser Ausdruck vielmehr dem englischen "his face fell" und beschreibt — ihm gleich — Enttäuschung und Niedergeschlagenheit.[21] Sie können mit dem Zorn eine Verbindung eingehen, wo das eigene Tun unverständlicherweise zurückgesetzt wird gegenüber dem scheinbar gleichen Tun eines anderen. Alle umsonst aufgewandte Mühe ist dem Zurückgesetzten in seiner Enttäuschung gegenwärtig und hält den einmal entbrannten Zorn wach. Der Anblick des Bevorzugten wird unerträglich und provoziert zu bösen Reaktionen, die weit gefährlicher sind als ein Zornesausbruch, weil sie nicht gleich erfolgen, sondern in Ruhe geplant werden (was etwa der Fall ist, wenn Abel nicht spontan niedergemacht, sondern erst später aufs Feld gelockt wird!).

---

[20] Gegen Westermann, S. 405, ist festzuhalten, daß unser Ausdruck nicht die Abwendung vom anderen meint, dazu hätte er präpositional ergänzt werden müssen (vgl. die von Westermann angeführten Beispiele aus Jer. iii 12 und Num. vi 26!).

[21] Die LXX kennt nur einen bekümmerten und niedergeschlagenen Kain; statt einer Vokabel für "zornig werden" gebraucht sie λυπεῖν bzw. περίλυπος.

Solche Phänomene kennt der Jahwist, "der große Psychologe unter den biblischen Erzählern" (von Rad, S. 11). Dieses Wissen verbindet ihn mit der alten und der jungen Weisheitsliteratur, die immer wieder das menschliche Angesicht in seinen verschiedenen Aussagemöglichkeiten beobachtet und als Spiegel des Inneren erfaßt.[22] Solche Beobachtungen gehen auch in die erzählenden Texte ein,[23] und es verwundert nicht, wenn sie in der Grundfassung der Geschichte von Kain und Abel auftauchen, eben in V. 5.

Genau an dieser Stelle, wo nach weisheitlicher Erkenntnis Gefahr im Anzug ist, schaltet sich Jahwe mit seinen Fragen ein. Sie wollen, wie schon angedeutet, zur Selbstbesinnung anleiten, sind keine "echten" Fragen. Diese hätte Kain leicht beantworten können, und wir Modernen wären sicher gespannt darauf, was Jahwe dann geantwortet hätte — wir suchen ja auch Antwort auf die dunkle Frage, warum es den einen gelingt und die anderen bei gleichem oder gar größerem Bemühen auf der Schattenseite des Lebens stehen. Darauf kann der Jahwist so wenig antworten wie wir. Aber er weiß, daß das Gelingen der einen die anderen gefährdet, weil sie zu Taten provoziert werden, die die Gemeinschaft zerstören — bis hin zum Brudermord. In solcher Situation, die mit seinen Fragen anvisiert ist, hat er ein zurechtbringendes Wort zu sagen. Es gilt nicht nur Kain, sondern jedem Menschen in gleicher Gefährdung, denn die Geschichte von Kain und Abel ist ja beim Jahwisten Menschheitsüberlieferung geworden, "Kain" immer wieder Gegenwart. "Viele heißen Kain",[24] viele können sich wiederfinden in Jahwes fragender Anrede und vielen gilt die ihr folgende Erläuterung.

Leider ist ihr Text stellenweise verderbt. Die Verderbnis ist alt, da sie von der hebräischen LXX-Vorlage geteilt wird. Diese bringt dazu noch eine zusätzliche Variante ein: statt *lappātaḥ* liest sie *lntḥ*.[25] Sonstige scheinbare Abweichungen der LXX beruhen auf einem anderen Verständnis des unpunktierten Textes (*ḥṭ't* = du hast gesündigt: ἥμαρτες; *rbṣ* = sei ruhig: ἡσύχασον). Es folgt aus der

[22] Belege sind Prv. xv 13 (ein fröhliches Herz macht das Angesicht heiter), xxi 29 (ein böser Mann tritt mit einem frechen Gesicht auf), ferner Prv. vii 13; Qoh. vii 3 und viii 1. Stolz, S. 437, erinnert an Sir. xiii 25:
καρδία ἀνθρώπου ἀλλοιοῖ τὸ πρόσωπον αὐτοῦ

[23] Z.B. Gen. xl 7 und xxxi 5.

[24] Titel eines Fernsehspiels der ARD.

[25] Da im Althebräischen n und p u.U. ähnlich aussehen, könnte sie eine durch den Opferkontext nahegelegte, sehr frühe Verwechselung innerhalb der hebräischen LXX-Vorlage darstellen. Sie verrät, daß schon Tradenten alter Zeit mit der "Tür" nichts anfangen konnten. "Was soll hier eine Tür?" fragt Procksch, S. 47.

durch die zusätzliche Variante nahegelegten Deutung von V. 7a: "Hast du nicht gesündigt, wenn du recht opferst, aber (das Opfertier) [26] nicht recht zerteilst?" Die Variante läßt als t.t. der Opfersprache auch *ś't* auf die Darbringung des Opfers bezogen werden, indem es von *jṭb*/hi. abhängig gemacht wird.[27] War am Anfang der Erzählung von einem abgelehnten Opfer Kains die Rede, so wird hier gedeutet: es wurde rituell inkorrekt vollzogen.[28] Im Duktus unseres Textes muß diese und jede an sie angelehnte Deutung zweifellos ausscheiden. Der Jahwist ist nicht am Opfer interessiert, sondern an der Reaktion Kains, und deshalb kann die folgende Erläuterung nur mit ihr etwas zu tun haben. Dem ist entsprochen, wenn *ś't* hier auf die Wendung *nś' pānīm* anspielt, die "zunächst Ausdruck des guten Gewissens" ist.[29] Dann wäre *jṭb*/hi. — wie auch sonst in Texten, die vom weisheitlichen Denken bestimmt sind (Jes. i 17; Jer. iv 22) — im Sinne von "gut, recht handeln" absolut gebraucht. Der zu Mißverständnissen Anlaß gebende Infinitiv[30] dürfte, da eine Erläuterung klar sein muß, aus einem ursprünglichen *tiśśā'* entstanden sein.[31] Dann sagt Jahwe zu Kain und zu jedem Menschen in gleicher Gefährdung: "Nicht wahr, wenn du dabei bist, recht zu handeln, erhebst du dein Angesicht (= hast du ein gutes Gewissen)". Dann — so darf weiter paraphrasiert werden im Anschluß an V. 6 — trägst du nicht deine jetzige Miene zur Schau. Sie verrät, daß du im Begriff bist, nicht recht zu handeln!

Letztere Aussage wird in einem Bild gemacht: Wie "Frau Torheit" in Prv. ix 14 sitzt die Sünde vor der Tür ihres Hauses, um die Vorübergehenden herbeizulocken (Prv. ix 15). Allerdings ist von einem "Sitzen" in unserem Text gerade nicht die Rede: sie "liegt", "ruht" macht sich also — im Gegensatz zu Frau Torheit — gerade nicht bemerkbar. Die hier gebrauchte Vokabel *rbṣ* beschreibt vorzugsweise das Lagern von Tieren.[32] Ein Tier ist dabei ständig, auch wenn es

[26] Da Kain von den Früchten des Feldes opfert (V. 3), *ntḥ* als Objekt des Opfers aber nur Tiere kennt (Ex. xxix 17; Lev. i 6, 12, viii 20; 1 Kön. xviii 23, 33) kommt es als ernst zu nehmende varia lectio nicht in Betracht.

[27] ὀρθῶς als Umschreibung für *jṭb*/hi. bei folgendem Infinitiv, der dann konjugiertes Verb wird, erscheint auch Deut. v 28 und 1 Kön. xvi 7.

[28] Die LXX ist also mit ihrer hebräischen Vorlage der erste Interpret, der die Ablehnung des Opfers zu begründen versucht!

[29] So Stolz S. 112 unter Verweis auf 2 Sam. ii 22 und Hi. xi 15.

[30] Das zeigt die LXX-Fassung; *jṭb* kann den Infinitiv auch ohne *l*^e regieren: Jes. xxiii 16; Ps. xxxiii 3.

[31] So u.a. Gunkel, S. 43, und Procksch, S. 45. Der Fehler beruht auf Buchstabenverwechselung.

[32] Gen. xxix 2, xxxix 9, 14; Jes. xi 6f., xiii 21 u.ö.

fest zu schlafen scheint, ansprechbar auf Reize von außen. Menschen einer Welt, die mit Tieren mehr Umgang hatte als wir, haben das zweifellos beobachtet. Diese Beobachtung bringt der Jahwist mit ein, wenn er die Sünde ruhen läßt wie ein auf Reize eingestelltes Tier. Der Reiz, den sie empfängt, ist die Reaktion, die Gesichter wie das Kains widerspiegeln und die auf gefährliche Vorgänge im Innern hinweist. Dadurch wird ihr leidenschaftliches Verlangen geweckt, sich mit ihnen zu verbinden, ein Phänomen, das mit derselben Vokabel *t^e^šûqā* angezeigt wird, die in Gen. iii 16 erscheint.[33] Wie Frau Torheit, aber auch wie Frau Weisheit, wird die Sünde als Frau gesehen, was durch den Anklang an diese Stelle besonders deutlich wird.

Die vorgetragene Interpretation unseres Versteils ist mit mehreren Textänderungen durchgehend leichter Natur verbunden: die umstrittene "Tür" wird beibehalten; der bei einer personalen Sicht der "Sünde" erforderliche Artikel wird ergänzt (er fiel durch Haplographie fort); die unmögliche maskuline Form von *rbṣ* wird durch ein vorgestelltes t zu einer 3. Sing. Fem. Impf. (gleichfalls Haplographie; vgl. schon Dillmann, S. 94); das maskuline Suffixpronomen bei *t^e^šûqā* (wohl bedingt durch das maskulin oder als Substantiv verstandene *rbṣ*) muß durch das feminine ersetzt werden: "Wenn du aber dabei bist, nicht recht zu handeln, dann 'ruht' 'die' Sünde vor der Tür und auf dich geht 'ihr' Verlangen".

Aus einer solchen Erläuterung folgt zwingend die — abermals an Gen. iii 16 anspielende = Aufforderung, mit der der jahwistische Zusatz schließt: "Du aber herrsche über 'sie'!" (mit Änderung des Suffixpronomens). Gib ihrem Verlangen nicht nach, erweise dich als königlicher Herr über die Sünde![34]

Die Funktion des jahwistischen Zusatzes als *Belehrung* der Vielen, die Kain heißen, ist evident.[35] Sie legt nahe, daß die Kürzung von

[33] Immer wieder hat die vermeintliche Selbstzitierung, dazu noch mit anderer Akzentuierung, Anstoß erregt (bei Wellhausen, S. 10, beginnend). Mit Recht wendet sich Dietrich, S. 99, Anm. 24, dagegen.

[34] Rein grammatikalisch könnte *timšol* auch potential wiedergegeben werden, doch dienen Fragen und Erläuterung sicher nicht nur der unverbindlichen Feststellung "du kannst über sie Herrschen".

[35] Bemerkenswerterweise läuft auch die so anders einsetzende LXX-Wiedergabe auf eine Belehrung hinaus. Kain ist bekümmert (Anm. 21!) und hat die Fassung verloren, sein Gesicht hat gewissermaßen einen Kollaps bekommen (συμπίπτειν). In dieser Situation wird er — echt griechisch (Bekümmernis gehört zu den Affekten, die man möglichst eindämmen muß!) — zur Ruhe aufgefordert, dann werde sein Gesicht zurückkehren (ἀποστροφή beruht auf einem mißverstandenen *t^e^šuqā*!) und er werde darüber Herr sein (αὐτοῦ Kann sich grammatikalisch nur auf πρόσωπου beziehen).

Erzählelementen zugunsten der Reden gleichfalls belehrender Intention entspricht. Damit wird Dillmanns Beobachtung, nach der in der Geschichte von Kain und Abel "die lehrhafte Bearbeitung eines besonderen Stoffes" vorliege (S. 86) neu bestätigt. Aber sie ist *nicht von vornherein* ein "Lehrstück", sie wird es erst *durch die gestaltende Hand des Jahwisten*. Sie wird es in besonderer Weise durch die beiden Verse 6 und 7, die wir als seine Erweiterung bestimmen.

Zunächst muß beeindrucken, was sie einem Kain — und mit ihm dem Menschen schlechthin — an Erkenntnis und Handlungsfähigkeit zutrauen. Sie lassen ihn nicht in seinen Affekten stecken bleiben, die ihn dahin treiben, die Hand gegen den Bruder zu erheben. Sie decken deren Gefahren auf, um Kain auf seine großen, ja, "königlichen" Möglichkeiten anzusprechen: Kain kann nicht nur gegen die andringende Sünde "kämpfen" (so Dillmann, S. 94) — er kann sie sogar beherrschen (*mšl*!). Nicht nur Herr über die Schöpfung ist der Mensch (Ps. viii 6f.; Gen. i 26), er darf nach Gen. iv 6 auch Herr über die Sünde sein — fraglos eine tiefgründige jahwistische Interpretation dessen, was wir Menschenwürde nennen. Wenn Kain *nach* einer solchen Belehrung seinen Bruder erschlägt, so hat er — furchtbar genug — nicht nur Jahwes Wort verworfen. Er hat zugleich seine eigenen von Jahwe aufgezeigten Möglichkeiten mit Füßen getreten. Damit wird zwangsläufig auch seine Tat anders qualifiziert. Das Problem des doppeldeutigen *ʿāwōn* in V. 13 kann darauf hinweisen: meint es in der Urfassung die Folgen der Sünde, also die Sünden*strafe*, so gewinnt es durch die jahwistische Überarbeitung den Sinn von Sünden*schuld* und Kains Klage wird "ein Ausdruck dumpfer Verzweiflung" (Procksch, S. 49). Sie ist das Beste, das Kain noch bleibt. Sie wird Jahwe sein bewahrendes Zeichen entlocken, das dann eine ähnliche Funktion übernimmt wie die von Jahwe in iii 21 gefertigte Kleidung. Es zeigt an, daß Jahwe den schuldig Gewordenen nicht läßt und sogar "im Lande Flüchtig" Macht entfalten kann.

Genesis iii und iv erhalten durch die jahwistische Erweiterung in iv 6-7 ihre eigentliche Klammer: in beiden Kapiteln scheitert der Mensch an dem, was ihm von Jahwe zugetraut wird. Unsere Verse geben dabei zu verstehen: Jahwe kommt auch dann nicht zum Ziel, wenn er die Lehre der Weisheit einsetzt. Sie erreicht mit ihren Argumenten — hier wird der Jahwist eminent weisheitskritisch — nicht mehr als das undurchschaubare "von dem Baum der Erkenntnis des Guten und Bösen darfst du nicht essen" (Gen. ii 17). Sie *kann nicht* mehr erreichen, denn "das Gebilde des Menschenherzens ist doch böse von Jugend an" (Gen. viii 21; vgl. vi 5; übersetzt nach von Rad, S. 90). Zweifellos besteht zwischen unseren Versen in Gen. iv 6-7 und dem vom Jahwisten formulierten Rahmen der Sintflutgeschichte ein direkter Zusammenhang: dessen Aussage vom menschlichen Herzen wird in ihnen vorbereitet.

Hat es aber dann noch Zweck, einen so gesehenen Menschen auf sein Erkennen und Handeln anzusprechen? Kann Kain, kann der Mensch, der im Begriff ist, Unrecht zu tun und mit dem es so schlimm steht, überhaupt noch Belehrung annehmen? Ist sie nicht von vornherein zum Scheitern verurteilt, die jahwistische Erweiterung in Gen. iv 6 und 7 sinnlos?

Es ist das Gewaltige an dieser so dunkel anmutenden Sicht des Menschen, daß sie ihn gerade *nicht* auf Bosheit und Versagen festlegt, sondern ihm seine gottgeschenkten Möglichkeiten vor Augen stellt. Hierin präludiert der Jahwist die prophetische Verkündigung des Jesaja, der — gleichfalls von der Weisheit Israels herkommend — noch an *Mörder* appellieren kann: "Lernet Gutes tun!" (Jes. i 17; vgl. dazu i 15 und 21). Wenn angesichts der offenkundigen Realitäten ein solcher Appell überhaupt ergehen kann, so hat das ausschließlich etwas mit *Jahwe* zu tun, der Zukunft neu eröffnet. Eben das bekennt der Jahwist, wenn er *Jahwe* in unseren Versen reden läßt, ihn, der als Gott Kains der Gott Israels und zugleich der Menschheit Gott ist. Wo Jahwe sich in Erinnerung bringt, werden Chancen aufgedeckt für Menschen. Der Jahwist hat das als erster unüberhörbar bezeugt.

DIE PRIESTERSCHRIFT UND DIE GESCHICHTE

von

NORBERT LOHFINK
Frankfurt am Main

Peter Charlier zum Gedächtnis

Die jüdische Tradition bezeichnet die 5 ersten Bücher der Bibel als das "Gesetz". Dasselbe tut allerdings auch das Neue Testament.[1] Die christliche Tradition neigt dazu, diese Bücher eher den bei ihr dann folgenden "historischen Büchern" zuzuordnen.[2] Das tat allerdings auch schon Flavius Josephus, *Contra Apionem* 1, 8 (Niese 38-40). Hinter diesem Unterschied stehen tiefgreifende Verstehensdifferenzen. "Gesetz" deutet auf eine gegebene, bleibende, zu bewahrende Ordnung. "Geschichte" dagegen meint eine zwar hochbedeutsame, aber doch vergangene Entwicklung. Sie schließt nicht aus, daß nach ihr doch ganz andere, neue Entwicklungen kamen, und daß sie mit Recht kamen.

Unsere Wissenschaft muß fragen, wie der Pentateuch sich selbst verstanden habe. Diese Frage wird man vor allem an die sogenannte Priesterschrift stellen müssen. Denn sie ist die quantitativ umfangreichste, nach üblicher Auffassung die zeitlich letzte und sicher auch die alles am meisten prägende Schicht des Pentateuch.[3] In der Tat ist während der eigentlich produktiven Phase der Pentateuchforschung, nämlich im vorigen Jahrhundert, die Deutung der Priesterschrift

[1] Mt. v 12, 18, vii 12, xi 13, xii 5, xxii 36, 40, xxiii 23, usw.

[2] Der jüdischen Tradition fehlte eine Versuchung für so etwas, da die Bücher Jos. - 2 Kön. mit den eigentlichen Prophetenbüchern zusammen die eine Gruppe der "Propheten" bildeten. Eine Unterscheidung dieser Gruppe in "frühere" und "spätere" Propheten ist erst seit dem 8. Jh. n. Chr. bezeugt, vgl. O. Eißfeldt, *Einleitung in das Alte Testament* (Tübingen, ³1964), S. 766. "Historische Bücher" als Büchergruppe werden zuerst in der Septuaginta greifbar, die jedoch den Pentateuch als eigene, im strengen Sinn allein kanonische Größe gesehen zu haben scheint, vgl. E. Sellin - G. Fohrer, *Einleitung in das Alte Testament* (Heidelberg, ¹⁰1965), S. 537.

[3] Die Abgrenzung, die sich im allgemeinen durchgesetzt hat, geht auf Th. Nöldeke, *Untersuchungen zur Kritik des Alten Testaments* (Kiel, 1869), S. 1-144 ("Die sogenannte Grundschrift des Pentateuch"), zurück. Dort S. 143f. eine Übersicht.

weithin vom Gegensatzpaar "Gesetz — Geschichte" bestimmt gewesen, auch wenn die Wörter wechselten.

Als erster ist de Wette 1807 in seiner "Kritik der Mosaischen Geschichte"[4] der Frage genauer nachgegangen. Er entdeckte das Gesetz wie die Geschichte und entschied sich nicht. Einerseits sprach er vom "Epos der hebräischen Theokratie" (S. 31). In ihm habe ein "Dichter" die "Entstehung und Ausbildung des Volkes Gottes und seiner heiligen Verfassung" gesungen, so wie später "Virgil die Entstehung der heiligen Roma" (S. 32). Andererseits sei dieser Dichter aber vor allem auf eines aus gewesen: Er wollte aus der Geschichte "die theokratischen Gesetze deduciren" (S. 51).

Das labile Gleichgewicht der beiden Aspekte zerbrach in der Folgezeit zu entgegengesetzten Positionen. Als Beispiele, die hier in Göttingen besonders naheliegen, seien Ewald und Wellhausen eingeführt, Lehrer und Schüler.

H. Ewald widmete dem von ihm so genannten "Buch der Ursprünge" im 1. Band seiner siebenbändigen *Geschichte des Volkes Israel*[5] 32 zusammenhängende Seiten und kam auch in der Folge mehrfach darauf zurück. Er beobachtete zwar, daß "der verfasser nur dánn auch mit unverkennbar wärmster theilnahme des eigenen herzens und in aller ausführlichkeit erzählt, wenn er einen gesetzgeberischen zweck verfolgen und rechtliche oder sittliche bestimmungen ... im rahmen der erzählung erläutern kann" (S. 123). Aber der "hauptzweck" (S. 117) dieses "herrlichsten aller Hebräischen geschichtswerke" (S. 116) sei es doch, "den gesamten geschichtlichen stoff im weitesten umfange zu übersehen und bis in die letzten anfänge alles werdens zurückzuverfolgen", genau so, wie es "die Griechen nach den Persersiegen" taten (S. 117). Dieses Geschichtswerk wolle alles "unter den begriff des entstehens und werdens" bringen (S. 121). Es deute auch eine Sinngestalt der Geschichte an. Denn als Aufbauprinzip seiner Darstellung benutzte der Verfasser die bei vielen alten Völkern verbreitete Theorie von den 4 Weltaltern. Er gliedere die Geschichte ja nach Adam, Noach, Abraham und Mose. Was bei Hesiod Gold, Silber, Bronze und Eisen symbolisierten, wolle auch das "buch der ursprünge" aussagen. Es erzähle von einer "in den-

---

[4] Die folgenden Zitate sind aus: W. L. M. de Wette, *Kritik der Israelitischen Geschichte*, Erster Teil: Kritik der Mosaischen Geschichte = ders., *Beiträge zur Einleitung in das Alte Testament*, 2 (Halle, 1807).

[5] Im folgenden zitiert nach der 3. Ausgabe (Göttingen, 1864); die 1. Ausgabe erschien 1843.

selben stufen sich äußerlich immer weiter ausbreitenden und in künsten fortschreitenden, innerlich aber sich immer schneller aufreibenden menschheit" (S. 118).[6]

Diese Deutung des Lehrers klingt noch nach in dem Siglum Q (quatuor), das J. Wellhausen, der Schüler, einzuführen versuchte.[7] Er rechnete mit 4 Bundessetzungen Gottes bei Adam, Noach, Abraham und Mose, die das Werk gliedern.[8] Doch von absteigenden Weltaltern konnte bei Wellhausen keine Rede mehr sein. Vielmehr komme der "Priestercodex" — wie er jetzt sagt — erst "mit der mosaischen Gesetzgebung in sein eigentliches Fahrwasser und erdrückt alsbald die Erzählung durch die Last des legislativen Stoffes" (S. 362). Auch alles, was vorher erzählt wurde, sei "legislativen Zwecken untergeordnet" (S. 361). Das "Gesetz" sei "der Schlüssel zum Verständnis auch der Erzählung des Priestercodex" (S. 383). In einem Wort: "Historisch ist nur die Form, sie dient dem gesetzlichen Stoff als Rahmen um ihn anzuordnen, oder als Maske, um ihn zu verkleiden" (S. 7).

Später hat man zwischen den Extremen zu vermitteln versucht, etwa durch den häufigen Gebrauch von Kuenens Formel von der "historisch-legislativen Schrift".[9] Die meisten von uns haben sich wohl schon eine Formel wie die von G. von Rad zu eigen gemacht, der als den Gegenstand der priesterlichen Geschichtserzählung "das Herauswachsen bestimmter kultischer Institutionen aus der Geschichte" bezeichnet hat.[10] Bei einer solchen Auffassung ist die erzählte Geschichte sicher mehr als nur "Rahmen" oder gar "Maske". Aber letztlich wird sie doch nur in "ätiologischer Absicht" erzählt, als "historische

---

[6] Ausführlicher dazu noch S. 368-73.

[7] "Die Composition des Hexateuchs", *Jahrbücher für Deutsche Theologie* 21 (1876), S. 392: "Abkürzung für Vierbundesbuch (quatuor), welchen Namen ich als den passendsten für sie vorschlage".

[8] *Geschichte Israels* 1 (Berlin, 1878), S. 356-60 = ders., *Prolegomena zur Geschichte Israels* (*Zweite Ausgabe der Geschichte Israels, Band I*) (Berlin, 1883), S. 358-61 (hiernach wird im folgenden zitiert). Das Siglum Q hat sich nicht durchgesetzt. Vgl. A. Kuenen, *Historisch-kritische Einleitung in die Bücher des alten Testaments hinsichtlich ihrer Entstehung und Sammlung* I, 1 (Leipzig, 1887), S. 62: "G I, 28-30 ist eigentlich kein Bündnis, sondern ein Segensspruch".

[9] Kuenen, *Einleitung* (wie Anm. 8), S. 78, und öfter. Am deutlichsten wird das vermittelnde Ausgleichen im Rahmen der Wellhausenschule vielleicht bei H. Holzinger, *Einleitung in den Hexateuch* (Freiburg i.B., 1893). Er nennt P eine "legislative Schrift in historischer Form und mit historischer Substruktur" (S. 335).

[10] *Theologie des Alten Testaments* 1 (München, 1957), S. 232. Vgl. ebd. S. 233: "P will allen Ernstes zeigen, daß der im Volke Israel historisch gewordene Kultus das Ziel der Weltentstehung und Weltentwicklung ist".

Legitimierung" eines späteren Israel.[11] So dürfte, selbst wenn wir keine Bedenken haben, zugleich von der priesterlichen Darstellung der "Heilsgeschichte"[12] zu reden, im ganzen doch seit Wellhausen das "Gesetz" den Sieg davongetragen haben. Das bedeutet aber, um in heute gängigere Kategorien zu springen: Wir tragen die Meinung mit uns herum, die Priesterschrift habe zwar auf die Geschichte zurückgegriffen, aber nur zu dem Zweck, die zu ihrer Zeit etablierten gesellschaftlichen Verhältnisse durch narrative Legitimation zu stabilisieren.[13] Sie wäre also fortschrittsfeindlich und gegen gesellschaftliche Veränderung.

Ich habe im folgenden nicht vor, innerhalb der so skizzierten klassischen Fragestellung einfach eine der in ihr vorgegebenen möglichen Positionen zu beziehen und neu zu begründen. Die Betrachtung läßt sich heute differenzieren. Es gibt inzwischen neue Fakten, Beobachtungen, Fragestellungen und Gesichtspunkte zum Thema "Priesterschrift und Geschichte". Die gilt es aufzuarbeiten und neu zu ordnen. Allerdings werde ich am Ende, wenn auch von neuen Gesichtspunkten aus, doch wieder notwendigerweise auf die klassische Fragestellung zurückkommen müssen.

Zunächst einmal sei auf einiges hingewiesen, was in den letzten Jahrzehnten die klassische Betrachtungsweise differenziert oder gar gesprengt hat. Die Aufzählung nennt nur das Wichtigste.

1. Die Unterscheidung zwischen einer eigentlichen priesterlichen Geschichtserzählung und dem restlichen, vor allem legislativen Material existiert zwar seit Wellhausen.[14] Aber eigentlich hat erst

---

[11] G. von Rad, *Die Priesterschrift im Hexateuch* (Stuttgart - Berlin, 1934), S. 187f.

[12] Wahllos herausgegriffenes Beispiel: J. Scharbert, "Der Sinn der Toledot-Formel in der Priesterschrift", in H. J. Stoebe u.a., *Wort - Gebot - Glaube* = Festschrift W. Eichrodt, (Zürich, 1970), S. 76, spricht für P von der "Heilsgeschichte, in welcher Segen und Verheißung von Zeit zu Zeit verdichtet werden, bis im hierarchisch gegliederten Gottesvolk sich die Gottesherrschaft Jahwes manifestiert".

[13] Dies gilt auch, wo man heute in der Nachfolge von Y. Kaufmann die Priesterschrift als vorexilisch betrachtet. Vgl. M. Weinfeld, "Pentateuch", in *Encyclopaedia Judaica* 13 (Jerusalem, 1971), S. 235: "The priestly material in Genesis serves only the priestly and sacred purpose of emphasizing the basis for the sanctity of Israel and its institutions".

[14] Wellhausen unterschied sowohl in der *Composition* (wie Anm. 7) als auch in den *Prolegomena* (wie Anm. 8) zwischen Q und RQ. Da ihm eine von den Gesetzen unabhängige Datierung von Q aber nicht leicht fiel, rückte er in den *Prolegomena* die beiden Größen doch wieder sehr zusammen. In der *Composition*, S. 455f., faßte er seine Analyse des "Priestercodex" so zusammen: "Sein Kern

M. Noth 1948 in seiner *Überlieferungsgeschichte des Pentateuch* (Stuttgart, 1948), unter wirklichem Absehen von P^s nach der Theologie von P^g gefragt.[15] Es ist von der Sache her aber unbedingt erforderlich, die Frage mindestens in einem ersten Schritt auf P^g einzuengen. Die Fixierung auf die Spannung "Gesetz — Geschichte" könnte ja gerade durch die Kombination von P^g mit P^s bedingt sein.[16]

2. Im gleichen Werk hat Noth die Ansicht geäußert, bei der Kultordnung Israels (deren Darstellung in der Sinaiperikope er weiterhin als das eigentliche Zentrum von P^g betrachtete) handele es sich eher

---

ist Q, aber dieser Kern hat sich vielfach erweitert, gewissermaßen in organischer und hypertrophischer Weise, sofern die Erweiterungen überall an den Kern anknüpfen und dorther ihre Tendenzen, Vorstellungen, Formeln und Manieren haben. Es ist der gleiche Boden des Zeitalters und der Kreise, woraus Q und die sekundären und tertiären Nachwüchse hervorgegangen sind".

[15] S. 7-9 (hier spricht er sogar einem großen Teil des legislativen Materials das Recht auf ein Siglum P^s ab) und 259-67. Natürlich haben Autoren wie Holzinger (*Einleitung*, wie Anm. 9) darauf geachtet, die in P^g "hervortretenden allgemeinen Anschauungen" vorgängig zur "Gesetzgebung" und zu den "sekundären Bestandteilen" von P zu untersuchen. Aber man hat nicht den Eindruck, daß sich das sehr ausgewirkt hat. G. von Rad, *Priesterschrift* (wie Anm. 11), S. 188, meinte sogar, der legitimierende Zusammenhang zwischen Geschichte und Gesetz trete in P deutlicher hervor als in P^s.

[16] Darauf weist K. Elliger, "Geschichtserzählung" (wie Anm. 19), S. 129, hin. Natürlich hängt einiges davon ab, wieviel man bei einer Unterscheidung von P^g und P^s auch P^g noch an "Gesetz" läßt. Noth ist in dieser Hinsicht in den mittleren Büchern des Pentateuch sicher radikaler gewesen als seine Vorgänger. Doch vielleicht muß man sogar noch radikaler als Noth sein, vor allem für den Bereich zwischen Gen. i und Ex. xiv. Vgl. für Gen. ix 4-6 S. E. McEvenue, *The Narrative Style of the Priestly Writer* (Rom, 1971), S. 68-71; für Gen. xvii 14 P. Grelot, "La dernière étape de la rédaction sacerdotale", *VT* 7 (1957), S. 176f. und 188; für Ex. xii 1-14 J. L. Ska, "Les plaies d'Égypte dans le récit sacerdotal (Pg), et la tradition prophétique" (erscheint demnächst), Excursus: "Ex 12, 1-14. 28 fait-il partie de Pg?" (negative Antwort). Dann bleibt an "Gesetzlichem" vor den Offenbarungen in der Wüste eigentlich nur noch die im Schöpfungstext begonnene Sabbatthematik, die aber erst in der Sinaiperikope ihren Höhepunkt erreicht, und die Beschneidung, die aber in die Thematik des Berit-Zeichens hineingenommen und insofern nicht selbständiges Thema ist. Zum Sabbat vgl. N. Negretti, *Il settimo giorno, Indagine critico-teologica delle tradizioni presacerdotali e sacerdotali circa il sabato biblico* (Rom, 1973), S. 147-251; N. Lohfink, "Die Sabbatruhe und die Freizeit", *Stimmen der Zeit* 194 (1976), S. 395-407; für die Sabbatstruktur der Sinaiperikope ferner: M. Oliva, "Interpretación teológica del culto en la perícopa del Sinaí de la Historia Sacerdotal", *Biblica* 49 (1968), S. 345-54. Erst in P^s gibt es den Sabbat als Gesetz, vgl. Negretti, ebd., S. 252-306. Zur Beschneidung in Gen. xvii aus letzter Zeit: E. Kutsch, "Ich will euer Gott sein", *ZThK* 71 (1974), S. 361-88; M. V. Fox, "The Sign of the Covenant", *RB* 81 (1974), S. 557-96; C. Westermann, "Gen 17 und die Bedeutung von berit", *ThLZ* 101 (1976), S. 161-70; W. Groß, "Berit in der Priesterschrift" (erscheint demnächst in der *Trierer Theologischen Zeitschrift*).

um eine "ideale" Kultordnung, um ein "Zukunftsprogramm".[17] Auf diese Weise zeigte er die Möglichkeit, eine literarische Verbindung von Geschichte und Gesetz als Ausdruck einer systemverändernden und nicht -stabilisierenden Tendenz zu sehen.[18]

3. Während Noth noch bei der traditionellen Meinung blieb, die priesterliche Erzählung erreiche "ihr eigentliches Ziel" mit der Darstellung "der am Sinai eingesetzten Ordnungen" (*Überlieferungsgeschichte* S. 8) hat K. Elliger in seinem Aufsatz "Sinn und Ursprung der priesterlichen Geschichtserzählung" ein nicht leicht zu widerlegendes Plädoyer dafür gehalten, daß das eigentliche Thema von P^g trotz der Breite, die die Sinaiperikope erreicht, gar nicht der Kult oder die Kultgemeinde, sondern das Land Kanaan sei. Der "Inbegriff der göttlichen Geschichtslenkung" sei "der Besitz des Landes Kanaan als der materiellen und ideellen Basis, auf der das Leben des Volkes und selbstverständlich der Kultus als wichtigste Funktion sich erst richtig entfalten kann".[19] Diese These ist umso überzeugender, als

---

[17] Noth, *Überlieferungsgeschichte* (wie Anm. 15), S. 260 und 263. Übersicht über Autoren, die in der Nachfolge Noths nicht mehr die nachexilische Gemeinde als Vorgegebenheit von P^g annehmen, bei W. Wood, *The Congregation of Yahweh: A Study of the Theology and Purpose of the Priestly Document*, Dissertation, Union Theological Seminary, Richmond, Virginia (1974), S. 30-39. Die Loslösung des "Priesterkodex" vom nachexilischen Tempel hat lange vor Noth jedoch schon Y. Kaufmann vollzogen, vgl. als erste Veröffentlichung J. Kaufmann, "Probleme der israelitisch-jüdischen Religionsgeschichte", *ZAW* 48 (1930), S. 42: "Mit der Wirklichkeit der nachexilischen Zeit aber hat das Werk des P gar nichts zu tun".

[18] Noth selbst gelangt am Ende zu der Theorie, P^g habe jedes eigene Interesse an Geschichte gefehlt. P^g wolle die "kultische Priestertradition" vom "Wohnen und von der Gegenwart Gottes im Tempel" durch das "numinose Element des Sinaigottes", der "nur erscheint", "ergänzen und korrigieren". Nur weil die Sinaitradition allein innerhalb des "großen Erzählungsganzen" der alten Pentateuchquellen gegeben war, sei der Verfasser dazu gezwungen gewesen, daß er "eine summarische Rekapitulation des ganzen alten Pentateuchstoffes aufbot" (*Überlieferungsgeschichte*, S. 266f.). Das ist wohl nichts anderes als Wellhausens "Rahmen" und "Maske", nur nicht mehr zugunsten des Gesetzes, sondern zugunsten einer bestimmten Theorie von Gottes Gegenwart, die propagiert werden soll. Es wird wohl kaum der großen Mühe gerecht, die P^g dann doch auf die "summarische Rekapitulation" der Pentateucherzählung gewandt hat, und auch nicht dem vorher gefallenen Wort vom "Zukunftsprogramm".

[19] *ZThK* 49 (1952), S. 129. Ähnlich dann vor allem R. Kilian, "Die Hoffnung auf Heimkehr in der Priesterschrift", *Bibel und Leben* 7 (1966), S. 39-51; E. Cortese, *La terra di Canaan nella storia sacerdotale del Pentateuco* (Brescia, 1972). Nach der Zusammenfassung von P. Diepold, *Israels Land* (Stuttgart, 1972), S. 7f., scheint G. D. Macholz, *Israel und das Land*, Diss. habil., Heidelberg (1969), eine Tendenz von P anzunehmen, Israels Existenz von seiner Bindung an das Land Kanaan zu lösen.

Elliger noch Noths literarkritische Annahme voraussetzt, P^g habe mit Moses Tod geendet und den Einzug ins Land nicht mehr dargestellt — eine meines Erachtens nicht notwendige Voraussetzung.[20] Im Gegensatz zum Kult, den P^g nur für Israel kennt, ist das Wohnen im eigenen Land etwas, was allen Völkern zukommt. Damit ist die Urgeschichte, die von allen Völkern handelt, wieder stärker in die Frage nach der Thematik von P^g hineingezogen — sie könnte mehr als bloßes Vorspiel sein.[21]

4. Durch Elligers These wird zugleich etwas anderes neu konkretisierbar, was eigentlich schon seit de Wette klar ist: In P^g machen Auswahl des Stoffs und Technik der Darstellung das Erzählte ständig "transparent" auf die angezielten Leser und ihre Situation; sie wollen das Denken des Lesers "auf Hintergründe lenken".[22] Elliger rechnete dabei mit Lesern im babylonischen Exil. Vielleicht ließe sich die Transparenz des priesterschriftlichen Erzählens noch besser aufweisen, wenn man auch die Bezüge des Textes zur exilischen und frühnachexilischen Prophetenliteratur, besonders zum Buch Ezechiel, mitberücksichtigte.[23] Auf jeden Fall tritt hier die Möglichkeit eines Geschichtsdenkens hervor, dem es vielleicht gar nicht mehr auf die kausale oder finale Zuordnung verschiedener Ereignisse auf der Linie der Zeit ankam, sondern auf so etwas wie in der Vergangenheit

---

[20] Näheres unten, Anm. 30.

[21] W. Brueggemann, "The Kerygma of the Priestly Writers", *ZAW* 84 (1972), S. 397-413, sieht ganz ähnlich wie Elliger als Botschaft von P, "that the promise of the land of blessing still endures and will be realized soon" (S. 41). Dagegen sucht er den Schlüssel dafür am Anfang von P, speziell in Gen. i 28. Von anderen Ausgangspunkten her kommt auch J. Blenkinsopp, "The Structure of P", *CBQ* 38 (1976), S. 276-92, zu einer viel engeren Verbindung von Urgeschichte und Geschichte Israels in P, als man gewöhnlich sieht. Vgl. dazu ferner L. Dequeker, "Noah and Israel", in: C. Brekelmans, *Questions disputées d'Ancien Testament* (Gembloux, 1974), S. 115-29.

[22] "Geschichtserzählung" (wie Anm. 19), S. 189. De Wette deutete diesen Sachverhalt dadurch an, daß er konstant von "Mythe", "Poesie" und "Epos" sprach. Für Wellhausen war es selbstverständlich, "daß auf die priesterliche Gestaltung der Erzvätersage die Verhältnisse des babylonischen Exils eingewirkt haben"; trotz "allem archaistischen Schein" gelange "die Gegenwart des Erzählers auch positiv in der Schilderung der Patriarchenzeit zum Ausdrucke" — so *Prolegomena*, S. 362. Doch steht bei den älteren Autoren der Gedanke des genaue Nachrichtenvermittlung verhindernden Einflusses der Abfassungszeit im Vordergrund, weniger der Gedanke einer kerygmatischen Intention des Verfassers.

[23] A. Eitz, *Studien zum Verhältnis von Priesterschrift und Deuterojesaja*, Dissertation, Heidelberg (1969), schöpft ihr Thema nicht aus. Wichtig wäre vor allem eine umfassende Untersuchung des Verhältnisses von P^g zum Ezechielbuch. Sie fehlt noch.

hervortretende paradigmatische Grundkonstellationen, die Bedeutung für die Gegenwart haben können.

5. In diesem Zusammenhang darf nicht unerwähnt bleiben, daß McEvenues Studie *The Narrative Style of the Priestly Writer* endlich eine beschämende Lücke ausgefüllt hat und uns überhaupt erst richtig in die Lage versetzt, die schriftstellerische Technik von P^g zu verfolgen und so den einzelnen Beobachtungen ihren Stellenwert im ganzen zu geben.[24] Dies gilt unbeschadet der Skepsis, die man gegenüber der Vermutung haben kann, es handle sich um so etwas wie israelitische Kinderliteratur.[25]

6. Eine höchstbedeutsame Parallele zumindest zur priesterlichen Urgeschichte, der Atraḫasīs-Mythus, ist, obwohl zu einem kleinen Teil schon lange bekannt, erst vor einigen Jahren in größerem Umfang zugänglich geworden.[26] Für die Interpretation von P^g scheint er mir noch nicht genügend zur Kenntnis genommen zu sein.[27]

7. In neuester Zeit mehren sich die Versuche, in den erzählenden priesterschriftlichen Texten nicht eine ursprünglich selbständige Schrift, sondern nur kommentierende und umdeutende Ergänzungen zu den älteren Pentateuchmaterialien zu sehen, oder auch die Hand

[24] Wie Anm. 16; ders., "Word and Fulfilment: A Stylistic Feature of the Priestly Writer", *Semitics* 1 (1970), S. 104-10; ders., "The Style of a Building Instruction" (noch unveröffentlicht). Vorher liegt noch eine unveröffentlichte Heidelberger Dissertation: R. Borchert, *Stil und Aufbau der Priesterschriftlichen Erzählung* (1956).

[25] Am deutlichsten ausgesprochen in "Building Instruction": "a document for the children of the exiles who were not to be allowed to become assimilated in Babylon". So schlagend die Ähnlichkeit des Stils zwischen P^g und moderner Kinderliteratur für Vorschulkinder ist und so wertvoll diese Beobachtung für unsere Einfühlung in die hinter der Sprache von P^g stehende Sichtweise werden kann, so offen bleibt doch die Frage nach Herkunft, Vorgeschichte und Funktion dieses Stils in der Priesterlichen Literatur. Eigentliche Kinderliteratur ist bisher nur als neuzeitliches Phänomen bekannt.

[26] W. G. Lambert und A. R. Millard, *Atra-Ḫasīs, The Babylonian Story of the Flood* (Oxford, 1969). Besprechungsartikel dazu: W. L. Moran, "Atrahasis: The Babylonian Story of the Flood", *Biblica* 52 (1971), S. 51-61. Weitere Literatur: vgl. die jährliche "Keilschriftbibliographie" der Zeitschrift *Orientalia*.

[27] Vergleiche mit biblischen Texten ignorieren entweder die Existenz von literarischen Schichten im Pentateuch, wie z.B. A. R. Millard, "A New Babylonian 'Genesis' Story", *Tyndale Bulletin* 18 (1967), S. 3-18; I. M. Kikawada, "Literary Convention of the Primaeval History", *Annual of the Japanese Biblical Institute* 1 (1975), S. 3-21 (Literatur!), oder konzentrieren sich auf nichtpriesterliche Stellen, wie z.B. ders., "Two Notes on Eve", *JBL* 91 (1972), S. 33-7. Für Vergleiche mit P^g weiß ich nur zu nennen N. Lohfink, "Die Priesterschrift und die Grenzen des Wachstums", *Stimmen der Zeit* 192 (1974), S. 435-50; ders., "Sabbatruhe" (wie Anm. 16); Blenkinsopp, "Structure" (wie Anm. 21), S. 282.

der eigentlichen Pentateuchredaktion.[28] Sie haben mich bisher nicht überzeugen können. Doch scheinen sie mir mindestens eines deutlicher bewußt zu machen: Auch eine ursprünglich selbständige priesterliche Geschichtserzählung darf vielleicht nicht einfach als unabhängige Paralleltradition zu den anderen, älteren Pentateuchtraditionen betrachtet werden; vielmehr ist sie vielleicht als bewußt Bezug nehmende und bewußt sich absetzende Neukonzeption zu betrachten. Ein solcher intentionaler Bezug auf die "alten Quellen" fordert allerdings nicht notwendig eine Ergänzungstheorie, sondern ist auch für eine selbständige Schrift denkbar, wenn die "alten Quellen" dem Verfasser und den Lesern nur bekannt waren.

Wenn ich von diesen und vielen anderen, nicht genannten Neuansätzen der letzten Zeit her Anregungen aufgreife, so möchte ich mich im folgenden doch nicht an eine bestimmte Position anhängen und von ihr aus weiterdenken, sondern die Sachfragen selbst sollen neu gestellt werden. Bevor ich damit beginne, schulde ich aber

[28] Als erster hat auch für die erzählenden Teile der Priesterschrift K. H. Graf in der letzten Wendung, die er seiner Theorie über die Abfolge der Pentateuchschichten gab, diese Sicht geäußert: es handle sich um eine Serie von "später zu dem 'jahwistischen' Werk hinzugekommenen Zusätzen". So in "Die s.g. Grundschrift des Pentateuchs", in A. Merx, *Archiv für die wissenschaftliche Erforschung des Alten Testaments* 1 (Halle, 1869), S. 474. Wellhausen setzte aber dann die Theorie von einer ursprünglich selbständigen priesterlichen Geschichtserzählung durch. Auf Grafs Linie, wenn auch meist ohne Kenntnis dieses Vorläufers, sind folgende Namen zu nennen: S. Maybaum, *Die Entwicklung des altisraelitischen Priesterthums* (1880), S. 107ff. (mir nicht zugänglich); B. D. Eerdmans, *Alttestamentliche Studien* I-IV (Gießen, 1908-1912); ders., "Ezra and the Priestly Code", *Expositor* 7. ser., 10 (1910), S. 306-26; R. H. Pfeiffer, "A Non-Israelite Source of the Book of Genesis", *ZAW* 48 (1930), S. 66-73; ders., *Introduction to the Old Testament* (New York, 1942); P. Volz, "P ist kein Erzähler", in P. Volz und W. Rudolph, *Der Elohist als Erzähler, ein Irrweg der Pentateuchkritik?*, *BZAW* 63 (Gießen, 1933), S. 135-42. Bisweilen wird in diesem Zusammenhang auch M. Löhr, *Untersuchungen zum Hexateuchproblem, I, Der Priesterkodex in der Genesis*, *BZAW* 38 (Gießen, 1924), genannt. Aber Löhr sieht in P eher den Redaktor vieler Einzeltraditionen (= Ezra), hält also eine Art Fragmentenhypothese. Als Endredaktor des Pentateuch wird P auch von I. Engnell gesehen. Die neueren, hier zu nennenden Autoren sind: F. M. Cross, "The Tabernacle: A Study from an Archaeological Approach", *BA* 10 (1947), S. 57f.; ders., *Canaanite Myth and Hebrew Epic* (Cambridge, Mass., 1973), S. 293-325; R. Rendtorff, "Der 'Jahwist' als Theologe? Zum Dilemma der Pentateuchkritik", in *Congress Volume Edinburgh 1974*, *SVT* 28 (Leiden, 1975), S. 158-66; ders., *Das überlieferungsgeschichtliche Problem des Pentateuch*, *BZAW* 147 (Berlin, 1977), S. 130-42 und 160-63; J. Van Seters, *Abraham in History and Tradition* (New Haven, Conn., 1975), S. 279; Blenkinsopp, "Structure" (wie Anm. 21), S. 280. Zur ganzen neuesten Diskussion um die Pentateuchquellen vgl. Issue 3 (July 1977), des *Journal for the Study of the Old Testament* mit verschiedenen Beiträgen.

wenigstens eine kurze Rechenschaft über meine literaturgeschichtlichen Annahmen, die ich notgedrungen hier einfach voraussetzen muß.

Ich gehe also davon aus, daß man im Hexateuch innerhalb des priesterschriftlichen Materials (P) eine fast vollständig erhaltene priesterliche Geschichtserzählung (P^g) abheben kann.[29] Sie reicht — gegen Wellhausen und Noth — mit ihren letzten Sätzen noch ins Buch Josua hinein.[30] Sie wurde ursprünglich als selbständige Schrift

[29] Gen. i 1 - ii 4a; v 1-27, 28*, 30-32; vi 9-22; vii 6, 11, 13-16a, 17a, 18-21, 24; viii 1, 2a, 3b-5, 13a, 14-19; ix 1-3, 7-17; 28f.; x 1-7, 20, 22f., 31f.; xi 10-27, 31f.; xii 4b, 5; xiii 6, 11b, 12*; xvi 1, 3, 15f.; xvii 1-13, 14*, 15-27; xix 29; xxi 1b-5; xxiii 1-20; xxv 7-11a, 12-17 ... 26b; xxvi 34f.; xxvii 46 - xxviii 9; ... xxxi 18*; xxxiii 18a; xxxv 6a, 9-15, 22b-29; xxxvi 1, 2a ... 6-8, 40-43; xxxvii 1f.; xli 46a; xlvi 6f.; xlvii 27b, 28; xlviii 3-6; xlix 1a, 28b-33; l 12f.; Ex. i 1-5, 7, 13f.; ii 23*, 24f.; vi 2-12; vii 1-13, 19, 20*, 21b, 22; viii 1-3 ... 11*, 12-15; ix 8-12; xi 9f.; xii 37a, 40-42; xiii 20; xiv 1-4, 8f., 10*, 15-18, 21*, 22f., 26, 27*, 28f.; xv 22*, 27; xvi 1-3, 6f., 9-12, 13* ... 14* ... 16*, 17, 18*, 19-21a, 22*, 23-26, 31a, 35b; xvii 1*; xix 1, 2a; xxiv 15b-18a; xxv 1-2, 8, 9*; xxvi 1-30; xxix 43-46; ... xxxi 18; xxxiv 29-32; xxxv 4, 5a, 10, 20-22a, 29; xxxvi 2-3a, 8*; xxxix 32-33a, 42f.; xl 17, 33b-35; Lev. ix 1*, 2f., 4b-7, 8*, 12a, 15a, 21b-24; Num. i 1, 2*, 3*, 19b, 21*, 23*, 25*, 27*, 29*, 31*, 33*, 35*, 37*, 39*, 41*, 43*, 46; ii 1*, 2, 3*, 5*, 7a, 10a, 12*, 14a, 18a, 20a, 22a, 25a, 27*, 29a, 34; iv 1* ... 2*, 3, 34*, 35f., 37*, 38-40, 41*, 42-44, 45*, 46*, 47f.; x 11-13; xii 16b; xiii 1-3a, 17*, 21, 25, 26*, 32; xiv 1a, 2, 5-7, 10, 26-28, 29*, 35-38; ... xx 1* ... 2, 3b-7, 8*, 10, 11b, 12* ... 22b ... 23*, 25-29; xxi 4*, 10f.; xxii 1; xxvii 12-14a, 15-23; xxxiv 1-18; Dtn. i 3; xxxii 48-52; xxxiv 1* ... 7-9; ... Jos. iv 19*; v 10-12; xiv 1, 2*; xviii 1; ... xix 51. Diese Abgrenzung ist aus der von Elliger entwickelt, mit der ich ursprünglich gearbeitet hatte. Vgl. Elliger, "Geschichtserzählung" (wie Anm. 19), S. 121f. Die Veränderungen gegenüber Elliger stützen sich z.T. auf eigene Beobachtungen und ältere Kommentare, z.T. auf folgende neuere Literatur: Blenkinsopp, "Structure" (wie Anm. 21), S. 249, Anm. 16, und S. 290f.; Cortese, *Canaan* (wie Anm. 19), S. 41-51; W. Groß, "Jakob, der Mann des Segens", *Biblica* 49 (1968), S. 335-7; D. Kellermann, *Die Priesterschrift von Numeri 1,1 bis 10,10 literarkritisch und traditionsgeschichtlich untersucht*, *BZAW* 120 (Berlin, 1970); S. McEvenue, "A Source-Critical Problem in Nm 14, 26-38", *Biblica* 50 (1969), S. 453-65; Negretti, *Settimo giorno* (wie Anm. 16), S. 173-9; ferner die in Anm. 16 genannten Arbeiten von Grelot, McEvenue und Ska. Man kann, wie schon Wellhausen oder in neuerer Zeit G. von Rad, W. Groß, P. Weimar und andere, mit Grund fragen, ob sich noch Vorstadien oder von P^g eingebaute Materialien erkennen lassen. An der Möglichkeit, Genaueres zu rekonstruieren, zweifle ich. Die folgenden Überlegungen fragen grundsätzlich nicht hinter die in dieser Anmerkung abgegrenzte Größe P^g zurück.

[30] Schon Wellhausen vertrat die Ansicht, P^g sei in Jos. nicht nachzuweisen, allerdings erst in *Prolegomena*, S. 379f., noch nicht in früheren Veröffentlichungen. Doch hat sich die Ansicht nicht durchgesetzt. Noth kam im Zusammenhang seiner Auffassung vom Deuteronomistischen Geschichtswerk zur gleichen Annahme. Vgl. vor allem *Überlieferungsgeschichtliche Studien* (Tübingen, ²1957), S. 182-90; ders., "Überlieferungsgeschichtliches zur zweiten Hälfte des Josuabuches", in *Alttestamentliche Studien F. Nötscher zum 60. Geburtstag gewidmet* (Bonn, 1950), S. 152-67. Alles, was in Jos. im Stil von P auftritt (irgendwelche

verfaßt, obwohl das, was ich im folgenden ausführe, sich mindestens teilweise auch bei einer Ergänzungs- oder Redaktionshypothese vertreten ließe.[31] Der Verfasser des Werks kannte nicht nur selbst

---

Listen gehörten sowieso nicht dazu), seien untereinander nicht zu verbindende Zusätze zu meist schon sekundär-deuteronomistischen Texten aus später Zeit. Aber selbst wenn man Noth in der Beurteilung des Listenmaterials folgt, bleibt die Frage, ob man schon deshalb kaum mit P^g rechnen könne, weil sich keine priesterliche Landeroberungserzählung nachweisen läßt. Wäre eine solche wirklich zu erwarten? McEvenue, *Narrative Style* (wie Anm. 16), S. 117-23, hat gezeigt, daß P^g aus der traditionell kriegerischen Kundschaftererzählung alle militärischen Aspekte entfernt hat. Nach A. Kuschke, "Die Lagervorstellung der priesterschriftlichen Erzählung", *ZAW* 63 (1951), S. 99f., ist auch das Lager Israels jedes militärischen Charakters entkleidet. In ganz P^g treten nur die Ägypter militärisch auf, aber selbst sie werden nicht in einem Krieg überwunden. P^g ist, wenn der Ausdruck erlaubt ist, "pazifistisch". P^g kann jedenfalls bei der Einwanderung in Kanaan genau so knapp gewesen sein wie beim Auszug aus Ägypten in Ex. xii 40-42. Man muß ferner auch nicht von der Erwartung ausgehen, P^g habe in Jos. in ähnlicher Weise wie vorher im Pentateuch die Basis der Redaktionsarbeit abgegeben und müsse daher in Jos. ähnlich lückenlos wie dort bewahrt sein, vgl. S. Mowinckel, *Tetrateuch - Pentateuch - Hexateuch*, *BZAW* 90 (Berlin, 1964), S. 51. So ist die angemessene Fragestellung nur die, ob die wenigen Texte im Stil von P, die sich mit Sicherheit in Jos. finden und vom Erzählungssystem von Jos. aus alle als nachträgliche Eintragungen betrachtet werden können, wirklich ihren jetzigen Kontext notwendig voraussetzen und — wenn nicht — wie weit sie vielleicht vom erzählerischen System von P^g her erwartet werden müssen. In der Tat ist Jos. xviii 1a als Hinweis auf den Ort, wo im Land das Heiligtum aufgeschlagen wurde, zu erwarten, und xviii 1b liefert die noch ausstehende Erfüllungsnotiz zu Gen. i 28 (dazu Näheres unten in Teil II!). Zu Jos. xiv 1 und xix 51 vgl. Num. xxxiv 16 (das Noth zu Unrecht P^g abspricht). Sind diese Verse für P^g wahrscheinlich gemacht, dann sind Notizen wie Jos. iv 19* und 5, 10-12 zu erwarten. Und schließlich wäre vielleicht doch zu überprüfen, ob nicht doch auch in den Listen einiges aus P^g erhalten ist. Doch muß das nicht sein, und selbst mit Listen dürfte der Schluß von P^g nach dem Tod Moses recht kurz gewesen sein und auf jeden Fall keine Szene mit Gottesrede mehr enthalten haben. Vgl. zum ganzen Blenkinsopp, "Structure" (wie Anm. 21), S. 287-91.

[31] Die neuere Argumentation gegen P^g als selbständige Erzählung läßt sich so zusammenfassen: 1. P ist, vor allem in der Patriarchengeschichte, zu knapp, um überhaupt als Erzählung gelten zu können. 2. Es würden unentbehrliche Inhalte der alten Quellen fehlen, etwa eine Ursünde oder ein Sinaibundesschluß. 3. P-Texte sind Überschriften auch zu älteren Materialien. 4. P-Texte hängen von JE-Texten ab, setzen sie also voraus. 5. Gerade für viele P zugeschriebenen Textsplitter, ohne die P keine fortlaufende Erzählung mehr wäre, sind die sprachstatistischen Beweise oft sehr fragwürdig. Dazu sei knapp bemerkt: Zu 1: Geht man bei dieser Überlegung nicht von einem Gattungspostulat aus, das nicht an sicheren P-Texten, sondern an den alten Quellen gewonnen wurde? Zu 2: Die hier unterstellten Tatsachen stimmen zum Teil nicht, z.B. kann man nicht einfach sagen, bei P fehle eine Ursünde. Ferner liegt ein nicht begründbares Postulat vor — P müsse alles erzählt haben, was JE erzählt hat. Zu 3: Überschrift- und Einleitungsfunktion von P-Texten zu gemischten Textbeständen sind durch redaktionelle Tätigkeit bei der Zusammenarbeitung von P und dem alten Pentateuchmaterial voll erklärbar. Zu 4: Selbstverständlich bildete JE die Haupt-

den vorpriesterlichen Pentateuch und zumindest Vorstufen der "früheren" und der "späteren Propheten", sondern setzte auch bei seinen Adressaten solche Kenntnisse voraus.[32] Er schrieb seine

---

vorlage von P^g, und der Verfasser von P^g konnte bei seinen Lesern auch Kenntnis von JE voraussetzen. Das genügt zur Erklärung der gemeinten Sachverhalte. Zu 5: Rendtorff, der dieses Argument ausarbeitet, legt zweifellos den Finger auf eine Reihe problematischer Stellen. Doch übertreibt er die Beweisanforderung und arbeitet zum Teil mit rhetorischen Argumenten. Umgekehrt sollte er sich jedoch unbedingt an die von ihm selbst geforderte "erneute sorgfältige Prüfung" machen, ob nicht doch "etwa andere als die hier vorgetragenen Gründe dafür sprechen, noch weitere Texte" jener "priesterlichen Schicht zuzurechnen", die er selbst zwischen Gen. i und Ex. vi als ein einheitliches Textsystem bestehen lassen mußte, und ob nicht dann doch noch viele andere Texte in diesen weiteren P-Bereich verzahnt sind. Zitate aus Rendtorff, *Pentateuch* (wie Anm. 28), S. 162, Anm. 16. Jede Ergänzungs- oder Redaktionstheorie, die eine vorangehende selbständige Existenz von P^g ablehnt, gerät vor Schwierigkeiten, auf die ihre neueren Vertreter nicht einzugehen pflegen: 1. Wie läßt sich in solchen Theorien die redaktionelle Technik der Zusammenarbeitung in manchen Texten, etwa in der Flutgeschichte oder in der Kundschaftererzählung, sinnvoll erklären? Solche subtile Verzahnung setzt mehrere präexistente Texte voraus. Wer einen Text interpretierend ergänzen will, arbeitet anders. 2. Die außerordentlich strenge Struktur von P^g kann nicht ursprünglich für den jetzigen Textbestand gedacht gewesen sein, denn sie wird durch den Zusammenhang mit den älteren Texten ja weitgehend unsichtbar gemacht. 3. Wichtige theologische Aussagen von P^g sind strukturabhängig (etwa die Berit-Theologie) und treten infolge der Verwischung der Struktur im jetzigen Textzusammenhang kaum noch hervor.

[32] JE — um bei diesem Kürzel zu bleiben — dürfte dem Verfasser von P^g schon in frühdeuteronomisch bearbeiteter Gestalt vorgelegen haben. Sie liegt schon Dt/Dtr voraus, vgl. dazu jetzt vor allem D. E. Skweres, *Die Rückverweise im Buch Deuteronomium*, Dissertation, Hochschule Sankt Georgen, Frankfurt a.M. (1976 — erscheint 1978 in der Reihe *Analecta Biblica*). Vor allem wenn man die Abrahams-Berit von Gen. xv, die Gen. xvii zweifellos voraussetzt, erst als frühdeuteronomisch betrachtet (wie das heute gern getan wird), muß man schon mit einem frühdeuteronomischen Pentateuch als Vorlage von P^g rechnen. Dessen Handlungsablauf muß für den Verfasser von P^g und seine Leser schon so etwas wie kanonische Geltung gehabt haben, denn bei aller Freiheit hält sich die Darstellung im wesentlichen doch daran. Auch für seine Leser: Das zeigen die vielen Abkürzungen der Darstellung, die Einführung neuer Personen und Handlungsrequisiten, als seien sie längst bekannt, die oft versteckten oder umdeutenden Anspielungen auf den Text der alten Quellen. Zumindest Teile aus den Bereichen der Bücher Jos. - 2 Kön. müssen ebenfalls bekannt gewesen sein, es sei nur als Beispiel das archaisierende Element der Himmelfahrt des erscheinenden Gottwesens in Gen. xvii 22 und xxxv 13 genannt, für das nur Ri. xiii 20 als uns noch bekannte Vorlage in Frage kommt. Für ähnliche Sachverhalte bezüglich mancher Prophetenbücher, vor allem Ez., vgl. z.B. M. Oliva, "Revelación del nombre de Yahweh en la 'Historia sacerdotal': Ex 6, 2-8", *Biblica* 52 (1971), S. 1-19; Ska, "Les plaies d'Égypte" (wie Anm. 16); L. Van den Wijngaert, "Die Sünde in der priesterschriftlichen Urgeschichte", *Theologie und Philosophie* 43 (1968), S. 35-50. Am unklarsten ist das Abhängigkeitsverhältnis zwischen P^g und Deuterojesaja, vgl. Anm. 25 zur Dissertation von Eitz. Die These von A. S. Kapelrud, "The Date of the Priestly Code (P)", *ASTI* 3 (1964), S. 58-64, scheint mir nicht sicher bewiesen zu sein.

Schrift am wahrscheinlichsten in der Zeit der beginnenden Rückkehrmöglichkeiten aus dem babylonischen Exil.[33]

[33] Ich stütze mich bei meiner Datierung vor allem auf die Abhängigkeit von exilsprophetischen Texten und auf die exils- und diasporaorientierte Paradigmatik. Die linguistische Diskussion, die wieder neu in Gang gekommen ist, hat zunächst zu teilweise gegensätzlichen Thesen geführt. Vgl. vor allem R. Polzin, *Late Biblical Hebrew. Toward an Historical Typology of Biblical Hebrew Prose* (Missoula, Montana, 1976); A. Hurvitz, "The Evidence of Language in Dating the Priestly Code. A Linguistic Study in Technical Idioms and Terminology", *RB* 81 (1974), S. 24-56. Ein Vergleich der beiden Untersuchungen findet sich bei Polzin, S. 168f. Der Typ der Kriterien von Hurvitz erlaubt leider keinen Vergleich mit eigentlich dtr Material. Ferner ist fraglich, ob etwas, was typologisch vor dem Ez-Buch liegt, notwendig auch schon vorexilisch ist. Wie Polzins Untersuchung zeigt, ist linguistisch der Unterschied zwischen P^g und P^s relevant. Hurvitz unterscheidet jedoch nicht zwischen beiden Korpora. Sein Material wäre daraufhin neu zu überprüfen. Wenn das Kapitel III bei Polzin nicht falsifiziert werden kann, wird man doch damit rechnen müssen, daß auf der Ebene der kultischen Terminologie P^g bewußt an der alten Sprache festhielt. Vielleicht liegt hier auch der Einfluß alter Vorlagen vor. Bis zur weiteren Klärung der linguistischen Diskussion hängt also doch alles an der sinnvollsten historischen Einordnung der Paradigmatik der Erzählungen von P^g und an der Frage der Beziehung zu exilischen Prophetenschriften. Da die Paradigmatik zur Not auch schon nach dem Fall Samarias denkbar wäre, hängt letztlich alles an der Beziehung zu Prophetenschriften. Wer hier nicht zu folgen bereit ist, sollte konsequenterweise für Thesen wie die von Y. Kaufmann offen sein. Bei der Frage der Beziehung von P^g zu Prophetenschriften stellt Deuterojesaja ein besonderes Problem dar. Die Entstehung von P^g muß früher angesetzt werden, falls Deuterojesaja P^g voraussetzt. Ist dies nicht der Fall, dann würde zu einem etwas späteren Zeitansatz vor allem das passen, was sich in meiner Untersuchung "Die Ursünden in der priesterlichen Geschichtserzählung", in G. Bornkamm und K. Rahner, *Die Zeit Jesu* = Festschrift H. Schlier (Freiburg, 1970), S. 38-57, ergab. Da im Kern eine Diaspora angesprochen ist, die schon heimkehren könnte, aber zögert, ließen sich jedoch auch noch spätere Abfassungssituationen denken. Doch darf man auch wieder nicht zu weit hinabgehen, da dann ja die Abfassung und Einfügung von H und alles, was wiederum daran hängt, noch später zu liegen käme. Vgl. N. Lohfink, "Die Abänderung der Theologie des Priesterlichen Geschichtswerks im Segen des Heiligkeitsgesetzes", in H. Gese und H. P. Rüger, *Wort und Geschichte* = Festschrift K. Elliger (Neukirchen-Vluyn, 1973), S. 129-36; A. Cholewiński, *Heiligkeitsgesetz und Deuteronomium* (Rom, 1976), vor allem S. 138f. Sowohl die neueren Argumente für vorexilischen Ansatz, etwa bei Y. Kaufmann und seiner Schule, als auch die für massiv nachexilischen Ansatz, etwa bei J. G. Vink, "The date and origin of the Priestly Code in the Old Testament", in *The Priestly Code and Seven Other Studies, Oudtestamentische Studiën* 15 (Leiden, 1969), S. 1-144, beziehen sich gewöhnlich auf eine allgemeine "priesterliche Literatur" ohne ausgearbeitete Schichtenunterscheidung oder auf einen fertigen "Priesterkodex", den näher zu analysieren man sich weigert. Man argumentiert dann entweder mit Argumenten, die in der Tat das Alter vieler Inhalte, Materialien, Traditionen, Vorlagen beweisen, aber nicht ohne weiteres die Abfassungszeit von P^g, oder mit Argumenten, die nur für letzte Zusätze und redaktionelle Überarbeitungen gelten. Y. Kaufmann ist im übrigen durchaus für die Möglichkeit später literarischer Arbeit am alten Gesetzesmaterial offen gewesen, wie noch gegen Ende seines Lebens bei der Auseinandersetzung mit E. Auerbach deutlich wird: vgl. "Der Kalender und das Alter des Priesterkodex", *VT* 4 (1954), S. 308f.

Diese Schrift soll also hinsichtlich der Geschichte befragt werden. Hat sie die Absicht, Geschichte zu erzählen? Welche Sicht der Geschichte hat sie? Die erste Frage ist die nach der vorhandenen historischen Aussageintention. Die zweite Frage ist die nach der alles tragenden Geschichtsphilosophie, wenn dieses Wort in solchem Zusammenhang erlaubt ist. Man könnte natürlich noch eine weitere Frage stellen, nämlich die, ob P^g dem modernen Historiker brauchbare historische Informationen vermittelt. Aber wir kennen ja im wesentlichen die Quellen von P^g, und so darf man für diese Frage jederzeit auf die Quellen verweisen und sie im Zusammenhang mit P^g vernachlässigen.

I. *Die Rückverwandlung der Geschichte in Mythus*

Eine Intention, Geschichte darzustellen, wäre nach unserem Verständnis ja wohl dann gegeben, wenn der Verfasser die Meinung hatte, er erzähle Dinge, die faktisch geschehen sind, und was er erzähle, sei in der Zeit auch so hintereinander geschehen und auseinander hervorgegangen, wie er es erzählt. Eine noch größere Annäherung an unser modernes Verständnis wäre gegeben, wenn der Verfasser gar Kategorien wie Kausalität, Entwicklung oder Fortschritt erzählerisch zum Ausdruck brächte. Aber es mag hier genügen zu fragen, ob der Verfasser darauf aus war, das mitzuteilen, was wirklich geschah, und ob er es als einen zusammenhängenden einsinnigen Ablauf in der Zeit erzählen wollte.

Die alten Pentateuchquellen, gleichgültig, wie man sie im einzelnen konzipiert, hatten zweifellos eine solche Absicht — trotz kerygmatischer Hintergedanken[34] und gattungsbedingter Sperrigkeit ihres eigenen Materials.[35] Sie wollten Israel über seine Vergangenheit informieren. Wollte der Verfasser von P^g das ebenfalls?

Er könnte eine Intention, in diesem Sinne Geschichte zu erzählen, gehabt haben, auch wenn die von ihm benutzten Quellen faktisch unzureichend waren und wir heute als Historiker das Ergebnis seiner schriftstellerischen Arbeit weithin verwerfen müßten. Es geht nur um seine Intention.

Zunächst will es scheinen, als habe der Verfasser von P^g wirklich

[34] Klassische Untersuchungen: H. W. Wolff, "Das Kerygma des Jahwisten", *EvTh* 24 (1964), S. 73-98; ders., "Zur Thematik der elohistischen Fragmente im Pentateuch", *EvTh* 29 (1969), S. 59-72.

[35] Vgl. hier etwa, was G. von Rad, "Offene Fragen im Umkreis einer Theologie des Alten Testaments", *ThLZ* 88 (1963), Sp. 410-14, zur Gattung der "Sage" geschrieben hat, von der ein großer Teil des Stoffs in JE bestimmt ist.

die Absicht, Geschichte zu erzählen. Er erzählt ja, wenigstens in groben Zügen, jene alte Pentateucherzählung nach, die diese Absicht hatte. Auch er beginnt bei der Schöpfung, kennt eine Urzeit und eine Flut, spricht von den Erzvätern Abraham, Isaak und Jakob, läßt ihre Familie dem Josef nach Ägypten folgen, schildert die Befreiung Israels aus Ägypten und die Jahre in der Wüste, hält sich dabei lange am Sinai auf und führt Israel schließlich in das den Vätern verheißene Land. Ist die Übernahme des Erzählungsfadens nicht notwendig auch Übernahme der mit ihm verbundenen geschichtlichen Aussageintention?

Der Verfasser übernimmt diesen auf geschichtlichen Zusammenhang ausgerichteten Erzählungsfaden nicht nur. Er bringt überdies Name, Zahl und Ordnung hinein. Name durch die Genealogien und die Völker- und Stämmetafeln,[36] Zahl durch ein wohlausgebautes chronologisches System,[37] Ordnung durch verschiedene Struktur-

---

[36] Genealogien: Gen. v 3-27, 28*, 30-32; ix 28f.; xi 10-26, 32; xxi 5; xxv 7, 8*, 26*; xxxv 28f., (22-26); xlvii 28, 33; (Ex. i 1-5). Das ist die Hauptgenealogie, die bei Jakob dann nicht mehr im sauberen Schema durchgeführt und von seinen 12 Söhnen, den Stammvätern des Volks an, auch nicht mehr weitergeführt wird, nachdem in Ex. i 7 die Erfüllung des Vermehrungssegens konstatiert ist. In diese Genealogie sind die erzählenden Notizen und ausführlichen Erzählungen eingehängt — vgl. z.B. für die Sintflut McEvenue, *Narrative Style* (wie Anm. 16), S. 36-41 —, ebenso genealogische Seitenbemerkungen. Neben die lineare Hauptgenealogie treten dabei als segmentierte Genealogien die Völker- und Stammestafeln. Sie finden sich in Gen. x 1-7, 20, 22f., 31f.; xxv 12f., 16; xxxv 22-26; xxxvi 40-43; Ex. i 1-5. Abgesehen von den Listen der Söhne Jakobs dienen diese dazu, die entsprechenden Nachkommen aus dem Darstellungsgang von P^g zu entlassen. Für Literatur vgl. C. Westermann, *Genesis 1-11* (Darmstadt, 1972), S. 55-67; ders., *Genesis I*, (Neukirchen-Vluyn, 1974), S. 436, 468, 662f. und 741. Wichtige neue Arbeiten: A. Malamat, "King Lists of the Old Babylonian Period and Biblical Genealogies", *JAOS* 88 (1968), S. 163-73; M. D. Johnson, *The Purpose of the Biblical Genealogies* (Cambridge, 1969), S. 14-28; R. R. Wilson, "The Old Testament Genealogies in Recent Research", *JBL* 94 (1975), S. 169-89.

[37] Ein durchlaufendes chronologisches Hauptsystem von P^g läßt sich aus den Angaben folgender Texte erarbeiten: Gen. v 3, 6, 9, 12, 15, 18, 21, 25, 28, 32; xi 10, 12, 14, 16, 18, 20, 22, 24, 26; xxi 5; xxv 26; xlvii 28 (hier kann man errechnen, wann Jakob nach Ägypten kam); Ex. xii 40f. (von Gen. xlvii 28 aus läßt sich hier das Jahr des Auszugs berechnen); Dtn. i 3; Jos. iv 19. Die Zahlen in MT, Sam und G sind zum Teil erheblich verschieden, und keine Zahlenreihe dürfte als ganze die ursprünglichen Zahlen spiegeln. Näheres dazu noch unten Anm. 61. Neben den oben angegebenen Texten gibt es noch eine Reihe redundanter Angaben, die P^s dann noch weiter vermehrt. Subsysteme, zum Teil bis in die Tage hinein, finden sich für die Schöpfung (Woche), die Sintflut (Sonnenjahr), das Leben Abrahams und Jakobs, die Zeit der Wüstenwanderung und des Einzugs in Kanaan (z.T. kultische Termine). Vgl. Johnson, *Genealogies* (wie Anm. 36), S. 28-36 und 262-5 (Lit.). Ferner die Literatur zum Kalender der Jubiläen und von Qumran.

systeme der Darstellung, die einander zum Teil einschließen, zum Teil überlagern. Die umfassendste Gliederung, die das ganze Werk in 10 wenn auch ungleich große Teile aufteilt, wird durch die Toledot-Formeln angezeigt.[38] Der zehnte Teil, die Toledot Jakobs, der quantitativ die ganze zweite Hälfte der Schrift ausmacht, wird nochmals gegliedert durch 8 Wandernotizen, die jeweils einen Abschnitt beenden und zum nächsten führen, der an einem anderen Ort spielt.[39]

Tafel I

Die Toledot-Aufteilung von P^g

Gen. ii 4	T. von Himmel und Erde	Erzählung	Segen
v 1	T. Adams	Genealogie	
vi 9	T. Noachs	Erzählung	Segen + *Berit*
x 1	T. von Noachs Söhnen	Völkertafel	
xi 10	T. Sems	Genealogie	
xi 27	T. Terachs	Erzählung	Segen + *Berit*
xxv 12	T. Ismaels	Stämmetafel	
xxv 19	T. Isaaks	Erzählung	Segen
xxxvi 1	T. Esaus	Stämmetafel	
xxxvii 2	T. Jakobs	Erzählung	Wanderungen

[38] Vgl. Tafel I. Ich rechne mit folgenden 10 ursprünglich zu P^g gehörenden Toledot-Formeln: Gen. ii 4 (Unterschrift); v 1; vi 9; x 1; xi 10, 27; xxv 12, 19; xxxvi 1; xxxvii 2. Als P^s betrachte ich Gen. xxxvi 9; Num. iii 1. Die ältere Literatur ist gründlich zitiert bei P. Weimar, "Die Toledot-Formel in der priesterschriftlichen Geschichtsdarstellung", *BZ* 18 (1974), S. 65-93. Weimar hat gezeigt, daß die Toledot-Formeln mitsamt den an sie anschließenden Formulierungen in P^g den Einsatz neuer Teile der Darstellung markieren. Unbeschadet ihrer begrenzteren Funktion in einer eventuellen Vorstufe von P^g leiten sie hier nicht nur Genealogien ein, sondern auch Notizen und Erzählung sind ihnen zugeordnet. Weimar selbst ist noch nicht ganz konsequent und rechnet nicht in jedem Fall damit, daß in P^g jede Toledot-Formel dem gesamten Text bis zur nächsten Formel (bzw. dem Ende des Werks) vorgeordnet ist. Mir scheint das die einzig mögliche Konsequenz aus seinen Beobachtungen zu sein. *tol^edot NN* meint dann in P^g so etwas wie: "das, was sich von NN aus ergab und ereignete". Gen. xxxvii 2 leitet also den gesamten Text von der Ausreise nach Ägypten bis zum Einzug in Kanaan ein. All dies ist "Jakobsschicksal". Das quantitative Mißverhältnis ist nichts, das dagegen spräche. Auch vorher hatten die einzelnen Toledot-Texte schon recht verschiedene Länge. Natürlich müssen die Jakobs-Toledot dann mit anderen Mitteln strukturiert werden. Dazu dienen die Wandernotizen, vgl. die nächste Anmerkung. Gegenüber allen anderen modernen Versuchen, den Aufbau des Werkes zu definieren, besitzen die Toledot-Formeln einen Vorteil: Es sind Struktursignale, die der Verfasser selbst seinem Werk eingegeben hat.

[39] Vgl. Tafel II. In den zu P^g gehörenden Wandernotizen in der Genesis sind *lqḥ*, *jṣ'*, *bw'* und *jšb* die typischen Verben. Vom Exodus Israels an erscheinen

Tafel II

Die Wanderungen Israels in P^g

Israel in Ägypten	Auszug aus Ägypten	Ex. xii 37a, 40-42, xiii 20
Vernichtung der Ägypter	Zur Wüste Sin	xv 22aα, 27, xvi 1
Offenbarung des Sabbats	Zur Wüste Sinai	xvii 1a, bα, xix 1, 2a
Offenbarung des Heiligtums	Zur Wüste Paran	Num. x 11-13, xii 16b
Sünde des Volks	Zur Wüste Zin	... xx 1aα
Sünde von Mose und Aaron	Zum Berg Hor	... xx 22b ...
Tod Aarons	In die Steppen Moabs	xxi 4aα, 10f., xxii 1b
Tod Moses	Einzug in Kanaan	... Jos. iv 19aβ, b, v 10-12, xviii 1

Tafel III

Die "theologischen" Textbereiche in P^g

Gen. i	Die Erschaffung der Welt
Gen. vi-ix	Flut und Noach-Berit
Gen. xvii	*Abraham-Berit*
Gen. xxxv	*Segen über Jakob*
Ex. vi-xi	Sendung Moses und Aarons, Wunder vor Pharao
Ex. xiv	Vernichtung Pharaos im Meer
Ex. xvi	*Wachteln und Manna: Offenbarung des Sabbats*
Ex. xxiv - Num. iv	*Sinai: Offenbarung und Errichtung des Heiligtums*, Lager
Num. xiii-xiv	*Erkundung des Lands: Sünde von Volk und Führern*
Num. xx	*Wasserspende in der Wüste: Sünde von Mose und Aaron*
Num. xx	Einsetzung Eleasars, Tod Aarons
Num. xxvii - Dtn. xxxiv	Einsetzung Josuas, Anweisung für die Landnahme, Tod Moses

---

neue Verbkombinationen, vor allem mit *nsʿ*, *bwʾ* und *ḥnh*. Einige Zuteilungen zu P^g sind nicht ganz sicher, aber doch wahrscheinlich. Einige Notizen sind nur noch verstümmelt bewahrt. Doch lassen sich auf jeden Fall 8 "Wanderungen" Israels feststellen. Abschluß einer Einheit durch Ortsveränderung ist ein uraltes episches Darstellungsmittel, das P^g hier aufgreift. In den sich ergebenden Abschnitten zeigt sich wieder ein klarer Bauwille mit Vorliebe für Paarungen, wie schon vorher bei den Toledot-Aufteilungen. Ausgewählte neuere Literatur: M. Noth, "Der Wallfahrtsweg zum Sinai", *PJ* 36 (1940), S. 5-28; E. Weidner, "Assyrische Itinerare", *ArOr* 21 (1966), S. 42-6; V. Fritz, *Israel in der Wüste* (Marburg, 1970), S. 33f.; G. W. Coats, "The Wilderness Itinerary", *CBQ* 34 (1972), S. 135-52; Cross, *Myth* (wie Anm. 28), S. 308-17; G. I. Davies, "The Wilderness Itineraries: A Comparative Study", *Tyndale Bulletin* 25 (1974), S. 46-81.

Großer Wert scheint auf diejenigen Texte gelegt zu sein, in denen Gott redend auftritt. Man könnte sie als die "theologischen Texte" von P^g bezeichnen. Sie sind jeweils paarweise einander zugeordnet.[40] Am Anfang des Werks, in Gen. i 28, findet sich eine Art Geschichtsprogramm, dessen Einlösung und Nichteinlösung dann unterwegs jeweils festgestellt wird.[41] Durch dies und, sobald man mehr ins Detail geht, noch durch vieles andere,[42] wird die in P^g geschilderte

---

[40] Vgl. Tafel III. Die "theologischen Texte" auf dieser Übersicht sind nur mithilfe der bisher erwähnten Struktursignale Toledot-Formeln und Wandernotizen sowie der Tatsache, daß Gott redend auftritt, gewonnen. In Ex. vi-xi und Ex. xxiv - Num. iv könnte man innerhalb dieser Texte noch einmal mehrere Einheiten unterscheiden. Als erster hat McEvenue, "Fulfilment" (wie Anm. 24), S. 105, auf den Sondercharakter dieser Texte hingewiesen. Innerhalb dieser "theologischen Texte" gibt es nochmals zwei Gruppen, deren eine auf der Übersicht durch Kursivdruck hervorgehoben ist. Nur sie enthält eigentliche Erscheinungserzählungen. Bei Abraham und Jakob erscheint Gott und fährt am Ende wieder zum Himmel auf (Gen. xvii 22, xxxv 13). Nach dem Auszug aus Ägypten erscheint die Herrlichkeit Jahwes, zuerst aus der Wüste, dann auf dem Sinai, dann im Heiligtum. Literatur: N. Lohfink, "Die priesterschriftliche Abwertung der Tradition von der Offenbarung des Jahwenamens an Mose", *Biblica* 49 (1968), S. 1-8; Oliva, "Interpretación" (wie Anm. 16); C. Westermann, "Die Herrlichkeit Gottes in der Priesterschrift", in H. J. Stoebe, *Wort - Gebot - Glaube*, Festschrift W. Eichrodt (Zürich, 1970), S. 227-49 (systematisiert zu stark und kommt dadurch mit Ex. xvi nicht zurecht); Oliva, "Revelación" (wie Anm. 32); H. Mölle, *Das "Erscheinen" Gottes im Pentateuch* (Bern-Frankfurt, 1973); M. Oliva, "Las revelaciones a los patriarcas en la historia sacerdotal", *Biblica* 55 (1974), S. 1-14.

[41] Näheres dazu unten in Teil II.

[42] Ich kann allerdings nicht, wie es immer wieder geschieht, die "Bundesschlüsse" in Gen. ix und xvii als darstellungsgliedernde Signale betrachten, so wichtig sie für die Theologie von P^g sind und so sehr feststeht, daß sie aufeinander bezogen sind. Dasselbe gilt von den verschiedenen Gottesnamen, die in P^g vorkommen. Hier sind im übrigen schon die Fakten komplizierter, als im allgemeinen angenommen wird. Der "Erzähler" gebraucht den Jahwenamen schon einmal an der wichtigen Stelle Gen. xvii 1 (es besteht kein Grund, hier eine redaktionelle Änderung zu postulieren). Bei den Patriarchen spricht er weiter von Elohim, und nur die erscheinende Gottheit und Menschen, wenn sie von dieser Erscheinung sprechen, gebrauchen den Gottesnamen El Schaddaj. Die Offenbarung des Jahwenamens in Ex. vi erhält nicht die Würde einer Erscheinungserzählung. G. von Rad, *Priesterschrift* (wie Anm. 11), S. 167-86, hat eine Struktur von "drei mächtige(n) konzentrische(n) Kreise(n)" durch Nacherzählung nachzuweisen versucht. Dazu hat Noth, *Überlieferungsgeschichte* (wie Anm. 15), S. 260f., festgestellt, diese "Gesamtanlage" sei "durch die Überlieferung schon festgelegt" gewesen, und die drei Kreise hätten sich "wohl weniger aus einer umfassenden Geschichtsschau als vielmehr aus verschiedenen Einzelheiten der älteren Überlieferung" ergeben. Struktursignale, die diese Dreiteilung tragen könnten, sehe ich nicht. Auch die Ausführungs- und Erfüllungsnotizen, auf die sich Blenkinsopp, "Structure" (wie Anm. 21), vor allem stützt, sind nicht eigentlich erzählungsgliedernd, so wichtige Aussagefunktionen ihnen auch in anderer Hinsicht zukommen.

Geschichte zu einem Ablauf, bei dem man jeden Punkt sauber in Zeit und Raum unterbringen kann.[43] Weist das nicht darauf hin, daß eine möglichst klare und zuverlässige historische Darstellung beabsichtigt war?

Leider wird etwas zuviel Ordnung hergestellt. Die Figuren und Ereignisse werden nach geradezu ästhetischen Prinzipien über Raum und Zeit verteilt. Daher kommen einem, je mehr man in diese Schrift eindringt, desto mehr Zweifel, ob hier noch jene Demut gegenüber dem Faktum vorhanden war, die für eine geschichtliche Aussageabsicht letztlich entscheidend bleibt.

Fast immer treten Paare auf. Schöpfung und Flut sind die beiden einzigen auserzählten Themen der Urzeit. Noach und Abraham sind die beiden Empfänger einer Berit. Abraham und Jakob sind die beiden Erscheinungsempfänger der Väterzeit. Mose und Aaron sind die beiden Führer Israels bei Befreiung und Wanderung. Die Manna- und die Sinaiperikope sind die beiden Kultstiftungsgeschichten, die eine für den Sabbat, die andere für das Heiligtum und seinen Gottesdienst. Zweimal wird gesündigt, bei der Kundschaftersendung und am wasserspendenden Felsen. Aaron muß sterben, und Mose muß sterben. Eleasar wird eingesetzt, und Josua wird eingesetzt. Und so gibt es noch viele Paare.[44] Dann gibt es Siebenerschemata: Sieben Tage der Schöpfung, sieben Tage, bis Mose auf den Berg ins Feuer gerufen wird. Oder es ist die Zahl 10: Zehn Generationen zwischen Schöpfung und Flut, zehn Generationen zwischen Noach und Abraham, zehn Toledot-Überschriften. Ist hier das Gefühl für die verwirrende und undurchsichtige Vielfalt geschichtlicher Faktizität nicht ausgetrieben, und erst recht das Gefühl für jene unberechenbaren und unvoraussagbaren Wendepunkte des Menschheitswegs, wo Freiheit und Zufall am Werk sind?

Die alten Pentateuchquellen, bei allem Abstand vom modernen Umgang mit Geschichte, hatten doch für all dies einigen Sinn. Er spiegelte sich im ungefügen Beieinander der aufgehäuften und nur

---

[43] Der "Raum" wird in Gen. i erstellt, die Völkertafel in Gen. x füllt ihn in einer ersten Annäherung mit Bewohnern (weitere Differenzierungen folgen später in den Stämmetafeln), die Wanderungen, von denen erzählt wird, beleben ihn. Meist haben sie mit einer Korrektur falscher Verteilungen der Menschen im Gesamtraum zu tun.

[44] Die Vorliebe für Paarungen zeigt sich auch mehr im Kleinen. So finden wir in den Toledot Terachs: Wanderung Terachs und Wanderung Abrahams, Geburt Ismaels (und Beschneidung) und Geburt Isaaks (und Beschneidung), Tod Saras (und Begräbnis) und Tod Abrahams (und Begräbnis). Als Trenner zwischen diesen kleineren Einheiten spielen Zeitangaben eine Rolle.

leicht bearbeiteten Traditionsmassen. Eine derartige Zurückhaltung hat sich P^g nicht auferlegt. Der Verfasser schuf schöne Gestalt, indem er seinen Vorlagen Gewalt antat. Er ließ aus, baute um, veränderte, fügte in souveräner Freiheit Neues ein.

Ich kann jetzt immer nur Beispiele bringen. Um die Zweiheit Abraham - Jakob herauszuarbeiten, strich er die Isaaks- und Josefsgeschichte zusammen. Weil er das Thema "Sünde" erst bei der Wüstenwanderung behandeln wollte, entfernte er in der Jakobserzählung den betrügerischen Erwerb des Vatersegens und die Feindschaft der Brüder (Gen. xxviii 1-45). Für den Zug Jakobs nach Osten fand er einen neuen Grund: Jakobs Eltern schickten ihn nach Paddan Aram, weil er keine kanaanäische Frauen heiraten sollte.[45] Das Motiv war keine neue Erfindung. Aber in den Vorlagen fand es sich bei Isaak.[46] So wurde Isaak nicht gebraucht, wohl aber ein Motiv aus seiner Sage, und das Motiv wanderte zu Jakob hinüber. Da war doch offenbar nicht mehr die Historie gefragt, sondern nur noch die Ereigniskonstellation und das in ihr sich aussprechende Problem: Wo man seine Frauen holen sollte, aus den Völkern oder aus dem eigenen Volk. Für derartige Verpflanzungen von Inhalten, die an sich einmal eine feste geschichtliche Stelle hatten, ließen sich noch viele Beispiele bringen: Kleinigkeiten, wie in Gen. xvii 17 die Umwandlung des Lachens Saras in ein Lachen Abrahams,[47] und auch Gewichtigeres, wie das theologisch wahrlich folgenreiche Schweigen bezüglich der Sinai-Berit.[48] Dies letztere zeigt, daß es

---

[45] Gen. xxvi 34f., xxvii 46, xxviii 1-9.

[46] Gen. xxiv. Dort zieht nicht Isaak selbst nach Osten, um sich eine Frau aus der Verwandtschaft zu holen, sondern der Knecht seines Vaters. Zum Hauptmotiv vgl. Gen. xxiv 3f. Es dürfte sich in Gen. xxv 20, der zu vergleichenden Passage von P^g, trotz ihres fragmentarischen Erhaltungszustands kaum befunden haben. Zur Gesamtbehandlung der Tradition in der Jakobserzählung von P^g vgl. Groß, "Jakob" (wie Anm. 29), S. 339f. Zum Umgang mit der Tradition in Bezug auf die Motive Schuld und Strafe in ganz P^g vgl. Lohfink, "Ursünden" (wie Anm. 33), S. 41-7.

[47] Alte Quellen: Gen. xviii 12-15. Zur Abhängigkeit von den alten Quellen vgl. zuletzt McEvenue, *Narrative Style* (wie Anm. 16), S. 145f.

[48] Dazu vgl. vor allem W. Zimmerli, "Sinaibund und Abrahambund", in: ders., *Gottes Offenbarung* (München, 1963), S. 205-16. H. Cazelles, der Ex. xix 3b-8 zu P rechnet, sieht hier trotzdem nur eine "Erneuerung" der Abrahams-Berit: "Alliance du Sinai, Alliance de l'Horeb et Renouvellement de l'Alliance", in H. Donner, *Beiträge zur alttestamentlichen Theologie* = Festschrift W. Zimmerli (Göttingen, 1977), S. 69-79. Man wird kaum mit Kutsch, "Gott" (wie Anm. 16), S. 386, sagen können, wenn P^g den Terminus *b^{e}rit* für die Sinai-Ereignisse nicht verwende, biete sie gegenüber der älteren Überlieferung "nichts Neues", denn die Vorstellung von einem Sinai-Bund habe es überhaupt "in Israel nicht ge-

bei all dem nicht nur einfach um die Ästhetik der Darstellung ging, sondern daß diese selbst wiederum Vehikel für genau überlegte theologische Aussagen sein sollte.

Ähnliches gilt von den Genealogien und der Chronologie. P^g wurde zu einer Zeit abgefaßt, als in Jonien schon die gelehrten Mythographen ihre Stammbaumsysteme entwarfen und einer von ihnen, Hekataios von Milet, schon zum erstenmal, mithilfe der Genealogien und eines Durchschnittswerts für eine Generation rückwärtsschreitend, eine absolute Chronologie für die Zeit der Heroen zu erstellen versuchte.[49] Eine Ähnlichkeit der chronologischen Technik läßt sich auch bei P^g nicht verkennen, wobei der Durchschnittswert für eine Generation 100 Jahre betragen zu haben scheint.[50] Aber im ganzen dürfte P^g auch in den Genealogien und Zahlen eher in der altorientalischen Tradition stehen.[51] Darauf weist die Anordnung der linearen Genealogien um die Flut als Mitte herum,[52] vielleicht auch die Rolle der Zehnzahl,[53] auf jeden Fall die ursprungsmythische Rückführung aller Fakten auf einen einzigen Anfang.[54] Im einzelnen weiß

---

geben". Denn selbst wenn, wie Kutsch annimmt, alle Belege für *b^erit* im nichtpriesterschriftlichen Teil der Sinaierzählungen dem "deuteronomisch-deuteronomistischen Bereich" zuzuordnen sind, können wir sie trotzdem schon der P^g vorgegebenen Überlieferung zurechnen. Ferner geht es ja nicht einfach um das Wort *b^erit*, sondern auch um die ältere Verbindung der Sinaitradition mit Rechtsverkündigung. Wie aufregend der Abbau des Sinaibundes selbst in priesterlichen Kreisen war, zeigt die recht bald erfolgte Rückgängigmachung durch den Einbau von H. Vgl. dazu Lohfink, "Abänderung" (wie Anm. 33).

[49] Zur griechischen Mythographie, deren Höhepunkt im 6./5. Jh. vor Christus lag, vgl. (mit weiterer Literatur) W. Speyer, "Genealogie", in *Realenzyklopädie für Antike und Christentum* 9 (Stuttgart, 1976), S. 1166-70. Das Werk des Hekataios von Milet trägt den Titel "Historiae", aber auch "Heroologia" oder "Genealogiae".

[50] Zur Generationenkalkulation zumindest des MT in P^g vgl. unten, Anm. 60.

[51] Vgl. die oben Anm. 36 zitierten Arbeiten sowie M. Ramlot, "Les généalogies bibliques, un genre littéraire oriental", *Bible et vie Chretienne* 60 (1964), S. 53-70. Eine weitere Dimension der Abhängigkeit von mesopotamischer Wissenschaft tut sich auf, wenn M. Barnouin mit seiner Rückführung der Zahlen in Gen. v und in den Musterungslisten von Num. auf babylonische Mathematik und Astronomie recht haben sollte. Vgl. M. Barnouin, "Recherches numériques sur la généalogie de Gen. V", *RB* 77 (1970), S. 347-65; ders., "Les recensements du livre des Nombres et l'astronomie Babylonienne", *VT* 27 (1977), S. 280-303.

[52] Das entspricht dem Aufbau der Sumerischen Königsliste. Zu ihr vgl. vor allem T. Jacobsen, *The Sumerian Kinglist* (Chicago, 1939).

[53] Daß 10 Generationen die ideale genealogische Tiefendimension darstellten, vertrat Malamat, "King Lists" (wie Anm. 36). Wilson, "Genealogies" (wie Anm. 36), widerspricht. Aus der Bibel wäre vor allem die 10 Generationen umfassende Ahnentafel Davids in Rut iv 18-22 zu vergleichen. Durch die Aufgliederung des Gesamtwerks in 10 "Toledot" präsentiert sich P^g vielleicht sogar als so etwas wie potenzierte "Toledot".

[54] Das geschah in der Antike allerdings selten mit solcher Konsequenz und

man gerade in diesem Bereich nie genau, wo von P^{g} übernommene Tradition, wo eigenes Konstrukt vorliegt. Nur: wenn Tradition übernommen ist, dürfte Wilsons Feststellung gelten, daß es aus der Völkerkunde keinen Beweis dafür gibt, "that genealogies are created for the purpose of making historical record",[55] und da, wo wir den Verfasser von P^{g} selbst am Werk sehen, zeigen sich andere als geschichtliche Intentionen. Der jahwistische Metuschael wird als Metuschelach geführt, damit er schon im Namen als Sünder erkennbar sei und deutlich werde, daß die Flut Folge von Sünde war.[56] Die Lebensalter vor der Flut sind so eingerichtet, daß Sünder wie Metuschelach in der Flut selbst umkamen,[57] und daß andererseits alle Urväter zugleich die Entrückung des vollkommenen Henoch miterleben konnten.[58] Alle Väter von Noach ab, im ganzen 10 Generationen, konnten zugegen sein, als Abraham das Licht der Welt erblickte, dann erst starben sie

---

Ausdrücklichkeit wie in P^{g}. Doch als Grundprinzip steckt es selbst in einem Werk wie in den Hesiod zugeschriebenen "Frauenkatalogen" oder "Ehoien", wo verschiedene große Geschlechter auf je verschiedene Ahnfrauen zurückgeführt werden, die aber alle Verkehr mit Göttern hatten.

[55] "Genealogies" (wie Anm. 36), S. 189.

[56] Metuschelach, Vater Lamechs, in Gen. v 21 P^{g} ist zweifellos identisch mit Metuschael, Vater Lamechs, in iv 18 J. Vielleicht hat der Verfasser von P^{g} nicht frei geändert, sondern es gab zwei Alternativformen des gleichen Namens. So M. Tsevat, "The Canaanite God Šälaḥ", *VT* 4 (1954), S. 41-9, der im zweiten Element den Namen des Unterweltsgottes sieht: *šelaḥ* oder *šeʾol*. Aber selbst dann dürfte P^{g} die Form Metuschelach ausgewählt oder gegen J bewahrt haben, weil diese den Bestandteil *šelaḥ* "Geschoß, Wurfwaffe" zu enthalten schien, was dazu paßt, daß die Flut, in der Metuschelach umkam, in *ḥamas* "Gewalttat" ihre Ursache hatte. Weiteres zu den Namensformen in den Genealogien von P^{g} immer noch gut bei K. Budde, *Die biblische Urgeschichte* (*Gen. 1-12,5*) (Gießen, 1883), S. 98-100.

[57] Nach den Zahlen des MT starb Metuschelach im Jahre der Flut (geboren *anno mundi* 687, Alter 969 Jahre; die Flut selbst trat ein *anno mundi* 1656). Nach den Zahlen von Sam. trifft dies überdies auch für Jered und Lamech zu, und das dürfte ursprünglich sein, vgl. unten Anm. 61. Dann besteht genau die zweite Hälfte der zehnköpfigen vorsintflutlichen Genealogie — Henoch und Noach natürlich ausgenommen — aus Sündern, die in der Flut umkommen. Man kommt kaum daran vorbei, daß in P^{g} der Einbruch der Sünde hierdurch ausgedrückt wird. Skepsis dagegen gebührt der immer wiederkehrenden Behauptung, die abnehmenden Lebensalter drückten die Zunahme der Sünde aus. Diese Behauptung läßt sich kaum am Text verifizieren, vgl. Van den Wijngaert, "Sünde" (wie Anm. 32), S. 36f. Zum ganzen vgl. Budde, *Urgeschichte* (wie Anm. 56), S. 92-103.

[58] Henoch wurde nach dem MT *anno mundi* 987 entrückt. In diesem Jahr lebten noch und schon alle vorsintflutlichen Väter außer Adam, der 930 gestorben war, und Noach, der erst 1056 geboren wurde. Nach dem Samaritanus, der vermutlich die ursprünglichen Zahlen hat, wurde Henoch 887 entrückt, und auch Adam, der 930 starb, und Noach, der schon 707 geboren wurde, konnten es miterleben.

nacheinander.[59] Durch die Zahlen werden also einfach bestimmte Gestalten und Ereignisse herausgestrichen. Die Gesamtchronologie im masoretischen Text setzt den Exodus in den *annus mundi* 2666. Das sieht nach zwei Dritteln eines Weltenjahrs von 4000 Jahren aus, und dieser *annus magnus et mirabilis* wäre, wenn man andere biblische und außerbiblische, in der Makkabäerzeit zugängliche Informationen zu Hilfe nimmt, nach unserer Zeitrechnung das Jahr 164 v. Chr., also das Jahr der Wiedereinweihung des Tempels.[60] Das kann natürlich nur ein in der Makkabäerzeit hineinretuschiertes System sein. Aber wir haben Grund anzunehmen, daß auch das ursprüngliche Zahlenwerk auf einen *annus mirabilis* hin durchsichtig war, vermutlich den Tempelbau Salomos.[61] Für das meiste Genealogische und Chronologische in P^g ist uns der Schlüssel verlorengegangen — doch die wenigen Türen, die wir öffnen können, führen uns nicht zur Geschichte.

Wenn das bei den Namen und Zahlen so ist, was ist dann von den Worten und Taten zu halten? Elliger hat von der Transparenz der priesterschriftlichen Darstellung gesprochen. Zwar wird in Vergangenheitsform erzählt. Aber das, was erzählt wird, entspricht Situationen, Möglichkeiten, Erfahrungen und Problemen der angezielten Leserschaft. Ihr bietet es im Gewand der Vergangenheit Lebenshilfen und Lösungsmöglichkeiten an. Der Sachverhalt läßt sich oft dadurch nachweisen, daß terminologisch auf prophetische Texte der Exilszeit angespielt wird.

Als Beispiel diene die Kundschaftererzählung in Num. xiii-xiv.[62]

[59] Nach dem MT, der hier die ursprünglichen Zahlen haben dürfte, wurde Abraham *anno mundi* 1946 geboren. Noach starb 2006, Sem 2094, Schelach 2124, Heber 2185, Peleg 1994, Regu 2014, Serug 2047, Nahor 1995, Terach 2098 — also alle nach Abrahams Geburt.

[60] Vgl. zuletzt Johnson, *Genealogies* (wie Anm. 36), S. 32f. Die 2666 Jahre bis zum Exodus lassen sich (für die letzten zweizweidrittel Generationen allerdings nur mithilfe der Levitengenealogie in Ex. vi 16-25 P^s) als die Zeit der 26 $^2/_3$ Generationen von Adam bis Eleasar bestimmen, falls man die Generation mit 100 Jahren ansetzt (als mögliche Basis dafür vgl. Gen. xv 13-16).

[61] Die mir plausibelste Rekonstruktion der ursprünglichen Chronologie von P^g stammt von A. Jepsen, "Zur Chronologie des Priesterkodex", *ZAW* 47 (1929), S. 251-3. Demnach wären für die Zeit vor der Flut die Zahlen des Sam., für die Zeit nach der Flut die des MT ursprünglich. Dafür lassen sich bei Vergleich der verschiedenen Zahlenreihen Gründe angeben. Dann wäre der Exodus *anno mundi* 2320 anzusetzen. Da der salomonische Tempelbau 480 Jahre nach dem Exodus begonnen wurde (nach 1 Kön. vi 1, einem Text, der P^g schon vorgelegen haben dürfte), kommt man auf den *annus mundi* 2800 als *annus mirabilis*.

[62] Zum folgenden vgl. vor allem McEvenue, *Narrative Style* (wie Anm. 16), S. 90-144, und Lohfink, "Ursünden" (wie Anm. 33), S. 52-4.

Die Sünde, die Israels Stammesvertreter und das ganze Volk in der Wüste Paran begehen, erhält einen genauen Namen: *dibbat ha'areṣ* "Verleumdung des Landes" (Num. xiii 32, xiv 36f.). Die Verleumdung wird auch zitiert, und die entscheidende Formulierung lautet: *'ereṣ 'okelet jošᵉbeha hi'* "ein Land, das seine Bewohner auffrißt, ist es" (Num. xiii 32). Nimmt man beide Formulierungen zusammen, dann wird man geradezu zwangsläufig zu Ez. xxxvi 1-15 geführt, der Prophezeiung "an die Berge Israels". Diese Berge sind verödet und in den Besitz anderer Völker gekommen. Sie sind hineingeraten in den *dibbat 'am*, in die "Verleumdung durch die Leute" Ez. xxxvi 3. Jahwe verheißt ihnen nun, er werde das Volk Israel in sie zurückbringen und dort wieder zahlreich und glücklich leben lassen. Wie hatten die Leute die Berge Israels verleumdet? Sie hatten, wie gegen Ende des Orakels zitiert wird, gesagt: *'okelet 'adam 'atti* "eine Menschenfresserin bist du".[63] Der Zusammenhang der beiden Texte dürfte deutlich sein.[64] Offenbar konnten die Leser von P^g ihn auch erkennen. Sie lebten in einem Augenblick, wo man wieder zurückkehren konnte. Aber vielleicht reizte viele die Rückkehr gar nicht. In solchem Zusammenhang wollte die Anspielung auf den Ezechieltext besagen, daß eine Verzögerung der Heimkehr und ihre Begründung durch abschätzige Äußerungen über das Land nichts anderes wären als sündige Übernahme des Urteils der anderen Völker.

Sieht man das, dann erkennt man auch den Sinn der Veränderungen, die P^g in der Kundschaftererzählung gegenüber deren älterer Gestalt vorgenommen hat. McEvenue hat gezeigt, daß P^g aus der alten Kundschafter- und Kriegserzählung alles Kriegerische ausgetrieben hat.[65] Eine friedliche Inspektion des zu beziehenden Landes wird erzählt. Auch das macht die Geschichte durchsichtig auf die Verhältnisse im Perserreich. Da mußte ja nichts erobert werden. Wohl aber ist es denkbar, daß zuerst einmal Delegierte vorausreisen mußten, um die Neuansiedlungsmöglichkeiten zu studieren, und daß dann erst größere Heimkehrerkarawanen organisiert wurden. Vieles hing natürlich an dem Urteil, das eine solche Delegation bei ihrer Rückkehr abgab.

---

[63] Ez. xxxvi 13; vgl. xxxvi 14.

[64] Die neueste Diskussion der Frage, ob P^g auch die Vokabeln des Fruchtbarkeitssegens (*prh* und *rbh*, in Gen. i 22 und oft) aus Ez. xxxvi 11 habe, findet sich bei M. Gilbert, "Soyez féconds et multipliez (Gn 1, 28)", *Nouvelle Revue Théologique* 106 (1974), S. 733.

[65] Zum "Pazifismus" von P^g vgl. noch oben Anm. 30.

Auf ähnliche Weise ließe sich auch bei vielen anderen Erzählungen und Motiven von P^g zeigen, wie wenig es um das vergangene Faktum, wie sehr dagegen um die möglichst große Durchlässigkeit der Darstellung für die Welt des Lesers ging. Auch die Urgeschichte wurde auf diese Weise mit der Gegenwart verbunden. Die Sintflut wurde ja heraufgeführt durch die Sünde von "allem Fleisch".[66] Diese Sünde, offenbar die menschliche Grundsünde überhaupt, erhält ebenfalls einen genauen Namen. Sie heißt *ḥamas* "Gewalttat".[67] Das bringt sicher die Sünde Kains und die Rachgier Lamechs auf den Begriff (Gen. iv 1-16, 23f.). Aber wieder liegt zugleich ein Verweis auf Ezechiel vor. Die Gesamtheit der in Gen. vi 9-13 zur Einleitung der Sintflut benutzten Begriffe schlägt die Brücke zu Ez. xxviii 1-19, dem dritten Wort gegen den König von Tyrus. Ich kann das hier nicht im einzelnen dartun. Jedenfalls ist in jenem Tyrus-Orakel ein alter Mythus vom Himmelsturz eines Urwesens verwertet. Dessen ursprüngliche Sünde, der Hochmut, wird dort im Hinblick auf das, was Tyrus getan hat, als *ḥamas* interpretiert.[68] In dieser Konkretisierung und unter Weglassung des ursprünglichen Hochmuts bietet P^g seinen Lesern den alten Sündenfallmythus subtil anspielend an. Das, was damals Gottes gute Schöpfung verdarb,[69] war jene Gewalttat, deretwegen auch jetzt noch prophetische Völkerorakel ergehen müssen. Auch heute müßte eigentlich die Flut wieder kommen — so sollen die Leser folgern. Sündenfall der Urmenschheit und ferne Sintflut am Morgen der Welt werden also über die Brücke eines Ezechielorakels aus der Vergangenheit heraufgeholt und zu etwas Heutigem gemacht.

Auf diese Weise könnte man fast ganz P^g durchkommentieren. Jedes Ereignis ist transparent erzählt. Was einmal war, kann also wiederkehren. Die Strukturkongruenz erhellt die Gegenwart des Lesers, ja vielleicht jede mögliche Gegenwart.

Wie soll man die Intention, die hinter solchem Erzählen steht, benennen? Sie geht auf schon Geschehenes. Doch bleibt es ihr dabei gleichgültig, wann etwas geschah, wie es mit allem vorher Geschehe-

---

[66] Für das Folgende vgl. McEvenue, *Narrative Style* (wie Anm. 16), S. 20-32 und 41f.; Lohfink, "Ursünden" (wie Anm. 33), S. 48-52; vor allem aber — trotz des Verdikts von Westermann, *Genesis I* (wie Anm. 36), S. 559: "hat im Text keinen Anhalt" — Van den Wijngaert, "Sünde" (vgl. Anm. 32), S. 40-48.

[67] Gen. vi 11, 13. Zum innerpriesterschriftlichen Bezug dieses Begriffs auf Gen. i 29 und ix 2f. weiter unten in Teil II.

[68] Ez. xxviii 16. Zum Wort vgl. H. J. Stoebe, "*ḥāmās* Gewalttat", in *THAT* I (München, 1971), Sp. 583-7.

[69] Vgl. die Wurzel *šḥt* in Gen. vi 11, 12, 13.

nen zusammenhängt, wie es alles Spätere beeinflußt. Wichtiger ist, daß alles, was irgendwann einmal geschah, zur Zeit des Lesers wiederkommen kann. Dadurch kann das Damalige das Jetzige erhellen. Dies ist ein Verständnis von Geschichte, für das es gewissermaßen einen Vorrat paradigmatischer Weltkonstellationen gibt, die alle schon da waren und die wiederkommen können. Es lohnt sich, von ihnen zu erzählen, denn wenn sie wiederkehren, kann ihre Kenntnis nützlich sein.

In Mesopotamien setzte die Omen-Literatur vermutlich ein ähnliches Geschichtsverständnis voraus.[70] Sie rechnete natürlich nicht nur mit einer Wiederholbarkeit von Weltkonstellationen, sondern dazu noch mit der Korrespondenz zwischen Welt-Großsituation und Omenbefund. Ferner disponierte sie ihr Material gewöhnlich nach anderen Gesichtspunkten als denen der zeitlichen Abfolge und ist in diesem Sinn doch noch einmal ganz anders situationsisolierend als die Priesterschrift. So scheut man sich schließlich doch, sie hier zum Vergleich heranzuziehen. Entferntere Beziehungen der Geisteshaltungen sind dennoch nicht ausgeschlossen. Auch in Israel waren die Priester mit Orakeln betraut, eine der letzten Dispositionen Gottes in der Priesterschrift ist die Unterordnung Josuas unter den Priester Eleasar, der das Urim-Orakel bedienen kann (Num. xxvii 21), und in P^g geschieht kaum etwas, was vorher nicht von Gott angesagt oder befohlen wurde.[71]

Sei dem wie immer — im folgenden sei ein anderer Weg versucht, die Intention, die in P^g hinter der Transparenz des Erzählens von der Vergangenheit steckt, zu bestimmen. Es ist der Vergleich mit der mythischen Rede, speziell mit dem Urzeitmythus.[72]

---

[70] Als Überblick vgl. A. L. Oppenheim, *Ancient Mesopotamia* (Chicago, 1964), S. 206-24. Wichtigste Veröffentlichungen bei H. Hirsch, "Akkadische Wahrsageliteratur", in *Kindlers Literaturlexikon* I (Zürich, 1965), Sp. 341-3. Wichtig sind für unseren Zusammenhang vor allem die "historischen Omina", die quantitativ allerdings ein Randphänomen darstellen. Zur Geschichtsauffassung vgl. H. Gese, "Geschichtliches Denken im Alten Orient und im Alten Testament", *ZThK* 55 (1958), S. 132: "Der Geschichtsbegriff ... ist folgender: Jede Situation oder Zeitart ist schon einmal in der unübersehbaren Abfolge der Situationen dagewesen, jede kehrt auch wieder, doch ist diese Abfolge als solche unbestimmbar ... Eine Entwicklung eines Zustands aus dem andern im Zeitverlauf wird hier nicht gedacht, geschweige denn, daß Geschichte Ziel und Abzweckung hätte".

[71] Hier wäre allerdings noch einiges zu differenzieren, vgl. McEvenue, "Fulfilment" (wie Anm. 24). Ferner wäre im Zusammenhang die mesopotamische Vorstellung von der Bestimmung des Schicksals durch die Götter hinzuzuziehen. Vgl. W. G. Lambert, "Destiny and Divine Intervention in Babylon and Israel", in *The Witness of Tradition*, *Oudtestamentische Studiën* 17 (Leiden, 1972), S. 65-72.

[72] Literatur zum Thema "Mythus und AT" ist zusammengestellt bei Dequeker, "Noah" (wie Anm. 21), S. 120, Anm. 19.

Dieser erzählt in der Überzeitlichkeit der Urzeit Dinge, die immer und überall gelten und so auch das Jetzt erklären können. Es kann vorkommen, daß auch historische Gestalten in den Mythus einsinken. Aber der Mythus ist nicht darauf angewiesen, daß seine Figuren einmal gelebt haben.

Die priesterliche Erzählung kommt demgegenüber — wenn man von der Urgeschichte der alten Quellen absieht — von ausgebreiteter historischer Substanz her. Sie bleibt ihr auch, bei aller Freiheit, etwa in der Abfolge der Hauptgeschehnisse, treu. Dennoch erzählt sie nun alles, als erzähle sie Mythen. Sie verwandelt gewissermaßen Geschichte in Mythus zurück. Deshalb muß man den Eindruck gewinnen, als handle es sich bei aller zeitlichen Abfolge letztlich um eine große, nach künstlerischen Prinzipien zusammengestellte Bildersammlung. Sie kommt von der Geschichte her, doch sie tendiert auf Paradigmata. Sie geht nicht so weit, diese völlig voneinander zu isolieren. Sie baut sogar die Genealogien aus und führt eine Chronologie ein, offenbar, um der Isolierungstendenz ihres Erzählens bewußt entgegenzuwirken und den Ereignisfaden auf keinen Fall reißen zu lassen. Aber Verkettungen von Einzelmythen gibt es in Urzeitmythen auch, etwa im Atraḫasīs-Mythus, von dem sofort zu sprechen sein wird. Vielleicht kann man als vorläufiges Ergebnis formulieren, in P^g ende die Urzeit nicht nach der Flut, sondern sie sei über die ganze erzählte Geschichte hin ausgedehnt worden.

II. *Die Ablehnung einer dynamischen Welt*

Auch einen Erzähler, der nicht Geschichte, sondern Paradigmata erzählen will, kann man fragen, was für eine Auffassung von Geschichte, was für eine "Geschichtsphilosophie" er habe. Auch er muß sich ja seinen Reim darauf machen, wie die Gegenwart seiner Adressaten sich zu Vergangenheit und Zukunft verhält. Er kann dies auch in seinen einzelnen Paradigmata oder in deren Gesamtkomposition zum Ausdruck bringen. Um wieviel mehr die priesterliche Geschichtserzählung, die ja von Geschichtswerken herkommt und trotz ihrer anderen Erzählintention diese Herkunft auch keineswegs verleugnen will.

In den alten Pentateuchquellen steckte Geschichtsphilosophie. Gen. xii 1-3 macht Abraham vor dem Hintergrund einer dem Fluch verfallenen Gesamtmenschheit zum Anfang eines neuen, von Gott her dynamisch sich ausbreitenden Segens für alle Völker.[73] Die Geschichte

[73] Vgl. vor allem Wolff, "Kerygma" (wie Anm. 34).

der Erzväter und — mindestens von einer frühdeuteronomischen Bearbeitung des Pentateuchs an — die gesamte Geschichte Israels bis zur Landnahme wird mit den Kategorien "Verheißung - Erfüllung" gedeutet.[74] Das Deuteronomium und das damit verbundene Geschichtswerk, dazu auch einiges in der Sinaiperikope, fügen noch die Kategorie eines "Vertrages" zwischen Jahwe und Israel als Deutungsprinzip hinzu.[75] Daher kann man die Frage nicht umgehen, wie P^g sich zu all dem gestellt habe.

Und eine andere Frage tritt sofort hinzu. Mindestens vieles in den paradigmatischen Perikopen von P^g hat ja mit exilischer und nachexilischer "Hoffnung auf Heimkehr" zu tun.[76] Dadurch vereint sich der Verfasser von P^g mit dem Chor der Propheten seiner Zeit, denn auch diese singen Hoffnung auf Heimkehr. Bei ihnen verbindet sich das nun aber mit dem, was man Dynamisierung der Geschichte nennen könnte. Die Zukunft wird größer sein als die Vergangenheit je war. Ein neues, alles Frühere übertreffende Handeln Jahwes steht bevor. Die Linie der Zeit steigt. Das Eigentliche steht noch aus. Vor allem Deuterojesaja dynamisiert auf diese Weise das Geschichtsverständnis. Aber nicht nur er. Ist auch P^g, weil Hoffnung auf Heimkehr verkündend, mit von der Partie?

---

[74] Gute Einführung (wobei allerdings P auf eine Linie mit JE gebracht wird) bei G. von Rad, *Theologie des Alten Testaments* 1 (München, [6]1969), S. 181-4. Die Kategorie zieht sich als Leitmotiv durch die Arbeiten, die bei C. Westermann, *Probleme alttestamentlicher Hermeneutik* (München, 1960), zusammengestellt sind. Die neuere Diskussion um die redaktionelle Zuordnung der Verheißungstheologie im Pentateuch wurde, mit einiger Spätzündung, durch J. Hoftijzer, *Die Verheißungen an die drei Erzväter* (Leiden, 1956), ausgelöst. Die Einschränkungen im Text sind im Hinblick auf Rendtorff, *Problem* (wie Anm. 28), gemacht. Doch vgl. auch J. Van Seters, "The Yahwist as Theologian? A Response", *Journal for the Study of the Old Testament* Issue 3 (1977), S. 17f. Daß die Theologie der Landverheißung an die Väter keineswegs einfach übernommen werden mußte, zeigt die Geschichtstheologie des "kleinen historischen Credo" von Dtn xxvi 5-9. Vgl. dazu: N. Lohfink, "Dtn 26,5-9: Ein Beispiel altisraelitischer Geschichtstheologie", in *Geschichte, Zeugnis und Theologie* = *Kerygma und Mythos* VI-7 (Hamburg-Bergstedt, 1976), S. 100-07.

[75] Ich sage bewußt "Vertrag", nicht "Bund" oder gar "Bestimmung", wie E. Kutsch, *Verheißung und Gesetz, Untersuchungen zum sogenannten "Bund" im Alten Testament*, *BZAW* 131 (Berlin, 1973), etwas zu sehr auf die Wortbedeutung von *b^{e}rit* fixiert, möchte. Trotz vieler Bedenken im einzelnen ist der Grundthese von einer ausgesprochenen Bundestheologie der dt/dtr Literatur zuzustimmen, die L. Perlitt, *Bundestheologie im Alten Testament* (Neukirchen-Vluyn, 1969), entwickelt hat. Zum Zusammenhang mit neuassyrischer Staatsideologie und zu dem wissenssoziologischen Prozeß, der zur Ausbildung dieser Vertragstheologie geführt hat, vgl. N. Lohfink, *Unsere großen Wörter* (Freiburg, 1977), S. 24-43, ders., "Deuteronomy", *IDBSuppl.* (Nashville, 1976), S. 231.

[76] Vgl. Anm. 19 und 21.

Die Frage lag fern, solange man in der von P^g erzählten Geschichte nur eine Legitimation der nachexilischen Kultgemeinde sah. Inzwischen ist sie aber schon in die Vermutung verdichtet worden, die priesterliche Kultgemeinde in der Wüste stelle vielleicht gar nicht eine Urgestalt, sondern ein Zukunftsideal, wenn nicht ein Eschaton dar.[77] Wie steht es damit?

Da der Verfasser von P^g das, was er sagen will, gewöhnlich auch deutlich sagt, sollten wir nach reflexen Äußerungen suchen. Dabei ist es angebracht, bei jener Geschichtsdeutung einzusetzen, die seine Vorlagen enthielten. Das Thema "Abraham als Beginn des Segens für alle Völker" hat er nicht aufgegriffen.[78] Die deuteronomische Bundestheologie hat er offenbar abgelehnt und deshalb eine andere Aussage an das Wort *b*^{e}*rit* gehängt.[79] Anders jedoch mit der Kategorie "Verheißung - Erfüllung". Sie spielt eine den gesamten erzählten Geschichtsverlauf übergreifende Rolle.[80]

Sie erscheint nicht erst bei den Patriarchen, sondern schon im Zusammenhang der Schöpfung.[81] Steck hat gezeigt, daß die Worte

[77] Eher aus einer Art Vollständigkeitsbedürfnis hat man auch in der Zeit der älteren Auffassung von P schon die Frage nach der "Wirksamkeit des messianischen Gedankens" in der Priesterschrift gestellt, allerdings ohne viel damit anfangen zu können. Vgl. Holzinger, *Einleitung* (wie Anm. 9), S. 388. Zur neueren Literatur vgl. oben Anm. 17.

[78] Es besteht Anlaß zur Annahme, daß der Verfasser von P^g seinen Lesern die Gelegenheit geben wollte, mitzuerleben, wie er dieses Thema elegant abwürgte. Denn er greift im Zusammenhang der Abrahamsverheißung das Stichwort "Völker" auf. Aber nur in dem Verstand, daß von Abraham eine Menge von Völkern abstammen sollen: Gen. xvii 4-6. Also schon ein "Völkersegen", aber nicht mehr für "alle" Familien oder Völker der Erde. Gen. xvii 16 stellt klar, daß dieser Segen nur die Nachkommen Saras betrifft, also sehr klar eingegrenzt ist. Zur Textkritik in diesem Vers vgl. N. Lohfink, "Textkritisches zu Gn 17, 5.13.16.17", *Biblica* 48 (1967), S. 439f. Gen. xvii 20 unterstreicht das, indem Ismael zwar zu einem großen, aber doch nur zu *einem* Volk werden soll. Jakob dagegen wird die Verheißung unterstrichen wiederholt: Gen. xxviii 3, xxxv 11, xlviii 3. Dabei macht das Nebeneinander von *goj* und *q*^{e}*hal gojim* in xxxv 11 klar, daß nichts anderes gemeint war als einfach das Volk Israel. So wird aus dem Segen für alle Völker der Erde langsam aber sicher die Zusicherung gemacht, aus Abraham solle das natürlich sehr zahlreiche Volk Israel abstammen. Zur traditionsgeschichtlichen Problematik dieser Formulierungen vgl. Groß, "Jakob" (wie Anm. 29), S. 326f.

[79] Vgl. Anm. 48. Ferner R. Clements, *Abraham and David* (London, 1967), S. 71-8.

[80] Wichtige stilistische Elemente in diesem Zusammenhang werden erfaßt durch McEvenue, "Fulfilment" (wie Anm. 24), und Blenkinsopp, "Structure" (wie Anm. 21).

[81] Zwar finden sich auch schon in den alten Quellen in der Urgeschichte einige Verheißungsmotive (vgl. Gen. iii 15, iv 15, viii 21f.), aber sie sind anderer Art und wirken sich gerade nicht literarisch greifbar in der späteren Geschichte Israels aus.

des Schöpfergottes in Gen. i nicht Befehle sind, die sich sofort ganz realisieren, sondern so etwas wie Entwürfe des von Gott angezielten Endzustands der Welt, wobei der Schöpfer in seinem schöpferischen Tun mehrfach nur einen Anfang setzt, aus dem sich dann im Lauf der Zeit der Endzustand ergeben wird.[82] Das gilt in besonderer Weise beim zweiten Werk des sechsten Tags, dem letzten und höchsten der gesamten Schöpfung. Hier gibt Gott im Segen über den Menschen, den Gen. i 28 enthält, einen Vorentwurf für die ganze Ereigniskette, die das Geschichtswerk dann schildert.[83] Diesem Segen, der teilweise auch im Gang der Darstellung wiederholt und wiederaufgenommen wird, entsprechen später auch Erfüllungsnotizen.[84] So

Tafel IV

Gen. i 28 als Vorentwurf von P^g

		BRK	*PRH*	*RBH*	*ML' 'RṢ*	*KBŠ 'RṢ*	*RDH* (Tiere)		
Segen	Gen. i 28	×	×	×	×	×	×		
	ix 1, 7	×	×	×	×				
	xvii 2, 6, 16	×	×	×					
	xxviii 3	×	×	×					
	xxxv 9, 11	×	×	×					
	xlviii 3f	×	×	×					
Erfüllung	xlvii 27		×	×					
	Ex. i 7		×	×	×				
	Jos. xviii 1					×			
								YR' +	*ḤTT*
Revision	Gen. ix 2							×	×

[82] O. H. Steck, *Der Schöpfungsbericht der Priesterschrift* (Göttingen, 1975).

[83] Insofern P^g sich um die anderen Schöpfungswerke (von ihrer Gefährdung bei der Sintflut abgesehen) nicht mehr weiter kümmert, sie also aus seiner Darstellung entläßt, liegt hier beim Menschen allerdings ein Spezialfall vor, der, wie Steck ebd. S. 129-58 ausführlich darlegt, die Gesamtgestaltung von Gen. i 26-31a tief beeinflußt hat. Die letzte Untersuchung zur hier vorliegenden Thematik ist Brueggemann, "Kerygma" (wie Anm. 21), der allerdings zu unvermittelt in Gen. i 28 eine Aussage über Israel und seine Hoffnung, aus dem Exil in sein Land heimzukehren, herausliest. Meine eigene Analyse von Gen. i 28 findet sich in N. Lohfink, " 'Macht euch die Erde untertan'?", *Orientierung* 38 (1974), S. 137-42; vgl. ders., "Die Priesterschrift und die Grenzen des Wachstums", in *Theologisches Jahrbuch 1976* (Leipzig, 1977), S. 223-48. Die dort gegebene Interpretation der Herrschaft des Menschen über die Tiere ist jedoch im Lichte dessen, was nun folgt, zu revidieren.

[84] Zum Folgenden vgl. jeweils Tafel IV. Dort sind jene Formulierungen nicht aufgenommen, die sich auf die Vermehrung der Tierwelt oder auf die Seitenlinien in der Nachkommenschaft Abrahams beziehen, ferner ist nur der Wortschatz von Gn. i 28 berücksichtigt.

fragen wir nun im Hinblick auf eine vermutete Eschatologie in P^g, ob in Gen. i 28 etwas angekündigt wird, dessen Erfüllung im Werk selbst nicht geschildert wird und, wenn möglich, auch in exilisch-nachexilischer Zeit noch ausstand.[85]

Nach Gen. i 28 soll zunächst einmal die anfänglich kleine Menschheit sich vermehren und über die Erdoberfläche ausbreiten: *p^eru ur^ebu umilʾu ʾet haʾareṣ*.[86] Dieser Segen wird nach der Flut, wo die Menschheit wieder am Anfang steht, wiederholt und dann insbesondere noch einmal Abraham und Jakob, aus denen das Volk Israel werden soll, gegeben. Die Erfüllung wird zweimal konstatiert, in Gen. xlvii 27 und in Ex. i 7. Zumindest die zweite dieser Erfüllungsnotizen meint den Segen über Abraham-Jakob und den Segen über die ganze Menschheit zugleich.[87]

Dem Vermehrungssegen schließt sich in Gen. i 28 der Segen dafür an, daß die durch die Vermehrung entstehenden Völker jeweils ihr Land in Besitz nehmen. Denn so scheint mir der Imperativ *kibšuha* verstanden werden zu müssen.[88] Dieses Verheißungs- und Segensmotiv erscheint von neuem von Abraham an, da jedoch unter anderem Vokabular: Es ist die Verheißung des Landes Kanaan an Abraham und Isaak und die ständige Bezugnahme auf sie im Fortgang der priesterlichen Erzählung.[89] Nachdem der Vermehrungssegen am Anfang des Buchs Exodus erledigt ist, bestimmt sie den Gang der Handlung, wie vor allem Ex. vi klarstellt. Israel ist noch nicht in seinem Land und muß in dieses Land gebracht werden. Daß dies wirklich die Ausführung von dem ist, was in Gen. i 28 zur ganzen

---

[85] Bei J zum Beispiel ist das der Fall. Denn die "Erfüllungen" von Gen. xii 1-3, die Wolff in der Patriarchengeschichte aufgewiesen hat, sind doch nur so etwas wie "Erfüllungen *in nuce*", und die volle Erfüllung des Völkersegens stand in der Zeit, in der J verfaßt wurde (gleichgültig, wie man diese ansetzt), auf jeden Fall noch aus.

[86] Hierzu vgl. vor allem noch Gilbert, "Multipliez" (wie Anm. 64).

[87] Daß eine Erfüllungsnotiz zweimal gegeben wird, muß nicht erstaunen, da P Wichtiges gern paarweise auftreten läßt. Daß die zweite Notiz *per modum unius* sich auch auf den Segen bei der Schöpfung bezieht, geht klar aus zwei Ausdrücken hervor, die sie hat, die aber nicht zum Abraham-Jakobssegen gehörten: *šrṣ* vgl. Gen. ix 7; *mlʾ* (Land) vgl. Gen. i 28, ix 1. Die Reihenfolge ist hier chiastisch zu Gen. ix 1, 7.

[88] Vgl. Lohfink, "Erde" (wie Anm. 83), S. 138f.

[89] Analyse der relevanten Texte bei Cortese, *Canaan* (wie Anm. 19). Die im Gegensatz zum Fruchtbarkeitssegen veränderte Terminologie hängt an der traditionellen Landverheißung und an speziellen priesterlichen Vorstellungen vom sakralrechtlichen Charakter des Landbesitzes Israels. Offenbar sollte hier doch nicht alles in den Bereich der Gesamtmenschheit übertragen werden, deshalb die andere Terminologie in Gen. i 28.

Menschheit gesagt wurde, macht einer der letzten Sätze von P^g deutlich. Denn in Jos. xviii 1 wird nun wieder die Vokabel von Gen. i 28 aufgenommen, die zwischendurch niemals gebraucht worden war: "Die volle Versammlung der Söhne Israels kam zusammen in Schilo, und dort errichteten sie das Zelt der Begegnung, als das Land in Besitz genommen vor ihnen lag" (*w^eha'areṣ nikb^ešah lipnehem*). Dies ist die literarische Klammer um das ganze Werk.

So bleibt aus Gen. i 28 nur noch ein Element, die menschliche Herrschaft über die Tiere.[90] Für sie fehlt in P^g jede Erfüllungsnotiz. Aber das liegt nicht daran, daß hier nun endlich ein noch ausstehendes Eschaton zu greifen wäre, so schnell sich uns hierfür vielleicht auch Parallelen vom messianischen Tierfrieden anbieten möchten,[91] sondern dieses Thema wird anders als durch Erfüllung innerhalb von P^g erledigt: durch eine Revision des Weltentwurfs. Im Blick auf die Herrschaft über die Tiere bekommt der Mensch, um mesopotamisch zu reden, noch einmal neu "sein Schicksal bestimmt".

Der unmittelbar auf Gen. i 28 folgende vegetarische Speisebefehl für Mensch und Tier in i 29 zeigt, daß die Herrschaft der Menschen über die Tiere auf jeden Fall als etwas ganz paradiesisch-Friedliches gemeint war. Genau dies zerstört jedoch die Sünde von *kol baśar* "allem Fleisch" — Mensch und Tier sind beide in diesem Ausdruck eingeschlossen —, welche die Sintflut heraufführt.[92] Sie ist ja *ḥamas* "Gewalttat". Menschen wie Tiere haben zu töten begonnen, offenbar um gegen Gottes Speiseordnung fleischliche Nahrung zu sich zu nehmen. Nach der Flut wird Gott Noach zusagen, nie mehr eine neue Flut zu senden.[93] Doch damit er dies machen kann, muß er vorher gewissermaßen das Maß möglicher Gewalttat vermindern. Das tut er, indem er den Menschen erlaubt, von nun an Fleisch zu essen. Das ist der Sinn jener mit der Sprache des heiligen Kriegs arbeitenden Einführung eines Kriegszustands zwischen Mensch und

[90] Zur Bedeutung von *rdh*, das man nicht von dem fragwürdigen Beleg Joel iv 13 her bestimmen darf, vgl. Lohfink, "Erde" (wie Anm. 83), S. 139.

[91] Etwa Jes. xi 6-9.

[92] Gegen A. R. Hulst, "Kol basar in der priesterlichen Fluterzählung", in *Oudtestamentische Studien* 12 (Leiden, 1958), S. 28-68, und ohne die komplizierte Erklärung von J. Scharbert, *Fleisch, Geist und Seele im Pentateuch* (Stuttgart ²1964), S. 53f., der Mensch als "Spitze" allen Fleisches sei gewissermaßen "alles Fleisch", weil die Tiere ja vom Gericht über den Menschen mitbetroffen seien.

[93] Gen. ix 8-17. Zur Analyse vgl. vor allem McEvenue, *Narrative Style* (wie Anm. 16), S. 72-8, und Groß, "Berit" (wie Anm. 16). Die meisten Arbeiten verbauen sich den Zugang zu diesem Text durch Nichtbeachtung des Tempussystems und der stilistischen Figuren.

Tier in Gen. ix 2: "Furcht und Schrecken vor euch (*mora'akem w^{e}ḥitt^{e}kem*) soll sich auf alle Tiere der Erde legen, auf alle Vögel des Himmels, auf alles, was sich auf der Erde regt, und auf alle Fische des Meeres. Euch sind sie in die Hand gegeben (*b^{e}jedkem nittanu*)".[94]

Auch das letzte Element von Gen. i 28 weist also nicht über jene Geschichte hinaus, die in P^{g} erzählt wird. Eine andere Verheißung, die sich nicht auch innerhalb ihrer Erzählung erfüllt, kommt nicht in Sicht. Die Verheißung, Abraham und Jakob seien Stammväter von Königen, ist mindestens für die Leser von P^{g} längst in Erfüllung gegangen.[95] Ebenso die, Jahwe werde ihr und ihrer Nachkommen Gott sein.[96] So können wir getrost sagen, P^{g} kenne kein Mehr, das über die in der geschilderten Geschichte beschriebenen Realitäten in Zukunft noch hinausgehen werde. P^{g} kennt keine dynamische, sich immer wieder selbst übersteigende und auf ein ungeahntes Eschaton hinsteuernde Geschichte, nachdem Israel einmal den Jordan überschritten hat.

Eher ist im Zusammenhang mit paradiesischem Vegetarismus und dessen Aufhebung nach der Flut eine absteigende Linie sichtbar geworden. Sollte Ewald doch recht gehabt haben, wenn er die im ganzen ja geschichtspessimistische Theorie von den vier Weltaltern zum Vergleich heranzog? Zwar wäre sie nicht selbst in P^{g} zu finden, wohl aber gäbe es auch nach P^{g} in der Geschichte einen analogen Abstieg aus einer besten Welt in eine neue, nur noch zweitbeste.

In gewissem Sinn scheint mir das zuzutreffen. Wir sind allerdings in der Lage, eine viel naheliegendere Parallele heranzuziehen als irgendeinen Text über einen Abstieg von einem goldenen zu einem eisernen Zeitalter. Es handelt sich um den Atraḫasīs-Mythus (vgl. Anm. 26).

Er steuert bekanntlich recht schnell auf die Erschaffung der Mensch-

---

[94] Zur Verbindung des Wortpaars *jr' + ḥtt* mit dem Krieg vgl. Dtn. i 21, xxxi 8; Jos. viii 1, x 25; 1 Sam. xvii 11; 1 Chr. xxii 13, xxviii 20; 2 Chr. xx 15, 17, xxxii 7. Zur Verbindung der sprachlichen Form mit dem Jahwekrieg vgl. Dtn ii 25, xi 25. Daß *ntn b^{e}jad* der feste Ausdruck des Heilsorakels im Krieg war, bedarf keiner Diskussion.

[95] Sie findet sich in Gen. xvii 6, 16, xxxv 11. Sie deutet an, daß die Abrahamsberit bei P^{g} sich in die Tradition der Natansverheißung stellt, die als Davidsberit verstanden wurde und zunächst nicht in deuteronomischen Kategorien zu denken war. Vgl. dazu Clements, *Abraham* (wie Anm. 79).

[96] Sie erfüllt sich am Sinai, wenn Gott kultisch in Israels Mitte Wohnung nimmt. Dies ist mit der bei P^{g} üblichen Wiederholungstechnik mit Ex. vi 7 als Brücke in Ex. xxix 45f. an strategischer Stelle der Sinaioffenbarung eindeutig zum Ausdruck gebracht.

heit zu, sein erstes großes Ereignis, und dann schildert er die Geschichte der Menschen und Götter bis kurz nach der Flut. In diesem Augenblick schließen die über der Flut und der Rettung des Sintfluthelden Atraḫasīs zerstrittenen Göttergruppen einen Kompromiß, in dem das Dasein der Menschen in der Welt neu geordnet wird. Was eigentlich zum Götterbeschluß, die Menschen durch eine Flut zu vernichten, geführt hat, ist unter den Assyriologen offenbar noch umstritten. War es menschliche Rebellion — so G. Pettinato [97] —, war es der Griff nach Höherem, als für den Menschen vorgesehen war — so z.B. W. von Soden [98] —, oder war es das rein biologische Faktum, daß die Menschen sich zu rasant vermehrten und deshalb zu zahlreich wurden — so A. D. Kilmer und W. L. Moran? [99] Vielleicht war es sowohl Sünde als auch Biologie. Doch wenn man sich an das halten will, was in dem uns zugänglichen Text deutlich zutage tritt, nämlich die Kompromißformulierungen nach der Flut, dann scheint sich doch vor allem die Übervölkerungsproblematik zu spiegeln. Denn der Kompromiß bezieht sich auf Maßnahmen, die dazu dienen, die Zahl der Menschen kleiner zu halten als vorher.[100] Auf jeden Fall wird nach dem Atraḫasīs-Mythus nach der Flut eine neue Welt eingerichtet, weil die erste sich nicht bewährt hat, und hierin scheint mir eine klare Parallele zur Priesterschrift vorzuliegen, so unterschiedlich die Gründe zu sein scheinen, deretwegen es in den beiden Werken zur Flut kommt.

Was bedeutet dies nun für das Geschichtsverständnis von P^g? Der

---

[97] "Die Bestrafung des Menschengeschlechts durch die Sintflut", *Orientalia*, N.S. 37 (1968), S. 165-200. Lambert und Moran haben sich dazu recht kritisch geäußert.

[98] "Der Mensch bescheidet sich nicht. Überlegungen zu Schöpfungserzählungen in Babylonien und Israel", in *Symbolae Biblicae et Mesopotamicae Francisco Mario Theodoro de Liagre Böhl dedicatae* (Leiden, 1973), S. 349-58.

[99] Moran, "Atrahasis" (wie Anm. 26); Kilmer, "The Mesopotamian Concept of Overpopulation and Its Solution as Reflected in the Mythology", *Orientalia*, N.S. 41 (1972), S. 160-77.

[100] Möglicherweise wird die Zahl der Menschen auf ein Drittel der bisherigen Menschheit reduziert. Als Mittel dazu dienen Unfruchtbarkeit mancher Frauen, der Paschittu-Dämon (Kindersterblichkeit) und die Institution kinderloser Priesterinnen. Der Text (Worte des Gottes Enki an die Muttergöttin Nintu) wird von Kilmer so übersetzt: "He opened his mouth to speak, saying to the Lady of Birth, the Mother-womb: O Lady of Birth, Creatress of the Fates, (Let there be for the peoples ...) (*etwa 5 weggebrochene Zeilen*) ... Moreover, let there be a third-category among the people (? *oder*: only one-third of the people?). (Let there be) among the people bearing women and barren women, Let there be among the people a *Pašittu*-demon, Let it seize the baby from the mother's lap. Establish *Ugbabtu*-priestesses, *Entu*-priestesses, and *Igiṣitu*-priestesses, they shall indeed be tabood, and thus cut off child-bearing" (S. 171).

Atraḫasīs-Mythus erzählt offenbar deshalb von einer bewegten, noch nach Endgültigkeit tastenden Phase der Welt, weil er eine jetzige, ruhig gewordene Welt in ihrem Sosein erklären will.[101] Nichts anderes tut die Priesterschrift. Nur durchläuft sie den Weg durch die Dynamik zur Statik zweimal. Ein erstes Mal parallel zum Atraḫasīs-Mythus, bis hin zu einer ersten Beruhigung nach der Flut. Jetzt steht das Weltgebäude, und es wird nicht mehr erschüttert werden. Doch für die menschlichen Bewohner des Gebäudes folgt noch einmal eine zweite Periode der Dynamik. Sie wird im wesentlichen an Israel exemplifiziert. Die Menschheit hat das, was ihr am Schöpfungsmorgen entworfen wurde, ein wenig revidiert, noch einmal als Aufgabe vor sich. Sie muß in ihre Zahl hineinwachsen, und jedes Volk muß dann das ihm zustehende Land in Besitz nehmen. Das ist wieder Dynamik, ist auf eine größere Zukunft hinstrebende Geschichte. Doch dann wird der von Gott entworfene Zustand erreicht. Hier bricht die Erzählung ab, so wie der Atraḫasīs-Mythus nach dem Kompromiß nach der Flut abbrach. Die Welt ist jetzt so, wie sie sein soll, und benötigt keine Veränderung mehr. Es fehlt auch nicht das erzählerisch-formale Element einer Katastrophe am Ende der zweiten dynamischen Phase und einer Revision der alten Ordnung durch Gottes Wort. Die Sünde des Volks in der Kundschaftererzählung und die Sünde der geistlichen Führer in der Erzählung von der Wasserspende führen in der Wüste zum Untergang einer gesamten Generation mitsamt ihrer Führungsspitze — wer denkt da nicht an die Flut am Ende der Urzeit? [102] Und in Num. xxvii werden für die Zeit von der Landnahme ab die Führungsverhältnisse in Israel umgebaut: In der dynamischen Phase verkehrte Mose mit Gott, und Aaron war ihm untergeordnet; jetzt wird Eleasar, der Priester, Josua, dem Nachfolger Moses, sagen, was Gott ihm durch Orakel mitteilt.[103]

Die Stabilität der in zwei Schüben von Gott in ihre endgültige Form gebrachten Welt wird garantiert durch die doppelte Berit. Die Berit mit Noach garantiert die Stabilität des Weltgebäudes, die Berit mit

[101] Diese Überlegungen sind breiter ausgeführt bei N. Lohfink, "Die Priesterschrift und die Grenzen des Wachstums", *Stimmen der Zeit* 192 (1974), S. 435-50.

[102] Man könnte sogar fragen, ob die Plagen- und Schilfmeerthematik nicht auch in diesen Zusammenhang gehören soll.

[103] Für diese Neuverteilung der Macht in Israel hatte man gewöhnlich nur den priesterlichen Machtanspruch in der nachexilischen Zeit als Erklärung parat. Der muß nicht gefehlt haben, aber warum wurden die Dinge dann nicht gleich von Anfang an so erzählt, daß die späteren Verhältnisse sich spiegelten? Dies sieht sich anders an, sobald man die Strukturanalogie zum Urzeitmythus einführt.

Abraham die Volkszahl, den Landbesitz und die Gegenwart Gottes im Heiligtum in Israels Mitte. In beiden Fällen handelt es sich um eine *b^erit ʿolam*, "eine ewige Zusage".[104] Ihre Geltung ist nicht mehr, wie die der deuteronomischen *b^erit*, von der Bundestreue der Menschen abhängig. Wenn eine menschliche Generation sündigt, fällt sie zwar heraus, es trifft sie die Strafe. Aber von Gott aus ist nichts zurückgenommen, und die nächste Generation kann wieder in die stabile Endgültigkeitsgestalt der Welt zurückkehren.

Auch das Israel im Exil, das heißt die Leser der priesterlichen Erzählung, ist herausgefallen. Die Wüstensituation ist wieder da, oder sogar die ägyptische Situation. Aber auch Hoffnung auf Heimkehr ist da, und sie gründet nicht in irgendeiner Eschatologie und nicht in der Erwartung neuer, alles Frühere übertreffender Setzungen Gottes in der Zukunft, sondern in dem, was seit dem Jordanübergang unsere Welt von Gott her immer schon hat und von ihm her auch nie verlieren kann. Daß die Geschichten, die P^g erzählt, paradigmatisch sind, hängt gerade damit zusammen, daß die Welt immer wieder aus ihrer Vollgestalt ins Unvollkommene des Werdens zurückfallen kann. Dann müssen die Wege der dynamischen Phase gewissermaßen nochmals gegangen werden. Dies verbindet die Ergebnisse des ersten Teils unserer Überlegungen mit dem, was hier im zweiten Teil zur Geschichtsphilosophie der Priesterschrift erarbeitet wurde.

Dieses Geschichtsverständnis leistet für das Israel im Exil genau das gleiche wie ein eschatologisch bewegter Prophet: Es gibt ihm Hoffnung. Dabei wirft es aber nicht jene unauslöschliche Unruhe in die Menschenherzen, die die Propheten geschaffen haben. Vielleicht ist das allein schon ein Grund, warum wir uns heute, da die Menschheit an den "Grenzen des Wachstums" angekommen zu sein scheint, etwas genauer mit der Vision einer statischen Welt beschäftigen sollten, die uns die priesterliche Geschichtserzählung bietet.

Diese Vision ist im übrigen so differenziert, daß die ehemalige Alternative "Gesetz oder Geschichte" nicht mehr existiert. Die erzählte Vergangenheit legitimiert keineswegs mehr einfach die bestehenden Verhältnisse. Die Leser der Priesterschrift leben ja gar nicht innerhalb der herrlichen und ruhigen Ordnungsgestalten, die von Gott her vorgesehen sind und herrschen könnten. Andererseits ist aber auch die Erwartung nicht auf ein neues, noch unbekanntes,

---

[104] Zur *b^erit*-Theologie von P^g, auf die hier nicht mehr weiter als in dieser formalen Aussage eingegangen werden kann, vgl. die Anm. 48 und 93 genannte Literatur.

völlig überraschendes Eschation hin dynamisiert. Die Idealgestalt der Welt war schon da und ist bekannt. Sie ist von Gott her immer da, und man muß nur zu ihr zurückkehren.

Man kann vielleicht fragen, ob die Überladung der priesterlichen Geschichtserzählung mit legislativem Material dann nicht doch die Gewichte zum "Gesetz" hin verschoben hat. Oder ob im endgültigen Pentateuch nicht doch das viel mehr "geschichtliche" Erzählen der alten Quellen oder die deuteronomische Bundestheologie durchschlagen, sodaß der eigentümliche Umgang von P^g mit der Geschichte dadurch nicht mehr sichtbar bliebe. Daher ist die Frage, mit der ich begonnen habe, jetzt am Ende immer noch offen. Sie muß ja überdies dann noch einmal vom Kanonverständnis her gestellt werden, dem jüdischen oder dem christlichen. Aber auf jeden Fall wird man ihr nur beikommen können, wenn man im Umgang mit so differenzierten Gebilden, wie es die priesterliche Geschichtserzählung ist, auf so unreflektierte Begriffe wie etwa den beliebten Begriff der "Heilsgeschichte" verzichtet.

ELOHIM BEIM JAHWISTEN

von

H. LUBSCZYK

Erfurt

Die Urkundenhypothese, die in der Zeit der literarkritischen Erforschung des Alten Testaments für lange Zeit die Vorherrschaft errungen hatte, und die für die überlieferungsgeschichtliche und redaktionsgeschichtliche Forschung die Grundlage bildete, ist Gegenstand neuer Überlegungen geworden, in denen die alten Ergebnisse einerseits aktualisiert, präzisiert und bestätigt [1] und anderseits völlig in Frage gestellt oder negiert werden.[2] Vieles, was einmal sicheres Ergebnis der kritischen Forschung zu sein schien, ist wieder in Fluß gekommen. Sicher ist es verdienstvoll, festgefahrene Positionen, die die freie Sicht blockieren, neu zur Diskussion zu stellen und auf ihre Gültigkeit zu überprüfen. Aber es ist für das Ansehen der kritischen Exegese sicher nicht vorteilhaft, wenn einerseits die Existenz der Pentateuchquellen heftig bestritten wird, und man anderseits sich doch immer weiter auf sie bezieht, und einigermaßen konkrete Vorstellungen von ihrer theologischen Eigenart fortbestehen. Es wäre wenig glücklich, wenn lange Perioden der Forschung als Irrwege beiseite geschoben werden müßten, ohne den Versuch, ihre Ergebnisse, wenn auch modifiziert, weiter zu berücksichtigen.

Es soll darum in diesem Vortrag das Problem der ältesten Pentateuchquellen noch einmal angegangen werden, und zwar von den

---

[1] O. Kaiser, *Einleitung in das Alte Testament* (Gütersloh, ²1970), S. 75ff., 85ff.; R. Kilian, *Die vorpriesterlichen Abrahamsüberlieferungen* (Bonn, 1966), S. 284ff.; H. Schulte, *Die Entstehung der Geschichtsschreibung im alten Israel* (1972); S. Mowinckel, *Erwägungen zur Pentateuch Quellenfrage*, *BZAW* 128 (1964), S. 65ff.; G. Wallis, "Die Seßhaftwerdung Israels und das Gottesdienstverständnis des Jahwisten im Lichte der elohistischen Kritik", *ZAW* 83 (1971), S. 14f.; H. Seebass, *Mose und Aaron, Sinai und Gottesberg*, (Bonn, 1962), S. 2. Vgl. a. H. Holzinger, *Einleitung in den Hexateuch* (Freiburg i.B., 1893), S. 108; O. Eißfeldt, "Die Komposition von Ex 1-12. Eine Rettung des Elohisten", *Kleine Schriften* II (Tübingen, 1963), S. 160-70.

[2] R. Rendtorff, "Der 'Jahwist' als Theologe? Zum Dilemma der Pentateuchkritik", *Congress Volume Edinburgh 1974*, *SVT* 28 (1975), S. 158-66 (166); ders., *Das überlieferungsgeschichtliche Problem des Pentateuch*, *BZAW* 147 (1976).

Gottesnamen her.[3] Wenn die Entdeckung verschiedener literarischer Schichten im Pentateuch bei den Gottesbezeichnungen ihren Anfang nahm, so ist das wohl darin begründet, daß die dargebotenen Traditionen von verschiedenen Gottesvorstellungen geprägt sind, so daß sich in den verschiedenen literarischen Schichten die Entfaltung der Gotteserfahrung Israels niederschlägt. So werden die Wurzeln des israelitischen Glaubensbewußtseins erkennbar, und verschiedene Phasen seiner Geschichte mit Gott treten in den Blick.

Grob könnte man sagen, daß mit dem Gottesnamen "El" Wesensaussagen verbunden sind.[4] "El" erscheint als der Ewige, der Allmächtige, der Höchste, der Schöpfer, der Lebendige, der Eifersüchtige, der Gott, der sich im Kult offenbart, der sieht und sich sehen läßt.

Mit "Elohim" dagegen werden Gottesbeziehungen von einzelnen oder von Gruppen ausgedrückt.[5] "Elohim" ist der Gott Jakobs, der Gott Abrahams und Isaaks, der Gott der Hebräer, der Gott Israels. Mit "Elohim" wird das Bundesverhältnis Israels ausgedrückt, das sich in den Formulierungen "mein Gott", "unser Gott", "ihr Gott" ausspricht.

"Jahwe" endlich bezeichnet den gegenwärtigen Gott,[6] der in der Mitte seines Volkes als Handelnder erfahren wird.[7] Mit dem Namen "Jahwe" steht der "Heilige Krieg" in Verbindung, der vielleicht die Urgestalt der geschichtlichen Gotteserfahrung darstellt.[8]

Die Synthese dieser verschiedenen Gottesvorstellungen und Gotteserfahrungen im biblischen Glaubensbewußtsein, die in der Erforschung der frühen Überlieferungen und Quellen im Pentateuch in

---

[3] Nach S. Mowinckel, *Erwägungen zur Pentateuch Quellenfrage*, S. 65, gibt es "in den nicht-priesterlichen Partien des Pentateuch Stücke", "wo man ohne eine 'Quellenscheidung' nicht auskommt" (Ex. xxxiv); H. Klein, "Ort und Zeit des Elohisten", *EvTh* 37 (1977), S. 247.

[4] O. Eißfeldt, "El und Jahwe", *Kleine Schriften* III (Tübingen, 1966), S. 395ff.; L. Köhler, *Theologie des Alten Testamentes* (Tübingen, [4]1966), S. 29.

[5] A. Alt, "Der Gott der Väter", in *Kl. Schr. z. Gesch. Isr.* I (München, 1953), S. 1ff., 51; H. Seebass, *Der Erzvater Israel BZAW* 98 (1966), S. 72; L. Köhler, a.a.O., S. 17ff.; R. Smend, *Die Mitte des Alten Testamentes* (Zürich, 1970), S. 56.

[6] M. Buber, *Moses* (Heidelberg, [2]1952), S. 107ff.; ders., *Königtum Gottes* (Heidelberg, [3]1956), S. 69f.; M. Noth, *Das zweite Buch Mose* (Göttingen, 1959), S. 30; Th. C. Vriezen, "*'Ehje ʾašer' ehje*", in *FS A. Bertholet* (Tübingen, 1950), S. 498-512.

[7] R. Smend, *Jahwekrieg und Stämmebund* (Göttingen, 1963), S. 28f.; W. Zimmerli, *Grundriß der alttestamentlichen Theologie* (Stuttgart, 1972), S. 49ff.

[8] F. Schicklberger, *Die Ladeerzählungen des ersten Samuel-Buches* (Würzburg, 1973), S. 187f.; G. v. Rad, *Der Heilige Krieg im alten Israel* (Zürich, 1951), S. 44f.

den Blick tritt,[9] zeigt die Eigenart und Komplexität des biblischen Gottesverhältnisses in seinen Ursprüngen und kann für die Erkenntnis der bleibenden Bedeutung des Alten Testaments und seiner Entstehungsgeschichte für unseren Glauben und die Theologie von eminenter Bedeutung sein.

Durch die Entwicklung der überlieferungsgeschichtlichen und redaktionsgeschichtlichen Methode sind auch in bezug auf die Möglichkeiten der literarkritischen Erforschung von Texten neue Verhältnisse geschaffen worden. Spannungen, die in einem Text festgestellt werden, müssen nicht auf verschiedene Quellen hindeuten, sie können auch in einem Wachstum des Stoffes in der mündlichen Überlieferung begründet sein. Doch wird man dort, wo die Verwendung verschiedener Gottesbezeichnungen in einem Text offensichtlich nicht darauf beruht, daß dem Verfasser mehrere Gottesnamen in gleicher Weise zur Verfügung stehen, und auch nicht in der verschiedenen Bedeutung der Gottesbezeichnungen begründet sein kann, vielfach nicht auf ein Wachstum des Textes in der mündlichen Überlieferung schließen können, sondern literarische Entwicklung annehmen müssen. Dort, wo größere Abschnitte, die nur "Elohim" gebrauchen, mit Abschnitten wechseln, in denen nur "Jahwe" vorkommt, wird man das kaum anders als mit der Annahme verschiedener Quellen erklären können. Aber auch hier brauchen nicht mehrere Erzählungsfäden redaktionell miteinander verknüpft zu sein. Es können auch schriftliche Vorlagen von einem Verfasser übernommen und seinem Werk eingegliedert sein, in der Weise, daß der Verfasser in dem übernommenen Text den dort vorgefundenen Gottesnamen stehen läßt, im übrigen aber die ihm selbst geläufige Gottesbezeichnung verwendet.

Wenn man mit dieser Möglichkeit rechnet, dann könnte der "Jahwist" schriftliche Quellen benützt haben, die "Elohim" verwenden, und die er in sein Werk aufnimmt und interpretiert.[10] Wenn diese Vermutung zuträfe, dann könnte sich zwar die Annahme einer durchlaufenden elohistischen Quelle als überflüssig erweisen,

---

[9] H. J. Zobel, "Das Selbstverständnis Israels nach dem Alten Testament", *ZAW* 85 (1973), S. 292; ders., "Ursprung und Verwurzelung des Erwählungsglaubens Israels", *ThLZ* 93 (1968), S. 1-12; H. W. Wolff, "Das Kerygma des Jahwisten", *EvTh* 24 (1964), S. 73-98 = *Ges. Stud. z. AT* (München, 1964), S. 345-73; H. Gese, "Bemerkungen zur Sinaitradition", *ZAW* 79 (1967), S. 144, 142f.

[10] A. Kuenen, *Historisch-kritische Einleitung in die Bücher des Alten Testaments* (Leipzig, 1887), S. 157.

aber viele Beobachtungen über das Verhältnis der elohistischen zur jahwistischen Tradition und Theologie blieben bestehen. Vielleicht ließe sich so das Problem lösen, daß ein Teil der elohistischen Texte offensichtlich jünger ist als der Jahwist, und vielleicht von ihm abhängig, während andere elohistische Texte ältere Traditionen enthalten,[11] als wir sie beim Jahwisten finden. Wir müßten so mit mehreren Übernahmen schriftlicher Quellen aus dem Raum rechnen, in dem "Elohim" verwendet wurde. Man könnte also, auch wenn man die Feststellungen ernst nimmt, die seit Volz und Rudolph bis zu Rendtorff gegen die Quellenscheidung gemacht wurden,[12] weiter von elohistischer und jahwistischer Tradition und Theologie sprechen.

Unsere Frage kann von zwei Seiten her angegangen werden: Einerseits von einer analogen Beobachtung in der Ladegeschichte, in der sich durch die Bezeichnungen *'aron ha'elohim* und *'aron jahwe* nicht verschiedene Quellen voneinander unterscheiden lassen, sondern sich eine Grunderzählung von ihrer späteren Erweiterung abhebt. Anderseits lassen sich mit Hilfe der Gottesbezeichnungen "Jahwe" und "Elohim" in der Vätergeschichte Makrostrukturen erkennen, die für die Abraham-Isaak-Überlieferung und für die Jakob-Joseph-Geschichte je andere Verhältnisse hervortreten lassen. Während in der Abraham-Isaak-Überlieferung die älteren Texte "Jahwe" verwenden, ist es in der Jakob-Joseph-Geschichte umgekehrt. Hier scheint eine elohistische Grundlage jahwistisch interpretiert zu sein.

I

In der Ladeerzählung [13] der Samuelbücher wird fast durchweg der Gottesname "Jahwe" verwendet. Diesem nahezu einheitlichen Sprachgebrauch stehen aber unterschiedliche Bezeichnungen der

---

[11] H. Seebass, *Der Erzvater Israel*, S. 21, 57; ders., *Mose und Aaron*, S. 142; vgl. A. Jepsen, "Zur Überlieferungsgeschichte der Vätergestalten", *WZ Leipzig* III. G 2/3, (1953/54), S. 265-81 (280); F. Bleek, *Einleitung in das Alte Testament* (Berlin, [5]1886), S. 93; M. Noth, *Überlieferungsgeschichte des Pentateuch* (Stuttgart, 1948), S. 248f.

[12] W. Rudolph, *Der "Elohist" von Exodus bis Josua*, *BZAW* 68 (1938), S. 12; R. Rendtorff, *Das überlieferungsgeschichtliche Problem des Pentateuch*, S. 148ff.; S. Mowinckel, *Tetrateuch-Pentateuch-Hexateuch*, *BZAW* 90 (1964), S. 6.

[13] A. F. Campbell, *The Ark Narrative* (*1 Sm 4-6*; *2 Sm 6*). *A. Form-Critical and Tradition Historical Study* (Missoula, Montana, 1975); R. Schmitt, *Zelt und Lade als Thema alttestamentlicher Wissenschaft* (Gütersloh, 1972); J. Jeremias, "Lade und Zion. Zur Entstehung der Ziontradition", in *FS v. Rad* (München, 1971), S. 183-98; O. Eißfeldt, "Lade und Stierbild", *ZAW* 58 (1940/41), S. 190-215.

Lade gegenüber. Wie J. Maier festgestellt hat, ist der älteste Titel der Lade *'aron ha'elohim*.[14] Nun läßt sich aber mit Hilfe der Bezeichnung *'aron jahwe* nicht eine zweite Quelle feststellen, sondern eine spätere Erweiterung.[15] Die beiden Entwicklungsstufen des Textes sollen kurz vorgestellt werden.

Die Eigenart der Grundschrift und ihrer Bearbeitung läßt sich in dem Bericht von der Übertragung der Bundeslade nach Jerusalem ziemlich deutlich erkennen. Mit den verschiedenen Ladebezeichnungen sind verschiedene Vorstellungen verbunden. Mit *'aron ha'elohim* tritt ein Grundbericht hervor, der in der Erzählung sonst durchweg "Jahwe" verwendet, und eine einfache Darstellung des Verlaufes ist. Die Abschnitte dagegen, die von der Lade Jahwes reden und die, die ihnen sprachlich verwandt sind, bieten eine Interpretation des Geschehens, die den Ladekult in Jerusalem offenbar schon voraussetzt.

Der Grundbericht lautet:

> Und David brach auf und zog mit dem ganzen Volk, das bei ihm war, nach Baala in Juda, um von dort die *Lade Gottes* zu holen ... Man stellte die *Lade Gottes* auf einen neuen Wagen und führte sie vom Hause Abinadabs, das auf dem Berge liegt, fort; und Ussa und Achio, die Söhne Abinadabs, führten den neuen Wagen. Ussa ging neben der *Lade Gottes* her, und Achio ging der Lade voran ... Und als sie zur Tenne Nachors kamen, griff Ussa nach der *Lade Gottes* und hielt sie fest, denn die Rinder brachen aus. Da entbrannte der Zorn Jahwes gegen Ussa, und es schlug ihn dort Elohim.[16] Und er starb dort neben der *Lade Gottes*. Und es entbrannte der Zorn Davids ... Und er stellte sie in das Haus des Obed Edom, des Gatiters. Und Jahwe segnete den Obed Edom und sein ganzes Haus. Und es wurde David gemeldet: Jahwe hat das Haus des Obed Edom und alles, was ihm gehört, gesegnet, wegen der *Lade Gottes*. Da zog David hin und holte die *Lade Gottes* aus dem Hause Obed Edoms in die Stadt Davids in Freude (2 Sam. vi 2ff., 7, 8, 10b, 11b, 12).

Der Grundbericht zeigt die Unverfügbarkeit der Lade. Sie kann nicht manipuliert werden. Zugleich kommt aber auch ein Verhältnis Davids zu Jahwe in den Blick, das erstaunlich ist. David antwortet

[14] G. v. Rad, "Zelt und Lade", *Ges. Studien* (München, 1958), S. 120f.

[15] Vgl. H. Lubsczyk, "Die katechetische Verwertung der Überlieferungen von der Bundeslade", *BiLe* 2 (1961), S. 206ff.

[16] Der Text ist nicht in Ordnung; darum kann der Gebrauch von "Elohim" nicht für eine ältere Schicht aus dem elohistischen Bereich in Anspruch genommen werden. Entsprechend 1 Chr. xiii 10 könnte der Text gelautet haben: "Und er schlug ihn dort, weil er seine Hand nach der *Lade Gottes* ausgestreckt hatte".

auf den Zorn Jahwes mit Zorn und schiebt die Lade in das Haus eines Nichtisraeliten ab. Dies kann von dem Interpreten, der schon den Ladekult im Tempel voraussetzt, nicht einfach so hingenommen werden. Er erklärt das Abschieben der Lade in der Furcht Davids vor dem Herrn: "Wie kann da die Lade Jahwes zu mir kommen?" Die Nachinterpretation fügt kultische Einzelheiten hinzu: die Opfer, die nach sechs Schritten der Träger der Lade Jahwes dargebracht werden (13), den Posaunenschall (15), den für die Lade bestimmten Platz im Zelt (17). Die Szene mit Michal, der Tochter Sauls, kann in ihrem Grundbestand zum alten Bericht gehören. Sie würde lauten:

> David drehte sich mit aller Kraft vor dem Herrn, mit einem Schulterkleid aus Linnen gegürtet. Michal, die Tochter Sauls, blickte durchs Fenster. Sie sah David vor dem Herrn hüpfen und sich im Tanze drehen und hegte Verachtung für ihn in ihrem Herzen. Michal, die Tochter Sauls, blieb kinderlos bis zu ihrem Tode (2 Sam. vi 14, 16, 23).

Hier würde mit dem Gericht über das Haus Elis [17] das Gericht über das Haus Sauls verbunden.

Wie sich somit in 2 Sam. vi in den wesentlichen Umrissen ein ursprünglicher Bericht unter der Interpretation durch die Ladebezeichnung erkennen läßt, so finden wir es auch in dem ersten Teil der Ladegeschichte im ersten Samuelbuch. Hier ist der Bericht vom Verlust der Lade ganz knapp. Er lautet:

> Israel zog gegen die Philister und schlug bei Eben Haeser ein Lager auf. Die Philister lagerten bei Aphek. Sie stellten sich gegen Israel in Schlachtordnung auf, der Kampf tobte heftig, und Israel wurde von den Philistern geschlagen. Fast viertausend Mann fielen in der Schlacht auf freiem Feld. Auch die *Lade Gottes* wurde erbeutet, und die beiden Helisöhne Hophni und Pinchas mußten sterben (1 Sam. iv 1b, 2, 11).

Dieser knappe Bericht schildert den Vollzug der Gerichtsdrohung, die Jahwe über das Haus Elis im vorausgehenden Kapitel, in dem die Lade ebenfalls den Titel *Lade Gottes* trägt, bei der Berufung des Samuel ausgesprochen hatte. In diesen Zusammenhang gehört der Tod Elis bei der Nachricht vom Verlust der Lade (iv 12-18) und die Geburt seines Enkels, der den Unheilsnamen Ikabod erhält (iv 19-22). In beiden Berichten erscheint je dreimal der Titel *'aron ha'elohim.*

---

[17] Das *'ikkabedah*, das unmittelbar vorhergeht, kann an den Unheilsnamen "ikabod" erinnern, der am Ende der Katastrophe des Hauses Eli steht. Vgl. L. Rost, "Die Überlieferung von der Thronnachfolge Davids", in *Das kleine Credo* (Heidelberg, 1965), S. 119ff.

Auch der Bericht von der Überführung der Lade in den Dagontempel (v 1f.) der Philister verwendet noch zweimal *'aron ha'elohim*.

Der ganze sich so ergebende Grundbericht handelt mit einer großen erzählerischen Farbigkeit und Straffheit von der Lade, von ihrer Unverfügbarkeit und Herrlichkeit. Dieser Schicht entspricht der Einspruch Natans in 2 Sam. vii gegen den Tempelbauplan Davids und die Zurücksendung der Lade durch David bei seiner Flucht aus Jerusalem in 2 Sam. xv 24f.

Demgegenüber vertritt die Nachinterpretation andere Anliegen. Der Einschub in den Kriegsbericht (1 Sam. iv 3-10) [18] zeigt, daß die Lade nicht mehr selbstverständlich im Krieg mitzieht wie in Jos. vii oder 1 Sam. xiv 18 und auch noch 2 Sam. xvi 24ff. Sie wird erst nach der Niederlage geholt, so daß ein zweiter Waffengang notwendig wird. Der Einschub zeigt unter Verwendung verschiedener Ladetitel in theologisch reflektierter Form die Bedeutung der Lade.[19] Die Blamage des Dagon in 1 Sam. v 3ff. enthält eine scharfe Spitze gegen den Götzendienst, die nicht streng zum Thema "Lade" gehört. Hier erscheint zweimal "Lade Jahwes".

Zusammenfassend können wir sagen: In dem alten Bericht ist der Weg der Lade von Silo über das Exil bei den Philistern bis nach Jerusalem dargestellt. Der Unverfügbarkeit Gottes, die die Grundschicht betont (Tod des Ussa, Verlust der Lade, Widerstand gegen den Tempelbauplan, Rücksendung der Lade durch David) stehen in der *'aron jahwe*-Erweiterung verschiedene Anliegen gegenüber: Erklärung von Schwierigkeiten (Davids Furcht vor Jahwe, die Verunehrung der Lade durch ihren Aufenthalt im Dagontempel), die kultische Ausgestaltung (2 Sam. vi 5, 9, 10a, 11a, 13ff.), sowie die theologische Deutung der Lade als Zeichen für die Gegenwart Jahwes in dem zweiten Waffengang mit den Philistern (1 Sam. iv 4-10).

Aus diesem Befund können wir folgende Schlußfolgerungen ziehen: Wir können durch den verschiedenen Gebrauch der Ladetitel "Lade Gottes" und "Lade Jahwes" nicht zwei Erzählungsfäden voneinander scheiden, sondern eine Grunderzählung von ihrer Interpretation. Damit kommen aber nicht nur zwei, sondern drei Überlieferungsschichten oder -bereiche in den Blick. Der Überlieferungsbereich der Grunderzählung, die neben *'aron ha'elohim* durchweg "Jahwe" verwendet. Die Interpretation, die nur "Jahwe" sagt, und jener

[18] Vgl. J. Maier, *Das altisraelitische Ladeheiligtum*, *BZAW* 93 (1965), S. 47ff.; F. Schicklberger, *Die Ladeerzählungen des ersten Samuel-Buches*, S. 74ff.

[19] J. Maier, *Das altisraelitische Ladeheiligtum* S. 49ff.

Überlieferungsbereich, in dem die Lade den Titel "Gotteslade" angenommen hat.

Es ergibt sich nun die Frage, ob aus diesem Bereich mit der Lade — oder auch getrennt von ihr — schriftliches Material nach Jerusalem gekommen ist, das uns noch im Pentateuch erhalten ist.[20] Dabei müßten wir mit einer doppelten jahwistischen Interpretation rechnen: mit der, die der *'aron ha'elohim*-Schicht entspricht und mit jener, die der *'aron jahwe*-Schicht verwandt ist. So ergibt die Analogie der Ladegeschichte in bezug auf die Verwendung der Gottesnamen im Pentateuch nicht nur ein Beispiel für jenes Phänomen der Verwendung und Interpretation schriftlicher Quellen, das wir für den Pentateuch vermutet haben, sondern auch einen Hinweis auf den möglichen Ursprung der elohistischen Tradition.

II

Wenn man die Väterüberlieferungen der Genesis in bezug auf den Gebrauch des Gottesnamens überschaut, dann ergibt sich ein verschiedenes Bild für die Abraham-Isaak- und die Jakob-Joseph-Tradition, die sich in der Mosetradition im Buche Exodus fortsetzt. Während in der Abrahamgeschichte (Gen. xii-xvi, xviii f., xxiv) die Gottesbezeichnung "Elohim" nicht vorkommt [21] und ebensowenig in der Isaaküberlieferung (Gen. xxvi), ist in der Jakobtradition in Kap. xxxi-xxxv (außer xxxii 10) [22] fast nur "Elohim" verwendet, und in der Josephgeschichte wird, mit Ausnahme von Kap. xxxix, wo in den Rahmenversen 1-5 und 21-23 insgesamt achtmal "Jahwe" erscheint, durchweg "Elohim" gebraucht.[23] Dieser Befund in der Genesis erweckt den Verdacht, daß auch in der Exodusüberlieferung die Elemente, die "Elohim" verwenden, in diesen Zusammenhang gehören können.

Bevor wir dieser Frage nachgehen, soll die elohistische Jakobgeschichte im Zusammenhang skizziert werden. Schon vom Stoff her erscheinen die elohistischen Elemente als die älteren.[24] Es geht

[20] A. Weiser, "Die Tempelbaukrise unter David", *ZAW* 77 (1965), S. 163ff.

[21] Eine Ausnahme bildet neben Gen. iif. der Fluch über Kanaan (Gen. ix 26f.).

[22] Nach O. Eißfeldt, *Hexateuch-Synopse* (Leipzig, 1922), 65* zu J. gehörig.

[23] Gen. xxxix 9, xl 8, xli 16, 25, 28, 32 (bis), 38, 39, 45, 51, 52, xlii 18, 28, xliii 32 (bis), 29, xliv 16, xlv 5, 7, 8, 9, xlvi 1, 2, 3 (bis), xlviii 9, 11, 15 (bis), 20, 21, l 17, 19, 20, 24, 25. Mit Ausnahme von xlvi 1ff. immer in direkter Rede der handelnden Personen; S. Mowinckel, *Erwägungen zur Pentateuch Quellenfrage*, S. 61.

[24] H. Seebass, *Der Erzvater Israel*, S. 57, Anm. 5.

um das Verhältnis Jakobs zu den Heiligtümern Sichem [25] und Betel [26] im Westjordanland und um die des Ostjordanlandes Mahanajim [27] und Penuel[28] Die Wanderung Jakobs von einem Heiligtum zum anderen ist in eine Familiengeschichte eingebettet, in der der Ursprung der Stämme Israels und die Trennung von den Aramäern behandelt wird.[29] Da auch die Versöhnung mit Esau zu diesem elohistischen Kern der Jakobgeschichte gehört,[30] muß zuvor das Unrecht Jakobs gegen Esau erzählt worden sein,[31] so daß der Beginn der Geschichte in der verschiedenen Charakterisierung der beiden Brüder und ihres verschiedenen Verhältnisses zu Vater und Mutter [32] sowie in der List des jüngeren, der sich den Segen des Vaters stiehlt, gesehen werden muß.[33] In dieser Erzählung hat Esau nichts mit Edom zu tun. Es geht, ähnlich wie in der Geschichte von Kain und Abel, um das Verhältnis zwischen Viehzüchtern und Jägern.

Auch in den Kap. xxv, xxvii-xxx ist zu erkennen, daß die elohistischen Teile die älteren sind. Das ist besonders klar in der Betelüberlieferung zu sehen. Hier bilden die jahwistischen Elemente keine zusammenhängende Geschichte,[34] sondern eine theologische Interpretation der ursprünglichen elohistischen Geschichte, die schon aus

---

[25] Gen. xxxiii 20. Hier nicht "Elohim", sondern *ʾEl ʾelohe jisrael.*

[26] Gen. xxviii 10-22, xxxv 1-7. Neben "Elohim" steht in xxxv 7 analog zu xxxiii 20 "El Betel". Es geht offenbar um die Identifizierung von El mit dem Gott Jakobs.

[27] Gen. xxii 1f. Erzählung und Deutung mit "Elohim".

[28] Gen. xxxiii 31. Deutung des Namens "Penuel" mit "Elohim".

[29] Gen. xxxi 44-54. Die Deutung des Namens "Mizpa" ist jahwistisch.

[30] Das Stück wird von Gunkel und anderen zum größten Teil zu J gestellt; doch kommt in ihm nur der Gottesname "Elohim" vor (xxxiii 5, 10, 11).

[31] A. Kuenen, *Hist.-krit. Einleitung*, S. 138: "Aus der Fortsetzung des E in G XXXII, XXXIII geht hervor, daß auch nach dieser Urkunde Jakob sich an Esau versündigt hatte und nach Haran geflohen war; ein Bericht über sein Vergehen muß sich deshalb wohl in derselben gefunden haben . . ."

[32] Gen. xxv 28; vgl. xxxvii 3.

[33] Nach Wellhausen sind zwei Erzählungen miteinander vermischt. Die List Jakobs wird in beiden erzählt; vgl. R. Smend, *Die Erzählung des Hexateuch* (Berlin, 1912), S. 68f.

[34] E. Otto, "Jakob in Betel", *ZAW* 88 (1976), S. 172f., 176f. Die Parallelen zwischen der elohistischen Vorlage und der jahwistischen Interpretation erklären sich darin, daß das Gelübde Jakobs, das ursprünglich auf die Erscheinung antwortete, nun durch ein Wort Jahwes vorbereitet wird. Schon A. Kuenen, a.a.O., S. 138f., sieht, daß auf V. 10-12 unmittelbar V. 17 folgen mußte. "Aus der Leiter schließt Jakob, daß Betel ein Ort ist, wo Himmel und Erde miteinander in Gemeinschaft stehen. In dem eingeschobenen Stück v. 13-16 steht Jahwe (v. 13, 16), in dem andern Bericht Elohim (v. 12, 17, 20, 22)". A. Jepsen, "Zur Überlieferungsgeschichte der Vätergestalten", *WZ Leipzig* III. G ^{2}/3 (1953/54), S. 265-81 (280).

zwei Teilen besteht, einer Heiligtumslegende von Betel (xxviii 11f., 17ff.), die mit einer Gelübdeerzählung (xxviii 20, 22) verbunden ist. Der Sinn der Heiligtumserzählung ist klar. Es geht um den Ort — fünfmal wiederholt sich *maqom*, der durch den Traum Jakobs in seiner Heiligkeit offenbar und durch das Gelübde zum Gotteshaus wird.

In der elohistischen Grundlage der Betelerzählung erscheint Jakob, wie in den Heiligtumslegenden von Mahanajim und Penuel, als Visionär. Das geschehen selbst ist stumm und wird erst von Jakob selbst gedeutet. In der Penuelerzählung gehören die Worte des mit Jakob Ringenden zum Geschehen; die Deutung folgt in xxxii 31. Die Umbenennung Jakobs in Israel gehört nicht zur Heiligtumslegende von Penuel.

In der Erzählung von der Geburt der Jakobsöhne ist ein elohistischer Kern jahwistisch gerahmt. In dem Block der Stämme Dan, Naphtali, Gad, Aser, Issachar, Sebulon, Joseph kommt in der Begründung der Namensgebung der Söhne nur die Gottesbezeichnung "Elohim" vor; dagegen ist in dem einleitenden Komplex, in dem die Stämme Ruben, Simeon, Levi und Juda genannt werden, die Benennung mit "Jahwe" verbunden. Wenn die Stämme, bei deren Namensdeutung keine Gottesbezeichnung steht (Levi, Gad, Aser) mit zu dem Komplex gerechnet werden, in dem sie stehen, stimmen die in dem elohistischen Kern genannten Stämme in etwa mit denen überein, die im Deboralied erscheinen und teilweise mit denen, die in Ri. i der Stämmekoalition von Groß-Juda gegenüberstehen.

Die elohistische Liste zielt auf Joseph hin.[35] Die Erweiterung des Jahwisten und vor allem die zweite Deutung des Namens Joseph mit "Jahwe" öffnet die Liste zu Benjamin und damit zum Zwölfstämmebund hin.[36] Sie zeigt, daß es sich um eine redaktionelle Erweiterung des älteren Textes handelt.

Ergibt sich so in Umrissen eine deutliche elohistische Grundlage der Jakobtradition, so ist die Frage, ob man auch in der Mosegeschichte eine frühere elohistische Darstellung erkennen kann.

In der Mosetradition findet sich eine mit dem Gottesberg (Ex. iii 1, iv 27, xviii 5, xxiv 13) und mit Midian (Ex. iv 19, ii 15f., iii 1,

[35] S. Lehming, "Zur Erzählung von der Geburt der Jakobsöhne", *VT* 13 (1963), S. 74ff. (79); H. Seebass, *Der Erzvater Israel*, S. 35, Anm. 118.

[36] S. Lehming, S. 79. Die Hinzufügung der jahwistischen Deutung ist nicht als "bewußte Mißachtung der Verherrlichung Josephs" zu beurteilen, sondern als Hinweis auf das Zwölfstämmesystem. Vgl. C. A. Simpson, *Composition of the Book of Judges* (Oxford, 1957), S. 167f.

xix 1) verbundene Schicht, die nur "Elohim" verwendet.[37] Es scheint sich ein nahezu geschlossener Erzählungszusammenhang zu ergeben.

Die Erzählung beginnt mit der Darstellung der Notsituation in Ägypten, die durch die Geburt und die Rettung des Retters in charakteristischer Weise beleuchtet wird (Ex. i 8-22, ii 1-10). Sie berichtet weiter von der Flucht des Mose nach Midian (ii 15), seiner Begegnung mit dem midianitischen Priester und der Aufnahme in seine Familie (ii 16-22).

Zu dieser elohistischen Eröffnung stimmen die elohistischen Elemente in der Berufungsgeschichte und ergeben einen geschlossenen Bericht, in dem Mose als Retter gesandt wird.[38] Gott verspricht ihm — wie Jakob — sein Mitsein. Das Ziel der Rettung ist die Wanderung zum Gottesberg und der dort stattfindende Gottesdienst. Die Darstellung der Befreiung selbst ist am Gottesnamen nicht zu erkennen, könnte aber in Texten enthalten sein, die meist dem Elohisten zugeschrieben werden und die im Dialog mit Pharao vom Gott Israels sprechen. In ihnen spielt Mose eine aktive Rolle bei der Befreiung, wie es der elohistischen Berufungsgeschichte entspricht, in der Mose der Herausführende ist.

Nach A. H. J. Gunneweg (S. 5) war der Jahwe von Sinai "in der Auszugstradition ursprünglich sowenig zu Hause, wie Gesamtisrael in Ägypten war". Nun wird aber die Lösung Gunnewegs, daß Mose nach Midian gehen mußte, um den Jahwekult und den Sinai mit dem Auszug zu verbinden, schwerlich dem Text gerecht. Die Beziehung des Mose zu Midian ist kaum zu erfinden. Darum ist es näherliegend, die elohistische Schicht als die literarisch frühere anzusehen, die nachträglich jahwistisch interpretiert wird.

[37] Ex. i 8-2, 25*; iii 1, 2b, 3, 4b, 5f., 9-14, iv 20, xviii 1a, 5, 12*, xix 3-6*, 7a, 16f., 19, xx 18-21, xxiv 3a (LXX), 5 (LXX), 8f., 11, 13f, xxxi 18b, xxxii 15f., xxxiii 7a, 9. Zur Quellenscheidung vgl. W. H. Schmidt, *Exodus* (Lief. 1, Neukirchen-Vluyn, 1974), S. 21, 56; A. H. J. Gunneweg, "Mose in Midian", *ZThK* 61 (1964), S. 7ff.

[38] Eine Quellenscheidung in Ex. iiif. wird von Mowinckel (*Erwägungen zur Pentateuch Quellenfrage*, S. 64f.) für unnötig erachtet. Doch kommt man über eine Wahrscheinlichkeit nicht hinaus. Wenn man annehmen darf, daß die Begegnung der Exodusüberlieferung mit dem Jahwismus schon lange vor dem "Jahwisten" geschehen ist, muß man auch mit einer dem Jahwisten eigenen Auszugsüberlieferung rechnen, die er nachträglich mit der schriftlichen Darstellung des Auszugs die ihm quellenhaft vorliegt verbindet. Die Verwandtschaft der Berufungserzählung des Mose mit Prophetenberufungen betrifft nur das Formale, dagegen ist die Analogie zur Berufung Gedeons (Ri. vi 11-14) und zur Königssalbung Sauls (1 Sam. ix, 16, x 1, 6f.) sowohl inhaltlich wie formal. Die jahwistische Fassung (iii 2aA, 4a, 6aB, 7f.) ergibt keinen parallelen Erzählungsfaden, sondern bleibt im Rahmen der Interpretation.

Wenn man das Opfer des Jetro und die Übertragung richterlicher Funktionen an auserlesene Männer als das Grundlegende dieser Begegnung ansieht,[39] dann ist diese Tradition und die damit gegebene Beziehung des Mose zu Midian durchaus als alte Überlieferung verständlich. Es erweist sich als unnötig, zwei Erzählungsfäden zu konstruieren,[40] weil die Grundschrift des Kapitels mit E identisch ist.[41] Es geht um die Bestellung von Richtern, die für die vorstaatliche Zeit von eminenter Bedeutung ist.

Die elohistischen Elemente der eigentlichen Sinaiperikope können dann als Ablösung des midianitischen Priestertums durch das allgemeine Priestertum Israels angesehen werden.[42] Dann wäre aber mindestens ein Teil des elohistisch eingeleiteten Adlerspruches (Ex. xix 3-6) unentbehrlich. Das Mahl der Ältesten auf dem Berg (xxiv 9, 11), das vielleicht durch das Opfer der Jungmannschaft vorbereitet wurde (xxiv 3-5 LXX),[43] wäre der Höhepunkt dieser Übertragung.[44]

Das Amt des Mose, der das Volk Gott entgegenführt (Ex. xix 17, 19) und der anstelle des Volkes mit Gott redet (xx 18-21), liegt nicht im Bereich des Priestertums, sondern der Wortverkündigung und Führung sowie der Verwirklichung des Rechtes. Die Forderung des Rechtes in Israel, die durch das Richteramt, das Mose auf Anraten des Jetro einsetzt, urgiert wird, ist gegenüber dem Priestertum und dem Opferkult das Primäre. So wird in Israel das Opfer, das in der Umwelt ein Priestertum erfordert, zu einer Sache des Volkes. In den Opfervorschriften des Bundesbuches ist dementsprechend von einem Priestertum nicht die Rede (vgl. Noth). Die mit "Elohim" verbundenen Gesetzestafeln (Ex. xxxi 18b, xxxii 16) und das ebenfalls mit "Elohim" verknüpfte Begegnungszelt (Ex. xxxiii 9b) könnten noch in diesen Zusammenhang gehört haben.

---

[39] R. Knierim, "Exodus 18 und die Neuordnung der mosaischen Gerichtsbarkeit", *ZAW* 73 (1961), S. 146ff.; H. Seebass, *Der Erzvater Israel*, S. 59.

[40] Die Begegnung des Mose mit seiner Frau und seinen Söhnen ist für die elohistische Grundschrift wohl deshalb wichtig, weil diese die Stammväter der späteren Ladepriesterschaft sind. Die jahwistische Interpretation muß betonen, daß Mose seine Frau zurückgeschickt hatte, weil sie bei J mit nach Ägypten ziehen mußte wegen des Beschneidungsritus von Ex. iv 24ff. Im übrigen dient die jahwistische Einfügung (xviii 8-11) der Identifizierung Jahwes mit dem Exodus-Gott. Das übrige ist einheitlich elohistisch.

[41] Vgl. H. Seebass, *Mose und Aaron, Sinai und Gottesberg*, S. 45, 84ff.

[42] H. Seebass, S. 99, spricht von "Demokratisierung".

[43] In LXX ist in xxiv 5 "Elohim" vorausgesetzt. Die Abweichungen der LXX vom MT scheinen nicht völlig willkürlich zu sein. H. Schmid, *Mose*, *BZAW* 110 (1968), S. 69, betrachtet den ganzen Abschnitt xxiv 3-8 als elohistisch.

[44] M. Noth, *Das zweite Buch Mose*, S. 160f., bringt das Opfer der "jungen Leute" mit dem Bundesbuch in Verbindung.

Die ganze elohistische Grundlage der Mosegeschichte hätte somit den Charakter einer Rettergeschichte, die am Gottesberge endet und die die Begründung des Gottesvolkes zum Ziel hat. Ob diese Geschichte als Heiligtumslegende der Lade bezeichnet werden kann, hängt mit davon ab, ob es denkbar ist, daß der Bericht über die Entstehung der Lade durch den Einbau der priesterlichen Entstehungsgeschichte der Lade verloren gegangen sein kann. Vielleicht war die Urgestalt des Berichtes von der Entstehung der Lade, bei der es möglicherweise mehr um den Inhalt als um den Behälter selbst ging, nicht mit der priesterlichen Darstellung zu verbinden und mußte deshalb wegfallen.

Bevor wir nach der jahwistischen Interpretation fragen, müssen wir untersuchen, ob die elohistische Mose-Gottesberg-Geschichte schon vorjahwistisch durch die Josephgeschichte mit dem elohistischen Kern der Jakobgeschichte verbunden war. Wenn die elohistische Mosegeschichte ein hieros logos der Lade war, dann wäre ihre Verbindung mit Betel, das Ausgang und Ziel der Jakobgeschichte bildet, für die Zeit verständlich und notwendig, in der die Lade in Betel stand.[45]

Nach Mowinckel ist die Josepherzählung, "wie überhaupt jede echt israelitische Überlieferung, nordisraelitischen Ursprungs, und daß der älteste der Brüder als Leiter auftritt, ist natürlich und selbstverständlich. In der judaisierten Form ist — in Übereinstimmung mit der davidischen 'großisraelitischen' Idée — Juda der Leiter und die sympathische Figur unter den Brüdern geworden; das ist auch natürlich und wohl verständlich".[46] Der scharfe jahwistische Eingriff in Kap. xxxix und die Hinzufügung der Ismaeliter in Kap. xxxvii, xxxix würden ebenfalls dieser Judaisierung zuzurechnen sein.

Die Grundthemen der elohistischen Josephgeschichte: Vorrang des Joseph, der Neid der älteren Brüder, die Unwandelbarkeit der Pläne Gottes mit Joseph, seine rettende Funktion gegenüber den Brüdern sind in der Zeit, in der die Josephgruppe in den mittelpalästinenischen Raum eintrat und den älteren Stämmen der Leagruppe womöglich schon bald an Macht überlegen wurde, wohl verständlich.[47] Wenn es diese Gruppe war, die die elohistische

---

[45] Vgl. dagegen J. Maier, *Das altisraelitische Ladeheiligtum*, S. 41, bes. Anm. 11.

[46] *Erwägungen zur Pentateuch Quellenfrage*, S. 62.

[47] O. Eißfeldt, "Jakob-Lea und Jakob-Rahel", *Kleine Schriften* IV (Tübingen, 1968), S. 170ff.; M. Weippert, *Die Landnahme der israelitischen Stämme* (Göttingen, 1967), S. 53; R. Smend, *Jahwekrieg und Stämme bund*, S. 74.

Mosetradition mitbrachte oder in der diese zuerst rezipiert wurde,[48] dann wäre mit ihr eine neue Phase in der Geschichte Israels eröffnet worden. Das wiederum würde verstehen lassen, daß die elohistische Josepherzählung die Brücke bildet zwischen Jakob- und Mosetradition, so daß die elohistische Darstellung einen Block bildet, der die Begründung Israels bis zur Jakobtradition zurückverfolgt.

Diese Verbindung der Traditionskomplexe würde zugleich bedeuten, daß der El von Betel, der zunächst mit dem Gott Jakobs identifiziert worden war, schon vor-"jahwistisch" mit dem Gott des Exodus gleichgesetzt wurde. Wenn diese Identifizierung auch Jahwe, den Gott Israels, mit einschloß, der wohl schon von dem früheren Stämmebund der Leastämme verehrt wurde,[49] dann wäre der Ladekult von Betel und später von Silo in bezug auf die Integration früherer Gottesvorstellungen ein Prototyp des religiösen Universalismus des späteren Jahwekultes in Jerusalem.

Auch hier in Betel wäre schon in einer Synthese verschiedener Gottesvorstellungen das Glaubensbewußtsein Israels geöffnet worden, nicht nur zur protoisraelitischen Vätertradition hin, sondern auch zur präisraelitischen El-Verehrung.[50]

III

Wenn der Jahwist einen so großen Überlieferungsblock seinem Werk eingegliedert haben soll, dann stellt sich die Frage nach seiner eigenen Überlieferung, nach dem Ursprung der geistigen und religiösen Kraft, ein so komplexes Ganzes seiner eigenen Tradition zu integrieren.

Wir müssen darum den anderen großen Komplex in den Blick fassen, der sich vom Gottesnamen her in der Genesis abzeichnet: die mit der jahwistischen Urgeschichte verbundene Abrahamüberlieferung.

Rolf Rendtorff hat die Existenz des Jahwisten und der älteren

---

[48] Man wird fragen dürfen, ob die Verbindung der Stämme Ephraim und Manasse zu Joseph eine sekundäre ist, die möglicherweise mit dem Eindringen der Moseschar in Verbindung steht. O. Kaiser, "Stammesgeschichtliche Hintergründe der Josephsgeschichte. Erwägungen zur Vor- und Frühgeschichte Israels", *VT* 10 (1960), S. 1-15.

[49] Dafür könnte die Verbindung mit den Kenitern sprechen, die sowohl für den Süden gegeben ist, dadurch, daß die Keniter zu Groß-Juda gehören (H. J. Zobel, "Beiträge zur Geschichte Groß-Judas in früh- und vordavidischer Zeit", *Congress Volume, Edinburgh 1974, SVT* 28 [1975], S. 262f.). Auch für den nördlichen Raum ist die Verbindung zu den Kenitern durch das Deboralied (Ri. v 24) belegt. Vgl. R. Smend, *Jahwekrieg und Stämmebund*, S. 74.

[50] O. Eißfeldt, "El und Jahwe", *Kleine Schriften* III (Tübingen, 1966), S. 391ff.

Pentateuchquellen überhaupt bestritten.[51] Nach ihm hat es keine durchlaufende vor "deuteronomistische" Pentateuchredaktion gegeben: Er stützt sich dabei — was den Jahwisten anbetrifft — auf die Feststellung, daß weder ein jahwistischer Stil noch eine jahwistische Sprache noch eine jahwistische Theologie erkennbar seien.[52]

Ich möchte zunächst versuchen, die Existenz eines Erzählungszusammenhanges zwischen der jahwistischen Urgeschichte und dem Großteil der Abrahamüberlieferungen, in denen "Elohim" nicht vorkommt, aufzuzeigen. Dann kann die Frage gestellt werden, ob sich dieser Zusammenhang in der Interpretation der ursprünglich elohistischen Stoffe in der Jakob-Joseph-Mosegeschichte fortsetzt. Wenn man in Rechnung stellt, daß der Jahwist auch in der Abraham- und Urgeschichte Überlieferungen und eventuell auch schriftliche Quellen verwendet, dann kann seine Theologie, sein Stil und seine Sprache nicht monolithisch und uniform sein. Die Eigenart des Jahwisten wird in der Komposition und im übergreifenden theologischen Anliegen deutlich, die an bestimmten Stellen auch sprachlich und stilistisch faßbar sind.

Daß der Ur- und Abrahamgeschichte ein geschlossenes Werk zugrunde liegt, läßt sich an drei Hauptthemen erkennen, die in der Zeit des davidisch-salomonischen Reiches aktuell waren.

1. G. v. Rad hat die Urgeschichte eine "Harmatiologie" genannt.[53] Der Sündenbegriff der Urgeschichte, der in der Geschichte vom Paradies und Sündenfall zum erstenmal erscheint und dann in dem Rhythmus: Sünde, Gericht und Gnade [54] die ganze Urgeschichte prägt, behält nicht nur in ihr, sondern auch in der Abrahamgeschichte eine grundlegende Bedeutung.[55] Es geht dabei um den Griff des Menschen nach dem, was ihm Gott nicht gegeben oder ausdrücklich verwehrt hat. Charakteristische Leitworte, wie: das *Gute* oder das *Schöne sehen*, *begehr*en und nehmen und eventuell weiter*geben*, oder die anklagende Frage: "Was hast du getan?", markieren einen ganz

[51] *Das überlieferungsgeschichtliche Problem des Pentateuch*, S. 109ff.; "Der 'Jahwist' als Theologe?", *Congress Volume, Edinburgh 1974*, *SVT* 28 (1975), S. 166.

[52] *Das überlieferungsgeschichtliche Problem des Pentateuch*, S. 86-112.

[53] *Theologie des AT* I^3 (München, 1961), S. 158.

[54] *Das erste Buch Mose* (Lizenzausgabe DDR, Berlin, 1955), S. 127ff.

[55] Nach v. Rad stehen die Inhalte von 1 Mose ii und namentlich iii "in auffallender Isolierung im AT" (S. 82f.). Man wird aber sagen müssen, daß, auch wenn diese Texte nicht ausdrücklich zitiert werden, das hier gegebene, durch bestimmte Leitworte gekennzeichnete Sündenverständnis die ganze Abrahamgeschichte beherrscht.

bestimmten Sündenbegriff.[56] Einige von den Leitworten und Leitvorstellungen kehren in der Perikope vom Aufruhr der Göttersöhne (Gen. vi 1-4) [57] und in der Geschichte von der Gefährdung der Ahnfrau in Ägypten (Gen. xii 10ff.) [58] wieder. Auch die Geschichte der Zeugung Ismaels (Gen. xvi) läßt denselben Sündenbegriff erkennen. Abraham hört wie Adam auf die Stimme seines Weibes, und Sara nimmt ihre Magd und gibt sie Abraham, wie einst Eva von der Frucht des Baumes nahm und sie Adam gab.[59]

Die Trennung Lots von Abraham steht in demselben Gedankenfeld. Es geht bei der Landnahme Lots bzw. der Landgabe an Abraham nicht so sehr um den Umfang des von ihnen jeweils in Besitz genommenen Landes, sondern um die Weise des Besitzes. Während Lot sein Land wählt und sich um seines Besitzes willen von dem Segensträger Abraham trennt, empfängt Abraham sein Land von Gott. Die Wiederkehr der Worte: "Ich gebe es dir" (Gen. xiii 15, 17) zeigt im Zusammenhang der Ur- und Abrahamgeschichte den entscheidenden Gesichtspunkt an, unter dem die Landwahl Lots als verfehlt und verderbenbringend erscheint.[60] Von daher wird die sich anschließende Perikope vom Kriegszug der Könige des Ostens mit der Gefangennahme Lots im Sinn der jahwistischen Vorstellung von Gericht und Gnade verständlich.[61] Lot wird in das Schicksal des von ihm gewählten Landes verstrickt, während Abraham sich mit einem Schwur weigert, von Sodom etwas anzunehmen. Das Grundverhältnis Lots zum Land bleibt auch nach der endgültigen Katastrophe von Sodom und Gomorra dasselbe. Lot flieht nicht ins Gebirge, wie ihm

[56] *Theologie* I, S. 159ff.

[57] Die Worte "das Schöne sehen und nehmen" entsprechen der Versuchungsgeschichte in Gen. iii.

[58] Die Erzählung ist im Sinne des Sündenfalls stilisiert. Die Worte "schön anzusehen", "deinetwegen" (Gen. iii 11), "sehen und nehmen", "dein Weib", "was hast du getan?", "vermelden" kehren z.T. mehrfach wieder und lassen das Verhalten Abrahams im Sinne des Jahwisten als Schuld erkennen. Wenn der Jahwist selbst diese ursprünglich von Isaak und den Philistern erzählte Begebenheit auf Abraham und Ägypten übertragen hätte, dann wäre darin seine Absicht zu erkennen, die "Hamartiologie" der Urgeschichte in der Abrahamgeschichte weiterzuführen.

[59] *Das erste Buch Mose*, S. 160. Die übliche Zuweisung von Gen. xvi 3 an P berücksichtigt nicht die Beziehungen zu dem Sprachfeld des Jahwisten.

[60] In der Beschreibung der Landwahl Lots kehren für die Sündenvorstellung der Urgeschichte typische Vorstellungen wieder. Die fruchtbare Ebene wird ausdrücklich mit dem Garten Jahwes verglichen.

[61] H. Lubsczyk, "Melchisedek. Versuch einer Einordnung der Melchisedek-Perikope (Gen 14) in den jahwistischen Erzählungszusammenhang", in *Einheit in Vielfalt, Festgabe f. H. Aufderbeck* (Leipzig, 1974), S. 106f.

von den Engeln befohlen wird, sondern bittet um Zoar, wo er sich dann noch nicht halten kann. Der Griff seiner Töchter nach der Nachkommenschaft charakterisiert nicht nur den Ursprung der Moabiter und Ammoniter, sondern ist im Zusammenhang der Abschluß des Lot-Dramas. Der vielfach variierte Sündenbegriff des Jahwisten begegnet uns auch bei der Landnahme in der Achangeschichte (Jos. vii) [62] und kehrt sogar in der Davidgeschichte wieder.[63] David, der auf dem Dach seines Hauses lustwandelt wie einst Jahwe im Garten des Paradieses, *sieht* eine *schöne* badende *Frau*. Er sendet hin und *nimmt* sie. Die sich anschließende Thronfolgegeschichte könnte wie die Urgeschichte eine Harmatiologie genannt werden. Auf die Sünde des Vaters folgen die Sünden der Söhne, Vergewaltigung und Brudermord.[64] So ist nicht auszuschließen, daß die jahwistische Darstellung ein Grundproblem der davidischen Dynastie vor Augen hat, und daß die Wiederkehr von Sünde, Gericht und Gnade in der Ur- und Abrahamgeschichte auf die Sünde Davids, auf das Gericht über ihn und auf seine Begnadigung hin erzählt sind.[65]

2. Gegenüber der Betonung der Besonderheit Israels in der elohistischen Jakob-Mose-Überlieferung ist die jahwistische Abraham- und Urgeschichte universalistisch zu allen Völkern hin offen. Daß Abraham zum Segen für alle Völker werden soll, prägt das Verhältnis Israels zu den Völkern des davidischen Reiches. Dabei wird eine Differenzierung sichtbar. In verschiedener Weise werden Kain (Gen. iv 1-13), Kanaan (Gen. ix 18-27), Moab und Ammon (Gen. xix 30-38), die Aramäer (Gen. xxiv), die Ismaeliter (Gen. xvi), Ägypten (Gen. xii 10ff.), Mesopotamien und Babel (Gen. xi 8) mit Israel in Verbin-

[62] In Jos. vii 19ff., ist das Wortfeld des Sündenfallberichtes in einer besonderen Vollständigkeit gegeben: "Vermelde mir", "was hast du getan?", "das Gute sehen", "begehren", "nehmen".

[63] Man braucht aus dieser Übereinstimmung nicht die Identität des Verfassers der Thronfolgegeschichte mit dem Jahwisten zu folgern. Doch gibt es noch manche anderen Berührungspunkte zwischen beiden, in der Tendenz und in der Sprache; vgl. H. Schulte, *Die Entstehung der Geschichtsschreibung im alten Israel*, S. 154ff., 181ff.; W. Brueggemann, "David and his theologian", *CBQ* 30 (1968), S. 156ff.

[64] Die Begnadigung Absaloms, der von 2 Sam. xiii 1 im Blick der Thronfolgegeschichte steht, wird auffällig mit der Kainsgeschichte in Verbindung gebracht (xiv 7). Die erzwungene Begnadigung, in der der Mörder im Gegensatz zu Kain, der vom "Angesicht Jahwes" verbannt wird, wieder das Angesicht Davids sehen darf (xiv 24.32), ist der Anfang der Empörung und damit Vorbedingung für das endliche Gericht über Absalom.

[65] In 2 Sam. xv 19-23, 24-27, xvi 5-12 wird sichtbar, daß David zu der Einstellung, die die gesamte Aufstiegsgeschichte kennzeichnet, zurückgekehrt ist: er überläßt sich wieder der Führung Jahwes.

dung gebracht.[66] Dabei geht es fast immer um einen Vorrang Israels, zugleich aber auch um ein verschieden gestuftes Verhältnis zu ihm.

3. Abraham, der Vater der Völker, ist nicht nur die verbindende Gestalt im weltpolitischen Zusammenhang, in dem Israel in der davidisch-salomonischen Epoche steht, sondern er bildet auch im religiösen Bereich eine Klammer zwischen verschiedenen mehr oder weniger heterogenen Elementen der Überlieferung.[67]

Die Identifizierung der Gottheiten, die nicht auf Israel beschränkt ist, sondern auch in der Umwelt häufig vorkommt,[68] soll die Einheit mehrerer Gruppen ausdrücken und fördern. Dabei stellt die Begegnung der Jahweverehrung mit dem El Eljon von Jerusalem einen Sonderfall dar.[69] Melchisedek erkennt und bekennt die von Jahwe bewirkte Rettungstat als Werk des El Eljon von Jerusalem. Die ausdrückliche Identifizierung des El Eljon mit Jahwe wird aber nur von Abraham ausgesprochen, der Melchisedek den Zehnten gibt und wegen dieser Identifizierung geben kann. Diese differenzierte gegenseitige Anerkennung ermöglicht die Einheit der Kanaaniter mit den Israeliten in Jerusalem.[70] Dagegen ist die Identifizierung Jahwes mit dem Gott Abrahams und Isaaks für den Jahwisten kein Problem mehr. Er nennt — wie die Lade- und die Davidgeschichte überhaupt und auch der Großteil der Geschichten des Richterbuches — Gott durchweg "Jahwe".

---

[66] H. J. Zobel, "Beiträge zur Geschichte Groß-Judas in früh- und vordavidischer Zeit", S. 276, kommt zu dem Ergebnis, "daß der Grundgedanke eines theologischen Gesamtverständnisses Israels zwar aus dem Nordreich stammt, der Grundgedanke der ethnischen Einheit Israels aber von dem Südreich zum gemeinsamen Selbstverständnis beigesteuert wurde"; vgl. a. O. H. Steck, "Genesis 12, 1-3 und die Urgeschichte des Jahwisten", in *FS v. Rad* (München, 1971), S. 525-54.

[67] Die Identifizierung der verschiedenen Gottesvorstellungen miteinander ist, wie wir gesehen haben, schon im mittelpalästinensischen Raum in einer sehr durchgreifenden Weise geschehen. Das Verhältnis Abrahams zu den Völkern ist in der jahwistischen Urgeschichte mit dem Segen verbunden, der von ihm für alle Völker ausgeht. Das aber bedeutet, daß die Identifizierung nicht nur im religiösen Bereich bleibt, sondern politisch wirksam wird. Von daher muß die Trennung Lots von Abraham gesehen werden. Es muß bedacht werden, daß Melchisedek, indem er Abraham segnet, selbst gesegnet wird (Gen. xii 3), und daß auch die zahlreiche Nachkommenschaft Hagars im Zusammenhang der jahwistischen Darstellung wohl auf ihrer Beziehung zu Abraham beruht.

[68] Man wird hier vor allem an die ägyptische Religionsgeschichte denken dürfen; O. Eißfeldt, "Israels Religion und die Religionen seiner Umwelt", *Kleine Schriften* V (Tübingen, 1973), S. 1-20.

[69] O. Eißfeldt, Silo und Jerusalem, *Kleine Schriften* III (Tübingen, 1966), S. 422f.; vgl. R. H. Smith, "Abraham and Melchizedek", *ZAW* 77 (1965), S. 129-53.

[70] Anders R. H. Smith, S. 149f.

Wenn man die Isaaküberlieferung mit der Abrahamsgeschichte vergleicht, dann fällt auf, daß hier die theologische Prägung, die der Abrahamüberlieferung beim Jahwisten eigen ist, in der Substanz der einzelnen Geschichten fast ganz fehlt. Es geht um das Verhältnis Isaaks zu seiner Umwelt. Die Probleme der Halbnomaden, die im Umkreis der philistäischen Stadtstaaten wohnen, beherrschen das Feld.[71] Die beiden Erscheinungen Jahwes mit der Verheißung von Land und Nachkommenschaft (Gen. xxvi 2ff., 24f.; vgl. xii 7) entsprechen auch sprachlich den vom Jahwisten gestalteten Verheißungen an Abraham,[72] so daß sich die alte stammespolitisch geprägte Überlieferung von ihrer Interpretation durch den Jahwisten abheben läßt. Die so vom Jahwisten interpretierte Isaaküberlieferung bildet eine Brücke zwischen der jahwistischen Abrahamerzählung und der jahwistisch rezipierten und interpretierten Jakobgeschichte.

Diese jahwistische Gestaltung der Isaaküberlieferung läßt vermuten, daß die theologische Dynamik der Abrahamgeschichte, die nicht ohne die Urgeschichte zu denken und zu verstehen ist, ein Werk des Jahwisten ist. Man wird darum fragen dürfen, ob der Jahwismus vor dem "Jahwisten" nicht sehr stark von den konkreten Nöten der Nomaden geprägt war, die auch den Kampf um das Land im Jahwekrieg bestimmten. Der sozial und national bestimmte alte Jahweglaube mit seinem Kampf um das Land wäre dann erst durch die Exodusgruppe mit ihrer neuen Erfahrung Gottes und neuen Gemeinschaft mit ihm vertieft worden, so daß er zu dem Universalismus des "Jahwisten" fähig wurde. Erst die Erfahrung des in der Befreiung handelnden Gottes hätte den Herrscherdrang nomadischer Eroberer zum Universalismus des Jahwisten geläutert und erhoben,[73] der die Heilung der zerbrochenen Einheit der Menschheit von dem in der Geschichte handelnden Gott erhofft.

IV

Es haben sich in Umrissen zwei große Komplexe ergeben: die jahwistische Ur-Abraham-Isaakgeschichte und die elohistische Jakob-Joseph-Moseüberlieferung. Die eine begründet das Erwählungs-

---

[71] G. Fohrer, "Der Vertrag zwischen König und Volk in Israel", *ZAW* 71 (1959), S. 1-22; H. J. Zobel, "Beiträge zur Geschichte Groß-Judas in früh- und vordavidischer Zeit", S. 271f.

[72] R. Rendtorff, "Der 'Jahwist' als Theologe?", S. 163.

[73] R. Smend, *Jahwekrieg und Stämmebund*, S. 89f., sieht die Möglichkeit des Übergreifens der Mosegestalt von der Herausführungstradition auf die übrigen Traditionskomplexe.

bewußtsein Israels, die andere seinen Universalismus. Beide Elemente des alttestamentlichen Glaubens haben bleibende Bedeutung.[74] Wir müssen uns nun die Frage stellen, ob es denkbar ist, daß der in der Ur- und Abrahamgeschichte erkennbare Jahwist die Jakob-Joseph-Mosegeschichte in sein Werk aufgenommen hat. Mit anderen Worten: Kann die jahwistische Interpretation der Jakob-Joseph Mosegeschichte dem "Jahwisten" zugetraut werden, dessen Werk von der Situation im davidisch-salomonischen Reich bestimmt ist?

Der Jakobüberlieferung wird die jahwistische Geschichte vom Streit der beiden Brüder im Schoße ihrer Mutter vorangestellt (Gen. xxv 21-23). In diesem kleinen Abschnitt wird viermal "Jahwe" gebraucht. Aus den beiden gegensätzlichen Brüdern werden hier zwei feindliche Nationen, Israel und Edom (xxv 30).[75] Damit wird die Völkerordnung, die ein tragendes Element der Ur- und Abrahamgeschichte darstellt, vervollständigt. Das Zurücktreten Edoms, des älteren Volkes und Staates vor Israel, ist im davidischen Reich aktuell und sicher für den judäischen Süden interessanter als für den mittelpalästinensischen Raum, in dem Jakob zu Hause ist.[76] In der Erzählung von der List Jakobs wird man nicht nur die Antwort auf die Frage Isaaks: "Wie hast du so schnell etwas gefunden, mein Sohn?" als jahwistische Interpretation ansehen dürfen, die die Schuld Jakobs verschärft [77] und damit das Thema "Sünde, Gericht und Gnade" weiterführt, sondern auch jene Zusätze zum Segen Isaaks, in denen "Jahwe" vorkommt. Die Zusätze, "das Jahwe segnet" (27bB) und "Völker werden dir dienen, und niederwerfen werden sich vor dir Nationen" (29a) sowie: "Wer dich verflucht, der sei verflucht, und wer dich segnet, sei gesegnet" (29bB), entsprechen der Theologie des Jahwisten.[78] Die Herrschaft über Nationen und der an Israel gebundene Segen können auf die Situation des davidisch-salomonischen Reiches hinweisen. Das für die elohistische Grundlage des

---

[74] Daß die jahwistische universale Sicht auf die Erwählung Israels hingeordnet ist, betont G. v. Rad, *Theologie* I, S. 168: "... daß nämlich die Urgeschichte als eines der wesentlichsten Elemente einer theologischen Ätiologie Israels verstanden werden muß".

[75] G. v. Rad betont, daß die Erzählung auffallend unanschaulich ist. "Der ganze Abschnitt V. 21-28 ist ja keine eigentliche Erzählung und beruht auch nicht auf einer in sich geschlossenen älteren Sage" (*Das erste Buch Mose*, S. 230).

[76] Vgl. H. Gunkel, *Genesis* (Göttingen, [6]1964), S. 298f.

[77] Gen. xxvii 20. Die Lüge Jakobs wird durch die Beziehung auf Jahwe, den Gott Isaaks, verschärft. Anders Gunkel, S. 311.

[78] H. Gunkel schreibt auch V. 29 dem Elohisten zu. Doch wird man aufgrund des Schlusses lieber das Ganze für jahwistische Interpretation halten.

Jakobssegen Verbleibende entspricht dann ziemlich genau dem mehr einem Fluch gleichkommenden Segen über Esau.[79]

In der Geschichte des Traumes Jakobs in Betel (xxviii 10-22) lassen sich, wie mehrfach festgestellt worden ist, nicht eine jahwistische und eine elohistische Version voneinander scheiden, sondern die jahwistischen Elemente stellen eine Nachinterpretation der Heiligtumslegende von Betel dar, die schon vorjahwistisch mit einer Gelübdeerzählung verbunden worden ist.[80] Vers 14 entspricht wörtlich den jahwistischen Vorstellungen (vgl. Gen. xv 5, xii 3, xiii 14). Die Zusammenfassung der früheren Verheißungen, die beim Jahwisten an Abraham ergangen sind,[81] deutet darauf hin, daß uns hier seine Hand begegnet (die Ersetzung der "Sterne" durch den "Staub der Erde" [82] scheint mir dagegen kein Einwand zu sein, da alles andere wörtlich übereinstimmt). Das weitere Vorkommen von "Jahwe" in V. 16b und 21b dient der Identifizierung Jahwes mit dem El von Betel und dem Gott Jakobs. Auch diese Identifizierung liegt in der Linie des Jahwisten.

Die jahwistische Rahmung der Geschichte von der Geburt der Jakobssöhne (Gen. xxix 31-xxx 24), in deren Kern nur "Elohim" verwendet wird, vervollständigt das Schema des Zwölfstämmebundes, wobei Benjamin, der erst später geboren wird, zunächst noch fehlt. Ob die Stämme Ruben, Simeon, Levi und Juda schon den Kern einer älteren Stämmegruppe bilden oder ob diese Zusammenstellung hier ein Werk des Jahwisten ist, kann vom Text allein her nicht entschieden werden.[83] Wenn die Leagruppe tatsächlich eine proto-israelitische Vereinigung von Stämmen war, dann würde der Jahwist den elohistischen Kern aufgrund älterer geschichtlicher

---

[79] Jakob:

Gott gebe dir vom Tau des Himmels
und vom Fett der Erde
und Überfluß an Korn und Wein (Gen. xxvii 28).

Esau:

Fern sollst du wohnen vom Fett der Erde
und vom Tau des Himmels droben.
Von deinem Schwerte sollst du leben (Gen. xxvii 39, 40aA).

[80] E. Otto, "Jakob in Betel", *ZAW* 88 (1976), S. 186, rechnet mit einer vorliterarischen Redaktion in Gen. xxv-xxxvi am Heiligtum von Betel.

[81] Vgl. Gen. xxviii 13 und xiii 15; xxviii 14a und xiii 16 und xxviii 14bA und xiii 14B und xxviii 14bB und xii 3b.

[82] So auch in Gen. xiii 16; vgl. J. Hoftijzer, *Die Verheißungen an die drei Erzväter* (Leiden, 1956), S. 9.

[83] H. Gese, "Bemerkungen zur Sinaitradition", in *Vom Sinai zum Sion* (München, 1974), S. 35ff.; M. Weippert, *Die Landnahme der israelitischen Stämme in der neueren wissenschaftlichen Diskussion* (Göttingen, 1967), S. 48.

Überlieferung ergänzen.[84] Daß es sich literarisch um eine Ergänzung handelt, zeigt die Verdoppelung der Deutung des Namens "Joseph". Neben die elohistische Version in V. 23, in der der ältere Kern sein Ziel findet, tritt die jahwistische (V. 24), die die Erzählung zur Geburt des letzten Sohnes Benjamin hin öffnet und damit das 12er Schema schon vollständig macht.

In dem nun folgenden elohistischen Erzählungsblock finden sich noch einige weitere jahwistische Einschübe.[85] Das Bekenntnis Labans, daß er durch Jakob gesegnet worden sei (xxx 27-30) und der Befehl, heimzukehren (xxxi 3), der das Gebet Jakobs (xxxii 10-13) vorbereitet, das man mit dem Gebet Davids (2 Sam. vii 18ff.) verglichen hat,[86] entsprechen der theologischen Linie des Jahwisten.[87] So scheint es, daß der Jahwist den großen Komplex der elohistischen Jakob-Joseph-Moseüberlieferung, der ihm schriftlich vorlag, durch kraftvolle Eingriffe an wichtigen Punkten seinem Werk eingegliedert und ihm seine Theologie aufgeprägt hat.

Wir müssen uns noch die Frage stellen, ob auch der jahwistische Eingriff in die Josephgeschichte in dieser Linie liegt. Daß Joseph Gnade findet in den Augen seines ägyptischen Herrn (Gen. xxxix 4, 21), entspricht einer durchgehenden Vorstellung des Jahwisten.[88] Ebenso, daß Jahwe das Haus des Ägypters um Josephs willen segnet (Gen. xxxix 5). Hier geht die Verheißung an Abraham (Gen. xii 3) schon z.T. in Erfüllung. Das Mit-Sein Jahwes mit Joseph wird hier mit *'et* ausgedrückt (xxxix 2f., 21, 23), im Gegensatz zur elohistischen Überlieferung, wo wir *'im* finden (Gen. xxviii 15, 20; Ex. iii 12).[89] Schließlich entspricht auch die Betonung, daß Joseph schön

[84] Das würde bedeuten, daß das theologische Gesamtverständnis von dem ethnischen Grund her aufgenommen und rezipiert wird; H. J. Zobel, a.a.O., S. 276f.; H. Gese, "Bemerkungen zur Sinaitradition", S. 36f.

[85] Der Gottesname "Jahwe" kommt noch in xxx 27, xxxi 3, xxxii 10 vor.

[86] L. Ruppert, *Die Josephserzählung der Genesis* (München, 1965), S. 215.

[87] Die Themen von Gen. xii 1-3 kehren wieder und stimmen auch in der Formulierung überein: Land (xxxi 3, xxxii 10); Nachkommenschaft (xxxii 13), Verwandtschaft (xxxii 13). Die Verwendung von *ḥol* in xxxii 13 spricht allerdings für eine spätere jahwistische Nachinterpretation (vgl. Gen. xxii 17).

[88] Gen. vi 8a, xviii 3, xix 19. Die Wendung ist aber auch ein Leitwort in der Geschichte der Versöhnung Jakobs mit Esau: Gen. xxxii 6, xxxiii 8, 10, 15. Man möchte darum das Motiv der Geschenke Jakobs für Esau einer jahwistischen Interpretation zuschreiben. Die Wendung findet sich auch öfter in der Davidgeschichte: 1 Sam. xvi 22, xx 3, 29, xxv 8, xxvii 5; 2 Sam. xiv 14, 22, xv 25, xvi 4. Vgl. dazu H. Holzinger, *Einleitung in den Hexateuch*, S. 97f.

[89] *'et* für das Mitsein Gottes findet sich auch Ri. i 19 J; Gen. xxi 20 E; Num. xiv 9 P und Gen. iv 1 J.

von Gestalt und Aussehen war (xxxix 6) einer Linie, die beim Jahwisten mehrfach auftritt (Gen. xii 11, 14, ii 9, iii 6).

Auch die Einfügung der Ismaeliter und Judas in die Grunderzählung ist als jahwistische Interpretation verständlich. Sehr kunstvoll ist in Kap. xxxvii Juda als der der Joseph wohlwollende Bruder eingefügt, ohne daß Ruben, der diese Rolle in der elohistischen Grundlage gespielt hatte, dadurch verdrängt wird.[90] Der in der jahwistischen Interpretation berichtete Verkauf des in der Grundüberlieferung von den Brüdern in die Zisterne geworfenen Joseph an die Ismaeliter bereitet die Enttäuschung Rubens vor, der ihn nicht mehr in der Zisterne findet. Die midianitischen Kaufleute ziehen jetzt Joseph nicht mehr aus der Zisterne heraus, sie ziehen vorüber, und die Brüder holen Joseph herauf, um ihn an die Ismaeliter zu verkaufen. Ebenso wird Juda im weiteren Verlauf der Geschichte als Anwalt Benjamins eingefügt, ohne Ruben ganz zu verdrängen. Daß Juda sich für Benjamin verbürgt und an seiner Stelle in der Gefangenschaft Josephs bleiben will, macht die Geschichte aus einer Fügungsgeschichte zu einer echten Bekehrungserzählung. Diese Bekehrung der Brüder hat nicht nur eine Analogie in der Bekehrung Davids, die bei seiner Flucht aus Jerusalem sichtbar wird,[91] sondern führt die gesamte Patriarchengeschichte im Sinne der jahwistischen Konzeption von Sünde, Gericht und Gnade weiter. Einst haben die Brüder Benjamin um die Liebe des Vaters beneidet, jetzt bietet sich Juda selbst an, in der Gefangenschaft zu bleiben, damit der Knabe zu seinem Vater heimkehren kann. Mir scheint, daß man diese neuen Akzentsetzungen dem Jahwisten durchaus zutrauen kann, so daß die Annahme, die elohistische Version habe ihm schon vorgelegen, möglich wird. In der elohistischen Grundlage wird die Schuld der Brüder von Gott dazu benutzt, seine Pläne, die er in den Träumen Josephs geoffenbart hatte, zu verwirklichen. Immer wieder wird betont, daß es Gott selbst war, der Joseph nach Ägypten gebracht hat, um seine Brüder am Leben zu erhalten. Über diesen einfachen Sinn der Grunderzählung geht die jahwistische Interpretation weit hinaus. Die Fügungsgeschichte wird zur Führungsgeschichte, die Sündengeschichte zur Geschichte von Sünde und Gericht, Gnade und Bekehrung, alles Themen, die nach der Sünde Davids in Jerusalem aktuell sind.

---

[90] S. Mowinckel, *Erwägungen zur Pentateuch Quellenfrage*, S. 62, meint, daß schon in der mündlichen Überlieferung Juda neben Ruben getreten ist.

[91] Beide Male zeigen Reden die Wandlung an, die eingetreten ist: Gen. xliii 3-5, 8-9, xliv 18-34 und 2 Sam. xv 19f., 25f., xvi 10, 11f.

Am Ende ergibt sich die Frage, ob auch in der Geschichte des Auszugs und des Bundesschlusses die Hand des Jahwisten, der im davidisch-salomonischen Reich schreibt, zu erkennen ist. In der Darstellung der eigentlichen Ursprünge Israels als Volk werden wir von vornherein erwarten müssen, daß auch spätere jahwistische Erweiterungen zu Wort kommen, die jener Schicht der Ladeerzählung entsprechen, die *'aron jahwe* gebraucht.[92] Welche Momente können dem Jahwisten der Genesis zugeschrieben werden?

Wir werden davon ausgehen können, daß die Heiligtumsgeschichte der Lade mit dem Bundesschluß am Gottesberge abschließt, und daß als letzte Elemente des Ladekultes, die Tafeln und das Zelt, zu erkennen sind. Der weitere Weg Israels wird mit Ausnahme der Bileamgeschichte [93] nicht mehr unter Verwendung von "Elohim" dargestellt. Hier ist nun die erste Frage, die sich stellt, ob der Jahwist in diesem Bereich nur Interpret der Tradition ist wie in der Jakob- und Josephgeschichte, oder ob er über eigene Traditionen verfügt, die er mit der Mosegeschichte verbindet. Das letztere ist zu erwarten, denn die Kraft des Jahwisten, die elohistische Tradition weiterführend zu interpretieren, muß ein Fundament haben, in dem sie gründet.

In der vielschichtigen, z.T. kultisch geprägten Stoffmasse, die "Jahwe" verwendet, lassen sich zwei tragende Elemente erkennen, die der jahwistischen Konzeption entsprechen können: einmal das Land als Ziel des Auszugs, wie es schon in der jahwistischen Interpretation der Berufungsgeschichte des Mose erscheint (Ex. iii 7f., 17), und dann das Gegenwärtigsein Jahwes in der Mitte des Volkes (Ex. xxxiv; Num. xiv). In der jahwistischen Interpretation der Berufungsgeschichte ist nicht mehr Mose der Herausführende, dem in der elohistischen Grundlage das Mitsein Gottes versprochen wurde, sondern Jahwe, der wie in der Urgeschichte vom Himmel herabsteigt. Es geht jetzt in der gesamten Darstellung des Auszugs nicht mehr um eine Rettergeschichte, die am Gottesberg endet, sondern um die Grundlegung des Heiligen Krieges, in dem Jahwe selbst der Handelnde ist und der die Besetzung des Landes zum Ziel

[92] Man kann an den Trompetenschall, die Absperrung des Berges, die kultischen Reinigungsriten denken.

[93] Meist nimmt man an, daß die beiden jahwistischen Lieder in Kap. xxiv älter sind als die in Kap. xxiii. S. Mowinckel, *Erwägungen zur Pentateuch Quellenfrage*, S. 98. In diesem Falle würde die elohistische Schicht der Bileamsüberlieferung dem Jahwisten gegenüber als jünger anzusehen sein, wie die elohistischen Teile der Abrahamgeschichte.

hat.[94] Hierhin würde dann auch das Meerwunder und das Lied am Schilfmeer gehören, in dem der Auszug in der Begründung des Heiligtums in Jerusalem sein eigentliches Ziel findet. Auch die jahwistische Stilisierung der ägyptischen Plagen würde verständlich, in der das Wirken Jahwes betont wird und Mose nur der Verkünder des Handelns Jahwes ist.

Im einzelnen ist noch zu verweisen auf die Begegnung zwischen Mose und Jetro am Gottesberge. Hier haben wir ein weiteres Beispiel für die Identifizierung der Gottheiten. Jahwe wird mit dem Elohim des Auszugs in ähnlicher Weise gleichgesetzt wie in Gen. xiv mit dem El Eljon von Jerusalem.[95] Die Preisung des rettenden Gottes für seine Heilstat ist beiden Abschnitten in gleicher Weise eigen.[96]

Einer weiteren jahwistischen Nachinterpretation, die der *'aron jahwe*-Schicht der Ladeerzählung entsprechen könnte, wird man die kultischen Erweiterungen zuschreiben dürfen, die uns speziell in Ex. xix begegnen. Es würde zu weit führen, sie im einzelnen darzustellen. Ich möchte aber noch kurz auf die elohistische Abrahamüberlieferung eingehen, die durch eine jahwistische Hand mit der Abrahamgeschichte des Jahwisten verbunden worden ist (Gen. xxi 1, 33, xxii 11, 14f.). Hier kann man in der elohistischen Darstellung jene Verfeinerung des Gewissens und jene Nähe zur Prophetie feststellen, die dazu geführt hat, den "Elohisten", in dem man alle elohistischen Stoffe vereinigen wollte, dem "Jahwisten" gegenüber als jünger anzusehen. In diesen elohistischen Stücken der Abrahamgeschichte sind die Ätiologien der alten Traditionen, die beim Jahwisten noch erkennbar sind, z.T. verwischt.[97] Abraham ist eine exemplarische Gestalt. Durch seinen Glauben und seinen Gehorsam weist er dem Leben des Israeliten den Weg. In der jahwistischen Nachinterpretation dieser Überlieferungen finden sich Erklärungen von Unverständlichkeiten wie in der *'aron jahwe*-Schicht

---

[94] Wenn unsere Vermutung Recht hat, dann könnte die Landverheißung schon vor dem Exodus mit der frühen Landnahme Israels verbunden sein. Die Synthese von Eroberungskrieg und Exodus und Bund würden dann beide Traditionen verändern.

[95] Der Unterschied besteht darin, daß in Ex. xviii die Identifizierung Jahwes mit "Elohim" durch Jetro geschieht, während sie in Ex. xiv nur im Munde Abrahams erscheint, der von Melchisedek im Namen des El Eljon gesegnet wird.

[96] Vgl. Ex. xviii 10f. mit Gen. xiv 20. Die ausdrückliche Identifizierung ist dem Schwur Abrahams (xiv 22) vorbehalten.

[97] Vgl. v. Rad, *Das erste Buch Mose*, S. 200.

der Ladetradition (Gen. xx 18, xxii 14).[98] Es ist auffällig, daß in der Wiederholung der Segensverheißung (Gen. xxii 16ff.) die universale Bedeutung Abrahams für die Völker mit dem hitpael ausgedrückt wird.[99] Das bedeutet, daß die Völker nicht in Abraham gesegnet werden, sondern sich segnen. Abraham ist Urbild und nicht mehr Quelle des Segens für alle Völker.

So kommen über den Jahwisten und seine elohistische Vorlage hinaus weitere Schichten der Überlieferung in den Blick. Eine jüngere, schon prophetisch beeinflußte Aktualisierung der Tradition und dann eine weitere jahwistische Redaktion, die die elohistischen Weiterentwicklungen aufnimmt und in das Ganze des Pentateuch einfügt und die im Gegensatz zu dem bewußten unbesorgten Universalismus des Jahwisten mehr die Größe der Erwählung Israels unterstreicht.

V

Die Konsequenzen der vorgelegten Hypothese lassen sich von einem einzelnen kaum übersehen. Aber es scheint doch, daß der literarische Befund auf diese Weise leichter erklärbar ist, und daß die bisher gemachten Beobachtungen umfassender berücksichtigt werden können als bei einer Annahme mehrerer vollständiger Erzählungsfäden oder einer Verlegung der ersten zusammenfassenden Redaktion in die deuteronomistische Epoche.

Wenn es sich bewahrheiten würde, daß die Elohimtradition die Tradition von Betel und der mittelpalästinensischen Heiligtümer ist, dann würde sich auch die mehrmalige Übernahme von schriftlichem Material aus diesem Bereich erklären.

Wenn weiterhin die jahwistische Tradition älter war als die Auszugstradition, dann würde klar, daß der Jahwismus — womöglich schon der Jahwismus eines älteren Israel — erst in der Begegnung mit der Exoduserfahrung und der darin begründeten neuen Bindung an den Gott des Exodus zu dem Jahwismus des "Jahwisten" und der Propheten geworden ist. Dann würde der Jahwekrieg womöglich schon von den früheren Stämmen geführt worden sein und er wäre nicht das letzte Element des Jahweglaubens, sondern würde in die Erfahrung der Rettung integriert und von ihr verändert worden sein. Es wäre auch damit zu rechnen, daß die nordisraelitische Tradition

[98] Zu Gen. xx 14 J2 vgl. H. Gunkel, *Genesis*, S. 224f.; dagegen gehört V. 12 zu E; vgl. Gunkel, S. 223.

[99] Rendtorff, "Der 'Jahwist' als Theologe?", S. 164.

der Taborkoalition schon vormosaisch als Jahwetradition zu verstehen ist.[100]

Man müßte dann natürlich vermuten, daß die Begegnung zwischen Jahwe und dem Exodusgott nicht erst ein Werk des "Jahwisten" ist, sondern daß sie schon lange vorher, vielleicht im Raum von Sichem oder im Norden, geschehen ist.[101]

Die Frage nach der Stellung der Leviten, zu denen Mose gerechnet wird, zu Jahwe könnte dann auch der Überlieferung des Alten Testaments entsprechend gesehen werden. Der jahwehaltige Name der Mutter des Mose wäre kein Hindernis. Der verschiedene Sprachgebrauch in bezug auf den Gottesnamen braucht nicht ein Nichtkennen der anderen Gottesbezeichnungen zu bedeuten. Es könnte sein, daß — ähnlich wie im christlichen Bereich — die Namen "Jesus" und "Christus" oder "Heiland" bekannt sind und doch jeweils der eine oder der andere in einem bestimmten christlichen Milieu bevorzugt wird.

Jedenfalls stellt sich am Ende unserer Überlegungen die verschiedene Bedeutung der Gottesnamen noch einmal anders dar. Die mit "Elohim" ausgedrückte Gottesbeziehung wird endgültig in der Rettung besiegelt und empfängt in der Begegnung mit dem älteren Jahwismus ihre theopolitische Kraft; die Gegenwart Jahwes bei seinem Volk beruht nicht mehr nur auf seinem Erscheinen vom Sinai her, um ihm zu Hilfe zu kommen wie im Deboralied und anderen poetischen Texten, sondern ist jetzt die Gegenwart des Gottes Israels in der Mitte seines Volkes, das ihn in der Rettung erfährt, das ihn kennt, sich für ihn entscheidet und seinen Willen erfüllt. Erst von dieser Synthese her wird der Jahwismus des Jahwisten möglich: Nicht mehr der mit den Kenitern gemeinsame Jahwe, sondern Jahwe, der Gott Israels, der Gott der Freiheit, der Gott aller Völker und aller Menschen.

Sicher wird man aber auch die vielschichtige Begegnung Israels mit

---

[100] Da der Jahwekrieg unlösbar mit dem Jahwe-Namen verbunden ist (R. Smend, *Jahwekrieg und Stämmebund*, S. 31), ergibt sich so die Möglichkeit, auch schon die frühen Phasen der Landnahme gemäß Ri. i als "Heiligen Krieg" zu verstehen. Von den beiden Schemata der Berichte, die W. Richter, *Traditionsgeschichtliche Untersuchungen zum Richterbuch* (Bonn, 1963), S. 177ff., feststellt, zielt das erste auf die Rettung Israels und steht in Analogie zur elohistischen Mosegeschichte. Das zweite zielt auf die Eroberung des Landes (Ri. i) und könnte zur Urform des Jahwekrieges gehören. Diesem Schema würde auch die Darstellung in Ri. ivf. zuzuzählen sein, die fest mit "Jahwe" verbunden ist.

[101] Vgl. H. Seebass, *Der Erzvater Israel*, S. 106f.

El,[102] besonders mit dem El Eljon von Jerusalem in ihrer Bedeutung nicht unterschätzen dürfen. Denn erst die schon vorgegebene Erkenntnis des Wesens Gottes, seiner Ewigkeit und Allmacht, seiner Herrschaft über die Welt läßt die Bedeutung der Beziehung zu ihm und seiner Gegenwart bei seinem Volk voll erkennen.

So zeigt sich, daß die drei Komponenten der Gotteserkenntnis, die durch die Namen "El", "Elohim" und "Jahwe" bezeichnet werden, erst in ihrer Synthese zu ihrer je eigenen Bedeutung kommen. Zugleich bedeutet jede dieser Komponenten eine bleibende Beziehung zu dem Gottesglauben und der Gotteserfahrung der Umwelt Israels, die auch für die, die das Alte Testament als Heilige Schrift ansehen, erhalten bleibt und die heutige Öffnung der Kirchen nicht nur zueinander, sondern auch zu den Religionen der Welt in einer Weise bestätigen kann, die nicht den Synkretismus fördert, sondern jeweils eine Wandlung der sich Begegnenden bedeutet, in der das eigene nicht überfremdet, sondern in seiner eigentlichen Bedeutung tiefer erkannt wird.

---

[102] Wie der Name "Israel" sagt, bestanden zu El "keine Spannungen". O. Eißfeldt, "El und Jahwe", *Kleine Schriften* III (Tübingen, 1966), S. 391ff.

DIE AUFFASSUNG VON DER PROPHETIE IN DER DEUTERONOMISTISCHEN UND CHRONISTISCHEN GESCHICHTSSCHREIBUNG (MIT EINEM EXKURS ÜBER DAS BUCH JEREMIA) *

von

I. L. SEELIGMANN

Jerusalem

Eine Untersuchung, die die Auffassung von der Prophetie in bestimmten Schichten der biblischen Historiographie zum Gegenstand hat, wird sich naturgemäß sowohl mit dem Begriff der Prophetie wie mit der Historiographie in der Bibel befassen müssen. Es sei daher gleich eingangs betont, daß die folgenden Ausführungen nicht in erster Linie den Anspruch erheben, neue Einsichten in die Prophetie zu eröffnen, vielmehr wollen sie einen Beitrag zur biblischen Historiographie liefern.[1] In der Entwicklung dieser Historiographie lassen sich bei einer ziemlich groben Einteilung zwei Hauptphasen unterscheiden: eine erzählerische, sozusagen prae-reflektierende und eine spätere, reflektierende [2] mit deutlich theologischer

* Während der Arbeit an dieser Studie waren mir die Gespräche mit Frau Z. Talschier und Dr. Y. Zakovitch von großer Hilfe. Manche Gedanken gehen auf ihre Anregung zurück.

[1] Trotz der Verschiedenheit in der Zielsetzung und in der Auswahl des Materials berührt sich der nachstehende Versuch mehrfach mit der Untersuchung von P. R. Ackroyd, "Historians and Prophets", *SEÅ* 33 (1968), pp. 18-54. Auf seine Ausführungen sei hier nachdrücklich verwiesen.

[2] In der Hauptsache findet sich die reflektierende Geschichtsschreibung in den redaktionellen Partien, mit denen jüngere Geschichtsschreiber wie P, Dtr und Chr den von ihnen überlieferten Stoff umrahmen. Jedoch ist die Reflexion auch älterem Erzählgut keineswegs fremd; das gilt namentlich von Prophetenlegenden u. dgl. Dabei ist die Entscheidung nicht immer leicht, wo es sich um einen späteren Zusatz oder echte, alte Bestandteile handelt. Um zwei entgegengesetzte Beispiele herauszugreifen (beide folgen einer weisheitlichen Erzählung!): Es kann kaum bezweifelt werden, daß 1 Rg. xii 15b mit seinem Verweis auf das Gotteswort Achijas an Jerobeam die Erzählung der Reichsspaltung unterbricht und also einen Einschub bildet. Dagegen gehört die oft behandelte Stelle 2 Sm. xvii 14b, laut der Gott es war, Der über Absalom das Verhängnis brachte, wohl der ursprünglichen Erzählung von Absaloms Aufstand an (trotz des von der Massora verzeichneten Bruchs im Vers): xvii 14b ist ja durch xv 31 (und 34) vorbereitet.

Absicht. Unsere Themastellung konzentriert sich, wie schon aus dem Titel hervorgeht, auf die reflektierenden Stadien des biblischen Denkens, nur gelegentlich wird älteres Erzählgut in den Kreis unserer Betrachtungen einbezogen werden müssen.

I

Wenn auch unser Hauptanliegen der Historiographie gilt, so dürfen doch zur Begründung des Folgenden einige Bemerkungen über die Art des Gotteswortes in der biblischen Gedankenwelt nicht fehlen.[3] Die Bibel weiß um die Macht des Wortes; als Beleg dafür kann ihre Konzeption vom schöpferischen Wort Gottes dienen,[4] sowie ihre Anschauungen von Segen und Fluch, den Eid eingeschlossen. Allen Auffassungen von der Prophetie liegt die Idee von der Wirksamkeit des göttlichen Wortes zugrunde. Diese Wirksamkeit findet ihren Ausdruck in zwei Hauptformen. Das Wort sagt die Zukunft an und bestimmt sie, es ist als solches unabänderlich. Oder aber es droht mit der Strafe Gottes, indem es zugleich den Sünder zur Umkehr mahnt. Wenn es dann seine Wirkung ausübt und die Umkehr erfolgt, so wird das Unheil abgewendet und damit das Wort gleichsam aufgehoben.

Die Vorstellung vom Wort Gottes (nur indirekt mit der Prophetie in Verbindung gebracht) als einer dynamischen Potenz, fast hypostatisch gedacht, findet wohl ihren treffendsten Ausdruck in Jes. lv 10-11: "(Denn so wenig Schnee und Regen, die aus dem Himmel herabgekommen sind, dorthin zurückkehren, ohne die Erde getränkt zu haben) so wenig kehrt Mein Wort, das aus Meinem Mund hervor-

[3] Material, das über die folgenden Andeutungen hinausgeht, findet sich in den Darstellungen von L. Dürr, *Wertung des göttlichen Wortes usw.* (Leipzig, 1938); O. Procksch in *ThWNT* 4 (1943), pp. 89-100; H. Ringgren, *Word and Wisdom* (Lund, 1947), spez. p. 158; vgl. jetzt auch: A. Rofé, "Isaiah 55, 6-11 The Problems of the Fulfillment of Prophecies and Trito-Isaiah" (hebräisch), *Proceedings of the Sixth World Congress of Jewish Studies*, Vol. I (Jerusalem, 1977), pp. 213-21.

[4] Vom schöpferischen Wort Gottes, das Er entsendet und durch das Er auf der Erde Schnee, Reif und Eis schafft und wieder schmelzen läßt, heißt es Ps. cxlvii 15: "Wie schnell läuft Sein Wort." Interessant ist in diesem späten Psalm die assoziative Fortsetzung (19): "Er verkündet Sein Wort (so *Kethīb* und LXX) an Jakob", in der das Wort in die Bedeutung von Gebot übergeht. Das *Qerē*: "Seine Worte" im Plural dürfte von den im Parallelstichos erwähnten "Satzungen und Rechten" beeinflußt sein. In der oft zitierten Schilderung vom Schlagen der Erstgeburt durch das von Gott entsandte Wort, Sap. Sal. xviii 14-16, ist das schöpferische Wort in ein verheerendes verwandelt worden. Es hat hier die Funktion des Verderbeengels Ex. xii 23 übernommen. Etwas abweichend neuerdings B. L. Mack, *Logos und Sophia* (Göttingen, 1973), spez. pp. 96 f.

geht, zu Mir zurück,[5] ohne gewirkt zu haben, was Ich beschlossen und das vollbracht zu haben, zu dem Ich es sandte." Dank der Vorliebe Deuterojesajas für kosmische Bilder ist hier hart vor dem Ausgang der klassischen Prophetie die Funktion des Gotteswortes allumfassend formuliert. Diese Funktion läßt sich durch die verschiedenen Stadien der Prophetie im Alten Testament verfolgen. Wir erläutern das anhand einiger zeitlich und sachlich auseinanderliegender Beispiele. In der Episode 1 Rg. xvii 17-24 tritt der Prophet Elia — es entspricht nicht ganz seinem Charakter — als miracle worker auf: [6] er erweckt das tote Kind der Frau, in deren Haus er in Sarefat wohnt, zum Leben. Als er dann das wieder lebendige Kind der Mutter übergibt, sagt sie: "Nun erkenne ich, daß du ein Gottesmann bist und daß das Wort Gottes in deinem Mund Wahrheit ist." Die Erwähnung des Gotteswortes kommt ziemlich unerwartet, sie paßt eigentlich nicht zur Situation; hat doch Elia während der beschriebenen Wunderhandlung kein Gotteswort vernehmen lassen. In dem Augenblick aber, wo er als Gottesmann charakterisiert werden soll, wird das Wort Gottes sein unerläßliches Attribut. Bemerkenswert ist zudem, daß dieses Wort als Wahrheit bezeichnet wird, wohl weil es als sich im Laufe der Zeit verwirklichend gedacht ist: [7] Das prophetische Wort ist seinem Wesen nach Ankündigung der Zukunft, als solches ist es nicht weit von dem Wort des Segens (oder des Fluchs) entfernt. In einer der Segnungen des inspirierten Weissagers Bileam (Num. xxiii 19) wird Gott als Künder und Lenker der Zukunft beschrieben: "Gott ist kein Mensch, daß Er lüge" (man be-

[5] Das Motiv vom Nicht-Zurückkehren des Gotteswortes (auch Jes. xlv 23) findet ein schönes Echo in dem Ausspruch des Rav Yehuda b Rosch ha Schana 17b: Ein ewiger Bund sichert den Gnadeneigenschaften Gottes (Ex. xxxiv 6-7), daß sie nie unverrichteter Dinge zurückkehren.

[6] Dr. A. Rofé macht darauf aufmerksam, daß die Szene 1 Rg. xvii 17-24 jünger ist als ihre Parallele in 2 Rg. iv 32-37 und wohl deren Nachbildung. In 1 Rg. xvii steht die Episode, eingeleitet von einer schablonenhaften Redaktionsformel, ziemlich unvermittelt da. Ein aufschlußreiches Indiz verschafft der Umstand, daß Elia 19b das tot gewähnte Kind heraufnimmt "nach dem Obergemach, wo er verblieb", eine eindeutige Entlehnung von der Unterbringung Elisas bei der reichen Frau in Sunem (2 Rg. iv 10). Die arme Witwe von 1 Rg. xvii 2 besaß kaum etwas derartiges, auch wenn sie in unserem Abschnitt (17) als "Eigentümerin des Hauses" erscheint. Offensichtlich hat die dominierende Figur des Elia — er wird sonst selten Gottesmann genannt — eine der Wundertaten Elisas an sich gezogen. Immerhin zeugt das Beten Elias (20-21) religionsphänomenologisch von einem höheren Niveau als die Zauberhandlung Elisas (2 Rg. iv 34 f.), was auch für ein späteres Entstehungsdatum von 1 Rg. xvii spricht.

[7] *ʾemet* bezieht sich auf die zukünftige Erfüllung eines Gotteswortes Jes. xliii 9 und wohl auch 2 Sm. vii 28.

achte den Gegensatz zur Wahrheit 1 Rg. xvii 24!), "kein Menschenkind, daß Ihn etwas gereue; sollte Er sagen und nicht tun, reden und es nicht erfüllen?" Hier ist Gott selber Subjekt des Wirkens, *ʿśh*, das Jes. lv 11 Seinem Worte zugeschrieben wurde. Wie die Prophetie dem Segen und dem Fluch nahesteht, so ist sie auch dem schöpferischen Wort Gottes verwandt: gegebenenfalls spricht sie nicht nur von der Zukunft, sondern sie schafft sie geradezu herbei. Das ist der Hintergrund von Am. ix 10. Dort heißt es: "Durch das Schwert werden alle Sünder meines Volkes sterben, die da sagen: bring doch nicht das Unheil über uns und führe es nicht an uns heran." Gewiß ist der negative Imperativ an den Propheten gerichtet. Im Glauben des Volkes zumindest ist sein Wort es, das den Untergang heraufbeschwört. Zur gestaltenden Kraft der Geschichte gelangt das Prophetenwort dann bei Deuterojesaja. Schon im Eingang der Sammlung von Sprüchen, die von dem Propheten der Exilswende stammen (xl 8b), ist vom ewigen Bestand des Wortes Gottes die Rede, das an frühere Geschlechter ergangen ist und dessen Erfüllung nun bevorsteht. Hier wird genau die gleiche Wurzel *qūm* verwendet, mit der in dem oben angeführten alten Orakel Bileams (Num. xxiii 19b) die zukünftige Verwirklichung eines Gotteswortes ausgedrückt ist. Dieselbe Wurzel findet sich dann wieder in der fast programmatischen Aussage xliv 26: "Der das Wort Seiner Knechte erfüllt und den Plan Seiner Boten vollbringt".[8] Die Prophetie, die die Jahrhunderte umspannt, dient hier als Vermittlerin des Gotteswortes, in dem die Wiederherstellung Judas und Jerusalems vorgegeben ist.

Diese Anschauung liegt nun einem Spruch über das Wesen der Prophetie zugrunde, der sich in unserem Bibeltext in Am. iii 7 findet, aber nach Form und Inhalt keineswegs in den dortigen Zusammenhang gehört. Zudem enthält er sprachlich ein typisch deuteronomistisches Element. Wenn wir ihn also mit der großen Mehrzahl der Forscher dem Amos absprechen, so dürfen wir ihn völlig für sich betrachten. Wir brauchen seinem jetzigen Kontext keine Rechnung zu tragen, freilich können wir seine örtliche und zeitliche Herkunft (bzw. sein chronologisches Verhältnis zu Jes. xliv 26) nicht genau

[8] Da an die Reihe der Propheten gedacht ist, ist für *ʿbdw* ohne Zweifel *ʿbdjw* zu lesen. Auch xliii 10 muß statt *ʿabdī* wohl *ʿᵃbādaj* punktiert werden. An beiden Stellen ist der geforderte Plural, sowohl im MT wie in den LXX, fälschlich durch den Singular ersetzt worden. Schon P. Volz, *KAT* (1932), p. 56, hat mit Recht den Einfluß der Perikopen über den Gottesknecht für die unrichtige Auffassung unserer beiden Stellen verantwortlich gemacht; vgl. schon B. Duhm, *HKAT*[3] (1917), p. 311, ad xliii.

bestimmen. Er lautet: "Denn der Herr Gott tut nichts, es sei denn Er habe Seinen Ratschluß Seinen Knechten, den Propheten, kundgetan!" [9] Der Spruch zeugt von einer gewaltigen Hochschätzung der Prophetie, er besagt (und geht damit über Jes. xliv 26 hinaus): kein Ereignis kann Geschichte werden, wenn es nicht vorher von einem Propheten angekündigt worden ist. Was wir heute Am. iii 7 lesen, könnte als Motto für die Auffassung von der Prophetie in der deuteronomistischen Geschichtsschreibung der Königsbücher dienen.

II

Während der letzten dreißig Jahre hat die Korrespondenz zwischen dem vorhersagenden Gotteswort und seiner Erfüllung in der Geschichte ein zentrales Problem in der Erforschung der deuteronomistischen Historiographie, namentlich der Königsbücher, gebildet.[10] Man hat in dieser Korrespondenz ein Grundelement der literarischen Darstellung und der theologischen Geschichtsauffassung der deuteronomistischen Schule erkennen wollen: früher oder später verwirklicht sich in der Geschichte von Mal zu Mal das vorher an einen Propheten ergangene Wort Gottes.

Wieviel Wahres diese Erkenntnis auch enthalten mag, so ist doch bei ihrer Auswertung eine doppelte Warnung zur Vorsicht am Platze,

---

[9] (Mit A. Ehrlich, *Randglossen* 5 [Leipzig, 1912], p. 234, ist wohl die Vokalisation *gillāh* als Piʿel dem Qal des MT vorzuziehen.) Diese Stelle ist sehr schön erörtert worden von W. H. Schmidt, *ZAW* 77 (1965), pp. 183-8, der (p. 187) auf den mythologischen Ratschluß Gottes aufmerksam macht, vgl. Jer. xxiii 18, 22. Für die Datierung der Stelle sollte berücksichtigt werden, daß sich die Verbindung "Seine (Meine) Knechte, die Propheten" nur in den Spätschichten des Dtr findet (2 Rg. xvii 13, xxi 10, xxiv 2; DtrJer., Sach., Esr., Dan.). 2 Rg. ix 7 fehlt "Seine Diener" in der lucianischen Rezension, vgl. 1 Rg. xviii 4, 13, xix 14.

[10] Schon 1859 hat K. H. Graf in seinem Aufsatz über "Die Gefangenschaft und Bekehrung Manasse's", *ThStKr* 32 (1859), p. 476, "den Brauch des Verfassers der Bücher der Könige eine Weissagung zu berichten...und ihre Erfüllung zu erzählen" mit einer stattlichen Zahl von korrespondierenden Stellen belegt. Eine vollständige Aufzählung hat dann G. von Rad in "Die deuteronomistische Geschichtstheologie in den Königsbüchern" versucht (ursprünglich Anhang zu seinen *Deuteronomium-Studien* [Göttingen, 1947], später auch in seinen *Gesammelten Studien zum AT* [München, 1958]). Alle Vorhersagen und Erfüllungsvermerke werden von W. Dietrich, *Prophetie und Geschichte* (Göttingen, 1973), eingehend analysiert, um die These einer späteren P-Schicht in Dtr zu beweisen. E. Würthwein hat sich in seinem Kommentar (*ATD*, 1977) der Theorie eines "zweiten Deuteronomisten" weitgehend angeschlossen. Dietrichs Analysen, namentlich in den Kapiteln 1 (Form) und 3 (Sprachgebrauch) sind reich an zutreffenden Beobachtungen und richtigen Folgerungen. Jedoch halte ich seine Handhabung des Schemas Vorhersage — Erfüllung für allzu starr, siehe im folgenden.

an der die Forschung es manchmal hat fehlen lassen. Zum ersten ist die antike Denkart nirgends — auch in der Bibel nicht! — so konsequent, daß man eines ihrer Grundmotive schematisch handhaben darf, in unserem speziellen Falle wäre es zudem falsch, die Korrespondenz Vorhersagung — Erfüllung immer erst für die deuteronomistische Redaktion in Anspruch zu nehmen.

Wir besitzen, um mit dem zweiten Punkt anzufangen, einige Beispiele, in denen der Verweis auf das Wort, "das Gott oder der Prophet gesprochen hatte", ohne Zweifel dem Bestand einer alten, volkstümlichen Erzählung angehört. So etwa 2 Rg. iv 42-44. Elisa tritt als Wuntertäter auf und befiehlt, mit einem Geschenk von zwanzig Gerstenbroten und einigem Getreide eine große Menge zu speisen. Sein Diener glaubt nicht an die Möglichkeit, daß das Brot für so viele Leute ausreichen würde. Trotzdem gehorcht er und setzt es den Leuten vor, da aßen sie und ließen noch übrig "nach dem Wort des Herrn". In einem anderen Fall, 2 Rg. ii 19-22, beklagen sich die Einwohner von Jericho darüber, daß das Wasser der ortsnahen Quelle schlecht sei und Ursache für Unfruchtbarkeit und Krankheit. Elisa wirft eine Schale Salz in die Quelle und verkündigt die Gesundung des Wassers, da wurde das Wasser gesund bis zum heutigen Tag "nach dem Wort, das Elisa gesprochen hatte".[11]

Es schließt sich eine weitere Beobachtung an, die für das Verhältnis von Vorhersage und Erfüllung relevant ist; wir begegnen dabei wieder dem Mangel an Konsequenz im antiken Denken, der oben gestreift wurde. Nicht selten stoßen wir auf Diskrepanzen zwischen einer Prophetie und ihrer Verwirklichung. Solche Unstimmigkeiten können die Folge verschiedener literarischer Darstellung sein, ihre Ursache kann auch darin liegen, daß eine Weissagung sich ursprünglich auf etwas anderes bezog als das Ereignis, auf das sie angewandt wurde. In derartigen Fällen waren die sukzessiven Stadien der Redaktion bestrebt, die Spuren einer Zwiespältigkeit zu verwischen; das wurde jeweils durch nachträgliche Ergänzungen und

[11] Hier wäre auch 2 Rg. vii 16b und 17b zu nennen, wo die Bestätigung zweier Voraussagungen Elisas am Anfang der gleichen Erzählung mit der üblichen Formel berichtet wird. 17 Schluß und 18-20 bilden eine ergänzende Variante zu 1-2: am Eingang der Erzählung kommt die Ankündigung Elisas völlig unvermittelt, in 17-20 ist etwas von der Situation sichtbar, in der sie an den König ergangen war. Man denkt auch an 2 Rg. i 17, freilich hat A. Rofé, "Baal, der Prophet und der Engel" (hebräisch), *Beer-Sheva* 1 (1973), pp. 222-30, Gründe dafür geltend gemacht, daß 2 Rg. i spät datiert werden muß.

Umgestaltungen des Textes erreicht. Diese Sachverhalte werden im folgenden an zwei Beispielen erläutert.[12]

Das subtile Verhältnis zwischen Vorhersage und Erfüllung und die komplizierten literarkritischen und traditionsgeschichtlichen Fragen, die sich daran knüpfen, können recht anschaulich an der Revolution Jehus 2 Rg. ix 1-10, 27 (28) dargestellt werden. Nimmt sie doch wiederholt Bezug auf frühere Prophezeiungen, namentlich auf die Ankündigung Elias vom Ende Ahabs und seines Hauses (vgl. 1 Rg. xxi 17 ff.). Wir müssen hier etwas weiter ausholen, wenn auch von einer Erschöpfung der Probleme nicht die Rede sein kann. Die Erzählung von 2 Rg. ix und x ist schwierig und uneinheitlich; die Bestandteile weisen verschiedene Interessen auf. Für unser Anliegen zentral sind die Worte Jehus in ix 25-26; nachdem er den König Joram erschossen und damit das dem Sohne Ahabs angesagte Schicksal (1 Rg. xxi 29) vollzogen hat, spricht er zu seinem Adjutanten Bidkar: "Nimm ihn und wirf ihn auf den Acker Naboths von Jesreel. Erinnerst du dich nicht, wie du und ich hinter seinem Vater Ahab herritten, als der Herr diesen Spruch über ihn tat: Fürwahr, das Blut Naboths und seiner Söhne habe Ich in der vergangenen Nacht gesehen, spricht der Herr, und Ich werde es dir vergelten auf diesem Acker!" Es ist unbestreitbar, daß hier altes Überlieferungsgut vorliegt und daß darin der Acker Naboths (gerade dort findet nach 21 durch einen "beabsichtigten Zufall" die Begegnung zwischen Joram und Jehu statt) eine bedeutsame Rolle spielt: offenbar war die Erinnerung an den dort begangenen Frevel noch lebendig.[13] Eben die Tatsache, daß 2 Rg. ix 25-26 und 1 Rg. xxi offenbar von den gleichen Ereignissen die Rede ist, läßt die Unterschiede in der Darstellung umso deutlicher erkennen. Sie sind wiederholt festgestellt und behandelt worden.[14] Das betreffende Grundstück heißt

---

[12] Eine ähnliche Problematik bietet 1 Rg. xvi 34 im Vergleich zu Jos. vi 26 und gewissermaßen auch 2 Rg. xxiii 16-18 in seinem Verhältnis zu 1 Rg. xiii 2 (ff.), doch wird hier von einem Eingehen auf die Probleme dieser Stellen abgesehen.

[13] Einer Beobachtung H. Ewalds (*G.V.I.* III³ [Göttingen, 1866], p. 492) folgend formuliert J. Wellhausen, *Composition*³ (Berlin, 1899), p. 282, der Justizmord habe "eine viel grössere Aufregung im Volke hervorgerufen und für das Haus Omri eine viel verhängnisvollere Bedeutung gehabt, als der Baalsdienst." Die treffende Bemerkung macht bewußt, daß immer von neuem die Frage gestellt werden muß, wie ein aus biblischem Erzählgut gewonnenes Geschichtsbild sich zu dem verhält, was einst Wirklichkeit war.

[14] z.B. Wellhausen, p. 281; H. Gressmann, *SAT* II 1² (1923), p. 272; O. H. Steck, *Überlieferung und Zeitgeschichte in den Elia-Erzählungen* (Neukirchen, 1968), pp. 32-40.

1 Rg. xxi 1-16 (17) konsequent *kerem* (zehnmal); das Wort fehlt in unserer Darstellung völlig, dagegen findet sich hier 21-25 viermal *ḥelqāh*. 2 Rg. ix läßt nicht vermuten, der Acker sei so nahe an dem (einem) Palast Ahabs gelegen (1 Rg. xxi 2), aus 21 würde man eher das Gegenteil schließen. Derjenige, der in 1 Rg. xxi 17 ff. die Begegnung zwischen Ahab und Elia beschreibt, ist sichtlich nicht daran interessiert, daß der Eindruck entsteht, andere wären bei ihr zugegen gewesen. In 2 Rg. ix 25-26 fehlt jegliche Anspielung auf die zentralen *dramatis personae* in den beiden Teilen von 1 Rg. xxi: Isebel (1-16) und Elia (17-29). Während in der Erzählung 1 Rg. xxi 1-16 Naboth allein hingerichtet wird, ist 2 Rg. ix 26 von dem vergossenen Blut Naboths und seiner Söhne die Rede; offenbar ist eine andere Situation vorausgesetzt. Eine schlagende Bestätigung dafür bietet schließlich der Umstand, daß in 2 Rg. ix 26 Gott als nächtlicher Zeuge des Mordes erscheint,[15] das läßt auf einen im Geheimen vollzogenen Meuchelmord schließen und nicht auf einen in aller Öffentlichkeit begangenen Justizmord, wie er in 1 Rg. xxi beschrieben wird. Es liegt also 2 Rg. ix 25-26 über das Schicksal Naboths eine von 1 Rg. xxi in jeder Hinsicht abweichende Überlieferung zugrunde, wobei man sich des Eindrucks nicht erwehren kann, 1 Rg. xxi, und zwar in seinen beiden Teilen, stelle eine bedeutend jüngere Formgebung dar.[16] Anders als in ix 25-26 gehören

[15] Das Schauen Gottes in der Nacht in 2 Rg. ix 26 wird am besten als "in der Verborgenheit der Nacht" erklärt. Die gleiche hebräische Vokabel *ʾemeš* erscheint Gn. xxxi 42 bei einem Richterspruch Gottes, der laut 24 ebendort (vgl. 29) in einer Traumoffenbarung Gottes an Laban stattgefunden hat.

[16] Der zweite Abschnitt des Kapitels enthält eindeutig Bestandteile verschiedener Herkunft, von denen manche sicher von redaktioneller (W. Dietrich: DtrP) bzw. noch jüngerer Hand stammen. Doch sind mit dieser Feststellung die eigentlichen literarischen Probleme des Kapitels nicht berührt. Deren erstes ist: Wo liegt die Grenze zwischen den beiden Teilen? Haben wir wirklich (wie E. Würthwein im Anschluß an den hier wiedergegebenen Vortrag ausführte) in xxi 1-16 eine in sich geschlossene Erzählung vor uns? Erwartet nicht jeder Leser nach 16 eine Fortsetzung? Diese wäre dann in 17-20bα enthalten (Šanda, *EHAT*, 1911). Die dramatische Begegnung zwischen Ahab und Elia käme sicher als der verlangte Abschluß in Frage, doch fällt das Fehlen jeder Anspielung auf Isebel, die treibende Kraft in 1-16, auf. Würde dann O. H. Steck Recht haben mit seiner Vermutung pp. 42, 52: wir hätten in 17-18a, 19-20bα das älteste Element aus 1 Rg. xxi vor uns? Der schneidende Vorwurf Elias: "Hast gemordet und nimmst jetzt in Besitz" hat wohl einen authentischen Klang. Das gilt aber keineswegs von der Wortereignisformel in 17! Übrigens sei, ganz abgesehen von der Frage der Zugehörigkeit von 17-20bα, betont, daß das Auftreten Elias im Geist eines klassischen Schriftpropheten nur noch in 2 Sm. xii 1-15a (einem sicher eingeschobenen Stück) seine Parallele hat. Wir kommen also über die Annahme nicht hinaus: 1-16 ist nicht in sich abgeschlossen, es ist aber sehr fraglich, ob 17-20a

die Stellen ix 36-37 und x 10b und 17 einer späten redaktionellen Bearbeitung, möglicherweise verschiedenen Bearbeitungen an.[17] Den drei Stellen ist gemeinsam, daß sie ausdrücklich das Wort Gottes an Elia erwähnen und seine Bestätigung durch den Verlauf der Ereignisse hervorheben. Hier ist das Streben der Redaktion nach Harmonisierung deutlich erkennbar.

Etwas anders gelagert ist ein weiteres Beispiel für den Mangel an Übereinstimmung der vermeintlichen Vorhersagung und ihrer Erfüllung, das noch in Kürze besprochen werden soll. Auch hier gehen wir am besten von der "Erfüllung" aus, obwohl, oder: eben weil es sich gerade bei ihr gewiß um einen sekundären Zusatz handelt. 1 Rg. ii 13-46 werden die Maßnahmen berichtet, mit denen Salomo nach seinem umstrittenen Regierungsantritt seine zu befürchtenden Gegner unschädlich macht. Adonja, Joab und Simei läßt er aus dem Weg räumen. Den Hohenpriester Ebjathar schont er, doch schickt er ihn in die Verbannung nach Anathoth, wo die elidischen Priester ihren Grundbesitz hatten. Diese Verbannung wird in einer kurzen Notiz 26-27 mitgeteilt. 27b lautet dann: "So wurde das Wort des Herrn erfüllt, das Er gegen das Haus Elis geredet hatte." Der Sturz der Eliden wird dadurch als seit langem von Gott verhängt dargestellt. Die Bemerkung stammt sichtlich von jemandem, der den Eliden nicht wohlgesinnt war und die Legitimität des neuen Priesterhauses der Zadokiden betonen wollte, dessen Einsetzung übrigens erst 35b nachgetragen wird. Sie bezieht sich auf die alte (?) Prophetie

---

die ursprüngliche Fortsetzung gebildet hat. Unser zweites, kaum weniger schwieriges Problem ist die Bestimmung des literarischen Charakters von 1-16. Schon 2 Rg. ix 25-26 stellt außer Zweifel, daß 1 Rg. xxi historische Ereignisse zugrundeliegen. Dennoch ist xxi 1-16 alles andere als Geschichtsschreibung. Sehen wir einmal von den Anfangsworten "Es geschah nach diesen Begebenheiten", einer üblichen Redaktionsklammer, ab, so macht alles Folgende den Eindruck einer kunstvoll gestalteten Erzählung. Schon die Eröffnung *kerem hājāh leNābōt* weist auf eine solche, sogar auf eine Art Gleichnis hin (vgl. z.B. Gn. iii 1; Hi. i 1; speziell 2 Sm. xii 2; Jes. v 1b), und in allem, was folgt, spürt man eine Atmosphäre der Unwirklichkeit und Stilisierung. Wir hätten also einen Fall, wo ein geschichtlicher Kern vom Spiel der literarischen Phantasie überlagert worden ist. Von hier aus bestätigt sich noch einmal der Bruch zwischen 1-16 und 17-20a. Zudem weist die ahistorische Erzählform auf ein spätes Entstehungsdatum hin. Dazu stimmt die Verwendung des nicht vor dem Exil belegten Wortes *ḥōrīm* in 8 und 11. Unsere Darlegung wäre auch eine Stütze für Stecks erwägenswerte These (spez. pp. 68-71), Isebels Machtstellung wäre erst nachträglich aus der Periode Jorams in die Ahabs retrojektiert worden.

[17] Über ix 36-37 vgl. Steck, pp. 36 f., x 17 ist, vielleicht mit Ausnahme der ersten Worte: "Er kam nach Samarien", ein störender Einschub, der den Zusammenhang zwischen 16 und 18 unterbricht.

1 Sm. ii 27 ff., in der es 35 in der Tat heißt: "Ich werde Mir einen treuen Priester bestellen, der nach Meinem Herzen und nach Meinem Sinn handeln wird, Ich werde ihm ein beständiges Haus bauen, und er wird für immer 'vor Mir' hergehen." Es ist kaum anzunehmen, daß diese Stelle wirklich die Gründung der Priesterdynastie Zadoks im Auge hatte. Vielmehr scheint eine Umdeutung stattgefunden zu haben. Das wird schon dadurch nahegelegt, daß in 35 das Wort *m^e^šîḥî* offenbar eingeschoben wurde, um das Amtieren eines Priesters in königlichem Dienst zum Ausdruck zu bringen. Bedeutet doch die genau gleiche Verbindung *hithallēk lipnē* in 30 wie an allen ähnlichen Stellen in der Bibel "wandeln vor Gott".[18] Thenius' Vermutung, die Prophetie habe ursprünglich Samuel im Auge gehabt, ist attraktiv und paßt recht gut in den Zusammenhang der ersten Kapitel von 1 Sm.; allerdings setzt sie ein Samuelbild voraus, in dem priesterliche Züge noch stärker vorherrschen, als es in dem uns überlieferten Samuelkomplex der Fall ist.[19]

In gewisser Hinsicht ist die Diskrepanz zwischen Vorhersage und Erfüllung dort am größten, wo von der Erfüllung einer Prophetie, die sich in dem früher Erzählten nirgends findet, berichtet wird. Das ist der Fall, wenn wir 2 Rg. xiv 25-27 lesen: "Er (Jerobeam ben Joasch) hat das Gebiet Israels wiederhergestellt von Hamath bis ans Tote Meer, nach dem Wort, das der Herr, der Gott Israels, durch Seinen Knecht, den Propheten Jona ben Amittai aus Gath Hefer, gesprochen hatte. Denn der Herr sah", so heißt es weiter, "daß das Elend Israels sehr bitter (?) war...denn noch hatte der Herr nicht entschieden, den Namen Israels unter dem Himmel auszutilgen, da rettete Er sie durch Jerobeam ben Joasch." Das ganze Bruchstück hat einen merkwürdigen, altertümlichen und schicksalhaften Klang.[20]

---

[18] Gn. xvii 1, xxiv 40, xlviii 15; 2 Rg. xx 3; Ps. (xxvi 3), lvi 14, cxvi 9, vgl. auch Gn. v 24 und vi 9. Diese Parallelen, vor allem aber der Vergleich mit 30, erheben m.E. zur Gewißheit, daß "der Gesalbte" in 35 zur Aktualisierung des Textes nachträglich eingefügt worden ist. Darin liegt ein entscheidendes Argument für das hier vertretene Alter der Prophetie 27 ff. (trotz etwaiger Geeninstanzen), speziell von 35. H. J. Stoebes Ausscheidung von 35 f. (*KAT* 1973, p. 118) leuchtet mir nicht ein.

[19] O. Thenius (Leipzig, 1842), p. 14. Für priesterliche Züge in der Gestalt Samuels vgl. 1 Sm. i 22, ii 18, vii 9, ix 12-13, x 8, xvi 5 (die Liste weicht von den von Thenius angeführten Stellen ab). Vielsagend ist b. Sira xlvi 13, wo Samuel als Nasir, Prophet, Richter und Priester bezeichnet wird.

[20] Es scheint unangebracht, 2 Rg. xiv 25 mit Dietrich a.a.O. (Anm.) als Formel (p. 111) oder gar als Erfüllungsvermerk (p. 35) von DtrP zu bezeichnen. Das Schicksalhafte, das dem hier erwähnten Wort Gottes eignet, ist von J. Hempel, *Festschrift Bertholet* (Tübingen, 1950), p. 230 = *Apoxysmata* (Berlin, 1961),

Es dürfte nach dem Untergang des Nordreiches im Rückblick formuliert worden sein. Nach allem, was im Vorhergehenden über altes und spätes Gut in den Äußerungen der Königsbücher über das Wort Gottes ausgeführt worden ist, steht nichts der Annahme im Wege, Jona ben Amittai sei ein Prophet gewesen, der in der ersten Hälfte des achten vorchristlichen Jahrhunderts die Ausbreitung Israels von Hamath bis zum Toten Meer vorausgesagt hatte, zumal in Am. vi 14 genau die gleichen Grenzen genannt werden, in unmittelbarem Anschluß an die Prahlerei der Großsprecher, die sich mit den Siegen Jerobeams ben Joasch brüsten.

Unser Anliegen war, wie oben formuliert, zu zeigen, welchen Bedenken die Annahme einer starren Korrespondenz zwischen Vorhersage und Erfüllung in der deuteronomistischen Geschichtsschreibung unterliegt. Die dazu angestellten Erwägungen haben darüber hinaus die Variabilität des Verhältnisses zwischen Überlieferung und Redaktion in unseren Quellen ins Licht gerückt. Im folgenden sollen nun einige Merkmale, die das Bild von Propheten und Prophetie in den Königsbüchern bestimmen, herausgearbeitet und kurz erörtert werden.

Wer die Königsbücher unter dem Aspekt des über Prophetie und Propheten Berichteten durchmustert, stößt bald auf zwei bemerkenswerte Tatsachen: Die Propheten treten bis auf die Zeit Jesajas durchweg im Nordreich auf; sie wenden sich mit ihren Worten an die Könige, nicht an das Volk und greifen auch aktiv in die Vorgänge am Hof und in der Dynastie ein. (In beiden Hinsichten hat die Geschichtsschreibung Erbgut aus den Prophetenlegenden übernommen.) Die zwei genannten Erscheinungen haben auf den ersten Blick wenig gemein. In Wirklichkeit aber besteht zwischen ihnen, wie sich ergeben wird, eine Verbindung, die ihrer streng gesonderten Darstellung einige Schwierigkeit bereitet. Natürlich ist die Beobachtung von großer Wichtigkeit, daß wie andere religiöse Ideen und Institutionen offenbar auch die Prophetie ursprünglich ein nordisraelitisches Phänomen war, das erst gegen Ende des achten Jahrhunderts in Juda Wurzel schlug. Doch ist diese Entwicklung bei näherem Zusehen verständlich genug. Sie hängt eben mit der Funktion der Propheten zusammen. Wir finden sie, wie angedeutet, an Revolutionen beteiligt. — S. Herrmann hat für die Propheten den Begriff

p. 316, m.E. richtig empfunden worden; freilich glaube ich nicht, daß 2 Rg. xiv 24 der gleichen Schicht angehört wie 25-27, was nach Hempels Formulierung von ihm offenbar vorausgesetzt wird.

"Königsmacher" geprägt.[21] Dieser kann auf Samuel, Nathan, Achija von Silo und den Prophetenjünger, der Jehu zum König salbt, angewandt werden. Hierzu gehört auch der dreifache Auftrag zur "Salbung", den Elia (1 Rg. xix 15-16) von dem ihm am Horeb erscheinenden Gott erhält.[22] In vielen Fällen jedoch verwerfen die Propheten eben die Könige, denen sie zum Aufstieg verholfen haben. Sie wenden sich an sie mit Drohsprüchen; das Element der Opposition in ihrem Auftreten kann nicht übersehen werden. Eine derartige Opposition konnte im Südreich, wo die von Gott für alle Zeit erwählte Dynastie Davids herrschte, schwer aufkommen; eine Funktion erhält die Prophetie in Juda erst, als die ewige Dynastie Davids als bedroht erscheint. Im Nordreich dagegen waren die Propheten von Anfang an die Begleiter der sich fortwährend wiederholenden Revolutionen.[23] — In dem Gesagten liegt ein Weiteres beschlossen, das mit einer Eigenart der Geschichtsschreibung in den Königsbüchern zusammenhängt: Die Könige stehen überall im Zentrum der Ereignisse, ihr Verhalten ist weithin entscheidend für den Gang der Geschichte und damit für das Geschick ihres Volkes.[24] Es ist also nicht

[21] S. Herrmann, *Ursprung und Funktion der Prophetie im alten Israel* (Opladen, 1976), pp. 21-4.

[22] Der Befehl 15-16 ist offenbar in Hinsicht auf die Fortsetzung 17-18 formuliert worden. Sein gedankliches und literarisches Verhältnis zu der vorhergehenden Gotteserscheinung ist nicht ohne weiteres durchsichtig. Dazu sind die Aufträge, jeder nach eigener Art, unrealistisch (alt sind die Verse keinesfalls). Umso bezeichnender ist die Formulierung von 15-16 für die Vorstellung vom Propheten, der Könige "salbt".

[23] In der spätdeuteronomistischen Redaktion sagen Ahia von Silo zu Jerobeam (1 Rg. xiv 7) und Jehu ben Hanani zu Baʿscha (1 Rg. xvi 2), Gott habe die revoltierenden Könige "aus dem Volke (bzw. aus dem Staube) erhoben." Der Ausdruck weist frappierende Ähnlichkeit auf mit dem judäischen Königspsalm Ps. lxxxix 20. Nun soll nicht in Abrede gestellt werden, daß 1 Rg. xiv 7 und xvi 2 das Produkt einer redaktionellen Stilisierung sind. Doch ist damit nicht ausgemacht, ob sie der judäischen Endredaktion oder einem älteren nordisraelitischen Stadium angehören bzw. die eine oder andere alte authentische Wendung aus der nordisraelitischen Prophetie enthalten, die dann ihren Weg in einen späten judäischen Königspsalm gefunden hätte. Aber sogar wenn nordisraelitische Prägungen an den Stellen in Rg. durchschimmern (und ich halte das für durchaus möglich), so würde der prophetische Hofstil keineswegs dazu berechtigen, mit A. Alt (*Kl. Schr.* II [München, 1953], p. 122) das Königtum im Nordreich als charismatisch-nicht-dynastisch und die Revolutionen als gottgewollt zu bezeichnen. Vergleiche gegen diese Theorie: T. C. G. Thornton, *JTS*, N.S. 14 (1963), pp. 1-11; G. Buccellati, *Cities and Nations of Ancient Syria* (Roma, 1967), pp. 200-08; E. Würthwein, *ATD* (1977), p. 145, Anm. 21.

[24] Es scheint mir schwer zu bestimmen, wo das "königzentrische" Prinzip der Propheten und der Geschichtserzählung in das dynastische der deuteronomistischen Historiographie übergeht, auch inwieweit sich dabei Einfluß der Annalen

verwunderlich, daß die Propheten sich nicht wie die klassischen Schriftpropheten an das Volk, sondern immer an den König wenden, mit der Anrede: "Höre!" und nicht: "Höret!".[25] Als selbstverständlich sagt der "König von Israel" schon in der Prophetenerzählung 1 Rg. xxii 8: "Ich hasse ihn (Micha ben Jimla), denn er sagt mir nie Gutes an, sondern nur Böses".[26] Diese Erzählung, in der Micha der Schar der etwa vierhundert als Chor auftretenden Propheten gegenübergestellt ist, läßt die Frage aufkommen, ob irgendein Zusammenhang bestehe zwischen den in den Königsbüchern beschriebenen Propheten und der alten Hofprophetie. Die Frage hat diesem oder jenem Leser vielleicht schon vorgeschwebt, als oben von der Rolle der Propheten bei dem Aufstieg der Könige die Rede war. Bei ihrer Beantwortung will aber bedacht sein, daß von wenigen Ausnahmen abgesehen (2 Rg. x 30, xiv 25) die Propheten der Königsbücher immer Unheil und Untergang verkünden.

In diesen Unheilsansagen, die den in der deuteronomistischen Geschichtsschreibung auftretenden Propheten in den Mund gelegt werden, vollzieht sich ein für die Auffassung von der Prophetie folgenschwerer Übergang: In das Wort der Vorhersage, wie wir es noch in den alten Prophetenerzählungen finden (1 Rg. xvii 1, xxii 6, 17), wird der Gedanke der Vergeltung eingebaut. Diese Vergeltung

---

geltend macht. Es ist nur natürlich, daß das dynastische Bewußtsein im davidischen Südreich stärker ausgeprägt ist (wo in den Annalen auch immer die Mutter des neuen Königs erwähnt wird). Eine Kombination der beiden Prinzipien kommt in unüberbietbarer Schärfe in 2 Rg. xxiii 25-26 zum Ausdruck, einer Stelle, von der im folgenden noch die Rede sein soll.

[25] Die einzige scheinbare Ausnahme wäre die Erzählung von der Prophetie "des Gottesmannes Semaja an Rehabeam, Juda, Benjamin und das übrige Volk" in 1 Rg. xii 22-24. Sie wird mit Recht allgemein als chronistischer Nachtrag angesehen.

[26] In den Prophetenworten des Buches Amos ist von der Dynastie Jehus oder vom Hause des Königs Jerobeam ben Joasch nirgends die Rede. Es fällt darum besonders auf, daß gerade das wenige Erzählgut im Buche, vii 10 ff., an eine Weissagung anknüpft, nach der Gott "sich wider das Haus Jerobeams mit dem Schwert erheben wird." Mein Kollege Prof. M. Weiß ist der Ansicht, daß es sich in 10-17 nicht um eine einheitliche Erzählung handelt, sondern um ein Fragment (10-11), dem eine Erzählung aus einer anderen Situation folgt (12-17). Das Fragment 10-11 bezieht sich auf einen Ausspruch des Propheten über das Königshaus. Über die Stellung von 9b zwischen Vision und Erzählgut wage ich kein sicheres Urteil; man hat den Eindruck, 9a bilde den Abschluß der Visionsprophetie, vgl. viii 3. Zu diesen Fragen siehe die Kommentare und neuerdings P. R. Ackroyd, "A Judgment Narrative between Kings and Chronicles? An Approach to Amos 7:9-17", *Canon and Authority* (Philadelphia, 1977), pp. 71-87, spez. pp. 76, 81; manchen seiner Thesen kann ich freilich nicht zustimmen.

betrifft König und Dynastie, doch zieht sie, wie aus dem oben Ausgeführten hervorgeht, das Volk in Mitleidenschaft. Hier müssen nun tiefgreifende Unterschiede zu der Verkündigung der klassischen Schriftprophetie beobachtet und betont werden. In den Königsbüchern kommt die Vergeltung über das Königshaus und seine Untertanen nicht wegen sozial-sittlichen Verhaltens, sondern wegen kultischer Verfehlungen,[27] namentlich der Verehrung fremder Götter.[28] Anders als bei den klassischen Propheten fehlt auch jeder Aufruf zur Umkehr.[29] (Dem ist 2 Rg. xvii 13 nicht entgegenzuhalten; der Vers steht in einem sehr späten geschichtstheologischen Exkurs ganz eigener Herkunft.) In der deuteronomistischen Historiographie verkünden die Propheten das von Gott wegen der Sünden der Könige beschlossene Unheil. Nicht genug damit, daß die Worte der Propheten in den Königsbüchern keinerlei Einfluß der klassischen Prophetie aufweisen — auch die Namen der Schriftpropheten und ihre Botschaft erscheinen hier nirgends.[30] Eine scheinbare Ausnahme bildet Jesaja, anerkanntermaßen aber ist die (nicht durchweg einheitliche) Gestalt des Propheten in den späten Legenden 2 Rg. xviii 13-xx 19 (vgl. Jes. xxxvi-xxxix) völlig verschieden von dem klassischen Jesaja und seinem Wort. Besondere Hervorhebung verdient das gänzliche Fehlen Jeremias am Ende der Königsbücher; schon der

---

[27] Die Tatsache ist eindringlich von Y. Kaufmann in seiner *Geschichte der israelitischen Religion* II 1 (Tel Aviv, 1942), p. 298, betont worden (hebräisch, vgl. die gekürzte englische Bearbeitung der Bände I-III von M. Greenberg, *The Religion of Israel* [Chicago, 1960]). E. Würthwein stellt in seinem wichtigen Aufsatz über "Die Josianische Reform und das Deuteronomium", *ZThK* 73 (1976), pp. 395 ff., "die Frage... wie angesichts des... Sündenverständnisses... der Dtr ja vorausgehenden Propheten eine solche Verengung auf das rituelle Gebiet in den dtr Partien des Königsbuches möglich war" (p. 422). Er versucht sie durch einen Hinweis auf die besonderen Verhältnisse der Exilszeit und der nachexilischen Gemeinde, aus der Dtr ja hervorging, zu erklären.

[28] Vgl. J. P. Floss, *Gott dienen — Göttern dienen* (Bonn, 1975), spez. pp. 408-42. Wichtig sind in dem Buch die semantischen Unterscheidungen von *ʿbd*, wie z.B. Herr-Knecht-Verhältnis und kultischer Dienst.

[29] Über den Aufruf zur Umkehr in der klassischen Prophetie vgl. unten Anm. 46.

[30] Ein markantes Beispiel für den Unterschied zwischen der Geschichtsdarstellung der Königsbücher und der prophetischen Anschauung Jesajas bietet ein Vergleich von 2 Rg. xvi 5, 7-9 und Jes. vii 1-17. Dort nur der historische Bericht, wie Ahas durch Bestechungsgeld aus dem Heiligtum in Jerusalem den König von Assur Tiglat Pileser dazu bewegt, Damaskus zu besetzen, so daß Aram und Israel die Belagerung von Jerusalem aufgeben müssen. Hier dient dieser historische Sachverhalt nur als Anlaß zu der Glaubenspredigt des Propheten Jesaja und seiner Drohung, daß am Ende Assyrien Juda überwältigen werde. Vgl. P. R. Ackroyd, "Historians and Prophets" (Anm. 1), pp. 22-7.

babylonische Talmud nahm anläßlich 2 Rg. xxii Anstoß daran.[31] Hat doch Jeremia als gerichtsandrohender und zur Buße mahnender Prophet kaum seinesgleichen; so hätte die Erwähnung seiner Predigt gegen Ende der Königsbücher wenigstens ein Element der Theodizee für den Untergang von Staat, Dynastie und Tempel abgegeben, auf den das deuteronomistische Geschichtswerk ausgerichtet ist. Es kommt hinzu, daß das Buch Jeremia selbst eine Bearbeitung in der deuteronomistischen Schule durchgemacht hat, die uns noch beschäftigen wird.

Mit dem Wort Theodizee ist soeben einer von zwei Aspekten berührt worden, die zum Abschluß dieses Versuches, die deuteronomistische Auffassung der Prophetie in ihren Elementen zu beschreiben, noch etwas näher beleuchtet werden müssen. Genau besehen handelt es sich dabei um eine doppelte Schranke, die dem Gehalt der Prophetie in der deuteronomistischen Historiographie gesetzt ist. Wir sahen früher, daß sich in der Prophetie der Königsbücher ein Übergang von der Vorhersage zu einer Vergeltung für den Abfall von Gott vollzieht. Diese Idee der Vergeltung enthält Ansätze zu einer Theodizee. Doch gelangen diese Ansätze im Rahmen der Prophetenworte nicht zur vollen Entfaltung (auf die Ausnahme 2 Rg. xxi 10-14 gehen wir unten ein), weil in ihnen jeder Aufruf zur Umkehr fehlt. Bemerkenswerterweise liegt eine selbständige, eigens zu diesem Zweck verfaßte Theodizee der Exilierung nur für das Nordreich vor, nämlich in dem schwierigen und nicht einheitlichen Abschnitt 2 Rg. xvii 7-23. Ein Gegenstück von gleichem Gewicht für Juda gibt es nicht; der Einschub 2 Rg. xvii 18b-20 kann nicht als solches gelten. Wohl wird das in diesen Versen angeschlagene Motiv "...und auch Juda" noch zweimal (2 Rg. xxi 11, xxiii 27) aufgenommen, eine Spätschicht, die uns gleich noch beschäftigen wird. Der größere Nachdruck, der in dieser Beziehung auf Nordisrael liegt, ist umso auffallender, als man eine Theodizee für den Untergang Judas, der Endpunkt und Ziel der deuteronomistischen Geschichtsschreibung bildet,[32] eher und dringlicher erwarten würde.

[31] Die verwunderte Frage, weshalb Josia, nach der Auffindung des Gesetzbuches, Boten zur Gottesbefragung nicht zu Jeremia, sondern zu Hulda schickt, wird b Meg 14b verschieden beantwortet.

[32] M. Weippert, "Fragen des israelitischen Geschichtsbewußtseins", *VT* 23 (1973), p. 435, möchte die ganze Geschichtsdarstellung von Ri. ii 11 (vgl. schon ii 2) bis 2 Rg. xvii bzw. xxv, die ihren Ausgangspunkt bei der Abwendung Israels von seinem Gott gleich nach der Landnahme nimmt und mit der Vertreibung aus dem Lande endet, "als eine einzige große Ätiologie des Landverlustes" bezeichnen.

Nun hat es in der deuteronomistischen Schule, als deutlich wurde, daß der Fall Judas bevorstand und nachdem er eingetreten war, nicht an Versuchen gefehlt, die etwaigen Heilszusagen Gottes gerade in bezug auf Juda mit dem wirklichen Ablauf der Geschichte in Einklang zu bringen. Zwei dieser Versuche haben ihre Spuren an mehreren Stellen in den Königsbüchern hinterlassen. Einmal werden in einer Reihe von späteren Nachträgen zu dem deuteronomistischen Geschichtswerk die Versprechen Gottes von der ewigen Fortdauer der davidischen Dynastie und der Unverletzlichkeit des Tempels als von vornherein bedingt hingestellt: Sie würden nur gelten, wenn die Könige (und das Volk) Gott und Seinen Geboten die Treue halten würden (1 Rg. ii 4, viii 25, vgl. vi 11-13, ix 6-7; 2 Rg. xxi 7-8).[33] Sodann werden in einer Sonderschicht gegen das Ende der Königsbücher die Untaten Manasses für alles Unglück verantwortlich gemacht (2 Rg. xxi 11-12, xxiii 26-27, xxiv 3, 4b). In 2 Rg. xxi 10-14 ist die theologische Reflexion in eine anonyme Prophetie eingedrungen (sie wird "Seinen Dienern, den Propheten" zugeschrieben), die auch sonst von den in den Königsbüchern üblichen Prophetenworten abweicht. Diese Prophetie ist von dem Bewußtsein getragen, daß nun auch Juda, das sich sicher wähnte, von dem Geschick Samariens ereilt wird d.h. ereilt worden ist.[34] Daß in den Prophetien der deuteronomistischen Geschichtsschreibung die Theodizee wenig zur Geltung kommt, wird durch einen weiteren Umstand ergänzt. Die Prophetenworte setzen, wie dargelegt, die Vergehen der Könige voraus, ohne zur Umkehr aufzufordern. Die Strafe, mit der gedroht wird, bekommt dadurch etwas Unausweichliches, man darf sagen: Schicksalhaftes. Wir berühren damit die Frage nach der Art der

[33] Schon der auf uns gekommene Text der Nathansweissagung enthält in 2 Sm. vii 14 eine leichte Einschränkung des Versprechens im Falle einer Verschuldung. Daß die Bedingung nachträglich eingeschoben worden ist, springt besonders 1 Rg. ii 4 in die Augen, wo sie in einem ungewöhnlich schönen Beispiel von "Wiederaufnahme" *lēʾmōr*... *lēʾmōr* erscheint. Ebenso vielsagend ist der Gebrauch des einleitenden *raq* in 1 Rg. viii 25 und 2 Rg. xxi 8. Man beachte weiter, daß die Bedingung an allen angeführten Stellen den nomistischen Charakter trägt, der nach R. Smend, "Das Gesetz und die Völker", *Festschrift von Rad* (München, 1971), pp. 494 ff., eine Spätschicht der deuteronomistischen Redaktion verrät. Über die Verwandlung der unbedingten Zusage in eine bedingte spricht auch W. H. Schmidt, "Kritik am Königtum", ebenda, pp. 445 ff. (freilich weicht seine Darstellung von der hier gegebenen etwas ab). Er führt auch Ps. cxxxii 12 und Sach. iii 7 an; an letztgenannter Stelle "übernimmt der Hohepriester die Verpflichtungen, denen der König unterworfen war".

[34] Genau vergleichbar ist die (spät)deuteronomistische Anschauung in Jer. vii 14-15.

schicksalhaften Momente, die den verschiedenen Formen der in der Bibel enthaltenen Prophetien anhaften. Eine rein fatalistische Atmosphäre beherrscht die Fremdvölkerprophetien, deren Sammlungen in den Büchern der großen Propheten eine alte Schicht bilden: hier wird den Völkern Unheil angesagt, das schicksalsschwer ist durch das Fehlen jeder Motivierung; man fühlt sich an die Stimmung der späteren Apokalyptik erinnert. Der Verkündigung der klassischen Schriftprophetie selber fehlt dagegen jedes Element des Fatalismus. Die in den Königsbüchern enthaltenen Prophetien nehmen sozusagen eine Zwischenstellung ein: das fatalistische Element ist dadurch abgeschwächt, daß das Unheil durch den Abfall der Könige begründet ist, allerdings nur in ihrem jeweiligen persönlichen Verhalten! Gleichwohl bleibt ein Hauch des Unwiderruflichen spürbar, wie wir das oben auch für die Heilsprophetie des Jona ben Amittai (2 Rg. xiv 25) und die daran geknüpfte nachdenkliche Betrachtung (26-27) schon beiläufig feststellten.

III

Wir wenden uns jetzt den Büchern der Chronik zu, in denen wir ganz anderen Anschauungen über Prophetie und Propheten begegnen werden.[35]

Unseren Darlegungen müssen wir aber ein paar Bemerkungen vorausschicken. Die erste bezieht sich auf die Frage der Glaubwürdigkeit des Verfassers und des von ihm Berichteten. Sie ist seit de Wettes wohl unübertroffenem "Kritischem Versuch" immer wieder und von recht verschiedenen Gesichtspunkten aus behandelt worden. Ganz allgemein sei hier gesagt: Wo von konkreten Ereignissen, wie Feldschlachten, Festungsbau und dergleichen die Rede ist, kann es (ich bin geneigt hinzuzufügen: ausnahmsweise) vorkommen, daß dem Verfasser Überlieferungen oder gar Akten vorlagen, die uns sonst

---

[35] Am Anfang dieses Abschnittes sei gleich betont, daß, wenn hier von dem Chronisten geredet wird, immer nur an den Verfasser der Chronikbücher gedacht ist. Hoffentlich setzt sich die Erkenntnis durch, daß die Bücher Esra und Nehemia von anderer Hand stammen. In neuerer Zeit siehe dazu u.a. S. Japhet, "The Supposed Common Authorship of Chronicles and Ezra-Nehemia...", *VT* 18 (1968), pp. 330-71 (aufgrund des Sprachgebrauchs), J. D. Newsome, "Toward a new understanding of the Chronicler...", *JBL* 94 (1975), pp. 201-17 (der auch auf die unterschiedliche Schätzung der Prophetie in Chr und E/N hinweist; freilich kann ich Bedenken gegen die Argumentation und die Frühdatierung der Chronik nicht unterdrücken), jetzt die überzeugende und allseitige Beweisführung bei H. G. M. Williamson, *Israel in the Books of Chronicles* (Cambridge, 1977), pp. 5-82.

nicht erhalten sind und die er in seinem Werk verarbeitete. Anders liegt die Sache, wo es sich um gedankliche oder religiöse Vorstellungen handelt. Dort ist er ganz Theologe. Fast von selbst macht er die auftretenden Sprecher zu Trägern seiner Ideen. Mit der letzten Feststellung berühren wir schon direkt unser eigentliches Thema; dieses bietet aber noch ein weitergehendes Beispiel für den Mangel an historischer Zuverlässigkeit des Autors. Wir sahen oben, daß die älteren Erzählungen von Propheten als Gründern von Dynastien, denen sie dann später den Untergang ansagten, im Nordreich beheimatet waren. Der Verfasser der Chronik konnte, weil er keine fortlaufende Darstellung von der Geschichte des Nordreichs geben wollte, die Überlieferungen über diese Propheten, die ihm aus seiner Quelle, den Königsbüchern, wohlbekannt waren, nicht in sein Werk aufnehmen. Stattdessen finden sich bei ihm Erzählungen von Propheten, die sich mit Ratschlägen und Mahnungen an die Könige von Juda wenden, deren Authentizität naturgemäß starken Bedenken unterliegt. Die zweite kürzere und etwas andersartige Vorbemerkung hängt mit der Neigung des Verfassers zusammen, die auserwählte Dynastie Davids, wenn nur immer möglich, zu verherrlichen. Es ist sicher kein Zufall, daß er seine programmatischen Abrisse gerade Königen wie Abia (2 Chr. xiii) und Hiskia (2 Chr. xxix-xxxi) in den Mund legt oder daß es Josaphat ist, der sich in einer Ansprache (2 Chr. xx 20) an ein so berühmtes Prophetenwort wie Jes. vii 9b anlehnt. Man hat mit Recht bemerkt, daß bei unserem Autor die Könige und ihre Reden nicht selten prophetische Züge tragen.[36] Wir werden darum im Laufe des Folgenden nicht nur Prophetenworte anführen, sondern gelegentlich auch Äußerungen von Königen in den Kreis unserer Betrachtung einbeziehen müssen. Doch fangen wir mit der Wertung von Propheten und Prophetenwort beim Chronisten an.

Der Chronist zitiert oft als Quellen für die Begebenheiten, die er beschreibt, Bücher, die von Propheten verfaßt sein sollen. Die Reihe solcher "prophetischen" Geschichtsschreiber läuft vom Propheten Samuel (1 Chr. xxix 29) bis Jesaja ben Amoz (2 Chr. xxxii 32); naturgemäß besteht für den Chronisten die Unterscheidung nicht, die wir zwischen klassischen und nicht-klassischen Propheten machen. Die ganze Vorstellung von prophetischen Quellen ist eine Fiktion. Eigentlich genügt für diese Feststellung die anachronistische Notiz 1

[36] Newsome, pp. 203 f.

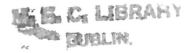

Chr. xxix 29, nach der die Worte des Propheten Samuel, des Propheten Nathan und des Sehers Gad, jede oder alle zusammen, eine schriftliche (!) Darstellung aller Taten Davids enthalten haben sollen. Sie läßt sich aber auch erhärten durch einen Vergleich von 1 Rg. xxii 46 mit 2 Chr. xx 34 und 2 Rg. xx 20 mit 2 Chr. xxxii 32. An beiden Stellen in den Königsbüchern werden als Quellen für die Taten Josaphats bzw. Hiskias die Annalen der Könige von Juda genannt. In 2 Chr. xxxii 32 wird ganz unvermittelt eine prophetische Quelle (Jesaja ben Amoz) danebengestellt; in 2 Chr. xx 34 ist sogar angedeutet, das Geschichtswerk Jehus ben Hanani sei in die königlichen Annalen aufgenommen worden. Eben dieser fiktive und gekünstelte Charakter seiner prophetischen Quellen zeigt nun, wieviel dem Chronisten an ihrer wiederholten Erwähnung gelegen war: prophetische Äußerungen besaßen für ihn kanonische Autorität.[37]

Ein weiteres Indiz für die kanonische Geltung, die der Prophetie für den Verfasser der Chronikbücher zukam, bietet die Streuung der Stellen aus den Büchern der klassischen Prophetie, die er in seinen Werken zitiert oder auf die er deutlich anspielt. Diese Stellen finden sich Jes. vii 9, xli 8; Jer. xxxi 15; Hos. iii 4; Sach. iv 10, viii 10, d.h. in sehr verschiedenen Prophetien aus vorexilischer, exilischer und nachexilischer Zeit. Es ist kaum Zufall, daß die Zitate und Anspielungen gerade und ausnahmslos in Reden und Ansprachen erscheinen, die vom Chronisten verfaßt sind und zu deren Sprecher er Propheten und einmal auch den König Josaphat macht; er war sich offenbar ihres rhetorischen Charakters wohl bewußt. Noch wichtiger für die Art der chronistischen Geschichtsschreibung ist es, daß die Zitate eine Umbiegung erfahren, durch die ihre ursprüngliche Bedeutung verändert und ganz der Gedankenwelt des Chronisten angeglichen wird. Diese Behauptung sei im folgenden durch eine Analyse zweier Beispiele erhärtet und verdeutlicht.[38] In dem berühmten Wortspiel Jes. vii 9b heißt es: *ʾim lōʾ taʾ^{a}mīnū kī lōʾ tēʾāmēnū*: "Wenn ihr nicht glaubet, so werdet ihr nicht standhalten." Eine ins Positive gewandte Variation dazu wird 2 Chr. xx 20b dem König Josaphat in einer

---

[37] Sogar die Einrichtung des Tempeldienstes durch David, das zentrale Anliegen des Chronisten, stammt nach 2 Chr. xxix 25 eigentlich von den Propheten Gad und Nathan, "denn die Weisung war Gottes mittels Seiner Propheten".

[38] Diese Beispiele wollen keineswegs einen Ersatz bilden für das bedauerliche Fehlen jedes Hinweises auf die Art, in der der Chronist seine Quellen umdeutet und aktualisiert, in meinem Aufsatz "Voraussetzungen der Midraschexegese", *SVT* 1 (1953), pp. 150 ff.; vgl. jetzt T. Willi, *Die Chronik als Auslegung* (Göttingen, 1972), speziell p. 53.

Ansprache an die Krieger vor einer Feldschlacht in den Mund gelegt: "Glaubet an den Herrn, euren Gott, und ihr werdet standhalten." Schon vor mehr als vierzig Jahren hat G. von Rad gesehen,[39] daß hier nicht nur die Form variiert ist, sondern auch eine Wandlung des Inhalts vorliegt. In der Fortsetzung der Worte Josaphats heißt es nämlich: "Glaubet an Seine Propheten und es wird euch gelingen." Hier tritt neben den Glauben an Gott der an Seine Propheten; die Propheten selber hätten einen solchen nie beansprucht, doch bilden sie für den Chronisten, wie gesagt, ein kanonisches Korpus. Ein vergleichbares Beispiel findet sich allem Anschein nach 2 Chr. xv 3. In den Worten des Asarja ben Oded heißt es: "Und lange Zeit wird für Israel vergehen, ohne den wahren Gott, ohne Priester und ohne Lehre." Wir dürfen hier eine bewußte chronistische Umbildung von Hos. iii 4 erblicken: Hosea hatte gesagt, daß Israel lange Zeit leben würde ohne König und Fürsten, ohne Opfer (d.h. Altäre) [40] und Denksteine, ohne Ephod und Teraphim. Der Chronist hingegen spricht von dem Fehlen der Verehrung des wahren Gottes mittels einer Lehre (Thora), die vom Priester-Lehrer verkündigt wird. In diesem Fall geht die Umdeutung recht weit, schon deshalb, weil Hosea eine Zeit voraussagt, in der Israel ohne die Größen leben wird, die vom Propheten ausnahmslos negativ beurteilt werden, während für den Chronisten der wahre Gott, der unterrichtende Priester und die Thora die höchsten Werte bedeuten.[41] Die Propheten besitzen also für den Verfasser der Chronik eine so große Autorität, daß er eine midraschartige Aktualisierung ihrer Worte vornimmt. Dieses Verfahren spricht, wie sich versteht, nicht eben für die geschichtliche Zuverlässigkeit des Autors.

Trotz der Verherrlichung der davidischen Dynastie ist der Chronist im Gegensatz zu der deuteronomistischen Geschichtsschreibung weit davon entfernt, den König als ausschließlichen Träger der Geschichte zu betrachten. Viel öfter als in den Königsbüchern berät sich [42] der

[39] G. von Rad, "Die levitische Predigt in den Büchern der Chronik", zuerst erschienen in der *Festschrift O. Procksch* (Leipzig, 1934), siehe dort p. 119.

[40] Daß neben *maṣṣēbāh* von Altären und nicht von Opfern die Rede war, wird (trotz LXX) schon durch einen Vergleich mit Hos. x 1-2, vgl. auch Ex. xxxiv 13; Dt. vii 5 und xii 3, sichergestellt.

[41] Für den Nachdruck, den der Chronist auf den Begriff Thora legt, führt T. Willi, *Die Chronik als Auslegung* (Göttingen, 1972), p. 125, als überzeugende Stelle 2 Chr. vi 16 an, wo das "vor Mir wandeln" in dem Gebet Salomos 1 Rg. viii 25 vom Chronisten durch "in Meiner Lehre wandeln" ersetzt worden ist.

[42] In 2 Sm. xvi und xvii sowie gehäuft in 1 Rg. xii lesen wir über den Rat, den sich ein König bei seinen Ratgebern einholt. In beiden Fällen handelt es sich um

König mit den Würdenträgern oder mit dem Volk; die Überführung der Lade von Kirjath Je'arim in die Davidsstadt wird ausdrücklich vom Volk gutgeheißen (1 Chr. xiii 1-4). Es ist nicht auszumachen, ob sich in dem Motiv des sich beratenden Königs — wie es der Zeit unseres Autors wohl entsprechen würde — Institutionen des persischen Hofes widerspiegeln, die historisch belegbar sind.[43] Jedenfalls tritt in der Chronik, auch von diesem Motiv abgesehen, neben den König von Juda des öfteren "das ganze Volk" oder "ganz Israel".[44] Dadurch wird nun die chronistische Historiographie wieder nahe an die klassische Prophetie gerückt. Diese richtet sich in Sonderfällen an den König, sonst aber durchweg an das Volk und zwar immer im Plural. Genau das gleiche trifft nun auf die Chronik zu. Geradezu auffallend ist in dieser Beziehung 2 Chr. xxxiii 10: Es ist deutlich, daß sich das mahnende Wort Gottes vor allem gegen den König Manasse richtet. Der Chronist jedoch läßt Gott zu Manasse und seinem Volk sprechen, sie aber hören nicht (beachte den Plural). Den Propheten und anderen Sprechern in der Chronik wird immer ein "Höret!" in den Mund gelegt, wie in der klassischen Prophetie und anders als in der deuteronomistischen Geschichtsschreibung. Besondere Beachtung verdient die Tatsache, daß das "Höre das Wort

weisheitliche Erzählungen, die aus dem Rahmen eigentlicher Geschichtsschreibung fallen, vgl. immerhin xvi 21-22 nach xv 16. In wirklich historischen Zusammenhängen ist von einer Beratung des Königs nicht direkt die Rede. (Nach 1 Rg. xii 26-27 heißt 28 wohl: der König ging mit sich zu Rate, faßte einen Plan.) Anders in der Chronik. Der Ratgeber des Königs ist hier ein offizieller Titel; sogar wenn man von 1 Chr. xxvii 32-33 als nicht zur Arbeit des Chronisten gehörig absieht, so bleibt doch 2 Chr. xxv 16, die höhnische Frage Amazjas an den ihn zurechtweisenden Propheten: Hat man dich "zum Ratgeber des Königs" bestellt? Im selben Vers wird die Wurzel *y'ṣ* mehrfach und in verschiedenen Schattierungen verwendet; gleiches geschieht bei der Schilderung der schlechten Einflüsse, denen Ahasja laut 2 Chr. xxii 3-5 ausgesetzt ist. Der König berät sich mit Würdenträgern oder dem Volk vor politischen oder kultischen Maßnahmen, vgl. 2 Chr. xxxii 3, xx 21, xxx 2 und 23. Besondere Beachtung verdient, daß dem Krieg des Amazja von Juda gegen Joasch von Israel laut xxv 17 eine Beratung (mit sich selbst?!) vorausgegangen sein soll, von der an der Parallelstelle 1 Rg. xiv 8 nichts erwähnt ist.

[43] Als feste Verbindung finden wir "den König und seine (sieben) Ratgeber" Esr. vii 14, 15, 28 und viii 25, ein romanhafter Nachklang Esth. i 13-15, wo 14 auch von den sieben Fürsten von Persien und Medien die Rede ist; siehe E. Meyer, *Geschichte des Alterthums* III (Stuttgart, 1901), p. 43 und vgl. noch Stellen wie Herodot vii 8 u.ä.

[44] Besonderes Gewicht kommt wieder den Stellen zu, an denen sich die Ausdrucksweise des Chronisten mit der seiner Vorlage vergleichen läßt wie 1 Chr. xi 4 und 2 Chr. i 3 in (bewußter) Abweichung von den Parallelen 2 Sm. v 6 bzw. 1 Rg. iii 4; vgl. noch 2 Chr. xv 2, xx 15 (xxx 2, 23).

des Herrn!" des Micha ben Jimla (1 Rg. xxii 19) in 2 Chr. xviii 18 durch ein "Höret das Wort des Herrn!" ersetzt worden ist, das (wiewohl auch von der LXX bezeugt) nicht so recht in den Zusammenhang paßt!

In der Chronik erscheinen die Propheten als Mahner und Warner, die zur Umkehr auffordern.[45] In unserem Zusammenhang kann nicht näher auf die Frage eingegangen werden, ob in der klassischen Prophetie der Aufruf zur Umkehr ein übergeordnetes oder ein untergeordnetes Motiv darstellt. Ich bin der Meinung, es handle sich um ein übergeordnetes, wenn auch keineswegs das einzige.[46] Unbestreitbar bleibt, daß die älteste Exegese: das Buch Jona, die deuteronomistische Bearbeitung des Buches Jeremia die Prophetie als Mahnung zur Umkehr verstanden hat — so auch die Chronik. Prägnant ist das formuliert, als nach dem Tode des Priesters Jojada der König Joasch und das Volk von Gott abfallen und fremde Götter verehren, 2 Chr. xxiv 19: "Da sandte Er Propheten zu ihnen, um sie zum Herrn umkehren zu lassen, und diese warnten [47] sie." Eine der-

---

[45] Vgl. jetzt S. Japhet, *The Ideology of the Book of Chronicles and its Place in Biblical Thought* (hebräisch) (Jerusalem, 1977), pp. 154-66.

[46] Schon oben wurde das Fehlen der Mahnung zur Umkehr in der deuteronomistischen Geschichtsschreibung als Unterschied von der klassischen Prophetie vermerkt. Man darf vielleicht sagen, daß in der klassischen Prophetie die Gewißheit des Kommens Gottes und der Aufruf zur Umkehr in einer gewissen Spannung nebeneinanderstehen. Allerdings wird dadurch die absolute Gültigkeit des Gotteswortes etwas beeinträchtigt, kann doch die Buße des Menschen das angedrohte Gericht abwenden. Bei Jesaja überwiegt die Ankündigung des Kommens Gottes, doch sollte dabei das Gewicht von vi 9-10 im Berufungsauftrag nicht übersehen werden: indirekt spricht hier das Bewußtsein, der Aufruf zur Umkehr sei der zu erwartende Inhalt der Prophetie gewesen, doch ist er durch die Unabwendbarkeit der Strafe aufgehoben worden. Das fünfmalige: "Ihr aber seid nicht zu Mir zurückgekehrt", Am. iv 6-11 setzt doch voraus, daß Gott die Strafe über sein Volk bringt, um es zur Umkehr zu bewegen. Ich kann H. W. Wolff nicht zustimmen, wenn er, zuletzt *Festschrift W. Zimmerli* (Göttingen, 1977), pp. 547 ff., dem Motiv der Umkehr zu Gott (und nicht zu der Vergangenheit) z.B. bei Hosea und Amos jede tragende Bedeutung abspricht. Hos. xiv 2 f. und Am. v 4, 6 reden direkt von der Umkehr. Auf Einzelheiten der Exegese von Hos. xiv 3, sowie von dem Komplex Am. v 13-16 muß hier verzichtet werden; keinesfalls darf Am. v 14 f. als Zusatz betrachtet werden.

[47] Siehe meine Erörterung in der *Festschrift W. Baumgartner*, *VTS* 16 (1967), pp. 265 f. Anders jetzt T. Veijola in seinem Beitrag *Ugarit-Forschungen* 8 (1976), pp. 343-51. Seine gelehrten und reichhaltigen Ausführungen scheinen mir überzeugender für die Grundbedeutung von *ʿēdūt* als für die Verbindung von *ʿēdūt* mit *hēʿīd*. Trotz der Assoziation an den (späten) Stellen 2 Rg. xvii 15 und Neh. ix 34 glaube ich, daß auch aus morphologischen und syntaktischen Gründen *hēʿīd b*...durchweg "warnen" heißt. Ich möchte auch an der ursprünglichen Bedeutung "Gott als Zeugen anrufen" festhalten. Die Stelle Sir. xlvi 19 (sie ist

artige Mahnung im prophetischen Stil, aber noch stärker kultisch ausgerichtet, wird dem König Hiskia in den Mund gelegt xxx 6: "Da zogen die Boten...durch ganz Israel und Juda und verkündeten nach dem Befehl des Königs: Ihr Kinder Israels, kehret um zu dem Herrn, dem Gott Abrahams, Isaaks und Israels...und kommt zu Seinem Heiligtum, das Er für immer geheiligt hat." Es ist vielleicht angebracht, darauf hinzuweisen, daß in 5-9 alle zentralen Themen, die dem Verfasser am Herzen liegen, zusammen auftreten: Ein frommer König aus dem Hause Davids fordert in der klassischen Prophetie entlehnten Wendungen ganz Israel, von Dan bis Beer Scheba, zum Kult in dem von Gott erwählten Tempel zu Jerusalem auf. Der Feldzug Sisaks gegen Jerusalem in der Zeit Rehabeams hat nach 2 Chr. xii seinen Grund in dem Abfall Judas von Gott. Diese Feststellung fand der Chronist nicht in seiner Quelle 1 Rg. xiv 25; er will durch sie seine eigene Anschauung zum Ausdruck bringen. Näher wird diese ausgeführt in den Worten des Propheten Semaja (5): "Ihr habt Mich verlassen, so habe Ich euch verlassen und euch in die Hand Sisaks gegeben." Der Umstand, daß der Prophet so völlig als Wortführer chronistischen Gedankenguts vorgestellt ist, legt den Verdacht nahe, der ganze hier berichtete Vorgang sei fingiert. Damit werden wir von neuem vor die wichtige Frage nach der Authentizität der chronistischen Prophetenerzählungen gestellt. Die Fortsetzung unserer Stelle lautet (6): "Da demütigten sich die Fürsten Israels und der König und sprachen: Der Herr ist gerecht." Darauf läßt Gott den Propheten sagen: "Weil sie sich gedemütigt haben, will Ich sie nicht vernichten." In dieser Prophetenerzählung ist die Ermahnung zur Buße erfolgreich: es findet eine kollektive Umkehr statt (vergleichbar ist 2 Chr. xxviii 9 ff.). In anderen Fällen aber, und sie bilden die Mehrzahl, prallt die prophetische Predigt an der Verstocktheit des Volkes ab. Die Fortsetzung der oben zitierten Stelle xxiv 19 lautet einfach: "aber die Leute hörten nicht auf sie". Drastisch erweitert wird diese Aussage 2 Chr. xxxvi 15-16, gegen Ende des Buches, wo wir lesen: "Und der Herr, der Gott ihrer Väter, ermahnte sie immer wieder durch Seine Boten, die Er früh und spät zu ihnen sandte, denn Er wollte Sein Volk und Seine Stätte wohl schonen. Sie aber verspotteten die Boten Gottes, verachteten Seine Worte und verhöhnten Seine Propheten, bis sich der Grimm

eine Exegese von 1 Sm. xii 5!) war mir 1967 entgangen; zudem vergleiche man Dt. xxx 19! Instruktiv ist, daß nach frührabbinischen Quellen der Zeuge eines Fehltritts verpflichtet ist, den Übeltäter zu warnen (MSanh. v 1; Makk. i 9).

Gottes gegen Sein Volk ins Unheilbare steigern mußte!" Hier erscheint das Motiv der Schmähung der Propheten und ihrer Worte (Neh. ix 26, 29 f.) [48] im Rahmen einer eindrucksvollen Theodizee. In 15 "früh und spät" lehnt sich der Chronist deutlich an das Buch Jeremia, so wie es ihm vorlag, an (vgl. den nächsten Abschnitt).[49] Das ist kaum Zufall, war doch im unmittelbar Vorhergehenden (12-13) erzählt, wie Jeremia vergeblich versucht, den König Zedekia von seinem schlechten Weg und dem Treubruch gegen den König von Babel abzuhalten. In 20-21 (dem ursprünglichen Abschluß des Buches) erscheint Jeremia dann wieder als der Prophet, der die siebzigjährige Dauer des Exils (Jer. xxv 11-12, xxix 10) vorausgesagt und damit auch die Aussicht auf Wiederherstellung erweckt hatte.[50] Ganz anders als in der Darstellung des Deuteronomisten steht die Gestalt Jeremias eindrucksvoll am Ausgang der chronistischen Historiographie, was den Einfluß der klassischen Prophetie auf den Verfasser noch einmal bestätigt.

In alten Geschichtserzählungen finden wir wiederholt die Wurzel *š‘n ‘l ni.* in der Bedeutung "sich stützen auf", z.B. auf einen Speer, auf jemandes Hand (2 Sm. i 6; 2 Rg. v 18, vii 2). Vom Propheten Jesaja wird die gleiche Verbalform in dieser Konstruktion übertragen gebraucht: "sein Vertrauen auf jemand stellen", vor allem x 20 (zweimal), auch xxx 12, xxxi 1, an den beiden letzten Stellen von dem falschen Vertrauen Judas auf Ägypten (dieser Gebrauch wird von Ezechiel xxix 6-7 für den gleichen Sachverhalt nachgeahmt!). Der Chronist verwendet nun *š‘n ‘l ni.* genau in der übertragenen Bedeutung, die wir bei Jesaja (bzw. Ezechiel) finden und die den älteren historischen Quellen fremd ist. Man ist geneigt, an eine Beeinflussung durch Jesaja zu denken, liest sich doch 2 Chr. xvi 7 fast als eine Umkehrung von Jes. x 20. Jes. x 20 lesen wir: "An jenem Tage aber werden sich der Rest Israels und was übrig ist vom Hause Jakobs nicht mehr stützen auf den, der sie schlägt, sondern sie werden in Wahrheit vertrauen auf den Herrn, den Heiligen Israels!" 2 Chr. xvi

[48] O. H. Steck, *Israel und das gewaltsame Geschick der Propheten* (Neukirchen, 1966), speziell p. 65, Anm. 6.

[49] Es ist vielleicht der Erwähnung wert, daß schon in xxxvi 12-14 ein Nachklang von Jer. xxxvii 2 erkennbar ist. (Es scheint abwegig, umgekehrt Jer. xxxvii 2 als chronistischen Einschub zu betrachten.)

[50] M. Weinfeld, *Deuteronomy and the Deuteronomic School* (Oxford, 1972), pp. 143-6, weist im Anschluß an R. Borger nach, daß die typologische Zahl ihre Vorbilder in den Inschriften Asarhaddons hat. Über die innerbiblischen Deutungen der siebzig Jahre vgl. noch O. Plöger, "Siebzig Jahre", *Festschrift F. Baumgärtel* (Erlangen, 1959), pp. 124 ff., zu unserer Stelle speziell p. 129.

7 spricht der Seher Hanani zum König Asa: "Weil du dich auf den König von Aram gestützt hast und nicht vertraut hast auf den Herrn, deinen Gott, darum ist das Heer des Königs von Aram deiner Hand entronnen!" — Die ältere Geschichtsschreibung (namentlich das Buch der Richter) erkennt im historischen Geschehen eine doppelte Kausalität: neben der Hilfe Gottes stehen menschliche Anstrengung und menschliche Kraft.[51] Für den Propheten und wieder namentlich für Jesaja handelt in der Geschichte nur Gott; nur auf Ihn soll man sich verlassen und nicht auf menschliche Kraft oder menschliches Heldentum. In diesem Zusammenhang ergibt sich bei einem nochmaligen Vergleich von Stellen in der Chronik mit solchen in den Königsbüchern eine interessante Beobachtung. An drei Stellen in den Königsbüchern (1 Rg. xv 23, xxii 46; 2 Rg. xx 20) wird, mittels eines Zitats aus den Annalen, gestorbenen Königen von Juda ihre Heldenhaftigkeit *g^ebûrāh* nachgerühmt. An den entsprechenden Stellen in der Chronik (2 Chr. xvi 11, xx 34, xxxii 32) fehlt jedesmal — so daß kaum von Zufall die Rede sein kann — diese Erwähnung der *g^ebûrāh*: Für den Chronisten sind Kraft und Macht keine menschlichen Eigenschaften, sondern ausschließlich Gott vorbehalten. Das kommt schon zum Ausdruck in den Gebeten Asas (2 Chr. xiv 10) und Josaphats vor der Feldschlacht (xx 6) und auch in dem Mahnwort des Gottesmannes an Amazja (xxv 8). Vor allem muß hier an das Loben Gottes durch David erinnert werden: "Dir, o Herr, gebühren Macht und Kraft...und in Deiner Hand sind Stärke und Kraft und in Deiner Hand steht es, einen jeglichen mächtig und stark zu machen." (1 Chr. xxix 11-12). In seinem Glauben, daß nur Gott Kraft eignet, ist der Chronist offenbar vom prophetischen Denken, speziell von Jesaja, beeinflußt. Freilich deutet David in seinem Lobspruch an, daß Gott von dieser Kraft auch Menschen verleihen kann. Daß gerade er dieser Möglichkeit Rechnung trägt, braucht nicht zu verwundern. Gibt es doch von der oben erwähnten Tendenz des Chronisten, heimgegangenen Königen *g^ebûrāh* abzusprechen, eine bezeichnende Ausnahme. Von David heißt es 1 Chr. xxix 29-30, seine Geschichte sei beschrieben von den Propheten Samuel, Nathan und Gad, "dazu auch seine königliche Macht und Kraft" (*g^ebûrāh*). Eben für diese Stelle hatte der Chronist in seinen wirklichen Quellen kein Vorbild. Er schuf sie frei. Hier sehen wir, daß der Chronist David, den Liebling Gottes, nicht mit menschlichen Maßstäben maß, hier findet aber auch

[51] Vgl. meinen Aufsatz, "Menschliches Heldentum und göttliche Hilfe", *ThZ* 19 (1963), pp. 385 ff., speziell pp. 408-10.

Wellhausens berühmtes Urteil über das Davidbild des Chronisten seine Grenze.[52]

IV

Die Entstehungsgeschichte des Buches Jeremia ist, entweder ganz oder teilweise, von der Forschung des zwanzigsten Jahrhunderts unablässig in Angriff genommen worden. Es stellt sich dabei immer deutlicher heraus, wie verwickelt die betreffende Problematik ist und wie schwierig es ist, hier zu einer Gesamtlösung zu gelangen, die sowohl den prophetischen Reden wie den biographischen Teilen und dazu ihren verschiedenen Bearbeitungen Recht widerfahren ließe. Der nachstehende Exkurs will nicht mehr als eine Erwägung zu einem Teilproblem vorlegen, die vielleicht zur Ergänzung der oben vorgetragenen Thesen dienen kann.

Auch in jüngster Zeit sind wieder Bedenken gegen die verbreitete Annahme einer deuteronomistischen Redaktion vorgebracht worden, doch läßt sich meines Erachtens ihre Existenz — jedenfalls für bestimmte Teile des Buches — nicht wohl leugnen.[53] Eine zentrale Frage für die Beurteilung des vorliegenden Textes ist, ob er selbständige und neugeschaffene deuteronomistische Stücke enthält, oder ob er eine deuteronomistische Bearbeitung von ursprünglichen Sprüchen des Jeremia darbietet. Beide Möglichkeiten schließen einander nicht aus: es dürften verschiedene Redaktionsprozesse neben- und nacheinander vor sich gegangen sein.

Jedenfalls scheint nachweisbar, daß sich in der Bearbeitung stellenweise echte Jeremiaworte verstecken. Die Forschung muß versuchen, solche authentischen Bruchstücke aus der Überlagerung herauszuschälen. Einen sicheren Anhaltspunkt bietet der Vergleich von xxii 1-5 mit xxi 12. In xxii 3 sind die offenbar echten Worte "und rettet den Beraubten aus der Hand des Gewalttätigen" in eine predigthafte Ansprache[54] hineingeraten, die voll ist von deuteronomistischen

[52] J. Wellhausen, *Prolegomena zur Geschichte Israels*[2] (Berlin, 1883), p. 189: "Was hat die Chronik aus David gemacht!...ein mattes Heiligenbild umnebelt von einer Wolke von Weihrauch."

[53] Als eine willkommene Grundlage für literarkritische Weiterarbeit am Buche Jeremia erweist sich noch immer die Zusammenstellung der "deuteronomistischen" Wendungen bei J. Bright, "Prose Sermons of Jeremiah. Appendix A", *JBL* 70 (1951), pp. 30-35.

[54] Der Ton des Stückes wird gleich von den Anfangsworten: "Übt Recht und Gerechtigkeit" bestimmt, genauso Ez. xlv 9. In beiden Fällen ist die Forderung an die Könige (Fürsten) gerichtet, nicht von ungefähr: wird doch gerade ihnen diese Tugend nachgerühmt 2 Sm. viii 15; 1 Rg. x 9; Jer. xxii 15. In Ezechiels

Wendungen. Kaum weniger eindeutig ist ein zweiter Fall. Bekannte Beispiele deuteronomistischer Komposition finden sich in der Tempelrede und dem Bericht über sie in Kap. vii bzw. xxvi.[55] In beiden Kapiteln wird nun die Zerstörung des Heiligtums in Silo, "wo Gott ehedem Seinen Namen hatte wohnen lassen", wiederholt erwähnt (vii 12, 14, xxvi 6 vgl. 9). Nun wird dieses Heiligtum in der ganzen Bibel (außerhalb der sich darauf beziehenden Erzählungen in den Büchern Richter und Samuel) nur noch einmal, Ps. lxxviii 60, genannt. Jeremia aber gehörte, das will bedacht sein, zu den Priestern in Anathoth d.h. dem Hause der Eliden, dessen letzter Priester Ebjathar dorthin von Salomo verbannt worden war (1 Rg. ii 27). Die Erinnerung an das Heiligtum in Silo war wohl ein Gesprächsthema, über das sich der Kreis, in dem Jeremia aufwuchs, manchmal unterhielt. Die Betonung seiner Zerstörung entstammt also sicher einem Ausspruch von Jeremia selbst. Eine weitere Beobachtung sei wenigstens zur Diskussion gestellt. Typisch für das Buch Jeremia und eben für seine deuteronomistischen Teile ist die Verbindung *haškēm w*[e]..., die besagen will, daß Gott immer aufs neue (und vergeblich!) Propheten gesandt hat, um zum Volk zu sprechen und es zu warnen. Sie findet sich in dieser Schicht elfmal, außerdem an einer offensichtlich vom Jeremia-Buch abhängigen Stelle (2 Chr. xxxvi 15); eine sonstige wirkliche Parallele gibt es nicht.[56] Der infinitivus absolutus *haškēm* soll den Eifer Gottes und Seiner Boten zum Ausdruck bringen. Man fragt sich, ob vielleicht der Gebrauch dieses Verbums in der täglichen, persönlichen Erfahrung des Jeremia seine Wurzel hat. Er wohnte in Anathoth und mußte jeden Morgen in Jerusalem sein, als die Stadt erwachte, der König ausritt und das Volk in den Tempel ging. Dazu stand er in aller Frühe auf, um den Weg von seinem Heimatort in die Hauptstadt zu machen.[57] Wenn die Vermutung zuträfe, hätten wir

---

Lehre über göttliche Vergeltung wird es dann zur Charakteristik jedes gerechten Menschen, Ez. xviii und xxxiii (siebenmal). So auch schon im Volkssprichwort der Weisheit Prv. xxi 3.

[55] Vgl. die schöne Behandlung bei W. Thiel, *Die deuteronomistische Redaktion von Jeremia 1-25* (Neukirchen, 1973), pp. 105-19.

[56] Eine entfernte Parallele wäre höchstens Prv. xxvii 14; hier scheinen das (seinen Mitmenschen) "mit lauter Stimme" bzw. "am frühen Morgen preisen" Varianten in einem Sprichwort zu sein, das — eine verbreitete Erscheinung — in verschiedenen Formen umlief. 1 Sm. xvii 16 gehört nicht hierher.

[57] N. haReübeni, *Neues Licht über das Buch Jeremia* (Tel Aviv, 1950), pp. 12 f. (hebräisch), freilich ohne jede literarkritische Implikation; einen Nachklang des Wegs, den Jeremia immer von Anathoth nach Jerusalem zu machen hatte, hört er auch aus dem elfmaligen "gehe hin" (*hālōk*) in den göttlichen Aufträgen an den Propheten heraus (p. 16).

ein weiteres Beispiel von der Art, in der der Stil der deuteronomistischen Predigt ein eigenes Wort von Jeremia aufgriff und gleichsam in Variationen verarbeitete. Als Bestätigung dieser Hypothese darf xxv 3 gelten, wo es heißt: "Seit dem dreizehnten Jahr des Josia... nun schon dreiundzwanzig Jahre lang...habe ich jeden Tag von neuem zu euch geredet" (*'aškēm wᵉdabbēr*).[58] Die eigene Erfahrung Jeremias wäre dann im später hinzugefügten Vers 4 in die geläufige Formel vom unablässigen Senden der Propheten durch Gott abgewandelt.

Wichtiger für unseren Zusammenhang als das an sich interessante Verhältnis zwischen dem Eigenwort Jeremias und der es umgestaltenden Hand des deuteronomistischen Redaktors ist die Frage, was sich über den Zweck und namentlich auch über das relative Datum der deuteronomistischen Bearbeitung von Jeremias Prophetien ermitteln läßt. Der Zweck läßt sich schwerlich eindeutig und in der hier gebotenen Kürze feststellen. In der Bearbeitung der Jeremiaworte gelangt der Aufruf zur Umkehr (wie ähnlich bei Ezechiel) zu einem Höhepunkt, wobei geradezu die absolute Geltung des Gotteswortes beeinträchtigt wird: Nicht das einmal ergangene Wort Gottes bestimmt den Lauf der Dinge, sondern das Verhalten der Menschen — tut ihr Buße, so tritt das Strafgericht nicht ein; [59] in der Ablehnung der Bußpredigt liegt eine Theodizee der Katastrophe. Damit berühren wir einen geschichtstheologischen Faktor, war es doch das Bestreben dieser Redaktionsschicht, Jeremia als Vertreter der deuteronomistischen Anschauungen über den Untergang und seine Ursachen hinzustellen.[60] Ein charakteristisches Beispiel bietet Jer. xv 4: "Ich werde

[58] Die hier mit Vorbehalt vorgetragene Exegese von xxv 3-4 setzt voraus, daß sich in 3 ein jeremianischer Kern versteckt. Beachtung verdient nun, daß in diesem Vers und nur in ihm die Form *'škjm* (in plene-Schreibform!) verwendet wird. Dies ist wohl als Aramaismus zu erklären. Doch kommt eine zögernde Frage auf: Vielleicht schimmert hier eine Textform durch, in der Jeremia von sich in der ersten Person des Imperfekts sprach?

[59] W. Thiel hat für diese Form die Bezeichnung Alternativ-Predigt vorgeschlagen (p. 117 u.ö.). Der Ausdruck Alternative findet sich schon in den trefflichen Analysen von S. Herrmann, *Die prophetische Heilserwartung*... (Stuttgart, 1965), pp. 162-204, siehe dort speziell p. 175. Die Relativierung der ursprünglichen Unabwendbarkeit des Gotteswortes (vgl. oben Anm. 46) ist herausgearbeitet worden in dem bedeutsamen Aufsatz von A. Rofé, "Studies on the Composition of the Book of Jeremiah" (hebräisch), *Tarbiz* 44 (1975), pp. 1 ff., speziell pp. 24-9.

[60] Die Absichten, die hier dem Bearbeiter zugeschrieben werden, weichen ziemlich stark von B. Duhms verärgerter Behauptung ab (*KHAT* 1901, p. XVIII), der Redaktor habe aus dem Propheten "soweit ihm etwas Menschliches bleibt... einen Thoralehrer" gemacht. Richtig ist zwar, daß in den Dt-Partien des Jeremia-Buches mehrfach von Geboten gesprochen wird, die Gott Israel befohlen hat,

sie zum Entsetzen für alle Königreiche der Erde machen wegen Manasses, des Sohnes Hiskias, des Königs von Juda, um dessentwillen, was er in Jerusalem getan hat." Wir erinnern uns, daß auch in einer Sonderschicht der Königsbücher (2 Rg. xxi 10 ff., xxiii 26 f., xxiv 3) Manasse, über all seine Nachfolger hinweg, für die endgültige Katastrophe verantwortlich gemacht ist. Bei Jeremia, der von dem späteren König Jojakim ein so abschreckendes Bild entwirft (xxii 13, 17 ff.), kommt das Verdikt über Manasse ziemlich unerwartet. Es ist kaum zu bezweifeln, daß wir hier die Hand des deuteronomistischen Bearbeiters erkennen können und daß seine Formulierung von den Stellen in den Königsbüchern beeinflußt ist; sie lagen ihm also schon vor. Wir folgern, daß die deuteronomistische Bearbeitung des Buches Jeremia nach dem Abschluß der Königsbücher stattgefunden hat. (Das schließt natürlich nicht aus, daß gelegentlich Ergänzungen in den Königsbüchern, z.B. in 2 Rg. xvii, noch später nachgetragen wurden.) Es will beachtet sein, daß der Topos von den vorüberziehenden Fremdvölkern, die ihrem Entsetzen über das Schicksal von Land, Tempel und Stadt Ausdruck geben und es durch den Abfall des Volkes von seinem Gott zu erklären versuchen,[61] in Dt. xxix 23 ff. und sicher in 1 Rg. ix 8-9 in einen mehr oder weniger organischen Zusammenhang zum Kontext gebracht worden ist. Ein solcher Versuch der Anpassung fehlt völlig für Jer. xxii 8-9 — es handelt sich um einen freien Zusatz des deuteronomistischen Bearbeiters —, was auch für ein späteres Datum der Version in Jeremia sprechen würde. Es gibt dafür noch andere Anzeichen. 2 Rg. xxiv 20 heißt es, bevor der eigentliche "historische" Anlaß für den Fall Jerusalems, der Aufstand Zedekias gegen Nebukadrezar, genannt wird: "Denn zum Zorn des Herrn war es in Jerusalem und Juda gewesen, bis Er sie von Seinem Angesicht fortschaffte." Jer. xxxii

als Er es aus dem Land Ägypten führte; der Bearbeiter lehnt sich oft buchstäblich an (ethische) Vorschriften aus dem Deuteronomium an; es findet sich auch eine Predigt über die Inachtnahme des Sabbats (xvii 19-27, für den Hintergrund der Stelle ist Neh. xiii 15 ff., speziell 19 vgl. x 32, wichtig). Duhms Urteil scheint deshalb überspitzt, er wird auch dem Abschnitt xxxi 31-34 über den "neuen Bund" (pp. 255-6) kaum gerecht. Mit diesen Bemerkungen soll in keiner Hinsicht das große Verdienst geschmälert werden, das der von ihm geleisteten Pionierarbeit für die Literarkritik des Jeremia-Buches zukommt.

[61] Der Topos von Frage und Antwort über das eingetretene Unglück hat Vorgänger in den Annalen assyrischer Könige; die Ursache ist dort, daß ein Volk seinen Vasalleneid gegen Assur gebrochen hat. Für den Rassamzylinder Assurbanipals hat schon D. H. Müller, *Ezechielstudien* (Wien, 1894), pp. 61 f., darauf aufmerksam gemacht. Weitere Beispiele, insbesondere in bezug auf den Kontext in Dt. xxix, bei M. Weinfeld, pp. 115 f.

31 lautet: "Denn zu Meinem Zorn und Ingrimm ist Mir diese Stadt gewesen, vom Tage an, wo man sie erbaut hat bis auf den heutigen Tag, so daß Ich sie von Meinem Angesicht wegschaffen will." Die Jeremiastelle bietet sichtlich eine jüngere, ausgeschmückte Stilisierung von 2 Rg. xxiv 20. Man hat auch sonst den Eindruck, daß die deuteronomistischen Wendungen im Jeremia-Buch eine bereicherte Spätform darstellen.

Weitere Beobachtungen kommen hinzu. Nicht weniger als siebenmal (vii 23, xi 4, xxiv 7, xxx 22, xxxi 1, 33, xxxii 38) findet sich die formelhafte Beteuerung: Ich werde euer Gott, ihr werdet Mein Volk sein. In dieser Prägung scheint sie mir eindeutig priesterlicher Herkunft [62] (sie wird auch von Ezechiel oft verwendet). Wir hätten also eine Verbindung von deuteronomistischen und priesterlichen Stilelementen. Ganz abgesehen von der Frage nach der Datierung von priesterlichem Sprachgut, darf doch sein Vorkommen in einer deuteronomistischen Schicht als sicheres Zeichen jüngeren Ursprungs gewertet werden. Eine andersartige Überlegung schließt sich an. Sie ist nicht sprachlicher, sondern mehr sachlicher Natur, erweist sich aber eben dadurch als bedeutsam für unser Problem. Häufig (vii 24, 26, xi 8, xvii 23, xxxiv 14, xliv 5) beklagen die Bearbeiter mit immer gleichen Ausdrücken die Unverbesserlichkeit des Volkes: Seitdem Gott sie aus Ägypten geführt hat, haben sie nicht auf Seine Stimme gehört, Seinem Willen ihr Ohr nicht geliehen und sind halsstarrig gewesen. Dieses Motiv, das vermutlich auf Eigenworte Jeremias zurückgeht,[63] ist nun typisch für die spätere Historiographie: 2 Rg. xvii 14; Neh. ix 16, 17; 2 Chr. xxxvi 13, vgl. xxx 8, auch Sach. i 4 u.a.; so erfährt auch hier unsere These, die Bearbeitung des Jeremia-Buches sei jung, weitere Unterstützung.

Gewichtige Argumente dafür, daß die deuteronomistische Rezension von Jeremia ein spätes Produkt, wenn nicht gar das späteste der deuteronomistischen Schule bildet, finden sich zudem außerhalb des Buches. Die Königsbücher stellen (2 Rg. xvii 13 ausgenommen) die Propheten nie als Mahner zur Umkehr dar. Sie vertreten damit, auch in ihren redaktionellen Teilen, eine andere und doch wohl

---

[62] Etwas anders freilich R. Smend, *Die Bundesformel* (Zürich, 1963), p. 5, und S. Herrmann, p. 165, Anm. 8.

[63] Wohl aus seiner eigenen prophetischen Erfahrung wirft Jeremia dem Volk vor, sein Ohr sei unbeschnitten und es höre nicht (vi 10 und 19); so wird das echte Wort (ii 25): "Du aber sagtest 'Nein, es ist vergeblich, denn Fremde liebe ich und ihnen will ich folgen' ", in xviii 12 vom Redaktor aufgenommen und deuteronomistisch neu formuliert.

ältere Auffassung von der Prophetie und dem Wort Gottes als die Bearbeitung des Buches Jeremia, die sich eher dem Theodizeebegriff der Chronik nähert. Entscheidend jedoch dürfte eine weitere Erwägung sein. Wir sprachen oben davon, daß Jeremia auffälligerweise am Schluß der Königsbücher gar nicht erscheint. Das ließe sich, wie erwähnt, zur Not dadurch erklären, daß die Gestalten der klassischen Propheten in der deuteronomistischen Geschichtsschreibung überhaupt fehlen. Wir sahen schon, daß gerade im Falle Jeremias diese Erklärung kaum ausreicht. Vollends unannehmbar würde sie, wenn der Verfasser von 2 Rg. xxv das Buch Jeremia schon in deuteronomistischer Überarbeitung gekannt hätte. Sollte er da den "Gesinnungsgenossen" Jeremia nicht erwähnt haben?

Wir wagen die Behauptung, daß wir in der Redaktion des Buches Jeremia, mit ihren vielfachen dringlichen Aufrufen zur Umkehr, eine Art Übergang zwischen der deuteronomistischen und der chronistischen Auffassung von der Prophetie vor uns haben.

WIE IST EINE ISRAELITISCHE LITERATURGESCHICHTE MÖGLICH?

von

MASAO SEKINE
Tokio

Eine israelitische Literaturgeschichte baut auf die Ergebnisse der Einleitungswissenschaft und zieht literaturwissenschaftliche Arbeiten des Alten Testaments heran.

Die Pentateuch- bzw. Hexateuchkritik, die historisch und sachlich gesehen, das Zentrum der alttestamentlichen Einleitungswissenschaft ausmacht, ist in der gegenwärtigen Forschung mit schweren Fragen belastet,[1] aber ich möchte im großen und ganzen bei den bisherigen Linien bleiben und meine israelitische Literaturgeschichte entwerfen.

Die literaturwissenschaftlichen Arbeiten am Alten Testament, die nach der modernen Methodik der Literaturwissenschaft durchgeführt sind, vermehren sich in den letzten Jahren ständig. Das ist die Lage, die unsere Zeit von der Gunkels, der als Erster eine israelitische Literaturgeschichte bewußt entworfen hat,[2] unterscheidet. Gunkels Plan, eine israelitische Literaturgeschichte als Geschichte der literarischen Gattungen und Formen darzustellen, reicht heute nicht mehr aus.

Eine israelitische Literaturgeschichte ist aber methodisch von einer literaturwissenschaftlichen Arbeit am Alten Testament streng zu scheiden und muß einen eigenen Weg gehen. Das kommt hauptsächlich daher, daß sie eine geschichtliche Darstellung sein muß, die mehr als die Summe der literaturwissenschaftlichen Einzelarbeiten beinhaltet. Nun erhebt sich die schwierige Frage, ob es überhaupt möglich ist, literarische Werke, die nur eine kanonische Auswahl aus der literarischen Hinterlassenschaft der Israeliten sein können, in der Form eines durchlaufenden geschichtlichen Vorgangs darzustellen.

---

[1] Vgl. H. H. Schmid, *Der sogenannte Jahwist* (Zürich, 1976); S. Tengström, *Die Hexateucherzählung* (Lund, 1976); R. Rendtorff, *Das überlieferungsgeschichtliche Problem des Pentateuch*, *BZAW* 147 (1977).

[2] H. Gunkel, "Die Grundprobleme der israelitischen Literaturgeschichte", *Reden und Aufsätze* (Göttingen, 1913).

Ist es nicht ein schöner Traum, den Prozeß zu rekonstruieren, um die literarischen Werke des Alten Testaments in die organische Reihenfolge der Geschichte zu bringen? [3]

Eine andere Schwierigkeit hängt mit der Frage zusammen, was man unter dem Wort "Literatur" im Alten Testament versteht. Wenn man das Wort im engeren Sinne, nämlich als schöne Literatur versteht, so ist kaum daran zu zweifeln, daß uns im Alten Testament viele außerliterarische Werke begegnen. Jedoch wage ich zu sagen, daß man bisher allzu streng zwischen der Literatur im engeren und weiteren Sinne unterschieden hat. Diese Unterscheidung ist im Grunde moderneuropäisch gedacht; sie muß im Blick auf die Literatur der alten Völker als unsachgemäß bezeichnet werden. Die Grenzen der Literarizität mancher Werke im Alten Testament müßten wohl als fließend aufgefaßt werden.

Die Anfänge der Literatur vieler Völker sind unmöglich von ihrer Religion zu trennen. Das ist z.B. bei der altjapanischen Literatur und der Literatur des Ainu-Volkes, das im Nordjapan noch heute lebt, der Fall. Ich möchte kurz die sogenannte Gästetheorie, die in der altjapanischen Literaturgeschichte weit anerkannt ist, berühren, um von daher die Frage des Grundtopos der israelitischen Literatur im neuen Licht sehen zu können. Man hat schon lange als eine interessante Tatsache beobachtet, daß ein Grundschema ziemlich weit und breit in der altjapanischen Literaturgeschichte ausfindig zu machen ist, nach welchem göttliche Gäste aus Übersee von Osten und Süden die japanischen Inseln besuchen, um nach einiger Zeit über das Meer wieder zurückzukehren. Folkloristisch verdient die Volkssitte auf dem Lande bei uns genannt zu werden, daß die Japaner Mitte Juli alljährlich noch heutzutage eine Art Totenmesse halten. Sie besteht darin, daß Geschenke und Gaben den Toten den Fluß hinabtreibend dargebracht werden. Denn die Toten werden nach der volkstümlichen Anschauung jenseits des Meeres als spirituelle Wesen lebend gedacht. Auch diese Volkssitte kann im Licht der oben genannten Gästetheorie gedeutet werden. Ein mehr oder weniger einheitlicher religiöser und kultureller Hintergrund im alten Japan hat den einheitlichen literarischen Topos, der durch die Gästetheorie geklärt worden ist, hervorgebracht. Ist es nicht möglich, in der israelitischen Literaturgeschichte, deren religiöser und kultureller Hintergrund als noch einheitlicher als im Fall Altjapans betrachtet werden dürfte, einen Grundtopos aus-

[3] Vgl. R. Smend, *Alttestamentliches Lesebuch* (Hamburg, 1974), S. 7.

findig zu machen? Wenn diese Möglichkeit besteht, so werden wir imstande sein, den ersten Schritt zu tun, um eine israelitische Literaturgeschichte nach diesem Grundtopos einheitlich zu gestalten. Während in der altjapanischen Literaturgeschichte göttliche Wesen aus Übersee als Gäste kommen, weil die japanischen Inseln vom Meer umgeben sind und diese Wesen mehr oder weniger vermenschlicht erscheinen, greifen die Gottheiten in der Wüste unversehens die Menschen an. Es geht hier bezeichnenderweise um Leben und Tod der angegriffenen Menschen. Solche Fälle begegnen uns typisch in Gen. xxxii 23-33 und Exod. iv 24-26. Es ist sehr bemerkenswert, daß das Element des Segens in der Erzählung des Kampfes Jakobs am Jabbok zum Vorschein kommt, während das Erlebnis Moses auf dem Rückweg von Midian m.E. im Grunde mit der Verfluchung durch die Gottheit zu tun hat. Denn Leben und Tod hängen im Alten Testament mit Segen und Fluch eng zusammen. Wenn wir aber in dem Segenswunsch an Rebekka (Gen. xxiv 60) schon literarisch geformte Verse — z.B. Rhythmus, Chiasmus und Parallelismus im weiteren Sinne — vorfinden, so dürfte hier schon von der literarischen Sprache die Rede sein. Ich möchte weiter im Spruch Lamechs (Gen. iv 23f.) eine Verfluchung mit der Absicht der Blutrache erblicken. Wie S. Gevirtz uns gezeigt hat,[4] kann man hier drei Stufen des Parallelismus erkennen, die eine Auflösung dieser alttestamentlich wichtigsten Formgebundenheit zeigen, was m.E. dem Wesen des Fluches entspricht, der nach J. Pedersen [5] die Auflösung der Seelenmacht verursacht. Auch anderwärts finden wir im Alten Testament machtbeladene Worte aus dem Munde der Menschen (z.B. Nu. xxi 17; Jos. x 26b), die rhythmisch geformt sind. Darum sind wir berechtigt, den Ursprung der literarischen Sprache im Alten Testament in den machtbeladenen Worten durch die Menschen und die Gottheit zu sehen. In dem Segenswunsch an Rebekka und der Verfluchung Lamechs geht es um Leben und Tod des Einzelnen und der Gemeinschaft. Alles in allem genommen komme ich zum Schluß, daß das Lebens- und Todesproblem den Grundtopos der israelitischen Literaturgeschichte ausmacht. Dementsprechend will ich die literarischen Werke des ganzen Alten Testaments durchmustern. Auch die alten Gesetze z.B. befassen sich weitgehend mit diesem Problem, da sie beabsichtigen, den Shalom des Einzelnen und der Gemeinschaft zu bewahren. Ich bin der Meinung,

---

[4] *Patterns in the Early Poetry of Israel* (Chicago, 1963), S. 25ff.
[5] *Israel I-II* (London-Copenhagen, 1926), S. 437, 440f., 451f.

daß nicht nur die einzelnen gesetzlichen Bestimmungen, sondern auch das Gesetzeskorpus — wie z.B. das Bundesbuch — in der israelitischen Literaturgeschichte behandelt werden können. Die israelitischen Gesetze, anders als die altorientalischen, sind anerkanntermassen im Grunde tief religiöser Natur.

Es läßt sich jedoch nicht bestreiten, daß eine israelitische Literaturgeschichte schöne literarische Werke im Alten Testament in den Vordergrund rücken muß. In diesem Sinne steht am Ausgangspunkt einer israelitischen Literaturgeschichte die Frage: wo empfanden die Israeliten das Schöne in der Literatur am stärksten? Meine Antwort darauf lautet: in der Krise, in der die Hauptfigur in der Erzählung um Leben und Tod vor Gott ringt, z.B. die Horebszene in den Eliageschichten (1 Kö. xix 13aβff.), Isaaks Opferung durch Abraham (Gen. xxii), die Berufungsgeschichte Jesajas (Jes. vi). Man kann und muß von dem Schönen in der Krise sprechen. Dabei gilt es, die Eigenart des Alten Testaments herauszuarbeiten. Auch in der Literatur anderer Völker kann von dem Schönen in der Krise die Rede sein, besonders soweit sie religiös gefärbt ist. Ich denke meinerseits an ein Beispiel aus der Dichtung unseres Haiku-Dichters, Matsuo Basho, dessen Werke als ein Schwanengesang aufgefaßt werden müssen. Aber der japanische Dichter sieht bei jedem Schritt mit tiefer Resignation dem Tode entgegen, einer Resignation, die unter dem Einfluß des Zen-buddhismus und des Laotse entstanden ist. Die Israeliten dagegen ringen um Leben und Tod vor ihrem lebendigen Gott. Weiter muß man beachten, daß die Israeliten das Lebens- und Todesproblem nur in der Gegenwart ihres lebendigen Gottes begreifen. So bedeutet für sie der Tod nicht nur das physische Ende, sondern das Fernsein von Gott, die damit bedingte Schwachheit von Leib und Seele; Erniedrigung und Verzweiflung liegen schon im Bereich des Todes. Wenn wir also von dem Schönen in der Krise sprechen, müssen wir diese Eigenart der alttestamentlichen Todesauffassung ins Auge fassen. Der Knecht Jahwes in Jes. liii kann als ein auffallendes Beispiel dafür angeführt werden, obwohl von ihm in V. 2 gesagt wird: er hatte keine Gestalt noch Schöne. Hier muß man freilich die Sache genauer ansehen. Wenn man von dem Schönen in der Krise spricht, muß die Errettung von der Krise irgendwie inbegriffen sein. Denn das Schöne kann nur etwas Positives sein. Mit anderen Worten: das Schöne in der Krise muß als Vorgang aufgefaßt werden. Mit dem Ausdruck "das Schöne als Vorgang" meine ich mehr als "das Schöne als Geschehendes", von dem v. Rad und Westermann gesprochen haben.[6] Andererseits kann man anhand der Wörter *japhe* und *ṭob* feststellen, daß das Schöne als Seiendes, z.B. an der menschlichen Gestalt zum Ausdruck kommt, hauptsächlich in den Schriften der salomonischen Zeit, nämlich dem Jahwisten, den älteren Teilen der Bücher Samuelis und dem Hohenlied einerseits, sowie in dem Buche Esther andererseits angetroffen werden kann.[7] Freilich ist im Alten Testament auch von der Schönheit in der geschaffenen Natur die Rede, die mit Gottessegen eng verbunden ist. Aber die Schönheitsauffassung in der salomonischen Zeit, genauer gesagt, in der Zeit, in der Israel mit dem Ostmittelmeer in Berührung kam, sowie in der hellenistischen Zeit, stellt eine Ausnahme dar. Ich denke z.B. an die Simsongeschichten, in denen uns merkwürdige Züge begegnen, die sich, wie Gunkel gelehrt hat, mit der Mittelmeerwelt verbinden.[8]

Nun müssen wir uns mit der schwierigsten Frage beschäftigen: wie können wir die literarischen Werke im engeren und weiteren Sinne, die uns im Lauf eines Jahrtausends vereinzelt und zerstreut im Alten Testament erhalten blieben, zu einer durchgehenden Literaturgeschichte ausgestalten? Die Frage ist allerdings nicht nur die Frage der Literaturgeschichte, sondern der Geschichte überhaupt. Es geht, genauer gesagt, um die Frage der Geschichtserkenntnis im allgemeinen. Die uns bekannten historischen Tatsachen sind besonders im Altertum notwendigerweise quellenmäßig sehr beschränkt. Es gilt, die Lücken auszufüllen, damit eine Geschichtsschreibung entstehen kann. Dies ist m.E. nur möglich, wenn man soziologische Erkenntnisse, die uns allgemeine Erfahrungsregeln zu erkennen geben, in die Geschichtswissenschaft integriert. Solches positives Wissen von Regeln des Geschehens nennt Max Weber "nomologisches Wissen", während unser Wissen von historischen Tatsachen "ontologisches Wissen" genannt wird.[9] Die Lücken in unseren historischen Erkenntnissen können durch soziologisches Wissen ergänzt und ausgefüllt

[6] G. von Rad, *Theologie des Alten Testaments* I (München, 1969^{6}), S. 375ff.; C. Westermann, "Das Schöne im Alten Testament", *Zimmerli-Festschrift* (Göttingen, 1977). Ich stehe von Rad näher als Westermann.

[7] Vgl. G. Gerleman, *Das Hohelied* (Neukirchen, 1963), S. 74, wo die Stellen im Blick auf den Gebrauch des Wortes *japhe* angegeben sind. Ich konnte feststellen, daß *ṭob* ungefähr in denselben Büchern wie *japhe* gebraucht wird, abgesehen davon, daß *japhe* im Buche Esther nur einmal, während *ṭob* viermal erscheint, und daß *ṭob* niemals in dem Hohenlied gebraucht wird.

[8] H. Gunkel, "Simson", *Reden und Aufsätze* (Göttingen, 1913).

[9] M. Weber, "Kritische Studien auf dem Gebiet der kulturwissenschaftlichen Logik", *Gesammelte Aufsätze zur Wissenschaftslehre* (Tübingen, 1968^{3}), weiter vgl. derselbe, *Wirtschaft und Gesellschaft* (Studienausgabe, Tübingen, 1972^{5}).

werden, indem unsere Phantasie unser nomologisches Wissen auf das ontologische Wissen anwendet.

Solche soziologische Erkenntnisse liefern uns auch das Gerüst zur israelitischen Literaturgeschichte. Dadurch können wir die Periodisierung im Blick auf sie vollziehen. Konkret gesagt, möchten wir als Arbeitshypothese die folgenden Perioden der israelitischen Literaturgeschichte annehmen, indem wir idealtypisch gedachte Gemeinschaften als Träger literarischer Produkte in dem Geschichtsablauf Israels nacheinander aufzählen: Literatur der Familiengemeinschaft, Literatur der Stämmegemeinschaft, Literatur der Gemeinschaft des Stämmebundes, Literatur der Staatsgemeinschaft und Literatur der religiösen Gemeinschaft. Jede Gemeinschaft besteht aus Sozialschichten, die wieder nicht realiter, sondern idealtypisch angenommen werden können.

Für die inhaltsbezogene Darstellung der israelitischen Literaturgeschichte ist es notwendig, einen Standpunkt zu gewinnen. Von diesem aus ist die Eigenart der literarischen Werke, die jede Periode vertreten können, herauszuarbeiten. Dieses Spezifikum möchten wir als literarische Grundstimmung bezeichnen, die sich ihrerseits in ihre Komponenten zergliedert, die wir Sentiments und Stile nennen wollen. Stimmung und Sentiment dürfen nicht mit Gefühlen verwechselt werden. Ich definiere: Gefühle verändern sich leicht und vergehen, während Stimmung und Sentiment mit einer bestimmten Idee und Sprachform verbunden sind und sich nicht leicht davon trennen lassen.

Die Gemeinschaften, von denen oben die Rede war, sind nicht imstande, von den Herrschaftsformen, unter denen sie stehen, getrennt zu werden. Das Kennzeichen des Gemeinschaftsbewußtseins nach innen unter der patriarchalischen Herrschaft kann mit Weber als Pietät bezeichnet werden. Diese Bezeichnung möchte ich als Bezeichnung der literarischen Eigenart verwenden. Zweifellos können wir in den Patriarchenerzählungen der Genesis Familiengeschichten im Sinne A. Jolles' [10] erblicken. Zugleich begegnet uns in den Familiengeschichten der drei Patriarchen überall die Grundstimmung der Pietät, d.h.: Pietät zwischen den Gliedern der Familie. Ich nenne nur ein Beispiel: in der oben berührten Erzählung des Kampfes Jakobs am Jabbok, die ich mit H.-J. Hermisson [11] traditionsgeschichtlich für sehr alt halten möchte, ist es beachtenswert, daß Jakob die Gottheit, mit der er rang, sehr pietätsvoll um Segen bat. Außerdem bin ich mit

---

[10] *Einfache Formen* (Studienausgabe, Tübingen, 1974⁵), S. 67ff.
[11] "Jakobs Kampf am Jabbok", *ZThK* 71 (1974), S. 239ff.

Roland Barthes in der Meinung einig, daß Jakob in der Gottheit doppelbildlich seinen Bruder Esau anerkannte.[12] Weiter möchte ich darauf aufmerksam machen, daß es in den Familiengeschichten der drei Patriarchen übereinstimmend um Leben und Tod der Hausgemeinschaft geht. Ebenso in den Mosegeschichten, aber nicht im Bereich der Hausgemeinschaft, sondern der Stammes- bzw. Stämmegemeinschaft, deren Grundstimmung als Strenge gekennzeichnet werden dürfte. Auch die Hausgemeinschaft unter der patriarchalischen Herrschaft steht unter der Autorität, die nach außen durch Solidarität geschützt wird. Dagegen tritt in der Mose- und Josuazeit, die unter der charismatischen Herrschaft steht, die strenge Autorität auch nach innen in den Vordergrund. Als Beispiele möchte ich die kurzen Szenen in Exod. iv 24-26 und Josua v 13-15 anführen. Hier werden Mose auf dem Rückweg von Midian durch die Gottheit angegriffen und Josua vor dem Kampf um Jericho durch den Heerführer Jahwes geweiht. Die Hausgemeinschaft der Patriarchenzeit und die Stämmegemeinschaft der Mose- und Josuazeit befindet sich unter der starken Regulierung der betreffenden Gemeinschaft; die Sozialschichten bleiben undifferenziert, nämlich als die der Halbnomaden und der Krieger. Deshalb möchten wir uns hypothetisch mit der Bestimmung der Grundstimmung begnügen. Wir wollen nur hinzufügen, daß die Bezeichnung Strenge auch der Theophanieschilderung der Mosezeit, den gesetzlichen Bestimmungen und den Stammessprüchen gilt. Was das Mirjamlied (Exod. xv 21), das in die Mosezeit zurückreichen kann, anbelangt, wollen wir es von einem anderen Standpunkt aus betrachten, der direkt mit der Frage der literarischen Sprache des Alten Testaments zu tun hat.

Es ist wohl weit anerkannt, daß die Sprache in der Literatur sich vieler Bilder und Metaphern bedient und sich in ihrer Mehrdeutigkeit von der alltäglichen Sprache unterscheidet. Die biblische Sprache zeigt sich der literarischen Sprache insofern verwandt, als sie sich von der Eindeutigkeit der alltäglichen Sprache scheidet. Sogleich muß hier hinzugefügt werden, daß die biblische Sprache jedoch im Grunde ganz anders geartet ist als die rein literarische. Denn es geht hier um Gott *und* Menschen, und soweit es immer gleichzeitig um beide geht, dürfte die Eigenart der biblischen Sprache als doppelbildlich aufgefaßt werden. Man könnte sie auch Ursprache nennen,

[12] R. Barthes, "La lutte avec l'ange: analyse textuelle de Genèse 32.23-33", *Analyse structurale et exégèse biblique* (Neuchâtel, 1971), S. 34.

zumal sie die menschliche Welt von der Urwirklichkeit Gottes her beleuchtet und beschreibt. Hauptsächlich dreht es sich dabei um die Eigenart dieser ursprachlichen Doppelbildlichkeit in jedem der literarischen Werke im Alten Testament. Anhand des Mirjamliedes im Vergleich mit dem Deboralied soll gezeigt werden, was damit gemeint ist. Im Mirjamlied fällt auf, daß sich hier die Gottestat direkt mit dem dadurch herbeigeführten Ereignis in der Geschichte verbindet: Gott warf Ross und Reiter der Ägypter ins Meer. Die Eigenart der Doppelbildlichkeit, die uns in diesem alten Hymnus überrascht, kann als Unmittelbarkeit, die Gott und die Welt miteinander in Beziehung setzt, charakterisiert werden. Was das Deboralied in Jud. v betrifft, so hat die Sache eine ganz andere Bewandtnis. Ich kann hier auf die viel diskutierte Frage der Gattungsbestimmung des Liedes nicht eingehen und muß auch die Frage des historischen Hintergrundes, die mit Kap. iv im Zusammenhang steht, ausklammern. Es handelt sich ohne Zweifel um das literarische Meisterstück aus der Zeit des Stämmebundes. Was uns jetzt beschäftigen muß, ist der Unterschied zwischen dem Mirjamlied und dem Deboralied. Während Gott in dem ersteren unmittelbar in die Geschichte eingreift, ist die Hand Gottes in dem letzteren nur durch die Menschen und die Naturerscheinungen mittelbar zu spüren. Das Auffallende in dieser mittelbaren Doppelbildlichkeit ist dies: die Mittel, die Gott und Ereignisse verbinden, sind wesentlich religiöser Art, nämlich das traditionalisierte, veralltäglichte Charisma der Prophetin Debora und der heilige Krieg als Institution. Es geht sowohl im Mirjamlied wie im Deboralied um Leben und Tod. Im Deborakrieg wird aber kein Wunder geschildert wie beim Durchzug durch das Schilfmeer, sondern Geschehnisse und Episoden, die etappenweise nacheinander folgen. Hier werden wir ein Kriegsepos erblicken können, obwohl sich z.T. lyrische und dramatische Elemente mischen. Damit hängt zusammen, daß wir die literarische Grundstimmung der Zeit des Stämmebundes als Ordnungsstimmung bezeichnen wollen. Sowohl die soziale Umschichtung, die zur allmählichen Sesshaftwerdung führte, als auch der Kultus im Kulturland spielen die entscheidende Rolle in dieser scheinbar sehr bewegten Zeit.

Mit der Entstehung des Königtums gehen wir auch literaturgeschichtlich einer ganz neuen Zeit entgegen. In der sog. Thronfolgegeschichte Davids findet man eine ganz paradoxe Doppelbildlichkeit. Bezüglich der Absicht dieser ersten Geschichtsschreibung in Israel ist jüngst viel diskutiert worden. Wahrscheinlich ist sie weder theologisch noch politisch.[13] Literaturgeschichtlich betrachtet, ist die "Schönheit in der Krise" von der Gestalt Davids untrennbar. Die Todesfälle der Davidssöhne werden sehr tragisch geschildert. Der Höhepunkt dieses Meisterwerkes aber kreist einmal um die Gestalt des Menschen David, der beim Aufstand Absaloms Jerusalem erniedrigt verläßt und weinend den Ölberg besteigt, verhüllten Hauptes und barfuß (2 Sam. xv 30), und zum anderen um die Gestalt des Vaters, der den Tod seines geliebten Sohnes beweint mit den Worten: "O wäre ich für dich gestorben! O Absalom, mein Sohn, mein Sohn" (2 Sam. xiv 1). Das Schöne in der Krise kommt hier durch die menschliche, allzu menschliche Natur Davids am stärksten zum Ausdruck. Hier hat die Menschengestalt zum ersten Mal ein literarisches Gewicht gewonnen. Zugleich bedeutet das die Entstehung des Lyrischen in Israel. Kein Wunder, daß David sich in seinem Bogenlied (2 Sam. ii 19ff.) und in seinem Klagelied über Abner (2 Sam. iii 34f.) als Lyriker zeigt. In den beiden Liedern sind drei Stufen des Lyrischen nach Kayser zu beobachten: nämlich lyrisches Nennen, lyrisches Ansprechen und liedhaftes Sprechen.[14] Vom Standpunkt der Doppelbildlichkeit muß gesagt werden, daß sich sowohl in der Thronfolgegeschichte als auch in den beiden Liedern Gott in der Verborgenheit befindet. Kausales Denken und Geschichtsimmanenz sind die Kennzeichen der Zeit der Staatsgemeinschaft. Neuderdings spricht man von der anthropozentrischen Geschichtsbetrachtung in der israelitischen Historiographie.[15] Alles das aber kann Gottes Handeln im Verborgenen nicht in Abrede stellen.

Meine Zeit erlaubt es nicht, das interessante Problem des Jahwisten ausführlich zu behandeln. Nur in Anknüpfung an die beachtenswerten Worte Jahwes nach der Sintflut in Gen. viii 21 sollen die wichtigsten Fragen hervorgehoben werden. In diesen Jahweworten "Ich will hinfort nicht mehr die Erde verfluchen usw." kommt die ambivalente Stellungnahme des Jahwisten in bezug auf das Lebens- und Todesproblem, die uns seit dem Anfang der Urgeschichte wiederholt auffällt, am deutlichsten zum Ausdruck. Die Gestalt der Schlange in Gen. iii zeigt schon die Eigenart der Ambivalenz, zumal sie einerseits ein von Gott geschaffenes Tier, andererseits ein mythisches Bild

[13] E. Würthwein, *Die Erzählung von der Thronfolge Davids — theologische oder politische Geschichtsschreibung?* (Zürich, 1974).

[14] W. Kayser, *Das sprachliche Kunstwerk* (Bern, 1961⁷), S. 339.

[15] H. Cancik, *Grundzüge der hethitischen und alttestamentlichen Geschichtsschreibung* (Wiesbaden, 1976), S. 212.

verkörpert.[16] Ich bin geneigt, mit Jolles' Schrift *Einfache Formen* "Mythe" im Alten Testament anzunehmen, wenn es sich um das einmalige Geschehen in der Urzeit und Endzeit handelt. Es wäre durchaus natürlich, daß wir, die wir das Lebens- und Todesproblem als Grundtopos unserer Literaturgeschichte vor uns stellten, die Gattung Mythe ernst nehmen. Sogleich müssen wir darauf hinweisen, daß uns im Alten Testament die Mythen, die bei allen Völkern der Welt am Anfang der Literaturgeschichte eine bedeutende Rolle spielen, am Anfang und Ende der Geschichte begegnen. Mit anderen Worten: im Alten Testament wird die Geschichte selbst mit dem ambivalenten Urfaktum des Lebens und Todes, des Segens und Fluches, des Heils und Unheils bewegt. Hier haben wir es nicht nur mit der jahwistischen und elohistischen Geschichtsschreibung, sondern schon mit dem Grundproblem der Propheten und der Apokalyptiker zu tun.

Nach der Entstehung der Staatsgemeinschaft müssen wir die Grundstimmung und ihre Komponenten in Zusammenhang mit den Sozialschichten, denen die Verfasser der betreffenden literarischen Werke angehörten, bestimmen. Die aufgeklärte Stimmung und das kultusfreie Sentiment der Thronfolgegeschichte Davids erklären sich von einem Verfasser, welcher der durch die Entstehung des Königtums entmächtigten Intellektuellenschicht zugehörte. Ich bin geneigt, anzunehmen, daß der Jahwist, aus Gründen, auf die ich hier nicht einzugehen imstande bin, dem Landlevitentum angehörte.[17] Die Geisteshaltung und die literarische Eigenschaft der Ambivalenz, die ich als Kennzeichen des Jahwisten hervorgehoben habe, stehen m.E. mit der Tatsache irgendwie im Zusammenhang, daß er selbst zu den Sozialschichten der Gerim gehörte, die ihrerseits als seine Leserschaft betrachtet werden können.

Ich möchte mich nun der Frage der Prophetie zuwenden, weil ich hier wieder methodisch neue Gesichtspunkte besprechen kann. Mein

---

[16] B. S. Childs, *Myth and Reality in the Old Testament* (London, 1960), S. 47f.; O. Loretz, *Schöpfung und Mythos* (Stuttgart, 1968), S. 118ff.

[17] Die Bestimmung, daß der Jahwist dem Landjudäertum zugehörte (O. H. Steck in *Probleme biblischer Theologie* [München, 1971], S. 552f.), reicht nicht aus. Die Verbindungslinien mit Jerusalem sind auch nicht ganz in Abrede zu stellen. Das Landlevitentum hatte, wie B. Mazar (*SVT* 7 [1960], S. 202) meint, zugleich mit dem Lande und Jerusalem in der salomonischen Zeit zu tun. Ich verweise auf die folgenden jahwistischen Stellen, wo auffälligerweise von dem Levitentum die Rede ist: Gen. xxxiv, Exod. ii 1, iv 14, xxxii 25-29. Der Noahspruch (Gen. ix 25-27) stammt m.E. aus der früheren Zeit des Stämmebundes Israels, mit dem das Levitentum eng verbunden war, und wurde vom Jahwisten aufgenommen.

Ausgangspunkt besteht in der Unterscheidung zwischen den Propheten der Handlung wie Elia und Elisa und den Propheten des Wortes, d.h. den Schriftpropheten. In der Zeit der Propheten der Handlung lag eine soziale Revolution im Bereich der Möglichkeit, da sich die obere und untere Schicht direkt gegenüber standen. In der Zeit der Schriftpropheten waren die Mittelschichten stark ausgebildet, die eine Vermittlerrolle zwischen beiden spielten und eine Revolution wie bei Jehu unmöglich machten. Das erklärt uns, warum die Schriftpropheten als Propheten des Wortes auftraten, die einerseits sozialkritisch redeten und andererseits eine eschatologische Veränderung der Gesellschaft mythisch wahrsagten. Im großen und ganzen entsprechen die Gattung "Berichte" den Propheten der Handlung und die Gattung "Prophetenworte" den Propheten des Wortes. Was die erste Gattung betrifft, so ist nicht zu bezweifeln, daß die Horebszene in 1 Kö. xix, wie schon erwähnt, als ein Meisterwerk bezeichnet werden kann. In ihm wird das Schöne in der Krise am bis zum Todeswunsch verzweifelten Elia wunderbar sichtbar. Wegen der begrenzt verfügbaren Zeit erlaube ich mir auf meine andernorts geschriebene Arbeit zu verweisen,[18] die durch die Anregnung R. Jakobsons entstanden ist, der m.E. die Frage des Parallelismus uns im neuen Licht zu sehen gelehrt hat.[19]

Literaturgeschichtlich ist die Struktur des Wortes bei den Schriftpropheten ungeheuer wichtig. Durch das Gerichtswort trennten die Propheten des Wortes Gott und Volk einmal gänzlich ab, um beide wieder aufs neue durch das Wort des Heils zu verbinden. Dadurch wird Gott zum Weltgott, während Israel zu einem Volk unter den Völkern wird. Man denke an Amos ix 7. Mit anderen Worten: die Entstehung des Weltgottes ist nur dadurch vorstellbar, daß Israel zu einem Volk in der Völkerwelt geworden ist, ohne daß Israel aufhörte, Gottes Volk zu sein. Dieses Paradoxon ist nur dadurch möglich geworden, daß die Propheten des Wortes als Träger des Wortes Gottes zwischen Gott und Israel standen. Sie waren ja nicht Individualisten im modernen Sinne, aber eben die Einzelnen, die nur mit dem Wort Gottes einsam zwischen Gott und Volk dastanden. Sie waren in

[18] M. Sekine, "Elias Verzweiflung", *Annual of the Japanese Biblical Institute* 3 (1977).

[19] R. Jakobson, "Grammatical parallelism and its Russian facet", *Language* 42 (1966), S. 399ff.; derselbe, "Linguistics and Poetics", *Style in Language* (New York-London, 1960), S. 350ff. Weiter vgl. derselbe, *Questions de poétique* (Paris, 1973). Mit der Bezeichnung "grammatischer oder generalisierter Parallelismus" scheint mir Jakobson die innere Strukturiertheit der Dichtung zu meinen.

ihrer Art die Menschen in der Krise, die sich transparent machten, um zu einem Spiegel zu werden, in welchem sich Gotteswille und Volksgestalt widerspiegeln. Die Doppelbildlichkeit, die ich als Eigenart der religiös-literarischen Sprache der Bibel charakterisierte, erhält also die reinste Form im prophetischen Wort.

Es ist kaum zu bezweifeln, daß die Schriftpropheten weder Schamanen noch primitive Ekstatiker, sondern reife Persönlichkeiten mit höchster dichterischer Begabung sind. Daraus ergibt sich, daß wir an sie mit der Methode der neuen Stilistik herantreten dürfen und müssen. Es ist nicht genug, daß wir die Prophetenworte z.B. des Amos und des Jesaja einerseits als dramatisch, diejenige des Hosea und des Jeremia andererseits als lyrisch kennzeichnen. Da es sich um die Eigenart der höchst persönlich entfalteten Dichterworte der Einzelpropheten handelt, die den differenzierten Sozialschichten angehörten, so tut es not, sie mit dem stilistischen Standpunkt, der die Persönlichkeitsmomente in Betracht zieht, zu behandeln. Der dramatische Stil eines Amos, der pathetisch und problematisch im Sinne Staigers [20] charakterisiert werden könnte, müsste weiter mit der Terminologie Busemanns [21] als Verbindung eines energischen Stils mit einem gedanklichen Stil, dagegen der lyrische Stil eines Hosea als Verbindung eines Fühlungsstils mit einem aktivischen Stil aufgefaßt werden. Es erübrigt sich, hier auf die Erklärung der Einzelheiten einzugehen. Mir liegt daran, zu zeigen, daß wir bei der Bestimmung der literarischen Eigenart in Werken der Staatsgemeinschaft nicht nur mit der Grundstimmung, sondern mit den Sentiments und Stilen zu tun haben, hauptsächlich weil Sozialschichten differenzierter werden. Ich möchte hinzufügen, daß die Literarizität besonders nach der Entstehung der Intellektuellenschichten in Israel mit der Geistesgeschichte Israels in enger Beziehung steht, so daß unsere Terminologie, obgleich wir damit zur Hauptsache literaturgeschichtlich gedacht haben, von dem geistesgeschichtlichen Hintergrund untrennbar wurde. Das wird bei der Terminologie Humor und Ironie, die in der literaturwissenschaftlichen Arbeit am Alten Testament oft gebraucht wird, der Fall sein.[22] Darauf können wir heute nicht mehr eingehen, ebensowenig auf die Besprechung der

---

[20] E. Staiger, *Grundbegriffe der Poetik* (Zürich, 1961⁵), S. 143ff.

[21] A. Busemann, *Stil und Charakter* (Meisenheim am Glan, 1948), S. 70ff.

[22] E. M. Good, *Irony in the Old Testament* (Philadelphia und London, 1965); vgl. weiter J. Hempel, *Althebräische Literatur* (Wildpark-Potsdam, 1930-1934), passim.

Einzelwerke in der Zeit der religiösen Gemeinschaft. Nur kurz möchte ich zusammenfassen, was mir die Eigenschaften der literarischen Werke in der Spätzeit zu sein scheinen. Vor allem fällt der Mischcharakter auf, der in ihnen überall sichtbar wird. Da ist zuerst die Vermischung der Prophetie mit dem Kultus, der Weisheit und der Apokalyptik zu nennen. Die Prophetengestalt bei den deuterojesajanischen Ebed-Jahwe-Liedern ist anders als die schon oben genannten zwei Typen. Ich möchte sie den Propheten der Existenz nennen, die mit ihrem Sein zwischen Gott und Israel bzw. der Welt dastand und sich selbst als Opfer darbrachte. Dieser Zug war schon teilweise bei Jeremia sichtbar. Das Loben des Gottessegens und die Klage der mit dem Tode bedrohten Existenz sind die Grundformen im Psalter, die sich nun durch die Verbindung mit den Elementen der Weisheit, des Gesetzes, der Prophetie [23] und der Apokalyptik mannigfaltigerweise verschieben. Die Geschichtsschreibung wird mehr oder weniger tendenziös und didaktisch. Dieselbe Eigenschaft herrscht mehr und mehr in den späteren Weisheitsbüchern des Alten Testaments. Es gilt die komplizierten Mischgebilde der Spätzeit zu analysieren und literaturgeschichtlich darzustellen.

Ich komme zum Schluß: die methodischen Gesichtspunkte, die ich an Beispielen hauptsächlich aus der vorexilischen Zeit klarzumachen versucht habe, mögen sich als brauchbar erweisen und imstande sein, sich zu bewähren.

---

[23] Ich denke an die neue Gattung, die M. Mannati herausarbeitete und "les psaumes d'exhortation prophétique contre les impies" nannte (Ps. lii, lviii usw.). Vgl. dazu M. Mannati, *Les Psaumes* 1 (Paris, 1966), S. 57ff.

LESSING UND DIE BIBELWISSENSCHAFT

von

RUDOLF SMEND
Göttingen

Was ich Ihnen, aufgefordert vom Herrn Präsidenten, vorzutragen habe, ist kein Beitrag zur Lessingforschung oder auch zur Wissenschaftsgeschichte im eigentlichen Sinn. Ich bin kein Lessing-Experte, und die meisten von Ihnen sind es, wie ich vermute, auch nicht, obwohl Ihnen allen, wie ich ebenfalls vermute, *Miss Sara Sampson* und *Minna von Barnhelm*, *Emilia Galotti* und *Nathan der Weise*, aber auch die *Literaturbriefe* und die *Hamburgische Dramaturgie*, *Laokoon* und *Die Erziehung des Menschengeschlechts* keine ganz fremden Namen sind. Meine Aufgabe ist, Ihnen auf diesem Hintergrund einige wenige Hinweise darauf zu geben, daß es auch für Bibelwissenschaftler, deren Arbeit dem Alten Testament gilt, sinnvoll ist, an diesem Ort des Mannes Gotthold Ephraim Lessing zu gedenken, der hier von 1770 bis zu seinem Tode 1781 Bibliothekar der Bibliotheca Augusta gewesen ist.[1]

Im September 1771 läßt die etwas intellektuelle Frau eines Dorfpfarrers, nicht in Wolfenbüttel, die schönen Nußbäume abhauen, die in ihrem Garten stehen. Sie nehmen ihr das Licht, und die Dorfkinder, die mit Steinen nach den Nüssen werfen, stören sie in tiefen Überlegungen. Sie beschäftigt sich nämlich mit der Untersuchung des Kanons und wägt Kennicott, Semler und Michaelis gegeneinander ab. So steht es zu lesen in einem Roman, der 1774 erschien. Seinem Autor war die damalige Bibelwissenschaft nicht ungeläufig, und damit konnte er offenbar auch beim lesenden Publikum rechnen. Der Autor hieß Goethe, der Roman *Die Leiden des jungen Werther*.

Im gleichen Jahr 1774 plante Lessing die Herausgabe einer Schrift mit dem Titel "Eine noch freiere Untersuchung des Kanons alten und neuen Testaments" — ein Plan, der nicht ausgeführt wurde. Schon dem Titel nach sollte es sich um eine Überbietung von J. S.

[1] Der Vortrag wurde während der Exkursion des Kongresses nach Wolfenbüttel am 24. August 1977 in der dortigen Trinitatiskirche gehalten (mit Kürzungen).

Semlers *Abhandlung von freier Untersuchung des Canon* handeln, die 1771 bis 1775 in vier Teilen erschien.[2] Wie kam der Dichter, Kritiker und Bibliothekar dazu, sich derart in die gelehrten Geschäfte der Theologen einzumischen?

Lessing legte Wert darauf, "nur Liebhaber der Theologie und nicht Theolog" zu sein.[3] Daß der Göttinger Walch in ihm zunächst einen "gelehrten Prediger" vermutete [4] und daß der Leipziger Ernesti ihm sogar den theologischen Doktorhut aufsetzen wollte,[5] konnte ihn nicht irremachen. Wie Faust hatte er, Sohn eines ebenso gelehrten wie frommen Pfarrers und Enkel eines Ratsherrn, der "De religionum tolerantia" disputiert hatte, "leider auch Theologie" studiert, aber nur kurz und durchaus nicht "mit heißem Bemühn". Daß er zum normalen Studieren nicht taugte, gilt allerdings nicht nur für seine kurze Gastrolle bei den Theologen. Er durchschaute früh ein Gelehrtentum, in dem ein Halbhundert überflüssiger Anmerkungen einen Philologen machen, und brachte dessen Karikatur als kaum neunzehnjähriger in seinem ersten Lustspiel [6] auf die Bühne. Gegen die "geschwornen Anmerkungsschmierer" [7] und das, was sie repräsentierten, zog er weiter zu Felde — nicht zugunsten der sogenannten großen Linie oder der gefälligen Form, hinter denen beiden sich allzuoft die Schludrigkeit verbirgt, sondern für unerbittliche Treue im Detail und gewissenhafte, aber auch lesbare Darstellung. "Unsere schönen Geister", so klagt er, "sind selten Gelehrte, und unsere Gelehrte selten schöne Geister. Jene wollen gar nicht lesen, gar nicht nachschlagen, gar nicht sammlen; kurz, gar nicht arbeiten: und diese wollen nichts, als das. Jenen mangelt es am Stoffe, und diesen an der Geschicklichkeit ihrem Stoffe eine Gestalt zu erteilen".[8] Die Alternative ist in Deutschland schärfer als in den beneidenswerten Ländern englischer und französischer Sprache. Zwar haben bei uns nicht wenige Histo-

---

[2] Vgl. Lessings Brief an seinen Bruder Karl vom 11.11.1774. Der Hauptteil wäre ein weiteres Fragment aus dem Nachlaß des H.S. Reimarus gewesen.

[3] *Werke*, ed. J. Petersen-W. v. Olshausen (im Folgenden: *PO*) XXIII, p. 164 (*Axiomata*). Dazu A. Schilson, *Geschichte im Horizont der Vorsehung. G. E. Lessings Beitrag zu einer Theologie der Geschichte*. Tübinger theologische Studien 3 (Mainz, 1974), pp. 35f.

[4] Vgl. Lessing an J. D. Michaelis 16.10.1754.

[5] Brief seines Bruders Karl an ihn vom 4.7.1771.

[6] *Der junge Gelehrte*, 1747 (*PO* III, pp. 43ff., *Werke*, ed. H. G. Göpfert, im Folgenden: *G*, I, pp. 279ff.). Der Satz über die Anmerkungen dort I, 2 (*PO* p. 51, *G* p. 289).

[7] *PO* VII, p. 65, *G* III, p. 514 (Des Herrn von Voltaire kleinere historische Schriften. Vorrede, 1751).

[8] *PO* IV, p. 152, *G* V, p. 185 (52. Literaturbrief, 23.8.1759).

riker schön geschrieben; bei den biblischen Exegeten ist es eine seltene Ausnahme geblieben. Lessing hat sich große Mühe gegeben, die Alternative zu überwinden; er hat von einem, der sich auf Stil verstand, attestiert bekommen, die theologische Polemik seiner späten Jahre sei "höchstwahrscheinlich sein schönstes Werk", ja noch mehr: "seine schönste Dichtung".[9]

Solche Lobsprüche fielen den Gelehrten meist schwer. Nicht ohne Veranlassung hatte Lessing "die Gabe, sich widersprechen zu lassen", eine Gabe genannt, "die unter den Gelehrten nur die Toten haben".[10] Und er hatte einigen von ihnen widersprochen, daß ihnen Hören und Sehen verging. Der Göttinger Chr. G. Heyne sah in ihm einen "Herkules mit der Keule", "der Schmetterlinge totschlägt",[11] und ein späterer, in Göttingen ebenfalls nicht unbekannter Heine, Heinrich, stellte im Rückblick fest: "Indem er seine Gegner tötete, machte er sie zugleich unsterblich"; "für ewige Zeiten" seien sie nun in Lessings Werken erhalten "wie Insekten, die sich in einem Stück Bernstein verfangen".[12] Nur so wissen wir von dem Laublinger Pastor Lange mit seiner Horazübersetzung, von dem Hallenser Professor Klotz mit seinen antiquarisch-archäologischen Arbeiten und dann dem streitbaren Hamburger Hauptpastor Goeze und seinem unbeholfeneren Amtsbruder, dem Wolfenbüttler Superintendenten Reß, der anonym gegen Lessing, den nicht Anonymen, schrieb und eine vernichtende Antwort bekam, die ihn vom Schloßplatz zur Marienkirche herüber unter raffinierter Wahrung und zugleich Aufhebung der Anonymität als einen "guten Nachbarn" und "vermutlichen Laien" anredete.[13]

Wogegen Lessing streitet, meist ohne Pardon und mit einer mindestens in Deutschland davor und danach kaum gekannten Virtuosität, das sind im Kleinen falsche Übersetzungen, Zitate aus zweiter Hand, mit denen man, wie wir alle wissen, immer ein Risiko eingeht, und all die Unterlassungs- und Verwechslungssünden, die Philologen und Historikern passieren,[14] und das sind im Grossen — aber gibt

---

[9] Thomas Mann, *Gesammelte Werke*, Frankfurter Ausgabe, IX, p. 241.

[10] *PO* XIV, p. 85, *G* III, p. 591 (*Rettungen des Horaz*, 1754).

[11] Brief an Lessing 28.6.1773.

[12] *Sämtliche Schriften*, ed. K. Briegleb III, p. 586 (*Religion und Philosophie in Deutschland* II).

[13] *PO* XXIII, pp. 56ff. (*Eine Duplik*), vgl. XXIII, pp. 194f., 254f. (*Erster und eilfter Anti-Goeze*).

[14] Vgl. etwa die Bemerkungen über Jöchers Gelehrtenelexikon im 25. "Brief" (*PO* VIII, pp. 177ff., *G* III, pp. 335ff.).

es hier streng genommen den Unterschied von klein und groß? in Lessings Sinn schwerlich — Unverstand und Voreingenommenheit, mögen sie auch noch so viel Material aufhäufen. Im Haus Nathans des Weisen gelten Bücher nicht allzu viel. "Mein Vater liebt", sagt Recha, "die kalte Buchgelehrsamkeit, die sich / mit toten Zeichen ins Gehirn nur drückt, / zu wenig".[15] Ganz ähnlich Lessings Selbstaussage: Er stellt dem "Ich bin kein Prophet" des Amos nicht nur sein "Ich bin kein Theologe" zur Seite, sondern auch dies: "Ich bin nicht gelehrt — ich habe nie die Absicht gehabt, gelehrt zu werden — ich möchte nicht gelehrt sein, und wenn ich es im Traum werden könnte. Alles, wornach ich ein wenig gestrebt habe, ist, im Fall der Not ein gelehrtes Buch brauchen zu können".[16] Der das sagte, wußte viele Bücher zu brauchen — und darum durfte er es sagen! —, aber er wußte auch, worauf es ankommt. Vom "Altertumskrämer" unterschied er den "Altertumskundigen". "Jener hat die Scherben, dieser den Geist des Altertums geerbet. Jener denkt nur kaum mit seinen Augen, dieser sieht auch mit seinen Gedanken. Ehe jener noch sagt: 'So war das!' weiß dieser schon, ob es so sein können".[17] Er weiß es aber nicht darum, weil er ohnehin immer alles schon weiß, weil es die Meinung seiner Richtung oder Schule ist, weil es ihm ins Bild paßt, sondern darum, weil hier, an dieser Stelle, auf diesen Gegenstand hin, seine Gedanken sehend sind. "Lessing hat einen Blick, wie ich noch nie gesehn habe, in seinen blauen Augen, einen rechten Geierblick", berichtet J. H. Voß, der Homerübersetzer.[18] Und Lessing weigert sich durchaus, mit anderen als diesen seinen Augen zu sehen [19] und eine andere Sprache als die seine zu reden.[20] Er ist ja kein Theologe, hat also auf kein System geschworen und bedauert "alle ehrliche Männer, die nicht so glücklich sind, dieses von sich sagen zu können".[21] Ein Freund hält ihm vor, er habe "gar keinen Grundsatz ... als diesen, gar keine Grundsätze zu haben".[22] Dafür aber hat er "Ehrgeiz und Neubegierde",[23] und so entdeckt er, teilt mit, rückt zurecht,

[15] *PO* II, p. 280, *G* I, p. 582 (*Nathan* V, 6).
[16] *PO* XXV, p. 156, *G* V, p. 788 (*Selbstbetrachtungen und Einfälle*).
[17] *PO* XVII, p. 341, *G* VI, p. 443 (*Wie die Alten den Tod gebildet*, 1769).
[18] Nach R. Daunicht, *Lessing im Gespräch* (München, 1971), p. 398, vgl. p. 400.
[19] Vgl. *PO* XXIII, pp. 98, 106 (*Eine Duplik*, 1778, Sechster und achter Widerspruch), auch etwa *PO* VIII, p. 116, *G* III, p. 278 (Vierter "Brief").
[20] *PO* XXIII, p. 164 (*Axiomata*, Anfang).
[21] Ebenda.
[22] J. A. Ebert an Lessing 27.1.1769.
[23] *PO* IV, p. 41, *G* V, p. 53 (11. Literaturbrief); vgl. den Brief an Elise Reimarus vom 7.5.1780.

verdirbt -isten und -ianern die Konzepte.[24] Es ist wie mit etwas anderem Hintergrund bei Herder auch kein Zufall, daß sich die gelegentliche Aussicht auf die relativ gebundene Stellung eines Universitätsprofessors nicht verwirklichte; freilich hatte er dann in Wolfenbüttel einen hohen Preis zu bezahlen. Seine Äußerungen über den Professorenstand sind meist nicht schmeichelhaft; doch er unterhielt mit manchem Vertreter dieses Standes — genannt seien Kästner in Leipzig, später Göttingen, und Reiske in Leipzig — achtungsvolle ja freundschaftliche Beziehungen.[25]

Die Gattung, in der es der gelehrte Nichtgelehrte früh zur Meisterschaft brachte, war die der "Rettungen". Er konnte sich hier an seinen Leipziger Lehrer J. F. Christ anschließen, der seinerseits von Pierre Bayle gelernt hatte.[26] Es handelte sich um die Rehabilitierung von mehr oder auch weniger bekannten Gestalten, die durch doktrinäre oder moralische Vorwürfe in ein falsches Licht gekommen waren, und darüber hinaus um die grundsätzliche Erörterung der durch jene Gestalten bezeichneten allgemeineren Probleme. Lessings Polemik ist in den Rettungen oft ebenso scharf wie das zugrundeliegende Motiv vornehm. "...wen glaubt man wohl, daß ich darinne gerettet habe? Lauter verstorbne Männer, die es mir nicht danken können. Und gegen wen? Fast gegen lauter Lebendige, die mir vielleicht ein sauer Gesichte dafür machen werden".[27] Lessing "rettet" in mehreren Provinzen des Geistes. Mögen die *Rettungen des Horaz* den Höhepunkt der Gattung darstellen,[28] so sind sie doch schon umgeben von gleichartigen Versuchen auf theologischem, genauer kirchengeschichtlichem Gebiet, an denen Lessing ebenso gelegen war. Und seine Kompetenz ist hier dieselbe gewesen.[29] "Keiner der großen deutschen

[24] Über seine Stellung zu den -isten vgl. das Gedicht "Wem ich zu gefallen suche, und nicht suche" (*PO* I, pp. 74ff., *G* I, pp. 102ff.).

[25] Über J. J. Reiske vgl. J. Wellhausen, *Enc. Brit.*, 10th edn, XX, pp. 354f., über Lessings Beziehungen zum Ehepaar Reiske H. Schneider, *Lessing* (Bern, 1950), pp. 110ff.

[26] Vgl. E. Schmidt, *Lessing* (4. Aufl., Berlin 1923) I, pp. 40ff. An Bayles *Dictionnaire historique et critique* schließt sich Lessing ausdrücklich an in der *Rettung des Cardanus* von 1754 (*PO* XX, p. 111, *G* VII, p. 10).

[27] *PO* VII, p. 39, *G* III, p. 522 (Vorrede zu *Schriften* III, 1754); vgl. *PO* XIV, pp. 85f., *G* III, pp. 591f. (*Rettungen des Horaz*, 1754).

[28] Vgl. K. S. Guthke, *Gotthold Ephraim Lessing*. Sammlung Metzler 65 (2. Aufl., Stuttgart, 1973), pp. 26f.

[29] "Bei seinem Studieren gab er keiner Wissenschaft aus Überlegung und Wahl den Vorzug, sondern hielt sie alle für gleich wichtig, überließ sich folglich ganz dem Zufalle und dem gelegentlichen Eindrucke. Denn er hatte keinen andern Hauptzweck als die Wahrheit; und sah mehr auf den allgemeinen Nutzen als

Klassiker — auch der Theologe Herder nicht — hat ähnlich imponierende theologische Fachkenntnisse, zumal auf dem Gebiet der alten Kirchengeschichte besessen wie Lessing, der sich rühmen konnte, die Kirchenväter der ersten vier Jahrhunderte mehrmals sorgfältig gelesen zu haben".[30]

In seiner Stellung zu den Theologen allerdings ist seine Distanz zu den Gelehrten insgemein noch potenziert. Einem durchreisenden Kandidaten der Theologie aus Dänemark sagt er 1777, "daß die Theologen eine Menschenklasse seien, mit denen er in aller Welt am allerwenigsten hätte übereinkommen können, sie schlössen in einem ewigen Zirkel".[31] 1771 beruhigt er seinen Bruder, er brauche nicht bange zu sein, daß "das schale Lob der Theologen" ihn verführen werde, sich "mehr mit ihren Quisquilien und Ungereimtheiten zu beschäftigen".[32] Als er dann 1774 jene "noch freiere Untersuchung des Kanons" plant, da soll das "eine kleine Komödie" sein, die er sich mit den Theologen macht.[33] Die Komödie nahm unerwartete Dimensionen an, und wenn er 1778 im Rückblick auf den Hauptteil des Streites von einer "Katzbalgerei" spricht, dann darf das nicht über den tiefen Ernst der inzwischen verhandelten Probleme hinwegtäuschen. Kurz danach kündigt Lessing aber sogar noch den Nathan damit an, er wolle den Theologen "einen ärgeren Possen" spielen "als noch mit zehn Fragmenten".[34] Wenn er in diesen Jahren sagt, es sei ihm "im Grunde" bei seinen "theologischen ... Neckereien und Stänkereien, mehr um den gesunden Menschenverstand, als um die Theologie zu tun",[35] dann deutet sich darin über die vordergründige Polemik hinaus einiges von seiner Stellung zur Theologie und ihrem Gegenstand an. Fast erleichtert nimmt man zur Kenntnis, daß diese Stellung bei den Literatur- und Theologiehistorikern nicht weniger umstritten ist als bei den Alttestamentlern Mose oder der

---

den seinigen, mehr auf *das* Verdienst, als auf *den* Verdienst. Die Theologie war ihm eben so wichtig, als die Antiquität, die Vorstellung der alten Griechen und Römer von dem Tode eben so forschenswert, als die Vorstellung der Christen von der Dreieinigkeit. Sobald eine Sache für ihn nicht mehr Reiz hatte, sobald ein gewisser dunkler Überdruß sich dabei einschlich, stand er mitten unter der Arbeit davon ab, und überließ sich einer andern Beschäftigung mit eben so viel Teilnahme und Eifer" (Lessings Bruder Karl bei Daunicht, p. 593).

[30] K. Beyschlag in: Lessing, *Werke*, ed. K. Wölfel, III, p. 593.

[31] A. C. Hviid bei Daunicht, p. 441f.

[32] An Karl Lessing 4.7.1771.

[33] An Karl Lessing 11.11.1774.

[34] An Karl Lessing 11.8.1778; vgl. damit die sehr andere Aussage im Brief vom 20.10.1778.

[35] An Karl Lessing 20.3.1777.

deuterojesajanische Gottesknecht. Das liegt zu einem guten Teil an Lessings Denk- und Ausdrucksweise. Nach einem Wort Kierkegaards gehört er nicht zu den "brüllenden und den dozierenden Subjektivitäten",[36] er stellt seine eigene Position ständig in Frage, macht sich, wie er selbst sagt, "gern allerlei Hypothesen und Systeme..., um das Vergnügen zu haben, sie wieder einzureißen",[37] würde nicht alles, was er γυμναστικῶς schreibt, auch δογματικῶς schreiben.[38] Er konnte nach dem Zeugnis von Ch. F. Nicolai "das Allzudecisive nicht wohl leiden, und pflegte in gesellschaftlichen gelehrten Unterredungen oft die Partie zu nehmen, welche die schwächere war, oder die, wovon jemand positiv das Gegenteil behaupten wollte";[39] dahin gehört auch, daß er in Sachsen die preußische, in Preußen die sächsische Sache zu verteidigen pflegte.[40] Die Wahrheit ist vielfach. "Jeder glaubt sie zu haben, und jeder hat sie anders".[41] Ihr Besitz ist viel weniger wert als der Trieb nach ihr.[42] Drastischer sagt es Moses Mendelssohn in bezug auf Lessings "Liebe zum Forschen": "Das Jagen behagte ihm mehr als das gejagte Wildbret".[43] Nimmt man hinzu, was die Taktik des Streits und auch die Vorsicht angesichts der stets drohenden Zensur geboten,[44] dann verwundert nicht, daß Lessing für seine Person die Bekenntnispflicht abgelehnt hat[45] und der ihm von Goeze ungeschickt gestellten Gretchenfrage nach seiner Religion geschickt ausgewichen ist.[46] Er liefert hier noch weniger als sonst etwas, was man "in einem Paragraphen einsalzen" kann.[47] Da

---

[36] S. Kierkegaard, *Abschließende unwissenschaftliche Nachschrift*, übers. von H. M. Junghans, I (Düsseldorf, 1957), p. 58.

[37] Brief an A. H. Reimarus 6.4.1778.

[38] An Karl Lessing 16.3.1778.

[39] Bei Daunicht, p. 587. Vgl. auch M. Mendelssohn ebenda, p. 583: "Geist der Untersuchung war bei ihm alles. Mit seichten Gründen behauptete Wahrheit, pflegte er zu sagen, ist Vorurteil; nicht minder schädlich, als offenbarer Irrtum, und zuweilen noch schädlicher..."

[40] Nicolai bei Daunicht, pp. 150f.

[41] *PO* I, p. 188, *G* I, p. 171 (*Die Religion*, 1751, Vorerinnerung).

[42] Vgl. die berühmten Worte in der *Duplik* von 1778 (*PO* XXIII, pp. 58f.).

[43] Bei Daunicht, pp. 577f.

[44] Zur Problematik der Annahme einer regelrechten Verstellung und des Begriffspaares exoterisch-esoterisch vgl. Schilson, l.c., pp. 201f.; ders., *Theologie und Philosophie* 47 (1972), p. 421.

[45] E. Hirsch, *Geschichte der neuern evangelischen Theologie* IV (Gütersloh, 1952), pp. 121f.

[46] *PO* XXIII, pp. 258f. (*Nötige Antwort auf eine sehr unnötige Frage des Herrn Hauptpastor Goeze in Hamburg*, 1778); dazu die Briefe an Elise Reimarus vom 9.8.1778 und an J. G. Herder vom 25.1.1780. Vgl. auch Beyschlag, l.c., p. 595.

[47] Vgl. Kierkegaard, l.c., p. 99.

es hier nicht meine Aufgabe ist, dieser Frage weiter nachzugehen, begnüge ich mich mit einem Hinweis auf E. Hirschs mir lehrreich scheinende Formel, daß Lessing "sich über die christliche Religion so hinausgekommen wußte wie Paulus über das Judentum".[48] Einen präzisen Anhaltspunkt gibt Lessing selber in dem erst nach seinem Tode veröffentlichen Satz: "Nathans Gesinnung gegen alle positive Religion ist von jeher die meinige gewesen".[49]

Von Nathan wäre nun ausführlicher zu reden, nicht nur unter dem Gesichtspunkt von Lessings Stellung zur Religion, sondern auch, weil es reizvoll wäre, die Weisheit dieser großen Dramenfigur [50] mit der Weisheit des Alten Testaments zu vergleichen, von der zumindest mittelbar manches in den Nathan eingegangen ist. Doch es wird Zeit, daß wir uns in der gebotenen Kürze einen Überblick über Lessings direkte Äußerungen und Beiträge zur Bibelwissenschaft verschaffen.

Zunächst ist zu sagen: der Mann kennt, darin den meisten Klassikern, leider nicht mehr den meisten heutigen Theologen zu vergleichen, die Bibel genau und weiß an passenden Stellen davon Gebrauch zu machen; und nicht erst der Mann, sondern nachweislich schon der dreizehnjährige Junge.[51] Für Bibelausgaben, besonders spanische — er hatte für Spanisches immer eine Vorliebe —, interessiert sich nicht erst der Bibliothekar.[52] In Hamburg läßt er sich 1769, vor dem Streit, vom Hauptpastor Goeze dessen Bibelsammlung zeigen und macht hinterher Notizen darüber und über das, was Goeze in der Textkritik gegen Semler bemerkt hat.[53]

Kenntnis, Interesse und vor allem guter Geschmack lassen Lessing in den Kritiken seiner früheren Jahre wiederholt für die Bibel gegen ihre Ausleger Partei ergreifen. Er findet, daß Bolingbroke "oft ziemlich cavalierement von der Bibel spricht",[54] verwahrt sich dagegen, daß man wie Wieland beim Übersetzen die Sprache der Bibel, statt sie "in ihrer edlen Einfalt" zu lassen, "durch affektierte Tiefsin-

[48] Hirsch, l.c., p. 124.

[49] *PO* II, p. 314, *G* II, p. 748 (Vorredenentwurf zum *Nathan*). Freilich ist das "gegen" verschiedener Deutungen fähig, vgl. Schilson, *Geschichte*, p. 96, n. 35.

[50] Vgl. F. Brüggemann, "Die Weisheit in Lessings 'Nathan' ", *Zeitschrift für Deutschkunde* 39 (1925), pp. 557ff. (Neudruck in G. und S. Bauer, *Gotthold Ephraim Lessing*. Wege der Forschung CCXI [Darmstadt, 1968], pp. 74ff.).

[51] Vgl. *PO* XXIV, pp. 89f., *G* III, pp. 677, 679 (Glückwünschungsrede bei dem Eintritt des 1743sten Jahres).

[52] Vgl. *PO* VIII, pp. 182ff., *G* III, pp. 341ff. (25. "Brief", Abraham Usque).

[53] *PO* XIX, pp. 163ff., *G* V, pp. 732ff. (Kollektaneen Hamburg IV).

[54] *PO* IV, p. 30, *G* V, p. 39 (4. Literaturbrief, 1759).

nigkeiten, durch profane Allusionen, verunstaltet"[55] und daß man die Auslegung in die Übersetzung hineinträgt, indem man etwa *ʾaelōhīm* in Gen. i 1 mit Dreieinigkeit übersetzt.[56] Überhaupt ist es mit der Auslegung eine schwierige Sache. "Die Bibel rate ich dir, ohne alle Hülfe zu lesen. Doch brauchst du nicht immer darüber zu liegen; aufs höchste bei garstigem und traurigen Wetter, oder wenn du von der Arbeit müde und zu andern Verrichtungen ungeschickt bist. Fliehe alle Ausleger; denn glaube mir, kein einziger ist von Vorurteilen frei... Die Bibel selbst aber lies mit Sorgfalt und Überlegung; nicht mit jener sinnlosen Ehrfurcht, die man Andacht zu nennen pflegt... Lies die Bibel nicht anders, als du Livius, Froschmäusler oder der Gräfin von Bembrok (Pembroke) Arkadien liesest. Einiges davon lobst du; einiges übergehst du; von einigem wolltest du, daß es lieber anders, als so heißen möge. Es steckt auch noch vieles in der Bibel, das noch niemand bemerkt oder an den Tag gebracht hat; und das entweder auf deine oder auf eines andern Hand wartet. Viele Stellen sollten ganz anders ausgelegt werden. Bei vielen folgt ein Schöps dem andern, und ein Ausleger dem andern".[57]

Aber auf gute Auslegung ist Lessing immer begierig, und er begrüßt einen Band des neutestamentlichen Kommentarwerks von Ch. A. Heumann in Göttingen als "eine der vollständigsten und lehrreichsten" Arbeiten "in ihrer Art" und fügt die bemerkenswerten Sätze hinzu: "Er ist so weit von der Art gemeiner Exegeten entfernet, daß bekannte Erklärungen, wenn sie nichts als das Alter und die Allgemeinheit vor (für) sich haben, niemals bei ihm von Ansehen sind, und daß ihn der Vorwurf erzwungener Neuerungen niemals abschreckt, mit seinen eigenen Augen zu sehen. Es wäre Schade, wenn er in der Auslegung dieser und jener Stelle einen allgemeinen Beifall erhalten sollte. Den Gottesgelehrten von Profession würde dadurch auf einmal ein fruchtbarer Stoff zu Zänkereien, worinne sie ihre Gelehrsamkeit eben so unwidersprechlich, als ihre Hartnäckigkeit zeigen können, benommen werden".[58] Bei Gelegenheit der mit Anmerkungen versehenen Übersetzung des Neuen Testaments von J. A. Bengel nimmt Lessing dessen Bemerkung auf, "daß diejenigen, welche

---

[55] *PO* IV, p. 36, *G* V, p. 47 (8. Literaturbrief, 1759).

[56] *PO* IX, pp. 74f., *G* III, pp. 24f. (Rezension von J. V. Zehner, 8.1.1751).

[57] Diese Sätze stehen in Lessings Wiedergabe des *Ineptus Religiosus* von 1754 (§§ 18.20, *PO* XX, p. 137, *G* VII, pp. 39f.). Man darf annehmen, daß Lessing sich mit ihnen ohne Ironie identifizieren konnte. — Ein Schöps ist im damaligen Sprachgebrauch ein männliches Schaf, genauer ein Hammel.

[58] *PO* IX, pp. 199f., *G* III, p. 77 (Rezension vom 18.11.1751).

das alte Testament vor die Hand nähmen, sehr dünne gesäet, und also desto höher zu schätzen wären. Dieses Geständnis", so fährt er fort, "wird bei jedem Rechtschaffenen den Wunsch erwecken, einem so nachteiligen Mangel je eher je lieber abgeholfen zu sehen"; man solle sich durch das Schicksal des Wertheimischen Übersetzers nicht abschrecken lassen.[59] Als Lessing diese Anregung im August 1766 gegenüber J. D. Michaelis in Göttingen wiederholte, fiel sie auf fruchtbaren Boden. Ein Zeuge der Unterredung in Michaelis' Studierzimmer in der heutigen Prinzenstraße erinnerte sich später "noch lebhaft, was Lessings spöttelnde Bemerkung, daß die Christen so wenig von dem erführen und benutzen könnten, was die Schriftgelehrten auf ihren Studierzimmern erfänden, in ihren Hörsälen vortrügen, und in ihren gelehrten meist lateinischen Schriften bekannt machten, für einen starken Eindruck auf Michaelis gemacht hat, und wie er von der Zeit an sich mit dem Plane zu einer Übersetzung der Bibel beschäftigt hat".[60] Wenige Jahre später, 1769, begann seine *Übersetzung des Alten Testaments, mit Anmerkungen für Ungelehrte* zu erscheinen.

Es überrascht nicht, daß Lessing sich in seinen frühen Jahren weder auf die Seite der Orthodoxie noch auf die der Neologie oder des Rationalismus schlägt. Für die Art mancher Moderner, die Bibel auf ihre Linie zu bringen, hat er nur Sarkasmus übrig. So angesichts der Dissertation eines Königsbergers mit Namen Weiß, der Abraham aufgrund eines λογισάμενος "er dachte", das Hebr. xi 19 von ihm gesagt wird, zu einem Logicus, einem Mann der Vernunft, kurz zu einem Rationalisten macht. Lessing gratuliert ironisch:

"Die Logik Abrahams? Wer hätte das gedacht?
Vielleicht daß Weiß sich bald an Sarens Physik macht".[61]

Natürlich schont Lessing auch die Orthodoxie nicht. Er rät, die Anzahl der sogenannten christologischen Weissagungen im Alten Testament, statt sie in immer neuen "Rettungen" um jeden Preis aufrecht-

[59] *PO* IX, p. 302, *G* III, pp. 196f. (Rezension vom 12.1.1754).

[60] J. C. F. Schulz in: J. D. Michaelis, *Lebensbeschreibung von ihm selbst abgefaßt*, mit Anmerkungen von Hassencamp (Rinteln und Leipzig, 1793), pp. 247f. (auch bei Daunicht, p. 209). Michaelis bestätigt die Schulzsche Darstellung mindestens nicht ausdrücklich. Er schreibt in der Vorrede zum 1. Band das Hauptverdienst an seinem Entschluß, das Werk zu beginnen, seinem Göttinger Kollegen G. Leß zu. Schon früher allerdings hätten "auswärtige Freunde von weltlichem Stande" ihm derartige Anregungen gemacht; dabei mag er an Lessing gedacht haben.

[61] *PO* IX, p. 323, *G* III, pp. 201f. (Rezension vom 2.5.1754).

zuerhalten, lieber zu verringern,[62] und führt in der Besprechung eines dogmatischen Lehrbuchs die Inspirationslehre ad absurdum, indem er auf ihre Konsequenzen hinweist.[63] Im ganzen allerdings ist ihm die Orthodoxie, die er ja wirklich nicht bejahen kann, vor allem in seiner späteren Zeit, die respektablere Partei. Sie verhält sich nach seinen Worten gegen "unsere neumodische Theologie", dieses "Flickwerk von Stümpern und Halbphilosophen", immerhin noch wie "unreines Wasser" gegen "Mistjauche", sie ist "im Grunde tolerant", die neue Theologie dagegen, die "uns unter dem Vorwande, uns zu vernünftigen Christen zu machen, zu höchst unvernünftigen Philosophen macht", "im Grunde intolerant". "Meines Nachbars Haus drohet ihm den Einsturz. Wenn es mein Nachbar abtragen will, so will ich ihm redlich helfen. Aber er will es nicht abtragen, sondern er will es, mit gänzlichem Ruin meines Hauses, stützen und unterbauen. Das soll er bleiben lassen, oder ich werde mich seines einstürzenden Hauses so annehmen, als meines eigenen".[64] So spricht der späte Lessing, der gelegentlich in Sorge ist, "ein wenig zu viel mit weggeworfen zu haben".[65] Ein alter Freund konnte sogar sagen, und es ist oft wiederholt worden, Lessing habe mit der Herausgabe der Fragmente der orthodoxen Partei einen Dienst erweisen wollen.[66] Es wäre freilich ein merkwürdiger Dienst gewesen, und jedenfalls haben ihm die Orthodoxen dafür nicht gedankt. Sie sahen nur, wie der unheimliche Nachbar daran war, ihr Haus abzutragen, und brachten kein Verständnis dafür auf; es wäre, wie sie und er nun einmal waren, auch viel verlangt gewesen.[67]

Lessing geht 1770 von Hamburg nach Wolfenbüttel in der Absicht, mit den ihm dort gegebenen Mitteln "so mancherlei Anschläge auszuführen".[68] Er kann bei diesen "Anschlägen" außer auf die Schätze der hiesigen Bibliothek auch auf viel Arbeit zurückgreifen, die er bisher, vor allem wohl in den produktionslosen — und gerade darum auf die Dauer besonders produktiven — Breslauer Jahren von 1760-65 geleistet hat [69] und der er nun neue Arbeit in einem Ausmaß

[62] *PO* IX, pp. 170f., *G* III, pp. 63f. (Rezension von Ch. Lilienthal, 24.5.1751).
[63] *PO* IX, pp. 218f., *G* III, pp. 146f. (Rezension von P. Ahlwardt, 16.12.1752); dazu K. Aner, *Die Theologie der Lessingzeit* (Halle, 1929), p. 175.
[64] Briefe an Karl Lessing vom 2.2.1774 und 20.3.1777.
[65] Brief an M. Mendelssohn vom 9.1.1771.
[66] Ch. F. Nicolai bei Daunicht, p. 379.
[67] "Es muß Ihnen sehr kirr däuchten, sich von Orthodoxen gesegnet zu sehen", schreibt Heyne an Lessing am 9.12.1770 anläßlich einer Rezension des *Berengar*.
[68] Brief an Nicolai vom 2.1.1770.
[69] Vgl. S. B. Klose bei Daunicht, p. 170f.

hinzufügt, von dem erst die — leider ganz ungenügende — Nachlaßveröffentlichung durch seinen Bruder ein ungefähres Bild ergeben hat. Die Positionen, die er nunmehr vertritt, lassen sich zu einem guten Teil schon in seine früheren Jahre zurückverfolgen und haben sich in wichtigsten Punkten bei ihm längst vor ihrer Publikation gebildet.[70] Am Anfang des Wolfenbüttler Jahrzehnts steht außer einer gewissen Verschiebung des allgemeinen Urteils [71] vor allem die so folgenreiche Beschäftigung mit der ihm schon in Hamburg bekannten *Apologie oder Schutzschrift für die vernünftigen Verehrer Gottes*, die der 1768 verstorbene Hamburger Orientalist und Schulrektor H. S. Reimarus als Manuskript hinterlassen hatte. Reimarus, Anhänger einer vernünftigen oder natürlichen Religion, bestritt in diesem umfangreichen Werk die Möglichkeit und Notwendigkeit von Offenbarung überhaupt und die Wirklichkeit der Offenbarung in der Bibel Alten und Neuen Testaments. Das riesige Material an Widersprüchen, unerfüllten Weissagungen, unmöglichen Wundern, moralischer Unvollkommenheit, ja Lug und Trug biblischer Personen, das er dafür zusammenstellte, war im wesentlichen, in Hamburg nicht ganz ungewöhnlich, Import aus England, wo sich Reimarus als junger Mann eine Weile aufgehalten hatte; die Verbindung mit dem dortigen Deismus und seiner Literatur war geblieben. Lessing beschreibt das Werk des Reimarus als einen "Hauptsturm auf die christliche Religion". "Es ist keine einzige Seite, kein einziger noch so versteckter Winkel, dem er seine Sturmleitern nicht angeworfen. Freilich hat er diese Sturmleitern nicht alle mit eigener Hand geschnitzt; die meisten davon sind schon bei mehrern Stürmen gewesen; einige derselben sind sogar ein wenig sehr schadhaft, denn in der belagerten Stadt waren auch Männer, die zerschmetternde Felsenstücke auf den Feind herabwarfen. — Doch was tut das? Heran kömmt nicht, wer die Leiter machte, sondern wer die Leiter besteigt, und einen behenden kühnen Mann trägt auch wohl eine morsche Leiter".[72]

---

[70] Vgl. W. Dilthey, *Das Erlebnis und die Dichtung* (Leipzig, 1906), pp. 77ff.; J. Schneider, *Lessings Stellung zur Theologie vor der Herausgabe der Wolfenbüttler Fragmente*, Diss. phil., Amsterdam, 1953.

[71] Vgl. den schon zitierten Brief an Mendelssohn vom 9.1.1771 sowie Beyschlag, l.c., pp. 599f.

[72] *PO* XXIII, p. 56 (*Eine Duplik*, 1778, I). Die *Apologie* wurde 1972 von G. Alexander in 2 Bänden erstmals vollständig herausgegeben. Zu ihrer Würdigung, die hier nicht die Aufgabe sein kann, vgl. D. F. Strauß, *Hermann Samuel Reimarus und seine Schutzschrift für die vernünftigen Verehrer Gottes* (Leipzig, 1862);

In diesen Sätzen schwingt eine leise Distanziertheit mit, ohne die Lessing nicht zum "Pflegevater der von dem Verfasser der Fragmente hinterlassenen Mißgeburt" geworden ist, wie sein Widersacher Goeze ihn liebevoll genannt hat.[73] Warum "stieß" er den Reimarus, der sein Manuskript aus guten Gründen für sich behielt, "in die Welt?" "... weil ich mit ihm nicht länger unter einem Dache wohnen wollte. Er lag mir unaufhörlich in den Ohren, und ich bekenne..., daß ich seinen Zuraunungen nicht immer so viel entgegenzusetzen wußte, als ich gewünscht hätte. Uns, dachte ich, muß ein Dritter entweder näher zusammen- oder weiter auseinanderbringen, und dieser Dritte kann niemand sein als das Publikum".[74] Lessing will die Öffentlichkeit,[75] und wie einst der assyrische Befehlshaber mit den Abgesandten des Königs Hiskia hebräisch und nicht aramäisch sprach, damit das Volk von Jerusalem ihn verstand, so weist er das Ansinnen zurück, den Streit in der lateinischen Gelehrtensprache zu führen.[76] Also gehen, fast durchweg in der Reihe *Zur Geschichte und Literatur. Aus den Schätzen der Herzoglichen Bibliothek zu Wolfenbüttel*, die "Fragmente" heraus, als "Papiere eines Ungenannten", dessen Anonymität bis lange nach Lessings Tod, 1814, gewahrt bleibt: zunächst 1774 *Von Duldung der Deisten*, dann 1777 gleich fünf Fragmente auf einmal: *Von Verschreiung der Vernunft auf den Kanzeln*, *Unmöglichkeit einer Offenbarung, die alle Menschen auf eine gegründete Art glauben können*, *Durchgang der Israeliten durchs rote Meer*, *Daß die Bücher A.T. nicht geschrieben worden, eine Religion zu offenbaren*, *Über die Auferstehungsgeschichte*, und schließlich 1778, am umfangreichsten, *Vom Zwecke Jesu und seiner Jünger*, dies schon in die Debatte hinein, die sich sogleich an jene fünf Fragmente und die ihnen von Lessing beigegebenen "Gegensätze des Herausgebers" angeschlossen und in wenigen Monaten zu großer Heftigkeit gesteigert hatte.

Matthias Claudius erdichtete damals eine Audienz, die der Kaiser von Japan dem Asmus aus Wandsbeck gewährt. Der Kaiser befragt den Asmus auch über die Einwendungen gegen die Religion in

W. Caspari, "Reimarus über alttestamentliche Literaturgeschichte", *Theologische Blätter* 5 (1926), pp. 273ff.; H. Graf Reventlow, "Das Arsenal der Bibelkritik des Reimarus", in *H. S. Reimarus* (Göttingen, 1973), pp. 44ff.

[73] Vgl. E. Schmidt (ed.), *Goezes Streitschriften gegen Lessing* (Stuttgart, 1893), p. 41.

[74] *PO* XXIII, p. 252 (*Eilfter Anti-Goeze*, 1778).

[75] Vgl. Dilthey, l.c., p. 11, über den Unterschied des Schriftstellers vom wissenschaftlichen Forscher.

[76] *PO* XXIII, pp. 209ff. (*Vierter Anti-Goeze*, 1778). Auf der Gegenseite z.B. Goeze, l.c., pp. 43.71.

Europa. Asmus antwortet: "Herr Lessing hat neulich ... verschiedene Zweifel eines Ungenannten bekannt gemacht, davon einige recht gelehrt und artig sind. Er hat sie aber widerlegt." Darauf der Kaiser: "Hat er sie widerlegt?" Asmus: "Nicht eben förmlich; denn er ist unparteiisch". Auf die weitere Nachfrage des Kaisers erläutert er: Lessing "meint, wer Recht hat, wird wohl Recht behalten; der soll's aber auch behalten und darf das freie Feld nicht scheuen! und also läßt er die Zweifel mit Ober- und Unter-Gewehr aufmarschieren: marschiert ihr dagegen! So'n Trupp Religionszweifel ist aber wie die Klapperschlange und fällt über den besten wehrlosen Mann her; das will er nicht haben, und darum hat er jedem Zweifel einen Maulkorb umgetan... Und, sagt er, ehrlich gegen den Feind zu Werk gegangen!" Darauf wieder der Kaiser, der gut zugehört hat: "Die förmliche Widerlegung der Zweifel ist also noch nicht gekommen". "Noch nicht", bestätigt Asmus, "so viel ich weiß, wird aber vielleicht noch kommen..." Der Kaiser fragt zurück: "Ihm scheint an dieser Widerlegung nicht sonderlich viel gelegen zu sein?" Darauf Asmus: "Gar nichts, Sire".[77]

Der Wandsbecker Bote hat klar gesehen, was Lessings Absicht ist.[78] Natürlich will er nicht den Orthodoxen einen Dienst tun oder irgendetwas dergleichen.[79] Er will die Wahrheit, und er glaubt, der Streit um die Fragmente werde ihr zugute kommen. Für diesen Streit sollen die "Gegensätze des Herausgebers" einstweilen Material und Gesichtspunkte liefern, bis auf beiden Seiten der Mann erscheint, "welcher die Religion so bestreitet, und der, welcher die Religion so verteidiget, als es die Wichtigkeit und Würde des Gegenstandes erfodert".[80] Der Advokat des Ungenannten ist Lessing durchaus nicht, vielmehr oft sein entschiedener Gegner; [81] er hängt ihm wirklich auch "Maulkörbe" um. Das Geschick, mit dem er sich zwischen den Fronten bewegt, hat damals und seither manche Verwirrung gestiftet. Es dürfte nur wenige geben, denen bei der Lektüre nicht

[77] *Asmus omnia sua secum portans oder Sämtliche Werke des Wandsbecker Boten* III (1778, Vorwort vom August 1777); die "Nachricht von meiner Audienz beim Kaiser von Japan" in der Ausgabe von U. Roedl (Stuttgart, 1954), pp. 158ff.

[78] Vgl. die Bestätigung in Lessings Brief an Claudius vom 19.4.1778.

[79] Vgl. aber K. Barth, *Die protestantische Theologie im 19. Jahrhundert* (Zollikon, 1947), pp. 221f.

[80] *PO* XXII, p. 188, *G* VII, p. 459 (Gegensätze).

[81] Vgl. *PO* XXIII, pp. 227ff., 251ff. (*Siebenter und eilfter Anti-Goeze*), ferner Lessings Brief an J. A. H. Reimarus vom 6.4.1778: die "Erziehung des Menschengeschlechts" "würde freilich das Ziel gewaltig verrücken, auf das mein Ungenannter im Anschlage gewesen".

zuweilen etwas unheimlich würde; es ist in mancher Hinsicht schwer, dem späten Lessing auf den Grund zu kommen.

Die "Gegensätze des Herausgebers", die die fünf "mittleren" Fragmente begleiten,[82] beginnen mit einer Feststellung über die Tragweite des Ganzen: den Christen, anders als den theologischen Apologeten, brauchten die Fragmente selbst dann nicht zu erschrecken, wenn sie völlig recht hätten. Denn "der Buchstabe ist nicht der Geist; und die Bibel ist nicht die Religion. Folglich sind Einwürfe gegen den Buchstaben, und gegen die Bibel, nicht eben auch Einwände gegen den Geist und gegen die Religion". Schon im "Gegensatz" zum ersten Fragment, von der "Verschreiung der Vernunft", taucht das Alte Testament auf: die Geschichte vom Sündenfall, Gen. iii, sagt mehr als der Fragmentist wahrhaben will: nämlich nicht nur daß "unsere ersten Eltern eben darum gefallen wären, weil sie ihrer Vernunft sich nicht bedient hätten", und daß wir es anders machen sollten, sondern: "die Macht unsrer sinnlichen Begierden, unsrer dunklen Vorstellungen über alle noch so deutliche Erkenntnis ist es, welche zur kräftigsten Anschauung darin gebracht wird. Von dieser Macht berichtet die Mosaische Erzählung entweder die erste traurige Erfahrung, oder erteilet das schicklichste Beispiel". Im "Gegensatz" zum zweiten Fragment, von der Offenbarung, fordert Lessing dazu auf, ihm ein Volk zu nennen, "in dessen Händen das anvertraute Pfund der Offenbarung wahrscheinlicher Weise mehr gewuchert haben würde, als in den Händen des Jüdischen". Daran schließt er die Sätze: "Dieses unendlich mehr verachtete als verächtliche Volk ist doch, in der ganzen Geschichte, schlechterdings das erste und einzige, welches sich ein Geschäft daraus gemacht, seine Religion mitzuteilen und auszubreiten. Wegen des Eifers, mit welchem die Juden dieses Geschäft betrieben, bestrafte sie schon Christus, verlachte sie schon Horaz. Alle andere Völker waren mit ihren Religionen entweder zu geheim und zu neidisch, oder viel zu kalt gegen sie gesinnt, als daß sie für derselben Ausbreitung sich der geringsten Mühewaltung hätten unterziehen wollen. Die christlichen Völker, die den Juden in diesem Eifer hernach gefolgt sind, überkamen ihn bloß, in so fern sie auf den Stamm des Judentums gepfropft waren". Was die eindrucksvolle Kritik des dritten Fragments an der Erzählung vom Durchzug durchs Rote Meer angeht, so relativiert Lessing zunächst das Gewicht der zweifellos viel zu

[82] *PO* XXII, pp. 186ff., *G* VII, pp. 457ff.

hohen Zahlen von Israeliten und Ägyptern. "Man hätte viel zu bezweifeln, wenn man an allen den alten Schlachten zweifeln wollte, bei welchen die Zahl der gebliebenen Feinde von dem einen Schriftsteller so, von dem andern anders, und von allen weit größer angegeben wird, als sich mit andern zugleich erzählten Umständen reimen läßt". Er fügt dann den schon vorhandenen natürlichen Erklärungen des Hauptvorgangs noch eine weitere hinzu, stellt aber dem Orthodoxen als die beste und unwiderleglichste Möglichkeit anheim, das Ganze mit allem Drum und Dran für ein Wunder zu erklären. Der wichtigste "Gegensatz" ist der gegen das vierte Fragment. "Daß die Bücher A.T. nicht geschrieben worden, eine (seligmachende) Religion zu offenbaren", hat der Ungenannte damit beweisen wollen, daß darin "von der Unsterblichkeit der Seelen, von der Belohnung und Bestrafung in einem zukünftigen ewigen Leben" nichts gelehrt wird. Dies räumt Lessing ein und fügt noch hinzu, "das A.T. oder doch das Israelitische Volk, wie wir es in den Schriften des A.T. vor den Zeiten der Babylonischen Gefangenschaft kennen lernen, habe nicht einmal den wahren Begriff von der Einheit Gottes gehabt". Aber auch das besagt noch nichts gegen "die Göttlichkeit der Bücher des A.T." "Denn diese muß ganz anders, als aus den darin vorkommenden Wahrheiten der natürlichen Religion erwiesen werden". Das unternimmt Lessing, indem er hier die erste Hälfte der dann 1780 vollständig veröffentlichen *Erziehung des Menschengeschlechts* einschiebt. Offenbarung ist danach Erziehung und das Alte Testament keine Darstellung der Religion in ihrer Vollkommenheit, sondern das — seitdem durch "das zweite bessere Elementarbuch" abgelöste (§ 64) — "Elementarbuch" für ein Volk im Kindesalter, "mit welchem Gott so ganz von vorn anfangen mußte . . ., um in der Folge der Zeit einzelne Glieder desselben so viel sichrer zu Erziehern aller übrigen Völker brauchen zu können. Er erzog in ihm die künftigen Erzieher des Menschengeschlechts. Das wurden Juden, das konnten nur Juden werden, nur Männer aus einem so erzogenen Volke" (§ 18). Schließlich der "Gegensatz" zum fünften Fragment, über die Auferstehungsgeschichte. Die vom Ungenannten zusammengestellten Widersprüche in den Evangelien bestehen. Doch es sind nicht "Widersprüche der Zeugen, sondern der Geschichtschreiber; nicht der Aussagen, sondern der Nachrichten von diesen Aussagen". Diese Widersprüche hätten nur durch "ein fortdauerndes Wunder" in den Jahrzehnten bis zur Aufzeichnung durch die Evangelisten verhindert werden können. Ein solches Wunder aber ist eine ganz unnötige Annahme; wer es annimmt, hat freilich alle Widersprüche in den Evangelien zu beheben — ein aussichtsloses, aber sogleich gegen den Ungenannten und nun auch Lessing gemeinsam versuchtes Unternehmen.

Denn jetzt rollt die Flut der Gegenschriften an.[83] Lessing antwortet noch im Winter 1777/78 öffentlich zwei Kontrahenten, dem Hannoverschen Lyceumsdirektor Schumann, der gegen das zweite, und dem Wolfenbüttler "Nachbarn" Reß, der gegen das fünfte Fragment geschrieben hat.[84] Schumann wird Adressat der Schrift *Über den Beweis des Geistes und der Kraft* [85] mit ihrer berühmten These, daß zufällige Geschichtswahrheiten nie der Beweis von notwendigen Vernunftwahrheiten werden können, und dem abschließenden Wunsch, es "möchte doch alle, welche das Evangelium Johannis trennt, das Testament Johannis [nämlich der apokryphe Satz: 'Kinderchen, liebt euch!'] wieder vereinigen!"[86] An Reß richtet sich die *Duplik* [87] in Sachen der Auferstehungsgeschichte. Lessing rechnet noch einmal genau die vom Ungenannten behaupteten und von Reß bestrittenen Widersprüche durch, die für ihn, wie auch immer das exegetische Einzelergebnis lautet, die Grundfrage doch nicht entscheiden. Denn hält der Ungenannte die Auferstehung für unglaubwürdig, weil sich die Nachrichten der Evangelisten widersprechen, Reß sie dagegen für glaubwürdig, weil sie sich nicht widersprechen, so weiß Lessing: "Die Auferstehung Christi kann ihre gute Richtigkeit haben, ob sich schon die Nachrichten der Evangelisten widersprechen".

Diese Auseinandersetzungen sind das Vorspiel für den großen Streit mit Goeze, den Mit- und Nachwelt mit Ärger und Ergötzen verfolgt haben — Vorspiel auch in dem Sinn, daß es meist die dort

---

[83] Verzeichnis bei S. Seifert, *Lessing-Bibliographie* (Berlin/Weimar, 1973), pp. 487ff.

[84] J. D. Schumann, *Über die Evidenz der Beweise für die Wahrheit der Christlichen Religion* (Hannover, 1778, Vorwort Sept. 1777); J. H. Reß, *Die Auferstehungs-Geschichte Jesu Christi gegen einige im vierten Beitrage zur Geschichte und Literatur aus den Schätzen der Herzoglichen Bibliothek gemachte Einwendungen verteidiget* (Braunschweig, 1777). Beide haben dann auch auf Lessings Gegenschriften geantwortet: Schumann, *Antwort auf das aus Braunschweig an ihn gerichtete Schreiben über den Beweis des Geistes und der Kraft* (Hannover, 1778; Lessing hatte anonym geschrieben); Reß, *Die Auferstehungs-Geschichte Jesu Christi ohne Widersprüche.* Gegen eine Duplik (Hannover, 1779).

[85] *PO* XXIII, pp. 45ff.

[86] Ausgeführt in *Das Testament Johannis. Ein Gespräch*, 1777 (*PO* XXIII, pp. 51ff.).

[87] *PO* XXIII, pp. 56ff.

angeschlagenen Themen sind, die nun immer neu variiert werden,[88] großartig vor allem in den *Axiomata*, die das in den "Gegensätzen des Herausgebers" über Bibel und Religion, Buchstaben und Geist Gesagte gegen Goezes Einwürfe verteidigen. Auf die Dauer — das Ganze währt freilich nur ein halbes Jahr, bis zur Aufhebung der Zensurfreiheit durch den Herzog von Braunschweig am 6.7.1778 — erfreuen die beiden Kämpen aber mehr den Rhetoriker als den Theologen. Der Theologe denkt angesichts dieses gänzlichen Nichtverstehens und Nichtverstehenwollens schmerzlich an das "Testament Johannis", und er sieht einiges Recht auch auf seiten des groben Goeze. Geist und Religion lassen sich schwerlich von Buchstaben und Bibel so trennen und gegen sie ausspielen, wie es bei Lessing geschieht; wenn die Bibelkritik des Fragmentisten, namentlich im Blick auf den "Zweck Jesu und seiner Jünger", zutrifft, dann kann das für den Glauben doch wohl nicht so folgenlos bleiben, wie Lessing behauptet.[89] Aber gegen die orthodoxe Inspirationslehre ist Lessing durchaus im Recht, und ebenso mit der Leugnung der Möglichkeit des historischen Beweises für den Glauben, nach all der Polemik am tiefsten und lebendigsten in der "Ringparabel" im "zwölften Anti-Goeze", dem *Nathan*. Einige Jahre früher hat Lessing den schönen Satz geschrieben, "daß das einzige Buch, welches, im eigentlichen Verstande, für die Wahrheit der Bibel, jemals geschrieben worden, und geschrieben werden könne, kein anderes als die Bibel selbst sei".[90] Über die Herkunft dieses Satzes[91] und über seine Bedeutung vor Lessing und bei ihm selbst ließe sich manches sagen, und auch wir hier würden ihn uns wohl nicht alle im genau gleichen Sinn zu eigen machen. Mir scheint aber, daß richtiger von der Bibel

[88] Auf Lessings Seite: *Eine Parabel. Nebst einer Kleinen Bitte und einem eventualen Absagungsschreiben an den Herrn Pastor Goeze in Hamburg*; *Axiomata, wenn es deren in dergleichen Dingen gibt. Wider den Herrn Pastor Goeze in Hamburg*; *Anti-Goeze. D.i. Notgedrungene Beiträge zu den freiwilligen Beiträgen des Herrn Pastor Goeze. Erster-Eilfter*; *Nötige Antwort auf eine sehr unnötige Frage*.., alle 1778 (*PO* XXIII, pp. 152ff.). Goezes Schriften in der Ausgabe E. Schmidts wurden schon genannt. Lessings und Goezes Sätze sind unter überwiegend literarisch-dramatischen Gesichtspunkten einander gegenübergestellt bei A. Schöne, "In Sachen des Ungenannten: Lessing contra Goeze", *Text + Kritik* 26/27 (2. Aufl., München, 1975), unter überwiegend theologischen Gesichtspunkten bei G. Isermann, *Lessing und Goeze*. Göttinger Quellenhefte für Unterricht und Arbeitsgemeinschaft 21 (Göttingen, 1975).

[89] Vgl. Hirsch, l.c., pp. 153f. Zur Problematik von Lessings Haltung gegenüber der protestantischen "Bibliolatrie" auch Aner, l.c., pp. 222f.

[90] *PO* XXI, p. 188, *G* VII, p. 224 (*Des Andreas Wissowatius Einwürfe wider die Dreieinigkeit*, 1773).

[91] Lessing gibt damit die Meinung Leibniz' wieder.

kaum gesprochen werden kann, und ebenso, wenngleich indirekt, von der Bibelwissenschaft, die damit von einer Last und einem Wahn befreit wird, unter denen sie nur schweren Schaden nehmen kann.

Lessing hat sich in den Jahren des Fragmentenstreits nicht nur zu den Prinzipienfragen von Bibel und Offenbarung geäußert, er hat auch, unter Rückgriff auf seine früheren Studien, exegetisch-historisch gearbeitet. Die Nötigung dazu verstärkte sich, als gewichtigere Gegner auf den Plan traten. "Endlich lassen sich", schreibt er im Dezember 1778, "die großen Wespen doch aus dem Loche sterlen. Die Göttingsche sumset nicht so arg, als sie zu stechen drohet. Wir werdens ja sehen".[92] Die Kommentatoren sind sich nicht einig, ob die Göttingsche Wespe G. Leß mit seinem Buch *Auferstehungs-Geschichte nach allen vier Evangelisten. Nebst einem doppelten Anhange gegen die Wolfenbütteler Fragmente von der Auferstehung Jesu; und vom Zwecke Jesu und seiner Apostel* oder Ch. W. F. Walch mit seiner *Kritischen Untersuchung vom Gebrauche der Heiligen Schrift unter den alten Christen in den ersten vier Jahrhunderten* gewesen ist. Beide Bücher erschienen 1779. Im selben Jahr meldete sich auch J. S. Semler mit einer *Beantwortung der Fragmente eines Ungenannten, insbesondere vom Zweck Jesu und seiner Jünger.* Semlers Schrift, von der sich Lessing besonders viel versprochen haben mochte, war langatmig und unergiebig; ein anonymer Anhang gab zu verstehen, daß Lessing nach Bedlam ins Irrenhaus gehöre. Lessing war erbost: "Der Schubiack Semler... Ich bekam sein Geschmiere, eben als ich noch den ganzen 5ten Akt am 'Nathan' zu machen hatte, und war über die impertinente Professorgans so erbittert, daß ich alle gute Laune, die mir zum Versmachen so nötig ist, verlor, und schon Gefahr lief, den ganzen 'Nathan' darüber zu vergessen". Weiter nennt er ihn einen Esel und nimmt sich vor, ihm aus Bedlam ein Briefchen zu schreiben, "daß er an mich denken soll".[93] Dazu ist es nicht gekommen, wohl aber zu Entwürfen für "sogenannte Briefe an verschiedene Gottesgelehrte" und anderen Ausarbeitungen, die sich im Nachlaß gefunden haben. Den höchsten Rang nimmt unter ihnen ein, was sich auf das Neue Testament und die alte Kirche bezieht und in engem Zusammenhang mit Lessings These von der Priorität der mündlichen Tradition und der Regula fidei vor dem Neuen Testament steht: die Stücke "Bibliolatrie" [94]

---

[92] An Elise Reimarus 16.12.1778.

[93] An Elise Reimarus 14.5.1779.

[94] Deutung des Wortes gegen Lessings ausdrückliche Erklärung bei Hirsch, p. 157.

und "Von den Traditoren" gegen Walch [95] und sodann die "Theses aus der Kirchengeschichte" und die "Neue Hypothese über die Evangelisten als bloß menschliche Geschichtschreiber betrachtet",[96] diese beiden etwas älter, die "Neue Hypothese" 1777/78 als Anfang einer geplanten Reihe von Schriften verfaßt und von Lessing selbst für besonders gründlich und sinnreich erachtet.[97] Ihr Inhalt, das verlorene Hebräerevangelium als Vorlage der Evangelien des Matthäus, Markus und Lukas, ließ sich, bei Lessing seltener Fall, "in Paragraphen einsalzen", wenn auch auf die Dauer nur in die Paragraphen der Wissenschaftsgeschichte.[98]

Doch es gibt auch Nachlaßfragmente, die dem Alten Testament gelten. Da ist "Meines Arabers Beweis, daß nicht die Juden, sondern die Araber die wahren Nachkommen Abrahams sind",[99] ein ganz kurzes Stück, das man "sehr Reimarisch" zu nennen pflegt [100] und von dem sich kaum noch sagen läßt, ob es nur "geistige Gymnastik" [101] ist oder einen tieferen Zweck verfolgt, und, wichtiger und aufschlußreicher, aber ebenfalls nicht ohne Rätsel, das größere Fragment "Hilkias".[102] Lessing tritt darin den Beweis an — leider hat er dessen Einzelheiten nicht zu Papier gebracht [103] —, daß das unter König Josia aufgefundene Gesetzbuch "das einzige oder eben so gut als das einzige Exemplar war". Dies und damit zu behaupten, "daß es dem Volke und den Priestern schon so unbekannt gewesen, daß sie von der Existenz eines solchen Buches gar nichts mehr gewußt hätten", hatte ein anderer, durchaus geschätzter Nachbar Lessings, J. F. W. Jerusalem,

---

[95] *PO* XXIII, pp. 307ff., 313ff., *G* VII, pp. 667ff., 672ff. Vgl. ferner die "Sogenannten Briefe an Herrn Doktor Walch", *PO* XXIII, pp. 319ff., *G* VII, pp. 677ff., worin der wichtige Stellungswechsel gegenüber dem 8. *Axioma* (p. 320 bzw. 680). Zum Wissenschaftsgeschichtlichen und zur Sache A. Harnack, *Beiträge zur Einleitung in das Neue Testament* V (Leipzig, 1912), pp. 6ff.

[96] *PO* XXI, pp. 244ff., XXIII, pp. 120ff., *G* VII, pp. 605ff., 614ff.; vgl. auch Historische Einleitung in die Offenbarung Johannis (*PO* XXIII, pp. 140ff., *G* VII, pp. 636ff.).

[97] Vgl. seinen Brief an den Bruder Karl vom 25.2.1778.

[98] Vgl. W. G. Kümmel, *Das Neue Testament. Geschichte der Erforschung seiner Probleme* (Freiburg/München, 1958), pp. 90ff.; Th. Zahn, *Einleitung in das Neue Testament* 2 (2. Aufl., Leipzig, 1907), p. 200; J. Wellhausen, *Einleitung in die drei ersten Evangelien* (2. Ausg., Berlin, 1911), p. 109.

[99] *PO* XXI, pp. 251f., *G* VII, pp. 605f.

[100] E. Schmidt II, p. 216. Treffender ist auch die Erinnerung an Bayle und Voltaire (G. Pons, *Gotthold Ephraïm Lessing et le Christianisme* [Paris, 1964], p. 317).

[101] E. Schmidt; vgl. auch H. Graf Reventlow, *Ev. Theol.* 25 (1965), p. 447.

[102] *PO* XXI, pp. 133ff., *G* VII, pp. 301ff.

[103] p. 136 (*PO*), 305 (*G*). Oder hat man sich, wie mehrere Herausgeber vermuten, dort nur den Bibeltext hinzuzudenken?

Abt von Riddagshausen bei Braunschweig, "die größte Unverschämtheit" genannt.[104] Nicht nur gegen ihn wendet sich Lessing, sondern gleich danach auch gegen H. Prideaux, der für die Zeit nach Josia eine große Anzahl von Abschriften des Gesetzes postulierte.[105] Lessing hält dafür, daß das josianische Exemplar das einzige war und blieb und daß es sich bei dem Gesetzbuch in der Hand des Esra um kein anderes als eben dieses gehandelt hat. Leider wissen wir nicht, worauf Lessing mit seiner These hinauswollte; wahrscheinlich gedachte er die Zweifel an der mosaischen Autorschaft des Pentateuchs zu verstärken.[106] Im Vorbeigehen setzt er das wiedergefundene Gesetzbuch mit den gesetzlichen Teilen des Deuteronomiums gleich — was später einmal zu der Frage geführt hat, "ob nun Lessing anstatt de Wettes als Vater der Deuteronomiumforschung zu gelten" habe.[107] Das wäre indessen eine fast noch unsinnigere Vaterschaft als die mancherlei ideologischen Vaterschaften, die ihm im Laufe der Zeit von rechten und linken -isten und -ianern für ihre theologischen oder politischen Ideen angesonnen worden sind. Lessings Beitrag zur alttestamentlichen Wissenschaft im engeren Sinn ist bescheiden und hätte wohl auch, wenn er weiter ausgeführt worden wäre,[108] nicht viel über das hinaus erbracht, was schon Hobbes und Spinoza gesehen hatten. Vielleicht hat Lessing sich in der *Erziehung des Menschengeschlechts* durch Herder anregen lassen,[109] aber die Anstöße, die in seiner Jugend, in dem für unsere Wissenschaft so wichtigen Jahr 1753, Astrucs *Conjectures* und Lowth' *De sacra poësi Hebraeorum* gaben, haben ihn, soviel wir wissen, nicht beschäftigt.

Das ist aber, wie ich hoffe Ihnen nicht ganz verdeckt zu haben, für uns Alttestamentler kein Grund, uns nicht mit ihm zu beschäftigen, vielleicht nicht zuletzt so, daß wir ihn, den unabhängigen Geist und

---

104 *Briefe über die Mosaische Schriften und Philosophie* (Braunschweig, 1762); in der 2. Aufl. (1772), p. 14.

105 *The Old and New Testament Connected in the History of the Jews* I (7th ed., London, 1724), p. 260; deutsche Übersetzung von A. Tittel I (2. Aufl., Dresden, 1726), p. 417.

106 Vgl. den fünften Absatz des Fragments und dagegen die *Briefe* Jerusalems.

107 J. Hempel, *ZAW* 51 (1933), p. 299, n. 1.

108 Der "Hilkias" dürfte zu Anfang der siebziger Jahre geschrieben sein, vermutlich im Zuge der Vorbereitungen auf die "noch freiere Untersuchung des Kanons alten und neuen Testaments"; vgl. zur Datierung L. Zscharnack, *PO* XXI, p. 17 und Pons, l.c., p. 335. Eine geplante Verwendung in den "Briefen an verschiedene Gottesgelehrten" (E. Schmidt II, p. 288) braucht das nicht auszuschließen.

109 Vgl. L. Zscharnack, *PO* XXIII, p. 42; Th. Willi, *Herders Beitrag zum Verstehen des Alten Testaments* (Tübingen, 1971), pp. 94, 130.

unbestechlichen Kritiker, als eine Art Instanz auch für unsere eigenen Bemühungen gelten lassen. So haben es zwei andere Außenseiter unserer Wissenschaft, deren Namen in ihren Reihen immer einen guten Klang hatten, Mendelssohn und Herder, mit ihm gehalten. Mendelssohn bekennt, er habe sich bei jeder Handlung, die er vorhatte, bei jeder Zeile, die er hinschreiben sollte, Lessing "als Freund und Richter" vorgestellt;[110] Herder fragte sich immer, wenn er eine Schrift herausgab, kurz und gut: "Was wird Lessing dazu sagen?"[111] Es könnte wohl nicht schaden, wenn auch wir uns möglichst oft diese Frage vorlegten. Was wir dann noch in *Vetus Testamentum* und an anderen Orten zu druckten wagten, würde wahrscheinlich besser, schöner und kürzer.

[110] Brief an Karl Lessing vom Januar 1781, bei Daunicht, p. 574.
[111] W. Oehlke, *Lessing und seine Zeit* II (München, 1919), p. 46.

THE "COMPARATIVE METHOD" IN BIBLICAL INTERPRETATION—PRINCIPLES AND PROBLEMS[1]

by

SHEMARYAHU TALMON

Jerusalem

I

Modern Old Testament studies, from the inception of the historico-literary or *literarhistorische* approach, constitute an illuminating example of interdisciplinary contacts and of the transfer of methods applied in one field of research to another. Thus, the principles underlying the analysis to which the ancient Hebrew literature has been subjected by modern scholarship, especially since the beginning of the nineteenth century—the days of de Wette, Ewald, Kuenen, Graf and Wellhausen, to mention only a few outstanding names—in essence were those formulated by students of classical Greek literature, which were then adopted and adapted by biblical scholars to meet the requirements posed by the particular character of the writings of the Old, and, for that matter, the New Testament.[2] A further illustration of the fructification of biblical studies by other disciplines is the overall complex of "oral tradition" and the "traditio-historical" method, which has freely emulated analytical and interpretative techniques and procedures developed by students of ancient Scandinavian lore and of the epic literature of Eastern European peoples.[3] Similary, *Werkinterpretation* or "close reading" and the like schools which crystallized in general literary criticism influenced and still

---

[1] I wish to thank my assistant, Mr. David Satran, for his help in the preparation of this article.

[2] For the history and survey of the literature, see H. F. Hahn, *Old Testament in Modern Research* (Philadelphia, 1954; 1956); H. J. Kraus, *Geschichte der Historisch-Kritischen Erforschung des Alten Testaments* (Neukirchen, 1956; 1969); R. Smend, *Wilhelm Martin Leberecht de Wettes Arbeit am Alten und Neuen Testament* (Basel, 1958).

[3] E. Nielsen, *Oral Tradition* (London 1954); I. Engnell, "Methodological Aspects of Old Testament Study", *SVT* 7 (1959), pp. 13-30; *id.*, "The Traditio-Historical Method in Old Testament Research", *Critical Essays in the Old Testament*, tr. J. T. Willis (London, 1970), pp. 3-11, to mention only a few relevant items.

influence heavily the contemporary study of Old Testament literature *qua* literature with concomitant repercussions on other areas of biblical research.[4]

The restating of these well-known facts may be likened to carrying coals to Newcastle, since the dependence of biblical scholarship on other humanistic disciplines and even on the natural sciences with respect to fundamental outlooks as well as tools of the trade is generally admitted and recognized. The perusal of any "History of Modern Biblical Study" or "Introduction to Biblical Literature" will prove the point. However, two considerations induce me to preface my paper with these cursory remarks of a very general nature. Firstly, the fact that a fully detailed, up-to-date analysis of this interdependence still remains a desideratum. And secondly, to remind us that the "comparative method", on which I wish to focus attention, did not emerge independently within the restricted frame of our discipline, but rather was devised and developed in other areas of historical and phenomenological research which gave comparative biblical studies their impetus. Again, this fact will be readily acknowledged by all, and likewise the legitimacy of applying to the biblical literature techniques worked out in quite disparate fields of scholarly endeavour.

Alas, there seems to be a decisive difference between these other disciplines and our own. Sociologists, anthropologists, ethnographers and historians bestow constant attention on the evaluation and re-examination of the conceptual modes by which they guide ther comparative investigations; it would appear that in the realm of the Old Testament, however, comparative studies concerning the ancient Hebrew society, its literature and world of ideas, deal preponderantly with particular cases of parallels found or assumed to be present in other cultural complexes. Scholars seem to be less concerned about scrutinizing their methods in the light of the experience gathered from their "field work" and seldom apply themselves to such basic questions as whether the comparative method intrinsically operates under the "assumption of uniformity", as one school advocates, or if the aim should be "a comparison of contrasts rather than a comparison of similarities", as another school would have it.[5]

---

[4] M. Weiss, "Die Methode der 'Total-Interpretation' ", *SVT* 22 (1971), pp. 88-112, provides a survey and bibliography.

[5] Cf. K. E. Bock, "The Comparative Method of Anthropology", *Comparative Studies in Society and History* 8 (1965/66), pp. 269-80; and E. R. Leach, "The Comparative Method in Anthropology", *International Encyclopedia of the Social Sciences* 1 (New York, 1968), pp. 339-45.

The even more fundamental dichotomy between comparativists and non-comparativists which is very much in the foreground of contemporary anthropology has barely found an echo in biblical scholarship.[6] Specifically, it may be said that so far as biblical studies have been affected at all by the vigorous forays of the structuralists against the comparativists, the impact came from social scientists like Mary Douglas and E. R. Leach (following C. Lévi-Strauss) who applied to biblical literature the structuralist concepts fashioned in the science of anthropology.[7]

Analogous to what was, and to a degree still is, the practice in other areas of comparative research—history, sociology, ethnography, anthropology, folklore etc.—so too in biblical studies two main approaches can be discerned. On the one hand we encounter what Marc Bloch defines as "the comparative method on the grand scale. . . the basic postulate of this method, as well as the conclusion to which it constantly returns, is the fundamental unity of the human spirit or, if you wish, the monotony and astonishing poverty of human intellectual resources during the course of history".[8] This generalizing trend, which catalogues rather than explains the phenomena under review, entails a "loss of uniqueness and variegation", and suggests a uniformity which does not really exist in social behaviour.[9] By fastening its attention on what is or appears to be identical or similar in diverse, even widely removed societies—historically and geographically—it lumps these features together, thus providing proof for

[6] A thorough discussion of the problem is presented by A. J. F. Köbben, "Comparativists and Non-Comparativists in Anthropology", in R. Naroll and R. Cohen (ed.), *A Handbook of Method in Cultural Anthropology* (New York, 1970), pp. 581-96. Köbben notes (p. 583) that the two trends—one following the principle of "specificity" and "specification", the other that of "homogeneity"—had already been differentiated by Kant in his *Critique of Pure Reason*: "This distinction shows itself in the different manner of thought among students of nature [and of culture, S.T.], some . . . being almost averse to heterogeneousness, and always intent on the unity of genera; while others . . . are constantly driving to divide nature [or society, S.T.] into so much variety that one might lose almost all hope of being able to distribute its phenomena according to general principles".

[7] A notable exception is J. W. Rogerson, *Myth in Old Testament Interpretation*, *BZAW* 134 (Berlin, 1974), especially his analysis of "The Structural Study of Myth" (pp. 101-27). A critical survey and full bibliography of Mary Douglas's research is provided by S. R. Isenberg and D. E. Owen, "Bodies, Natural and Contrived: The Work of Mary Douglas", *Religious Studies Review* 3 (Jan. 1977), pp. 1-17. For Edmund Leach, and his critics, see p. 339, n. 28.

[8] "Two Strategies of Comparison", in A. Etzioni and F. L. Dubow (ed.), *Comparative Perspectives: Theories and Methods* (Boston, 1970), p. 41.

[9] Köbben, p. 582.

the axiomatic basic likeness of men and their societies which serves as a philosophical launching pad for the comparative method on the grand scale. At the same time, and in full consciousness, it completely loses sight of what makes cultures, societies and men ready objects for comparison, namely the peculiar and sometimes particularistic traits which one developed independently of and in distinction from others.

In the frame of Old Testament studies, this approach is represented by J. G. Frazer's classical multi-volume work *Folklore in the Old Testament* (1918) which may be considered an offspring of his even more comprehensive opus *The Golden Bough*, first published in 1890 and subsequently republished in constantly expanding editions. These works constituted the summation of scholarly endeavours in the second half of the nineteenth century and concomitantly provided the momentum for numerous less ambitious studies which issued forth from the school of social scientists whose foundations were laid by that eminent British scholar. The comparative approach "on the grand scale" in Old Testament research, as still practised by researchers who like to find resemblances between biblical stories and narrative motifs in other cultures, and in doing so lean heavily on Frazer's work, therefore received its major impetus from the outside. It echoes the emphasis laid on the method in a wide range of general disciplines, primarily but not exclusively in the social sciences, including the study of religion and literature. It tallies with the evolutionist theory which had had a pronounced impact on the sciences generally up to the first half of this century and, nearer home, on modern critical Old Testament research as well. Scholars of various disciplines who adopt this approach in their comparative endeavours meet therefore on shared philosophical premises, in spite of the diversity of their pursuits.

The comparative method on the grand scale will concede that the fundamental equality in thought processes, social organization and societal progress is more decidely an outstanding characteristic of the "primitive" stages of human development than of the structures and the philosophical horizons of "higher" societies. However, it presumes that the intrinsic unity of mankind yet manifests itself in relics from those early phases which can be identified, and then compared, in societal and conceptual moulds of more developed historical peoples, even unto modernity. Comparisons can be drawn, therefore, between any two (or more) cultures and social organisms which exhibit some similar features, though they be far-removed from one another in time and space. Given this underlying persuasion of the intrinsic equality of men and their societal structures, any extensive investigation of diverse cultures will bring to light parallels in social customs, ritual and lore in as distinct and disparate settings as those of the South American Indians and the Kings of France, the Teutons and ancient Egypt, Tiv law and British law, biblical Israel and Arab Nomads. Accords and agreements of this kind are the more readily detected the more atomistic the approach, i.e. the more pronounced the discussion of the compared phenomena in isolation from their overall cultural and civilizational context. For example, if we should consider modern by-laws against spitting on the floor in vehicles of public transport or other public places without reference to the pertinent context of contemporary *mores* and attitudes toward hygiene, they could be compared with the prohibition of spitting in the solemn assemblies of the Judean Covenanters for which a parallel can be found in Essene customary law. But to derive from this comparison a similarity in meaning in such diverse cultural contexts produces staggering and indeed nonsensical results. Bronislaw Malinowski's classic stricture, namely that "in the science of culture to tear out a custom which belongs to a certain context leads nowhere", can be enlarged to include clusters of customs or groups of phenomena which may turn up in different cultures.[10]

This criticism which in the main is aimed at the Frazer school is well taken; as will yet be made explicit, random comparison without reference to the general structure and profile of the overall scale of values and beliefs of the societies involved can only mar and distort. Seemingly identical phenomena which may occur in different cultures are often quite differently weighted in the one in comparison with the other. When dealing comparatively with separate features of social and religious life, or with single concepts, motifs and idioms, it is imperative, to view them in relation to the total phenomena of the groups involved. As Emile Durkheim observed, "Social facts [in the widest sense of the term, S.T.] are functions of the social system of which they are a part; therefore they cannot be understood when they are detached. For this reason, two facts which come from two different societies, cannot be fruitfully compared merely because they seem to resemble one another".[11]

[10] As quoted by Köbben, p. 584.
[11] *Apud* Köbben, p. 590.

Of a different scope and character is another type of comparative procedure that has become prominent in Old Testament research since the thirties of the present century in the wake of momentous developments in ancient Near Eastern archaeology which have significantly broadened the outlook of scholars with regard to those social and religious phenomena, modes of thought, literary achievements and linguistic habits distinguishing biblical culture. This comparative method has carved itself a secure niche in contemporary biblical research. Again we observe a parallelism between developments in comparative study generally and in the domain of the Old Testament. Marc Bloch defines this method as one "in which the units of comparison are societies that are geographical neighbours and historical contemporaries, constantly influenced by one another. During the historical development of such societies, they are subject to the same over-all causes, just because they are so close together in time and space. Moreover, they have, in part at least, a common origin" (loc. cit.). While the comparative method in the grand manner may be likened to general linguistics which deal with all human languages, the historically and geographically circumscribed method is closer to comparative philology which is concerned with "language groups within which signs of a common historical origin can be detected",[12] for instance the Indo-Germanic or the Semitic language families.

It would be difficult to grade the importance of geographic proximity, historical propinquity and other factors for the application of comparative analysis. However, we would tend to accept as a basic rule, *mutatis mutandis*, the scale proffered by James Barr with reference to comparative philology: sources closer to the Old Testament in time take pride of place over considerations of geographic proximity; because of the latter, though, even features observed in relatively late sources may retain traces of earlier common cultural conditions. Thus *date* appears to be more important than *place*. Within this framework, a general closer *affinity* should decide on the actual investigative procedure, i.e. the decision as to which two out of an available selection of compared features, culled from different cultural settings, are most likely to represent a common basic phenomenon. It appears that in dealing not only with linguistic issues but with a wider array of cultural traits which are to be compared, the

[12] J. Barr, *Comparative Philology and the Text of the Old Testament* (Oxford, 1968), p. 77.

maxim to be followed is M. J. Herskovits's characterization of the comparative method as pertaining to "the analysis of cultures *lying within a given historic stream*", since it takes adequately into consideration the aspects of historical and geographical proximity as well as those of cultural affinity.[13]

The historically and geographically defined method of comparison successfully removed biblical Israel from the cultural and conceptual seclusion imposed upon it by the isolationist ideology which characterizes generally the biblical, and particularly the prophetic, outlook. Careful observation, classification and interpretation of the new information which excavators made available to the historian and the sociologist, to the student of literature and of religion, disclosed an elaborate network of channels which had linked ancient Israel with the nations—and the cults and cultures of those nations—in whose proximity, indeed midst, she dwelt: from Egypt in the south, throught the Canaanite expanse on both sides of the Jordan, and on to Mesopotamia in the north-east. A synoptic view of the ever increasing information brought to light from the archives of Ugarit, Nuzu, Mari and the Hittite lands made it exceedingly clear that in the two millennia before the common era the peoples of the ancient Near East indeed lived within a "historic stream" created and maintained by the geographic-historical continuity which made possible a steady transfer and mutual emulation of civilizational and cultural achievements. The existence of propitious physical means such as a well developed network of roads which opened up the area and furthered communication in times of war and peace and the availability of a *lingua franca*, in addition to the basic linguistic affinities between the languages spoken in the region, made that part of the ancient Near East a veritable market place for the exchange of ideas in the realm of cult, culture and their literary concretizations.

Propelled by these internal developments, even more than by the momentum provided from without the discipline, Old Testament scholars proceeded to assemble a veritable host of facts which witnessed to the interweaving of Israel in that fabric of concepts, customs and social structures in which other peoples of the area were enmeshed. The rapidly growing efforts along the lines of the historico-geographical comparative method brought on a wave of publications demonstrating parallels between Israelite culture and the cultures of her

[13] *Apud* S. C. Thrupp, "Editorial", *Comparative Studies in Society and History* 1 (1958/59), p. 3.

neighbours, drawn from a multiplicity of aspects—language, literary conventions, articles of belief and of ritual, social and political organization. The sheer bulk and compass of these materials wrenched biblical Israel from the position which Old Testament ideology had ascribed to her, that of "a people dwelling alone and not reckoning itself among the (other) nations" (Num. xxiii 9).

With specific regard to the cult, this vigorous scholarly endeavour reached its peak in the "myth and ritual" school. While the question of the origin and identity of the sources of this approach in biblical studies is still under discussion, J. W. Rogerson is most probably correct in presuming that three factors played a decisive role in its evolution: "the emergence of the ritual theory of myth, the publication of certain Babylonian and Assyrian texts about the New Year Festival, and the diffusionist anthropology which apparently dominated England in the 1920's" (p. 67). S. H. Hooke and his followers who initiated the myth and ritual position construed it to prove the existence of a common Canaanite and Mesopotamian cultic pattern (also containing Babylonian elements) to which biblical Israel was a partner. In fact, they did not stop short at the discernment of a general cultic pattern, but rather widened the scope of the comparative inquiry so as to give it a more comprehensive range and to include within its frame of reference conceptual and societal phenomena which cannot be accomodated under the rubric "cult" in the restricted sense of the term. Thus it is presumed, on the basis of comparison, that the specific configurations of the myth and ritual pattern were affected by general societal phenomena and developments: the originally *agricultural* Canaanite version of the shared basic cult supposedly turns up in Israel in a typically *urban* variant, possibly influenced by the Babylonian pattern which also was urban in character.

Again, there is no need on this occasion to go into the intricacies of the issue under discussion as they have been adequately dealt with in recent publications, most extensively and profoundly by Rogerson. What is of present concern is the emergence of a "pattern of culture" school that operated under the premises worked out by the "myth and ritual" position. The method adopted by the "pattern" school for the analysis of myth—namely "to break it down into small units and to find out where these units occur and what combinations they build up"—a method whose legitimacy was defended recently by H. Ringgren, was in fact not only applied to the science of mythology whence it originated, but became the part taken as well by scholars who analysed phenomena of a completely different nature.[14] For this reason, and not simply for the application of such analysis to myths, the school came under heavy criticism from quarters that insisted on the existence of individual patterns of culture among the diverse peoples of the ancient Near East. It is somewhat difficult to concur with Ringgren in the argument that "both parties are right", because they employed the term "pattern" in different ways. While it is true that a synoptic view of the discussion discloses a discrepancy in the use of the term "pattern", the division between these schools of thought remains much more fundamental: it derives from the unbridgeable dichotomy between an "atomistic" and a "holistic" approach.

The "myth and ritual" as well as "pattern of culture" schools, which received their initial impetus from the "historical-geographical stream" method of comparison, proceeded to disclose their Frazerian philosophical underpinnings. The fundamentally non-functionalist position in fact represents a cloaked, and more scientifically acceptable, return to the comparative approach "on the grand scale". While the pattern school in the Hooke tradition is not satisfied with comparing elements alone, it views more comprehensive configurations *sub specie* "combinations", i.e. not as original self-contained units, but rather as secondary cultural constructions. In contrast, the holistic method tries first to understand a cultural configuration in its entirety. Without disregarding resemblances between constitutive elements in two different civilizations from the same "historic stream", it emphasizes the individuality and dissimilarity conferred upon these identified components by their very existence within specific organic cultural totalities. Scholars like Th. Jacobsen and H. Frankfort are much more interested in what B. Landsberger defined as the *Eigenbegrifflichkeit* of the diverse cultures, predominantly based on a religiopolitical circumscription, than in their presumed similarity or similarities. Coming from scholars whose expertise is the study of ancient Near Eastern cultures—archaeologically, historically, sociologically, linguistically and phenomenologically—this insistence on the particularity of the Hebrew culture and its dissimilarity from neighbouring cultures should serve students of the Old Testament as a guideline in their comparative studies.

---

[14] "Israel's Place among the Religions of the Ancient Near East", *SVT* 23 (1972), p. 6.

The diversity and the comprehensiveness of biblical phenomena that invite a comparison with their likenesses in other ancient Eastern cultures will not allow for a full presentation of the problems involved. Nor will it be possible to cover all the different aspects of the material which can be and indeed are submitted to comparative study and which in practice constitute, separate subdisciplines in Old Testament research. One could argue in favour of a synoptic view which conceives of these diverse aspects as one continuum and thus would submit complex rather than simple structures to comparative analysis. In the present context, however, it appears advisable to approach the matter in accord with the stratified treatment it is given in contemporary research. Again, selection is imperative. Therefore, we shall illustrate some shortcomings of the procedures often followed by comparativists, and what appear to be necessary rectifications, by examples drawn from essentially two domains of Old Testament study: 1. socio-political institutions, with some reference to matters pertaining to cult and myth; and 2) issues of a philological or literary nature—textual emendations based on external parallels; literary imagery which signifies concepts and modes of thought; literary forms or *Gattungen*.[15] The order of presentation chosen is meant to place increasingly in relief the prevalent atomizing or isolationist approach in comparative research, in contrast to the required investigation of total phenomena, i.e. of single features in relation to their cultural context and their function in more comprehensive organic structures or, with Rowton, "organic processes".[16]

II. *Socio-political Institutions*

A) *Nomadic Survivals*

In introducing this necessarily sketchy discussion of what I tend to view as an unqualified application of the comparative method to socio-historical aspects of biblical Israel, I wish to dwell shortly on the presumed presence of a "nomadic ideal" in the ancient Hebrew

[15] The ensuing presentation aims at viewing concisely, and in a more comprehensive framework, several issues which I have discussed elsewhere in greater detail. For this reason, I absolve myself from adducing here full documentation either for opinions approvingly offered of for those critically assessed.

[16] The structural approach is well-employed by M. B. Rowton in an interesting series of articles (in process) on "the role of dimorphic structure and topology in the history of Western Asia"; for a full listing see *Oriens Antiquus* 15 (1976), p. 17, n. 4.

world of ideas.[17] The issue hinges on the basic assumption of the comparative approach in the evolutionist tradition that early stages in human, and especially in societal development will reveal themselves in vestigial form in higher and later phases of the societies under review. Adopting this line of thought, K. Budde, P. Humbert and their followers discerned in the social web of Israel in the settlement period, and even in the phase of advanced urbanization under the monarchy, residues of nomadic *mores* which decisively affected Hebrew society throughout Old Testament times. Furthermore, primitive nomadic life with its simplicity and direct trust in God, unencumbered by cultic paraphernalia, showed to advantage against the background of the corrupted city society which progressively crystallized in Israel after the establishment of the monarchy. Not urban comfort and civilization, not even the agriculturist's life polluted by his unavoidable attachment to pagan fertility cults, are the ideal to which the spiritual leaders of Israel—*lege* the prophets—aspired; but rather the ascetic life style to which the Rechabites adhered, shunning all forms of settlement, whom Jeremiah assumedly extolled and held up as a socio-economic and religious paradigm for all Israel to emulate (Jer. xxxv). The Rechabites are represented, without sufficient material evidence, as the best known group to organize a return to the desert and to the nomadic ideal. This ideal supposedly transcends the confines of the Old Testament. It still appears, we are told, in the ideology of some constituent groups of postbiblical Judaism, such as the Qumran Covenanters and the Essenes with whom one tends to identify them. In fact, there are scholars who perceive the Qumran community as a late offshoot of the early, possibly pre-monarchic clan of the Rechabites, again on the basis of "similarity" and without being able to produce any evidence for the presumed historic continuity.

It must be put on record that some scholars indeed sounded a warning note. In his discussion of the "nomadic ideal", R. de Vaux exhorts us to beware of hasty comparisons "which may overlook essential differences". But having said this, he nevertheless concurs with the opinion that after having first lived as nomads or semi-nomads, when the ancient Israelites came to settle down as a nation,

---

[17] Cf. S. Talmon, "The 'Desert Motif' in the Bible and in Qumran Literature", in A. Altmann (ed.), *Biblical Motifs—Origins and Transformations* (Cambridge, Mass., 1966), pp. 31-63; *id.*, "Wilderness", *The Interpreter's Dictionary* of the Bible—*Supplementary Volume* (Nashville, 1976), pp. 946-9.

they still retained some characteristics of that earlier way of life.[18] When investigated in detail, this statement does not stand up to scrutiny. We could regard this as simply referring to an assumed internal development of the Israelite society, somewhat along the lines which determine the development of most societies in the ancient Near East, and assumedly also in other parts of the world and in other historical settings. At this juncture, however, the comparative approach on the grand scale comes into play, and the issue at hand assumes much wider proportions: since Arabs of pre-Islamic times and even of today either are full-fledged nomads or at least exhibit nomadic habits and traits, reasons de Vaux, "what we know of pre-Islamic, modern and contemporary Arab life can help us to understand more clearly the primitive organization of Israel" (p. 3; French, p. 15).

This comparability of ancient Israel and Arab society, according to some, applies not alone to social organization but also to the constitutive characteristics of the Yahwistic faith. In his *Beduinentum und Jahwismus* (Lund, 1946), S. Nystroem summarized and systematized features and parallels which some of his predecessors (e.g. J. Wellhausen, A. Causse, and M. Buber) already had pointed out. How tenuous the comparison of ancient Israelite with Arab culture is, on how slim a foundation it rests, is illustrated by the contrasting statement of I. Engnell with reference to issues of a literary character: "comparing Israelite material with relatively far-distant lands and cultures—India and Iran, for instance—actually can be more fruitful than comparing it with closer regions, such as Arabia. As a matter of fact, the latter even can be characterized as distinctly dangerous." [19] One wonders on what proved or provable evidence one view bases itself, and on what opposing evidence the other is founded. Is it not perhaps that both derive from intuitive insights and personal predilections, rather than from inquiries and investigations carried out according to appreciably objective criteria?

The issue is further complicated if one brings into account the view first expressed by W. F. Albright and C. H. Gordon that the patriarchal society exhibits characteristics of *tamkaru* life and that the fore-

[18] R. de Vaux, *Ancient Israel—Its Life and Institutions*, tr. by J. McHugh, (London, 1961), p. 12ff. = *Les Institutions de l'Ancien Testament* 1 (Paris, 1958), pp. 28ff.

[19] "Traditio—Historical Method", p. 8.

fathers of Israel could be more readily likened to "merchant princes" than to Bedouin Sheikhs. One realizes that even in the traditions about the historically hazy "Desert Period", Israel is not actually depicted as a typical desert people; so too the Bedouin characteristics discovered in the traditions pertaining to her settled life as a nation are questionable. In short, the exceeding shakiness of the "nomadic theory" and of the comparison with pre-Islamic or Islamic Arabic society is set in full relief.

Even more disturbing than the over-eager search for "similarities" to nomadic societies (with which biblical Israel is assumed to lie in the same historic stream) is the disregard for internal analysis as a means to elicit from the biblical literature itself the ancient Hebrews' concept of the ideal life. Even a cursory survey of the sources shows that nomads and desert-dwellers are abhorred and that the wilderness is conceived of as the abode of ghoulish spirits, wild beasts of prey and roaming marauders. The vast expanses of parched earth are shunned as the embodiment of all that is dangerous and evil. In contrast to this haunted world, Israel's societal ideal is portrayed in the visions of "the latter days" which are modelled in a restorative fashion on the idealized *Urzeit*, the days of the kingdom of David and Solomon when "Judah and Israel dwelt in safety, from Dan even to Beersheba, every man under his vine and under his fig tree" (1 Kings v 5).[20] A comparison of the essential features of the hoped for *Endzeit*, even of the vocabulary and imagery employed in its portrayal, with the above summary of Solomon's reign makes manifest the distortion which inheres in the attribution of a "nomadic desert ideal" to ancient Israel and to the biblical prophets. Thus Micah conceives of that blissful age: then all the nations "shall beat their swords into mattocks and their spears into pruning-knives; nation shall not lift sword against nation nor ever again be trained for war, and each man shall dwell under his vine, under his fig-tree, and no one shall frighten (them)" (Mic. iv 3-4; cp. 1 Kings v 5). The internal analysis of the Israelite conception of the ideal life produces results which are indeed different from those which ensue from the comparison with desert cultures and societies, be it on the "grand scale" or geared to the "historic stream" approach.

---

[20] See S. Talmon, "Typen der Messiaserwartung um die Zeitwende", in H. W. Wolff (ed.), *Probleme Biblischer Theologie, Gerhard von Rad zum 70. Geburtstag* (München, 1971), pp. 571-88.

B) *Democratic Institutions*

Scholarly endeavours to interpret the term *ʿam ha'areṣ* and to arrive by way of an analysis of the extant references at a satisfactory characterization of the social group or groups so designated are severely hampered by the apparent inconsistency in the employment of the term in biblical literature. The problem is compounded by the absence of any inner-biblical attempt to define the conceptual framework within which the term should be understood, beyond the mere recording of some events in history in which the *ʿam ha'areṣ* had been actively involved. This silence on principles and the lack of systematization is the rule rather than the exception and possibly reflects some basic attitudes and ancient Hebrew modes of thought, which seem to have been more empirical, fastening on concrete facts, than analytical and tending towards abstract syntheses. It is for these reasons that the suggestions offered in explanation of the term *ʿam ha'areṣ* and its content differ widely. We should go too far afield if we tried to survey the discussion of the issue in detail; such a review is not required for our present purposes and is moreover easily accessible in recent publications, of which I wish to mention three, since they seem to represent views which differ on principles of analysis and method. E. W. Nicholson, who bases himself almost exclusively on the biblical material, concludes his study of the *ʿam ha'areṣ* with the statement that "the term has no fixed and rigid meaning but is used rather in a purely general and fluid manner and varies in meaning from context to context".[21] This appears to be a counsel of despair which helps in elucidating neither the etymological meaning of the term nor, what is more important, its societal content.

In contrast, H. Tadmor and the present writer have proposed solutions to explain the entire range of usages of the term, though assuming synchronic differences and diachronic developments in its employment. However, despite accord with regard to the circumscribed diversity of meanings inherent in the term *ʿam ha'areṣ* and their diachronic variance, Tadmor and I arrive at different characterizations of the group or groups thus designated within the framework of the biblical polity. This difference arises from the diverse paths taken in the attempt to offer a solution. Tadmor addresses the issue within the wider context of the relation between " 'The People' and

[21] "The Meaning of the Expression *ʿam ha'areṣ* in the Old Testament", *JSS* 10 (1965), pp. 59-66.

the Kingship in Ancient Israel", comparing what he considers to be parallel phenomena in Ephraim and Judah.[22] He further broadens the scope of his investigation in order to compare the Hebrew term and its signification with parallel expressions in other historical and societal contexts, such as *'am ha'areṣ* in Byblos, and *niše māti* in Assyria. Adopting a much more restricted approach, I dealt with the Judean *'am ha'areṣ* exclusively in historical perspective, leaving aside, at least for the time being, any comparative considerations.[23]

The differing procedures result in quite disparate conclusions. Tadmor subtitles his essay "The Role of Political Institutions in the Biblical Period", thus revealing his intent to present the *'am ha'areṣ* and similar phenomena as constituted representatives of the populace *vis à vis* the king, i.e. institutions whose intervention in matters of the body politic apparently was regulated by mutually aknowledged rules. The references to institutions which acted on behalf of "the people" both in Ephraim and in Judah, albeit with different degrees of frequency, recur in the summarizing paragraph of the essay, culminating in the statement: "... when powerful social groups, such as army commanders, decided upon questions of state, they derived their authority from 'the people', and drew their power from the people's traditional institutions" (p. 66).

What appears to be implied in this presentation—especially by the choice of such terms as "decided upon questions of state", "derived authority", "the people", and "the people's traditional institutions"—is a situation in which the ascription of roles and the division of power between the monarchy and "the people" in ancient Israel was formally and legally regulated by what amounts to a constitution. Contrast with this view my conclusion that "Contrary to the insitutionalizing tendencies which haunt biblical research, the *'am ha'areṣ* of Judah can not be viewed as a democratic or otherwise constitutionally circumscribed institution. Rather is it a body of Judeans in Jerusalem that rose to some power and importance which was ultimately derived from their loyalty to the Davidic dynasty. The *'am ha'areṣ* in fact constitutes a sociological phenomenon that belongs to and illustrates a power structure which appears to be typical of a hereditary monarchy without clearly defined constitutional foundations. The readily given support of a group like the *'am ha'areṣ* helps in maintaining the political equilibrium by counteracting the possible eroding impact

[22] *Journal of World History* 11 (1968-9), pp. 46-68.
[23] *Fourth World Congress of Jewish Studies—Papers* 1 (Jerusalem, 1967), pp. 71-6.

of an ascending class of courtiers and ministers. Unwavering loyalty arising from kin ties balances a pragmatic allegiance rooted in vested interests" (p. 76). Again, while both authors draw attention to the sporadic nature of the intervention of the *'am ha'areṣ* (and other such groups, according to Tadmor), the manner of its going into action is differently conceived. According to Tadmor, "the people's institutions convened and acted only sporadically—when the dynastic continuity was disturbed" etc. (p. 68). Against this, I maintain that "The *'am ha'areṣ* never was formally convened or called upon by the king or some other agent", because "this body was not an institution at all, but a fairly loosely constituted power group", etc. (p. 75).

What concerns us in the present context is the divergence on principles: on the one hand there is the tendency to identify "institutions", of a more or less "democratic" character, which played an important role in the Israelite body politic. In the case of the *'am ha'areṣ* this was done most succinctly at the beginning of the century by M. Sulzberger in his book *The Am ha-aretz—The Ancient Hebrew Parliament* (Philadelphia, 1909) and was repeated some decades later by E. Auerbach who defined it as the "great national council", the democratic representation of the nation *vis-à-vis* the king. At the other end of the spectrum is the "non-institutional" explanation of the term with its application to ever-widening circles: *Landadel*, landed gentry or "lords of the land" (M. Weber, R. Kittel, A. G. Barrois, R. Gordis, S. Daiches, et al.) or even *Die Gesamtheit der Judaeischen Vollbuerger—l'ensemble des nationaux* (M. Noth and R. de Vaux).

I have presented this controversy in some detail not in order to prove, what does not really require proof, that the same biblical evidence can be interpreted quite differently by different scholars and lead to disparate conclusions. The crux of the matter lies in the method applied. The institutionalist who buttresses his arguments by comparable or assumedly comparable material from extra-biblical sources and non-Israelite political organisms never asks the fundamental question, viz. whether or not ancient Israel at all was inclined to solidify political institutions within the framework of the monarchy or before its inception. Phrased differently: does what we know from the sources at our disposal concerning the intrinsic structure of biblical society and biblical social thought recommend the suggestion that public opinion ever expressed itself in "institutionalized" forms and bodies, even of the variety found in "primitive democracies"? To answer this question adequately a deep and comprehensive analysis of biblical society is required. However, I would venture the suggestion that such an analysis will produce a negative answer. It will prove that with the exception of the institutionalized kingship and priesthood the social components of the ancient Israelite society expressed themselves and their preferences in a form of power play in which pragmatically, sometimes *ad hoc*, consolidated groups were the prime actors.

When we look at the wider sociological context, we are concerned with the correspondence that exists between diverse types of political structures and the forms in which divergent or dissenting opinions assert themselves against the established leadership. In every instance, this or the other particular element will have to be judged and defined not in isolation, but with a view to its functional relation to the totality of the social phenomena, and especially against the background of the "deep" principles of the societal structure. Old Testament scholars will be well advised to pay heed to the criticism levelled by E. Leach against ethnographers and anthropologists who approached their own materials in a similarly "atomistic" fashion: "The classical comparative method, the diffusionist reconstructions of the cultural historians, and the various styles in cross-cultural statistical analysis all rested on the proposition that 'a culture' ('a society', etc.) is to be conceived of as an assemblage of traits which can be separately compared. Functionalist social anthropology rejects this view. Societies are systems which can be compared only as wholes" (p. 343).

The same considerations apply to another controversy of the "institution versus non-institution" category. In discussing the internal historical events which occurred in Israel after the death of Solomon, A. Malamat attempted to show that, when challenged by the people to reduce the burden of taxes that Solomon had imposed upon them, Solomon's son and successor to the throne, Rehoboam, put the matter to a council which represented the people opposite the king. Rehoboam, in fact, took counsel with two bodies. One, constituted of the "elders" (*zeqenim*), is often referred to in biblical literature, and therefore well known. The other, that of the "young men" (*yeladim*), is never mentioned apart from the events described in 1 Kings xii 1-17. Discarding other possibilities with regard to the composition and nature of this group, the author arrives at the conclusion "that the assemblies of elders and 'young men' of Rehoboam are not mere spontaneous gatherings of the populace; but they constitute rather formal bodies of official standing in the kingdom" (p. 250).[24] He then goes on to compare this official "bicameral" Israelite assembly with a parallel institution which emerges from the Sumerian "Gilgamesh and Agga" epic, equating the Hebrew *zeqenim* with the Sumerian *abba uru*, "elders of the city", and the *yeladim* with their assumed Sumerian counterpart *guruš*, "council of men". Both bicameral bodies are evidence of a "political system which has been aptly named 'primitive democracy' by Thorkild Jacobsen. This form of government rested on *representative institutions* [my italics, S.T.] which functioned alongside of the central powers" (p. 250). Without overlooking "the different circumstances in Sumer and Israel and the individual character of each of the sources", Malamat nevertheless insists that "both of the examples are similar from a typological point of view" and therefore it is of minor importance whether the Sumerian assembly of *guruš* and the Israelite council of the *yeladim* "differed in their very essence and subsequently in their respective functions" (p. 252).

In his criticism of Malamat's thesis, D. G. Evans draws attention to "the difficulties which confront us in discussing political bodies (and indeed others) in the ancient Near East. Not only does the slenderness of the evidence oblige us to make the most of it to a dangerous extent, but it increases the risk, which is always present in studies of the remote past, of importing into our sources modern constitutional ideas and practices which have no place in them".[25] He then analyses the biblical tradition in detail, as Malamat had done. However, his reading of the sources leads to the statement that "To conclude that the *zᵉqēnīm* and *yᵉlādīm* at Shechem were political bodies of official standing in the kingdom seems to me more than the evidence will support", since neither of the councils at Shechem, if indeed there were two and not one, enjoyed sovereignty but at most acted in an advisory fashion. Decisions were taken and put into practice by the people's assembly or the king. Although in the biblical tradition the term *zeqenim* often indicates a group of men that has a specific standing in the body politic, in the instance under review it

[24] "Kingship and Council in Israel and Sumer: A Parallel", *JNES* 22 (1963), pp. 247-53.

[25] "Rehoboam's Advisers at Shechem, and Political Institutions in Israel and Sumer", *JNES* 25 (1966), pp. 273-9.

would appear that the word is not be understood in this technical sense. The opposition to *yeladim*, which is never employed as a socio-political term, rather suggests a contrast which is purely internal to the story; the reasons for Rehoboam's preference of one group over the other should be sought in the "generation gap" which existed between men who belonged to the father's generation, on the one hand, and to the son's, on the other.

It appears that in this case too the comparison of two literary units with some, albeit quite disparate, socio-political import, discussed in isolation from the intristic structures of the two societies involved, results in an identification of formal political institutions in Israel of the monarchic period which lacks proper foundation. The present writer would certainly opt for a non-institutional explanation.

C) *Divine Kingship*

Our final example pertaining to the socio-political dimension concerns the position of the king in the Israelite body politic. There is a widespread tendency among students of the Old Testament and the ancient Near East to discern in the biblical literature a concept of monarchy which invests the king with the status of divinity or at least accords him aspects of sanctity which elevate him above the position of a mere human being. This idea seems to derive from an over-simplified literary interpretation of idioms and expressions which extol the greatness of kings in terms culled from the realm of the divine. The comparison of such terminology, as well as the conceptual modes to which these idioms assumedly give expression, with parallels found in ancient Near Eastern literatures leads scholars to perceive an identical notion of divine kingship in the biblical world of ideas. The impact of the "pattern" school comes into full relief in the "divine kingship" theory, precisely because the phenomenon combines fundamental features of "myth and ritual" with wider aspects of a "pattern of culture". The "divine kingship" theory demonstrates a fusion between two quite diverse aspects of Israelite culture: the world of myth and cult as an expression of ancient Near Eastern religiosity coalesces here with the political and social dimension in which tangible history expresses itself. It is most likely this facet of comparative biblical studies that led to the application of structural analysis, which was initially applied exclusively to non-historical phenomena, also to the interpretation of biblical historical events and situations. In the biblical studies mentioned above, the anthropologist Edmund Leach took his departure from the Genesis stories considered as myth.[26] This attempt was regarded by professional Bible scholars with tolerance, equanimity or a mild lack of interest. Subsequently, though, Leach transferred his attention to the historical books of Samuel and Kings in the endeavour to lay bare "Some Structural Aspects of Old Testament History" in the traditions about Solomon's succession to the throne of David.[27] He claims to discern in these historical traditions structural patterns of a general character which usually are applicable to mythical lore. While acknowledging the challenge which issues forth from Leach's studies for a reconsideration of the traditional work on biblical materials, professional Bible scholars have been very reluctant to endorse the indiscriminate application of myth-oriented structural analysis to reports of actual historical events.[28]

Let me turn now to a critical review of the established "divine kingship" theory, and its inherent "patternism", through an examination of the meaning which adheres to the act of "anointing" the king.[29] The practice of anointing the ruler was well established in ancient Near Eastern societies but in Israel obviously was an innovation of the monarchic regime. It is never mentioned in the preceding period of the Judges or "Saviours", nor in the days of Joshua, Moses or the Patriarchs. Anointing, however, was known to the Hebrews from the context of the cult. Not only were cultic implements anointed, thus to confer upon them a degree of sacredness (Gen. xxxi 13; Ex. xxx 26, xl 9-11; Num. vii 1, 10, 84, 88), but also the special standing of certain cultic functionaries and other persons of renown was symbolized by the pouring of oil on their heads. There is one biblical report about anointing a prophet, as Elisha is thus appointed by Elijah to become his successor (1 Kings xix 16). It is of interest to observe that this act is juxtaposed with Elijah's being commanded concurrently to anoint Jehu ben Nimshi king over Israel. This very conjunction of prophet

[26] *Genesis as Myth and Other Essays* (London, 1969), pp. 7-23.

[27] pp. 25-83.

[28] See especially the aforementioned discussion by Rogerson, (n. 7); critical studies by A. Malamat, M. Pamment, and R. C. Culley are reviewed in J. A. Emerton's treatment of the issue in "An Examination of a Recent Structuralist Interpretation of Genesis XXXVIII", *VT* 26 (1976), pp. 79-98.

[29] See S. Talmon, "Kingship and the Ideology of the State", *The World History of the Jewish People—The Age of the Monarchies* (Jerusalem, 1977), part 2, pp. 3-26 (forthcoming). For a comprehensive survey of the issue, cf. E. Kutsch, *Salbung als Rechtsakt*, *BZAW* 87 (1963).

and king with reference to anointing can also be found in Ps. cv 15: *ʾl tgʿw bmšyḥy wlnbyʾy ʾl trʿw*, and in 1 Chron. xxix 22 with reference to Solomon and Zadok the priest.

Anointing was especially practised with regard to the High Priest (Ex. xxviii 41, xix 7, 36, xl 13-15; Lev. viii 10, 12; Num. iii 3, xxx 25, et al.), who therefore could be designated *hkhn hmšyḥ* (Lev. iv 3, 5, 16, vi 15).

Explicit references to the anointing of kings are found in the Bible only in certain instances: David (1 Sam. ii 4, v 3; Ps. lxxxix 21), Solomon (1 Kings i 39), Jehu (2 Kings ix 1ff.), Joash (ib. xi 12). Accordingly opinions are divided as to whether anointing was an indispensable feature of the rites of enthronement or was applied only when special circumstances, such as an interruption of normal dynastic succession, required a renewed affirmation of the king's assumedly sacral status. Without attempting here to arrive at a definite conclusion it may nevertheless be said that the familiar term *mšḥ lmlk* in the meaning of "to enthrone" (Jud. ix 8, 15; 2 Sam. ii 4; 1 Kings xix 15, et al.) and the recurring designation of kings as *mšyḥ yhwh* (1 Sam. xxiv 6, 16, xxvi 9, 11, 16, 23, et al.) seem to suggest that every king (in Judah and in Ephraim) was anointed, even when our sources are silent about the fact. The dimension of sacredness which adheres to the act of "anointing" with "holy oil" (*šmn hqdš*), which was kept at first in the Tabernacle (Ex. xxv 6, xxxvii 29; Lev. viii 2) and subsequently in the Temple (1 Kings i 39), makes it natural that the rite was performed by a priest (1 Kings i 39) or by a prophet (1 Sam. x 1ff., cp. ix 16; xvi 12-13; 2 Kings ix 6ff., cp. 1 Kings xix 15-16) on divine command. What calls for some explanation, however, is the fact that the rite of anointing the king is sometimes reported to have been executed by the "people" or possibly by the people's representative(s). According to 1 Chron. xxix 20-22 "they (i.e. the assembly of all Israel)... appointed Solomon, David's son... and *anointed him* as the Lord's prince, and Zadok as priest".

In a similar instance concerning the coronation of Joash the son of Ahaziah, king of Judah, 2 Kings reports that "they (either the people or the temple-guards) made him king, and *anointed him*, and they (LXX + the people) clapped their hands, and shouted 'Long live the King'" (2 Kings xi 12), whereas the parallel version in 2 Chron. xxiii 11 reads "Jehoiada (the priest) and his sons anointed him". Again we are told in 2 Kings xxiii 30 that "the *ʿam haʾareṣ* took Jehoahaz the son of Josiah, and they anointed him, and made him king in his father's stead". Lastly, in 2 Sam. xix 11, the people propose to rally around David after Absalom's death had brought an end to his rebellion, since "Absalom whom *we anointed over us* died in war". These references seem to imply that while "anointing" indeed was considered a sacral ritual act, which by definition must be carried out by a prophet or a priest, it more decisively bore sociopolitical significance. Even though conceptually the act of anointing conferred the immunity of sanctification upon the king, in actuality the rite gave concrete expression to the king's dependence on the people (and/or the priest and the prophet as the representatives of the divine sphere). In historical reality, the ritual of anointing was a ceremonial manifestation of the checks and balances which inhered in the Israelite monarchy. Through the granting or withholding of anointing, either of the above-mentioned agents—people or prophet/priest—could effect an important measure of control over the ruler.

When Israelite kingship is viewed in the context of biblical social institutions, and against the background of preceding forms of government, instead of being defined predominantly by means of assumed similarities which comparative research discovers in other ancient Near Eastern societies, the basic singularity of the biblical concept of the monarchy is accentuated. Contrary to widespread scholarly opinion, the presumedly sacral-ritual act of anointing did not enhance the Israelite king's status and power but rather circumscribed it. He was, in fact, more vulnerable than the earlier non-monarchical rulers. Before the establishment of the monarchy, a leader of the people—like the Judge, who was divinely inspired but not anointed—was never deposed once he had been established in office, even if he was found to be failing. Neither the mission of Samson, who angered his parents by marrying a Philistine woman (Judg. xiv 3; cp. Gen. xxvi 34-35, xxvii 46), nor that of Gideon, who by erecting the Ephod in Ophra sinned and caused others to transgress (Judg. viii 27), was terminated before it had run its course. As the first king, however, Saul is also the first appointed leader of Israel to be dethroned by the prophet who had anointed him (1 Sam. xiii 13-14, xv 26-28). Because Solomon sinned by marrying foreign wives (like Samson), and set up objectionable cultic places (like Gideon), the rule over ten tribes was divested from his dynasty (1 Kings xi 1-13) and assigned to Jeroboam ben Nebat (*vv.* 29-39). Ahab's transgressions caused his son to be deprived of the throne, and Jehu ben Nimshi was made king over Ephraim (2 Kings ix).

The very possibility that the rule of a king could be terminated *de iure*, and not only *de facto* in the wake of rebellions, strongly suggests that kingship was not considered sacrosanct and that the king himself was not believed to have acquired such status. The very possibility that a king's mission could be revoked—whether by God's emissary, a prophet (as in the case of Saul, Solomon and Ahab) or by the people (as in the case of Rehoboam)—evidences a concept according to which kingship was firmly confined within the human sphere.

A functional analysis of biblical traditions about the monarchic period, undertaken in cognizance of the traditions which portray the pre-monarchic times, proves that biblical idioms, imagery and motifs which appear to disclose an underlying conception of the Israelite king as being imbued with "divinity" are mere figures of speech, a *façon à parler*, which were adopted into the Hebrew vocabulary after having lost their original mytho-cultic significance. The apparent similarity with ancient Near Eastern royal terminology is external and should not be construed to indicate the existence of a shared cultural pattern of cultic "divine kingship". In his discussion of the supposed divinity of the Israelite kings, H. Frankfort succinctly makes the point: "Much is made nowadays of Canaanite and other Near Eastern elements in Hebrew culture, and a phenomenon like Solomon's kingship conforms indeed to the type of glorified native chieftainship which we have characterized... But it should be plain that the borrowed features in Hebrew culture, and those which have foreign analogies, *are least significant*. In the case of kingship they are externalities, the less important since they did not affect the *basic oddness* of the Hebrew institution" [my italics, S.T.].[30]

In concluding this part of the discussion, I wish to stress again that my present interest does not lie in the assessment of the accuracy of this or another specific theory, but rather in illustrating the assertion that in dealing with fundamental issues concerning the social and religious history of biblical Israel, scholars often revert to a comparison with external "parallels" without the prerequisite definition of a methodology of procedure and before examining the phenomena under consideration in their inner-biblical context.

One cannot but concur with the strictures Ringgren has voiced concerning this approach: "Comparative research in the Biblical

[30] *Kingship and the Gods* (Chicago, 1948), p. 339.

field has often become a kind of 'parallel hunting'. Once it has been established that a certain biblical expression or custom has a parallel outside the Bible, the whole problem is regarded as solved. It is not asked, whether or not the extra-Biblical element has the same place in life, the same function in the context of its own culture. The first question that should be asked in comparative research is that of the *Sitz im Leben* and the meaning of the extra-Biblical parallel adduced. It is not until this has been established that the parallel can be utilized to elucidate a Biblical fact" (p. 1).

III. *Philological and Literary Aspects*

A) *Comparative Philology* and Textual Emendation

Probably the most spectacular development in comparative biblical studies can be observed in the domain of "language" in the widest sense of the term. One takes note that in linguistics the endeavour to define exact rules for scholarly investigation has borne more fruit than in other areas. According to J. Barr, comparative linguistics concern "the comparative study of language groups within which signs of a common historical origin can be detected" and which can be fitted into "an historical common scheme" (loc. cit.) In the explanation of linguistic facts, the historical analysis is supplemented by a synchronic or structural examination of the material at hand from a "holistic" point of view, rather than in the "atomistic" fashion.[31] While in actual practice these guidelines are not always followed, it nevertheless can be said that linguistic scholarship has been placed on firmer theoretical ground than other fields of biblical research. The closer the affinity of one language to another, in structure and other basic features which point to a common historic origin, the wider the scope for the comparison of their respective vocabularies. Comparative philology can help in the explanation of *hapax legomena* or rare words and idioms in one language, which in a sister language are more widely used and better understood. Comparativists can point to impressive achievements in the interpretation of some difficult biblical texts, predominantly, though not exclusively, through the utilization of Ugaritic material. However, alongide with the salutary effect it has exercised, the Ugaritic-biblical comparative research increasingly has laid itself open to severe criticism.

---

[31] See M. H. Goshen-Gottstein, "Linguistic Structure and Tradition in the Qumran Documents", *Scripta Hierosolymitana* 4 (Jerusalem, 1958), pp. 101-37.

The more scholars engage in the search for parallels, the more "atomistic" the approach; personal inspiration often takes the place of systematic investigation, and impressionistic *déja vu* insights substitute for the required procedural principles. The results are a mixed blessing. Together with many "good figs", to use Jeremiah's simile, scholars, and more critically, students are fed from an ever growing bag of "bad figs". Handled with care and the necessary restraint, the collecting of Ras Shamra Parallels [32] can be, and indeed often is, illuminating. But when imagination is given free reign, the resulting "parallelomania" gives Old Testament studies a bad name and puts in question the reliability of biblical lexicography and comparative research generally. To be sure, it would be futile and counterproductive to advocate a radical purism which would abstain altogether from the application of the comparative method to biblical literature, as a result of some doubtful hypotheses and questionable textual emendations. What is to be demanded is that attention be paid to a given set of rules of which one shall be mentioned at this juncture: the solution of a crux in the biblical text should be attempted first and foremost, by reverting to the immediate context and to synonymous expressions in similar contexts, with direct and "distant parallelism" holding out special promise for the elucidation of opaque or obscure expressions. Comparison with extra-biblical material should be brought into play only when a properly executed inner-biblical analysis does not produce satisfactory results. Even then it would be wise to pay heed to the warning sounded by Y. Muffs, namely that "only after new meanings emerge naturally from the context of one language should comparative material be brought into the picture".[33]

The comparison of biblical literature with Ugaritic writings presents a particular problem. The similarity of the two languages and the obvious contacts Hebrew cultures had with Ugaritic/Canaanite culture—both lying within a single "historic stream"—have caused scholars to consider the two literatures to be of one cloth. Thus H. L. Ginsberg opined that "from the philological point of view... the Hebrew Bible and the Ugarit texts are to be regarded as one literature, and consequently a reading in either may be emended with

---

[32] L. R. Fisher (ed.), *Ras Shamra Parallels*, 1-2 (Rome, 1972-1977).

[33] "Two Comparative Lexical Studies", *The Gaster Festschrift*, *JANES* 5 (1973), p. 296.

the aid of a parallel passage in the other".[34] However, one wonders whether this sweeping statement can pass unchallenged. Methodological considerations and some comparative techniques which resulted from this dictum would have one judge the situation less sanguinely. Two literatures, such as the biblical and the Ugaritic, which emanated from different cultures, akin as they may be, can never be identified so unreservedly lest we be prone to consider the Semitic cultures to exhibit "the monotony and astonishing poverty of human intellectual resources" which the old-style comparative method on the grand scale took as a fundamental postulate. Paraphrasing a statement by A. L. Kroeber,[35] I would say that in comparative studies generally our concern is and should be with differences as much as with likenesses. The particularity of Hebrew literature on the one hand, and of Ugaritic writings on the other, must not be blurred so as to facilitate and legitimize their being judged as one cultural whole. In his aforementioned essay, Y. Muffs quotes one instance, the explanation of the common word *ʿoz* in Eccl. viii 1, for which H. L. Ginsberg proposed a novel interpretation, namely "anger", by working out the meaning innerbiblically and relating it subsequently to Akkadian *ezzu*, "anger, wrath". Here Ginsberg followed the recommended procedure. However, in other cases, predominantly where assumed Ugaritic parallels are involved, because of the posited "identity" of Hebrew and Ugaritic literature, one sometimes observes a significant departure from this rule. Occasionally Ginsberg will emend a difficult biblical text on the ground of a Ugaritic parallel, without attempting first to solve the problem inner-biblically.[36] Unfortunately, lesser luminaries in the field of comparative Semitic philology are prone to emulate his technique with less than satisfactory results. A case in point is Ginsberg's famous and widely acclaimed emendation of the puzzling ending of one line in David's lament over Saul and Jonathan: *hry bglbʿ ʾl ṭl wʾl mṭr ʿlykm wśdy trwmṭ* (2 Sam. i 21).

Numerous proposals had been put forward for the restoration of the assumed original reading underlying the awkward expression *wśdy trwmt* which does not make sense in the context, some utilizing the ancient versions, others resorting to conjectures. None was

[34] "The Ugaritic Texts and Textual Criticism", *JBL* 62 (1943), pp. 109ff.

[35] *Apud* Köbben, p. 590.

[36] See S. Talmon, "On the Emendation of Biblical Texts on the Basis of Ugaritic Parallels", *Ginsberg Volume*, *Eretz-Israel* 12 (Jerusalem, 1978), pp. 117-24 (Hebrew).

convincing enough to gain general support. By contrast, there was an almost immediate acceptance of Ginsberg's suggestion to read *šrʿ thmt*—"waters of the abyss"—derived from a line in the Dan'el epic which appeared to be the exact equivalent of the above Hebrew phrase, being set in a functionally identical context: *bl ṭl bl rbb bl šrʿ thmtm* (CTA 19 = 1 Aqht 1.44). Despite reservations subsequently entertained by critics, this emendation of a biblical crux by means of a Ugaritic parallel is still recognized as a classic.

However, the rare attestation of *šrʿ* in the Ugaritic vocabulary where it may well be a *hapax legomenon*, which moreover has no counterpart in the Hebrew Bible, detracts from the appeal of the proposed emendation. There also arose some doubts concerning the correct reading of the passage in the Dan'el epic.

The "waters of the abyss" hardly constitute a proper parallel to "dew" and "rain". In biblical, as in Ugaritic imagery, the "abysmal floods" always carry a negative not a positive connotation, such as is required in the context under review. For all these reasons it seems preferable to conceive of *śdy trwmt* as a parallel to *hry bglbʿ*, both referring to "heights" or mountains on which men are killed in battle. This is a *Leitmotif* in David's elegy which is often employed in other biblical descriptions of wars. A similar idiom is present in the Song of Deborah which exhibits striking affinities with David's lament with respect to genre, function and setting. There, the tribes of Zebulun and Naftali are extolled by the singer for having "risked their very lives... on the heights of the battlefield" (Judg. v 18; NEB). The crucial Hebrew expression is *ʿl mrwmy śdh*. On the strength of this phrase, it seems plausible to suggest that *wśdy trwmt* in 2 Sam. i 21 is a synonymous idiom in which the sequence of components has been inverted. It should be understood as *(w)trwmt śdh*, with *trwmh-trwmt* being derived from *rwm-rmh* as a byform of *mrwm-mrwmym*, denoting here "height", and not "offering" or "contribution" which is its prevalent connotation in biblical Hebrew. *Śdh*, probably identical with Akk. *Šadu*, here as in many other biblical passages, is equivalent to *hr*—mountain.

Another variant of *mrwm-trwmh* in combination with *śdh/hr* turns up in Lam. iv 9 in a literary and situational context which is almost identical with that in which David's lament is set. There we encounter the expression *mtnwbt śdy* in relation to Jerusalemites or Judahites slain in battle. Translations of the crucial passage—*šhm yzwbw mdqrym mtnwbt śdy*—such as "for these pine away, stricken through, for want of the fruits of the field" (RSV), or "these wasted away, deprived of the produce of the field" (NEB) make no sense in the context. The meaning of the stich must be determined by the parallel in the first half of the verse which has been correctly rendered: "They that be slain with the sword are better than they that be slain with hunger" (RSV), or "Those who died by the sword were more fortunate than those who died of hunger" (NEB). It appears obvious to translate the second line accordingly: "for they shed their (blood), speared on the height of the mountains". I suggest that *mtnwbt* resulted from a misreading of *mtrwmt*, still extant in 2 Sam. i 21. Therefore, the latter verse is not to be translated "Ye mountains of Gilboa, let there be no dew or rain upon you, neither fields of offering" (RSV); nor, following Ginsberg's emendation, "Hills of Gilboa, let no dew or rain fall on you, no showers on the uplands" (NEB); but rather, assuming an elliptic-chiastic parallelism, "Hills of Gilboa, no dew and no rain upon you, mountain heights".

I wish again to emphasize that the analysis presented here is not intended merely to prove or disprove the validity of an emendation suggested on the ground of a presumed external parallel. Rather, it is meant to illustrate the need for a definition of the proper procedure to be followed in the comparative philological study of biblical texts and to adduce proof for the maxim that the inner-biblical analysis always should precede the comparison with extra-biblical texts.

B) *Literary Imagery*

As has already been stated, biblical thinking seldom if ever expresses itself in a conceptual system. The Hebrews' ideas and concepts rather can be gauged from events narrated and from the narrators' attitudes which can be elicited, to a degree, from an analysis of the text. Recurring idioms, phrases and imagery are of considerable help in the discernment of matters and reflections with which the writers' minds were preoccupied; they constitute a form of capsule descriptions which substitute for the detailed presentation of intricate thought processes. On the cognitive level literary images can be employed as concretizations of abstract notions and thus facilitate the transmission of ideas, e.g. in the realm of myth and religious thought. In view of these remarks, it can cause no surprise that literary imagery is a ready object for comparative research (both on the grand scale, and in the "historic stream" manner) often in detachment from the immediate literary or cultural context. In some instances, such research comes into contact with comparative linguistics or philology; indeed the method has special appeal when treating texts or expressions whose connotation cannot be established with the help of the biblical lexicon or through etymology.

A case in point is the speculation about cosmogony and the conception of the world which hinges on the mythic-existential notion of the center of the world, as captured in the idea and the image of the *omphalos*.[37] Essentially the term and the imagery which it signifies point to a representation of the world in the form of a human body. Its centre is marked by a tall mountain representing its navel from which issues forth an imaginary umbilical cord, the *vinculum*, which links our world with the higher spheres, the world of the gods, just as the embryo is bound to his mother's body by the navel cord. W. Roscher, the innovator of modern *omphalos* research, proved the widespread existence of this idea in the classical world and showed that the principal sanctuaries of ancient Greece—Delos, Epidaurus, Paphos, Branchides, Miletus and Delphi—were each considered by their respective adherents to be at the centre of the earth, i.e. to constitute its navel. Roscher further demonstrated that the image of an imposing mountain as the center of the earth was already current among the nations of the ancient Near East. His hypothesis was developed by Wensinck who assembled impressive evidence that the *omphalos* idea persisted in post-classical Greek thought as well as in Jewish-Hellenistic and rabbinic sources.

The term *omphalos* twice appears in the Septuagint as the translation of the Hebrew term *ṭabbūr hā'āreṣ*. One of these occurs in Judg. ix 37 in the Abimelech story and is there connected, in one way or another, with the area of Shechem; the other mention is set in Ezekiel's vision of the onslaught of Gog on the People of Israel who have been gathered into their land (Ez. xxxiii 10-12). *Ṭabbūr* thus far has evaded precise etymological determination, nor can its biblical connotation be definitively established. That the LXX and the Vulgate (*umbilicus terrae*) reflect an understanding of *ṭabbūr* as "navel", in perfect accord with its meaning in mishnaic Hebrew, is beyond doubt. However, it remains open to discussion whether the existence of the pre-or extra-biblical "navel of the earth" mythic concept in the ancient Near East as well as the post-biblical notion of a "centre of the

[37] See S. Talmon, "The 'Navel of the Earth' and the Comparative Method", *Scripture in History and Theology, J. Coert Rylaarsdam Jubilee Volume* (Twin Cities, 1977), pp. 243-68.

world" designated *ṭabbūr-ṭibbūr* or *omphalos* indeed are decisive proof for the presence of that very same concept in the biblical world-view. The paucity of the evidence for the assumed existence of a biblical *omphalos* concept—two solitary mentions of the unexplained term *ṭabbūr hā'āreṣ*,—appears to neutralize its import, when compared with the prevalence of the concept in other, both earlier and later, cultures. Furthermore, the absence in the above-mentioned biblical passages of any reference to a sanctuary, a feature which is integral to the classical Greek as well as the most significant ancient Near Eastern examples of the "navel of the earth" myth, surely constitutes negative evidence. This deficiency, however, is "remedied" by postulating that since the events related in the Judges passage take place in the vicinity of Shechem and reference is made to "the tops of the mountains" (Judg. ix 36), the mention of *ṭabbūr hā'āreṣ* certainly must pertain to holy Mount Gerizim on the top of which the Samaritan temple stood during later periods. Likewise, one construes the recurrent mention of *hārē yiśrā'ēl* in Ezekiel's Gog of Magog vision (Ez. xxxviii-xxxix) as synonymous with Jerusalem. Thus *ṭabbūr hā'āreṣ* in that context is understood as an attribute of the holy city and her sanctuary.

Despite the frailty of this argumentation, Old Testament scholars have endorsed the identification of biblical *ṭabbūr hā'āreṣ* as "navel of the earth" on the basis of the above parallels. In this they were joined by phenomenologists, who now could add ancient Israelite culture to the group of cultures in which the *omphalos* myth was present, thus buttressing the proposition that the idea of a cosmic center was a universal component of the human conception of the world. Furthermore, some patternists attempted to elicit from the biblical sources evidence for the former existence of an Israelite *omphalos* myth. By infusing an abundancy of imagination into the comparative procedures, the *omphalos* myth was placed at the very center of Israelite religion, nay was made the "navel" of her conceptual world. S. Terrien's paper "The Omphalos Myth and Hebrew Religion", *VT* 20 (1970), pp. 315-38, serves as an example of the snowballing effect of this search for similarities by which distinct civilizations can be forced into one "pattern of cult" and "culture".

The contemplation of the *ṭabbūr hā'āreṣ* issue in the context of and in relation to the bases of the ancient Hebrew religion, instead of or even concomitant with its review in the comparative manner, should have convinced scholars of the improbability that the Mesopotamian, Jebusite or Canaanite mythic principle of the *omphalos* could have served as a pillar of ancient Israel's spiritual world. While vestiges of pagan beliefs certainly filtered into the popular cult and religion, it is far-fetched to assume that they were emulated by authoritative biblical authors, like the prophet Ezekiel. Terrien's insistence that "In all probability, the myth of the navel of the earth, far from being an incidental aspect of worship at the temple of Jerusalem, constitutes in effect the determining factor which links together a number of its cultic practices and beliefs that otherwise appear to be unrelated" (p. 317) appears baseless if one bears in mind the fragility and questionability of the evidence on which this claim rests. Indeed the treatment of the issue by the comparativists fully bears out the critical description and evaluation of their procedures by E. Leach: "The practitioners displayed a prodigious range of erudition in that they were familiar with an extraordinary variety of ethnographic facts. . . the ethnographic evidence was always used to exemplify general propositions with the implication that such propositions are validated by an accumulation of positive evidence. Neutral or negative evidence was never considered" ("The Comparative Method", p. 342).

From this discussion emerges a very simple, but fundamental rule which should be observed in the study of biblical texts and their conceptual import: when linguistic aspects provide but unclear and difficult hints toward the explanation of textual cruxes one should not depend on the forced testimony of assumed external parallels, ferreted out by the comparative method. Rather, the elucidation of difficult terms and ideas must be achieved from the biblical books themselves, since they are the only reliable first-hand evidence which mirrors, albeit fragmentarily, the conceptual horizon of ancient Israel and the linguistic and literary modes in which it found its expression. For this reason, internal parallels are of greater help than external ones; their identification can be achieved in a more systematic fashion than the pinpointing of similarities in extra-biblical sources. It appears to be quite appropriate at this juncture to bring forward the exegetical principle formulated by E. J. Kissane which has lost nothing of its force but, alas, often is lost sight of by Old Testament exegetes: "The context is the guide to interpretation, and disregard of the context leads to chaos" (Engnell, p. 5).

In the case under review, the significance of the rare expression *ṭabbūr hā'āreṣ*, the application of this procedure produces results which are quite different from the thesis put forward by the comparativists. A contextual analysis of the Ezekiel passage, and to a lesser degree of obviousness of the relevant passage in the Book of Judges, makes it evident that in both occurrences the term *ṭabbūr hā'āreṣ* has no mythic implications whatsoever, but rather describes an open place of settlement—*'ereṣ perāzōt*—where people live peacefully, assured of their safety without the need of fortifications and ramparts. This idea is clearly the tenor of Ezekiel's oracle about Gog. It sounds a warning to the enemy of his imminent fall and gives assurance to the people of Israel who have returned to their homeland to live there in tranquility. The *Leitmotif* of the oracle is "dwell in security", reiterated in a series of expressions one of which is "dwell on the *ṭabbūr hā'āreṣ*". The equation of *ṭabbūr hā'āreṣ* with "secure place", as the most tangible historico-geographical meaning which can be elicited from a close reading of the Ezekiel passage, is applicable also to the reference in the Abimelech tradition. It can be buttressed by a comparison of the situation described in the Gog oracle with similar descriptions of inimical onslaughts on a peaceful population. The most noteworthy example is found in Jud. xviii 7, 27-28 which depicts the attack of the Danites on the people of Laish. There phrases are employed which are synonymous with those used in the Gog oracle:

> "they dwell in security . . . quiet and safe . . . and quarrel with no one . . . (living) in a wide open land . . . in the valley next to (the city of) Bet Rehob" (cp. further 1 Chron. iv 40; Jer. xxxix 31-32; et al.)

In summary, the elucidation of the twice used term *ṭabbūr hā'āreṣ* by means of a contextual analysis and an inner-biblical comparison with synonymous expressions in functionally similar settings suggests that no mythic element whatsoever adheres to the term. There is no need or justification to saddle it with a mystic import by means of eisegesis based on the comparative method in the "pattern of cult" tradition.

C) *Literary Gattungen*

I turn now to the problem of the comparability of biblical literary forms or *Gattungen*. Once more our interest will focus on Ugaritic literature because of the proven similarity of its structures, imagery and phraseology with those found in biblical writings. Before presenting a specific example, it may be useful to make a preliminary remark: *per definitionem*, a literary *Gattung* has a specific *Sitz im Leben*, i.e. a well-circumscribed anchorage in the cultic and cultural structure of the society which produced it; it is the formalized literary expression of ideas, social concepts and cultic values which that society fostered. Therefore, the identification of a *Gattung* evidenced in the literature of one society also in the creative writings of another requires the additional proof that in both it had the same *Sitz im Leben*. This means that a comparative study of *Gattungen* must take into account the social context in which specific literary types and forms arise. What must be shown is that this *Gattung* and what it expresses indeed finds its place in the cultic and conceptual framework of both societies. A *Gattung* cannot be contemplated in isolation from the overall socio-cultural web of a society.

Our present concern will be with the application of these thoughts to the question whether there ever existed on Israelite national epic.[38] There can be no doubt that we have no evidence of an epos in biblical literature. U. Cassuto, to whose discussion of the question we shall return, states quite unequivocally that neither the epic nor the epic song proper is found in the biblical books. This statement will achieve common consent, unless one were to maintain that the Hebrew Bible in its entirety constitutes the national epic of the ancient Hebrews. There remains, though, the consideration of the *Vorgeschichte* of the present canon of biblical writings. It is correctly assumed that, in the stages before its crystallization in the form of books, Hebrew literature was current as only loosely connected, preponderantly oral traditions. It is within these earlier, no longer extant stages of this literature that the search for lost epic cycles has been conducted. Scholars concentrated their attention on the supposedly tangible remnants of and references to epic songs submerged in the present prose texts, especially the obscure *spr mlḥmt yhwh* (Num. xxi 14, with a barely intelligible quotation from that work), and the twice mentioned *spr hyšr* (Josh. x 13: 2 Sam. i 18, again with quotations).[39] With the exception of Tur-Sinai who took *spr* to mean "oral transmission" or "recitation" of God's mighty deeds,[40]

[38] See S. Talmon, "Did There Exist a Biblical National Epic?", Proceedings of the *Seventh World Congress of Jewish Studies*, (Jerusalem, 1977) [forthcoming].

[39] The proposed retroversion of ἐν βιβλίῳ τῆς ᾠδῆς mentioned in a Greek addition to 1 Kings viii 53 (13) and also found in one witness of the Vetus Latina into *spr hšyr*, and the latter's identification with *spr hyšr* (by inversion), is rather questionable in view of the apparent dissimilar content of these two compilations.

[40] N. H. Tur-Sinai, "Was there an Ancient 'Book of the Wars of the Lord'?", *BIES* 24 (1960), pp. 146-8 (Hebrew).

it is unanimously held that what the sources refer to indeed are epics which were yet known at the time of the historiographers who quote from them.

With S. Mowinckel the hypothesis achieved its fullest form.[41] According to him, the surmised *Israelitische Nationalepos* had successfully fused heroic epic tales, portraying the historical exploits of the Israelites and their God in the post-Davidic period, with an epic of cosmogony which rightfully belongs in the category of myth. Central to our present concern is the closing section of Mowinckel's essay which widens the scope of the inquiry—until then based altogether on biblical material *sensu strictu*—as the author turned to ancient Near Eastern epic literature in order to support the postulated existence of a Hebrew national-religious epic.

The employment of the comparative method in search of the lost biblical epic reached a new height in the writings of Umberto Cassuto, at whose disposal lay the newly-discovered Ugaritic literature.[42] Cassuto collected a good number of isolated expressions and word combinations scattered in biblical prose texts which bear the stamp of poetry, or even are reminiscent of specific literary turns in Ugaritic epics. The evidence which he assembled certainly strengthens the case for the generally accepted notion that biblical Israel had been imbued with vestiges of Ugaritic/Canaanite culture, including elements borrowed from epics of which the Hebrew authors must have known sizeable portions. Yet to jump from the collation of such obviously borrowed materials to the supposition that they help to prove the existence at one time of an originally Hebrew epic (or epics) is a far cry indeed. It is interesting to observe that Cassuto was almost compelled to make this assumption by this correct insight that biblical Israel hardly would have taken over lock-stock-and-barrel the polytheistic literature of the Canaanites. The antagonistic attitude toward the pagan cult and ritual with which the Ugaritic epics are intimately connected, simply ruled out such a transfer. Therefore, he maintains that as far as remnants of epic literature are recognizable in the biblical writings, they perforce must derive from original Hebrew epic songs.

It is at this state of our survey that we encounter once more the

---

[41] "Hat es ein israelitisches Nationalepos gegeben?", *ZAW* 53 (1935), pp. 130-52.

[42] "The Israelite Epic", *Biblical and Oriental Studies* 2, tr. I. Abrahams (Jerusalem, 1975), pp. 69-109.

issue of method. The combined evidence marshalled by scholars from their survey of biblical literature cannot provide a sound basis for positing the existence of full-fledged Hebrew epics in the biblical period. The evidence as a whole is circumstantial. It is based on inference from observations about the assumed developmental process of national literatures generally, and ancient Near Eastern and foremost Ugaritic literature especially. In addition, the presumed ancient Hebrew epic is discussed in complete isolation from other forms or *Gattungen* extant in the biblical writings. There can be no doubt that in the historiographies, the narratives, Psalms and even in the prophetic books we do encounter features which are characteristic of the epic genre: poetic rhythm, parallelistic structure and formulaic language. However, these features are found also in literature to which the designation "epic" cannot be applied. We still have to ask ourselves the fundamental question "what makes an epic an epic", and in what way can it be clearly distinguished from other forms of narrative "epic-type" literature. Not one of the scholars who engaged in the study of the issue attempted to provide a clear definition of the "epic" as a special *Gattung*, nor was a satisfactory definition offered by students of the history of general literature and of literary criticism.

Of even greater import is the following fact: the outstanding predominance in the Bible of straightforward prose narration which fulfils the functions for which other literatures revert to the epic genre: heroic tales, historiography, even myth and cosmogony. The phenomenon is too striking to be coincidental. I would propose that the ancient Hebrew writers purposefully nurtured and developed prose narration to take the place of the epic genre which by its content was intimately bound up with the world of paganism and appears to have had a special standing in the polytheistic cults. The recitation of the epics was tantamount to a re-enactment of cosmic events in the manner of sympathetic magic. In the process of total rejection of the polytheistic religions and their ritual expressions in the cult, epic songs and also the epic genre were purged from the literary repertoire of the Hebrew authors. Together with the content, its foremost literary concretization fell into disrepute and was banished from the Israelite culture. The epic elements which did survive—preponderantly in the literature of the monarchic period, i.e. from a time when the prophets were active—were permitted to infiltrate as building blocks of other forms of biblical literature, because they had lost their pagan import and had been neutralized. These survivals constitute examples of figurative language whose original connotations had been so diluted that they no longer evoked objection. However, the initial rejection of the epics and the epic genre seems to have been so thorough that they could never be reintegrated into the technical apparatus of the Hebrew *literati*. It can be surmised that the closure of biblical literature against the epic was helped along by the progressive falling into desuetude of this genre in the Semitic world from about the second quarter of the first millennium B.C. The following observation may be added: it would appear that in the framework of the cult, the Hebrew writers developed the historiographical psalm as a substitute for the epic. The great acts of God in the creation of the world and in history thus were related and possibly recited in a specifically and originally Israelite genre.

In summing up this discussion it can be said that the epic is not simply a *Gattung* which can be identified by a given number of literary techniques such as were specified for example, by W. Whallon.[43] It is rather the expression of a specific societal *Gestalt*. Its presence can be empirically established in those societies which did produce epics and in which it has a special *Sitz im Leben*.[44] It cannot be reconstructed where it does not exist. With reference to the epic as a specific literary genre, Israel presents a deep societal structure which is quite different from those of her neighbours. The cosmological epic requires a rich background of myth for its development; Israel was lacking that background, having rejected myth from the outset. The historical epic has been shown by D. F. Rauber to have flourished in societies in the heroic stages of their development.[45] It is therefore striking that biblical literature did not record even Israel's heroic age—the days of the Judges and the early kings—in the form of epics. Comparativists generally, and in the field of biblical studies especially, would do well to pay heed to differences between cultures and not only to likenesses. Adequate attention must be given to the interpretation of the dissimilarities from other cultures of the ancient Near East which made biblical civilization the peculiar and particular phenomenon it was. These considerations lead us to answer in the negative the question posed by Mowinckel and echoed by Cassuto—

[43] *Formula, Character, and Context—Studies in Homeric, Old English, and Old Testament Poetry* (Cambridge, Mass., 1969).

[44] Cf. the interesting observations on the position of the epic poet in Homeric Society in S. C. Humphreys, " 'Transcendence' and Intellectual Roles: the Ancient Greek Case", *Daedalus* 104 (1975), pp. 91-118.

[45] "Observations on Biblical Epic", *Genre* 3 (1970), pp. 318-38.

"Hat es ein israelitisches Nationalepos gegeben?" Biblical Israel did not produce epics nor did it foster the epic genre.

IV

In closing this presentation, I wish to return to the issue of procedure to which reference was made in the introductory part and to stress once more the need for the definition of a set of rules which should serve biblical scholars as guidelines in their pursuit of comparative studies. It must be emphasized that the formulation of a methodology of comparative research in matters pertaining to ancient Israelite culture and the Old Testament literature, because of the comprehensiveness and the variety of issues to which this research applies itself, is a task which transcends the framework of this paper and which cannot be carried out single-handed. It demands an interdisciplinary and synoptic grasp, thus requiring the co-operation of experts in diverse areas: philology, literature, folk-lore, theology, sociology, history, and the history of ideas. All that could be attempted here was the delineation of some basic—not always necessarily new—principles which should be followed in the intercultural comparative study of biblical phenomena. These can be summarized as follows:

The interpretation of biblical features—whether of a socio-political, cultic, general-cultural or literary nature—with the help of inner-biblical parallels should always precede the comparison with extra-biblical materials. In the evaluation of a societal phenomenon, attention should be paid to its function in the developing structure of the Israelite body politic before one engages in the comparison with parallel phenomena in other societies. Such comparisons can be applied to societies which lie in the same "historic stream" as biblical Israel. Comparisons on the "grand scale" are better avoided. In this respect, the methodological concerns expressed by Walter Goldschmidt are most pertinent: "Because each culture defines its own institutions there is always an element of falsification when we engage in institutional comparisons among distinct cultures".[46]

In any such study the full range of the available evidence must be taken into consideration: the "holistic" approach always should be given preference over the "atomistic". The abstraction of a concept, an aspect of society, cult or literature from its wider framework, and its contemplation in isolation, more often than not will result in distortion; its intrinsic meaning ultimately is decided by the context, and therefore may vary from one setting to another.

---

[46] *Comparative Functionalism* (Berkeley, 1966), p. 131.

ZUR THEOLOGIE DES PSALMS CXXXIX

von

SIEGFRIED WAGNER
Leipzig

I

Der Psalm cxxxix gehört zu den theologisch interessantesten Texten des alttestamentlichen Psalters, wenn nicht überhaupt des gesamten Alten Testaments. Es ist darum kein Wunder, wenn er immer wieder zum Gegenstand der verschiedenartigsten Untersuchungen gemacht wurde. Textkritische Analysen, literarkritische Beobachtungen, form- und gattungsgeschichtliche Studien, religionswissenschaftliche Vergleiche und theologische Exegesen haben seinen Geheimnissen auf die Spur zu kommen versucht.[1] Es hat den Anschein, als habe dieses Stück alttestamentlicher Literatur die Lösung seiner Rätsel noch nicht preisgegeben und als sei die alttestamentliche Wissenschaft noch immer gefordert, eine Antwort auf die Fragen zu suchen, die der Psalm nach verschiedenen Seiten hin aufgibt. Die textliche Überlieferung ist an einzelnen Stellen verderbt oder zumindest unsicher. Es fehlt nicht an Lösungsvorschlägen, von denen freilich bislang keiner allgemeinere Zustimmung erfahren hat. Die formale Gestaltung des Psalms ist nicht in allen seinen Teilen durchsichtig, Glossierungen werden in einigen Versen nicht ausgeschlossen. Allerdings gelingt es nicht, überzeugende Gründe für ihre Abgrenzung beizubringen. Nach wie vor umstritten ist die Zuordnung des Psalms zu einer bestimmten Gattung, deren "Sitz im Leben" beschrieben werden

---

[1] Neben den gängigen Kommentaren (z.B. von H. Gunkel, R. Kittel, A. Weiser, H.-J. Kraus u.a.) sind zahlreiche kürzere und längere Stellungnahmen zu Ps. cxxxix zu berücksichtigen, die letzthin H. Schüngel-Straumann, "Zur Gattung und Theologie des 139. Psalms", *BZ*, NF 17 (1973), S. 39-51, in ihrer 1. Anmerkung bibliographisch zusammengestellt hat. Darüberhinaus s. ferner: R. Lapointe, "La Nuit est ma Lumière", *CBQ* 33 (1971), S. 397-402; J. Krašovec, "Die polare Ausdrucksweise in Psalm 139", *BZ*, NF 18 (1974), S. 224-8; D. Sölle, "*Psalm 139*", *Die Hinreise. Zur religiösen Erfahrung. Texte und Überlegungen* (Stuttgart, 1975), S. 155-64, sowie neuere Dissertationen und Monographien zu Einzelthemen in den Psalmen, wie z.B. R. Albertz, *Weltschöpfung und Menschenschöpfung. Untersucht bei Deuterojesaja, Hiob und in den Psalmen* (Stuttgart, 1974), S. 118-21 mit den entsprechenden Anmerkungen.

könnte. Hier hat die heutige Exegese noch immer Anteil an der Ratlosigkeit, die die Gattungsforschung Gunkels schon diesem cxxxix. Psalm gegenüber empfand. Hymnus, geistliches Lied, Gebet, Gebet eines Angeklagten (und im Zusammenhang damit die Annahme von Unschuldsbeteuerung, Reinigungseid, Ordal, Gerichtsbescheid, Dank und Bekenntnis), Vertrauens- und Danklied wie schließlich das Zugeständnis von Mischformen werben in der Gattungszuweisung um Anerkennung. Die Annahme einer kultisch-rechtlichen Verwurzelung dieses Textes in den Institutionen von Tempel und Sakralrecht streitet mit der einer privaten Frömmigkeitsäußerung, die Psalm cxxxix darstellen soll. Dementsprechend differiert die Auffassung des in den Versen sich aussprechenden "ich" als kollektives (grundsätzliches) oder individuelles (persönliches, biographisches) "ich". Leider ist nicht einmal das Problem des ursprünglichen Umfangs von Psalm cxxxix geklärt. Die *v.* 19-24 stehen bekanntlich in einer gewissen Spannung zum Inhalt der *v.* 1-18. Man hatte dies schon sehr lange empfunden und für die Auflösung der Spannung sehr unterschiedliche Vorschläge unterbreitet, von der Umstellung der *v.* 19-24 vor die *v.* 1-18 bis hin zur Ablösung dieses Psalmteils vom Gesamttext. In der Tat könnten die *v.* 19-24 ein in sich geschlossenes eigenes Gebet darstellen, das nur zufällig an die *v.* 1-18 geraten ist. Dem Psalm fehlte nichts, wenn sie weggeschnitten würden. Indes rechnen die meisten neueren Untersuchungen und Kommentierungen dieses Psalms auf Grund gewisser textlicher und inhaltlicher Übereinstimmungen und Anspielungen mit der Zusammengehörigkeit der 24 Verse. Sie müssen sich dann allerdings zu dem Verhältnis der beiden in Spannung zueinander stehenden Teile äußern. Es ist leicht einzusehen, daß die Klärung dieses Problems Einfluß auf die Gattungsbestimmung hat. Wer den *v.* 19-24 eine Schlüsselfunktion für das Verständnis des Psalms als ganzen zubilligt (wie z.B. E. Würthwein), kommt hierin zu anderen Ergebnissen als derjenige, der den *v.* 1-18 ein starkes eigenes Aussagegewicht zumißt. Daß in den genannten Bereichen (Text, Umfang, Redaktion, Gattung) offenbar bis jetzt keine Eindeutigkeit erzielt werden konnte — ein Tatbestand, der in sich interpretabel sein dürfte, etwa in der Richtung, daß eine starke Beschäftigung mit der inhaltlichen Materie bis in späte Zeiten hinein angenommen werden könnte, — braucht nicht den Verzicht auf die Erhebung der Aussageinhalte zu bedeuten. Es hat im Gegenteil den Anschein, als sei es trotz der erwähnten Schwierigkeiten gut möglich, die theologischen Aussageabsichten des Psalms zu erfassen und zu beschreiben. Daß theologische Grundüberzeugungen für eine bestimmte Situation in Dienst und Pflicht genommen werden, ist im Alten Testament immer wieder zu beobachten (Schöpfungs-, Geschichts-, Bundestheologie). Schwierig zu entscheiden ist die Frage, ob für unseren Psalm einst eine bestimmte Situation zur Formulierung seiner theologischen Grundanschauungen geführt hat, oder ob der vorliegende Text nicht vielmehr das Ergebnis eines weitergegangenen Nachdenkens über theologische Sachverhalte widerspiegelt, das sich von dem ursprünglichen "Sitz im Leben" entfernt hat. Es braucht nicht Zufall zu sein, daß für diesen Psalm ein klassischer "Sitz im Leben" nicht mehr zu ermitteln ist. Dem Exegeten bleibt zunächst keine andere Wahl, als den Versuch zu unternehmen, die theologumena des Psalms ohne sichere Einsicht in dessen literarische und formale Gestaltung zu orten und bewußt werden zu lassen. Dabei sollte Ausgangspunkt und Voraussetzung der gesamte überlieferte Textbestand und im wesentlichen auch die vorliegende Textgestalt sein, welche nicht ohne zwingenden Grund geändert werden dürften. Freilich ganz ohne erkennbare formale Gestaltung ist der Psalm auch wieder nicht. Vom Inhalt und Gedankenfortschritt her gesehen läßt sich nicht nur zwischen den *v.* 18 und 19 eine Zäsur erkennen, sondern auch nach *v.* 6 und *v.* 12, so daß sich eine relativ ebenmäßige Gliederung von *v.* 1-6; 7-12; 13-18; 19-24 ergibt, wobei darauf verzichtet werden soll, alle stichoi und metrischen Akzenteinheiten auszuzählen und gegebenenfalls auszugleichen. Der Gestaltungswille ist erkennbar, nicht mehr unbedingt das exakte Gestaltungsergebnis.

II

Auffällig ist zunächst die stark individualistisch-existenziale Version der Glaubensüberzeugung von Jahwes Omniscienz, Omnipotenz und Ubiquität. Diese stellt offenbar eine grundsätzliche Reflektion über das Verhältnis Gott-Mensch und Mensch-Gott dar, welches auch unabhängig von einer denkbaren konkreten Situation besteht, die z.B. durch Angeklagtsein des Menschen, vergebliche Flucht und Gottesgerichtsurteil bestimmt ist.[2] Erst die *v.* 19-24 lassen die Vermutung zu, daß der gesamte Psalm aus den Nöten eines grundlos Verdächtigten und unschuldig Angeklagten heraus formuliert sein könnte. Diese Grundsatzüberlegungen stehen nicht im Interesse

---

[2] Wie so anders ist das Gebet eines Angeklagten in Ps. lv; vgl. auch den Unterschied zu Ps. xxvi und xliii 1 (u. ff.). In Ps. cxxxix 1-18 fehlt die Bitte "richte mich!", "schaffe mir Recht!" usw.

dogmatischer Lehrentscheidungen, sondern zeugen für existenzielle Betroffenheit dessen, der sich auf diesen Gott, von dem in Ps. cxxxix die Rede ist, eingelassen hat. Die Formulierungen (Jahwe im Vokativ vorangestellt, die Anrede eines "du" durch ein "ich") gehen im Gebetsstil einher, bringen aber keine Bitten oder Lobpreisungen vor, sondern treffen Feststellungen, die die Beziehungen zwischen diesem "du" Jahwes und dem "ich" des Sprechers betreffen. Die Form erinnert an ein Gebet, der Inhalt an das corpus eines Hymnus, doch es ist weder das eine noch das andere. Man gewinnt keineswegs den Eindruck, daß das, was von Jahwes Seite her berichtet wird, das jubelnde Lob des Sprechers hervorruft. Jahwe hat jenes "ich" durchmustert und durchforscht (Jahweh *ḥaqartanij*), so daß bei Jahwe nunmehr ein Wissen über dieses "ich" besteht (*watteda*ʿ).[3] Der Aspekt der vollendeten Handlung (Perfekt und Imperfekt+waw consec.) verbindet sich mit dem Aspekt des seither bestehenden Zustandes, dem sich das "ich" konfrontiert sieht und dem es sich nicht zu entziehen vermag. Das "ich" ist von dem "du" in den verschiedensten Situationen seines Lebens betroffen worden (*v.* 1+2). Die Sphäre der Beweglichkeit ist dem Wissen des anderen ausgeliefert. Es gibt keine Phase des Lebensablaufes, weder beim Verbleiben noch beim Aufbruch, die nicht jenem "du" vertraut (*jada*ʿ) wäre. Selbst der Weg in die innere Emigration, in die Welt des Gedankens und des ungesagten Wortes ist kontrolliert und dem "du" erschlossen (*v.* 2, 3, 4). Die polare Ausdrucksweise, deren sich der Psalm bedient, möchte die Totalität der beschriebenen Beziehung kennzeichnen.[4] Im einzelnen gelingt es dem Sprecher, die Absolutheit und Unausweichlichkeit der von ihm geschilderten Situation durch die Ausmalung grotesker Sachverhalte zu unterstreichen. Der von dem "ich" erst zu gehen beabsichtigte Weg ist von dem "du" bereits aus- und abgemessen (*v.* 3, *ẓerah*), um alle einzuschlagenden Pfade des "ich" hat sich das "du" schon besorgt (*hiskin*), der tief innen gefaßte Gedanke ist schon von ferne bemerkt (*bijn meraḥoq*, *v.* 2). Das "ich" kommt in Bezug auf sich selber dem "du" gegenüber immer schon zu spät. Kein Wunder, wenn es sich von dem "du" bedrückt und bedrängt empfindet. Im *v.* 5 findet dieser Zustand seinen

[3] Das in der Literatur erwogene Verständnis von *ḥaqartanij* als perfectum precativum und die im Anschluß daran vorgesehene Umpunktierung von *watteda*ʿ zu *weteda*ʿ (Jussiv) steht im Interesse der Wiederherstellung einer reinen inclusio (*v.* 1 und 23), s. J. Holman, "Analysis of the Text of Ps 139", *BZ*, NF 14 (1970), S. 37ff., 198ff. (bes. 39f.).

[4] S. die instruktiven Ausführungen dazu bei J. Krašovec, a.a.O.

Ausdruck in plastischen Formulierungen, die die Omniscienz, Omnipotenz und Ubiquität des anderen eher als Belastung denn als Befreiung kennzeichnen: "von vorn und von hinten bedrängst du mich und legst deine Handfläche auf mich". *ṣur* heißt "belagern", "bedrängen", "umzingeln" (im militärischen Sinne), und *'al* kann im feindlichen Sinne von "gegen" gebraucht werden. Die Anwesenheit dieses "du" im Lebensvollzug des "ich" kommt einer Belagerung und einer Beschlagnahme gleich, obwohl aktiv keine entsprechende Handlung von seiten Jahwes vorgenommen worden ist. Es wurde kein Weg verbaut, kein Gedanke verhindert und kein Wort verwehrt — und doch dieses Fazit! In der Schlußfolgerung (*v.* 6) aus diesen bewußt gewordenen Tatbeständen macht sich ein stark reflektierendes Element geltend. Diese Vorfindlichkeit möchte der Sprecher gedanklich bewältigen. Er beschäftigt sich mit diesem Problem, ohne zu einer ihn befriedigenden und befreienden Antwort zu gelangen. Er muß kapitulieren. Dies übersteigt seine rationalen Potenzen, es ist metarational. Die bei solchem Sachverhalt denkbaren Konsequenzen lassen sich rational in ein schlüssiges Menschenbild nicht verrechnen. Daß es solche Umschlossenheit gibt, ist unbegreiflich. Unausgesprochen schwingt der Wunsch mit, solcher Umklammerung zu entfliehen. Die Grundsatzfrage nach dem Verhältnis Gott-Mensch bricht auf. Was ist der Mensch im Gegenüber zu Gott? Freiheit und Selbständigkeit des Menschen stehen in Gefahr.

Der zwanghafte Charakter dieser Gott-Mensch-Beziehung erinnert an das zwanghafte Geschehen prophetischen Berufenseins und Erlebens. Die Vorstellung von der auf dem "Berufenen" schwer liegenden und lastenden Jahwehand gehört bei Ezechiel zur Beschreibung des Offenbarungsvorganges (i 3, iii 22 u.ö.). Das nachherige Bekenntnis zum Geschaffensein durch Jahwe (Ps. cxxxix 13ff.) läßt an einen Vergleich mit der Berufung des Jeremia denken (Jer. i 5), bei welcher ähnlich wie hier von der Umschlossenheit der pränatalen Existenz des zu Berufenden durch Jahwe die Rede ist. Der Komplex der Fluchtvarianten (Ps. cxxxix 7-12) könnte das typische Zurückweichen des Berufenen vor der Berufung repräsentieren (Jes. vi 5; Jer. i 6; Ex. iii 11, iv 10; 1 Sam. ix 21 u.a.m.). *jada'* würde in diesem Zusammenhang (zumindest in Ps. cxxxix 1) Erwählungsterminus sein können (vgl. *jada'* in Jer. i 5). "Jahwe, du hast mich durchschaut (erforscht, durchmustert, um deine Wahl zu treffen, *watteda'*, *v.* 1) und hast gewählt (erkannt)". Es ist nicht schwierig und auch nicht unmöglich, die nachfolgenden Verse in den

Kontext eines solchen Berufungsgeschehens zu ordnen und darin subjektive Reflektionen und Feststellungen des Betroffenen zu erkennen, die in den Berufungsgeschichten fehlen bezw. nur angedeutet sind. Daß sie gänzlich verloren gegangen sein sollten, will nicht recht einleuchten. Umgekehrt ist freilich nicht zu erweisen, daß in Ps. cxxxix eine solche Reaktion eines Berufenen tatsächlich vorliegt. Eine solche Verständnisvariante ist lediglich auf ihre Möglichkeit und Wahrscheinlichkeit hin einmal durchzuspielen. Anhaltspunkte für eine derartige Interpretation sind jedenfalls nicht von der Hand zu weisen.

III

Mit *v.* 6 war ein gewisser gedanklicher Einschnitt erreicht worden, so daß man nicht fehlgehen wird, mit *v.* 7 eine neue Sinneinheit beginnen zu sehen. Es ist schwer zu sagen, ob sich darin eine poetische strophische Gliederung zu erkennen gibt. Wert gelegt werden soll hier nur auf den thematischen Neueinsatz, der sich auch in formaler Hinsicht feststellen läßt. Sprachen die *v.* 1-5 von der Du-ich-Beziehung, so leitete der *v.* 6 über zur Ich-Reflektion, zur Tatbestandsaufnahme darüber, wie das betroffene "ich" sich zur Du-ich-Beziehung verhalten solle, bis schließlich die *v.* 7ff. dazu übergehen, von der Ich-du-Bezie hung zu sprechen. Inhaltlich knüpfen die *v.* 7ff. an den vorangehenden Abschnitt insofern an, als zumindest die *v.* 7-12 das Thema erörtern, wie der Umklammerung durch Jahwe zu entkommen sei. Zugleich erschließen sich neue Bereiche der intellektuellen Durchdringung der Gottesproblematik. Das Textstück als ganzes erfährt seinen Gedankenfortschritt. Das sogenannte Fluchtmotiv (im Zusammenhang mit dem Gottesgerichtsmotiv) hat in dieser Passage eigentlich keinen konkreten Bezug. Der Sprecher ist weder von außen noch von innen her angeklagt, und auch von Gottes Seite ist eine vorgesehene strafrichterliche Verfolgung nicht auszumachen. Sollten solche Hintergründe ursprünglich einmal bestanden haben und bestimmte Formulierungen noch aus solchen Formulierzwängen stammen, so wären die ursprüngliche Situation weit zurückgelassen und bestimmte typische Redewendungen nur noch als Ausdrucksmittel genutzt worden. Was aus dem Text selber als Motiv zur Flucht bezeichnet wird, ist die Anwesenheit Gottes, *v.* 7: "wohin soll ich gehen vor deinem Geist und wohin soll ich fliehen vor deinem Angesicht?" *ruaḥ* und *panim* (im parallelismus membrorum gebraucht) sind gewiß Umschreibungen für das in den *v.* 1-6 beschriebene bedrängende und betroffen machende Dasein Jahwes im Lebensvollzug des Sprechers. Trotzdem müßten dieser parallele Gebrauch und die spezielle Verwendung von *ruaḥ* in unserem Zusammenhang gesondert untersucht werden. Es könnte sein, daß eine Spiritualisierung mit der Benennung von *ruaḥ* beabsichtigt ist. Die Wohin-Fragen in *v.* 7 werden unter dem Druck der Ausführungen in den nachfolgenden Versen zu rhetorischen Fragen. Es gibt keine Fliehmöglichkeit. Die polare Ausdrucksweise steht erneut im Dienst von Totalitätsaussagen:[5] Himmel und Hölle, Morgen und Abend, Ost und West, Licht und Finsternis, Tag und Nacht, überall ist jenes "du". Auffällig ist die Mehrdimensionalität, es sind nicht allein geographische Lokalitäten, sondern auch kosmische und mythische genannt. Bei allem Zugeständnis an die poetische Sprachgestaltung und typisch vorderorientalische Ausmalungskunst hinterlassen diese Verse nicht letztlich den Eindruck des Metaphorischen. Es sind irrationale Regionen bezeichnet. Mag bei *šamajim* und bei *še'ol* an "oben" und "unten" gedacht sein, so doch dann aber auch — das gegenwärtige Leben transzendierend — an Leben und Tod schlechthin. In die *še'ol* gelangt ein alttestamentlicher Mensch ja wohl mit seinem Tode, wie aber nach *šamajim*? Daß Jahwes Anwesenheit in *šamajim* (*šam 'attah*) angenommen werden muß, ist genauso anfragbar wie Jahwes Dasein in *še'ol* (*hinneka*). Diese Vorstellungen haben zur Voraussetzung, daß Jahwe als Himmelsgott, aber auch als Unterweltsgott verstanden wird. Die Erwägung der Möglichkeit, dorthin zu entkommen, legt den Schluß nahe, daß Jahwe ursprünglich dort nicht anwesend war oder zumindest dort nicht vermutet wurde. Und in der Tat ist wenigstens für den Bereich der Toten- und Unterwelt die zögernde und späte alttestamentliche Bezeugung der Herrschaft Jahwes über Tod und Totenreich zuzugestehen.[6] Für den Sprecher unseres Psalms ist Jahwe aber nunmehr dort zugegen, ja vielmehr schon zugegen, da er dort bereits bei seinen Fluchtversuchen auf Jahwe stößt. In den *v.* 9-10 mögen die geographischen Extrempunkte des Ostens und des Westens vom Standpunkt des Palästinensers oder des Mesopotamiers[7] aus gesehen

---

[5] J. Krašovec, a.a.O.

[6] Das Verhältnis zwischen Jahwe und *šamajim* müßte noch einmal präzise untersucht werden, wobei die Frage Berücksichtigung zu finden hätte, ob die schöpfungstheologische Verhältnisbestimmung die einzig mögliche ist. Schon die Verwendung von *šamajim* in Gen. i ist bekanntlich unterschiedlich: liegt in *v.* 1 ein abstraktes, so in den *v.* 6ff. ein konkretes Verständnis vor.

[7] Nicht auszuschließen ist die Möglichkeit, daß Ps. cxxxix aus der (babylonischen) Diaspora stammt; s. dazu auch Frz. Delitzsch, *Die Psalmen* (Leipzig, [5]1894), S. 785.

angesprochen sein, für die der Psalmist eine Überbrückung zu wissen scheint, und wenn es der unaufhaltsame Fluchtweg der Sonne wäre, die niemand in ihrer Bahn zu stören vermöchte, aber auch hier könnte bewußt transzendiert die Flucht in die Mythologeme und Theologeme der Umwelt gemeint sein, in die sich der Problematiker von Psalm cxxxix hineinvertieft hat, um Jahwe zu entgehen. *Jam* und *Šaḥar* sind kanaanäische Gottheiten, und die majestätische Sonne, sollte ihre Tageswende mit *v.* 8 beschrieben sein, bedeutete nach altorientalischer Überzeugung eine mächtige Gottheit, der man sich vor nachstellenden Göttern hypothetisch durchaus anvertrauen könnte. Überdies wäre Schamasch zugleich eine Himmels- und Unterweltsgottheit.[8] Doch auch diese Wege erweisen sich als vergeblich, weil auch dort Jahwe anzutreffen ist; ja vielmehr noch: die Vorstellung von *v.* 9 geht über das bloße Dasein Jahwes hinaus, das allein schon potenzgeladen genug gewesen wäre. Jahwe muß den Sprecher mit seiner (linken) Hand dort führen (*gam šam*) und mit der rechten fassen, damit dieser in jenen Regionen nicht strauchelt oder vom Wege abkommt. Dem Verbum *naḥah* eignet ein fürsorglicher Ton.[9] Die Änderung von *tanḥenij* zu *tiqqaḥenij* ermäßigte die (wohl beabsichtigte) Groteske, die darin besteht, daß der Sprecher von Ps. cxxxix auf der Flucht vor Jahwe in seinem Fluchtgebiet von Jahwe geleitet werden muß, damit er sich durchfinden kann und nicht auf der Strecke bleibt. Auch hinter einer solchen Aussage muß die Überzeugung stehen, daß dem den Psalmisten betreffenden und betroffen machenden Gott auch durch andere Religionen und deren Götter keine Grenzen gesetzt sind. Sein Machtbereich überschreitet Religionsgrenzen, die durch politische Macht und ökonomischen Einfluß gezogen sind, obwohl er selber weder durch ökonomische noch durch politische Macht gedeckt ist. Man begegnet einem sehr konsequenten Durchdenken der Gottesfrage: wenn Gott überhaupt ist, dann nur so! Das ist nicht mehr Definierung des Monotheismus, sondern Praktizierung des definierten Monotheismus. Das ist von der Basis deuterojesajanischer Theologie aus weiter gedacht. Und ist dieses Verständnis der *v.* 7-12 als gedankliche Beschäftigung mit der Gottesfrage unter Einbeziehung der Um-

---

[8] Daß Schamasch zugleich Himmels- und Unterweltsgottheit ist, kann nur im sukzessiven Sinne verstanden werden, Schamasch ist es nacheinander.

[9] Vgl. *ThHAT* II, s.v. *naḥah* und den parallelen Gebrauch von *naḥah* und *ʾaḥaz* in Ps. lxxiii 23f. (freilich steht als dritter paralleler Terminus dort auch *laqaḥ*).

welts-Mythologeme und -Theologeme richtig, dann hätte diese Passage auch Bedeutung für die Offenbarungsproblematik im Alten Testament: Jahwes *ruaḥ* und Jahwes *panim*, d.h. doch Jahwes Anwesenheit in den Religionen der Umwelt Israels wäre proklamiert! Sicherlich darf dies nicht im Sinne einer steilen Theologie der natürlichen Offenbarung verstanden werden, obwohl es ganz gewiß etwas mit natürlicher Offenbarung zu tun hat, sondern vielmehr im Sinne der Gedankenführung des Psalms, daß Jahwe bei allen Versuchen, ihm zu entkommen, nicht aus dem Feld zu schlagen ist. Er ist bei der Morgenröte und am Ende des Meeres, im Himmel und in der Unterwelt. Die Reflektion darüber, wer dort noch ist oder gewesen ist, aber offenbar keine Jahwe verdrängende Gewalt mehr hat, liegt vor dem Ausspruch des Sprechers.[10]

Ganz ins Ungegenständliche führen die Worte der *v.* 11 und 12, wobei die Gestalt des Textes nicht unversehrt geblieben zu sein scheint (s. die Rekonstruktionsversuche in den Kommentaren und in der Literatur). Trotzdem ist es gut möglich, den Inhalt zu erfassen. Es geht um das Sichverbergen in der Finsternis mit Hilfe eines Machtwortes oder Zauberspruches (*v.* 11: "spräche ich..."), wie sie antikorientalischen Menschen zur Verfügung standen. Der Fluchtwillige rekurriert auf Praktiken, wie sie Israel wohl verboten waren, aber aus der Umwelt wahrscheinlich Eingang in die Volksfrömmigkeit gefunden hatten. Doch auch diese Dimension ist unausschreitbar. Die Aktionen gelangen nicht zu ihrem Ziel. Die Finsternis verfinstert sich nicht vor Jahwe, und die Nacht strahlt auf wie der Tag. Jahwe steht außerhalb der Funktionalitäten von Licht und Finsternis, sie haben auf ihn keine Wirkung. Der letzte stichos des *v.* 12 (der für gewöhnlich als Glosse gestrichen wird) zieht die theoretische Summe aus diesem Sahverhalt: "wie das Finstere entsprechend das Lichte".

---

[10] In der Literatur werden immer wieder die religionsgeschichtlichen Parallelen genannt und besprochen. Die Tendenz, ihnen wenig Gewicht für das Verständnis von Ps cxxxix zuzubilligen, ist zu begrüßen. Die Unterschiede sind bei Berücksichtigung aller temporalen und kulturellen Kontexte doch stärker als die Übereinstimmungen, vgl. neben anderen K.-H. Bernhardt, "Zur Gottesvorstellung von Psalm 139", *Kirche, Theologie, Frömmigkeit* (FS Gottfried Holtz) (Berlin, 1965), S. 20-31, bes. S. 26-8. Viel diskutiert wird auch die alttestamentliche Parallele Amos ix 1-4. Doch dürften auf Grund des Kontextes auch in ihr die Unterschiede in Funktion, Nutzung und Aussageziel gegenüber Ps. cxxxix nicht unterschätzt werden, wieder richtig K.-H. Bernhardt, S. 28-30. Die Deportationsvorstellungen im Amosbuch rechnen doch wieder mit der Gleichsetzung von Ausland = Elend = gottfernes, unreines, von anderen Mächten bestimmtes Land, z.B. Amos vii 17.

Der Dualismus, der Gegensatz zwischen Licht und Finsternis ist bei Jahwe aufgehoben, ist neutralisiert. Jahwe ist den Bedingungen dieser Koordinaten, die das Leben des Menschen bestimmen, nicht unterworfen. Alle Licht- und Dunkeltheorien geraten gegenüber Jahwe in eine grundsätzliche Krise. Jahwe ist anders als die Umweltsgottheiten. Neben die Bildlosigkeit und Ausschließlichkeit Jahwes tritt seine Außerweltlichkeit, die aber nicht als Weltlosigkeit verstanden werden darf. Seine Natur- und Weltbezogenheit ist gerade in diesen Versen anschaulich und plastisch bezeugt. Dies kennzeichnet die Fremdheit des israelitischen Gottesglaubens in seiner Umwelt. Auf einen solchen Gott bezogen zu sein, ist keineswegs einfach und leicht, sondern ist im Kontext der vorderorientalischen Religionen kompliziert und beschwerlich. Es funktioniert nichts, was sonst eigentlich funktioniert.[11]

Alle diese Erwägungen und Überlegungen bleiben innerhalb des Psalms cxxxix streng bezogen auf das Verhältnis jenes "ich" zu dem "du", um das es in den *v.* 7-12 ging, ein Verhältnis, dem das "ich" in seiner Betroffenheit durch das "du" nicht zu entkommen vermag, so große Anstrengungen (denkerischer Art) es auch unternimmt. Die Situation gegenüber der ersten Sinneinheit (*v.* 1-6) ist eigentlich noch aussichtsloser geworden und die Ratlosigkeit noch größer. Diesem Gott ist nicht zu entkommen, aber man muß sich zu ihm ja verhalten, will man weiterleben.

IV

Die Lösung der in den ersten beiden Aussage-Einheiten aufgezeigten bedrückenden existenziellen Problematik scheint in den *v.* 13-18 zu erfolgen. Inhaltlich wie formal beginnt mit diesen Versen ein neuer Sinnabschnitt. Sowohl was den Text als auch was die Textanordnung anlangt, scheint dieser Psalm-Teil nicht mehr richtig überliefert zu sein. Sehr viel Wahrscheinlichkeit für sich buchen kann eine schon in der älteren Exegese vorgeschlagene Umstellung der *v.* 13 und 14.[12] Es leuchtet ein, daß *v.* 13 sich glatter an *v.* 15

---

[11] Man mag überlegen, ob hinter den Aussagen von *v.* 11 + 12 das Nachdenken über die alten Traditionen von der Jahwe-Theophanie steht, wie sie beispielsweise in den in der Berufungsgeschichte des Jesaja (vi 3) verwendeten Vorstellungen von dem die ganze Erde anfüllenden *kebod Jahweh* begegnet.

[12] Die Umstellung schlägt auch H. Gunkel vor (*Die Psalmen* [Göttingen, ⁴1926], S. 591) unter Rückverweis auf F. Hitzig und J. Wellhausen, schneidet aber von *v.* 14a, b den Versteil 14c ab und ordnet die Verse wie folgt: 14a, b, 13, 14c, 15, wobei 14c noch eine textliche Veränderung erfährt (*me'od* soll zu

anschließt als an *v.* 14. Der Begründungssatz von *v.* 13 fügt sich gut an die Bekenntnisformel von *v.* 14 an. Wenn man will, könnte man in den *v.* 14, 13, 15-18 einen Hymnus sehen, dessen Introitus allerdings lediglich durch das *'odeka* vertreten würde ("ich will dich preisen", "ich will dir danken", "ich will dich bekennen"), während das corpus (mit *kij* bezw. *'al kij* eingeleitet) ausführlicher erhalten geblieben wäre. Indes könnte man auch im Blick auf den Inhalt an ein credo (Bekenntnis) denken, *jadah* (hi) ist darauf Hinweis. *v.* 14 ist im einzelnen schwierig, doch sein Inhalt ist verstehbar. Die Lösung des von Jahwe umschlossenen und Jahwe überall begegnenden Sprechers ist sozusagen die Flucht nach vorn, die Flucht aus der Du-ich-Betroffenheit in die Ich-du-Beziehung des Bekenntnisses, des Dankes und des Lobpreises, die Flucht zu Jahwe selber, die Anerkenntnis dieses "du", nicht die Anerkenntnis der Vorfindlichkeit seiner Situation, sondern des Subjekts, das ihm diese Vorfindlichkeit bereitet. Der Psalmist bleibt nicht bei der Omniscienz, Omnipotenz und Ubiquität Gottes stehen, sondern dringt vor zu Jahwe selber, zu dem "du", zu dem Herrn seiner Unentrinnbarkeit, die dieser Herr aufrecht erhalten, aber auch aufheben kann. Nicht der Jahwe an sich, sondern der auf das "ich" bezügliche Jahwe ist Zielpunkt der Flucht: "ich bekenne dich!" Und im folgenden beschreibt der Psalmist Jahwes Dasein und Agieren als: "darum daß du dich schaurig wundersam erweist, deine Werke sind wunderbar; ich weiß darum sehr wohl" (ich = *nafšij*; *joda'at*).[13] Der Partizipialstil gibt im vorliegenden Text Zustand und Dauer an. *jada'* ist mit seinen Funktionseigentümlichkeiten zu berücksichtigen, so daß man übersetzen sollte: "meine Seele erfährt (dies) sehr wohl", "ich muß damit sehr wohl vertraut bleiben". Vom Konsonantenbestand her gesehen könnte *joda'at* auch als *jada'ta* punktiert werden. Die Stelle müßte dann heißen: "meine Seele kennst du sehr wohl", wobei das vorangestellte Objekt *nafšij* als stark betont akzeptiert werden müßte. Aber der masoretische Text gibt auch in der vorliegenden punktierten Form einen guten Sinn: dem Jahwe *ḥaqartanij watteda'*, dem Wissen jenes "du" entspräche nunmehr, daß auch beim Betroffenen, bei dem "ich" ein Wissen um

---

me'aẓ und *joda'at* zu *jada'ta* geändert werden), a.a.O., S. 585f., 591. In den vorliegenden Ausführungen wird davon ausgegangen, den gesamten *v.* 14 unverändert (dies zusätzlich gegen *BHS* und *BHK*³ und E. Würthwein, "Erwägungen zu Psalm cxxxix", *VT* 7 [1957], S. 179, Anm. 1) vor *v.* 13 zu stellen.

[13] *nora'ot* = Furchtbarkeiten, Schauriges, hier adverbial gebraucht. *nifletij* ist mit den meisten zu *nifleta* zu ändern (s. auch *BHS*).

Jahwe besteht. *jada'* brauchte wie in *v.* 1 kein Objekt zu haben, was manche Exegeten bemängelt haben. Zurück zu dem *'odeka*: Die Lösung des Psalmsprechers überrascht: aus seiner verzweifelten Situation macht er einen Lobgesang, einen Hymnus, ein Bekenntnis! Er bekennt, daß dieser Jahwe Wunderbares, d.h. der rationalen Erfassung Entzogenes, tut. Und gedanklich erschließen sich ihm Berechtigung und Möglichkeit des "du" zu dieser Du-ich-Bezogenheit, deren er sich in seinem Nachdenken über Gott bedrückt bewußt werden mußte, in der Tatsache des eigenen Geschaffenseins durch diesen Gott, durch eben dieses "du". Auch hierin bleibt der Sprecher sich konsequent. Es ist nicht die Schöpfungstheologie an sich, die freilich schon Realgrund genug gewesen wäre, das Handeln Jahwes an ihm zu begründen, sondern die existenziale Interpretation der Schöpfermacht Jahwes. Nicht Mensch, Welt, Kreatur an sich sind geschaffen, sondern jenes "ich" bekennt sich als von diesem "du" erschaffen und in Existenz gesetzt. Das "du" hatte es sozusagen schon von Anfang an (gleichsam manuell) mit dem "ich" zu tun gehabt. Es war dem "du" schon Gegenstand der Aufmerksamkeit und Beachtung, noch ehe das "ich" in den Zustand der Ich-Bewußtheit getreten war (*v.* 13, 15). Das Recht des Schöpfers an seinem Geschöpf begründet das Recht Jahwes, den Psalmisten zu erforschen und zu durchmustern und um ihn zu wissen, begründet die Unentrinnbarkeit des Menschen vor Gott. Das Betroffensein durch Jahwe an allen Orten und in allen Situationen und Dimensionen kann im Blick auf die Schöpferqualität Jahwes kein Problem mehr sein. Es ist vorverlagert in die Schöpfungsproblematik, die hier vom Glaubenden in das Bekenntnis aufgehoben wird. Nicht über die Geschichtstheologie und auch nicht über die Kulttheologie, sondern über die Schöpfungstheologie erschließt sich dem Psalmisten der Zugang zu diesen theologumena.[14] Es sei dahingestellt, ob in der Tatsache des Geschaffenseins ein tröstliches Moment im Gedankenfluß von Ps. cxxxix erkannt werden darf, so wie das offenbar in Hiob x 8ff. argumentativ gegen Gottes vermeintlich grundloses Strafgericht in Anspruch genommen

[14] Ein Streit darüber, ob man von Schöpfungsglauben oder besser vom Schöpfungswissen des altorientalischen Menschen sprechen sollte, ist unnötig. Auch wenn es zum Grund*wissen* und zur Grundüberzeugung des antiken Orientalen gehört haben sollte, daß Welt, Mensch und Kreatur als von Gott geschaffen gelten (C. Westermann), so wird zu diesem Grundwissen noch sehr viel mehr gehört haben, was heute anstandslos unter die Kategorie des Glaubens subsummiert wird, — etwa, daß da Götter sind, zu denen Menschen sich zu verhalten haben (mit Gebet, mit Opfer, mit ethischen Entscheidungen usw.).

zu werden scheint.[15] Es bedarf in diesem Zusammenhang nicht der Einzelinterpretation der Verse, bezüglich welcher in den Kommentaren und in den verschiedensten Analysen und Voten sehr viel Treffliches gesagt ist. Wichtig ist wahrscheinlich nur der Gedanke, daß dem Schöpfer Geheimnisse offenkundig sind, die dem Geschöpf verborgen bleiben. In diese denkerische Konsequenz der existenziell verstandenen Schöpfungstheologie führen die Aussagen von *v.* 16 hinein. Jahwes Augen haben gesehen, was der Ersehene selber nicht hat sehen können, nämlich sich als Embryo. Keiner kennt sich im embryonalen, im pränatalen Zustand. Diese Vorstellungen führen an die Grenze des Absurden (ähnlich wie in den *v.* 7-12), entbehren aber nicht der Konsequenzhaftigkeit. Die zweite Aussageabsicht des *v.* 16 kreist um die Kategorie der Geschichte. Auch wenn die syntaktische Struktur der Versteile 16 b+c kompliziert und schwierig ist, entläßt sie aus sich doch einen vernünftigen Sinn: "Auf dein Buch wurden sie alle geschrieben, nämlich Tage, die geschaffen worden waren, (und zwar zu einem Zeitpunkt) als noch nicht einer bei ihnen existent war". Der Sprung von der Kategorie des Biologischen zur Kategorie von Zeit und Geschichte ist in diesem Zusammenhang nicht schwierig. Ging es in *v.* 16a um die pränatale Existenz des menschlichen Lebens, die von Jahwe bereits erfaßt und umgriffen wird, so in den beiden anderen Teilen des Verses um die Vor-Geschichte, um das Ante-Historische, das durch Jahwe bereits gebunden wird, bevor es existent wird. jamim werden geknetet, geformt, geschaffen, die Zeit ist geschaffene Zeit. Kein Mensch vermag in die Regionen des Pro-Histo-

---

[15] Die schöpfungstheologische Parallele in Hiob x 8ff. (man darf allerdings auch *v.* 3 und *v.* 18ff. nicht außer Acht lassen) steht im Dienste des Appells an Gottes Schöpfergüte, die das geschaffene Werk nach Meinung des Sprechers nicht zugrunde gehen lassen dürfte. Es wird der Versuch unternommen, den Widerspruch einsichtig zu machen, der darin besteht, daß ein Schöpfer zunächst ein Werk erstehen läßt, um sich hernach zu ihm nicht mehr zu bekennen und es der Zerstörung preiszugeben. Die Auffassung ist die, daß es für diesen Fall sinnvoller gewesen wäre, dieses Werk gar nicht erst zu erschaffen. Der positive Aussageertrag läuft darauf hinaus zu hoffen, daß der Schöpfer doch zu seinem Werk stehen möchte. Zusätzlich spielen in dem Komplex noch Gedanken der Schuldlosigkeit des sprechenden Hiob und der deswegen zu erwartenden (und vielleicht sogar zu fordernden) Straflosigkeit eine Rolle. Der Unterschied zu Ps. cxxxix ist deutlich, auch wenn in schöpfungstheologischer Hinsicht darin Übereinstimmung zu erkennen ist, daß auch Hiob sich persönlich als von Gott geschaffen bekennt und bezeichnet. Doch die Funktionen, die die schöpfungstheologischen Aussagen für jedes Stück haben, sind verschieden. In Ps. cxxxix stehen sie als Argument für die Berechtigung der Anwesenheit Gottes im Lebensvollzug des Psalmisten, in Hiob x als Appell an den Schöpfer, das Geschöpf zu erhalten, und damit als Ausdruck der Hoffnung.

rischen vorzudringen, Jahwe allein ist es möglich, und er fixiert Zeit, indem er sie registriert, notiert, aufschreibt, protokollarisch festhält, kodifiziert, noch bevor sie in den Raum der Geschichte tritt. Jahwe verfügt über ungeborenes Leben und über ungeborene Geschichte. Er steht jenseits und diesseits von Zeit und Geschichte. Die streng individualistisch-existenziale Interpretation der Gottesbeziehung erlaubt es, auch jamim auf den Sprecher des Psalms zu beziehen, ohne daß jamim zu jamaj geändert werden müßte. Zugleich ist aber auch deutlich, wie sich die Ausführungen über das Individuell-Persönliche hinausheben zu Grundsatzerklärungen, zum Paradigmatischen. Man sollte vorsichtig sein mit dogmatischen Begriffen wie Prädestination und Determination, doch gelangt der Sprecher von Ps. cxxxix zweifellos in diese Richtung. Er kann sich offenbar nicht anders behelfen, als den Gottesgedanken in diese Konsequenz zu bringen. Ubiquität, Omniscienz und Omnipotenz Gottes auf der einen Seite und die Unentrinnbarkeit des Menschen auf der anderen Seite gründen in der Schöpferpotenz Gottes. Die Schöpfermacht Gottes umgreift die pränatale und prohistorische Existenz menschlichen Lebens und Erlebens und gibt ihr ihre Termination. Im Blick auf *v.* 8 muß hinzugefügt werden, daß dieser Gott auch die posthistorische menschliche Existenz in der *še'ol* umschließt. Es gibt temporal und lokal keinen Jahwe-freien Raum mehr. Die einzig angemessene Haltung solchen Erkenntnissen und Erfahrungen gegenüber ist die des Lobpreises und Bekenntnisses zu diesem Gott, der auf Grund dieses Zirkels, eines unauflösbaren Zirkels, auf den Menschen bedrängend bezogen bleibt. Eine andere Lösung scheint es nicht zu geben, es sei denn die der Verzweiflung (*v.* 7).

V. 17+18 stellen so etwas wie ein Fazit aus dem Vorangehenden dar. Wollte man die *v.* 13-18 als einen Hymnus (mit stark reduziertem Introitus und ausgeführterem corpus) verstehen, so könnten *v.* 17+18 als Abgesang begriffen werden. Inhaltlich muß die neue durch die *v.* 14, 13, 15, 16 gegebene Situation in der Ich-du-Relation noch einmal auf das "ich" bezogen durchdacht werden. "Was mich nun anbetrifft..." (*welij*), so steht die Kapitulation in Gestalt der rhetorischen Fragen als Bekenntnis da: es ist zu schwer, diese Gedanken und Absichten (*re'æka*) zu begreifen, und es ist zu umfänglich, um ihrer Herr zu werden. Quantität und Qualität sind nicht zu bewältigen. Der Psalmist muß sich als unzuständig erklären. jaqar meint nicht nur die Kostbarkeit und Unerschwinglichkeit,[16] sondern auch im Blick auf

[16] Der Übersetzungsvorschlag "unerschwinglich" steht bei H. Schüngel-Straumann, a.a.O., S. 45, Anm. 66.

Dan. ii 11 die unerreichbare Höhe und unlösbare Schwierigkeit. Sie zu bewältigen wäre Überforderung. Neben dem Aspekt der Schwierigkeit wird der Gesichtspunkt der Unermeßlichkeit geltend gemacht mit dem altbekannten Bild von der Unzählbarkeit der Sandkörner, deren Summe durch die Unermeßlichkeit der Gedanken Gottes noch übertroffen wird. Der letzte Satz von *v.* 18 schiebt gleichsam alle Überlegungen beiseite und zieht den Schlußstrich:[17] "käme ich doch in irgendeiner Form zu einem Ende", *we'odij 'immak*, "ich wäre immer noch bei dir", d.h. "ich wäre deiner Anwesenheit in meinem Lebensvollzug immer noch nicht entflohen". Wahrscheinlich ist die innere Konsequenz des gesamten Psalms auch für das Verständnis dieses Passus leitend. Ehe man von der Unmöglichkeit spricht, Gottes Gedanken, Absichten, Pläne (*re'im*) zu erfassen, zu begreifen, zu bewältigen, sollte von der unabweisbaren Anwesenheit des "du" Gottes beim "ich" des Menschen die Rede sein; dies jedoch mit dem Hinweis auf die bemerkenswerte Umkehrung "ich noch bei dir", während die Betroffenheit ja immer durch die Verhältnisbestimmung "du bei mir" bezw. "du-mich" zum Ausdruck gekommen war. Vielleicht mag darin etwas Tröstliches erkannt werden, daß sich in dieser Umkehrung der Formulierung die bewußte Annahme des "du" durch das "ich" ausspricht, die in dem Bekenntnis und Lobpreis ihren Grund hat. Man wird Jahwe nicht los, Jahwe ist nicht aus dem Bereich des menschlichen Lebens zu drängen, seiner Anwesenheit ist nicht zu entfliehen. Ist das erst einmal gesagt, dann darf sicherlich auch weiter ausgeführt werden, was dieses we'odij *'immak* theologisch noch zu bedeuten hat: alles Nachdenken über Gott führt zu Jahwe. Es gibt nichts, was Jahwe verstellen, was einer Begegnung mit Jahwe entgegen stehen könnte. Alle philosophischen, mythologischen, religiösen Aufarbeitungs- und Bemächtigungsversuche scheitern an Jahwe, vermögen Jahwe nicht beizukommen, können Jahwe nicht überwinden (*v.* 6 *lo' 'ukal lah*). Man muß vor Jahwe stehen bleiben, man muß Jahwe aushalten, Jahwe ist nicht objektivierbar.[18] Man kann sich Jahwe gegenüber nur als Betroffener verhalten, der der Duch-ich-Betroffenheit in dem Ich-bekenne-dich-Verhältnis begegnet. In alledem ist unausgesprochen und ohne direkte Worte vernehmlich von der Größe und Gewalt, letztlich sachzutrefflich

[17] Die Herleitung des als Prädikat verwendeten Verbums von *qaṣaṣ* (hi) = "zu Ende kommen" hat viel Wahrscheinlichkeit für sich, vgl. auch *BHS*.

[18] Das Schlagwort von der "Nichtobjektivierbarkeit Gottes" nimmt auch H. Schüngel-Straumann, a.a.O., S. 49 auf.

von der Gottheit Gottes die Rede. Anderes wäre nicht Gott. Der Psalmsprecher kann es sich und demjenigen, der seinen Reflektionen folgt, nicht ermäßigen. Wenn Gott überhaupt ist, dann nur so!

V

Ist das bis zu *v.* 18 vorgetragene Verständnis richtig, so zeigte sich bei der Aufweisung der Gottesproblematik eine erstaunliche Geschlossenheit und Konsequenz in der Gedankenführung, die im Aufeinanderbezogensein der vorgetragenen Reflektionen auch einen möglichen und einsichtigen Gedankenfortschritt bedeutete. Aus diesem Rahmen brechen die *v.* 19-24 völlig aus. Sie sind durch nichts inhaltlich vorbereitet. Es ist verständlich, wenn in der Exegese immer wieder ihre Fremdheit und im Gefolge davon ihre Nichtzugehörigkeit zu diesem Psalm empfunden worden ist. Formal geben sie sich — wie schon oben ausgeführt — als Gebet, als ein Vernichtungs-, als ein Rachegebet und e contrario als eine Unschuldsbeteuerung, die für Orthodoxie und gegen Apostasie auftritt. Bisher ging es allein um jene Du-ich- und Ich-du-Beziehung, in welche der Psalmist das gott-menschliche und mensch-göttliche Verhältnis geordnet sieht, eine dritte personale Größe hatte darin keinen Platz Geprägte Formulierungen sind zusammengestellt mit singulären und selteneren Ausdrucksweisen. Die Erinnerung an die Situation des Angeklagten und damit auch formal an das Gebet eines Angeklagten ist durchaus gegeben. Doch sollte man auch die Unterschiede nicht übersehen, die zwischen der in den *v.* 19-24 vorausgesetzten Situation und der Lage eines unschuldig Verfolgten bestehen. So könnte auch der Eindruck berechtigt sein, daß in den *v.* 19-24 ein Zusatz vorliegt, mit welchem die Gedanken der *v.* 1-18 durch einen Späteren adaptiert sind, so wie etwa in Ps. xix die kühnen Gedanken der *v.* 1-7 durch den Torah-Hymnus der *v.* 8-15 angenommen und vor Mißverständnissen geschützt werden sollten. Es besteht ja durchaus die Möglichkeit, daß bestimmte theologumena des Ps. cxxxix noch keineswegs Allgemeingut der theologischen Überzeugungen jener Zeit gewesen sind, aus welcher der Psalm stammt. Es müßte der Versuch unternommen werden, den Psalm redaktionsgeschichtlich zu analysieren. Wollte man an der Zusammengehörigkeit aller Verse festhalten, so gäbe es schließlich auch den Lösungsvorschlag, daß der Psalmist vor sich selber und vor seinen abgründigen Reflektionen sich mit geprägtem Gebetsgut zu dem Gott seiner Väter schlägt, auf dessen Seite er unter allen Umständen verbleiben möchte. Sicherheit ist in dieser Frage nicht zu gewinnen, es gilt, Wahrscheinlichkeitswerte festzuhalten. Die Frage des Verhältnisses der beiden Psalm-Teile zueinander ist im Gegensatz zu der heute vorherrschenden Annahme ihrer Zusammengehörigkeit noch nicht geklärt.

VI

Es unterliegt wohl keinem Zweifel, daß die nachgezeichneten theologischen Konzeptionen des Ps. cxxxix eine differenziertere theologie- und geistesgeschichtliche Entwicklung voraussetzen und somit in der nachexilischen Zeit angesiedelt sind. Ein spätes Sprachgut scheint diese Annahme zu stützen. Der deuterojesajanische Monotheismus muß den Reflektionen voraufliegen, die Nähe zu weisheitlichem Denken ist zurecht immer wieder beobachtet worden.[19] Überraschend sind die sprachlichen und gedanklichen Übereinstimmungen mit vielen Passagen des Hiobbuches,[20] doch wird man die Unterschiede nicht ignorieren dürfen. Das Problem, von Gott unschuldig geschlagen. und verlassen zu sein, ist gerade nicht das Problem des Psalmisten. Ihn bedrückt die Anwesenheit, nicht die Abwesenheit Gottes in seinem Leben. Ihm wäre eine Abwesenheit Jahwes zuweilen lieber. Gottes "Handeln" besteht in Ps. cxxxix weitgehend lediglich im überraschenden und unvermuteten und wohl eben nicht immer willkommenen Dasein Jahwes in Lebens- und Denkvollzügen des Psalmisten.[21] Jahwe ist dem Denker im Psalm ärgerlich, weil man Jahwe nirgendwo loswerden kann. Indes mag die sprachliche und gedankliche Nähe zu Hiob (und auch zu anderen späten und weisheitlichen Texten des Alten Testaments) den geistigen Ort nachweisen, in welchem Ps. cxxxix wurzelt, die spätnachexilische israelitische Weisheit. Aufbau und Gestaltung der *v.* 1-18 können durchaus im Interesse einer weisheitlichen Didaktik vorgenommen worden sein. Das reflek-

[19] Neben J. Holman, J. Krašovec, H. Schüngel-Straumann, s. H.-P. Müller, "Die Gattung des 139. Psalms", *ZDMG* Suppl. 1 (1969), S. 345-55, bes. 349ff.; J. L. Koole, "Quelques Remarques sur le Psaume 139", *Studia Biblica et Semitica Theodoro Christiano Vriezen Dedicata* (Wageningen, 1966), S. 176-80; G. v. Rad, *Weisheit in Israel* (Neukirchen-Vluyn, 1970), passim.

[20] Auf sie hat zuletzt eindrücklich H. Schüngel-Straumann, a.a.O., hingewiesen, doch müßten auch die stark auseinandergehenden Aussageintentionen untersucht werden, die zwischen Hiob und Ps. cxxxix bestehen.

[21] Man wird in Bezug auf Jahwe wohl trotzdem nicht von ontischen Kategorien sprechen dürfen, obwohl es dringend erforderlich wäre, neben den zweifellos prominenten Tunskategorien im Gottesbild Jahwes Phänomenen mehr Aufmerksamkeit zu schenken, die als Seinskategorien verstanden werden können (Erhabenheit, Heiligkeit, Majestät, Glanz, Licht, Unvergleichlichkeitsformeln usw.).

torische Element ist in den Ausführungen ja nicht zu verkennen. Nicht unerwähnt bleiben soll das Zurücktreten kultischer und geschichtlicher Traditionen. Bemerkenswerterweise begegnet der Psalmsprecher Jahwe offenbar nicht im Raum der Geschichte (oder höchstens im Raum der Kleinfeldgeschichte seines eigenen persönlichen Lebens) und nicht in den Gottesdiensten seines Volkes, sondern vielmehr in seinen Reflektionen. Möglicherweise darf dies als Hinweis darauf gewertet werden, daß Geschichts- und Kulttheologie für ihn nicht mehr aktuell gewesen sind, vielleicht sogar umstritten oder nicht tragfähig genug. Auch dies könnte auf die spätnachexilische als auf eine als nachgeschichtlich empfundene Periode hindeuten. Beachtet werden sollte die Nutzung von Schöpfungstheologie für Begründung und Argumentation. Der Schöpfungsglaube hilft die Probleme lösen. Die Schöpfungstheologie erfährt eine individualistisch-existenziale Ausprägung (wohl noch konsequenter und anders als in der ähnlichen Stelle bei Hiob x). Der durch die Vernachlässigung von Geschichts- und Kulttheologie bedingte Verlust des universalistischen Aspekts im Gottesbild Jahwes wird durch die konsequente auf Präexistenzielles und Prohistorisches angewandte Schöpfungstheologie auf- und eingeholt. An die Stelle von Geschichts- und Kultmächtigkeit Jahwes ist in der theologischen Überlegung dieses Psalms dessen Omniscienz, Omnipotenz und Ubiquität getreten, die in der Individualbeziehung Gott-Mensch und Mensch-Gott konkret werden. Die Verhandlung solcher Themen gehört wie das Hiob-Thema (unschuldiges Leiden des Gerechten, Durchbrechung des Tun-Ergehen-Zusammenhanges) in die Diskussion spätisraelitischer weisheitlicher Schulen. In dieser Zeit liegt die Auflösung und Umformung klassischer literarischer Gattungen (vgl. dieselbe Erscheinung in der nachexilischen Prophetie oder schon bei Deuterojesaja), weswegen eine bestimmte literarische oder gattungstypische Gestaltung nach herkömmlichen Formen (etwa individuelles Klagelied, Vertrauenslied, Hymnus, Gebet eines Angeklagten usw.) in diesem Psalm nicht erwartet werden sollte. Andererseits ist aber auch wieder nicht der Bezug zur (auch literarischen) Tradition gänzlich aufgegeben. Doch werden diese in dem Psalm noch erkennbaren Formelemente zu eigenen Aussageabsichten genutzt und entfernen sich dadurch von ihrem ursprünglichen "Sitz im Leben". Sie erhalten einen neuen "Sitz im Leben". Dieser ist innerhalb der Weisheitsliteratur nicht immer und sofort und unmittelbar zu bestimmen, was aber nicht bedeutet, daß es keinen gegeben hätte. Welchen "Sitz im Leben" hatte beispielsweise die Hiob-Dichtung? Man wird auch nicht sagen dürfen, daß in Ps. cxxxix eine "neue" formale Gestaltung verneint sei. Die ebenmäßige Gliederung (wie auch immer sie im einzelnen ausgesehen haben mochte) ist äußerlich noch registrierbar und inhaltlich als Reflektion, vielleicht besser sogar noch als Meditation, als Bekenntnis und als Gebet bestimmbar. Man könnte in diesen Stücken Elemente des Frömmigkeitsvollzugs nachexilischer weisheitlich geprägter Frommer sehen.

Die mögliche Aufnahme von Traditionen, die der Berichterstattung über ein Berufungsgeschehen zugehören, zeigt die Breite der Rückbeziehung auf Überliefertes durch die Weisheit, wobei noch gar nicht ausgemacht ist, ob sich alttestamentliche Weisheit nicht in gewisser Weise als Kontinuum und Erbe alttestamentlicher Prophetie begriffen hat, so daß sich ein Weisheitslehrer ähnlich wie ein Prophet als von Jahwe betroffen und berufen hätte verstehen können, so wie es die prophetischen Berufungsberichte beschreiben. Die oben aufgezeigte Parallelität des Ps. cxxxix zu Gedanken und Formulierungen aus den Berufungsberichten bei Jeremia und bei Ezechiel sollte nicht ignoriert werden.

Die anspruchsvolle Intellektualität, die sich ja auch in der Hiobdichtung zeigt, zeugt für eine enorme geistige Höhenlage. Die Angehörigen der spätnachexilischen israelitischen Weisheitsschulen müssen intellektuell hochstehend gewesen sein. Gegenstand ihres Nachdenkens ist, wie eben auch Ps. cxxxix aufweist, immer wieder die Gottesproblematik gewesen, hier speziell das Verhältnis Jahwes zu den Mythologemen und Theologemen der Umwelt. Dabei scheint das Gottesproblem auch unter Absehung spezifischer israelitischer Theologie (etwa der Geschichtstheologie) durchvariiert worden zu sein. Die Überlegungen des Ps. cxxxix haben darin fast einen philosophischen Charakter und gewinnen erst in dem Bekenntnis (*v.* 14, 13, 15ff.) ihren theologischen Charakter zurück. Es geht um die Gottheit Gottes und damit um die Gottheit Jahwes. Die Extrapolation Jahwes in seinem Tun und in seinem Sein aus dem typischen, überschaubaren berechenbaren, erwarteten Tun und Sein orientalischer Götter, läßt Jahwe wirklich zu Gott werden und Gott sein. Eigentlich gilt: wer sich bei *šaḥar* aufhält, kann nicht zugleich bei *jam* sein, und wer in *šamajim* seine Bleibe aufstellt, kann sich nicht zugleich in die *še'ol* betten, und wer im Finstern ist, kann nicht zugleich im Lichte stehen. Für Jahwe gelten diese Begrenzungen nicht. Jahwe ist kein orientalischer Gott mehr, Jahwe ist überhaupt kein religiöser Gott mehr, sondern Jahwe ist Gott schlechthin! So könnte man im Ps. cxxxix auch von der Gottwerdung Jahwes sprechen.

Natürlich ist es vorstellbar, daß eine so weit ausgreifende Thematik, ein so kühner theologischer Gedankenflug den Autor der Skepsis und der Verdächtigung, der Gefahr des Isoliertwerdens aussetzte. Denker hatten es im Kontext einer "Normalfrömmigkeit" wohl immer schwer und gerieten oft genug in den Geruch der Gottlosigkeit, des Abfalls und des Unglaubens. Man darf fragen, ob es schon Allgemeingut des israelitischen Glaubens war, daß Jahwe in der *še'ol* anwesend ist, dort seine Herrschaft ausübt und die *še'ol* zu zwingen vermag, die Beute herauszugeben!? War es israelitisch integrierbar, von Geschichts- und Kulttheologie abzusehen? Ist die Nutzung von Schöpfungstheologie in ihrer Deduktion auf Präexistenzielles und Prohistorisches erlaubt gewesen? Konnte nicht der Vorwurf des Abweichens vom althergebrachten Wege (*derek 'olam*) entstehen, demgegenüber sich der Psalmist durch das Gebet und das darin implizit enthaltene Bekenntnis zu dem traditionellen Glauben schützen, wobei er mit Hilfe von geprägten Formulierungen sozusagen "auf Sicherheit gehen" wollte? Es ist schließlich auch vorstellbar, daß der Problematiker von Ps. cxxxix sich selber bei seinen ungewohnten Gedanken durch dieses Gebet in den Schutz dessen stellen wollte, über den er nachgedacht hat. So gesehen kann das Gebet am Schluß des Psalms seinen guten und einsichtigen Sinn haben und behalten. Trotz geprägter Formulierungen ist aber auch in diesem Stück (*v.* 19-24) nicht das reflektorische Element zu verkennen. Die Verse stellen nicht eine direkte Übernahme des Gebets eines Angeklagten oder eines Rachgebets dar, so daß auch nicht ein kultisch-rechtlicher Akt als "Sitz im Leben" für dieses Stück vorausgesetzt werden muß. Geprägtes Gut ist verarbeitet und auf den Sprecher selber zugeordnet.[22] In Ps. cxxxix begegnen Meditation (Reflektion), Bekenntnis und Gebet, offenbar Frömmigkeitsäußerungen des intellektuell regsamen Gottesfürchtigen in der spätnachexilischen jüdischen Gemeinde der sich bestimmten weisheitlichen Schulen angeschlossen haben mag.

---

[22] G. v. Rad, S. 60, 71, rechnet Ps. cxxxix zur sogenannten "Auseinandersetzungsliteratur". Der Terminus ist in der Ägyptologie gebräuchlich (Nachweis bei G. v. Rad).

DIE NACHTGESICHTE DES PROPHETEN SACHARJA

Zur Idee einer Form

von

GERHARD WALLIS
Halle/Saale

Die Nachtgesichte des Propheten Sacharja bieten der alttestamentlichen Forschung durch ihre Eigenart ein besonderes Problem. Zwar ist ihre formale wie inhaltliche Gestaltung nicht einzigartig und bietet mancherlei Anknüpfungsmöglichkeiten in der alttestamentlichen Prophetie.[1] So sieht der Prophet Amos eine fressende Heuschrecke (vii 1) oder einen ⟨Mann⟩ mit einem Bleilot in der Hand (s. *BHS* z.St. vii 7), einen Korb mit reifem Obst (viii 1). Jeremia sieht im Zusammenhang mit seinem Berufungserlebnis einen Mandelbaumzweig (i 11-12) und einen siedenden Topf (i 13-14).

Zweierlei ist zu diesen Erlebnissen zu sagen: 1) In jedem der Fälle handelt es sich offensichtlich um eine reale Wahrnehmung, die eine Deutung oder ein Zwiegespräch mit Jahwe im Gefolge hat. 2) In allen Fällen wird die hebräische Wurzel *rā'âh* verwendet und nicht die Wurzel *ḥāzâh*.

> Ähnlich steht es mit der Erfahrung des Propheten Ezechiel, der aus der Deportation im Zweistromland nach Jerusalem entrückt wird und dort die religiösen Verirrungen seines Volkes mit ansehen muß (viii 1-18), der andererseits von dem ihn begleitenden Wesen durch den überirdischen Tempel geführt wird, um dessen Ausmaße genau studieren zu können (xl-xlii, s. xl 2 *rā'âh*).

In diesen Darstellungen sind die Nachtgesichte des Propheten Sacharja teilweise schon vorgezeichnet. Die Propheten sehen etwas, sei es in visionärer Schau oder vielmehr mit ihrem leiblichen Auge, was zumindest bei Amos und Jeremia anzunehmen ist. In keinem der Fälle ist jedoch davon die Rede, daß es sich um Erfahrungen während der Nacht handelt. Vielmehr setzt auch dort das Sehen *rā'âh* das Licht

---

[1] Chr. Jeremias, *Die Nachtgesichte des Sacharja. Untersuchung zu ihrer Stellung im Zusammenhang der Visionsberichte im Alten Testament und zu ihrem Bildmaterial* (Göttingen, 1977).

des Tages voraus. Beim Propheten Sacharja dagegen wird das Sehen *rā'âh* während der Nachtzeit ausdrücklich hervorgehoben (i 8). Dies könnte vermuten lassen, daß es sich um nächtliche Erfahrungen, also um Traumerlebnisse, handeln soll.

Dagegen spricht aber die gesamte Darstellungsweise. Der Prophet äußert sich so, daß er seine "Augen aufhebt" *nāśâ' 'ēnajim* (ii 1, 5, v 1, 5, vi 1), was im Alten Testament zwar nicht ausschließlich, aber in weit überwiegender Mehrzahl der Fälle als Bezeichnung für das reale leibliche Sehen, ja das suchende Ausschauen verwendet wird. Es tritt auch immer in Verbindung mit *rā'âh* auf, nie verbunden mit *ḥāzâh*, das auch in den Nachtgesichten sicher nicht zufällig gemieden wird.

Schließlich beschreibt der Prophet, daß er offensichtlich zwischendurch einmal eingeschlafen ist und vom *angelus interpres* aufgeweckt werden mußte (iv 1). Die hierbei verwendete Wurzel *'ûr* III Hiph. bedeutet "munter machen, aufstacheln". Der Prophet möchte also mit Nachdruck auf seinen Wachzustand hinweisen. Es handelt sich damit nicht um ein Traumerlebnis, ganz offenbar auch nicht um eine Vision in dem im Alten Testament geläufigen Sinne. Der Prophet hätte dies sicher deutlicher erkennen lassen. Bezeichnenderweise geht E. L. Ehrlich in seiner Monographie über den Traum im Alten Testament [2] auf das Phänomen der Nachtgesichte auch gar nicht ein.

Weiterhin ist auch etwas ganz anderes als in Gen. xlvi 2 gemeint, wo dem Ahnvater Israel in einem Inkubationsorakel *mar'ôt hallaijlâh* die Zukunft seiner Nachkommenschaft gedeutet wird.[3] Die deutsche Sprache trägt diesem besonderen Offenbarungserleben Sacharjas dadurch Rechnung, daß sie speziell für dieses die Bezeichnung "Nachtgesichte" verwendet, die ungefähr seit der Mitte des vergangenen Jahrhunderts in unseren deutschen Sprachgebrauch eingedrungen ist.[4] Dieser Terminus ist eigentlich eher die Wiedergabe von *ḥazôn laijlâh*, *ḥäzjôn laijlâh*.[5] Dennoch hat dieser Ausdruck mehr und mehr die besondere Erfahrungsform des Propheten Sacharja bezeichnet und die Vermittlung durch den *angelus interpres* in den Nachtgesichten zu charakterisieren begonnen.

Es kann also zusammengefaßt werden: Um einen Traum handelt

---

[2] *Der Traum im Alten Testament*, *BZAW* 73 (1953).

[3] Ehrlich, S. 34.

[4] Nach meiner Beobachtung verwendet Michael Baumgarten, *Die Nachtgesichte Sacharjas* I/II (Braunschweig, 1859), zum ersten Mal diesen Begriff grundsätzlich.

[5] *ḥāzôn*/*ḥäzjiôn*/*ḥäzjônôt laijlâh* s. Hi. iv 13, xx 8, xxxiii, 15; Jes. xxix 7; alle Aussagen beziehen sich jedoch auf Träume.

es sich nicht. Dieser muß bekanntlich im Wachzustand erst gedeutet werden. Eine direkte Begegnung zwischen Gott und dem Menschen hat hier auch nicht stattgefunden. Somit grenzen sich die Nachtgesichte deutlich von den übrigen Prophetenerlebnissen des Alten Testaments ab, auch denen des Sacharja-Buches, welche der Gestalt des *angelus interpres* nicht bedürfen.

Damit ergibt sich die Frage, was für eine Art des aktuellen Erlebens hinter der gesamten Darstellung überhaupt steht. Zur Beantwortung dieser Frage bietet sich eine Einzelbeobachtung an: L. Koehler hat in einem kurzen Beitrag zur alttestamentlichen Wortforschung "Hebräisches *jāṣā'* und Markus 8, 11" [6] für die gelegentlich absolute Verwendung der Wurzel *jāṣā'* im Sinne von: "erscheinen, in Erscheinung treten, auftreten"; engl. "to appear (as someone), to enter"; franz. "paraître, entrer (en scène)" vorgeschlagen. So ist Mk. viii 11 καὶ ἐξῆλθον οἱ φαρισαίοι zu übersetzen: "und es traten die Pharisäer auf". Demzufolge ist im Sacharja-Buch ii 7 *w^ehinneh hammal'âk haddōbêr bî jōṣê'* zu übersetzen mit: "Siehe da trat der Bote auf, der mit mir redete", und daran anschließend die Wendung *ûmal'âk 'aḫêr jōṣê' liqrâ'tô*: "und ein anderer Bote trat (auf) ihm entgegen". Damit ist die Schwierigkeit behoben, die entstünde, wenn man *jāṣā'* mit "heraustreten" übersetzte, weil dann nämlich die adverbielle Bestimmung des Ortes vermißt wird, von dem beide Boten herkommen. Eine Emendation in *'āmad* (LXX εἱστήκει), wie sie J. Wellhausen, E. Sellin und K. Elliger zur Stelle vorgeschlagen haben, ist damit entbehrlich. Ebenso ist in v 5 *wajjēṣê' hammal'âk haddōbêr bî* zu übersetzen: "Und der Bote, der mit mir redete, trat auf". Gleichfalls gewinnt vi 1 (5) einen guten Sinn, wenn man *'arba' markābôt jōṣ^eôt mibbên š^enê hähārîm* wiedergibt mit: "Vier Wagen erschienen zwischen den beiden Bergen".[7]

Für ein deutsches Ohr verbindet sich mit dem Wort "auftreten" die Assoziation des dramatischen Ablaufes eines Vorganges besonders im Theater, auf der Bühne. Dies kann konkret in unserem Text nicht

---

[6] *ThZ* 3 (1947), S. 471.

[7] Auf anderen Wegen haben dies auch L. G. Rignell, *Die Nachtgesichte des Sacharja* (Lund, 1950), z.St.; W. A. M. Beuken, *Haggai-Sacharja 1-8. Studien zur Überlieferungsgeschichte der frühnachexilischen Prophetie* (Assen, 1967), S. 248, Anm. 3; W. Rudolph, *KAT* XIII 4 (1976), S. 83, z.St.; Chr. Jeremias, s.o. Anm. 1, S. 119, Anm. 5, festgestellt; s.a. *KBL*³ 1974, 407b, Nr. 3. Es wäre zu erwägen, ob man nicht beispielsweise auch Gen. i 24 in ähnlicher Weise interpretieren sollte: "Die Erde soll auftreten lassen lebendiges Wesen nach seiner Art...", denn aus der Erde hervorgehen sollen die lebendigen Wesen sicher nicht.

gemeint sein. Aber die Tatsache, daß in den kleinen hier beschriebenen Szenen Menschen oder Realien in Erscheinung treten, in Bewegung und miteinander in Beziehung geraten, handeln, reden oder etwas erleiden, läßt doch die Vermutung zu, daß dem Propheten solche kleinen dramenartigen Vorgänge vor Augen gestanden haben. Ganz besonders ist dies in dem Nachtgesicht der Fall, das freilich aus formalen Gründen von der modernen Exegese ausgesondert wird, im Nachtgesicht über die Investitur des Hohenpriesters Josua (iii 1-7), in dem allerdings die Wurzel *jāṣâ*' nicht verwendet wird. Man darf annehmen, daß der Prophet die literarische Form der Nachtgesichte nicht gänzlich neu geschaffen hat, sondern derartige Darstellungen gekannt hat, die seine Formensprache befruchtet haben. Auf welchem Wege dies geschehen ist, kann mit Sicherheit nicht gesagt werden.

Wenn wir nach vergleichbaren Vorbildern suchen, fällt unser Blick verständlicherweise zunächst auf die griechische Tragödie; dies umso eher, als wir von den vielfältigen Beziehungen zwischen Syrien-Palästina und den Ländern der Mittelmeerwelt zu jener Zeit einiges wissen. Diese Berührungen dürften durch Handel und Wandel, nicht zuletzt auch durch die seinerzeit schon verbreitete jüdische Diaspora sehr stark ausgeprägt gewesen sein. Dennoch können wir von dorther für die Interpretation der Nachtgesichte wenig Hilfe erwarten, denn das große Dreigestirn der griechischen Dramatik: Aischylos, Sophokles und Euripides gehört erst in das 5. vorchristliche Jahrhundert hinein. Sie kommen mit ihren Werken als Leitbilder für die Nachtgesichte also nicht in Frage. Bleibt uns nur noch der Versuch, aus den Vorstufen des griechischen Theaters für die Nachtgesichte des Propheten Sacharia einige Verständnishilfen zu gewinnen.

B. H. Stricker hat in seinem Aufsatz: "The Origin of the Greek Theatre" [8] einen sehr ideen- und hypothesenreichen Vorschlag unterbreitet. Nach ihm erwächst das griechische Theater aus dramatischen Szenen, die als sakral betrachtet wurden. Solche Aufführungen fanden zunächst in der Nähe des Tempels statt. Erst vom 4. vorchristlichen Jahrhundert an sind Reste von Steinbauten des Theaters nachweisbar. Ursprünglich bietet das Zelt, die σκηνή, den Hintergrund; das λογεῖον war die Plattform vor der Bühne, während die ὀρχέιστρα die Fläche für den Tanz gewesen ist, die mit Häcksel ausgestreut war. Auf diese

[8] *The Journal of Egyptian Archaeology* 41 (1955), S. 34, 47.

Weise läßt sich als Ursprung der Szenerie die Dreschtenne (engl.: "threshing-floor", franz.: "aire") erkennen, auf der sich das frühantike Theater ebenso wie manche Vorgänge des täglichen, auch des kultischen Lebens [9] abgespielt haben. Mit diesem Hinweis auf die Dreschtenne und ihre szenische Bedeutung versucht Stricker seine These von der Keimzelle des griechischen Theaters zu unterbauen.

Es ist nicht unsere Aufgabe, die Vermutungen Strickers im einzelnen auf ihre Haltbarkeit hin zu überprüfen. Der Ursprung des griechischen Theaters liegt überhaupt völlig im Dunkel. Die Griechen selbst haben sich um Herkunft und Wesen ihres Theaters erst zu kümmern begonnen, als es schon voll entwickelt gewesen ist und die Quellen der Anfänge nur noch schwach zu erkennen waren.[10] Unter anderen hat hier Aristoteles in seiner "Poetik" klärend zu wirken versucht. Er hat die Wurzeln des griechischen Dramas im dithyrambischen Chorlied gesucht, das auf den Festen zu Ehren des Dionysos vorgetragen wurde. Zur Tragödie, τραγωδία, dem Bocksgesang, ist das Chorlied erst herangereift, nachdem der Gesang das Stadium des Satyrspiels durchlaufen hatte; und dieser Vorgang ist nur so zu erklären, daß dem Chor ein Einzelsänger, ἐξάρχων, gegenübergestellt wurde.[11] Wann dies geschehen ist, ist strittig. Nach Aristoteles soll dies schon Arion um 600 vor Christus vorgenommen haben. Andere schreiben eine maßgebliche Entwicklung des griechischen Theaters dem Thespis zu, der um 530 vor Christus gewirkt hat und die Maske eingeführt haben soll.

Es dürfte nach allen diesen Erwägungen nicht geraten sein, die Nachtgesichte des Sacharja mit der Entstehung des griechischen Theaters in irgendeine Beziehung zu setzen, da dieses zu Sacharjas Zeit sicher noch nicht so entfaltet war, daß es auf die Gestaltung einer literarischen Form im syrisch-palästinischen Raum einen Einfluß hätte ausüben können; und auf Vorstufen des griechischen Theaters zurückzugreifen, scheint nicht geraten, da diese Vorstufen so wenig verläßlich überliefert sind und damit keinen soliden Grund für eine Folgerung abgeben. Was sicher aus der Frühgeschichte des grie-

---

[9] vgl. P. Volz, *Biblische Altertümer* (1914), S. 337; J. Gray, "Goren and City Gate", *PEQ* 85 (1953), S. 120; G. A. Ahlström, "Nathan und der Tempelbau", *VT* 11 (1961), S. 115-16.

[10] A. Lesky, *Die tragische Dichtung der Hellenen* (Göttingen, ²1964), I. Ursprungsprobleme, S. 11-39; ders., *Geschichte der griechischen Literatur* (Bern-München, ³1971), S. 260ff.; D. P. Kallistow, *Antikes Theater* (dt., Leipzig, 1974), S. 54ff.

[11] A. Lesky, *Geschichte der griechischen Literatur*, S. 260.

chischen Theaters erkennbar ist, steht zu den Nachtgesichten und ihrer Gestaltung übrigens in einer so losen Beziehung, daß wir uns gänzlich auf den Boden der Hypothese begeben würden, wollten wir daraus irgendwelche Schlüsse herleiten.

Bestenfalls könnte auf das erste Nachtgesicht etwas Licht fallen, in welchem der Reiter auf dem bräunlichen Pferd (der Einzelsänger?), die Botschaft der verschiedenfarbigen Pferde (!) — so wörtlich im Text i 8b, 11aαb — entgegennimmt, daß sie die ganze Welt durchstreift hätten und überall schon Ruhe vorgefunden hätten. Dabei handelt es sich an dieser Stelle nicht um bocksgestaltige Sänger (den Chor?), sondern um pferdegestaltige, die uns auch in den sogenannten Silenen der griechischen Dionysien begegnen.[12] Dies wäre zwar auffällig und beleuchtet das erste Nachtgesicht ein wenig, ist aber in dieser Art singulär. Daher müssen wir darauf verzichten, diese Spur weiterzuverfolgen. In den übrigen Nachtgesichten findet sich jedenfalls kein Anhalt mehr für irgendwelche Beziehungen zwischen dem frühen griechischen Drama und den Nachtgesichten des Sacharja. Festzuhalten wäre lediglich, daß die Keimzelle des griechischen Theaters die sakrale Kultausübung gewesen ist. Selbst wenn die Nachtgesichte Sacharjas eine Affinität zum Kultus aufweisen, wie K. Seybold[13] meint, haben wir doch vorerst daraus keine Folgerungen bezüglich der Form der Nachtgesichte zu ziehen.

Wir kommen zu dem Schluß, daß von dem Geist der griechischen Tragödie her die Idee der Nachtgesichte nicht zu beleuchten ist. Auch der Versuch B. H. Strickers, in die dunkle Frühgeschichte des griechischen Theaters Licht zu bringen, kann uns nicht wesentlich bei der Deutung der Nachtgesichte weiterhelfen. Auch die Form der Dithyramben in der Gestalt des Einzelsängers und des ihm gegenüberstehenden Chors läßt keine Verwandtschaft mit den Nachtgesichten erkennen. Hat man aber den Versuch, die Nachtgesichte des Propheten Sacharja von der dramatischen Gestaltung her zu deuten, aber erst einmal unternommen, liegt es nahe, weiter nach früheren Belegen solcher dramenartigen Literaturzeugnisse zu suchen.

Es kann nicht überraschen, daß diese Quellen auch wieder aus dem sakralen Bereich stammen, nun jedoch von sehr hohem Alter sind. Es handelt sich um den sogenannten Dramatischen Ramesseum-Papyrus (DRP), welchen G. E. Quibell bei seiner Grabung für den *Egyptian Research Account* in den Jahren 1895/96 in den hinteren Räumen des Ramesseum im westlichen Theben, in einer Grabanlage

---

[12] A. Lesky, *Die tragische Dichtung der Hellenen*, S. 22ff.

[13] *Bilder zum Tempelbau. Die Visionen des Propheten Sacharja* (Stuttgart, 1974), S. 76ff.

des Mittleren Reiches, aufgefunden hat.[14] Nachdem der Berliner Papyrologe Hugo Ibscher in genialer Weise die unzählig vielen Papyrusfragmente zusammengesetzt hat und damit einen zusammenhängenden Text herstellen konnte, konnte Kurt Sethe ihn bearbeiten und in den *Untersuchungen zur Geschichte und Altertumskunde Ägyptens* im Jahr 1928 publizieren. Seine Interpretation ist im wesentlichen anerkannt, so daß sie noch heute zu Grunde gelegt werden kann.

Zur äußeren Gestalt des Papyrus sollen schnell einige informative Bemerkungen gemacht werden. Der mehrfach zusammengeklebte Papyrus hat eine Länge von über 2 m und eine Höhe von 26-27 cm. Der Schriftspiegel ist im Durchschnitt 18,5 cm hoch und hat 138 senkrechte Schriftzeilen. Unter diesem Schriftspiegel befindet sich ein Bildfeld in der Höhe von 4,6-4,8 cm Höhe.[15] Daß die Schriftzeilen und die Bilder zueinander gehören, braucht nicht besonders betont zu werden. Im gegenwärtigen Zustand sind sowohl die senkrechten Zeilen in ihrer Reihenfolge untereinander gestört wie auch in ihrem Verhältnis zu den Bilddarstellungen. So bedarf es einiger Überlegungen, in welcher Reihenfolge die einzelnen Szenen des Rituals des Sed-Festes vorgetragen worden sind. H. Altenmüller [16] hat im Gefolge von W. Helck [17] den Versuch unternommen, eine richtige Abfolge wiederherzustellen.

Danach ergibt sich folgendes Bild. Das gesamte Spiel besteht aus 46 Szenen, die durch 31 Bilder illustriert werden. Dem Inhalt nach wurde das Ritualspiel auf dem Sed-Fest Sesostris I (1971-1925 v. Chr.) aufgeführt, nicht, wie ursprünglich von Sethe angenommen, zum Fest seiner Inthronisation.[18] Der Text ist nach Sethes Interpretation jedoch älter als Sesostris I, was an Schrift und Sprachgebrauch erkennbar ist. Der auf uns gekommene Papyrus seinerseits stammt aus einer Grabanlage der 12. Dynastie, also 2 Jahrhunderte später als Sesostris.[19] Wie dieses Exemplar in das Grab eines Privat-

---

[14] K. Sethe, *Dramatische Texte zu ägyptischen Mysterienspielen* (Leipzig, 1928) = *Untersuchungen zur Geschichte und Altertumskunde Ägyptens* (*UGAÄ*) 10, S. 85.

[15] H. Altenmüller, "Zur Lesung und Deutung des Dramatischen Ramesseumpapyrus", *Jaarbericht Ex Oriente Lux* (*JEOL*) 6 [Nr. 19] (1967), S. 421f.

[16] Vgl. H. Altenmüller, S. 422.

[17] "Bemerkungen zum Ritual des Dramatischen Ramesseum-Papyrus", *Or.*, N.S. 23 (1954), S. 388ff.

[18] *UGAÄ* X, S. 98.

[19] Vgl. beispielsweise: E. Otto, *Das ägyptische Mundöffnungsritual* (Wiesbaden, 1960) = *Ägyptol. Abhandlungen* 3; W. Helck, *Die Ritualszenen auf der Umfassungsmauer Ramses' II in Karnak* (Wiesbaden, 1968) = *Ägyptol. Abhandlungen* 18; K. Sethe, "Das 'Denkmal memphitischer Theologie'. Der Schabakostein des

mannes gelangt ist, in dem es die Zeiten überdauert hat, kann jedoch nicht mehr geklärt werden.

Es ist anzunehmen, daß alle Szenen dieses Papyrus als Einzelteile des gesamten Rituals real vorgeführt worden sind. In ähnlicher Weise zerlegen ja auch das ägyptische Mundöffnungsritual und die Ritualszenen auf der Umfassungsmauer Ramses II in Karnak [20] ein Zusammenspiel in einzelne Bilder und dazugehörige Texte, die sicher eine Abfolge von Einzelszenen eines Gesamtrituals darstellen sollen. Die Bedeutung jedes Bildes wird dabei durch den Text jeweils erklärt.

Das Ritualspiel des DRP war ursprünglich mythenfrei, ist aber später durch den ägyptischen Göttermythus des Osiris-Horus-Kreises untermalt worden. Bei dieser Unterlegung ist dann eine Kommentierung vorgenommen worden, die zu der auf uns gekommenen Gestalt des DRP geführt hat. In der Gesamtdarstellung des Rituals möchten wir uns der Anordnung anschließen, die Altenmüller [21] im Anschluß an Helck [22] hergestellt hat. Danach besteht das Ritual aus vier Hauptstücken: Zunächst wird die Königsstatue in die Kapelle eingeführt, was die Apotheose des verstorbenen Königs bedeuten soll. Sodann wird die symbolische Krönung des Königs vorgenommen, die mit der Huldigung der Hofbeamten verbunden ist. Danach wird der Djed-Pfeiler errichtet, dem ein Umtrieb des Viehs um die Mauer folgt. Und schließlich wird im Anschluß an die Feierlichkeit eine Schlachtung vorgenommen. Das ganze läuft auf eine sakrale Mahlzeit hinaus, die mit dem *ḥnkt*-Ritual verbunden ist.

Die einzelnen Teile werden durch vielfältige dramenartige Kleinszenen sinnfällig gemacht: Herbeibringen von Speisen und Getränken zur Opfermahlzeit, durch die Applikation von beiden Standarten, Übergabe von Kosmetika und Schmuckstücken. Das Ritual beschließen die Ausstattung der Hofbeamten, die gemeinsame Investitur, nachdem der verstorbene König bestattet worden war, Spiel und Gesänge. Alles läuft auf die Ausstattung des Königsschiffes und die Beladung der Begleitboote und deren Abfahrt hinaus. Ich möchte es mir ersparen, hier das umfangreiche Ritual in allen Einzelheiten zu behandeln, was den gegebenen Rahmen sprengen würde.

Britischen Museums", *UGAÄ* 10 (1928), S. 1-80, ist dem DRP zwar sehr verwandt, kann aber für die Interpretation der "Nachtgesichte" nicht herangezogen werden.

[20] s. Anm. 15.

[21] s. Anm. 16.

[22] *UGAÄ* 10, S. 210.

Methodisch ist es wohl am besten, die Darstellung durch sinnfällige Einzelbeispiele zu beleben. Als erstes Beispiel sei hier die von Sethe [23] als 32. und von Altenmüller [24] als 18. gezählte (Z. 97-100) Szene zitiert, zu der das Bild 21 gehört:

97 Es geschah, daß Brothälften gegeben wurden den Großen von Ober- und Unterägypten. Horus ist das, der die Augen zählt und die Köpfe (der Götter) ihnen wiedergibt.

98 Horus spricht Worte zu Thot: "Man gebe ihnen ihre Köpfe wieder!" // die Köpfe den Göttern (wieder)geben // den Großen von Ober- und Unterägypten die Brothälften geben.

99 Thot spricht Worte zu den Kindern des Horus und zu den Gefolgsleuten des Seth: "[Gnädig ist] euch Geb, und er gibt euch eure Köpfe (wieder)" // die Köpfe den Göttern (wieder)geben // ein *ḥtp-dj-nśw.t* ("gnädig ist der König und gibt")-Mahl // Ibisgau.

100 [Horus] spricht [Worte zu den Kindern des Horus und zu den Gefolgsleu]ten [des Seth:] ["gebt mir] mein Auge, damit ich zufrieden sei [mit ihm" // Das Auge] // [ein *ḥtp*-Mahl // ....]

Diese am Schluß etwas gestört überlieferte Szene weist eine kurze Handlung auf. Sie wird im erzählenden Tempus dargestellt und erfährt gleichzeitig offenbar vom Deutepriester eine verbale Interpretation, nicht auf den König, sondern zunächst auf seine "Söhne", die Großen von Ober- und Unterägypten, die Beamten. Diese erhalten Brothälften zugeteilt. Dieser dramenartige Vorgang wird so erklärt: Diese Teile von Brotfladen sind Stücke des Auges des Horus, was wohl nichts anderes als die Herrschaft des Königs von Ober- und Unterägypten bedeuten soll. Den Großen werden also diese Brotstücke übergeben, was ihnen besagt, daß sie ihre Köpfe, ihre Machtposition, zurückerhalten haben. Diese zunächst unmythische Szene wird dann mythisch unterlegt. Der König ist Horus, der Gott von Ober-, aber auch der von Unterägypten; seine Hofbeamten sind dann seine Söhne, die Horuskinder. Sein Auge ist seine Allmacht und die Repräsentanz der Einheit von Ober- und Unterägypten. Thot fungiert hier als Zeremonienmeister, der die Anweisungen erteilt. Auch diese Rolle hat im dramatischen Vollzug sicher ein Priester gespielt.

[23] s. Anm. 15.
[24] *UGAÄ* 10, S. 210.

Die Söhne des Horus werden in Z. 99 als Gefolgsleute des Seth angesprochen, was hier sicher nichts anderes als ebenfalls die Beamten des Königs bedeuten soll, zumal Horus und Seth bisweilen gemeinsam die Einheit von Ober- und Unterägypten darzustellen pflegen, wenngleich Seth an anderen Stellen als Gegner des Horus gedacht ist. Den Göttern — sprich den königlichen Beamten — wird dann das Mahl gereicht, das die Huld des Königs garantiert.

Am Ende der Z. 99 findet sich die unvermittelte Bemerkung "Ibisgau". Sethe [25] bemerkt dazu, daß dieser szenische Hinweis eine Anspielung auf das Zeichen des Gottes Thot, den Ibis, ist, vielleicht aber auch als der Ort gemeint ist, an dem die Handlung als vollzogen gedacht wird. Auf ähnliche Weise werden auch andere Szenen dieses Rituals lokalisiert. Unser Bild wird abgeschlossen durch die Bitte des Horus, sein Auge auch wiederzuerhalten, was die Vollendung seiner Repräsentanz als König von Ober- und Unterägypten bedeuten soll.

Nach Altenmüller [26] folgt dieser Szene dann Szene 19, welche von Sethe [27] in der Reihenfolge des DRP als 25. Szene (Z. 80-81) gezählt wird. Zu ihr gehört das 16. Bild. Behandelt wird das *ḥtp*-Mahl des Königs. Damit zeigt sich dann auch, daß die von H. Altenmüller vorgeschlagene Reihenfolge den Gang der Handlung richtig nachzeichnet. Hier wird nämlich die abschließend in Z. 100 von Horus geäußerte Bitte um Rückgabe seines Auges erfüllt:

80 Es geschah, daß das *ḥtp*-Mahl dem König aufgetragen wurde durch den Kellermeister. Thot ist das, der das Auge des Horus ihm zuträgt.

81 Thot spricht Worte zu Horus: "Ich reiche dir dein Auge, sei zufrieden mit ihm!" //
Das Geben des Auges des Horus an ihn // [Das Geben] des Mah[les] //.

(81) Die Horus [kinder] sprechen Worte zu Horus: "Ich hebe [es] dir (in) dein Gesicht". // Auftragen des Auges //.

Diese szenische Darstellung schließt, wie oben schon angedeutet, an die vorher behandelte nahtlos an. Hatte dort der König um sein Horusauge gebeten, so wird es ihm hier in der Gestalt des *ḥtp*-Mahles dargereicht, das die erneute Übernahme des Herrschaft über Ober-

[25] s. Anm. 15.
[26] s. Anm. 14.
[27] s. Anm. 17.

und Unterägypten symbolisieren soll. Diese Deutung ist wahrscheinlich ebenfalls von einem Priester vorgetragen worden. Der mythologische Hintergrund, der hier zu erkennen ist, beruht darauf, daß dem König/Horus von Thot, dem alten Mondgott und Gott der Weisheit, das Vollmondauge wieder verliehen wird, das während des abnehmenden Mondes und Neumonds geschwunden ist oder ihm — mythisch gesprochen — vom Gegengott Seth geraubt worden ist. Mit der Rückgabe des Horusauges erst wird der König als der Garant der Vollkommenheit und Einheit seines Reiches von Ober- und Unterägypten in seiner ganzen Herrschaft und Herrlichkeit bestätigt und dargestellt. Erst jetzt ist er vollständig ausgestattet.

Lassen Sie mich die kurze Auslegung des Textes hier abschließen. Auf eine umfassende Exegese, die erst den tieferen Sinn dieses Ritualspiels erheben würde, muß hier verzichtet werden. Formal ist jedoch ganz deutlich zu erkennen, daß von einer festgelegten sakralen Handlung berichtet wird, die auch bildlich am unteren Rande des Papyrus dargestellt wird. Im Ablauf dieser Szene werden Worte vorgetragen, so daß Handlung und Rede einander ergänzen und deuten. Diese Reden werden weitgehend Thot in den Mund gelegt. Das gesamte Ritual nimmt Bezug auf die Bestätigung des Königs als des Repräsentanten von Ober- und Unterägypten am Sed-Fest. Szenische Vermerke weisen darauf hin, daß die Handlungen auch wirklich ausgeführt worden sind und welche Bedeutung sie haben sollen.

Damit kann nun eine formale Brücke geschlagen werden zwischen dem DRP und den Nachtgesichten des Propheten Sacharja. Bei Sacharja werden die Szenen verbal dargestellt, eine bildliche Darstellung fehlt hier verständlicherweise. Aus diesem Grunde ist die erzählerische Darbietung bei dem Propheten auch etwas ausführlicher als im DRP. In den Nachtgesichten nimmt der *angelus interpres* die Aufgabe der Deutung wahr, die in gewisser Weise Thot oder der seine Rolle spielende Deutepriester übernimmt.

Aber auch der Unterschied zwischen den Nachtgesichten und dem DRP soll hier nicht übergangen werden. In den Nachtgesichten *fragt* der *angelus interpres* den Propheten oder umgekehrt nach dem Sinn des geschauten Bildes. Erst auf die Unfähigkeit des Propheten, die Wahrnehmung sich selbst richtig zu deuten, geht der *angelus interpres* ein, indem er die Bedeutung des Bildes klarstellt. In dem Nachtgesicht mit den vier Hörnern und den vier Schmieden (ii 1-4) und dem ⟨Mann⟩ mit der Meßleine (ii 5-9) wird die Handlung auch noch ein wenig weitergeführt. In diesem Sinne ist das Nachtgesicht von der Investitur des Hohenpriesters Josua (iii 1-7) am stärksten ausgeprägt, wodurch es im Zusammenhang der Nachtgesichte auch etwas fremdartig wirkt und von der Exegese ausgeschieden wird.

Gegen dieses Schema sträubt sich das Nachtgesicht von dem Leuchter und den beiden Ölbäumen (iv 1-6, 11-14). Hier findet gar keine Handlung statt; hier wird vielmehr nur ein Stilleben vorgeführt, ein stehendes Bild, das dann symbolisch gedeutet wird. Desgleichen bilden die überdimensional große fliegende Buchrolle (v 1-4) und das Epha, das die sündige Dirne enthält (v 5-11) und von den zwei Frauen mit den Storchenflügeln davongetragen wird, ein eigenes Problem. Wie sollte man sich diese beiden Bilder überhaupt real in Szene gesetzt vorstellen können?

Diese Feststellungen bewahren uns vor dem unbedachten Schluß, daß die Nachtgesichte des Propheten Sacharja den Szenen des DRP nachgestaltet seien. Immerhin aber haben diese mit den Szenen des DRP eines gemeinsam: Mit den Bildern wird dem geistigen wie dem leiblichen Auge etwas vorgestellt, was über den Bereich des Dargestellten und Darstellbaren im Wesen hinausgeht. Die augenfällige, szenische Handlung initiiert einen Vorgang, der dem menschlichen Handlungsraum schlechterdings völlig entzogen ist. Damit aber befinden wir uns im Bereich des Ritus.

Alle diese Szenen sind aber nur verständlich von dem Prinzip der Identität des dargestellten Symbols mit der intendierten Wirklichkeit her selbst, der Identität von Bild und Sache. Auf diese Weise wird das Problem der Gegenwartsbewältigung im DRP gelöst: Die innere Begründung der Repräsentanz des Königs von Ober- und Unterägypten als des Garanten der Einheit des Reiches. In den Nachtgesichten des Propheten Sacharja geht es dagegen um die Darstellung des neuen Jerusalem als des Garanten der Herrschaft Gottes über sein Volk und die gesamte Welt.

Wollen wir aber trotz aller Einwendungen auf diese Weise den sachlichen Bezug zwischen den Szenen des DRP und den Nachtgesichten des Propheten Sacharja sicherstellen, bleibt nun aber noch eine Frage offen. Ist nicht der zeitliche Abstand zwischen beiden literarischen Zeugnissen zu groß, als daß eines zum Verständnis der Form mit dem anderen in formale oder inhaltliche Beziehung gesetzt werden könnte? Wenn nun auch keine genealogische Abhängigkeit der Nachtgesichte von den Szenen des DRP postuliert werden soll und kann, so muß doch zumindest eine zeitliche Kontinuität vorausgesetzt werden können.

Nun wurde bereits von Sethe festgestellt, daß der Text aus der Zeit Sesostris I einerseits erheblich älteren Datums, der Papyrus andererseits in einem Grab deponiert war, das zwei Jahrhunderte später angelegt worden ist, was für dies Ritual eine Lebensdauer schon vor und über Sesostris hinaus beweist. Das allein spricht dafür, daß das Ritual nicht zeitlich punktuell gebunden gewesen ist, sondern mit der Existenz des Sed-Festes eine überdauernde Aktualität besessen hat.

Eine andere Beobachtung führt uns nun aber noch weiter: Die Szenenabfolge ist im DRP, wie schon oben bemerkt wurde, gestört, ebenso der Zusammenhang mit dem Bildfeld. Helck [28] hat bemerkt, daß in dem Grab der Cheriuf in Theben das Sed-Fest-Ritual des Amenophis' III (1402-1363 v. Chr.) in Bildern dargestellt sei. Altenmüller [29] hat auf Grund dieser Bilder die ursprüngliche Reihenfolge wiederhergestellt, die im wesentlich späteren Dokument aus der Zeit Amenophis' III nachgewiesen ist, während die Folge im DRP sicher durch eine falsche Abschrift entstanden ist. Auf Einzelheiten der Argumente Helcks und Altenmüllers hier einzugehen, ist nicht nötig. Wichtig ist hier nur, daß das gleiche Ritual auch noch in der Zeit des 15./14. vorchristlichen Jahrhunderts gepflegt worden ist, also mehr als ein halbes Jahrtausend nach Sesostris I. Altenmüller geht wohl mit Recht davon aus, daß dieses Repräsentationsritual ständig zum Sed-Fest wiederholt und damit als Jubiläums-Festritual angesehen worden ist. Damit ist dann dem Ritual eine Lebensdauer zuzuschreiben, die auch noch über Amenophis III hinausgereicht haben wird.

Möglicherweise hat Altenmüller [30] auch darin recht, daß er die Szene 10 (Z. 117-119), nach Sethe Szene 38, jenem gegenüber als Prügelszene der Priester deutet, die noch Sethe als "Das symbolische Bilden der Leiter für die Himmelfahrt des Königs" angesehen hatte.[31] Diese Szene folgt nach Altenmüllers Rekonstruktion der von der Herbeitragung der Königsstatue, Szene 9 (Z. 114-116), nach Sethe Szene 37. Das besagt im vorliegenden Zusammenhang, daß der verstorbene Vater des Königs in Gestalt der Statue zu seiner Grabstätte geleitet wurde. Die Begräbnisstätte ist im Ritual zweifellos die Kapelle, an dessen Eingang Gefolgsleute des Seth stehen und dem zum Gott aufgestiegenen verstorbenen König den Einlaß in den Tempel verwehren. Prügelnd erst müssen sich die Gefolgsleute des

---

[28] *JEOL* 6 [Nr. 18] (1967), S. 271-79.
[29] *UGAÄ* X, S. 223.
[30] s. Anm. 15, S. 433; *JEOL* 6 [Nr. 18] (1967), S. 273ff.
[31] s. Anm. 14.

Horus/Königs den Zugang zu den inneren Gemächern des Tempels verschaffen.

Altenmüller verweist in diesem Zusammenhang auf eine Darstellung des Herodot (II, 63), der von folgendem zu berichten weiß: "Nach Heliupolis und Buto pilgern sie nur, um dort zu opfern. Auch in Papremis opfern sie und feiern sie wie anderswo. Wenn aber die Sonne untergeht, machen sich einige wenige Priester bei dem Bild zu schaffen, während die meisten sich mit hölzernen Keulen am Eingang des Tempels aufstellen und mehr als tausend Männer, die ihr Gebet verrichten, auch mit Knüppeln bewaffnet, an der anderen Seite auf einem Haufen stehen. Das Bild, das sich in einem vergoldeten hölzernen Schrein befindet, wird am Vorabend des Festes in einen anderen Tempel gebracht. Nun spannen sich die wenigen Priester, die bei dem Bilde geblieben sind, vor einen vierrädrigen Wagen, auf dem der Schrein mit dem Bilde steht, um es wieder in den Tempel zu ziehen; die anderen aber, die am Eingang stehen, lassen sie nicht herein. Dann kommt die Beter dem Gotte zu Hilfe und schlagen auf sie ein, weil sie ihn nicht hereinlassen wollen. Da kommt es dann zu einer Prügelei, wobei sie sich die Köpfe einschlagen, und ich glaube, auch manche an ihren Wunden sterben. Die Ägypter freilich behaupten, es sei noch nie jemand ums Leben gekommen".

Wenn auch Herodot dieser Szene eine andere Deutung unterlegt, als sie durch das Sed-Fest-Ritual gegeben wird, so ist doch offensichtlich die Prügelszene des DRP gemeint. So haben wir hier den Beleg für eine Einzelszene dieses Rituals noch im 5. vorchristlichen Jahrhundert. Damit ist nun auch die zeitliche Brücke zu Sacharja geschlagen. Es könnten also solche oder ähnliche Rituale nicht nur in Ägypten, sondern auch in Syrien-Palästina bekannt gewesen sein.

Es liegt mir hier nicht daran, wie schon oben betont, Form und Anlage der Nachtgesichte aus den Szenen des DRP unmittelbar abzuleiten. Sicher aber ist, wie dies sowohl bei der Entstehung des griechischen Theaters zu beobachten, als auch bei den Szenen des DRP offensichtlich ist, daß solche Darstellungen ihre Wurzeln im Ritual des Kultes haben. Hier wurde eine Anzahl kurzer Einzelszenen, die über einen kultischen Vorgang Aussagen machen sollten, aneinandergefügt und ergaben dann, zwar inhaltlich selbständig, gemeinsam ein einigermaßen geschlossenes Bild.

Woher der Prophet Sacharja die Gestalt der Nachtgesichte im einzelnen entlehnt hat, kann nicht mehr mit Sicherheit gesagt werden. Man muß übrigens neben der Übernahme von geistigen Anregungen auch mit der eigenschöpferischen Leistung des Autors rechnen. Daß aber ein Ritual ähnlich dem des DRP bei der Form der Nachtgesichte Pate gestanden hat, mag an zwei Eigenschaften dieser Nachtgesichte erkennbar sein. Der Prophet legt Wert darauf, daß er nicht im Traum- oder Trancezustand diese Bilder gesehen hat, sondern im Bewußtseinszustand, den ja die Mysterienspiele auf jeden Fall voraussetzen. Zweitens verweisen die Rituale zur Beisetzung des verstorbenen Königs von sich aus auf die Abend- oder Nachtstunden (Herodot II 63). Möglicherweise stammt daher die auffällige Zeitangabe und die gewollte Geschlossenheit der sieben oder acht Gesichte.

Am Rande kann noch auf eine weitere Ähnlichkeit verwiesen werden. Gelegentlich kommen im DRP Ortsangaben vor, die den Damaligen sicher verständlich gewesen, uns Heutigen aber nicht mehr identifizierbar sind. Dies erinnert daran, daß der Mann im ersten Nachtgesicht zwischen den Mythen im Talgrund gestanden habe (i 8), während die vier Wagen zwischen den zwei Bergen aus Erz erscheinen (vi 1).

Kultrituale wollen eine supranaturale Realität herstellen; sie lassen eine gläubig erhoffte und angenommene Wirklichkeit schon gegenwärtig werden. Wenn ich recht sehe, so hat der Prophet Sacharja mit seinen Nachtgesichten nichts anderes tun wollen als gerade dies. Und darin trifft sich schließlich die Intention der Nachtgesichte mit der des DRP ebenso wie mit der des griechischen Theaters. Darin sind die allgemein-menschlichen Bemühungen zu erkennen, die gegenwärtige, sichtbare und erkennbare Welt mit all ihren Begrenztheiten, Problemen und Belastungen transparent werden zu lassen für einen tieferen Sinn, der hinter allem liegt, sowie für die Zukunft, die diese gegenwärtige Welt in sich birgt.

Ich möchte hier nicht weiter eingehen auf die Bewegung, die die Nachtgesichte des Propheten Sacharja ausgelöst haben, in welcher Geschichtsdeutungen in der Gestalt von dramatischen Darstellungen dargeboten werden. Sicher ließe sich von daher allein die Quelle der Apokalyptik nicht finden. Auffällig aber ist die Tatsache, daß die Apokalyptiker gern die Form der mehr oder weniger kurzen, verschlüsselten szenarischen Vorgänge gewählt haben, um einen geschlossenen Zeitablauf darin darzustellen, der dem Unwissenden und Ungläubigen verborgen bleiben muß. In diesen Bildern aber wird die erhoffte Zukunft zur tröstlichen Gewißheit. Sollte mein Deutungsversuch richtig sein, so dürfte auf die apokalyptische Form der Gegenwartsbewältigung neues Licht fallen.

TEXT HISTORY AND TEXT CRITICISM OF THE SEPTUAGINT

by

JOHN WM WEVERS
Toronto

Proper use of the Septuagint for text critical purposes presupposes the fact that it is a translation document.[1] Once a translation exists its independent scribal history is irrelevant for Hebrew text criticism except so far as contact with the original language still obtains in either an immediate or a mediate context. The text history of a translation document is of interest only so far as it constitutes an aid to the recovery of the original text; in other words what a particular ms reads is of relevance only in that it reflects the autographon, since only the original text reflects the parent text of the translator.

Unfortunately, this statement by itself is quite inadequate, since the influence of the Hebrew text remained a factor in the text history of the LXX in at least three ways. First of all, up until the time that the LXX became a purely Christian canon its text history was the product of Jewish scribes who were undoubtedly bilingual. Many of these bilingual copyists may well have known their Hebrew text better than the Greek; in any event the Hebrew text was the normative one and undoubtedly resulted in "corrections" of the Greek text towards the Hebrew text known to the scribes. Such corrections may have been simply sporadic as in the case of the pre-Christian Fouad papyrus 848 or recensional as in the case of the so-called *kaige* text.

Another type of Hebrew influence on LXX text history is that of Christian recensional activity. According to the well-known state-

[1] Textual scholars are of course aware of this problem. Particularly helpful is the important article of M. H. Goshen-Gottstein, "Theory and Practice of Textual Criticism: The Text-critical Use of the Septuagint", *Textus* 3 (1963), pp. 130-58. His study is especially relevant since he was facing the practical problem of recording Greek evidence for his own edition of Isaiah (Jerusalem, 1975). For a recent article presupposing many of the observations made in this paper see Emanuel Tov, "On 'Pseudo-Variants' Reflected in the Septuagint", *JSS* 20 (1975), pp. 165-78.

ment of Jerome [2] three such recensions were made during the third and early fourth centuries, that of Hesychius for Egypt, that of Origen for Palestine, and that of Lucian for Asia Minor. Very little is known about the Hesychian recension; it is not even known whether the revision was influenced by the Hebrew; it may have been simply a stylistic revision.

The Antiochian or Lucianic recension has been clearly identified in the Prophetic Canon; it is still problematic for the Pentateuch as a whole. There is some evidence of non-hexaplaric recensional activity influenced by the Hebrew text in the closely related groups which I have isolated as the *d* and *t* families; it is not impossible that these represent Lucian, though it remains an inexplicable fact that the quotations by Chrysostom and Theodoret do not represent this text.

The most influential recension was the hexaplaric. Origen's work is easily recognized in the Pentateuch and is best represented by three Greek mss (G 376 and 426) and by the Syrohexaplar, though its influence was of course much wider. According to his own testimony he only filled in lacunae, i.e. added from other translations text lacking in his LXX but present in his Hebrew. Such additions he marked with an asterisk. For the opposite situation, i.e. Greek text without a counterpart in the Hebrew, he did not delete the text but marked it with an obelus. Though he says nothing about any other kind of change at all, the nature of the Hexapla made changes in word order to fit the Hebrew unavoidable as well, and the evidence of the hexaplaric mss of the Pentateuch confirm this as fact.

A third factor contributing Hebrew influence to the LXX text tradition is indirect. Catena mss show the Church Fathers often quoting other Greek translations, notably those of Aquila, Symmachus and Theodotion, in discussing Biblical texts. Certain Biblical mss contain a number of such non-LXX readings on the margins, and even occasionally in the text itself. It must be said, however, that direct influence of these versions on LXX text tradition is minimal.

By now it should be fully clear that simply citing the LXX represents an inadequate use of the version. On the other hand, the citation of Greek evidence should always be made on the presupposition that it is or might be relevant for the text criticism of the Hebrew text.

---

[2] Jerome, Praef. in libro Paralipomenon.

In the course of preparing the edition of Deuteronomy for the Göttingen *Septuaginta* I had occasion to subject the text critical notes in the Deuteronomy fascicle of the *Biblia Hebraica Stuttgartensia* (*BHS*) [3] to critical review. This was a sobering experience. I can find no scientific principles underlying the motley collection of citations of the Greek evidence; worthless variants are chosen, important ones are disregarded. Many citations are incorrectly given, even more are quite misleading; a large number are irrelevant.[4]

What I propose to do in this essay is to examine these citations in some detail not in order to criticize the late editor but rather through an examination of some instances of misuse of the Greek of Dt. to establish certain general guidelines for its proper use in the text criticism of the Hebrew text.

1. My first observation concerns the *need for formal correctness*, i.e. the information given must be factually correct. Thus at i 15b Greek minuscules are cited as omitting the conjunction in the phrase "and captains of fifties"; this is incorrect. Some mss omit the entire phrase but no witness omits only the conjunction. At xiii 8a it is said about the phrase "which are around you (plural)" that Greek minuscules read the singular, but no Greek text reads the singular at all. The note is incorrect. At xxiv 21a it is said that the phrase "to the poor and" occurs before "to the alien and to the orphan" in the Washington ms and some minuscules. The fact is that these mss have "the poor" as the second item reading "to the alien and to the poor and to the orphan." For xxx 16 the LXX has a longer text. It begins with "but if thou shouldst obey the Lord thy God," a clause not found in the Hebrew. The Greek is incorrectly cited without the initial ἐὰν δέ äs but only with a και variant. At xxxiii 12d for the phrase "upon him" the note cites the Greek ὁ θεός in support of a proposed emendation. The fact is the Greek has καὶ ὁ θεός. xxix 5a concerns the clause "that I am Yahweh your God". Codex Vaticanus is cited as reading "that

[3] J. Hempel (ed.), *Liber Deuteronomii*, *BHS* fasc. 3 (Stuttgart, 1972).

[4] Many scholars have been severely critical of the footnotes in the editions of the Kittel *Biblia Hebraica* which *BHS* is intended to replace, but probably none as forcibly and trenchantly as H. M. Orlinsky; see especially his "The Textual Criticism of the Old Testament", in G. E. Wright (ed.), *The Bible and the Ancient Near East*: *Essays in honor of William Foxwell Albright* (Garden City, N.Y., and London, 1961), pp. 114-16, now reprinted in *Studies in the Septuagint*: *Origins, Recensions, and Interpretations, Selected Essays with a Prolegomenon by Sidney Jellicoe* (New York, 1974), pp. 239-58.

this is the Lord your God". The fact is that this 3rd person reading of the original LXX is uniquely corrected by Vaticanus to read "that I am the Lord your God". Or at xxx 5b it is said that the Greek except for Vaticanus and one ms add ἐκεῖθεν after the phrase "thy God". Precisely the reverse is true; it is Codex B that adds the word whereas no other witness does.

2. My second plea concerns *clarity of citation*. If a reader does not understand a note he can hardly use it for the serious exercise of text criticism. At iv 45a for the noun in the phrase "these are the testimonies (*hā'ēdōt*)" the emendation *hā'ēdūt* is proposed with the note cf the Greek τὰ μαρτύρια as the Greek of 2 Kgs xvii 15. The comment baffles me. Μαρτύρια is a well known equivalent for our Hebrew text (cf. also vi 17, 20) and is never used to render *hā'ēdūt* in Dt., and what is more renders exactly the same word in the cited 2 Kgs passage as it does here. Readers of note ix 16b must also be puzzled by the comment. It is said that the word for "quickly" is omitted in certain uncials but is present in the hexaplaric recension under an asterisk for an intended obelus. Since the word is present in the Hebrew the comment makes no sense. Actually ms G originally had an obelus but quite rightly corrected it to an asterisk. The comment at xii 7a is also not clear and therefore misleading. It concerns the word "your hand" in the phrase *bəkōl mišlaḥ yedkem* ("in all that you undertake"). The comment states that the LXX less B and some minuscules read for "your hand" "your hands" and that the Hexapla has it with the asterisk. The facts are that the LXX quite adequately rendered the phrase by "wherever you cast hands" to which Origen added the 2nd plural pronoun. It would be difficult if not impossible to have obtained this information from the note. Comment xv 11c concerns the word for "thy hand" and states that the LXX less the Washington ms, the Hexapla and some minuscules read the plural. This note is not clear since both "hand" and "thy" are singular. The facts are that the LXX reading is "thy hands" later corrected by Origen to "thy hand", i.e. all witnesses have the singular pronoun. And to mention but one more, xviii 16d is indexed in the text twice, and the note consists of two comments, the first of which applies to the second indexed word and the second to the first.

3. A third criterion for the correct use of Greek materials is *adequacy*, i.e. notes must give all the relevant facts pertaining to the Greek tradition. It is not sufficient simply to cite an omission by the LXX when Origen is known to have added it in the Hexapla as often

obtains in the Dt. apparatus (as in i 15a, 25a, ii 31b, iv 11a, xi 14b, xiv 6a, 27b, xv 2c, xvi 18a and xvii 5e), since the full information potentially gives us knowledge about the Hebrew at two periods of its text history, the time of the original translation and the time of Origen almost a half millennium later.

3.1. Furthermore, *inadequacy of information can be highly misleading.* The final phrase in ii 30 reads *kayyōm hazze(h)* "as at this day". The note (d) on the first word states that B 963 and some minuscules read ἐν τῇ ἡμέρᾳ equaling *bayyōm*. (Actually it is the corrector of B and not the original B that has this reading.) The fact is that the LXX rendered our phrase by ὡς ἐν τῇ ἡμέρᾳ ταύτῃ, and the reading in question is obtained by omitting ὡς, probably a simple stylistic improvement, and not presupposing *bayyōm* at all. So too the information given in xiii 10bcd is inadequate. Notes b and c concern the phrase *yādᵉkā tihye(h)* for both of which B and some minuscules are cited as witnessing a plural expression, viz. "thy hands shall be". For the subject of the next clause *yad* the last note cites the LXX less the Washington ms Lucian Origen and minuscules as reading the plural. The fact is that most of the large number of witnesses that witness to the plural in the last instance also have the earlier plural expression. What was overlooked was that the LXX read "and thy hands shall be" but B and some minuscules omit the conjunction. The notes are thus misleading. xiv 26a is a comment on *ūbayyayin* "and of wine" and states that the Washington ms and some minuscules read "or of wine" = *'ō bayyayin*. What is inadequate is the failure to state that the LXX had no conjunction at all. Nor is the stated retroversion correct. The Hebrew word is part of a list all joined with the conjunction *wa* which are rendered throughout by "or" and not by "and", i.e. the stated variant actually equals the Masoretic text. Note xvi 19c states that one of the 2nd person singular verbs appears in the Greek as 3rd plural. This is factually the case but a glance at the Greek shows that all three of the coordinate verbs are in 3rd plural. The note is thus misleading. And to cite another example I refer to xxiii 17a. The comment concerns the text reading "in thee in the place which he shall choose in one of thy gates". The note cites only the text of Codex B which reads "in you he shall dwell wherever it pleases him". The note is factually correct but quite misleads the reader since B is the only Greek witness which omits the phrase "in every place" of the LXX text. Furthermore "in every" was placed under the obelus showing that it was not present in the Hebrew of Origen's time. Also of importance is the fact that two text families (*b* and *d*) omitted the verb "he shall dwell", i.e. corresponding to the Hebrew text. And finally the Hexapla added under the asterisk the clause "which he shall choose in one of thy gates". All of the further facts I have mentioned are of importance to the Hebrew text critic; the one variant shown in the note is not.

3.2. Finally *adequacy should mean citing all variants which could be relevant to the text critic*. It is difficult to determine the rationale underlying the selection of LXX notes in the Dt. fascicle unless it be simply random selection. I cite but one example of an important variant which might well be based on a different parent text. The last two verses of ch. xxiii are reversed in the LXX text and corrected in the Hexapla, but this fact is not noted in the notes.

4. A further observation on the proper use of Greek evidence for Hebrew text criticism concerns the *text tradition and its proper presentation*. Many variant readings are supported by textual families and ought to be designated as such. Recensions when identified should be correctly and consistently set forth. Particularly misleading is the individual citation of uncial mss over against minuscule mss as though the latter were an amorphous group whose evidence needs no analysis. Let me illustrate this by once again referring to the Dt. notes. The evidence of the Washington ms is singled out for special citation, though it is only one member of a group of six mss, even when it has a reading at variance with and clearly secondary to the united evidence of the other five mss of the *n* group. In such instances the reading of the five mss might be important, whereas that of the Washington ms is of no possible interest to the Hebrew text critic. The fact that a ms is written in uncial script gives it no special value.

This undue reverence for uncials can at times lead to false conclusions. Thus xiv 25c gives us the incorrect information that th original hand of B adds the phrase "for his name to be called there" at the end of the verse. The phrase is actually in B^{mg} from the hand of a corrector, thus many centuries later than B, and chronologically no earlier than the minuscules cited in support of the variant. Similarly at xxxi 15c the original hand of B is cited as omitting the word "pillar" from the phrase "in a pillar of cloud". Actually B omitted the entire sentence and more by mistake and it was added centuries later by a corrector who indeed omitted the word for "pillar". Such failure to discriminate and correctly record the evidence often hides important information. Thus note xxiii 25a informs us that for *tābō'* minuscules read ἐπέλθῃς and all others read εἰσέλθῃς. I do not understand the *raison d'être* for supplying this information since either reading would substantiate *tābō'* as parent text, but the information ought at least to be correct. The ἐπέλθῃς reading should be attributed to 957, a second century B.C. papyrus, which uniquely reads the επι compound; 957 is of course not a minuscule text at all but an uncial.

In the case of the known recensions of the Greek text it is particularly important that their evidence be properly identified and presented, since these recensional texts may give some indication of the status of the Hebrew text at the time when these recensions were made. The Dt. notes identify two such recensions, the hexaplaric and the Lucianic. The identification of the Lucianic recension in Dt. is still highly problematic, though some kind of non hexaplaric recensional activity seems to be present in the two related groups which I have named *d* and *t*. An analysis of the actual evidence underlying the citation of the Lucianic text in the Dt. notes, however, shows that the editor had no clear idea what this text represented. On the whole it seems that the readings supported by *d* and *t* are called Lucian, though at times it is the one group and at times the other. But sometimes the editor cites Lucian when no *d* or *t* ms has the reading. Thus xxxiv 5a states that the Lucianic recension omits the word for "there". The fact is that the shorter text is an old variant already found in B and not in any *d* or *t* ms. Thus the shorter text is not "Lucianic". In the following verse we are informed (in note c) that the Lucianic text omits the phrase "in the land of Moab". Again this is not true; major support obtains for the shorter text in B and the groups *C b n* and *s*, but no *d* or *t* witness omits the phrase. In fact this kind of variant is not generally speaking the kind of text one would expect from Lucian, since his text tended to be longer rather than shorter.

Neither is the hexaplaric text always correctly identified. Hexaplaric recensional activity was on the whole limited to filling in lacunae in the Greek text, identifying materials in the Greek text without correspondence in the Hebrew, and change in word order of the Greek to make it correspond to the Hebrew. Possibly Origen changed the spelling of some proper nouns to fit the Hebrew more closely. Other types of variants, particularly omissions of words corresponding to the MT are most unlikely to be hexaplaric in origin. It is thus surprising to find the Hexapla supporting numerous omissions in the Dt. notes (as e.g. xxxiv 7c). But it is also necessary to identify hexaplaric readings correctly. Thus at viii 8b for "and fig trees" it is said that the Greek less Origen supports the omission of the conjunction. The fact is that the shorter text is indeed LXX but all *O* witnesses support that shorter text. The addition of καί may have been recensional but it was not hexaplaric. In vi 23a we are informed that the hexaplaric text has added the subject "the Lord our God" to the verb "he swore". Since the subject is not expressed in MT this is surprising. The fact is that this longer text is supported by a substantial number of witnesses but not by the two best hexaplaric witnesses among the mss to the hexaplaric text nor by the Syrohexaplar. The statement of hexaplaric support is clearly incorrect.

Furthermore, if the readings of the *d* and *t* groups are indeed recensionally distinct from the hexaplaric they must not be confused in the notes. Note xvi 1a states that the Greek except for the O recension reads "thou didst go out" for the Hebrew "Yahweh thy God brought thee out". It is, however, the *d* and *t* groups only who have a text corrected to correspond to the Hebrew, i.e. the note should have read Greek less Lucian. At xvii 9b we are told that both the Hexapla and Lucian read "or to" for the Hebrew "and to". But all the hexaplaric witnesses read καί (πρός); in fact only the *d n* and *t* groups have the variant text. It is also misleading to give only part of the recensional picture. ix 10 ends in Hebrew with "from the midst of the fire in the day of assembly". Two notes obtain; the first note states that some Greek witnesses omit "from the midst of the fire" but that it was added under the asterisk by Origen. The second note states that some Greek witnesses omit "in the day of assembly". The fact is that the entire text was omitted by the LXX and was restored by Origen under the asterisk. It must be emphasized that the text tradition must be not only understood but fairly presented.

5. It must also be stated that the proper use of the Greek evidence presupposes an *avoidance of the irrelevant.* There is little point in recording as is done in xii 13a that *b^ekol māqōm* is rendered in Greek by ἐν παντὶ τόπῳ, an exact and literal rendering. The comment is irrelevant.

5.1. Furthermore, irrelevant notes may be engendered also by *the failure to recognize the demands of the target language.* Note ii 24b informs us that for the imperative "inherit" the Greek reads the infinitive "to inherit". Of course it does since it modifies the verb "begin". Hebrew expresses this by successive imperatives, i.e. "begin! inherit!" But this would be peculiar Greek indeed; Greek normally says "begin to inherit". The note is irrelevant. The comment at iv 21d is also irrelevant. It states that for *bō'* Greek read εἰσέλθω = *bō'ī*. But the translator rightly chose a purposive construction demanding an inflected verb. The reading does not prove the retroversion given in the note in any way; it is this reading because it's Greek.

5.2. Irrelevancy can also obtain *when a variant is taken out of context*; it is then not only irrelevant, it is misleading. xxx 18b is a note on the negative particle in the clause "not shall you live long" stating that the negative is omitted by a Greek ms. Since the clause is paralleled by "you will certainly perish" this is surprising. The fact is that the Greek uses the double negative οὐ μή and ms 59 omits only the οὐ and the intent of the Greek remains negative. The comment misleads. Note xxxi 18c states that ms 44 omits "they have done" from the phrase "the evil which they have done". If this is correct it would result in an impossible text since "the evil which" by itself is gibberish. Actually ms 44 omits the relative as well. By citing only part of the omission a variant is produced which is irrelevant.

5.3. Irrelevant notes may also be created *by the failure to exercise text critical judgements on the Greek text*. Variants produced by inner Greek error are useless for the Hebrew text critic. It is at this level that the most blatant errors occur in the Dt. notes. Thus again and again—(in ch. i alone there are six instances: 26a, 28a, 29b, 30a, 32a and 33a) notes inform us that 2nd plural pronouns occur in Greek witnesses as 1 plural or vice versa. Since these are homophonous in Greek from Hellenistic times down to the present scribal confusion is bound to create the variant. The confusion of ὑμῶν / ἡμῶν over and over again in the Greek mss is simply due to the fact that both were pronounced as / *himon* /. Since these pronouns in both bound and free forms cannot be confused in Hebrew but are commonly so in Greek the conclusion is inescapable: the variant is totally irrelevant for the Hebrew text critic.

So too parablepses due to homoioteleuton in the Greek text are irrelevant for the Hebrew text. Thus the omission of "and thou shalt know today" in iv 39a by some Greek witness is due to inner Greek error and is irrelevant. The note xii 6a calls attention to a lengthy omission in Codex B by homioteleuton. But again one asks: then why cite it? It is irrelevant. (Cf. also xv 8d, xvi 19a, xvii 9a, xxviii 22b, and 48c.) Failure to understand the process of inner Greek error not only creates irrelevant notes; it can also mislead. At xxix 25b we are told that the second occurrence of *'ᵉlōhīm* is omitted by the

Greek less Lucian, but added by the Hexapla under the asterisk. But this reference to Lucian must be based on a misreading of the evidence. The *d* tradition has omitted part of the verse—including this word—by homoioteleuton. The note could only mean that Lucian had the word, but this is false. Or to give but one more example I refer to x 4b. The note states that the phrase "in the day of assembly" is omitted by the Greek minus Codex M and Lucian but was added by Origen under the asterisk. Furthermore, it is said that the Washington ms has "in the desert". The facts are that the Hexapla added ἐν τῇ ἡμέρᾳ τῆς ἐκκλησίας. So did the *n* group of mss of which the Washington ms is a member. The Washington scribe misread ἡμέρᾳ as ἐρήμῳ, i.e. "desert". What is not said in the note is that W^I actually reads "in the desert of the assembly". Here the failure to exercise elementary text critical judgement misinforms the reader since the reading "in the desert" would by itself actually make sense in the context.

5.4. And finally irrelevant notes can result from *failure to investigate the translation technique of the translator*. When a Greek rendering is cited which superficially might appear to presuppose a variant Hebrew text but in actual fact follows the normal translation pattern of the translator it is irrelevant and misleading. A few examples should make this clear. Note xix 16a calls attention to the variant *w^ekī* for *kī* and adds cf the Greek δέ. The protasis of the Dt. casuistic laws normally begins with *kī* or at times with *w^ekī*, but in the Greek translation this always occurs as ἐὰν δέ; in other words the δέ is always used. The occurrence of δέ is therefore irrelevant as far as the Hebrew text is concerned. (Cf. also xxii 22a.) At xiii 6d occurs the comment on the clause "and thou shalt burn the evil from thy midst" viz. that the Greek minus B and some minuscules read the plural. The fact is that the comment is relevant only for the verb. The phrases "the evil from thy midst" as well as "the evil from your midst" occur in Dt., but the translator always rendered the prepositional phrase by ἐξ ὑμῶν αὐτῶν. At xiii 15c the variant ἐν Ἰσραήλ is retroverted into *bqrb yśr'l*. Actually this phrase occurs elsewhere in Dt. only in xvii 20 (but cf also xi 6), whereas *byśr'l* occurs commonly. Both phrases are rendered by ἐν Ἰσραήλ, and the retroversion is irrelevant. The Hophal of *mwt* occurs three times in xxiv 16. For each occurrence we are told that the Greek presupposes the Qal form. Now it is true that the Greek reads "they/he shall die", but then the translator always rendered the Hophal as well as the Qal in this way. The Hophal occurs seven times in Dt. (cf also xiii 6, xvii 6 bis, xxi 22) and is always rendered by ἀποθανεῖται, (or the plural). The Greek evidence is irrelevant to the question whether the Hebrew text had a Hophal or Qal stem.

If to many I have seemed to belabour the obvious, to have simply verbalized what common sense should dictate, I apologize. In self-defense I must say that the formal criteria which I have set forth are violated far more often than observed by Hebrew text critics, and that their verbalization may serve a useful purpose.

WIE VERSTAND MICHA VON MORESCHET SEIN PROPHETISCHES AMT?

von

HANS WALTER WOLFF

Heidelberg

Die Frage nach dem Amtsverständnis der klassischen Schriftpropheten ist immer noch umstritten. Nur die extremen Antworten können heute als überholt gelten. Man will sie im allgemeinen weder als revolutionäre Einzelgänger noch als institutionell gebundene Kultusbeamte ansehen. Aber wie ist dann ihr soziologischer Standort zu bestimmen? In der gegebenen Forschungslage empfiehlt sich die gezielte Einzeluntersuchung.

Es gehört meines Erachtens zum Schwierigsten in der Prophetenforschung, aber auch zum Wichtigsten und Schönsten, den je besonderen Standort und die Verwurzelung der einzelnen Propheten aufzuspüren. Wer war der, den das lodernde Charisma des Prophetischen überkam? Die soziologische Herkunft der Traditionen, die im Feuer des Prophetischen aufgingen und es auch nährten, sind zu erfragen.

Suchen wir, für Micha von Moreschet Klarheit zu gewinnen! Ich gehe methodisch von den Texten aus, in denen sein eigenes Ich zur Sprache kommt. Darüber hinaus beschränke ich mich auf denjenigen Teil des Michabuches, der seit Bernhard Stade [1] als kritisch gesichertes Minimum echter Micha-Überlieferungen gilt, also auf Kap. i-iii. Vielleicht liefert das Ergebnis nebenher Kriterien zur Beurteilung der Ich-Aussagen im übrigen Michabuch.[2]

Die fraglos wichtigste Stelle (iii 8) kann uns bei Beachtung ihres Kontextes in Kap. iii zu einer Arbeitshypothese anleiten. Sie wird dann an den sonstigen Selbstaussagen Michas zu überprüfen sein. Nach dem ursprünglichen [3] Text ruft Micha:

---

[1] "Bemerkungen über das Buch Micha", *ZAW* 1 (1881), S. 161-72; vgl. J. L. Mays, *Micah* (Philadelphia and London, 1976), S. 13.

[2] vii 1ff., 7 (iv 14, vi 4f.).

[3] S.u. Anm. 12.

Dagegen ich, ich bin erfüllt
mit Kraft, .. Recht und Mut,
Jakob sein Verbrechen vorzuhalten
und Israel sein Unrecht.

Kräftig adversativ führt Micha sein Ich ein (*we'ûlām 'ānokî*), wie es im Redegefecht geschieht (vgl. Ijob ii 5, v 8, xiii 3). Der Satz will also zunächst vom vorangehenden Spruch (V. 5-7) her verstanden werden. Micha wirft sich selbst "den Propheten, die mein Volk verführen", entgegen (V. 5). Deren Schwäche setzt sein "kraftstrotzendes Rühmen" [4] voraus. Worin besteht deren Schwäche? Nach dem Anklagewort in V. 5 in der würdelosen Abhängigkeit von den Zuwendungen ihrer Hörer; nach dem Drohwort (V. 6-7) darin, daß sie ohne jede Gottesantwort im Finstern tappen. Dagegen trumpft Micha mit Kraft und Mut auf, die ihn unabhängig und überlegen machen, und mit der festen Orientierung, die er am "Recht" hat.

Auffällig ist nun, mit welchen Worten im einzelnen er sich selbst von den anderen Propheten abhebt. In V. 5-7 hatte er deren Sprüche über die Zukunftsaussichten kritisiert und ihnen angekündigt, daß Gott ihnen kein Wort mehr anvertrauen werde. Danach wäre zu erwarten, daß er von sich sagte: Mir aber ist Jahwes wahres Wort vom Künftigen anvertraut. Stattdessen aber spricht er von *mišpāṭ*, dem Recht, das ihn erfüllt. Der Unterschied ist deutlich. Thema jener Propheten ist Heil oder Krieg, also das, was Gott künftig herbeiführen möchte. Dem stellt Micha als sein Thema Recht und Unrecht entgegen, also das, was der Mensch gegenwärtig tun sollte und tatsächlich tut. Die Fortsetzung in V. 8b sagt ja klar, wozu er mit *mišpāṭ* erfüllt ist: "um Jakob sein Verbrechen vorzuhalten und Israel sein Unrecht".

Mit *mišpāṭ* aber steht Micha weniger in ausdrücklicher Konkurrenz zu den anderen Propheten als vielmehr zu "den Häuptern Jakobs und den Führern des Hauses Israel", die er als solche in iii 1 zur Eröffnung seines großen Jerusalemer Auftritts und unmittelbar nachher in iii 9 anspricht. Denn die Häupter und Führer fragt er in V. 1b: "Ist es nicht eure Sache, den *mišpāṭ* zu kennen?" In V. 9b klagt er dieselben an als die, "die den *mišpāṭ* verabscheuen". Und noch einmal heißt es in V. 11a: "Ihre Häupter treffen nach Bestechung Rechtsentscheide (*jišpoṭû*). Über die schamlos abhängigen Propheten hinweg stellt sich

[4] G. von Rad, *Theologie des Alten Testaments* II (München, [4]1960), S. 211.

Micha also genau den politisch Verantwortlichen als Verrätern des Rechts entgegen, wenn er von sich sagt, daß er mit Kraft und Mut für das Recht eintritt.[5]

Daß er sein Selbstverständnis in bewußter Konfrontation zu den Jerusalemer Häuptern und Führern ausspricht, geht auch daraus hervor, daß er die Adressaten seiner Vorhaltungen in V. 8b genauso "Jakob" und "Israel" nennt, wie er jene als "Häupter (des Hauses) Jakob und Führer des Hauses Israel" anspricht. Er braucht die Termini des alten Stämmeverbands statt der offiziellen politischen Benennung Juda und Jerusalem (vgl. Mi. i 1, 9; Jes. iii 1, 8). Diese Bestimmung ihres Funktionsbereichs ist für die Jerusalemer Politiker ebenso wenig selbstverständlich wie die Benennung *rā'šîm* und *qeṣînîm*. *rā'šîm* heißen in älterer Zeit die Sippen- und Großfamilienhäupter; die Verbindung *r'š* und *qṣjn* kommt im Alten Testament nur noch ein einziges Mal vor, und zwar für den Richter Jiftach in Ri. xi (6, 8) 11.[6] Warum spricht Micha nicht den König und seine Beamten an? Warum benennt er die verantwortlichen Jerusalemer mit den Titeln des altisraelitischen Sippenverbandes? Wir lassen die Frage noch offen.

Zuvor beobachten wir eine weitere Eigenart der Wortwahl in der Selbstaussage Michas. Er sagt, daß er "voll ist" von Kraft, Recht und Mut. Auf welchen Vorgang deutet *mālē'tî* hin? Die Kommentatoren denken oft an die Berufung zum Propheten; sie wollen sogar in iii 8 die Hauptelemente der sonstigen Berufungsberichte wiederfinden.[7] Doch da erscheint mir Vorsicht geboten. In prophetischen Berufungsberichten erscheint *ml'* nie. Ein einziges Mal beschreibt das Wort das Ergebnis einer Amtsübertragung von Mensch zu Mensch im späten priesterschriftlichen Bericht Dt. xxxiv 9: Josua "war erfüllt (*mālē'*)

---

[5] Die Reihung der drei Nomina *koaḥ ûmišpāṭ ûgebûrā* ist als Hendiatreis zu verstehen; vgl. A. S. van der Woude, *Micha* (Nijkerk, 1976), S. 116. Dabei bezeichnen "Kraft" und "Mut" die Qualität des Einsatzes, "Recht" aber sein wesentliches Kriterium. *mišpāṭ* meint weder das subjektive Rechtsbewußtsein noch ein bestimmtes Rechtskorpus, sondern jene einfache und doch alles entscheidende Grundordnung, die zwischen "gut" und "böse", zwischen "aufrichtig" und "verdreht" zu unterscheiden lehrt; vgl. iii 1f. und 9!

[6] Vgl. ferner *qāṣîn* in Jos. x 24, Prv. vi 7, xxv 15. Jesaja spricht wohl von "Führern" (*qeṣînîm*), aber nicht von "Häuptern". "Häupter" sind in älterer Zeit vornehmlich die Großfamilienväter, die Sippenältesten und Stammesführer (Num. xxv 4; 1 Kön. viii 1; vgl. H. P. Müller, *THAT* II, S. 705f.).

[7] J. L. Mays, S. 84f.; vgl. W. Rudolph, *KAT* XIII/3 (1975), S. 73, und A. S. van der Woude, S. 116.

vom Geist der Weisheit, da Mose seine Hand auf ihn gestützt hatte".[8] Wenn sonst vom Erfülltsein eines Menschen gesprochen wird, dann wird nie auf den Vorgang der Begabung oder gar der Berufung reflektiert, sondern stets vom Zustand des Voll-seins aus auf dessen Auswirkung.[9] Insbesondere wird an die Auswirkung gedacht, wenn das Vollsein sich auf einen Redevorgang bezieht. Elihu kann nach Ijob xxxii 18 nicht weiterhin schweigen, weil er "voll von Worten ist".[10] Jer. vi 11 steht Mi. iii 8 im prophetischen Bereich am nächsten "Ich aber bin ganz voll vom Zorn Jahwes, ich kann ihn nicht zurückhalten".[11] Die beiden letzten Stellen bringen wie Mi. iii 8 als einzige die Selbstaussage in der 1. sg. *mālēʾtî*; alle drei Stellen sprechen sachlich von der Unmöglichkeit des Schweigens, meinen also Vollsein nicht im Sinne eines (durch Berufung) Erfülltwordenseins, sondern im Sinne eines Übervollseins, eines unvermeidlichen Überfließens. In der derben Sprache Michas wäre etwa zu übersetzen: "Ich aber platze vor Kraft, Recht und Mut, Jakob sein Verbrechen anzuzeigen, Israel sein Unrecht". So zeigt *mālēʾtî* hier nicht mehr und nicht weniger an, als daß durch Micha jetzt geschieht, was bei den Häuptern und Führern Jerusalems geschehen sollte, nämlich *daʿat ʾæt hammišpāṭ* (iii 1), d.h. Sich-Kümmern um das Recht, was jene aber tatsächlich "verabscheuen" (V. 9). Nichts weist also in Mi. iii 8 auf einen Berufungsvorgang zurück; vielmehr stellt die gesamte Aussage nur die unvermeidbare Anklagepflicht heraus, deren zwingende Voraussetzung das gegenwärtige Erfülltsein mit Kraft, Recht und Mut ist.

Diese Sicht wird dadurch bestätigt, daß im ursprünglichen Text mit keiner Silbe der berufende Gott erwähnt wird. Seit Wellhausen ist erkannt und Symmachus' Übersetzung bestätigt es noch, daß *ʾaet-rûaḥ jhwh* ein späterer Nachtrag ist.[12] Für den Ergänzer war das völlige Fehlen des Gottesnamens an dieser Stelle anscheinend aufregend und unerträglich, für Micha selbst war er offenbar gut entbehrlich. In der Tat wäre der Hinweis auf Jahwe unverzichtbar, wenn Micha hier etwas über seine Berufung zum Propheten hätte sagen

[8] Darüber hinaus spricht P gelegentlich von der Begabung der Kunsthandwerker am Heiligtum durch Jahwe; dann braucht er *mlʾ* pi. (Ex. xxviii 3, xxxi 3, xxxv 31, 35. Vgl. ferner 1 Kön. vii 14, wo *mlʾ* ni. die Begabung zu allerlei Erzarbeiten beschreibt.

[9] Mi. vi 12: "Ihre Reichen sind voll Gewalttätigkeit"; Ps. xlviii 11: Jahwes "rechte Hand ist voll Gerechtigkeit"; Ijob xx 11: "Sein Gebein ist voller Jugendkraft"; Ps. x 1: "Ihr Mund ist voll Lug und Trug".

[10] Zur Defektiv-Schreibung s. *BHS*.

[11] Vgl. noch Jer. xv 17bβ im Zusammenhang von V. 10-11 und V. 15-18.

wollen. Jeder Berufungsbericht und jeder Hinweis auf einen prophetischen Sendungsauftrag betont nichts so sehr wie eben Jahwe als den unwiderstehlich sendenden Gott (vgl. nur Am. iii 8, vii 14f.; Jes. vi 8ff., viii 11; Jer. i 5ff., xxiii 9).

Wie erklären sich nun die Eigentümlichkeiten der Selbstaussage von iii 8, daß Micha zur Hauptsache konkurriert mit denen, die Recht wahrzunehmen hätten und daß er sie Häupter in Jakob und Führer in Israels Haus nennt? Wie erklärt es sich, daß er in dieser Sache nicht an seine spezielle Bevollmächtigung erinnert und Jahwes Namen überhaupt nicht eigens erwähnt? Ich suche die Antwort in der Arbeitshypothese, daß Micha selbst von Haus aus ein *zāqēn* von Moreschet war. So wird verständlich, daß er die Verantwortlichen Jerusalems in der Terminologie des alten Sippenverbandes anspricht und also mit ihnen gleichsam auf kollegialer Amtsebene verkehrt.[13] Als Ältester von Moreschet ist er selbst dem Recht verpflichtet; als solcher bedarf er zur Anzeige des Unrechts keines besonderen Berufungsauftrags. Als Ältester von Moreschet muß er nicht betont von Gottes Recht sprechen; denn in diesem Amt muß ihm alles nur an der konkreten Unterscheidung von "gut" und "böse" (iii 2a), von "gerade" und "verkehrt" (iii 9b) liegen. *mišpāṭ* ist gleichsam terminus technicus der Berufspflicht des Ältesten und Sippenhauptes.[14] Aus der Sippenweisheit mag dem Ältesten von Moreschet vertraut sein, daß "ein Weiser 'mächtiger ist als ein Starker' und ein Verständiger 'mehr als ein Kraftmensch' ".[15] Als *ʾîš daʿat mišpāṭ* weiß er sich kräftig überlegen. Wenn er sich als Ältester von Moreschet für seine Leute verantwortlich weiß, dann wird auch verständlich, daß er gegen die Propheten spricht, "die mein Volk verführen", und diejenigen Häupter anklagt, die "das Fleisch meines Volkes fressen" (iii 5 und 3).

[12] Die wichtigsten Gründe sind insgesamt zwingend: 1. Die Wortgruppe ist ohne Kopula eingeschoben. 2. Die Konstruktion mit *ʾaet* stößt sich mit den anderen Objekten. 3. Die Stellung zwischen *ko^{a}ḥ* und *ûmišpāṭ* befremdet. 4. Auch auf die gestörte Symmetrie der Doppeldreier kann hingewiesen werden. 5. Zu Symmachus vgl. J. Ziegler.

[13] *rāʾšîm* kann als Synonym zu *z^{e}qēnîm* gelten; vgl. 1 Kön. viii 1; Num. xxv 4, 5; Dtn. i 15, v 23, und R. de Vaux, *Das Alte Testament und seine Lebensordnungen* I (Freiburg i. Br., Basel, Wien, 1960), S. 245f. = *Les Institutions de l'Ancien Testament* I (Paris, 1958), S. 235f.; G. Chr. Macholz, "Zur Geschichte der Justizorganisation in Juda", *ZAW* 84 (1972), S. 317ff., 325; Conrad, *ThWAT* II, S. 645.

[14] Vgl. außer Mi. iii 1 auch 2 Chron. xix 6; Anm. v 15 und Hos. v 1, dazu H. W. Wolff, *Hosea*, *BK* XIV/1 (^{3}1976), S. 123.

[15] Prv. xxiv 5 zum Text s. *BHS* und B. Gemser, *Sprüche Salomos*, *HAT* I/16 (^{2}1963). Man beachte die Wortstämme *gbr* und *kḥ* analog zu Mi. iii 8a und *daʿat* analog zu iii 1.

So spricht doch nur ein amtlich Verantwortlicher, ein *ro'š hā'ām* (Num. xxv 4 J) von "seinem Volk" als von den ihm anvertrauten Landsleuten.

Wir prüfen unsere Hypothese an einigen weiteren Beobachtungen.

1. Wie kommt der Mann aus Moreschet nach *Jerusalem* (vgl. iii 10, 12)? Jerusalem liegt immerhin 35 km nordostwärts von Moreschet, wenn der Ort mit dem *tell ed-ǧudēde* identisch ist.[16] In der Königszeit muß eine rege Verbindung zwischen der Hauptstadt und den Landstädten im Südwesten Judas geherrscht haben. Nicht weniger als fünf Festungsstädte (nach der Liste Rehabeams 2 Chron. xi 7-9) lagen innerhalb eines Umkreises von 10 km um Moreschet: Aseka im Norden, Socho im Nordosten, Adullam im Osten, Marescha im Süden und Lachisch im Südwesten. Offiziere und Verwaltungsbeamte werden für einen lebhaften Verkehr nach Jerusalem gesorgt haben. Dabei kann mancher Landarbeiter aus Moreschet und Umgebung nach Jerusalem verschleppt und dort arbeitsverpflichtet worden sein. So wird verständlich, daß sich Micha in Jerusalem für "sein Volk" einsetzt, vor allem aber, wenn er das in der Residenz und in der Umgebung von Moreschet als *zāqēn hā'āraeṣ* tut. Denn ein Ältester hat nicht nur für die innere Ordnung und die Rechtswahrung an seinem Ort zu sorgen (Rt. iv), sondern er vertritt auch sein Gemeinwesen nach außen. So werden die Ältesten Judas als Stadtälteste auch zu wichtigen Staatsakten nach Jerusalem zusammengerufen.[17] In 1 Kön. viii 1-3 werden die *ziqnê jiśrā'ēl* den *rā'šê hammaṭṭôt* gleichgesetzt und den Sprechern der Großfamilien. Auf diesem Hintergrund wird verständlich, daß der *zāqēn* von Moreschet die *rā'šîm* in Jerusalem, die dort inzwischen einen Teil der Oberschicht und Funktionäre der königlichen Verwaltung darstellen, auf seine Landsleute hin anspricht.

2. Unsere Hypothese verdeutlich auch, warum im Prozeß gegen Jeremia (xxvi 17-19) "*Männer aus den Ältesten des Landes*" mit der Erinnerung an Michas Verkündigung als Entlastungszeugen auftreten. In diesen Kreisen wird der Vertreter der Landstadt Moreschet als nennenswertes Mitglied auch zuerst den Beinamen *hammorašti*

---

[16] Joachim Jeremias, "Moreseth-Gath, die Heimat des Propheten Micha", *PJB* 29 (1933), S. 42-53. Ein besserer Vorschlag liegt bis heute nicht vor.

[17] Vgl. 1 Kön. viii 1-3; 2 Kön. xxiii 1 und schon 1 Sam. xi 3, xvi 4, xxx 26; 2 Sam. xix 12f.; 1 Kön. xx 7; S. J. Conrad, *ThWAT* II, S. 645f. Wahrscheinlich stellen die "Ältesten des Landes" nicht ein ständiges Kollegium dar, "sondern eine bei Gelegenheiten zusammenkommende Repräsentanz" (M. Noth, *Könige*, *BK* IX/1 [1968], S. 177, und ders., *Geschichte Israels* [Göttingen, ³1956], S. 104).

erhalten haben (so Jer. xxvi 18 wie Mi. i 1). Innerhalb der landjudäischen Ältestenkreise können Michas Sprüche auch zuerst tradiert worden sein, und zwar mit Sorgfalt, wie das ziemlich genaue Zitat[18] von Mi. iii 12 in Jer. xxvi 18, dem Wort zur Zerstörung Jerusalems, zeigt.

3. Wir fanden in iii 8 keinerlei Hinweise auf eine besondere prophetische Berufung. Dem entspricht es, daß dort von Gottes Wort für die Zukunft überhaupt nicht die Rede ist. Dabei gipfeln doch seine Worte in der Regel mit einer Drohung (ii 3ff., iii 4, 6f., 12). Auch hätte das unmittelbar vorangehende Wort vom Erlöschen der seherischen Kraft bei den anderen Propheten (V. 6f.) ihn zu einer gegensätzlichen Äußerung über sich selbst veranlassen können. Stattdessen weist er nur darauf hin, daß er seine Berufspflicht kräftig wahrnimmt, die darin besteht, "Jakob sein Verbrechen aufzudecken und Israel sein Unrecht". Eben das aber gehört zu den ersten Amtspflichten eines Ältesten auf Grund des überlieferten Rechts. Nicht ums *Ganze* des prophetischen Amtes geht es hier also, geschweige denn um das eigentlich charakteristisch *Prophetische* in diesem Amt,[19] — die Ankündigung von Gottes Gericht —, sondern um das, was er selbst in dieses Amt einbringt. Das aber ist die Rechtspflege des Stadtältesten.

4. Auch in der übrigen Verkündigung Michas tritt der Name *Jahwe* ganz auffällig zurück. Die Botenformel *kō ʾāmar jhwh* kommt überhaupt nur zweimal im überlieferten Text vor und ist vielleicht an beiden Stellen erst redaktionell nachgetragen. Das gilt mit hochgradiger Sicherheit von iii 5.[20] Denn der Botenformel folgt hier überhaupt keine Ich-Rede Jahwes; hingegen spricht V. 7bβ in 3. Person von Gott ("es gibt keine Antwort von Gott"). Die Partizipien, mit denen die Propheten in V. 5 charakterisiert werden, lassen eher an ein ursprüngliches *hôj*-Wort denken, wie es in ii 1f. vorliegt. Auch wäre denkbar, daß der Spruch ähnlich wie iii 1 und 9 mit dem Aufruf "Höret doch!" begonnen hätte, denn auch in diesen Fällen folgen Partizipien (vgl. V. 2 und V. 9b-10). Keinesfalls aber liegt ein eigentlicher Botenspruch als Gottesrede vor, sondern eine Prophetenrede, wie sie denn ja auch in der Ich-Rede Michas (V. 8) gipfelt.

---

[18] Zur kleinen Differenz zwischen Mi. iii 12 und Jer. xxvi 18 s.u. S. 410f.

[19] Vgl. W. H. Schmidt, *Zukunftsgewißheit und Gegenwartskritik* (Neukirchen, 1973), S. 55ff. und H. W. Wolff, "Die eigentliche Botschaft der klassischen Propheten", *Beiträge zur alttestamentlichen Theologie, Festschr. W. Zimmerli* (Göttingen, 1977), S. 547-57.

[20] So mit Th. Lescow, "Redaktionsgeschichtliche Analyse von Micha 1-5", *ZAW* 84 (1972), S. 46-85 (S. 48), jetzt auch J. L. Mays, S. 81.

Etwas schwieriger ist die Entscheidung bei dem anderen Vorkommen der Botenformel in ii 3. Auch hier denkt Th. Lescow [21] an einen redaktionellen Zusatz. Nun ist zwar nicht zu bezweifeln, daß ii 3-5 auch sonst stark redaktionell erweitert wurde; [22] es sei nur auf das doppelte *lākēn* in V. 3 und V. 5 hingewiesen, auf die Verknüpfungsformel *bajjôm hahû'* in V. 4 und auf die Spannung zwischen der ursprünglich wirkenden Anredeform (2. pl. in V. 3b) und der Angabe des Adressaten in 3. Person ("über diese Sippe da") in V. 3a, wobei übrigens der Betroffene ebenso mit *'al* eingeführt wird wie in iii 5a. Schließlich bleibt auch hier zu beachten, daß in V. 5 von Jahwe nur in 3. Person die Rede ist. Dagegen fällt jedoch schwer ins Gewicht, daß zunächst auf die Botenformel in V. 3a eine Ich-Rede Jahwes folgt ("Siehe, ich plane Unheil"). Th. Lescow meint aber, *hinenî* gehe an dieser Stelle auf ein ursprüngliches *hinnē jhwh* zurück. Nach unseren Beobachtungen zu III 5 können wir auch für ii 3 den redaktionellen Charakter der Botenformel (und die entsprechende Änderung von *hinnē jhwh* in *hinenî*) nicht unbedingt ausschließen.

Am meisten ist zu beachten, daß bei allen sonstigen Übergängen von der Anklage zur Strafandrohung die Botenformel bei Micha fehlt. Ich verweise vor allem auf die Ankündigung des Untergangs Jerusalems in iii 12. Nachdem Micha in V. 9-11 die Richter, Priester und Propheten angeklagt hat, fährt er in V. 12 fort:

Darum wird euretwegen
  Zion zum offenen Felde umgepflügt,
Jerusalem zum Trümmerhaufen
  und der Tempelberg dem 'Wild' [23] des Waldes übergeben werden.

Sollte man nicht zur Eröffnung dieser Gerichtsansage (vor allem von Amos und Jesaja her) ein *kō 'āmar jhwh* erwarten? In der Tat ist bemerkenswert, daß es schon von den Alten vermißt wurde. Denn nach Jer. xxvi 18 führen die Ältesten im Verfahren gegen Jeremia das Michawort mit *kō 'āmar jhwh* ein. Das ist doch sehr bezeichnend! Umso beachtlicher bleibt, daß Micha selbst hier und in allen ähnlichen

---

[21] S. 51.

[22] Jörg Jeremias, "Die Deutung der Gerichtsworte Michas in der Exilszeit", *ZAW* 83 (1971), S. 330-54 (333-5).

[23] L. *lebahamôt* nach A. B. Ehrlich, *Randglossen zur hebräischen Bibel* 5 (Leipzig, 1911), S. 280, W. Rudolph, S. 68, und A. S. van der Woude, S. 122 (vgl. Mi. v 7 und Thr. v 18).

Fällen überhaupt nicht auf Jahwe verweist. Der Prophet selbst folgert: "Darum wird euretwegen Zion umgepflügt..." (*lākēn biglalkäm* weicht bei Jer. der Botenformel).

Man muß darüber hinaus überrascht feststellen, daß Micha fast nur da von Jahwe spricht, wo er den Gottesnamen seinen Gegnern in den Mund legt. In ii 7 wehren sie sich gegen Michas Drohwort mit dem Satz: "Hat Jahwe etwa die Geduld verloren?" In iii 11bβ schleudern sie ihm die Frage entgegen: "Ist Jahwe denn nicht in unserer Mitte?" Zu Michas Anklage gehört es, daß sie sich in solcher Weise "auf Jahwe stützen" (V. 11bα), und zu seiner Drohung, daß "sie zu Jahwe schreien werden, er sie aber nicht erhören wird" (iii 4). Je mehr seine Hörer "Herr, Herr!" sagen, aber den Willen Gottes nicht tun (Mt. vii 21), desto zurückhaltender ist er selbst mit dem Jahwenamen. Wenn ich recht sehe, kommt in sicher echten Michaworten außer an den genannten Stellen, die alle auf die Gegner bezogen sind, Jahwe nur noch ein einziges Mal vor in i 12 ("Unheil fährt herab von Jahwe auf Jerusalem"). Auch die Ich-Rede Jahwes bleibt eine Seltenheit. Außer der unsicheren Stelle ii 3 ist hier nur noch das fragmentarische Wort gegen Samaria in i 6 zu erwähnen: "Ich mache Samaria zum Trümmerfeld, ... ich schütte seine Steine zu Tal ...; ... *weśamtî* ... *wehiggartî*. (Die Ankündigung des Kommens Jahwes in der Theophanieschilderung i 3-4 gehört m.E. zu einer kultischen Redaktion.)

Wie erklärt sich dieses merkwürdige Zurücktreten des Jahwe-Namens und auch des pronominalen Ich Gottes bei Micha? Eine Besonderheit mag uns weiterführen. Wenn Amos, Hosea oder Jesaja *ʿammî* ("mein Volk") sagen, dann geschieht das zumeist innerhalb der Botenrede und meint dann Jahwes Volk. Wie verhält es sich bei Micha? In i 9 trauert er, weil der Schlag Jahwes "bis ans Tor meines Volkes, nach Jerusalem" gelangt; ii 4aβ — wahrscheinlich sekundär [24] — spricht vom "Ackeranteil meines Volkes". Typisch für Micha sind die folgenden Stellen. ii 8 spricht — bei allen textlichen Schwierigkeiten — doch wohl deutlich die an, die "als Feinde gegen mein Volk aufgetreten" sind; denn ii 9 fährt fort: "Die Frauen meines Volkes vertreibt ihr aus ihren geliebten Häusern". iii 3 klagt die Verantwortlichen in Jerusalem an: "Das Fleisch meines Volkes fressen sie" und iii 5 die Propheten, "die mein Volk verführen". Immer spricht Micha also mitleidend von seinem Volk, insbesondere

[24] So Jörg Jeremias, S. 334.

von seinen geschundenen Landsleuten und Sippenangehörigen, nie von Jahwes Volk als solchem.[25] Kann man diese Weise, *ʿammî* zur Sprache zu bringen, besser verstehen, als wenn man an einen Ältesten aus Moreschet denkt? Er setzt sich in erster Linie für seine bedrängten Sippenangehörigen und damit für sein ganzes leidendes Volk ein. Heilsgeschichtliche Traditionen und theologische Erwägungen, wie sie von seinen Jerusalemer Gegnern gepflegt werden (ii 7, iii 11), liegen ihm fern. Alles setzt er daran, mit Kraft und Mut *mišpāṭ* zu praktizieren. Damit, daß er Jahwes Namen so selten ins Feld führt, erinnert er eher an die entsprechende Zurückhaltung in weisheitlichen Traditionen. Weisheitlichem Denken entspricht es auch, den Tun-Ergehen-Zusammenhang ohne ausdrücklichen Hinweis auf Jahwe aufzudecken; so knüpft er wiederholt an seine Scheltworte mit einfachem *lākēn* die Ankündigung kommenden Unheils an (iii 6, 12; vgl. ii 3, 5, i 14). Gegenüber den Jerusalemer Amtsträgern, die stark dem Kult verbunden sind, zeigt er eine eher akultische Redeweise, wie sie einem Ortsältesten ansteht, dem die Rechts- und Weisheitspflege in der Sippe anvertraut ist (vgl. Prv. xxxi 23).

Wie dem auch sei, es ist ein äußerst erstaunliches Phänomen innerhalb der klassischen Prophetie, wie sparsam Micha von sich aus auf Jahwe hinweist. Er ist offenbar skeptisch gegenüber dem kultischen Mißbrauch des Gottesnamens.

5. In die gleiche Richtung der akultischen Redeweise in den Sippen weist die große Trauerklage in i 8-16. Zur Eröffnung spricht sich Michas Ich ein weiteres Mal aus:

> Ich muß wehklagen, heulen muß ich,
> barfuß und nackt muß ich gehen.
> Ich übe Wehklage wie Schakale
> und Trauerwimmern wie Strauße.

Das Heulen der Schakale und das Wimmern der Strauße wird laut, wo in der Zerstörung menschlicher Wohnstätten die Wüste wächst. Dann ruft Micha eine Vielzahl benachbarter Orte zu Riten der Untergangsklage auf, in Erwartung eines überlegenen Feindangriffs. Nichts erinnert da an kultische Klage; da dringt kein Flehen zu Jahwe vor; nichts erinnert im Wortlaut an ein Heiligtum.[26] Es geht um das

[25] Ganz anders dagegen der spätere Text Mi. vi 3, 5 (16?). Vgl. Th. Lescow, S. 53: "*ʿām* sind immer die von Mi. verteidigten Kleinbauern".

[26] A. S. van der Woude, S. 21ff., erwägt, daß der Text im Heiligtum zu Lachisch verkündigt wurde.

militärische Geschick der Ortschaften und die Zukunft ihrer Bewohner. Micha stellt sich in i 8 selbst in einer symbolisch gesteigerten Ausdruckshandlung an die Spitze aller Betroffenen. Seine Trauermanifestation kündigt an, was "auf allen Plätzen und in allen Straßen" nachzuvollziehen ist (Am. v 16). So mag am ehesten ein Ältester des Landes sprechen, wenn ihm prophetisches Wissen um die Katastrophe anvertraut ist.

Die Aufnahme des *hôj* — Rufs in ii 1 bestätigt es. Denn daß dieses *hôj* ursprünglich zur Leichenklage in der Sippe gehört, ist nach 1 Kön. xiii 30; Jer. xxii 18, xxxiv 5 unbestritten, gleichgültig, ob man an eine direkte Übernahme durch die Propheten des 8. Jahrhunderts denkt oder ob man eine Zwischenstufe weisheitlicher Warnrufe in der Pädagogik der Sippen postuliert.[27]

6. Eine letzte Ich-Aussage bleibt noch zu beachten. Den Sprüchen in Kap. iii ist ein *wāʾomar* vorangestellt. Fraglos gehört es nicht zu einem der mündlich verkündigten Sprüche, sondern zur literarischen Redaktion. Aber wenn die 1. Person des masoretischen Textes ursprünglich ist ("aber ich sprach"),[28] dann muß danach eine erste Niederschrift der Sprüche Michas auf ihn selbst zurückgehen. Daß diese Redaktionsnotiz adversativ zu verstehen ist, ergibt sich aus ihrer Anknüpfung an die vorangehende Diskussionsniederschrift in ii 6-11.[29] Man soll in den folgenden Sprüchen lesen, worin Micha sich von den Lügenpropheten (ii 11) unterscheidet. *wāʾomar* in iii 1 ist gleichsam die literarische Voranzeige seiner expliziten Konfrontation in iii 8. Daß wir so Micha auch als literarischen Autor anzunehmen haben, deutet verstärkt auf seine Zugehörigkeit zur obersten Bildungsschicht in Moreschet hin.[30]

7. Von iii 1 aus bedenken wir nun noch *formgeschichtlich* die kontrastierende Selbstvorstellung Michas in iii 8. Wo gibt es Vergleichbares für diese Form des Selbstbewußtseins? In der Prophetie müssen wir es schlechterdings singulär nennen.

Ich aber, ich bin erfüllt von Kraft, Recht und Mut,
Jakob sein Verbrechen anzuzeigen und Israel sein Unrecht.

---

[27] Vgl. zur umfassenden Diskussion zuletzt H. J. Zobel, *ThWAT* II, S. 382-8 (Literatur) und Chr. Hardmeier, *Kritik der Formgeschichte auf texttheoretischer Basis am Beispiel der prophetischen Weheworte*, Diss. Heidelberg (1975).

[28] *G* und *S* setzen die Vokalisation *weʾāmar* voraus.

[29] Andere, wie jüngst A. S. van der Woude, S. 100f., sehen hier die Entgegnung auf Worte falscher Propheten in 2, 12f. eingeführt.

[30] Hier könnte auch noch die Kunst der Wortspiele bei Micha angeführt werden; vgl. vor allem i 10-16 und ii 4, 11.

Muß man solche Selbstaussage nicht geradezu der Gattung der Prahlsprüche zuordnen? Erinnert dieses Kraftbewußtsein nicht wenigstens in seiner Struktur an das Prahlen Lamechs mit seiner ungeheuerlichen Vergeltung (Gen. iv 23f.)? Rühmt Micha nicht sein Ich in seiner Überlegenheit ähnlich wie David gegenüber der Schmährede Goliats: "Du kommts zu mir mit Schwert, Lanze und Krummschwert, ich aber (*we'ānōkī*) mit dem Namen Jahwes der Heere, des Gottes der Schlachtreihen Israels, den du geschmäht hast" (1 Sam. xvii 45)? Nur daß Micha hier nichts von Jahwe sagt! Zum Prahlwort gehört immer das kontrastierende Herausstellen des eigenen Ich und das Vergleichen mit dem Resultat der eigenen Überlegenheit. Solches Sich-Brüsten hat in der Regel die Funktion, die Feinde abzuschrecken.[31] Man muß sich wohl klarmachen, daß Micha derartigem Prahlen strukturell wie funktionell sehr nahekommt. Doch thematisch ist Michas Wort von den beiden genannten Prahlsprüchen weit entfernt.

Dagegen erinnert merkwürdigerweise Michas Art der Selbstvorstellung an die Selbstempfehlungen der Weisheit. Sir. xxiv 1 zeigt gleich im Eingang, daß zwar auch der Selbstruhm der Weisheit nicht weit von den Prahlreden entfernt ist:

Die Weisheit lobt sich selbst,
und inmitten ihres Volkes rühmt sie sich.
haḥākmā tehallēl nāpšāh ûbetôk 'ammāh titpā'ar

Aber stofflich steht Mi. iii 8 den beiden ersten Strophen von Prv. viii am nächsten.[32] Die wichtigsten Topoi, in denen die beiden sonst so verschiedenen Texte übereinstimmen, erscheinen mir beachtlich. Wie Micha sein Ich den Betrügern entgegenwirft, so empfiehlt die Weisheit in Prv. viii ihr Ich gegenüber der finsteren Verführungsmacht, die im vorangehenden Kapitel vii zu Worte kam. (viii 12:) "*Ich*, die Weisheit, bin Nachbarin der Klugheit". (V. 14:) "Bei *mir* ist Rat und Erfolg, *ich* bin die Einsicht, bei *mir* ist *Mut*" (*gebûrā* wie in Mi. iii 8). Wie Micha, so ist die Weisheit ihrer Überlegenheit gewiß; deren Basis ist das Recht (V. 16): "Durch *mich* regieren Amtsträger und Edle, alle gerechten Richter". (V. 20:) "*Ich* schreite auf dem Weg der Gerechtigkeit, mitten auf den Steigen des *Rechts*" (*mišpāṭ* wie Mi.

[31] C. Westermann, *Genesis*, *BK* I/1 (1974), S. 442, 456f.
[32] Vgl. H. Gese, "Der Johannesprolog", *Zur biblischen Theologie* (München, 1977), S. 177ff.

iii 8). Wie Micha (iii 1, 9) so ruft die Weisheit deshalb zum Hören auf: *šimʿû* (V. 6; vgl. V. 32 *šimʿû lî* "Hört auf mich!"). Wie Micha die Häupter anklagt, daß ihnen "die *Einsicht* (*daʿat*) in das *Recht*" fehlt (iii 1b) und daß "sie alles *Gerade verdrehen*" (iii 9b *kål-haješārā*), so erklärt die Weisheit, daß in ihren Worten "nichts Verkehrtes und *Verdrehtes* (*ʿiqqēš* viii 8b) ist, daß sie vielmehr "gerade(*ješārîm*) sind für die, die Einsicht (*daʿat*) finden". Wie Micha anprangert, daß "die Häupter nach Bestechung richten, die Priester um Lohn lehren und die Propheten um Silber (*bekäsäp*) wahrsagen" (iii 11), so empfiehlt die Weisheit: "Nehmt meine Zucht und nicht Silber (*ʾal käsäp*), und Einsicht (*daʿat*) statt kostbaren Goldes!" (viii 10).

Gerade wenn man damit rechnet, daß Prv. viii und Mi. iii zeitlich weit auseinanderliegen und auch funktional recht verschieden sind, setzt die Fülle von Überschneidungen wichtiger Begriffe in Erstaunen, nicht weniger der ähnliche Grundtenor der Selbstempfehlung der Weisheit und des Propheten sowie der weitgehende Verzicht beider, ausdrücklich auf Jahwe zu verweisen (erst in der 3. Strophe von Prv. viii, in V. 22, erklärt sich die Weisheit als Erstling der Geschöpfe Jahwes). Darf man den Schluß umgehen, daß beide Selbstempfehlungen letztlich auf dem gleichen Mutterboden, im gleichen geistigen Raum der Weisheit gewachsen sind, einer Weisheit, die nicht nur in den großen höfischen und hauptstädtischen Schulen, sondern in einfachen Formen notwendig auch unter den Sippenältesten der Landstädte zu pflegen war? Man wird dann auch Micha nicht mit den Prahlworten Lamechs u.ä. vergleichen, da es bei ihm wie bei der weisheitlichen Selbstempfehlung nicht um seine Person geht, sondern um die völlige Selbsthingabe an das Recht. Viel eher ließe sich mit G. von Rad von einem "Jauchzen im Geist", "einem herrlichen Aufschäumen seines Charismas" sprechen.[33] Nur darf man die Kampfsituation nicht vergessen, in der Micha den Machthabern mit der ihm eigenen Vollmacht begegnet. Im weitesten formgeschichtlichen Horizont wird man die weisheitliche wie die michanische Selbstrühmung auf halbem Wege zwischen den alten Prahlsprüchen und den Ich-bin-Worten Jesu im Johannesevangelium einordnen.

Wir fassen zusammen, was sich zur Frage nach dem soziologischen Standort Michas aus seinen Selbstaussagen ergeben hat. Sie werden weder verständlich, wenn Micha ein armer Landarbeiter war, der sich durch religiöse Impulse zum prophetischen Einzelkämpfer entwickelt

---

[33] S. 184.

hat, noch wenn man ihn einer kultischen Institution in Jerusalem oder Lachisch verpflichtet sieht. Vieles spricht dafür, ihn als einen Ortsältesten von Moreschet anzusehen, der mit den "Ältesten des Landes" auch in Jerusalem aus- und einging und dort in diesem Kreise als "der Moreschetiter" bekannt wurde. Man hat ihn den Propheten der Armen genannt, der seine göttliche Berufung im Notschrei gequälter Menschen fand.[34] Aber sein Einsatz für die Bedrängten war weniger Ursache als vielmehr Auswirkung seiner Verpflichtung dem "Recht" gegenüber, die er als Ältester wahrzunehmen hatte. So kann das Ältestenamt als die Basis seines Wirkens gelten. Von ihm her trat er seinen Jerusalemer Kollegen, den Häuptern und Richtern, aber auch den Priestern und Propheten entgegen. Und dabei bezog er sich kaum auf spezielle Aufträge Jahwes.

Er selbst scheint auf den Titel eines Propheten keinen Wert gelegt zu haben. Und doch war der Moreschetiter weit mehr als irgendeiner der Ältesten des Landes. Das besondere war einmal die ungewöhnlich kraftvolle und mutige Wahrnehmung des Ältestenamtes im Einsatz für das Recht und im Kampf gegen das Unrecht. Zum anderen weitete er seinen Amtsbereich über seine engere Heimat und die dortigen Einzelfälle aus speziell zur Hauptstadt hin. Zum dritten erfüllte ihn die echt prophetische Grundgewißheit, daß Juda und vor allem Jerusalem einer totalen Katastrophe entgegengehen. Insofern also transzendiert sein Wirken das gewöhnliche Ältestenamt wesentlich.[35] In der gezielten Direktheit und im Umfang seiner Drohungen läßt er Stil und Inhalt der Rechtsentscheidungen und Belehrungen eines durchschnittlichen Sippenhauptes weit hinter sich. (Von einer Mahnung zur Umkehr ist mit keiner Silbe die Rede. Ganz im Gegenteil kündigt er ein Unheil an, aus dem die Bedrohten ihren Nacken nicht herausziehen können, ii 3. Micha hat so wenig wie Amos die Zukunft Israels in die Hände der Menschen gelegt, auch wenn er das Ich Jahwes längst nicht so direkt zur Sprache bringt wie die, die ihre bösen Machenschaften hinter ihrem selbstsicheren Glauben an Jahwe verstecken).

In diesem Überschuß des eigentlich Prophetischen entspricht seine Verkündigung weithin der Verkündigung der drei anderen klassischen Propheten des 8. Jahrhunderts. Doch erscheint es mir für diesmal wichtig zu sehen, daß das prophetische Charisma soziologisch

---

[34] J. M. P. Smith, *Micah*, *ICC* (1911), S. 18.

[35] Zur Kombination der Institution des Ältesten-Amtes mit dem prophetischen Charisma vgl. auch Num. xi 14-17, 24-30.

eine recht verschiedene Basis haben kann. So sehen wir Hosea im Nordreich auf dem Hintergrunde einer levitisch-prophetischen Oppositionsgemeinschaft,[36] Jesaja auf dem Hintergrunde der höfischen Weisheitsschule Jerusalems;[37] Amos muß in mancher Hinsicht Micha nach seiner sozialen Herkunftsschicht am ähnlichsten gewesen sein.[38] Nur hat Amos sich bei seinem Auftreten im Nordreich immer wieder auf Jahwes speziellen Auftrag bezogen, während Micha die Berufung auf Jahwe weitgehend bei seinen Gegnern hört und sie eben damit hinsichtlich der Durchsetzung des Rechts desavouiert findet. Insofern ist Micha ein hervorragender Vorweg-Interpret des Wortes Jesu: "Nicht jeder, der zu mir ruft: Herr, Herr!, wird in das Himmelreich kommen, sondern nur, wer den Willen meines Vaters im Himmel tut" (Mt. vii 21).

---

[36] H. W. Wolff, "Hoseas geistige Heimat", *Gesammelte Studien zum AT* (München, ²1973), S. 232-50.

[37] J. Fichtner, "Jesaja unter den Weisen", *ThLZ* 74 (1949), Sp. 75-80; vgl. J. W. Whedbee, *Isaiah and Wisdom* (Nashville und New York, 1971).

[38] Vgl. H. W. Wolff, *Joel und Amos*, *BK* XIV/2 (²1975), S. 107f. Meinen Vorschlag, manche Aussagen des Amos von der altisraelitischen Sippenweisheit her zu verstehen, möchte ich von Micha her präzisieren. Beide sollte man sich als zum Kreise der Ältesten des Landes zugehörig denken, als Sippenhäupter je ihres Ortes. Es scheint mir geradezu schwer vorstellbar, daß sie diese Funktion nicht von Haus aus gehabt hätten. Als *zᵉqēnîm* hatten sie vor allem *mišpāṭ* zu wahren, im Prozeßverfahren wie in der sippenweisheitlichen Lehrtradition. Beider Ältestenamt aber mußte in den Dienst des außerordentlichen prophetischen Charismas treten, das sie nötigte, weit über ihren Heimatort hinaus Jahwes umfassendes Gericht zu verkündigen.